Transformative Work Design

THE SIOP ORGANIZATIONAL FRONTIERS SERIES

Series Editors: Brad Bell and Georgia Chao
Former Series Editors: Kevin Murphy and Angelo Denisi

For other books in the series, please visit:
https://www.siop.org/Research-Publications/Organizational-Frontiers-Series

Transformative Work Design: Synthesis and New Directions
Sharon K. Parker, Caroline Knight, Florian E. Klonek, and Fangfang Zhang

Transformative Work Design

Synthesis and New Directions

Edited by

SHARON K. PARKER
CAROLINE KNIGHT
FLORIAN E. KLONEK
FANGFANG ZHANG

OXFORD
UNIVERSITY PRESS

Oxford University Press is a department of the University of Oxford.
It furthers the University's objective of excellence in research, scholarship,
and education by publishing worldwide. Oxford is a registered trade mark of
Oxford University Press in the UK and in certain other countries.

Published in the United States of America by Oxford University Press
198 Madison Avenue, New York, NY 10016, United States of America.

© Society for Industrial and Organizational Psychology 2025

Editorial correspondence should be directed to
Oxford University Press, 198 Madison Avenue, New York, NY 10016.
Orders, sales, license, and permissions inquiries should be directed to
Oxford University Press, 198 Madison Avenue, New York, NY 10016

All rights reserved. No part of this publication may be reproduced, stored in a retrieval system, transmitted, used for text and data mining, or used for training artificial intelligence, in any form or by any means, without the prior permission in writing of Oxford University Press, or as expressly permitted by law, by license or under terms agreed with the appropriate reprographics rights organization. Inquiries concerning reproduction outside the scope of the above should be sent to the Rights Department, Oxford University Press, at the address above.

You must not circulate this work in any other form
and you must impose this same condition on any acquirer.

CIP data is on file at the Library of Congress

ISBN 9780197692561

ISBN 9780197692554 (hbk.)

DOI: 10.1093/oso/9780197692554.001.0001

Paperback Printed by Marquis, Canada

Hardback Printed by Bridgeport National Bindery, Inc., United States of America

Contents

List of Contributors   viii

INTRODUCTION

Transformative Work Design: An Integrative Framework   3
Sharon K. Parker, Caroline Knight, Florian E. Klonek,
and Fangfang Zhang

PART 1. FOUNDATIONS OF WORK DESIGN

The Evolution of Work Design Theory and Research   29
Anja Van den Broeck, Lorenz Verelst, and Hans de Witte

Multi-Level Work Design: Integrating Work Characteristics
Across Individual, Team, and Organizational Levels of Analysis   55
Cory M. Eisenhard and Frederick P. Morgeson

PART 2. OUTCOMES OF WORK DESIGN

Job Design and Well-Being: A Review of the Empirical Evidence   97
Sabine Sonnentag

Work Design and Performance   147
Sandra Ohly and Laura Venz

Work Design and Identity: Taking Stock of What We Know
and Charting Pathways for Future Research   175
Giverny De Boeck, Maïlys M. George, and Aušrinė
Vyšniauskaite

What You Do Makes Who You Are: The Role of Work
Design in Personality Change   191
Chia-Huei Wu and Ying Wang

Methodology in Work Design Research: The Past, Present,
and (Longitudinal) Future   207
Anita C. Keller and Iustina C. Armasu

vi CONTENTS

PART 3. ANTECEDENTS OF WORK DESIGN

Global and National Factors Shaping Work Design 237
David Holman and Anthony Rafferty

Shaping Work Design: The Influence of Occupational,
Organizational, and Work Group Factors 259
*Daniela M. Andrei, Amy Wei Tian, Florian E. Klonek, and
Lander J. G. Vermeerbergen*

On the Creation of Developmental Jobs 285
Irene de Pater

PART 4. TOP-DOWN WORK REDESIGN

How and Why Do Top-Down Work Redesign Interventions
Impact Well-Being and Performance? 305
Caroline Knight and Florian E. Klonek

Implementing and Sustaining Work Redesign 335
*Kevin Daniels, David Watson, Rachel Nayani, and Helen
Fitzhugh*

Unleashing Magic: A PARRTH to Participatory Work Redesign 359
Sharon K. Parker

Understanding the Outcomes of Work Transformations:
Evaluation of Organizational Interventions 385
Karina Nielsen

PART 5. BOTTOM-UP WORK REDESIGN

Job Crafting Theory and Perspectives 415
Maria Tims and Melissa Twemlow

Job Crafting Interventions 439
*Evangelia Demerouti, Maria Peeters, and Machteld van den
Heuvel*

It Pays to Play: Playful Work Design 465
Arnold B. Bakker and Yuri S. Scharp

CONTENTS vii

PART 6. FUTURE WORK

Artificial Intelligence: How It Changes the Landscape for
Work Design Research and Practice 483
Nadine Bienefeld and Gudela Grote

Reimagining Work Design in Contemporary Employment:
The Disruptive Rise of the Gig Economy 505
James Duggan and Jérôme Sulbout

The Perils of Algorithmic Management for Work Design 531
Xavier Parent-Rocheleau

Understanding Why, When, and How Virtual Work Works
through the Lens of a Work Design Perspective 545
Bin Wang, Xiang Fang, and Yi Zhao

Designing Work to Retain an Aging Workforce 569
Robin Umbra and Ulrike Fassbender

Text Analysis Using Artificial Intelligence as a Tool for Job
Analysis and Job Design 609
Emily D. Campion and Michael A. Campion

CONCLUSION

Where is the Future of Work Design Research Heading?: A
Roadmap for Key Topics To Be Investigated 629
*Fangfang Zhang, Caroline Knight, Florian E. Klonek, and
Sharon K. Parker*

Index 651

List of Contributors

Daniela M. Andrei, Associate Professor, Curtin University

Dr Iustina C. Armasu, University of Groningen

Arnold B. Bakker, Professor, Erasmus University Rotterdam

PD Dr Nadine Bienefeld, ETH Zürich

Emily Campion, Assistant Professor, University of Iowa

Michael Campion, Professor, Purdue University

Kevin Daniels, Professor, University of East Anglia

Giverny De Boeck, Assistant Professor, IESEG School of Management, UMR 9221 – LEM – Lille Economie Management, F-59000 Lille, France

Evangelia Demerouti, Professor, Eindhoven University of Technology

Anja Van den Broeck, Professor, KU Leuven

Machteld van den Heuvel, Assistant Professor, University of Amsterdam

Hans de Witte, Professor, KU Leuven & Optentia Research Unit – North West University

Irene de Pater, Professor, Edith Cowan University

Dr James Duggan, University College Cork

Cory M. Eisenhard, Michigan State University

Ms. Xiang Fang, Shanghai University

Dr Helen Fitzhugh, University of East Anglia

Maïlys M. George, Assistant Professor, IESE Business School, Universidad de Navarra

Gudela Grote, Professor, ETH Zürich

David Holman, Professor, University of Manchester

Anita C. Keller, Associate Professor, University of Groningen

Dr Florian E. Klonek, Deakin University

Dr Caroline Knight, University of Queensland

Frederick P. Morgeson, Professor, Michigan State University

Rachel Nayani, Associate Professor, University of East Anglia

Karina Nielsen, Professor, University of Sheffield (deceased)

Sandra Ohly, Professor, University of Kassel

Xavier Parent-Rocheleau, Professor, HEC Montreal

Sharon K. Parker, John Curtin Distinguished Professor; Curtin University

Maria Peeters, Professor, Utrecht University; Eindhoven University of Technology

Anthony Rafferty, Professor, University of Manchester

Yuri S. Scharp, Assistant Professor, Tilburg University

Sabine Sonnentag, Professor, University of Mannheim

Dr Jerome Sulbout, University of Liège

Maria Tims, Professor, Vrije Universiteit Amsterdam

Melissa Twermlow, Assistant Professor, Erasmus University Rotterdam

Dr Robin Umbra, University of Hohenheim

Laura Venz, Professor, Leuphana University of Lüneburg

Lorenz Verelst, Assistant Professor, Radboud University

Lander J. G. Vermeerbergen, Assistant Professor, Radboud University

Aušrinė Vyšniauskaitė, KU Leuven

Bin Wang, Associate Professor, Shanghai University

Ying Wang, Associate Professor, RMIT University

Dr David Watson, University of Essex

Amy Wei Tian, Professor, Curtin University

Chia-Huei Wu, Professor, King's College London

Dr Fangfang Zhang, Curtin University

Mr. Yi Zhao, Shanghai University

INTRODUCTION

Transformative Work Design

An Integrative Framework

Sharon K. Parker, Caroline Knight, Florian E. Klonek, and Fangfang Zhang

> *You're being tracked by a computer the entire time you're there . . . You're keenly aware there is an algorithm keeping track of you, making sure you keep going as fast as you can, because if there is too much time elapsed between items, the computer will know this, will write you up, and you will get fired.* (The Guardian, 2020)

This comment indicating poor work quality comes from someone working in an Amazon warehouse—a context that is renowned for intense job demands arising from the use of surveillance and other such control systems. Recently in France, Amazon was fined $32M Euro for excessive employee surveillance causing unreasonable work pressures and safety hazards (Webber, 2024). Such concerns about work quality have existed for more than 100 years. In the earliest issue of the *Journal of Applied Psychology* in 1917, one of today's leading journals on work issues, G. G. McChesney asked: *"Is there no inspiration in labor? Must the man who works go on forever in a deadly routine, fall into the habit of mechanical nothingness, and reap the reward of only so much drudgery and so much pay?"*

Work design is about the content and organization of one's tasks, activities, relationships, and responsibilities, either for an individual job or role, or for a group of jobs or roles (Parker, 2014). Decisions about work design, such as who does which tasks within a team, are often manifested in "work characteristics," or people's perceived experience of psychologically and physically important dimensions of work. In the case of the Amazon worker, the tasks are tightly controlled by algorithms, creating for workers low job autonomy and high workload—two key work characteristics that we know from research can have a profound impact on outcomes like mental health and absenteeism. Understanding which work characteristics are important for whom, and with

---

Sharon K. Parker et al., *Transformative Work Design*. In: *Transformative Work Design*. Edited by: Sharon K. Parker et al., Oxford University Press. © Society for Industrial and Organizational Psychology (2025).
DOI: 10.1093/oso/9780197692554.003.0001

4 TRANSFORMATIVE WORK DESIGN

what impact, has been a key focus of work design research for many decades (Parker et al., 2017).

Synthesizing this considerable body of research is our first goal with this book. If research findings are to be applied practically, and expanded theoretically, we must understand core theories and findings regarding what work design impacts. The book therefore provides a comprehensive overview of existing research and theory on work design, bringing together what we know in one volume, and highlighting the implications that derive from this knowledge. Our second aspiration for this book, however, is to go beyond what we know to delve into under-explored yet important emerging areas of research. For example, we focus in this book on some new and quite transformative outcomes of work design, such as identity and cognition. We also consider the neglected topic of the antecedents, or drivers, of work design—a critical issue if we want to create better quality work at scale. We give much more attention to the process of redesigning work than is typically focused on in research. Further, we focus on emerging issues for work design in the future, against the backdrop of the growth in hybrid models, altered career structures, new tasks and occupations due to technological change, demographic shifts, and other related profound contemporary changes. We seek to lay out an agenda for what new knowledge needs to be generated to create better quality work in the future.

There are six parts to this book: Foundations, Outcomes, Antecedents, Top-down Interventions, Bottom-up Interventions, and Future Work Issues. In this introductory chapter, in the spirit of synthesis, in the first section we first offer an *integrative framework* that encapsulates the ideas and scholarship captured across the six parts. In the second section of this chapter, we *sequentially overview each chapter within each of the six parts* to create a more detailed road map for the reader. Throughout, author names in bold refer to authors of book chapters in this volume.

An Integrative Framework

Figure 1.1 shows an integrative framework of work design that captures the key ideas covered in the book. The framework depicts that work characteristics—which are the traditional "heart" of the topic of work design (and in the middle boxes in our model)—can be considered at multiple levels: the individual level (Box A2), the team level (Box B2), and the organizational level (Box C2). Sometimes work characteristics are considered an even lower level of analysis (i.e., within-persons), but we do not depict this level for simplicity. Most commonly studied are work characteristics at the individual level, as indicated by the thicker line around this box. We draw on the SMART Work Design model (Parker & Knight, 2024) to summarize the key individual work characteristics that have been identified and investigated.

Of course, work characteristics at each of these levels are only worth worrying about if they have some consequence for people, teams, or organizations. Box A3 depicts some key and well-understood individual outcomes of work design (e.g., motivation, job performance, job satisfaction and other well-being indicators, and learning), as well as some of the outcomes for which evidence is emerging, such as cognition, identity, and even personality change. At the team level, work characteristics, such as team autonomy, have been shown to predict important team outcomes (Box B3) but there is little research on organizational outcomes (Box C3). It is also relevant to observe that, although it is rarely studied systematically, as indicated by the arrows linking outcomes at different levels (e.g., from A3 to B3/C3; and from B3 to C3), effects of work design at one level can potentially aggregate up to effects at higher levels. For instance, some studies suggest that the benefits of work design for individual and team engagement and related outcomes have culminated in organization-wide benefits such as lowered costs and reduced absenteeism. Also important, the link between work design and outcomes can be moderated by individual and contextual factors (not depicted in the figure for simplicity). One example of a potential moderating factor is age, as will be discussed later.

Importantly, work characteristics do not come out of thin air. As indicated by A1, A2, and A3, there are individual-, team-, and organizational-level antecedents of, or influences on, work design. For example, at the individual level (Box A1), people's proactivity and self-efficacy can increase job crafting and engagement in developmental challenges and hence can improve work design; at the team level, Box B1 highlights the role of leaders and managers, amongst other factors, in shaping the work design of teams by facilitating or constraining team-level work characteristics. Outcomes of work design can also recursively shape work design, such as when job autonomy leads people to be more proactive, which in turn leads them to take on more job autonomy. Importantly, our integrative model indicates that, beyond within-level antecedents, there can be cross-level antecedents, as depicted by the downward arrows from higher-level to lower-level work elements in the model. For example, an empowering supervisor (team level) can increase the level of autonomy of a subordinate (individual level); and a hierarchical organizational structure (organizational level) makes the implementation of self-managing teams (team level) almost impossible. These cross-level effects are not always straightforward, such as when group autonomy reduces individual-level autonomy (e.g., Langfred, 2000).

Understanding the antecedents of work design provides knowledge that can be leveraged to change work design. In other words, work can be redesigned. As depicted by the large block arrows in Figure 1.1, and as discussed in Part 4, work design can be changed or "redesigned" via top-down interventions, such as when an organization is re-structured and self-managing teams

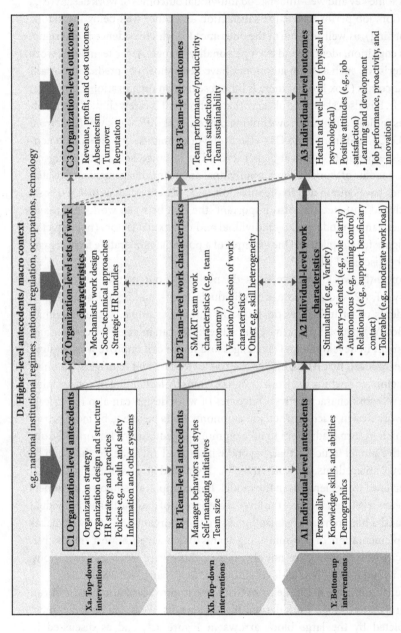

Figure 1.1 Integrative Framework of Work Design

Note: Thicker boxes and arrows indicate greater research evidence. This model excludes moderators, recursive links, and a lower level of analysis (within-person effects) for ease of depiction.

are implemented (Block Arrow Xa) or when a manager implements a job rotation scheme (Block Arrow Xb). Although top-down, most often these interventions benefit from involving workers in the change process. Work can also be redesigned by individuals themselves, via bottom-up interventions (Block Arrow Y), such as when workers self-initiate changes to their work to better fit their needs and preferences (an example of "job crafting").

Finally, the model indicates that work design always occurs within a wider macro context (Box D), shaped by higher level influences, which might be the occupation or sector that one is working within, the country, or even a particular time in history. This macro context shapes work design directly and indirectly. For example, occupational factors can shape work design as the roles, responsibilities, and tasks carried out in one's job vary according to occupation, as can higher-level and macro-factors, such as national health and safety regulation, the presence of trade unions, institutional regimes, and global advances in technology. The period in history also matters. For instance, academic interest in creating more enriched jobs was spurred as a direct result of the job simplification implemented during the first industrial revolution. Now we are in the fourth (and some argue fifth, or even sixth) revolution, and we are seeing new ways that technology and technologically enabled business models, as well as demographic change, have important implications for work design (as shown in the quote at the outset).

In sum, the integrative model in Figure 1.1 helps to bring together the key ideas and research covered in this book—and indeed in work design literature generally—and highlights where there is substantial and less substantial evidence for the proposed relationships. In what follows, we unpack this model in more detail and describe how each part of the book covers the key elements of the model.

Elaboration of the Model in Relation to Each of the Six Parts of the Book and Its Chapters

Part 1: Foundations of work design

Let us return to the topic of work characteristics, which tend to be at the heart of the research on work design, and hence are depicted in the center of our model (Box A2, B2, C2). By far the most attention has been given to individual work characteristics (Box A2), or how individuals perceive psychologically and physically important dimensions of their work. In Chapter 2 of the book, Key Foundations, **Anja Van den Broeck**, **Lorenz Verelst**, and **Hans de Witte** outline how, historically, people became interested in creating work with more

8 TRANSFORMATIVE WORK DESIGN

positive work characteristics because scientific management (Taylor, 1911), with its focus on "efficiency," led to simplified and dehumanized work. People's negative reactions to such work led to the development of models of work design such as the Job Characteristics Model (JCM) (Hackman & Oldham, 1975), the Demand-Control Model (Karasek, 1979), and the Job Demands-Resources (JD-R; Demerouti et al., 2001) model. These models identify various individual work characteristics that create meaningful work that is optimal for individual health and well-being—a focus that remains a critical concern today.

However, as Van den Broeck, Verelst, and De Witte describe in their chapter, the number of individual work characteristics (including job resources and job demands) considered within these models has proliferated to include more than 30, demonstrating the complexity of designing quality work and the need to take context into account when applying work design principles. One way to make sense of this complexity is through the SMART Work Design model (Parker & Knight, 2024), which—based on a higher-order factor analysis of 16 discrete work characteristics—identifies five categories of work characteristics: stimulating (including task variety, skill variety, problem solving, and information processing), mastery (including job feedback, feedback from others, and role clarity), autonomy (including scheduling, method, and decision-making autonomy), relational (including task significance, social support, and beneficiary contact), and tolerable (low levels of role overload, role conflict, and work-home conflict). This model is comprehensive, including motivational aspects from the traditional JCM (Hackman & Oldham, 1975), relational aspects from relational models of work design (e.g., Grant, 2007), and demands from the Job Demand-Control Model (Karasek, 1979). It has parallels with the JD-R model (Demerouti et al., 2001), but it is more nuanced, breaking "job resources" down into four major clusters (SMAR). We propose the five higher-order SMART dimensions as a useful way to summarize work design from an individual perspective (Box A2).

As then discussed by **Cory M. Eisenhard** and **Frederick P. Morgeson** in Chapter 3, whilst individual work design theory is well advanced, more conceptual and methodological attention needs to be given to team-level work characteristics (Box B2, Figure 1). Typically, team work characteristics are not a simple aggregation of individual work characteristics, and thus should not be conceptualized or measured this way. For example, SMART work characteristics at the team level should be assessed using items with a team-level referent (e.g., "we have sufficient decision-making influence in our team"), with an assessment as to whether perceptions of work characteristics are shared within the team. As Eisenhard and Morgeson discuss, other conceptualizations might also be important. For example, team skill variety might be extended to capture not just the total number of unique skills needed to complete the team's work, but also dimensions, such as how much skills overlap (or skill homogeneity versus heterogeneity) and how skills are combined amongst team members.

Importantly, Eisenhard and Morgeson argue there is insufficient attention to work design at the organizational level (Box C2), which they define as "the systematic deployment of sets of work characteristics to achieve desired outcomes." The authors identify several broad types of organizational work designs: *mechanistic work design* (e.g., Toyota Production System, lean production), *socio-technical systems approaches* (e.g., self-managing organizations), and *strategic HR approaches* (e.g., high performance work systems). Eisenhard and Morgeson argue for the importance of more research on work design at the organizational level *"because it can shape the meaning of work at the lower levels"*; a perspective that resonates with a later but somewhat different approach in Chapter 10 in which the authors unpack how organizational factors—such as organizational design—can shape individual and team work design.

Part 2: Outcomes of work design

Work characteristics—at each level—are only worth worrying about if they have some consequence for people, teams, or organizations. Indeed, considerable research shows that work design is associated with a myriad of health, well-being, and performance outcomes. We begin Part 2 with a focus on the more well-established outcomes. With the "mental health crisis" that is occurring in many countries, it is increasingly recognized that designing quality work can prevent mental ill health and promote well-being. In Chapter 4, **Sabine Sonnentag** comprehensively reviews how work design shapes both hedonic and eudaimonic well-being, using the SMART work design model as an organizing framework. A range of evidence—from longitudinal studies to laboratory studies to meta-analyses and even some field intervention studies, stimulating, mastery, autonomous, relational, and tolerable work characteristics are associated with well-being, especially eudaimonic outcomes. However, important nuances are highlighted. As one example, while stimulating work is consistently predictive of positive hedonic well-being outcomes such as satisfaction and engagement, as well as eudaimonic well-being indicators like meaningfulness, it is only weakly related to outcomes like anxiety or burnout and, as observed by Sonnentag, stimulating work can even become overtaxing.

Just because there is very good evidence that work design shapes well-being, this doesn't mean work design interventions invariably improve workers' health or well-being. Sonnentag shows positive evidence of benefits in some primary studies, especially for feedback (Mastery) and control (Autonomy), but also

10   TRANSFORMATIVE WORK DESIGN

some contrary evidence. She calls for quality studies: including sufficiently powered intervention studies, and theoretically chosen time lags.

Work design is not solely a vehicle for improving worker well-being, important though that is. As **Sandra Ohly** and **Laura Venz** outline in Chapter 5, work design can also affect workers' job performance. Performance, an umbrella term for an array of behaviors that contribute to organizational goals, is a perennially important topic as organizations strive to be competitive in a changing world. The authors organize their review around the performance model by Mark Griffin and colleagues (2007), which includes proficiency, adaptivity, and proactivity, with safety as an additional outcome. They identify three core mechanisms by which work characteristics can affect these outcomes: motivation (e.g., engagement, prosocial motivation), learning (e.g., skill development, knowledge gain), and cognitive capacity (e.g., memory, attention). As an example of the latter process, if work design fosters positive affect, this may broaden cognitive processes, such as flexible thinking, leading to the implication that job resources like autonomy and support may be especially important in contexts where problem-solving and other forms of proactivity are required.

Overall, whilst there is solid evidence linking work characteristics and both proficiency and proactivity through these mechanisms, Avshalom Caspi (2005; see also Andrei & Parker, 2018, on this topic) and relatively few others have focused on the link between work characteristics and safety. The authors call for more research on these outcomes, as well as new outcomes such as IT safety and security. Overloaded employees may, for instance, be more likely to click on harmful links lowering IT safety performance. Throughout their chapter, Ohly and Venz recognize the importance of distinguishing primary or core tasks (the focus of proficiency) from secondary tasks (e.g., adapting to interruptions), with performance often being enhanced when work structures allow individuals to focus their attention onto the primary tasks without too much disruption from the latter.

To this point, this book shows that work imbued with positive work characteristics like job autonomy can promote job satisfaction, organizational commitment, mental health, and job performance. But it can also be transformative—as per the book's title. Transformative means "causing a marked change in someone or something" (Oxford University Press, 2024). One area where there might be a marked change as a result of work design is identity. Work is a rich source of social connection and meaning, and many of us spend much time at work, thus **Giverny De Boeck**, **Maïlys M. George**, and **Aušrinė Vyšniauskaite** advocate, in Chapter 6, for the need to better understand how work design might influence individuals' sense of self, or their identity. Identity captures how individuals see themselves, or their answers to the question "Who am I?." From the authors' review of 28 papers, identities investigated in relation to work design include organizational, occupational, career, entrepreneurial, volunteer, and broader self-identities. There is emerging evidence that work design shapes people's identities. For instance, one study (Sweet et al., 2016) showed that less stimulating and autonomous work design explained why work was less important to women's sense of identity compared to men's, although women also had stronger relational work design which partly compensated for this effect.

Perhaps even more surprising, we see that work design can also affect broader aspects of identity, showing its transformational power. For example, one study (Jurek and Besta, 2021) showed that relational aspects of work design fostered employees' self-expansion, enhancing their self-growth and identity development. Importantly, work design not only affects identity but the reverse is true. De Boeck, George, and Vyšniauskaite also show some studies in which identity misfits prompt bottom-up work design in the form of job crafting.

In Chapter 7, **Chia-Huei Wu** and **Ying Wang** outline research showing that work design can shape personality, providing more evidence of the transformational impact of work design. This perspective builds on emerging evidence that personality traits can change over a person's lifespan. Theoretically, a job requires role taking or other situational demands, which invoke specific patterns of thoughts, feelings, and behaviors. Over time, these patterns are reinforced and consolidated such that an individual's personality gradually evolves to better meet the requirements of the role.

Wu and Wang review evidence that positive aspects of work design can shape change in people toward personality maturation, a process in which an individual becomes "more planful, deliberate, and decisive, but also more considerate and charitable" (Caspi et al., 2005, p. 469). From the Big Five perspective, this means becoming more emotionally stable, conscientious, and agreeable. For example, over multiple years, job autonomy can increase people's internal locus of control, proactive personality, and self-directedness. On the other hand, demanding jobs can increase neuroticism and decrease extraversion, although one study suggests that job demands can promote individuals actively mastering their environment, thereby fostering positive personality change. The impact of demands on personality change is likely to be moderated in important ways, just as it often is in short-term studies. As well as raising several fascinating questions for further exploration, such as the role of job crafting in individuals actively enacting personality change, methodological challenges in this domain are discussed. Researchers mostly rely on secondary longitudinal data, especially in Western countries, but there would be real value in designing a study to specifically look at these processes.

Although not covered in this book, another key outcome of work design is cognition (Box A3). Work design can contribute to workers' learning in the short to medium term, and potentially even affect cognitive functioning over the

12 TRANSFORMATIVE WORK DESIGN

much longer term, including the level of fluid and crystallized cognitive abilities. Sharon K. Parker, M. K. Ward, and Gwenith G. Fisher (2021) provide a multidisciplinary review of this perspective.

Methodologically, establishing the link between work design and outcomes requires longitudinal studies, as well as theorizing about the causal dynamics. In Chapter 8, **Anita C. Keller** and **Iustina C. Armasu** focus on the methods used to understand work design. Focusing on articles on the topic in six premier journals over the past 10 years, their analysis is quite striking—showing that a surprisingly large number (42 percent) of the 436 studies employed cross-sectional designs. Fortunately, it seems the number of such designs appear to be declining, whilst longitudinal designs—currently making up 34 percent of the studies—are growing in prevalence. A smaller number of studies employed a dyadic or team design (13 percent), 9 percent had an experimental design, and just 2 percent were qualitative. With respect to measures, about half of the studies (54 percent) used self-reports only, although many of these employed multiple assessments over time, reducing some of the problems of this approach. Non-self-report forms of data used in contemporary studies include occupational codes such as O*NET, HR data, or supervisor ratings. A small number of work studies are using biomarkers such as cortisol or heart-rate variability to assess stress and health outcomes of work design, and some have used objective measures to assess cognitive outcomes. Overall, it seems the methods and measures used in work design research appear to be improving, although Keller and Armasu advocate that "the future is longitudinal" and make many insightful recommendations for this future, such as that researchers need to pay more attention to temporal processes and change dynamics, and that there is an urgent need for intervention studies. As just one example, Keller and Armasu summarize intriguing evidence of asymmetry, such as that losing positive work characteristics has a stronger negative impact on well-being than gaining positive work characteristics does on positive well-being.

Part 3: Antecedents of work design

As articulated in Part 3 of the book, although traditionally a topic that has had less attention than outcomes (Parker et al., 2019), one can theorize and unpack *antecedents of work design*. This is an important topic because poor quality jobs persist, and understanding the factors that influence or constrain the design of jobs is critical to shaping how work design evolves, and how it can be crafted or redesigned.

There is increasing recognition that "macro" influences affect work design (Box D, Figure 1.1). Understanding these influences is crucial for helping nations to create appropriate policy and infrastructure to support quality work, and so we can recognize that micro and meso influences are often constrained by the wider context in which they exist. In Chapter 9, **David Holman** and **Anthony Rafferty** review how national institutions, institutional regimes (national configurations of institutions), the national economy, and global factors, such as supply chains, shape work design. In a fascinating chapter, these authors outline emerging evidence for a positive role of workplace safety regulations and national employment policies (such as hiring and firing laws and active labor market policies) in creating or supporting better quality work. The role of trade unions is mixed: trade unions in theory can influence organizations to create better quality work, as well as shaping good work indirectly through related policies. Certainly, there is evidence of the positive value of trade unions for quality work design, but also the reverse can be true, with the authors concluding the ability of trade unions to shape work design depends on the extent of union involvement in workplace decision making, union aims, employer behavior, and the role of regulation and the state in supporting unions.

The idea that a set of factors might be needed to positively shape work design comes to the fore in the authors' discussion of the effects of institutional regimes. Research consistently identifies the existence of better work design in social democratic regimes (the Nordic countries such as Denmark and Sweden). These regimes include highly influential trade unions, high union membership, extensive welfare benefits, active labor market policies, and national training policies which appear to operate together to create a "Nordic advantage" when it comes to work design. Altogether, despite their importance, research on macro influences is much less prevalent than that on individual and even organizational influences, and we fully concur with the authors that more inquiry is needed in this space, especially against a backdrop of changing migration patterns and climate change, global forces that will also affect work quality.

Daniela M. Andrei, **Amy Wei Tian**, **Florian E. Klonek**, and **Lander J. G. Vermeerbergen** in Chapter 10 continue the discussion of macro-level factors, considering the role of occupational antecedents. Different occupations require individuals to engage in different tasks, responsibilities, and roles, and adhere to occupational standards and regulations. Research shows that occupation accounts for a large amount of variance in role requirements, demonstrating its strong impact on shaping work design. Occupations also require individuals to hold different sets of values and norms. Indeed, research shows that as individuals become socialized into and identify with a particular occupation, they increasingly align their values with those of their occupation.

Andrei, Tian, Klonek, and Vermeerberge then consider organizational antecedents (Box C1), managerial antecedents (Boxes CI, B1) and workgroup antecedents (Box B1). Organizational factors, such as the degree of

14 TRANSFORMATIVE WORK DESIGN

centralization and control systems, human resource management (HRM) strategy, policies and procedures (e.g., flexible working, task distribution, involvement in decision-making, systems of control), organizational restructuring, and technological systems all impact the design of work and are themselves interlinked. For example, organizations aiming to be competitive through differentiation are likely to engage in practices promoting employee empowerment, skill development, and participation, creating work designs which are stimulating, autonomous, and allow individuals to gain mastery over their work. Leaders and managers have a crucial role to play in shaping employees' work design, both directly, such as by writing job descriptions and altering objective and structural work characteristics like autonomy and social interactions, and indirectly, through their behaviors and attitudes, such as encouraging or thwarting employee attempts to job craft. The chapter authors discuss the tension between research which shows that teamwork autonomy can benefit individuals through increased individual autonomy, task variety, and reduced demands, and research which suggests the opposite. This suggests nuanced and complex relationships and underlying mechanisms which still need to be teased out, particularly in terms of longitudinal dynamics.

In Chapter 11, **Irene de Pater** focuses on the antecedents of developmental challenge in work—a type of stimulating work design in which the job involves novel and demanding activities that require and build employees' abilities and motivation. Individual factors (Box A1) similar to those identified as antecedents of job crafting, such as proactive personality and self-efficacy, make people more likely to engage in developmental challenges. However, also important are team and leader processes (Box B1), as demonstrated in an intriguing discussion on gender differences in developmental challenge. Research shows that—despite having similar preferences for stimulating work—compared to men, women have less opportunity for developmental challenges and, when they exist, they are often different to those experienced by men (for example, women's challenges are more often related to obstacles). As to why, research has identified a range of different explanations, including that women choose these tasks less often than men when their performance might be evaluated, that in teams men tend to take on the more challenging tasks, and that male supervisors are less likely to assign challenging tasks to women. de Pater speculates on stereotypes about men being more competent than women may play into these dynamics. More generally, this discussion highlights the need to consider, from a work design perspective, how teams divide tasks amongst themselves, as well as how leaders allocate tasks to different team members. Both are important influences on people's work design yet neglected in research.

Part 4: Top-down work redesign

Work redesign does not receive much attention in the literature. However, especially now that work design seems to have come of age in organizations seeking solutions to worker burnout, early retirement, artificial intelligence (AI), and other such challenges, it is vital to foster practice that is based on evidence. Thus, in Part 4, we address this imbalance with a focus on top-down work redesign (Arrow Xa, Figure 1.1). Top-down work redesign interventions are manager-led, and often quite comprehensive in scope, covering the whole or a large part of the organization. These interventions are important because they shift the onus of responsibility away from the individual and have the potential to bring about considerable and systemic change in work design.

To begin, **Caroline Knight** and **Florian E. Klonek** (Chapter 12) discuss key top-down work redesign strategies and their impact. Drawing on two seminal reviews—one focused on the effect of interventions on well-being (Daniels et al., 2017) and one on performance (Knight & Parker, 2021)—Knight and Klonek conclude that job enrichment, job enlargement, and relational work redesign typically have positive effects on performance and usually on well-being, with overall positive albeit slightly less consistent evidence of positive impacts for self-managing teams. System-wide interventions have also been shown to sometimes have positive effects on performance, and to consistently improve worker well-being.

As these authors discuss, there is more to an intervention that just "what" it is, with the "fit" of the intervention to the context also being crucial. In the case of self-managing teams (SMTs), for example, Knight and Klonek discuss how SMTs might be most beneficial in high tech industries in which innovation is crucial ("where"), in contexts where uncertainty and interdependence is high ("when"), and for teams in which there are few fault-lines ("for whom"). Unpacking these more nuanced boundary conditions is an important contribution of this chapter, yet one that is sorely lacking in work design research overall. As the authors argue—and as raised multiple times in the book—we need more intervention studies to learn more about how to consistently create high quality work for individuals, teams, and organizations.

In a complementary chapter (Chapter 13) also focused on top-down work redesign, **Kevin Daniels**, **Rachel Nayani**, **David Watson**, and **Helen Fitzhugh** pick up on the relatively greater success, at least for well-being, of system-wide work redesign interventions. They focus especially on the question of how to sustain work redesign over the longer period; a challenging question to answer given most research investigates short-term effects of work redesign only. Sustainability, the authors argue, invariably lies in connecting the work design intervention to the other "moving parts" of the organization via three

16 TRANSFORMATIVE WORK DESIGN

distinct processes. Grafting, the path of least political resistance, means adapting the work redesign to be compatible with existing systems (e.g., not using self-managing teams in a context where there is individual pay for performance). Fracturing involves questioning and challenging other systems or practices when they are not compatible with work design, such as how flexible work scheduling might require efforts to challenge managers who locally do not allow flexibility. Gestalting is about bringing work design and other organizational elements into alignment, under a common purpose. Ultimately, the authors suggest that the emphasis on common purpose or seeking to achieve benefits for both workers and the organization, may be an authentic basis for the long-term success of work redesign.

A further intriguing set of ideas developed by the authors is how achieving and sustaining work design might come from a multi-stakeholder, multi-organization change process. A case in point is the "Good Jobs Project" (Fitzhugh et al., 2023) being conducted in Norwich, UK, led by researchers, the city council, and a civic society group. Simple resources have been developed to help the mostly untrained managers in low skilled, low pay seasonal work to create better quality work. For example, in one of "Four Boosts to Frontline Work," managers are encouraged to "make me part of the conversation" in a bid to increase employee autonomy. A full evaluation of this specific change is not yet available, but it might be these sorts of multi-organization approaches offer an alternative way forward for achieving sustainable work redesign (see also Parker & Jorristma, 2021).

Two further chapters then go deeper into various elements of top-down interventions. In Chapter 14, **Sharon K. Parker** discusses the importance of engaging those whose work is being redesigned in the process of redesign. She introduces the PARRTH Model, which includes the phases of Prepare, Assess, Reflect, Redesign, Track, and Habituate. As she discusses, this is a top-down approach involving support and endorsement from managers, but also involves involving workers codesigning their work, reminiscent of a form of collective crafting. This chapter provides evidence-based guidance to those who want to execute work redesign in their organization or a part of the organization.

In Chapter 15, **Karina Nielsen** goes deeper into the evaluation of work redesign interventions. She argues against continuing to use randomized control designs, in which individuals or teams are randomly allocated to an intervention versus control group, as the gold standard for evaluation. This approach is not only mostly impossible to execute in organizational settings, but it also does not capture—or indeed inform—the "how" of interventions which, as previously discussed, is considered crucial for success. Nielsen describes instead a new framework, Framework for Reporting and Assessing the Quality of

Organizational Interventions (FRAQOI), based on realist evaluation and implementation literatures that seek to answer the question of "what works for whom in which circumstances."

In FRAQOI, *prior to implementation*, details about the design of the intervention, the implementation strategies, the rationale for design choices, and the detailed evaluation plan should be reported (e.g., How were people recruited? What is the theory of change?). Once the work redesign is being *implemented*, the action planning process and content should be described, along with the possible mechanisms and boundary conditions necessary for successful implementation of action plans (e.g., Are the plans for action plan development followed and if not, why not?). Whether the implementation plan and the evaluation strategy are being adhered to should be reported, along with aspects such as whether evaluation is influencing the implementation (e.g., Are results being fed back to participants, and if so, with what consequence?). Finally, in the *post-implementation phase*, the focus is on assessing how the implementation process and content have affected multiple outcomes, including whether any effects sustain over time (e.g., Did dropout occur, and how did this affect the outcomes?). As Nielsen observes, evaluation of this kind will not only benefit researchers, but also organizations because the knowledge generated is fed into the process to help build capability for continuous improvement in work.

Part 5: Bottom-up work redesign

In Part 5, we move to a bottom-up perspective on work redesign, an approach that allows individuals to proactively create work that suits themselves and the context. Top-down work redesigns may overlook the unique needs and preferences of individuals, whereas these attributes are directly harnessed in job crafting and related interventions.

Maria Tims and **Melissa Twemlow** (Chapter 16) introduce the topic of job crafting, or the self-initiated behaviors that employees, and indeed teams of employees, take to actively shape their jobs. Job crafting has been linked with a series of positive outcomes such as employee well-being, work engagement, and performance. But as the popularity of the topic has grown, so too have the number of different types of crafting that have been considered. Tims and Twemlow discuss these many variations, concluding that a core distinction can be made between approach and avoidance crafting (or, very similar, promotion and prevention- focused crafting), with most evidence showing benefits of approach (promotion) crafting, consistent with a gain spiral, and showing negative effects of avoidance (prevention) crafting, consistent with a loss spiral. The authors also recognize that crafting does not occur in isolation: there

18　TRANSFORMATIVE WORK DESIGN

are often peers present who observe, and react to, the crafting of others. Parallel with the effects on crafters themselves, mostly it seems that co-workers who observe approach crafting consider it quite favorably, whereas avoidance crafting is often viewed negatively by coworkers, perhaps because of the negative attributions made about this behavior.

A second contribution by Tims and Twemlow is to consider job crafting across contexts. Interestingly, their analysis shows that crafting has most often been reported in healthcare, followed by education and then manufacturing. In all these settings, it seems that approach forms of crafting have benefits, whereas avoidance crafting is mostly negative (sometimes specific features, such as having empowering leaders buffered these negative effects). However, the antecedent conditions vary somewhat across the sectors. For instance, in education and manufacturing, studies focused more on commitment and attachment as predictors for approach crafting, whereas supportive leadership was focused on more in healthcare. What is clear across all contexts is that job crafting interventions can make a positive difference. In each sector, there is at least one compelling intervention study—suggesting positive change from crafting interventions is possible.

Chapter 17, by **Evangelia Demerouti**, **Maria Peeters**, and **Machteld van den Heuvel,** delves more deeply into crafting interventions, focusing on how individuals can be trained to shape their job to fit their needs and preferences by seeking resources and challenges (expansion-oriented crafting) and by reducing or optimizing job demands (reduction-oriented crafting). Although interventions vary, the approach recommended by the authors involves an interview phase to understand the context and the suitability of job crafting; a job crafting workshop, lasting from two hours to two days; individuals engaging in their crafting goals whilst in their work over a few weeks; and then a reflection session to review progress. Thus, interventions not only draw on models, like the job demands-resources model, but also theories such as those relating to goal setting, experiential learning, and the theory of planned behavior.

As to the question of impact, in their chapter the authors summarize evidence from a recent review of 33 studies, with two-thirds of the interventions shown to improve job crafting, 42 percent showing positive effects on work-related attitudes like engagement, and 30 percent showing an improvement in mental health. Further positive outcomes included task and adaptive performance, and employees' ability to deal with change. The authors conclude, and we concur, that *"the job crafting intervention is a promising tool to help organizations to support and maintain employee well-being and (to a somewhat lesser extent) performance, even during times of organizational change."* However, this review, an earlier meta-analysis, and various primary studies identify important moderators of job crafting interventions' effectiveness, such as the type of goals people set and their level of workload. Most studies also only focus on short-term effects and exclude mediating processes other than crafting.

Finally, in Chapter 18, **Arnold B. Bakker** and **Yuri S. Scharp** introduce the interesting notion of playful work design, a proactive cognitive-behavioral orientation aimed at fostering fun and challenge when doing one's work tasks. An example of this type of bottom-up work redesign is when a retail security guard tries to predict customer behavior, or a professor uses a curious word in a boring meeting to invigorate herself and colleagues. Such playful work design is self-initiated, and so is distinct from various forms of gamification that are sometimes introduced in organizations. Playful work design also focuses attention on the task, and is indeed embedded into the task, rather than diverting focus away from work, such as playing ping pong at lunch time. The authors differentiate playful work design from crafting because it is not about changing aspects of the job, but is about how one approaches specific tasks, either designing fun or designing competition into the tasks.

Playful work design, especially when it involves both designing fun and designing competition, leads to greater engagement, creativity, and task performance. A unique benefit of playful work design is that it seems especially protective of well-being in demanding contexts, such as in the case of platform workers who are often confronted with tough working conditions, workers during the height of the COVID-19 pandemic, or university professors facing high demands. The authors conclude with the observation that playful work design might be very powerful, but also quite volatile, and hence that "*the most sustainable use of playful work design would be to complement this strategy with other JD-R strategies, such as job design and job crafting.*" This is an apt way to conclude this section on work redesign.

Part 6: Future work

Reflecting on changes in the macro-context (Box D, Figure 1.1), the nature of work has shifted markedly in recent years, with an increase in digitalization, automation, remote work, and on-demand work. This theme has emerged in several of the chapters in this book up to this point. For example, in their chapter on performance, Ohly and Venz speculated that job complexity is likely to increase in many AI applications, with greater complexity being on the one hand motivating yet on the other hand cognitively taxing, therefore having mixed effects on performance. In Part 6, we delve more deeply into streams of research in relation to work design and future work.

In Chapter 19, **Nadine Bienefeld** and **Gudela Grote** make a strong case that work design theory and research can be used to proactively shape future

AI-enabled work. Consistent with Parker and Grote (2020), the authors argue there is a need to better investigate how AI and related technologies affect work design aspects, such as job autonomy, skill variety, and relational work, including understanding why the effects are sometimes positive and sometimes negative, depending on contingencies. The knowledge generated from such research can then be channeled into creating better quality human work when AI technologies are introduced.

Compellingly, Grote and Bienefeld urge us to consider even wider implications of AI for work design. The authors argue we need to examine how AI is changing whole occupations, not just jobs. For example, there has been a huge growth in the number of data scientists, yet there is also the possibility that AI might eventually make data scientists redundant. Such dramatic change highlights the importance of work designs that foster learning to help re-skill workforces so they are prepared not just for job transitions but occupational transitions. The scope of change with AI also raises questions as to how people maintain meaning if they ultimately need to work many fewer hours, what combinations of paid and unpaid work might arise, or what sorts of jobs will matter if people's livelihoods are secured by an unconditional basic income. Finally, the authors invite us to consider the work design of technology developers, especially given that technology is increasingly opaque, even for the developers themselves.

There have been radical shifts in employment paradigms, as unpacked in the comprehensive Chapter 20 by **James Duggan** and **Jérôme Sulbout**, with a vast growth in non-standard work arrangements, such as gig work in which digital platforms connect freelance workers with short-term task opportunities. Duggan and Sulbout delve deeply into the impacts for work design of two types of gig work: app-work and crowdwork. App-work occurs when workers provide on-demand services in local markets, such as Uber drivers or repair-services (e.g., TaskRabbit), whereas crowdwork occurs when workers provide remote and computer-based services, such as graphic design, anywhere in the world (e.g., Fiverr, Amazon Mechanical Turk). These types of gig work share some work design challenges. In both, for instance, the constant evaluation of performance and the pressure to maintain rankings undermines workers' autonomy in selecting tasks.

However, the different types of gig work also have unique challenges. For example, crowdwork is designed to be completed from anywhere in the world which can be socially isolating; and app-work, more so than crowdwork, is heavily directed by controlling algorithms in stark contrast to the promised autonomy of "being your own boss." Duggan and Sulbout discuss how the imperative to improve work quality is unlikely to come from the platform organizations themselves: "what represents *strategic value and innovation* for platform organizations, instead represents *complexity and injustice* for gig workers," although active resistance from workers, regulatory change, and more nuanced research may help to move the dial toward forms of gig work that benefit organizations and workers, preventing the emergence of a "new form of digital Taylorism."

Continuing this theme, **Xavier Parent-Rocheleau** (Chapter 21) turns to the implication of a specific type of digitalization, algorithmic management—a system of control in which algorithms are given the responsibility for making and executing decisions usually made by managers, such as task allocation and provision of performance feedback. While notorious in contexts like call centers, warehousing, and gig work, algorithmic management is spreading rapidly to manufacturing, transport, retail, care work, hotels, banking, engineering, and more, with evidence that as many as 35 percent of workers in Spain have at least some exposure to this form of automated management. One of the reasons this prevalence matters is because such systems significantly affect work design. Expanding on an earlier review of 50 work design studies by Parent-Rocheleau and Parker (2022), Parent-Rocheleau comes to a similar conclusion reached in the previous two chapters: that the effects of algorithmic management on work design are mixed and non-deterministic.

The author advocates the need to create better forms of algorithmic management through improved organizational choices, such as adopting a sociotechnical approach to designing technology (e.g., with more transparency and explainability), co-designing systems with workers, and supporting job crafting. In themes reminiscent of the chapter by Holman and Rafferty, as well as by Duggan and Sulbout, societal, political, and economic factors also influence design in this context. Improving policy and regulation, addressing issues such as whether workers in these systems are employees, self-employed contractors, or platform users (with different rights associated with each), and engaging in research and advocacy are identified as important ways forward.

Remote and hybrid work has increased massively in recent times due to the COVID-19 pandemic, as well as advances in technology. As **Bin Wang**, **Xiang Fang**, and **Yi Zhao** describe in Chapter 22, people increasingly no longer see virtual work as a "privilege" but as a right. In a comprehensive review, the authors discuss which work characteristics link the effects of virtual work practices with employee outcomes, or what they refer to as the *why* question. Continuing the theme of this part of the book, virtual work has upsides and downsides for work design, such as, on the one hand, reducing commuting demands and allowing more boundary control for managing home and family responsibilities, but on the other hand, increasing technology-related demands and often leading to inter-role conflict when home and work boundaries blur. These mixed effects imply moderators and boundary conditions, so, via a question about *when*, the authors review how different types of work are more or less suitable for virtual working. One example moderator is job complexity, with greater benefits of virtual work emerging for those who need time to concentrate to solve complex problems. But interdependence also matters—if those problems need to be solved collectively, then the value of virtual work can be reduced.

A further important shift in the literature is that instead of asking "Is virtual work effective?" or even "When is it effective?" scholars increasingly ask "How can effective virtual work be achieved?". To address this *how* question, the chapter's authors recommend proactively reconfiguring aspects of work design, the technology itself, and/or the capabilities of workers. For example, additional technical features could be designed for ICT systems to better support the coordination of interdependent virtual workers. These suggestions highlight the importance of adopting a longitudinal perspective to understand virtual work. Thus, over time, the effects of interventions to build virtual work capabilities or to change virtual work design need to be monitored, alongside naturally emerging external changes (such virtual work becoming the norm) to fully understand how to "make virtual work work."

So far, the focus of this part has been on changes in work brought about by technology and other forces. But the workforce is also changing. An aging population has long been a concern worldwide as individuals are living longer. People need to work longer to sustain a productive economy. In Chapter 23, **Robin Umbra** and **Ulrike Fassbender** focus on how work design can help to retain and support older workers in the workplace. In a systematic literature review of 158 distinct articles, the authors identified two overarching meta-theoretical perspectives on the topic. The first is the *retention-push approach*, focusing on changes *within an individual* that stimulate an older worker to either continue working or leave the workforce. As an example, some evidence supports the selection, optimization, and compensation framework, showing that older workers adapt as they age, such as by optimizing how they use their resources, thereby accommodating within-person changes. The second perspective is that *retention-pull perspective*, which is concerned with how situational factors—including work design—motivate older workers to continue working. Evidence supports this perspective as well, showing the role of job autonomy, job complexity, task characteristics, work context conditions, social support, feedback, and the interaction between demands and resources, for retaining older individuals.

What is striking from Umbra and Fassbender's review, however, is how rarely age has been systematically incorporated into models as a moderating factor. There is some evidence that positive work characteristics, like job autonomy, become more important as people age, but these studies are rare and, in the authors' terms, "only minimally reproducible." We know little about whether there are unique work design issues for older workers.

In Chapter 24, **Emily Campion** and **Michael Campion** turn the discussion of AI on its head and consider how AI can be applied to support the processes of job analysis and job design. Job analysis is the systematic identification of the tasks/activities people do in their work, as well as what skills, knowledge, abilities, or other attributes are needed to do those tasks and activities. As discussed in the chapters on work redesign, job analysis is often an important starting point prior to work redesign. But it is a labor-intensive process, involving synthesizing large amounts of information from observations, interviews, focus groups, surveys, and open-source job descriptions. Campion and Campion describe multiple diverse ways in which AI can assist in reviewing information, identifying subject matter experts, collecting job information, analyzing the data, and creating products (e.g., job descriptions). One simple example is that AI can be used to obtain and analyze data about tasks and skills from open-source archives of job data such as O*NET, from job advertisements, or from social media sites like Glassdoor.

Text analysis can also be applied to help understand how well work is designed, or how jobs might be redesigned. For example, dictionary approaches can be applied to job descriptions, open-ended text in surveys, or transcribed interviews to assess whether a job contains pertinent work characteristics or even whether people are engaging in various types of crafting. Text analysis may even surface inductively new work characteristics not currently captured on the basis that what people write and talk about tends to be what matters to them. Altogether, as Campion and Campion have observed, there is great potential for using text analysis and related methods for work design research and practice.

Conclusion

Finally, to conclude the book, the editorial team (**Fangfang Zhang**, **Caroline Knight**, **Florian E. Klonek**, and **Sharon K. Parker)** close the book by synthesizing some key ideas for future research. Each individual chapter includes recommendations for future research that relate to these key ideas and this final chapter synthesizes these and looks at some global suggestions for future research.

As we have shown, work design can be transformative, and it is this potential that we especially seek to understand, celebrate, and promote, in this book. We hope that the chapters contained herein inspire and guide your research and practice such that, in the next 100 years, we are not still lamenting an all-too-common phenomenon of poorly designed work.

References

Andrei, D. M., & Parker, S. K. (2018). Work design for performance: Expanding the criterion domain. In N. Anderson, D. S. Ones, H. K. Sinangil, & C. Viswesvaran (Eds.), *The SAGE handbook of industrial, work & organisational psychology: Organisational psychology* (pp. 357–377). SAGE.

Caspi, A., Roberts, B., & Shiner, R. L. (2005). Personality development: Stability and change. *Annual Review of Psychology 56*, 453–484.

Daniels, K., Gedikli, C., Watson, D., Semkina, A., & Vaughn, O. (2017). Job design, employment practices and well-being: A systematic review of intervention studies. *Ergonomics 60*(9), 1177–1196.

Demerouti, E., Bakker, A. B., Nachreiner, F., & Schaufeli, W. B. (2001). The job demands-resources model of burnout. *Journal of Applied Psychology 86*(3), 499–512. https://doi.org/10.1037/0021-9010.86.3.499

Fitzhugh, H., Woodard, R., & James, A. (2023). Recognising tensions, barriers and strategies for widening acceptance to public sociology engagement with businesses in the Good Jobs Project. British Sociological Society Conference, Manchester.

Grant, A. M. (2007). Relational job design and the motivation to make a prosocial difference. *Academy of Management Review 32*, 393–417. https://doi.org/10.5465/AMR.2007.24351328

Griffin, M. A., Neal, A., & Parker, S. K. (2007). A new model of work role performance: Positive behavior in uncertain and interdependent contexts. *Academy of Management Journal 50*(2), 327–347. https://doi.org/10.5465/AMJ.2007.24634438

The Guardian. (2020, 5 February). "I'm not a robot": Amazon workers condemn unsafe, grueling conditions at warehouse. https://www.theguardian.com/technology/2020/feb/05/amazon-workers-protest-unsafe-grueling-conditions-warehouse

Hackman, J. R., & Oldham, G. R. (1975). Development of the job diagnostic survey. *Journal of Applied Psychology 60*(2), 159–170. https://doi.org/10.1037/h0076546

Jurek, P., & Besta, T. (2021). Employees' self-expansion as a mediator between perceived work conditions and work engagement and productive behaviors. *Current Psychology 40*(6), 3048–3057.

Karasek, R. A., Jr. (1979). Job demands, job decision latitude, and mental strain: Implications for job redesign. *Administrative Science Quarterly 24*(2), 285–308. https://doi.org/10.2307/2392498McChesney

Knight, C., & Parker, S. K. (2021). How work redesign interventions affect performance: An evidence-based model from a systematic review. *Human Relations 74*(1), 69–104. https://doi.org/10.1177/0018726719865604

Langfred, C. W. (2000). The paradox of self-management: Individual and group autonomy in work groups. *Journal of Organizational Behavior 21*(5), 563–585.

McChesney, G. G. (1917). The psychology of efficiency. *Journal of Applied Psychology 1*(2), 176.

Parent-Rocheleau, X., & Parker, S. K. (2022). Algorithms as work designers: How algorithmic management influences the design of jobs. *Human Resource Management Review 32*(3), 1–14.

Parker, S. K. (2014). Beyond motivation: Job and work design for development, health, ambidexterity, and more. *Annual Review of Psychology 65*(1), 661–691. https://doi.org/10.1146/annurev-psych-010213-115208

Parker, S. K., & Grote, G. (2020). Automation, algorithms, and beyond: Why work design matters more than ever in a digital world. *Applied Psychology*. https://doi.org/10.1111/apps.12241

Parker, S. K., Andrei, D. M., & Van den Broeck, A. (2019). Poor work design begets poor work design: Capacity and willingness antecedents of individual work design behavior. *Journal of Applied Psychology 104*(7), 907–928. https://doi.org/10.1037/apl0000383

Parker, S. K., & Jorritsma, K. (2021). Good work design for all: Multiple pathways to making a difference. *European Journal of Work and Organizational Psychology 30*(3), 456–468. https://doi.org/10.1080/1359432X.2020.1860121

Parker, S. K., & Knight, C. (2024). The SMART model of work design: A higher order structure to help see the wood from the trees. *Human Resource Management 63*(2), 265–291.

Parker, S. K., Morgeson, F. P., & Johns, G. (2017). One hundred years of work design research: Looking back and looking forward. *Journal of Applied Psychology 102*(3), 403–420. https://doi.org/10.1037/apl0000106

Parker, S. K., Ward, M. K., & Fisher, G. G. (2021). Can high-quality jobs help workers learn new tricks? A multidisciplinary review of work design for cognition. *Academy of Management Annals 15*(2), 406–454. https://doi.org/10.5465/annals.2019.0057

Sweet, S., Sarkisian, N., Matz-Costa, C., & Pitt-Catsouphes, M. (2016). Are women less career centric than men? Structure, culture, and identity investments. *Community, Work & Family 19*(4), 481–500.

Taylor, F. W. (1911). Principles and methods of scientific management. *Journal of Accountancy 12*(2), 117–124.

Webber, A. (2024, 24 January). Amazon fined €32m for "excessive" employee monitoring. Personnel Today. https://www.personneltoday.com/hr/amazon-employee-monitoring-france/

PART 1

FOUNDATIONS OF WORK DESIGN

The Evolution of Work Design Theory and Research

Anja Van den Broeck, Lorenz Verelst, and Hans de Witte

Job design has a rich historical background, stretching back to the early days when people organized themselves for hunting, gathering food, or building monumental structures like the Aztec Temples. Wherever people collaborate to achieve a particular goal, they need to dissect the labor process into activities and tasks, integrate them into jobs, and divide these jobs between all workers (Puranam et al., 2014). In short, they need to design work. From a scientific point of view, work design can be defined as the content and organization of one's work tasks, activities, relationships, and responsibilities (Parker, 2014).

Within the current chapter, we aim to complement other excellent overviews of the work design literature (e.g., Parker, 2014; Parker, Holman, et al., 2017) by particularly focusing on the past and future of theory and research regarding motivational work design. First, we outline the background of motivational work design. We start by describing how scientific management, which is denoted as the first scientific study of work design, has led to the evolution of the social, organizational, and motivational research approaches in the literature on work design. We then elaborate on arguably the three most important motivational work design models that have dominated the work design literature: the Job Characteristics Model of J. Richard Hackman and Greg Oldham (1976), the Job Demand-Control Model of Robert Karasek (1979) and the Job Demands-Resources Model of Evangelia Demerouti and colleagues (2001). We then discuss how the principles behind these models may be critically evaluated and further extended to study the design of contemporary work from a motivational perspective.

Background of Motivational Work Design

To understand our current thinking on motivational work design, we need to go back to understand its background. We start off with explaining how the first

---

Anja Van den Broeck, et al., *The Evolution of Work Design Theory and Research*. In: *Transformative Work Design*. Edited by: Sharon K. Parker et al., Oxford University Press. © Society for Industrial and Organizational Psychology (2025). DOI: 10.1093/oso/9780197692554.003.0002

scientific approaches to work design, that were mostly mechanical in nature, gave rise to research examining work design from a social and organizational, as well as a motivational perspective.

Scientific management: Efficiency through alienation

Scientific management aimed to adopt a science-based approach to work to enhance efficiency. It flourished during the first Industrial Revolution, when technological revolutions enabled the automation of various job functions. Inspired by the work of Adam Smith (1776) who advocated for the division of labor, Frederick Winslow Taylor (1911) argued—as one of the advocates of scientific management—that ideal jobs should consist of single, highly simplified, and specialized activities that were repeated throughout the workday, minimizing wasted time and energy in between tasks (Campion & Thayer, 1988). Under this approach, employees were regarded as complementary components of the machinery and easily replaceable. Selection and training processes ensured a match between job demands and employees' abilities, and the set-up of tasks enabled employees to learn fast how to perform specific tasks according to prescribed procedures and standards. Supervisors were responsible for monitoring employees' actions, leading to a clear division between thinking and doing. Skilled managerial tasks done by management were separated from unskilled labor provided by employees. Employees' performance was rewarded based on their output (e.g., piecework), aligning their goal to earn money with the organization's goal of making profit. Because of the corresponding boost in efficiency, Taylorism soon found its way into administrative jobs. This movement opened the gates for bureaucracy characterized by high specialization, hierarchy, and formalization (Fayol, 1949; Mintzberg, 1980; Weber, 1978). Even today, mechanistic work design continues to influence the design of both manufacturing and service jobs in numerous organizations (Brandtner et al., 2024; Cordery & Parker, 2007; Monteiro & Adler, 2022).

One drawback of this mechanistic approach to work design was the decline in employee morale, and more mental and physical fatigue, as well as boredom, resulting in instances of sabotage (e.g., damaging a machine or withholding effort) and absenteeism (Linstead, 1985; Walker & Guest, 1952). The negative effects of scientific management eventually spurred the development of alternative, less mechanistic approaches to work design, focusing more on social and motivational factors.

Hawthorne studies: The importance of attitudes and social relations

To further investigate the implications of Taylorism, Elton Mayo (1933) did some experimental studies among a team of Western Electric Company workers, also known as the "Hawthorne studies." One of the key findings was that Tayloristic interventions aimed at determining optimal illumination levels or ideal working hours did not yield significant improvements in individual employee performance. In contrast, even when illumination levels were adjusted to the level of moonlight, production increased and continued to do so throughout the study period. This surprising outcome was attributed to the fact that the research team consulted and involved the employees. The sustained cooperation within teams and their open expression of ideas and feelings to management led to improved employee morale and efficiency. This underscores the influential role of individuals' attitudes and group norms in shaping employee behaviors, suggesting that they can have a strong impact on productivity, even stronger than individual rewards.

Socio-technical systems theory: The importance of systems and organizational structures

A comparable conclusion to the Hawthorne studies was drawn in the 1950s when researchers from the Tavistock Institute observed workers within the United Kingdom's coal mining industry. Contrary to the expected increase in productivity because of heightened operational efficiency, these scholars found that the introduction of the longwall machine—a high-power coal mining, cutting, and transporting system—did not increase productivity at all. In contrast, because it created very specialized jobs, mine workers no longer saw themselves as craftsmen, causing problems and errors that actually slowed down the mining process. The key takeaway of these studies is that technical aspects cannot be disentangled from the social or "human" aspects of work. These insights also form the fundamentals of socio-technical systems (STS) theory developed by Eric Trist and Ken Bamforth (1951) and further modernized throughout the years (Benders et al., 2000; de Sitter et al., 1997). Central to this theory is the idea of creating "simple" organizations and "complex" jobs. "Simple" organizations refer to minimizing hierarchy, internal control, and coordination needs, while "complex" jobs lead to meaningful work by re-integrating "thinking and doing." Ultimately, STS theory principles led to the development of autonomous working groups (also referred to as self-managing teams) in which employees are responsible for a whole range of tasks, with minimal coordination between these groups. STS theory has been applied in different settings, such as manufacturing (e.g., in Swedish car manufactories) and services (e.g., the healthcare sector) and provides valuable information for work design because it points out that technical systems (e.g., operation methods) can be seen as an antecedent of work design (Parker, Holman, et al., 2017). Nevertheless, STS theory has also been criticized, for example, because the dominant focus on groups or teams fails to capture the "uniqueness" of the individual employees, such as their needs and capabilities.

Herzberg's 2-factor Theory: The importance of individual employees' motivation

Around the same time as socio-technical thinking emerged in the United Kingdom, Frederick Herzberg developed an alternative to scientific management in the United States. He argued that people should be motivated from within and stated: "If I kick my dog, he will move . . . And when I want him to move again, what must I do? I must kick him again. But it is only when he has his own generator that we can talk about motivation" (Herzberg, 1968, p. 88). Herzberg then studied which factors in the context of work stimulate such internal motivation. He asked 200 engineers and accountants—relatively new jobs at the time—about the moments in their job that were either very satisfying or very unsatisfying.

Results revealed that dissatisfaction and satisfaction were two different states of mind. First, hygiene factors correspond with Abraham Maslow's lower-order needs that many species share, such as the need for security and social contact. They relate to company policies and administration, (relationship with the) supervisors, subordinates and colleagues, but also the work conditions, salary, status, and security. When these factors are absent or of poor quality, employees feel dissatisfied, while the presence of these factors may lead to a neutral situation. Interestingly, these factors are more extrinsic to work and some of them are more materialistic in nature. Second, the motivators correspond with Maslow's growth need of strength—unique to humans—and include feelings of achievement, recognition, the work itself, responsibility, advancement, and growth. Their presence leads to feelings of satisfaction among workers, while their absence associates with a neutral state. Motivators are intrinsic to work and are expected to be closely linked to the quality of one's work experience and one's work performance.

Herzberg proposed that jobs could be made more motivating by introducing job enlargement, job rotation, and, most notably, job enrichment. When jobs are enlarged, they are horizontally expanded, such that the core tasks of the employees are supplemented with tasks of similar difficulty. In the case of job rotation, the range of tasks per job is maintained, but people alternate between different jobs. This leads to more variety and less specialization or simplicity in the overall job experience. In the case of job enrichment, jobs are expanded vertically such that more difficult tasks or tasks with more responsibility are added. For example, in a grocery store, the job of a shelf stocker can be enlarged by making the person responsible for additional aisles, such that the employee gets to know other products. Job rotation may imply that workers rotate from one aisle to another or work some days a week in the bakery of the store, ensuring some variety and fostering further understanding of how the store operates. Finally, the job could be enriched by monitoring stock levels and making sure that products are ordered when stock is low and arranged in the best interest of the store. This will not only make the bakery workers' jobs more varied but also increase job autonomy and feedback.

Three Motivational Work Design Models

Over the course of the years, different motivational job design models have been developed. These tended to build or complement each other, leading to our current insights in what makes work truly motivational. Although various models have been documented, three have dominated the literature: the Job Characteristics Model of J. Richard Hackman and Greg Oldham (1976), the Job Demand-Control Model of Robert Karasek (1979), and the Job Demands-Resources Model of Evangelia Demerouti and colleagues (2001).

Hackman and Oldham's Job Characteristics Model

Hackman and Oldham (1975, 1976) developed the Job Characteristics Model (JCM) as a practical framework helping to assess the potential of jobs to motivate employees. They assumed that five job characteristics are important for employee outcomes because they foster three psychological states. These five core job characteristics are (1) *skill variety*, which pertains to the degree to which the job requires the use of different knowledge, skills, and talents; (2) *task identity*, which considers whether the job requires a worker to execute a task from the beginning to the end: (3) *task significance*, which is the degree to which a job has an impact on the work or life of other people inside or outside the organization; (4) *autonomy*, which refers to the degree to which the job offers freedom, independence, and the opportunity to make decisions (e.g., in how to execute one's tasks); and (5) *feedback*, which pertains to whether the job itself (rather

34 TRANSFORMATIVE WORK DESIGN

than a third party, such as a supervisor or customer) provides clear information to the employee about their level of effectiveness.

According to Hackman and Oldham, the five core job characteristics lead to three critical psychological states: experienced meaningfulness, experienced responsibility, and knowledge of results. Skill variety, task identity, and/or task significance lead to experienced meaningfulness, autonomy leads to experienced responsibility, and feedback from the task ensures knowledge of results. These critical psychological states then, first and foremost, increase employees' internal motivation, quality of work performance, and job satisfaction, and decrease absenteeism and turnover. Later versions shifted the focus from performance to efficiency and from absenteeism and turnover to growth satisfaction. However, it remains clear that Hackman and Oldham were not only concerned about employee well-being, but also with performance and bottom-line outcomes, such as absenteeism and turnover when designing the JCM.

Initially, the motivation potential of a job was seen as a multiplicative function based on a score on each core job characteristic. These scores were calculated via the Job Diagnostic Survey (1975), a measurement tool developed by Hackman and Oldham. Specifically, it was determined that jobs should contain feedback and autonomy, as well as at least one of the three remaining aspects (i.e., skill variety, task identity, and task significance). However, later it was found that the motivating potential of a job can also be captured by averaging the scores for all the different job characteristics. While in the first model, jobs with low autonomy would automatically be considered not motivating, in the latter model low levels of autonomy could be compensated for by high levels of task feedback.

Notably, Hackman and Oldham also acknowledged that not everyone would benefit equally from experiencing the core job characteristics. For employees who have a low growth need strength and thus are less eager to develop themselves through work, the job characteristics have a lower impact on the critical psychological states, which in turn are less strongly related to the outcomes. The same holds for employees who have low skills, knowledge, ability, and overall satisfaction with the work context.

Meta-analytic studies have provided support for the model's fundamental principles, demonstrating that motivational job characteristics lead to favorable attitudinal and behavioral outcomes through the critical psychological states (Fried & Ferris, 1987; Humphrey et al., 2007). The JCM spurred the research and interventions on how to make jobs more motivating. Their sole focus on motivation, however, caused them to neglect all the demanding aspects of work that may affect employees. This eventually inspired the formulation of a new highly influential work design model.

Karasek's Job Demand-Control (Support) Model

During his PhD, Karasek was surprised to see theoretical models talking about motivation and models considering work stress developed independently from each other. He sought a way to integrate both in his Job Demand-Control Model (JDCM) (Karasek, 1979), which was later expanded to the Job Demand-Control Support Model (JDCSM) (Karasek & Theorell, 1990). The JDCM assumes that stress and growth can be understood by looking at the interplay of job demands and job control.

Karasek's category of "job demands" is mostly known for including the amount of work that needs to be done in a specific time period (workload or time pressure). However, this category also includes conflicting role demands, being interrupted, cognitive demands, being unable to progress work because one must wait for others, some physical demands (e.g., heavy lifting, awkward positions), and job insecurity (e.g., job security and career opportunities). The category of positive job aspects is simplified to "job control," which includes decision or task authority (having the freedom to make one's own decisions), skill discretion (i.e., the degree to which one can use and develop one's skills at work) and task variety. In studies, the JDCM has mostly been limited to studying workload (as a demand) versus task autonomy (as job control). According to Karasek, high and low levels of job demands and job control may combine into four different types of jobs. When both job demands and job control are high, jobs are active and stimulate growth and learning. Managers and academics typically have such active jobs. In contrast, low job demands and low job control result in "passive jobs," such as those of security guards at the entrance of a residential palace. Such jobs require only few efforts from people, but also do not allow them to use their skills and/or exercise autonomy. Low demands and high job control, in contrast, result in low strain jobs, characterized by autonomy and skill utilization without high levels of workload. Successful writers may, for example, decide on their pace of publishing while simultaneously using their full skill potential. Finally, high demands and low job control are determinants of high strain jobs, typical for factory workers on assembly lines.

Going from passive to active jobs allows one to move on the learning axis, leading people to grow by exercising their skills and learning new things and competencies ("growth hypothesis"). Low strain and high strain jobs are situated on a strain axis, with high strain jobs causing physical and psychological illness ("strain hypothesis"). These two may also influence each other over time, such that learning and development may help to inhibit strain (perceptions), while the accumulation of strain forestalls learning over time. Interestingly, the interplay between job demands and job control may open several opportunities to redesign work. In high strain jobs, job demands may

36 TRANSFORMATIVE WORK DESIGN

be lowered to decrease employee strain but may lead to passive jobs in which growth is forestalled. Increasing job control in such jobs may help to shift into active jobs, in which employees are better equipped to deal with job demands. However, the empirical studies suggest that the effects of job demands and job control should be studied from an additive (i.e., their joint main effects, which are expected to be independent) rather than a multiplicative perspective (i.e., studying their interaction effect) (Häusser et al., 2010; van der Doef & Maes, 1998).

Later, Karasek, in collaboration with Tores Theorell, added a social dimension and considered the importance of social support (Karasek & Theorell, 1990). Such support could come from the supervisor taking a people-oriented (e.g., showing concern) or task-oriented (e.g., good organizer) perspective while not displaying negative behaviors (e.g., being hostile) or it could come from colleagues providing practical (e.g., when coworkers collaborate) or emotional (e.g., being friendly) support and refraining from asocial behavior (e.g., not being hostile). Receiving such support has a beneficial impact and may buffer the adverse effects of high demands and low control (Karasek & Theorell, 1990).

The JDCM spurred quite a bit of research and has been dominant in the field of occupational health psychology and medical sciences for decades. Systematic reviews and meta-analyses generally show consistent evidence for the strain hypothesis, suggesting deterioration of health and well-being among high strain jobs (de Lange et al., 2003; Häusser et al., 2010; Stansfeld & Candy, 2006; van der Doef & Maes, 1998). Studies have dominantly examined the strain hypothesis, whereas the growth hypothesis received considerably less research attention, which stimulated the emergence of a new model.

Bakker and Demerouti's Job Demands-Resources Model

The Job Demands-Resources (JD-R) model was developed from the PhD of Demerouti and her supervisors, Arnold B. Bakker and Wilmar Schaufeli (Demerouti et al., 2001). Throughout the years, the model grew into what is now coined as "Job Demands-Resources Theory" (Bakker & Demerouti, 2017). The JD-R model started from the observation that work design research either adopted an a theoretical laundry list of job characteristics or worked with a fixed and rather limited set of variables put forward by two dominant work design models: the JDCM of Karasek, previously described, and the effort–reward imbalance model (Siegrist, 1996). This latter model assumes that stress—often evidenced in terms of cardiovascular problems—arises when employees receive few rewards (i.e., money, esteem, and job security/career opportunities) for the efforts they need to put into the work (i.e., the job demands and/or imposed obligations), particularly when employees are overcommitted to work.

At its core, the JD-R model assumes that it is important to study both employees' health and well-being and that these may be influenced by a diverse range of work characteristics, depending on the job and profession. However, across this wide variety of work characteristics, some general theoretical principles can be applied. First, Bakker and Demerouti assume that work characteristics can be divided into two categories: job demands and job resources. *Job demands* are defined as the physical, psychological, social, or organizational aspects of work that require sustained physical, cognitive, or emotional efforts of workers and are therefore associated with certain physiological and/or psychological costs (Bakker & Demerouti, 2007). They can be situated at the level of the task (e.g., interruptions), work (e.g., workload), team (e.g., role conflict), and the organization (e.g., reorganizations). *Job resources* are defined as those physical, psychological, social, or organizational aspects of work that buffer the job demands and their psychological and physical costs, are extrinsically motivating because they are functional in achieving work goals, build self-efficacy as well as social exchange, and/or are intrinsically valuable because they stimulate growth, learning, and satisfaction of the basic psychological needs of autonomy, competence, and relatedness. Also job resources can be found at the level of the task (e.g., feedback), work (e.g., autonomy), team (e.g., social support), and the organization (e.g., career possibilities).

Another general theoretical principle of the JD-R model is that job demands and resources explain two different processes. First, job demands lead to a *health-impairment process*. Building on other models, such as the stress adaption model (Selye, 1956) and the state regulation model of compensatory control (Hockey, 1997), the health-impairment process describes how job demands require increased effort, which might deplete workers' physical, emotional, and cognitive resources. In turn, this elicits a stress process. Unsurprisingly, job demands can be seen as the main cause of burnout, which is typically regarded as a syndrome composed of three different aspects: exhaustion (i.e., being mentally extremely fatigued), cynicism (i.e., taking a distant attitude toward work), and reduced personal efficacy (i.e., not feeling competent anymore) Maslach et al., 2001). Notably, job demands are not necessarily negative, but they become stressful when they exceed employees' capacities and when employees can no longer recover from putting in extra effort to face these demands. Second, job resources spark a *motivational process* as they help to satisfy workers' basic psychological needs and boost work engagement. The latter is defined as a positive affective-cognitive state of fully functioning, characterized by vigor (i.e., high

38   TRANSFORMATIVE WORK DESIGN

mental energy and resilience), dedication (i.e., high involvement and sense of significance), and absorption (i.e., total involvement and forgetting everything around) (Schaufeli et al., 2002).

In line with the conservation of resources theory (Hobfoll, 1989), the JD-R model further assumes that job demands and job resources have a multiplicative impact on workers' well-being (such as burnout and work engagement). First, job resources buffer (the detrimental impact of) job demands on stress as they reduce the health-impairment process. For example, workers who have sufficient autonomy will be better able to handle colliding deadlines as they can reprioritize as necessary. Second, job demands boost the positive effect of job resources on work engagement. For example, training, feedback, and opportunities for recovery (as job resources) will be more 'useful' when workers are regularly confronted with job demands.

Another theoretical proposition of the JD-R model is that personal resources impact the role of job demands on workers' well-being. Personal resources are defined as malleable, lower-order, cognitive-affective, personal aspects relating to resilience and contributing to individuals' potential to successfully control and influence the environment (Hobfoll et al., 2003). In terms of personal resources within the JD-R model, researchers have mainly investigated self-efficacy, optimism, resilience, or organizational based self-esteem. Personal resources may function as antecedents of (the perception of) job demands and job resources, explain why job resources give rise to engagement (i.e., mediation), and buffer for (the negative consequences of) job demands (Xanthopoulou et al., 2007). For example, studies have shown that having a lot of job resources increases people's hardiness, which then associates with more engagement and lower levels of burnout (Coso-de-Zuniga et al., 2020).

Throughout the years some major theoretical advancements have been made within the JD-R model. Although the JD-R model initially put burnout and work engagement as focal outcomes, various other outcomes have been tested. These include aspects of employee health and well-being (e.g., depression, psychosomatic complaints), job attitudes (organizational commitment, change readiness) and work-related behavior (performance, absenteeism) (Van den Broeck et al., 2013). Moreover, more recently, researchers have started paying attention to how employees themselves may proactively optimize their job demands and job resources via job crafting, or how workers may engage in maladaptive self-regulation activities when job demands are too high. Finally, researchers have also started describing gain and loss cycles: work engagement may foster proactive behaviors (such as job crafting), providing more resources (gain cycle), while high stress might lead to even more job demands through increased self-undermining.

Key insights from the motivational work design models

The three work design models described have arguably dominated the literature on motivational work design. These models offer distinct yet complementary insights into the important aspects of work design and its implications for employee motivation, well-being, and performance. Hackman and Oldham's JCM emphasizes the role of specific job characteristics in fostering critical psychological states, ultimately enhancing motivation, satisfaction, and behavioral outcomes. Karasek's model explores the interplay between job demands and control, categorizing jobs based on their potential for strain and growth. Finally, Bakker and Demerouti's JD-R model introduces the overarching categories of job demands and resources, primarily elucidating their differential effects on burnout and work engagement. Together, these models provide a comprehensive framework for understanding the multifaceted nature of work design and its impact on individuals and—ultimately—organizations. Yet, they all individually and collectively also suffer from several limitations. In the next section, we further discuss these limitations and those of the motivational work design literature in general.

Future Directions for Motivational Work Design Theory

This section casts a critical eye on the current state of the motivational work design literature and provides suggestions for future work. First, we suggest that the work design literature may benefit from a more careful study as to whether everyone may indeed benefit from motivational work design. Second, we elaborate on the current scope of the studied work characteristics and suggest how this scope can be expanded. Third, we tap into how the outcomes and processes can be broadened to further understand the impact of motivational work design on workers' functioning. Fourth, we hint at the role of personal characteristics within motivational work design theory and discuss how our current approach may overlook important individual influences. Finally, we outline how the study of the antecedents of work design may be a valuable paradigm shift to help us understand how work design may emerge.

Clarifying the assumptions of the benefits of motivational work design

The traditional work design models build on the assumption that employees are inherently growth-oriented, active, and willing to put aside their own

40 TRANSFORMATIVE WORK DESIGN

self-interest for the benefit of more collective goals, such as those of the organization. This perspective aligns with Douglas McGregor's (1960) Theory Y and stands in sharp contrast to the Theory X perspective assuming that employees are inherently lazy and solely driven by self-interest, which is the working hypothesis underlying mechanistic work design. Mechanistic work design heavily relies on (monetary) rewards and punishments, such as layoffs, to stimulate employees. In contrast, a Theory Y perspective emphasizes creating a stimulating environment. Applying the principles of motivational work design is considered crucial for fostering people's inherent growth nature, as suggested by motivational work design theory. Starting from Herzberg's 2-factor theory, the work itself was seen as a strong source of motivation. Everyone is thus assumed to benefit from well-designed motivational work. Moreover, the JDCM and the JD-R model even suggest that motivating jobs may lead to an automatic growth spiral in which employee motivation and growth development lead to ever-increasing feelings of mastery. In turn, these feelings have the potential to offset stress.

As such, these models cannot explain the common understanding among non-experts and researchers that motivational characteristics, such as social support or autonomy, may not always be beneficial (Biron & van Veldhoven, 2016; Deelstra et al., 2003). However, such findings align with research providing evidence for a "too much of a good thing effect" in the workplace (Pierce & Aguinis, 2013). This idea is also corroborated in terms of work design by Peter Warr (2013) in his vitamin model. Within this model, Warr suggests that some work characteristics, metaphorically labeled as "vitamins," may after a certain point become toxic such that with a further additional increase, detrimental effects prevail. These "additional decrement" (AD) vitamins include several work characteristics, including, among others, motivational aspects such as the opportunity for personal control, skill use and acquisition, variety, and contact with others. In addition, according to Warr, other job characteristics may lose their motivational potential after a certain point, such that an increase has no longer beneficial effects. These work characteristics—which thus have a constant effect on employee functioning after a certain point—include motivational aspects such as availability of money, supportive supervision, and career opportunities and equity. Where exactly these variables reach their inflection point depends on individual characteristics, such as overall job satisfaction.

Even though Warr's vitamin model has appeared in textbooks on work design (e.g., Peeters et al., 2013), it is less prominent in the research on work design. Research in the realm of this model could, however, shed more light on the interesting question of whether (increases in) motivational work characteristics are always beneficial. Such studies seem warranted given the laymen's assumption that some employees may prefer and benefit from mechanistic work designs (e.g., executing relatively simple tasks and relinquishing control).

Broadening the scope of the studied job characteristics

In general, the (research in the realm of the) classic motivational work design models restrict themselves to a limited set of job characteristics that are deemed most influential for employee well-being and productivity. Although this adds to the simplicity of the models, some valuable other aspects are neglected. First, it is interesting that some aspects featured in particular models have become neglected in subsequent models. For example, the JCM included a rich variety of motivational characteristics. However, when the JDCM integrated this motivational approach with the stress perspective, it reduced the number of motivational factors being studied to what fits the broader category of job control. Herein, for example, only one determinant of experienced meaningfulness (i.e., variety) was included, while others (i.e., task identity and task significance) were neglected. This is unfortunate because meaningful work, broadly defined as work that is personally significant and worthwhile (e.g., Pratt & Ashforth, 2003), is an important aspect of people's working lives (Rosso et al., 2010). Meta-analytical results indicate that meaningful work strongly relates to various aspects of workers' well-being (e.g., work engagement), attitudes (e.g., commitment), and behaviors (e.g., organizational citizenship behaviors), and spills over to the experience of life satisfaction and general health (Allan et al., 2019). By no longer paying as much attention to task identity and significance as identified by the JCM, we may miss out. Indeed, although meaning in work may be experienced in various ways (Lysova et al., 2019), having jobs that are consciously designed to promote a sense of purpose and positive impact on others is a substantial contributor to experienced meaning (Allan, 2017; Grant, 2008, 2012). Trying to enhance experienced meaning through work design may be an even better alternative than leaders trying to convey the added value of one's work, as such an input may be too abstract, distant, or vague, while the effects of task significance are more direct (Lysova et al., 2019). As such, this is an excellent example of how work design might be a substitute for leadership, or might be even more beneficial (Kerr & Jermier, 1978).

Second, it is noteworthy that work design research predominantly concentrates on a general set of job characteristics related to the content of work, while comparatively less emphasis has been placed on aspects less directly connected to the work content. For example, empirical studies within the work design literature mainly focus on traditional job demands and resources, which are already featured in Karasek's model (i.e., workload, autonomy, skill use) (Van den Broeck et al., 2013). However, aspects concerning social relations, remuneration, and work environmental aspects have been relatively overlooked. This is intriguing given that classic motivational work design models do mention these aspects. For example, although Herzberg (1968) argued that factors related to the content of work were most influential in increasing employee satisfaction, taking care of the other aspects was deemed essential to avoid employee malfunctioning. Hackman and Oldham (1976) followed this route. They stressed the importance of the work content at the core of their model yet assumed in their quintessential paper that social support matters too. In turn, the JD-R model aimed to expand this line of work by suggesting that job demands and job resources can be related to one's tasks and thus the content of the work but can also be related to factors at the level of one's roles, teams, and even the wider organization. Taking this to heart would allow future research to take a broader view of which factors influence employee outcomes, for example, by also considering aspects such as ergonomic hazards, privacy in the workspace (Haapakangas et al., 2018), leadership (Inceoglu et al., 2018), and organizational support (Zhou et al., 2022).

Interestingly, other—perhaps less well-known—models and questionnaires in addition to these classic models have substantially broadened and innovated the scope of work characteristics studied, while also accounting for the changing world of work (e.g., Grant et al., 2011; Humphrey et al., 2007, Morgeson & Humphrey, 2006). For example, Adam Grant and colleagues (2011) and Stephen E. Humphrey and colleagues (2007) also pay attention to cognitive factors (e.g., information processing, job complexity, problem-solving) and social characteristics (e.g., interdependence and interactions outside the organization), which are increasingly important within contemporary jobs. Moreover, by measuring autonomy in terms of work scheduling, decision making, and work methods, Frederick P. Morgeson and Humphrey (2006) provide an example of how job characteristics may be measured in a more nuanced way. An excellent example in this regard is also the recently developed SMART model of work design (Parker & Knight, 2024). Based on the described motivational work design models, the SMART model identifies five higher-order types of work characteristics: stimulating work characteristics (task variety, skill variety, information processing requirements, and problem-solving requirements), mastery work characteristics (job feedback, feedback from others, and role clarity), autonomous work characteristics (decision-making autonomy, timing autonomy, and method autonomy), relational work characteristics (social support, task significance, and beneficiary contact), and tolerable work characteristics (low levels of role overload, work–home conflict, and role conflict). This model allows the study of a broad range of job characteristics in a comprehensive way.

Third, it is intriguing to see that, for decades, work design research has, more or less, been centered around the same work characteristics. This raises the vital question of whether our theories and measurements can capture "new" work characteristics that have emerged due to the technologization of work processes (e.g., AI, robotics, big data, etc.) and work itself (e.g., telework, platform work) (Parker & Grote, 2022). Some scholars seem to suggest that the work characteristics featuring in the classic work design models previously noted can indeed explain the impact of fundamental technological changes in the workplace (e.g., telework [Gajendran & Harrison, 2007], communication technology [Wang et al., 2020], or AI [Tursunbayeva & Renkema, 2023]). Yet, others suggest that we need to take a (slightly) different approach when we want to understand how technological changes impact work design. For example, Monideepa Tarafdar and colleagues (2019) suggest that the stressful impact of technology should be understood by examining specific factors, such as techno-overload, techno-uncertainty, techno-insecurity, techno-invasion, and techno-complexity, rather than more general work characteristics (e.g., workload, job insecurity). Accordingly, future work can pay more attention to the question of whether existing work design models can still capture work characteristics of newly emerging jobs or changing jobs, or whether newer work design models should include different or other work characteristics. Such research could use the two-step approach as advocated by Demerouti and colleagues (2001): first examine which (new) job characteristics are at stake in a particular situation using qualitative, exploratory research designs, then tap into the relative importance of these job characteristics using quantitative methods.

Finally, we might have missed out on novel insights into which job characteristics matter and why not all work design theories and models have received research attention on a global level. Specifically, only a few—and dominantly Western—models are researched by scholars throughout the world. For example, models such as the JDCM and the JD-R model have been more influential in European literature, while the JCM has arguably been more dominant in American literature. In addition, some models have never been embedded within the international work design literature. For example, the Demand Induced Strain Compensation Model (DISC) was developed in the Netherlands and Germany by Jan de Jonge and Christian Dormann (2003). One of the core propositions of this model is that job demands and job resources are most likely to interact if they match. For example, emotional resources (e.g., emotional support) are more powerful in buffering emotional demands (e.g., difficult customers) compared to cognitive resources. The model further states that this buffering effect is most likely to have a substantial impact on emotional outcomes (e.g., emotional exhaustion) compared to other outcomes. Although the model received empirical support for its core propositions (de Jonge et al., 2004), it has not been widely used in the work design literature.

44   TRANSFORMATIVE WORK DESIGN

Moreover, even though the current work design models have been shown to be relevant across the globe, a more international non-Western voice would be welcome so that we do not miss out on job characteristics that may have primordial importance within other cultures. A more culturally diverse perspective on work design may enable us to take a more inclusive view (Holtbrügge, 2013). Future work could, for example, look at the value of "ubuntu" (i.e., one's orientation to the broader community prominent in South Africa) or could examine whether the Asian "guanxi" (i.e., as a way to relate to others based on trust and reciprocity [Zhang et al., 2017]) can be considered as a job resource or a job demand (Tauetsile, 2021). As a third example, future work design research may try to understand whether people adopting the Indian "jugaad principle" (i.e., seeing unconventional frugal innovation where others do not see opportunities) are more likely to recognize job resources where others do not (Sivarajan et al., 2021).

Reconsidering the scope of work design outcomes: Going beyond well-being

The work design literature may also benefit from a broader perspective regarding the outcomes and processes leading to them. Throughout the evolution of the work design models, various outcomes have been studied. While Hackman and Oldham (1976) discussed a comprehensive set of outcomes, including attitudes (e.g., job satisfaction) and behaviors (e.g., performance, turnover, absenteeism), the JDCM limited this set of outcomes to a general measure of growth, as well as strain as the most important outcome from prior stress models (Karasek, 1979). Within the JD-R model (Demerouti et al., 2001), well-being again occupies a central position: burnout and work engagement are considered essential mediating mechanisms to which job demands and job resources may impact other outcomes (i.e., performance, turnover, and absenteeism).

Regrettably, the focus on well-being in the literature on work design seems to have pushed other relevant outcomes of the design of work to the background. This is unfortunate because it may lead to the erroneous conclusion that changing work design may benefit predominantly (if not only) the well-being of employees, and is less relevant for other outcomes, such as employees' learning and development, ambidexterity (i.e., the possibility to perform well and look for new opportunities for growth [Parker, 2014]), and performance (Knight & Parker, 2021). These latter outcomes may be a primordial concern for organizations and can be considered as distal to work design (e.g., Grant et al., 2011). To encourage organizations to pay closer attention to the design of work, more scholarly work is needed on the relevance of work design for a broader set of outcomes including work performance.

Investigating work performance as outcome of motivational work design assumes a different approach compared to investigating performance in scientific management (Cerasoli et al., 2014). In particular, in scientific management, performance is typically the result of small repetitive behaviors of employees and operationalized as the number of produced goods or services. Such performance is typically not dependent upon unique characteristics or talents of the individual employee, but mostly determined by technology. It can be evaluated by counting discrete outputs such as piecemeal work (e.g., the number of references checked). Within motivational work design, the focus is more on types of performance linked to complex work (e.g., writing a paper) which is determined more by employees' personal investment, and needs to be evaluated primarily by paying attention to the quality of performance (e.g., creativity, lack of errors made). While the quantity of performance was primordial in scientific management where employees operated alongside machines, the quality of performance has gained importance in Western economies that shifted from production work to knowledge and service work (Gittell & Bamber, 2010).

Focus on the individuals: Personal characteristics affecting the impact of job characteristics

The various motivational work design models acknowledge that employees' personal characteristics (e.g., resilience, self-esteem) influence the impact of job characteristics. For example, as mentioned earlier, personal characteristics are studied as antecedents of job demands and resources (in the JD-R), mediators of the impact of job resources (in the JD-R), and moderators of job demands (in the JD-R) or motivational characteristics (in the JCM), or outcomes (in the JDCM). Yet, we see at least three ambiguities in the current literature that future research could address. First, some roles may be neglected. Over the years, various scholars extended the roles of personal resources by assuming they may also intensify the effect of job demands and attenuate the impact of job resources (e.g., act as a personal demand [Vander Elst et al., 2019]) or boost the impact of job resources (Van den Broeck et al., 2015) or mediate the impact of job demands (Van den Broeck et al., 2018). In short, the classic work design models seem to underestimate the roles that people's personal traits may play in the experience and effects of job characteristics. Second, it remains unclear which personal characteristics may be related to work design and within what specific timeframe. Existing studies have shown that work characteristics may not only impact individuals' fluctuating traits (e.g., optimism), as assumed by the JD-R model and the JDCM, but also their more stable personalities. Chia-Huei Wu and colleagues (2020), for example, reported that chronic job insecurity was associated with higher neuroticism and lower agreeableness over the course of four years. In line with this study, future research could further unravel what other personal characteristics may affect work design and within what timeframe.

Second, a particularly promising avenue for future research may be the notion that a worker's appraisal of an objective work situation influences their perceived job characteristics. One reason why the objective environment may lead to divergent perceptions of work characteristics builds from stress appraisal theory (Lazarus & Folkman, 1984). According to this theory, employees may continuously evaluate whether a situation is irrelevant, benign, or stressful. When relevant, a situation can subsequently be appraised as either a challenge, suggesting that one can learn from the situation, or as a stressor, indicating that the situation is likely to be harmful and employees should invest in trying to cope with it. Depending on this evaluation, job characteristics may then have rather benign or rather detrimental effects. These assumptions are echoed within the challenge-hindrance framework (Crawford et al., 2010; LePine, 2022). Originally, this framework assumed that some job characteristics (e.g., red tape, role conflict) were hindrances or energy-consuming roadblocks that hinder goal achievement, while other job characteristics (e.g., workload, cognitive demands) were job challenges, or issues that require sustained effort but also offer opportunities to learn and develop (Van den Broeck et al., 2010). Further developments of this framework showed that employees' appraisals differ and matter for how these job characteristics influence employee functioning. When employees appraise job characteristics such as role ambiguity or workload as hindering, there is a negative impact on work-related outcomes. In contrast, when employees appraise a situation as a challenge, it may not be that detrimental to their functioning (Webster et al., 2011). All this highlights that an objective work environment may not be inherently positive or negative, but that personal factors may play a role in how the situation is perceived and impact employee functioning. It would be interesting to see whether personal factors may also help employees perceive more motivational work characteristics by appraising the objective work environment as highly positive and benign. For example, it would be interesting to uncover whether personal characteristics may help employees to see opportunities for skill use in any assigned task and autonomy when supervisors provide little guidance.

Changing the view: Studying the antecedents of work design

The classic work design models all focus on how job characteristics impact employee functioning. However, how these job characteristics themselves emerge is less clear. In overviewing the literature, Sharon K. Parker, Anja Van den Broeck and colleagues (2017) proposed a model of the potential antecedents of work design. This model illustrates that such influencing factors occur at all levels including the individual employee (e.g., age, gender), team (e.g., leadership, group norms), organization (e.g., HR systems, technology, structure), occupation (e.g., law, values) levels, as well as at the level of the national (e.g., national economy and culture) and international (e.g., globalization, market liberalization) environment. While technology—as one of these influencing factors—has received considerable research attention (Parker & Grote, 2022; Wang et al., 2020), there is still a lot to learn about the other influential factors, such as the structure of the organization.

Importantly, these influencing factors may not have a deterministic impact on workers. In contrast, their effects are likely to be influenced by the actions of the employees themselves, as well as managers and supervisors who can alter the work design of their employees. While there is a rich body of literature on how employees (re)design work (e.g., Tims & Bakker, 2010; Wrzesniewski & Dutton, 2001), research on the role of managers in job (re-)design is still in its infancy. This is regrettable, as Herzberg pointed to the role of managers to improve employee work design many years ago. In his 1968 work, he mapped out a step-by-step plan on how managers could consider ways to enrich people's work, but that feelings of discomfort and anxiety may prevent them from doing so.

Leaders matter when investigating the antecedents of job characteristics. Employees who perceive their leaders, for example, as transformational (Piccolo & Colquitt, 2006) or autonomy-supportive (Sarmah et al., 2022) report more motivational job characteristics and fewer demanding aspects of work. The processes through which this occurs are less clear: leaders might influence either employees' perceived or objective job characteristics, or both. On the one hand, following social information processing theory (Salanic & Pfeffer, 1978), leaders may influence employees' evaluations and perceptions of their job characteristics by managing the social construction of work and the sensemaking processes that inform their judgement (Maitlis & Lawrence, 2007). For example, leaders might help employees see a newly assigned project as an additional opportunity for development, rather than just an addition to one's workload. On the other hand, leaders may also influence employees' objective job characteristics by allocating tasks differently. For example, leaders might assign a greater or fewer number of projects to a particular employee, or carefully target projects that offer new learning opportunities to a particular subordinate. Indeed, leaders have formal decision-making power around the division of work and task allocation, either strategically or on an ad-hoc basis.

48 TRANSFORMATIVE WORK DESIGN

The paucity of research adopting this perspective, however, shows that people are not predominantly inclined to make work more motivational. Rather, the contrary turns out to be true: students (Campion & Stevens, 1991) as well as professionals (Parker et al., 2019) tend to develop rather simple jobs. This is because people see such an approach as the more logical or rational thing to do. However, in some cases, participants in these studies did create motivating work. This is especially the case when people have expertise and knowledge in work design, task autonomy, and/or are open to experiences. Yet, more research is needed to investigate whether these factors also apply to leaders, or whether other factors might come into play. More insights would also be welcome on how managers mitigate the aforementioned multi-level, more distal antecedents of work design such as technology and globalization.

Conclusion

Mechanistic work design marked the beginning of the scientific study of work design. The way it treated people resulted in several different counter-movements that focused on deeply human aspects such as attitudes and social relations (i.e., developed from the Hawthorne studies), the importance of autonomy within organizational structures and processes (i.e., outlined in STS theory), and employee motivation (i.e., as marked by the 2-factor Theory of Herzberg). The latter approach gave rise to a whole set of motivational models such as the JCM of Hackman and Oldham (1976), the JDCM of Karasek (1979) and the JD-R model of Demerouti and colleagues (2001). These models provide a rich perspective of how work can be made more stimulating (and less demanding). Although Maureen Ambrose and Carol Kulik stated many years ago, in 1999, that we know all there is to know about work design, many issues are left untapped today. Traditional models were rich, but the way in which the work design literature evolved may not always have done justice to the original research, and changes in the world of work open up opportunities for new research avenues. We hope that the classic motivational work design models may still be "old friends," but that new insights in the exiting area of work design research may provide us with "new faces" as well.

References

Allan, B. A. (2017). Task significance and meaningful work: A longitudinal study. *Journal of Vocational Behavior 102*, 174–182. https://doi.org/10.1016/j.jvb.2017.07.011

Allan, B. A., Batz-Barbarich, C., Sterling, H. M., & Tay, L. (2019). Outcomes of meaningful work: A meta-analysis. *Journal of Management Studies 56*(3), 500–528. https://doi.org/10.1111/joms.12406

Ambrose, M. L., & Kulik, C. (1999). Old friends, new faces: Motivation research in the 1990. *Journal of Management 25*(3), 231–292. https://doi.org/10.1016/S0149-2063(99)00003-3

Bakker, A. B., & Demerouti, E. (2007). The Job Demands-Resources model: State of the art. *Journal of Managerial Psychology 22*(3), 309–328. https://doi.org/10.1108/02683940710733115

Bakker, A. B., & Demerouti, E. (2017). Job demands–resources theory: Taking stock and looking forward. *Journal of Occupational Health Psychology 22*(3), 273–285. https://doi.org/10.1037/ocp0000056

Benders, J. H., Doorewaard, H., & Poutsma, E. (2000). Modern socio-technology: Set by de Sitter. In M. Beyerlein (Ed.), Work teams: Past, present, and future (pp. 169–180). Kluwer Academic. https://doi.org/10.1007/978-94-015-9492-9_10.

Biron, M., & van Veldhoven, M. (2016). When control becomes a liability rather than an asset: Comparing home and office days among part-time teleworkers. *Journal of Organizational Behavior 37*, 1317–1337. https://doi.org/10.1002/job

Brandtner, C., Powell, W. W., & Horvath, A. (2024). From iron cage to glass house: Repurposing of bureaucratic management and the turn to openness. *Organization Studies 45*(2), 193–221. https://doi.org/10.1177/01708406231200727

Campion, M. A., & Stevens, M. J. (1991). Neglected questions in job design: How people design jobs, task-job predictability, and influence of training. *Journal of Business and Psychology 6*(2), 169–191. https://doi.org/10.1007/BF01126707

Campion, M. A., & Thayer, P. W. (1988). Job design: Approaches, outcomes and trade-offs. *Organizational Dynamics 15*(3), 66–79. https://doi.org/10.1016/0090-2616(87)90039-8

Cerasoli, C. P., Nicklin, J. M., & Ford, M. T. (2014). Intrinsic motivation and extrinsic incentives jointly predict performance: A 40-year meta-analysis. *Psychological Bulletin 140*(4), 980–1008. https://doi.org/10.1037/a0035661

Cordery, J., & Parker, S. K. (2007). Organization of work. In P. F. Boxall, J. Purcell, & P. M. Wright (Eds.), *Oxford handbook of human resource management* (pp. 187–209). Oxford University Press.

Crawford, E. R., Lepine, J. A., & Rich, B. L. (2010). Linking job demands and resources to employee engagement and burnout: A theoretical extension and meta-analytic test. *Journal of Applied Psychology 95*(5), 834–848. https://doi.org/10.1037/a0019364

Deelstra, J. T., Peeters, M. C. W., Schaufeli W. B., Stroebe, W., Zijlstra, F. R. H., & van Doornen, L. P. (2003). Receiving instrumental support at work: When help is not welcome. *Journal of Applied Psychology 88*(2), 324–331. https://psycnet.apa.org/doi/10.1037/0021-9010.88.2.324

Demerouti, E., Bakker, A. B., Nachreiner, F., & Schaufeli, W. B. (2001). The Job Demands-Resources model of burnout. *Journal of Applied Psychology 86*(3), 499–512. https://doi.org/10.1108/02683940710733115

de Sitter, L. U., den Hertog, J. F., & Dankbaar, B. (1997). From complex organizations with simple jobs to simple organizations with complex jobs. *Human Relations 50*(5), 497–534. https://doi.org/10.1023/A:1016987702271

Fayol, H. (1949). *General and industrial management*. Pitman.

Fried, Y., & Ferris, G. R. (1987). The validity of the job characteristics model: A review and meta-analysis. *Personnel Psychology 40*(2), 287–322.

Gajendran, R. S., & Harrison, D. A. (2007). The good, the bad, and the unknown about telecommuting: Meta-analysis of psychological mediators and individual consequences. *Journal of Applied Psychology 92*(6), 1524–1541. https://doi.org/10.1037/0021-9010.92.6.1524

Gittell, J. H., & Bamber, G. J. (2010). High-and low-road strategies for competing on costs and their implications for employment relations: International studies in the airline industry. *International Journal of Human Resource Management 21*(2), 165–179. https://doi.org/10.1080/09585190903509464

Grant, A. M. (2008). The significance of task significance: Job performance effects, relational mechanisms, and boundary conditions. *Journal of Applied Psychology 93*(1), 108–124. https://doi.org/10.1037/0021-9010.93.1.108

Grant, A. M. (2012). Leading with meaning: Beneficiary contact, prosocial impact, and the performance effects of transformational leadership. *Academy of Management Journal 55*(2), 458–476. https://doi.org/10.5465/amj.2010.0588

Grant, A. M., Fried, Y., & Juillerat, T. (2011). Work matters: Job design in classic and contemporary perspectives. In S. Zedeck (Ed.), *APA handbook of industrial and organizational psychology* (pp. 417–453). American Psychological Association. http://dx.doi.org/10.1037/12169-013

Haapakangas, A., Hallman, D. M., Mathiassen, S. E., & Jahncke, H. (2018). Self-rated productivity and employee well-being in activity-based offices: The role of environmental perceptions and workspace use. *Building and Environment 145*, 115–124. https://doi.org/10.1016/j.buildenv.2018.09.017

Hackman, J. R., & Oldham, G. R. (1975). Development of the Job Diagnostic Survey. *Journal of Applied Psychology 60*(2), 159–170. https://doi.org/10.1037/h0076546

Hackman, J. R., & Oldham, G. R. (1976). Motivation through the design of work: Test of a theory. *Organizational Behavior and Human Performance 16*(2), 250–279. https://doi.org/10.1016/0030-5073(76)90016-7

Häusser, J. A., Mojzisch, A., Niesel, M., & Schulz-Hardt, S. (2010). Ten years on: A review of recent research on the Job Demand-Control (-Support) model and psychological well-being. *Work and Stress 24*(1), 1–35. https://doi.org/10.1080/02678371003683747

Herzberg, F. (1968, January). One more time: How do you motivate employees? *Harvard Business Review.* https://hbr.org/2003/01/one-more-time-how-do-you-motivate-employees

Hobfoll, S. E. (1989). Conservation of resources: A new attempt at conceptualizing stress. *American Psychologist 44*(3), 513–524. https://doi.org/10.1037/0003-066X.44.3.513

Hobfoll, S. E., Johnson, R. J., Ennis, N., & Jackson, A. P. (2003). Resource loss, resource gain, and emotional outcomes among inner city women. *Journal of Personality and Social Psychology 84*(3), 632–643. https://doi.org/10.1037/0022-3514.84.3.632

Hockey, G. F. (1997). Compensatory control in the regulation of human performance under stress and high workload: A cognitive-energetical framework. *Biological Psychology 45*, 7393. https://doi.org/10.1016/S0301-0511(96)05223-4

Holtbrügge, D. (2013). Indigenous management research. *Management International Review 53*(1), 1–11. https://doi.org/10.1007/s11575-012-0160-1

Humphrey, S. E., Nahrgang, J. D., & Morgeson, F. P. (2007). Integrating motivational, social, and contextual work design features: A meta-analytic summary and theoretical extension of the work design literature. *Journal of Applied Psychology 92*(5), 1332–1356. https://doi.org/10.1037/0021-9010.92.5.1332

Inceoglu, I., Thomas, G., Chu, C., Plans, D., & Gerbasi, A. (2018). Leadership behavior and employee well-being: An integrated review and a future research agenda. *Leadership Quarterly 29*(1), 179–202. https://doi.org/10.1016/j.leaqua.2017.12.006

De Jonge, J., & Dormann, C. (2003). The DISC model: Demand-induced strain compensation mechanisms in job stress. In M. F. Dollard, A. H. Winefield, & H. R. Winefield (Eds.), *Occupational stress in the service professions* (pp. 43–74). Taylor & Francis. https://doi.org/10.1201/9780203422809.ch2

De Jonge, J., Dormann, C., & van Vegchel, N. (2004). Taakeisen, Hulpbronnen en Psychische gezondheid: Het Demand-Induced Strain Compensation (DISC)-Model. *Gedrag & Organisatie 17*(1), 59–79.

Karasek, R. A. (1979). Job demands, job decision latitude, and mental strain: Implications for job redesign. *Administrative Science Quarterly 24*(2), 285. https://doi.org/10.2307/2392498

Karasek, R. A., & Theorell, T. (1990). *Healthy work: Stress productivity and the reconstruction of working life*. Basic Books.

Kerr, S., & Jermier, J. M. (1978). Substitutes for leadership: Their meaning and measurement. *Organizational Behavior and Human Performance 22*(3), 375–403. https://doi.org/10.1016/0030-5073(78)90023-5

Knight, C., & Parker, S. K. (2021). How work redesign interventions affect performance: An evidence-based model from a systematic review. *Human Relations 74*(1), 69–104. https://doi.org/10.1177/0018726719865604

de Lange, A. H., Taris, T. W., Kompier, M. A. J., Houtman, I. L. D., & Bongers, P. M. 2003. "The very best of the millennium": Longitudinal research and the demand-control-(support) model. *Journal of Occupational Health Psychology 8*, 282–305. https://psycnet.apa.org/doi/10.1037/1076-8998.8.4.282

Lazarus R. S., & Folkman, S. (1984). *Stress, appraisal, and coping*. Springer.

LePine, M. A. (2022). The challenge-hindrance stressor framework: An integrative conceptual review and path forward. *Group and Organization Management 47*(2), 223–254. https://doi.org/10.1177/10596011221079970

Linstead, S. (1985). Breaking the "purity rule": Industrial sabotage and the symbolic process. *Personnel Review 14*(3), 12–19. https://doi.org/10.1108/eb055518

Lysova, E. I., Allan, B. A., Dik, B. J., Duffy, R. D., & Steger, M. F. (2019). Fostering meaningful work in organizations: A multi-level review and integration. *Journal of Vocational Behavior 110*, 374–389. https://doi.org/10.1016/j.jvb.2018.07.004

Maitlis, S., & Lawrence, T. B. (2007). Triggers and enablers of sensegiving in organizations. *Academy of Management Journal 50*(1), 57–84. https://doi.org/10.5465/AMJ.2007.24160971

Maslach, C., Schaufeli, W. B., & Leiter, M. P. (2001). Job burnout. *Annual Review of Psychology 52*(1), 397–422. https://doi.org/10.1146/annurev.psych.52.1.397

Mayo, Elton. (1933) *The human problems of an industrial civilization*. Macmillan.

McGregor, D. (1960). Theory X and theory Y. In D. S. Pugh (Ed.), *Organization theory* (pp. 358–374). Penguin.

Mintzberg, H. (1980). Structure in 5's: A synthesis of the research on organization design. *Management Science 26*(3), 322–341. https://doi.org/10.1287/mnsc.26.3.322

Monteiro, P., & Adler, P. S. (2022). Bureaucracy for the 21st century: Clarifying and expanding our view of bureaucratic organization. *Academy of Management Annals* 16(2), 427–475. https://doi.org/10.5465/annals.2019.0059

Morgeson, F. P., & Humphrey, S. E. (2006). The Work Design Questionnaire (WDQ): Developing and validating a comprehensive measure for assessing job design and the nature of work. *Journal of Applied Psychology 91*(6), 1321–1339. https://doi.org/10.1037/0021-9010.91.6.1321

Parker, S. K. (2014). Beyond motivation: Job and work design for development, health, ambidexterity, and more. *Annual Review of Psychology 65*, 661–691. https://doi.org/10.1146/annurev-psych-010213-115208

Parker, S. K., Andrei, D., & Van den Broeck, A. (2019). Why managers design jobs to be more boring than they need to be. *Harvard Business Review*. https://hbr.org/2019/06/why-managers-design-jobs-to-be-more-boring-than-they-need-to-be

Parker, S. K., & Grote, G. (2022). Automation, algorithms, and beyond: Why work design matters more than ever in a digital world. *Applied Psychology 71*(4), 1171–1204. https://doi.org/10.1111/apps.12241

Parker, S. K., Holman, D., & Johns, G. (2017). One hundred years of work design research: Looking back and looking forward. *Journal of Applied Psychology 102*(3), 403–420. https://psycnet.apa.org/doi/10.1037/apl0000106

Parker, S. K., & Knight, C. (2024). The SMART model of work design: A higher order structure to help see the wood from the trees. *Human Resource Management 63*(2), 265–291. https://doi.org/10.1002/hrm.22200

Parker, S. K., Van den Broeck, A., & Holman, D. (2017). Work design influences: A synthesis of multilevel factors that affect the design of jobs. *Academy of Management Annals 11*(1), 267–308. https://doi.org/10.5465/annals.2014.0054

Peeters, M. C., De Jonge, J., & Taris, T. (2013). *An introduction to contemporary work psychology*. John Wiley & Sons.

Piccolo, R. F., & Colquitt, J. A. (2006). Transformational leadership and job behaviors: The mediating role of core job characteristics. *Academy of Management Journal 49*(2), 327–340. https://doi.org/10.5465/AMJ.2006.20786079

Pierce, J. R., & Aguinis, H. (2013). The too-much-of-a-good-thing effect in management. *Journal of Management 39*(2), 313–338. https://doi.org/10.1177/0149206311410060

Pratt, M. G., & Ashforth, B. E. (2003). Fostering meaningfulness in working and at work. In K. Cameron, J. E. Dutton, & R. E. Quinn (Eds.), *Positive organizational scholarship: Foundations of a new discipline* (pp. 308–327). Berrett-Koehler.

Puranam, P., Alexy, O., & Reitzig, M. (2014). What's "new" about new forms of organizing? *Academy of Management Review 39*(2), 162–180. https://doi.org/10.5465/amr.2011.0436

Rosso, B. D., Dekas, K. H., & Wrzesniewski, A. (2010). On the meaning of work: A theoretical integration and review. *Research in Organizational Behavior 30*, 91–127. https://doi.org/10.1016/j.riob.2010.09.001

Salanic, G. R., & Pfeffer, J. (1978). A social information processing approach to job attitudes and task design. *Administrative Science Quarterly 23*(2), 224–253. https://doi.org/10.2307/302397

Sarmah, P., Van den Broeck, A., Schreurs, B., Proost, K., & Germeys, F. (2022). Autonomy supportive and controlling leadership as antecedents of work design and employee well-being. *BRQ Business Research Quarterly 25*(1), 44–61. https://doi.org/10.1177/23409444211054508

Schaufeli, W. B., Salanova, M., Gonzalez-roma, V. A., & Bakker, A. B. (2002). The measurement of engagement and burnout: A two sample confirmatory factor analytic approach. *Journal of Happiness Studies 3*, 71–92. https://doi.org/10.1023/A:1015630930326

Selye, H. (1956). *The stress of life.* McGraw-Hill.

Siegrist, J. (1996). Adverse health effects of high-effort/low-reward conditions. *Journal of Occupational Health Psychology 1*(1), 27–41. https://psycnet.apa.org/doi/10.1037/1076-8998.1.1.27

Sivarajan, R., Varma, A. M., & Reshmi. (2021). To jugaad or not? How Mumbai's gig workers thrive against psychological contract discrepancies. *South Asian Journal of Human Resources Management 8*(1), 103–132. https://doi.org/10.1177/2322093721995311

Smith, A. (1776). *An inquiry into the nature and causes of the wealth of nations.* W. Strahan and T. Cadell.

Stansfeld, S., & Candy, B. (2006). Psychosocial work environment and mental health—a meta-analytic review. *Scandinavian Journal of Work, Environment & Health 32*(6), 443–462. https://www.jstor.org/stable/40967597

Tarafdar, M., Cooper, C. L., & Stich, J. F. (2019). The technostress trifecta—techno eustress, techno distress and design: Theoretical directions and an agenda for research. *Information Systems Journal 29*(1), 6–42. https://doi.org/10.1111/isj.12169

Tauetsile, J. (2021). Employee engagement in non-Western contexts: The link between social resources Ubuntu and employee engagement. *International Journal of Cross Cultural Management 21*(2), 245–259. https://doi.org/10.1177/14705958211007874

Taylor, F. W. (1911). Principles and methods of scientific management. *Journal of Accountancy 12*(2), 117–124.

Tims, M., & Bakker, A. B. (2010). Job crafting: Towards a new model of individual job redesign. *SA Journal of Industrial Psychology 36*(2), 1–9. https://doi.org/10.4102/sajip.v36i2.841

Trist, E. L., & Bamforth, K. W. (1951). Some social and psychological consequences of the longwall method of coal getting. An examination of the psychological situation and defences of a work group in relation to the social structure and technological content of the work system. *Human Relations 4*(1), 3–38. https://doi.org/10.1177/001872675100400101

Tursunbayeva, A., & Renkema, M. (2023). Artificial intelligence in health-care: Implications for the job design of healthcare professionals. *Asia Pacific Journal of Human Resources 61*, 845–887. https://doi.org/10.1111/1744-7941.12325

Van den Broeck, A., de Cuyper, N., de Witte, H., & Vansteenkiste, M. (2010). Not all job demands are equal: Differentiating job hindrances and job challenges in the job demands-resources model. *European Journal of Work and Organizational Psychology 19*(6). https://doi.org/10.1080/13594320903223839

Van den Broeck, A., Schreurs, B., Guenter, H., & van Emmerik, H. (2015). Skill utilization and well-being: A cross-level story of day-to-day fluctuations and personal intrinsic values. *Work & Stress 29*(3), 306–323. https://doi.org/10.1080/02678373.2015.1074955

Van den Broeck, A., Van Ruysseveldt, J., Vanbelle, E., & De Witte, H. (2013). The job demands–resources model: Overview and suggestions for future research. *Advances in Positive Organizational Psychology 1*, 83–105. https://doi.org/10.1108/s2046-410x(2013)0000001007

van der Doef, M., & Maes, S. (1998). The job demand-control (-support) model and physical health outcomes: A review of the strain and buffer hypotheses. *Psychology & Health 13*(5), 909–936. https://doi.org/10.1080/08870449808407440

Vander Elst, T., Secru, M., Van den Broeck, A., Van Hoof, E., Baillien, E., & Godderis, L. (2019). Who is more susceptible to job stressors and resources? Sensory-processing as a personal resource and vulnerability factor. *PLoS One 14*(11), e0225103. https://doi.org/10.1371/journal.pone.0225103

Walker, C. R., & Guest, R.H. (1952). *The man on the assembly line.* Harvard University Press. https://psycnet.apa.org/doi/10.4159/harvard.9780674599949

Wang, B., Liu, Y., & Parker, S. K. (2020). How does the use of information communication technology affect individuals? A work design perspective. *Academy of Management Annals 14*(2), 695–725. https://doi.org/10.5465/annals.2018.0127

Warr, P. (2013). Jobs and job-holders: Two sources of happiness and unhappiness. In I. Boniwell, S. A. David, & A. C. Ayers (Eds.), *Oxford handbook of happiness* (pp. 733–750). Oxford University Press. http://dx.doi.org/10.1093/oxfordhb/9780199557257.013.0054

Weber, M. (1978). *Economy and society: An outline of interpretive sociology.* University of California Press.

Webster, J. R., Beehr, T. A., & Love, K. (2011). Extending the challenge-hindrance model of occupational stress: The role of appraisal. *Journal of Vocational Behavior 79*(2), 505–516. https://doi.org/10.1016/j.jvb.2011.02.001

Wrzesniewski, A., & Dutton, J. E. (2001). Crafting a job: Revisioning employees as active crafters of their work. *Academy of Management Review 26*(2), 179–201. https://doi.org/10.5465/AMR.2001.4378011

Wu, C. H., Wang, Y., Parker, S. K., & Griffin, M. A. (2020). Effects of chronic job insecurity on Big Five personality change. *Journal of Applied Psychology 105*(11), 1308–1326. https://doi.org/10.1037/apl0000488

Xanthopoulou, D., Bakker, A. B., Demerouti, E., & Schaufeli, W. B. (2007). The role of personal resources in the job demands-resources model. *International Journal of Stress Management 14*(2), 121–141. https://doi.org/10.1037/1072-5245.14.2.121

Zhang, X., Zhou, J., & Kwan, H. K. (2017). Configuring challenge and hindrance contexts for introversion and creativity: Joint effects of task complexity and guanxi management. *Organizational Behavior and Human Decision Processes 143*, 54–68. https://doi.org/10.1016/j.obhdp.2017.02.003

Zhou, T., Xu, C., Wang, C., Sha, S., Wang, Z., Zhou, Y., Zhang, X., Hu, D., Liu, Y., Tian, T., Liang, S., Zhou, L., & Wang, Q. (2022). Burnout and well-being of healthcare workers in the post-pandemic period of COVID-19: A perspective from the job demands-resources model. *BMC Health Services Research 22*(1), 1–15. https://doi.org/10.1186/s12913-022-07608-z

Multi-Level Work Design
Integrating Work Characteristics Across Individual, Team, and Organizational Levels of Analysis

Cory M. Eisenhard and Frederick P. Morgeson

Work design research has one of the longest histories in the organizational sciences. From its foundational works (Babbage, 1835; Gilbreth, 1911; Smith, 1776; Taylor, 1911) to its modern empirical science (Parker et al., 2017), work design has engaged scholars and impacted the lives of workers. Thousands of books and journal articles have documented how individual jobs can be designed to achieve a host of important outcomes (Humphrey et al., 2007). Studies focusing on job design represent the majority of research on work design. Such a focus on the individual level of analysis makes sense given the historical importance of individual jobs and the individual workers who perform those jobs.

The progress made in work design at the individual level of analysis is most clearly reflected in the work characteristic approach to work design. In fact, the Job Characteristic Model (JCM) (Hackman & Oldham, 1975, 1976, 1980) is the most well-known theory in work design and among the most cited theories in organizational behavior and human resource management (HRM) research (Parker et al., 2017). Scholars across disciplines have continued to develop the work characteristic approach, debating and expanding the scope of work characteristics under examination (Morgeson & Campion, 2003; Parker et al., 2001). A contemporary work characteristic approach yielded the Work Design Questionnaire (WDQ), a taxonomic approach to individual work characteristics that examines 18 work characteristics spanning the task, knowledge, social, and contextual domains of work (Morgeson & Humphrey, 2006).

Somewhat independently from research that explored the work characteristic approach, organizational scholars began to articulate the advantages of adopting a multi-level perspective (House et al., 1995; Roberts et al., 1978). This research suggested that focusing on (and ultimately integrating) different levels of analysis would produce more useful and accurate theoretical and empirical models. Reflecting on work design approaches that might span levels, Frederick

---

Cory M. Eisenhard and Frederick P. Morgeson, *Multi-Level Work Design*. In: *Transformative Work Design*. Edited by: Sharon K. Parker et al., Oxford University Press. © Society for Industrial and Organizational Psychology (2025). DOI: 10.1093/oso/9780197692554.003.0003

P. Morgeson and Stephen E. Humphrey (2008, p. 42) noted that "the literatures on job and team design have evolved somewhat independently. This is unfortunate, as these literatures share many of the same constructs, suggesting a similarity that is not represented in current models of work design." Today, there is substantial research that has integrated job and team design constructs with enough studies for meta-analysis in some domains (e.g., Byron et al., 2023; Courtright et al., 2015; Ryu et al., 2022).

Less attention has been paid to work design at the organizational level of analysis. This is in part because of the lack of clarity about what constitutes work design at the organizational level. To address this gap, we reexamine several organizational work design approaches that present systematic principles for the deployment of sets of work characteristics. For example, the Toyota Production System (TPS) (Ohno, 1988) deploys autonomy and work simplification to achieve efficiency and quality outcomes (Campion, 1988; Campion & Thayer, 1985). Although little work design research to date has been conducted that invokes the organizational level of analysis, it is potentially important.

We seek to understand the nature of work design at the individual, team, and organizational levels of analysis. To accomplish this, we first draw from past research to define the range of work characteristics studied at the individual level of analysis (Morgeson & Humphrey, 2006). Focusing on the range of task, knowledge, social, and contextual work characteristics provides an integrating framework across levels. We offer definitions of each work characteristic at the individual level. Second, we perform a selective narrative review of the work design literature at the team level of analysis. The team level has received significant attention from work design researchers throughout its history which helps us recognize the important ways that the meaning of the individual work characteristics changes at the team level. We offer a definition of each work characteristic at the team level that reflects a dual concern for the existing definition at the individual level and the ways that researchers have conceptualized the work characteristics differently at the team level of analysis.

Finally, we clarify what work design represents at the organizational level of analysis. To do so, we reexamine organizational design research that discusses work characteristics. The individual and team work characteristics represent the building blocks for organizational work design. We identify organizational design approaches that systematically deploy sets of work characteristics to achieve specific outcomes, potentially bridging the micro-oriented individual and team level work design scholarship with the macro-oriented organizational level. We focus on three approaches to organizational design that have been particularly influenced, and at times guided, by work design: mechanistic approaches focused on the technical processes of the organization (e.g., scientific management), socio-technical systems approaches focused on the joint optimization of technical and social processes, and strategic HR approaches that focus on bundles of HR practices that can achieve organizational performance outcomes.

This chapter makes four contributions to multi-level work design research. First, we clarify the meaning of work design at the organizational level of analysis. Second, we review the work design literature at the team level of analysis and offer insights into how the meaning of work characteristics changes at the team level versus the individual level. We define work characteristics at the individual level and then selectively review work design research that has expanded our understanding of the work characteristics at the team level. Third, we reassess the organizational design literature to identify sets of work characteristics that are deployed to achieve specific outcomes, connecting work characteristics across the individual, team, and organizational levels of analysis. Fourth, we conclude by identifying gaps in the work design literature at the higher levels of analysis. Although some have suggested that there is little new to learn about work design, we identify many opportunities for theoretical and empirical contributions at the team and organizational levels of analysis.

From the Individual and Team Levels to the Organizational Level of Analysis

Work design scholars have integrated the individual and team levels of analysis into a holistic conceptualization of work design that spans these levels (Morgeson et al., 2020; Morgeson & Humphrey, 2008; Parker, 2014). For example, Morgeson and Humphrey (2008, p. 42) defined work design as the "study, creation, and modification of the composition, content, structure, and environment within which jobs and roles are enacted." Despite this, it is unclear how these conceptualizations apply at even higher levels of analysis. As such, it is important to clarify what work design means at the organizational level beyond being the environmental context in which work is designed for individuals and teams. To clarify work design at the organizational level of analysis, we consider work design's role in the organizational design literature (Donaldson, 2001).

Following research on the organizational contingencies in which certain work design principles are more appropriate than others (Parker et al., 2001), we start by examining the role of work design from the contingency theory perspective on organizational design (Donaldson, 2001). Tom Burns and George M. Stalker (1961, pp. vii–viii) first articulated this contingency view, stating that, "if the form of management is properly to be seen as dependent on the situation the concern is trying to meet, it follows that there is no single set of principles for 'good organization,' an ideal type of management system which can serve as a model to which administrative practice should, or could in time, approximate."

This perspective is appropriate for discussing work design at the organizational level given the many unique outcomes organizations seek to achieve by accomplishing work (e.g., efficiency, quality, satisfaction, financial performance). The work of Michael A. Campion and colleagues (Campion, 1988; Campion & McClelland, 1993; Campion & Thayer, 1985; Morgeson & Campion, 2002, 2003) explicates the breadth of outcomes that different work design approaches influence, identifying potential tradeoffs associated with choosing one approach over another. Organizations may be concerned with efficiency, motivation, or health, among many other outcomes and combinations of outcomes (Campion & Thayer, 1985). Each desired outcome indicates a different approach to work design that is reflected in a set of work characteristics (e.g., low job complexity and high autonomy to achieve efficiency and quality outcomes). In this view, work design at the organizational level is an element of organization design (i.e., one of several processes of structuring the organization), specifically where sets of work characteristics are systematically deployed to achieve desired outcomes. Therefore, we define work design at the organizational level as sets of work characteristics focused on achieving desired organizational goals.

To situate work design at the organizational level relative to the individual and team levels, we suggest that the design of individual jobs and roles reflects organizational design principles relating to the implementation of "rules and programs" for "job-related situations that can be anticipated in advance and to which an appropriate response can be identified" (Galbraith, 1973, pp. 10–11). In situations where organizational complexity is high, planning takes the form of "specifying outputs, goals, or targets . . . employees select behaviors that lead to goal accomplishment" (Galbraith, 1974, p. 29). Work design at the organizational level of analysis is part of this type of planning. Organizational managers bring attention to, shape, align, and coordinate work design throughout the organization by identifying desired outcomes (Katz & Kahn, 1966; March & Simon, 1958).

The selection and implementation of work design principles at the organizational level is a strategic imperative, with certain principles being beneficial or harmful given the specific organizational contexts (Delery & Doty, 1996). Moreover, these are strategic decisions that managers must make. Work design is often an implicit role of the manager that is not always articulated (Morgeson & Campion, 2003). For example, an organizational design decision to create a C-level purchasing director role may indirectly remove autonomy from individual purchasing jobs, although the decision does not explicitly invoke the design of work in any way.

The following sections on work design at the individual and team levels of analysis define the "raw material" of work design from which sets of work characteristics can be constructed at the organizational level. These sets of work characteristics are combinations of work characteristics that are deployed together to achieve desired goals. Although earlier work design and work redesign research considered a narrow set of task characteristics at the individual level, later research expanded this perspective to increase the raw material of work design to incorporate knowledge, social, and contextual characteristics (Morgeson & Campion, 2003) and team roles (Morgeson & Humphrey, 2008). We articulate and integrate these insights across domains and levels to introduce a multi-level framework of work design across individual, team, and organizational levels of analysis.

Work Design at the Individual Level of Analysis

Work design research at the individual level of analysis is at a mature stage of development. The work characteristic approach to work design is well established (Hackman & Oldham, 1975, 1976, 1980) and has expanded its focus into the broader context of work (Morgeson & Campion, 2003; Morgeson & Humphrey, 2006). The empirical database is considerable, with hundreds of empirical tests and multiple meta-analyses of the broad consequences of the work characteristics (Carter et al., 2024; Fried & Ferris, 1987; Humphrey et al., 2007). Because of its mature standing and the existence of many excellent reviews, we have chosen to define the work characteristics at the individual level of analysis in Table 3.1 rather than repeat past reviews.

Importantly, work design research at the team level of analysis is relatively less mature than at the individual level. In some cases, the teams literature discusses constructs that are clearly the same as constructs at the individual level, with the referent shifted from the individual to the team. At other times, researchers have added important conceptual developments to the work characteristics at the team level, changing their meaning and nature. Table 3.1 offers definitions for the work characteristics at the individual and team levels. We indicate where we see both literatures using the same definitions but different referents (i.e., a referent shift). Additionally, we indicate when research has provided insights that have expanded our understanding of how specific work characteristics change at the team level of analysis (i.e., conceptual development). As work design at the team level of analysis is less mature, we offer a historic narrative and selectively review this literature in the following section.

60 TRANSFORMATIVE WORK DESIGN

Table 3.1 Individual and Team Work Design: Defining Work Characteristics at the Individual and Team Levels of Analysis

Work Character-istic	Individual Level Definition	Team Level Definition	Referent Shift or Conceptual Development?
Autonomy	The freedom that a job offers regarding scheduling, decision-making, and methods used to perform work.	The freedom the team has regarding scheduling, decision-making, and methods used to perform work.	Referent shift
Task variety	The range of activities associated with a job.	The range of activities a team is responsible for.	Referent shift
Task significance	The degree to which a job is meaningful and impacts people.	The degree to which the work a team performs is meaningful and impacts people.	Referent shift
Task identity	The degree to which a job involves a complete unit of work, the result of which is easy to identify.	The extent to which a team completes a whole piece of work.	Conceptual development
Feedback from the job	The degree to which a job provides knowledge of how well work was performed.	The degree to which a team's work provides knowledge of how well work was performed.	Referent shift
Job complexity	The difficulty associated with the skills and knowledge required to perform a job.	The difficulty associated with the skills and knowledge that must be integrated to complete a team's work.	Conceptual development
Skill variety	The number of skills required to perform a job.	The breadth of unique skills needed within the team, including skills that emerge by combining team members' skills, that are required to complete work.	Conceptual development
Specialization	The depth of knowledge and skills required to perform a job.	The extent of specialized tasks that the team performs.	Conceptual development
Problem solving	The amount of creative, innovative, and unique ideas required to perform a job.	The amount of creative, innovative, and unique ideas required to perform the team's work.	Referent shift

Work Character-istic	Individual Level Definition	Team Level Definition	Referent Shift or Conceptual Development?
Information processing	The amount of data that is examined and processed to perform a job.	The amount of data that is managed to accomplish the team's work.	Conceptual development
Inter-dependence	The extent to which a job relies on others and the extent that others rely on the job to be completed.	The extent to which a team must coordinate its efforts and resources to accomplish work, the extent to which workers must set goals and receive feedback and rewards as a team, and the extent to which the team must rely on others and is relied on by other others to accomplish its work.	Conceptual development
Social support	The opportunities for advice, assistance, and friendship that a job provides.	The degree to which the relational structure of the team offers opportunities for assistance, conflict management, and leadership support.	Conceptual development
Feedback from others	The extent that others within the organization provide knowledge about how well the work was performed.	The extent to which the team receives feedback from its members, as well as leaders and coworkers throughout the organization.	Conceptual development
Interaction outside the organiza-tion	The extent to which a job requires interaction with people external to the organization.	The extent to which the team's work requires interaction with people external to the organization.	Referent shift
Ergonomics	How well a job allows for healthy posture and movement.	How well a team's work allows for healthy posture and movement.	Referent shift
Physical demands	The amount of physical activity and effort associated with a job.	The amount of physical activity and effort associated with a team's work.	Referent shift

continued

62 TRANSFORMATIVE WORK DESIGN

Table 3.1 *continued*

Work Character-istic	Individual Level Definition	Team Level Definition	Referent Shift or Conceptual Development?
Work conditions	The health, safety, and comfort of the environment associated with a job.	The health, safety, and comfort of the environment associated with a team's work.	Referent shift
Equipment use	The variety and complexity of the technology, equipment, and tools used in a job.	The variety and complexity of the technology, equipment, and tools used to accomplish a team's work.	Referent shift

Work Design at the Team Level of Analysis

Evidence for the use of work teams dates back deep into the ancient world (e.g., Cuneiform Tablets circa 3000 BCE; Englund, 1991). The earliest work design research discussed the division of labor (Babbage, 1835; Smith, 1776), and specialized, simplified tasks (Taylor, 1911). These work design principles had implications for how workers related to one another that went largely unstated. For example, highly specialized workers could perform only a small part of a larger, interdependent task. It would not be until the Hawthorne studies that these implications would be recognized in the management literature (Roethlisberger & Dickson, 1939). Observations of informal groups during the Hawthorne studies revealed that the social context of work had significant consequences, suggesting that work design might benefit by purposefully designing work in ways that consider "teamwork and cooperation" (Mayo, 1949, p. 82).

Explicit discussions of teams as a work design phenomenon came from socio-technical systems (STS) theory (Trist & Bamforth, 1951). STS research identified the autonomous work group as a critical unit of analysis for work designers (Parker & Wall, 1998). Work teams have continued to increase their popularity in practice and research (Hackman, 1987; Hackman & Oldham, 1980), both trends that continue to this day (Mathieu et al., 2019).

Campion and colleagues (1993) greatly advanced work design research at the team level, connecting many work and team characteristics to important outcomes. Although not the first to study team and work design (e.g., earlier research was performed on autonomous work groups [Hackman, 1987, Wall et al., 1986]), Campion and colleagues made many contributions by generating measures, dealing with level of analysis issues, and offering empirical data. Further integrations of team and work design have continued the development of this literature (Morgeson & Humphrey, 2008), alongside other major advancements that embed work design in the broader context of work (Humphrey et al., 2007; Morgeson & Humphrey, 2006; Parker et al., 2017).

Task characteristics

Task characteristics have received the most attention at the team level of analysis. Team and task design elements have been studied in isolation but share many similarities (Morgeson & Humphrey, 2008). Indeed, J. Richard Hackman and Greg R. Oldhamf (1980) argue that task characteristics will have the same impact on a host of behaviors and attitudes at the team level of analysis as they have at the individual level of analysis. Their perspective, alongside STS research on autonomous work groups (Cherns, 1976; Cumming, 1978; Trist & Bamforth, 1951), led to the early trajectory, and a continuing focus at the team level on autonomous teams and task characteristics generally.

This focus is reflected in team level work characteristics being examined on their own, as well as research that has combined sets of task characteristics into a single construct to represent the context of work that teams are embedded within. For example, a set of work characteristics reflects the context in which team empowerment occurs (Maynard et al., 2012; Seibert et al., 2011; Spreitzer, 2008). Similar research suggests that a combination of autonomy, flexibility, job enrichment, and task complexity will reflect a supportive work context and will be related to higher psychological safety (Frazier et al., 2017). Moreover, M. Lance Frazier and colleagues (2017) found that team autonomy and team interdependence as individual constructs were both positively related to psychological safety. Indeed, although we organize our review of this literature by the constructs in isolation, it is important to acknowledge that some research has theorized and tested their interactive and combined effects.

Autonomy. Team autonomy has received more attention than any other work characteristic at the team level of analysis. The considerable amount of research has generated several different conceptualizations and empirical representations of what autonomy means at the team level. Examining early discussions of autonomous work groups in STS research (Trist & Bamforth, 1951; Trist et al., 1963), Hackman (1976, p. 3) articulated a conceptualization of team level autonomy that reflects the group's authority "to make decisions about methods for carrying out the work, scheduling various activities, assigning different individuals to different tasks, and (sometimes) deciding which individuals will be permitted to join the group as new members." This approach to team autonomy suggests that autonomy is a structural characteristic of the team, granted by the organization.

Around the same time, another approach to team autonomy grew out of the aggregation of individual autonomy within teams (Hackman & Oldham, 1980). Conceptual clarity was improved by shifting the referent from the individual to the team before aggregation (Campion et al., 1993). Although there is nothing necessarily wrong with either approach, it is important to recognize the theoretical differences between them, and between individual and team autonomy (Langfred, 2000, 2005, 2007). Team autonomy reflects a characteristic of the team that is distinct from the autonomy experienced by individuals within the team. Claus W. Langfred (2005, p. 514) states that "any team can thus be described in terms of both the level of team autonomy that the team has and the average level of individual autonomy that members of the team have." This is important because, for example, increased individual autonomy within a team is associated with higher individual motivation but reduced team cohesiveness (Langfred, 2000).

Team autonomy has been connected to outcomes across all three levels of analysis. Early research most often connected team autonomy to team performance (Stewart, 2006). Recently, Kameron M. Carter and colleagues (2024) produced a meta-analysis examining 394 studies, connecting team work design with team performance. Their meta-analytic test showed that autonomy was positively related to performance, but that the effects were relatively small. Their moderation analysis showed that industry had a profound effect on the relationship, and when considering the high-tech industry, autonomy had an outsized impact on performance.

Moreover, team autonomy is expected to have broad behavioral and attitudinal outcomes as well. Indeed, a recent meta-analysis was performed on team autonomy as an antecedent of team performance and attitudes (Ryu et al., 2022). J. Woon Ryu and colleagues (2022) found that team autonomy predicts team performance and attitudes, showing that these relationships were mediated by team functioning (task and relational functions; Courtright et al., 2015). Moreover, they identified moderators that showed why autonomy sometimes had inconsistent results, finding some evidence that when tasks were routine, the relationship between team autonomy and task functions was weaker; further, when tasks were routine the relationship between team autonomy and attitudes was weaker as well.

Autonomy has received attention under several other terms as well. One example comes from Helen M. Williams, Sharon K. Parker, and Nick Turner's (2010) study of autonomy in teams using a novel measure and a novel term called team self-management (or similarly, team self-managing behavior; Rousseau & Aubé, 2010). Williams and colleagues (2010) found that team self-management mediated the relationship between proactive personality and performance. Greg L. Stewart and Murray R. Barrick (2000) considered team autonomy under the guise of team self-leadership, showing that it interacted with task type such that it improved performance on conceptual tasks and worsened performance on behavioral tasks (i.e., executing work). Collective timing and method control (Jackson & Mullarkey, 2000) was developed using earlier individual level autonomy measures (Jackson et al., 1993). Paul R. Jackson and Sean Mullarkey's (2000) examination of a shift away from traditional functional manufacturing work design toward a lean production approach showed the importance of collective autonomy relative to individual autonomy for predicting job strain and satisfaction. Although representing a small sample of the team autonomy literature, these examples show the manifold discussions this important construct has provoked.

The conceptual development of team autonomy research suggests a definitional clarity that is largely not present elsewhere at the team level in work design (Cordery et al., 2010; Hackman, 1987; Ryu et al., 2022). We define team autonomy as the amount of freedom the team has regarding scheduling, decision-making, and methods to complete tasks.

Task variety. Task variety could be conceptualized as task routines at the team level (Langfred & Moye, 2004; Rousseau & Aubé, 2010). Routine tasks represent predictable situations, whereas nonroutine tasks represent situations with changing demands and unique methods or procedures (Rico et al., 2008). Task variety at the team level is important because teams are uniquely capable of approaching exceptional cases, given the potential for having breadth of skills within the team. Although the team task routines research is not a perfect analog to task variety at the individual level of analysis, it does provide one avenue for exploring task variety at the team level. Team task variety reflects the range of activities a team is responsible for.

Task significance. Studies on team task significance have often used individual level measures, reflecting Hackman and Oldham's (1980) assertion that significance (along with skill variety and task identity) predicts the experienced meaningfulness of work for teams in the same way they predict experienced meaningfulness for individuals. Indeed, Stewart's (2006) meta-analysis shows that team task meaningfulness, defined in this way, has a positive relationship with performance. Bradley L. Kirkman and colleagues (Kirkman and Rosen, 1999, 2000; Kirkman et al., 2004) suggest that task significance at the team level of analysis reflects the intrinsic meaningfulness of the team's work and team's contributory impact on achieving those tasks. When experienced alongside autonomy and potency, teams are expected to feel empowerment (Kirkman et al., 2004). Although these studies have approached significance in seemingly different ways, underlying each definition is the meaningfulness of work, closely matching the definition at the individual level. Team task significance reflects the degree to which the work a team performs is meaningful and impacts people.

Task identity. Thomas G. Cummings (1978) and Hackman (1976) suggest that task identity is a common, if not essential, trait of self-managing teams. In this view, teams are designed to complete an entire piece of work. On the other hand, Campion and colleagues (1993, 1996) suggest that task identity may be confusing at the team level of analysis because the team as an entity accomplishes a complete unit of work, yet the individual workers are unlikely to see this larger complete piece because their work is reflected in a smaller part of the whole. This phenomenon is further clarified in research on lean production teams where the team is responsible for a standardized part that will be worked on further within another organizational structure (Jackson & Mullarkey, 2000). Individual team members' ability to identify their personal efforts or the team's efforts is de-emphasized here. Therefore, it is important to recognize the limitations of task identity at the team level as a predictor of consequences for individuals and teams. Still, recognizing the historic conceptual development for task identity in self-managing teams is important. The team is responsible for completing a "whole and meaningful piece of work" (Hackman & Oldham, 1980), even if identifying the effort involved in completing that work is difficult (Campion et al., 1993). Team task identity reflects the extent to which a team completes a whole piece of work.

Feedback from the job. Given the combined effort associated with work completed by teams, feedback from the job has received little attention. Instead, research on feedback from the job has largely focused on the team performance feedback, which has been reflected in feedback from others about how the team performed its combined work. This research has focused on general measures of feedback available to teams, largely decontextualized from its source (i.e., the job or others; Patterson et al., 2005). Given this overlap, we review this relatively small literature together and suggest that feedback from the job should reflect a referent shift until more research is performed. Therefore, team feedback from the jobs reflects the degree to which a team's work provides knowledge of how well work was performed.

Knowledge characteristics

Knowledge characteristics, more than task characteristics, change in meaning at the team level of analysis. One reason for this is that teams are created in large part to combine the knowledge and skills of workers to "align members' competencies with task demand" (Mathieu et al., 2019). Several knowledge, skills, and abilities (KSAs) emerge at the team level of analysis, largely relating to teamwork

(Stevens & Campion, 1994, 1999). These KSAs are reflected in a broader scope of knowledge characteristics at the team level. KSAs relating to interpersonal interaction (e.g., conflict resolution, communication, collaboration, coordination) and self-management (e.g., goal setting, performance management, task planning, task coordination), are critical considerations in work design at the team level (Stevens & Campion, 1999).

Job complexity. Job complexity at the team level is more commonly discussed in terms of task complexity or its opposite, task simplicity. When task complexity is high, scholars have argued that it is appropriate, and often required, to approach the task with teams (Sundstrom et al., 1990), and for the most complex tasks, multiteam systems (Zaccaro et al., 2012). Task complexity articulates the relationships between KSAs, complexity arising from the team social environment, and multi-level considerations like teamwork that can each increase complexity. Scholars have suggested that teams are formed to approach task complexity because the breadth of KSAs necessary to complete complex tasks does not exist within a single worker (Bligh et al., 2006; Pearce & Manz, 2005). Indeed, Jessica R. Mesmer-Magnus and Leslie A. DeChurch (2009, p. 543) suggest that "highly complex task domains typically require specialized, nonredundant experts with dissimilar training and background characteristics to integrate information in order to reach a quality solution." Team task complexity has become an increasingly important topic as teams become larger and work becomes generally more complex and interdependent.

Additionally, task complexity emerges from the skills of teamwork itself (Humphrey & Aime, 2014; Stevens & Campion, 1994, 1999). Research in this domain emphasizes the dynamic nature of teamwork, identifying how complexity emerges from coordinating interdependent work and integrating multiple workers' skills and knowledge (Vashdi et al., 2013). Some evidence suggests that teamwork KSAs will mediate the positive relationship between team autonomy and performance as well as the negative relationship between autonomy and stress (Leach et al., 2005).

Meta-analyses on task complexity have had inconsistent results. Task type complexity, as a moderator of the relationship between conflict and performance, has shown mixed results. For example, Carsten De Dreu and Laurie Weingart (2003) found that complex task types strengthened the negative relationship between conflict and performance, whereas Frank R. C. de Wit, Lindred L. Greer, and Karen A. Jehn (2012) found that task type complexity had no effect. In a similar way, task complexity as a moderator of shared leadership and performance received mixed results. For example, Danni Wang, David A. Waldman, and Zhen Zhang (2014) found that task complexity strengthened the relationship between shared leadership and performance, whereas Lauren D'Innocenzo, John E. Mathieu, and Michael R. Kukenberger (2016) found

68   TRANSFORMATIVE WORK DESIGN

that task complexity weakened the relationship between shared leadership and performance.

Although task complexity has received limited attention at the team level of analysis, there has been significant construct development. Early research found that teams facing simple, routine tasks are expected to improve many team level outcomes because the difficulty of these tasks was low (Campion et al., 1993; Rousseau & Aubé, 2010). As described, recent research has offered a more nuanced assessment where performance is less easy to predict. Task complexity (i.e., team job complexity) is defined as the difficulty associated with the skills and knowledge that must be integrated to complete a team's work.

Skill variety. Workers in teams are believed to require broader skills to flexibly shift to perform emergent work tasks (Hackman, 1987; Sundstrom et al., 1990). Most models of teamwork suggest that some skill homogeneity is to be expected within teams (i.e., overlapping skills), but that the heterogeneity of KSAs available to the team will improve performance (Gladstein, 1984). Indeed, skill diversity has received considerable attention in the team diversity literature (van Knippenberg et al., 2004, van Knippenberg & Schippers, 2007). Diverse KSAs are believed to give teams more potential options for overcoming challenges, especially non-routine challenges (van Knippenberg et al., 2004). "Having high variety on KSAs provides the team with the necessary raw materials for performing and then adapting to changes in performance requirements" (Harrison & Humphrey, 2010, p. 332).

Broadly, diversity in teams has been theorized to be a "double-edged sword" (Milliken & Martins, 1996) and to have an inconsistent main effect (van Knippenberg & Schippers, 2007). In contrast, skill diversity has received more consistent results. There is significant evidence that KSA diversity has has a larger relationship with performance and conflict within teams (Pelled et al., 1999; Simons et al., 1999), relative to other forms of diversity that are less relevant to work (Pelled, 1996). An important caveat is that, invariably, larger teams face lower cohesion and satisfaction, and higher coordination costs (Gully et al., 1995). As such, including more team members to improve skill variety has significant tradeoffs.

Team skill variety has important extensions beyond its conceptualization as an individual work characteristic. Although the total number of unique skills required to complete the team's work as a unit remains essential to the definition of team skill variety, several other important facets of the work characteristic become clear at the team level. Specifically, overlapping skills (i.e., skill homogeneity versus heterogeneity) and the combining of skills to accomplish work both suggest that this work characteristic deserves additional conceptual development. To this end, team skill variety is defined as the breadth of unique skills needed within the team, including skills that emerge by combining team members' skills.

Specialization. Specialization at the team level reflects the team's type and the purpose for the team's creation (Cohen & Bailey, 1997; Sundstrom et al., 1990). In this view, specialization refers to the specific organizational needs that the team addresses, and the specialized knowledge and skills that the team uses to address those needs. Categorical titles, such as project team, cross functional team, and top management team indicate some information about the strength of specialization in these teams (Cohen & Bailey, 1997; Michel & Hambrick, 1992). Although most studies have focused on the variety of knowledge and skills held by individual team members, by identifying the specialized purposes that teams have in organizations we have gained some insight into how specialization is reflected at the team level of analysis. Team specialization reflects the specialized task that the team performs.

Problem solving. Little research has directly approached problem solving as a team level work design construct, but team problem solving has been broadly examined in the context of team creativity and innovation. Creativity and innovation in teams have been approached most often as the performance of a creative task, such as creating new products and procedures (Paulus et al., 2012). Some scholars have suggested that this explicit focus on a creative task is not required, and that team creativity and innovation can also reflect the introduction of ideas that are novel to the team (van Knippenberg & Schippers, 2017).

These two perspectives help inform team problem solving by suggesting that both creative outputs and the generation and implementation of creative and innovative ideas within the team are within the purview of extant research. The team creativity and innovation literature has historically focused on individual creative outcomes (Hülsheger et al., 2009), but a more recent meta-analysis suggests that this trend is changing, and multi-level outcomes of team creativity are becoming more common (Byron et al., 2023). Team problem solving reflects the amount of creative, innovative, and unique ideas required to perform the team's work.

Information processing. One theory of teams suggests that they are information processors (Hinsz et al., 1997; Martins & Sohn, 2022). This view has two contributions. First, teams must surface information. Second, they must combine the information, processing the surfaced information in a way that transforms it into something useful to the team (Hinsz et al., 1997). Teams often monitor a much larger set of information than individuals are capable of, especially in teams where worker expertise is heterogeneous, and multiple experts must combine their knowledge to perform a task (De Dreu et al., 2008).

TRANSFORMATIVE WORK DESIGN

Information processing at the team level has been approached from the perspective of how the team examines information about the task (Laughlin, 1980; Stasser & Stewart, 1992) and the way information is discussed by the team (Henningsen & Henningsen, 2003). Information processing has received considerable attention in the teams literature as a predictor of performance. This relationship has been tested through meta-analysis (albeit with few studies), with evidence suggesting that this relationship is mediated by information sharing (Mesmer-Magnus & DeChurch, 2009). Team information processing reflects the amount of data that a team must manage to accomplish its work.

Social characteristics

Work design scholars have come to recognize the important role of the social environment surrounding jobs and teams (Morgeson & Campion, 2003). The clear connection between teams and social characteristics has led to conceptualizations of multi-level work design that consider the social environment as a higher level of analysis than the job or task in work design (Morgeson & Humphrey, 2008).

Interdependence. The term "interdependence" is found in many definitions of work teams (e.g., Kozlowski & Bell, 2003; Kozlowski & Ilgen, 2006; Salas et al., 1992). It makes sense then that a large amount of work design research at the team level has been performed on interdependence (Campion et al., 1993; Courtright et al., 2015; Gully et al., 2002). A sustained interest in team interdependence has led to significant conceptual development of the construct and its integration with the teams literature. These conceptions of interdependence go beyond interdependence as an individual level work characteristic and are reflected at the team level by a smaller literature on the external interdependence between the team and individuals, teams, and organizations external to the team (Gladstein, 1984).

Early research (e.g., Thompsons, 1967) on team interdependence focused on task interdependence. This perspective emphasized the structural nature of interdependence, relating to stable structural design decisions like team, task, and process design (Campion et al., 1993; Wageman, 1995). James D. Thompson (1967) conceptualized team interdependence as workflow patterns that reflected how taskwork was divided, which is largely static (i.e., structural); interdependence is high when multiple team members' work is integrated, and low when team members complete work independently and then have their efforts pooled. Moses N. Kiggundu (1981, 1983) expanded this conceptualization of task interdependence to incorporate the extent to which team members rely on one another for resources, including skills, information, and materials to complete work. Additionally, there is a process of task interdependence that has gained more recent attention. Rather than a stable feature of the team, process-oriented research emphasizes the dynamic emergent states of the team (Marks et al., 2001).

Another conceptualization of interdependence that has received substantial research is outcome interdependence. First conceptualized as "goal interdependence" and "interdependent feedback and rewards," outcome interdependence reflects the degree to which teams, versus individuals, have goals and receive rewards (Campion et al., 1993; Wageman, 1995). Rewarding team outputs (versus individual contributions) is a design decision that is expected to encourage individuals to perform behaviors that benefit the group as a whole (Campion et al., 1993; Guzzo & Shea, 1992). Edward J. Lawler (1981) suggested that outcome interdependence in teams is critical to prevent competition between team members. A recent meta-analysis on team interdependence examined the consequences associated with task and outcome interdependence in conjunction (Courtright et al., 2015).

Stephen H. Courtright and colleagues' (2015) meta-analysis suggests that both task and outcome interdependence are related to team performance, and both are partially mediated by task team functions (i.e., transition/action processes, collective efficacy) and relational team functions (i.e., interpersonal process and cohesion), with task interdependence more strongly predicting task functions and outcome interdependence more strongly predicting relational functions. Team interdependence has been commonly used to influence several other team outcomes as well. Other meta-analyses have used interdependence to predict team innovation (Hülsheger et al., 2009), and to strengthen the relationship between trust and performance (DeJong et al., 2016).

One additional form of interdependence, interpersonal interdependence (Marks et al., 2001), is not covered in this review. Although this construct has been named using the interdependence moniker, it is more clearly an interpersonal process construct which is not clearly related to work design.

The vast conceptual development of the interdependence construct at the team level of analysis has generated several important conceptual differences between work design research at the individual level and team levels of analysis. We highlight three domains of interdependence research that relate to team interdependence as a work characteristic: task interdependence, outcome interdependence, and external interdependence. Given this conceptual development, we define team interdependence as the extent to which a team must coordinate its efforts and resources to accomplish work, the extent to which workers must set goals and receive feedback and rewards as a team, and the extent to which the team relies on others and is relied on by other others to accomplish its work.

72 TRANSFORMATIVE WORK DESIGN

Social support. One interesting development related to social support at the team level concerns its outcomes. Many studies have adapted organizational citizenship behavior (OCB) measures from the individual level to the team level (Nohe & Michaelis, 2016). Several studies emphasize the important interactions between the individual and team levels, suggesting that OCBs at the team level are the consequence of socially supportive behavior, especially from the leader (Kirkman et al., 2004; Nohe & Michaelis, 2016). Other important research relating to social support at the team level are team managerial support (Shea & Guzzo, 1987) and shared liking or attraction within the group (Evans & Jarvis, 1980). Social support takes on an expanded role at the team level, reflecting the critical role of interpersonal relationships between team members, including leaders. Team social support is defined as the degree to which the relational structure of the team offers opportunities for assistance, conflict management, and leadership support.

Feedback from others. Feedback from others largely reflects feedback from leaders inside and outside of the team (Kirkman & Rosen, 1999; Wageman, 2001) and from others more generally (Patterson et al., 2005). Leader feedback is expected to be related to the location of the leader as internal or external to the team (Morgeson, 2005). Internal leaders are expected to be focused on day-to-day team management, whereas external leaders are better able to provide feedback (Komaki Desselles & Bowman, 1989). Seeking feedback from others throughout the organization has been identified as an important role within teams (Ancona & Caldwell, 1988).

Autonomous teams are believed to require performance feedback to align their goals with organizational goals and to avoid a state of disorder (Katz & Kahn, 1966). Research has shown that autonomy and feedback have an important interactive effect, referred to as "channeled autonomy," which can create alignment between the team and the organization, ultimately leading to improved team performance (Gonzalez-Mulé et al., 2016). Team feedback from others reflects the extent to which the team receives feedback from its members, as well as leaders and coworkers throughout the organization.

Interaction outside the organization. Although many teams must work interdependently with individuals, teams, and organizations that are external to the organization, there is little research that explicitly focuses on this. Rather, many studies have focused on interaction outside the team with other parts of the organization and boundary-spanning behaviors between teams (Ancona & Caldwell, 1988, 1992; Choi, 2002; Sundstrom & Altman, 1989). There is some research on how teams assess (i.e., "scan") the environment for information outside of the organization (e.g., marketing trends), although, this largely is outside of the social nature of the work (Ancona & Caldwell, 1992). Team interaction outside the organization reflects the extent to which the team's work requires interaction with people external to the organization.

Contextual characteristics

Because contextual characteristics at the team level of analysis have received little empirical research attention, this section highlights the potential for incorporating contextual features into team level work design research. Indeed, much of the work on context at the team level of analysis has been outside of the characteristics examined in the WDQ, with many studies focusing on novel contextualizations of the work environment (Johns, 2018).

Ergonomics. One aspect of the environment is the physical space that is available to the team. Ergonomics are affected by the size of physical space, potentially crowding teams of workers (Altman, 1975). At the team level of analysis, more research has considered the psychological impingement of physical spaces than the ergonomics of the space (Sundstrom et al., 1990). For example, researchers have considered how the physical environment creates opportunities for privacy, communication, and social behavior (Sundstrom et al., 1980; Sundstrom et al., 1990). Less research has considered how the physical environment affects the team's ability to move and maintain healthy positions, although some applied ergonomics research has discussed this work characteristic as an outcome (e.g., musculoskeletal discomfort outcomes in teams; Robertson et al., 2008). Team ergonomics reflects how well a team's work allows for healthy posture and movement.

Physical demands. Physical demands in teams have received some attention in the context of the job demands-resources model with the same predicted demands effects as the individual level (e.g., burnout risks; Bakker & Demerouti, 2007). Physical demands in teams have also received some attention in the applied ergonomics literature and are predicted to have the same deleterious effects as those predicted at the individual level (e.g., Fritzsche et al., 2014). Physical demands reflect the amount of physical activity and effort associated with a team's work.

Work conditions. Little research has considered work conditions as a characteristic of work in teams (cf., Fritzsche et al., 2014). Team health and safety have largely been considered from a climate perspective (Hofmann et al., 2017; Hofmann & Morgeson, 1999; Salas et al., 2020) or a training (KSA) perspective (Salas et al., 2008). Comfort has received some attention in teams, specifically noise and other unwanted external intrusions (Sundstrom et al., 1994; Sundstrom & Altman, 1989). Work conditions reflect the health, safety, and comfort of the environment associated with a team's work.

74   TRANSFORMATIVE WORK DESIGN

Equipment use. Although equipment use has received little research attention at the team level of analysis, the increasing complexity of technology has led to teams operating technology in contrast to earlier technologies which were more often operated by individuals. Importantly, equipment use in teams is argued to change the nature of teamwork (e.g., equipment use enables team virtuality; Larson & De Church, 2020). Equipment use reflects the variety and complexity of the technology, equipment, and tools used to accomplish a team's work.

Work Design at the Organizational Level of Analysis

Work design at the organizational level of analysis reflects the systematic deployment of sets of work characteristics to achieve desired outcomes. Sets of work characteristics are believed to have the potential to generate synergistic and interactive effects in combination (Morgeson & Humphrey, 2008), potentially altering the predictable relationships between work characteristics and outcomes. Campion's interdisciplinary research identified four models of work design, each focused on unique, and often conflicting, outcomes (Campion & Thayer, 1985). Implicit in this research is the idea that thematically related work characteristics (e.g., mechanistic, motivational) can produce distinctive outcomes, with some sets of work characteristics leading to important tradeoffs in outcomes (e.g., between satisfaction and efficiency; Campion & McClelland, 1993; Morgeson & Campion, 2002).

Although our focus at the organizational level of analysis is to identify sets of work characteristics and outcomes associated with them, organizational work design is contextualized by other aspects of organizational design. Work design in the organizational design literature is often construed as an element of organizational design (e.g., Adler et al., 1999; Gibson & Birkinshaw, 2004). One common theme when work design scholars explore the higher levels of analysis is that outcomes are often not predicted accurately by the work characteristics in isolation (Parker et al., 2001). Organizational design decisions infuse work characteristics with organizational context through organizational structures such as size and centralization (James & Jones, 1976; Oldham & Hackman, 1981). Indeed, organizational context is often impactful because information in the broader work environment changes the nature of work (Johns, 2006, 2018; Morgeson et al., 2006; Morgeson et al., 2010). We review organizational design research that presents sets of work characteristics, desired outcomes, and organizational context, summarizing the reviewed approaches by highlighting their work characteristics and desired outcomes in Table 3.2.

MULTI-LEVEL WORK DESIGN 75

Table 3.2 Organizational Work Design: Deploying Sets of Work Characteristics to Achieve Desired Outcomes

Organizational Design Approach	Work Design Approach	Set of Work Characteristics	Desired Outcomes
Scientific Management	Mechanistic	Low autonomy, task variety, identity, job complexity, skill variety	Efficiency
Toyota Production System	Mechanistic	High autonomy, low job complexity	Efficiency, quality
Lean Production	Mechanistic	High autonomy, task variety, feedback from the job, task identity, skill variety, information processing, interdependence	Efficiency, job satisfaction
Socio-Technical Systems Theory	Sociotechnical Systems	High autonomy, feedback from the job, task identity, interdependence	Efficiency, job satisfaction
Self-Managing Organizations	Sociotechnical Systems	High autonomy, feedback from others	Employee empowerment
Balance Theory of Job Design	Sociotechnical Systems	High autonomy, feedback from the job	Safety
High Performance Work Systems	Strategic HR	High autonomy, significance, interdependence	Organizational performance

Mechanistic approaches

Scientific management. Although scientific management is often associated with the mechanistic approach to designing individual jobs (e.g., time-and-motion studies; Gilbreth, 1911), Frederick W. Taylor's (1911) vision was for a totalizing mechanistic approach to organizational design. In this vision, the concept of work design should be organization-wide, with every individual job designed in an interlocking system of mechanistic cooperation. Taylor (1911,

p. 140) stated, "it is no single element, but rather this whole combination, that constitutes scientific management." Scientific management sought to program every conceivable action at work in the "one best way" (Taylor, 1911, p. 41).

To achieve this goal, the mechanistic approach to work design is focused on broadly reducing the task and knowledge characteristics of work, with the ultimate goal of increasing efficiency outcomes. There are many unintended and undesirable consequences of designing work this way, which have largely been articulated by motivational approaches to work design (Herzberg et al., 1959; Hackman & Oldham, 1975). Implicit in the scientific management approach is the increasing interdependencies of low autonomy, highly specialized workers (March & Simon, 1958). As individual workers perform smaller, more specialized parts of larger tasks, they rely on and are relied on by other workers and teams within the organization to complete the entire work task. Additionally, these small and specialized tasks are not reflective of entire pieces of work, resulting in very low task identity.

The properties of this scientific management system, specifically relating to job simplification, made sense in the context of early efforts at mass production and industrialization as reflected in Ford Motor Company's moving assembly lines in the early 1900s. As machines and automation became increasingly important facets of the work environment, worker knowledge and skill receded from prominence. Although still practiced today, even expanding with the advent of artificial intelligence (AI) and algorithmic management (AM) (Parent-Rocheleau & Parker, 2022; Parker & Grote, 2022), highly mechanistic approaches tend to appear less attractive because of the recognition of their many undesirable, unintended consequences, such as low motivation and job satisfaction, and increased absenteeism. Moreover, as the organizational environment becomes more variable and dynamic, unpredictable contingencies require coordination between interdependent but siloed workers (March & Simon, 1958).

New organizational and work designs emerged following the Hawthorn studies (Roethlisberger & Dickson, 1939). These new organizational designs recognized that informal organizational structures existed in every organization (Mintzberg, 1979) and that overly formalized and mechanistic work may be unpleasant or unhealthy for workers (Likert, 1961). These insights in research were mirrored in changes across organizational design practice, changing the trajectory of work design away from purely mechanistic approaches and toward approaches that considered human experiences.

Toyota Production System. The TPS (Ohno, 1988) represents a reflection and advancement on organizations designed using scientific management principles. The TPS added worker autonomy to mechanistically designed jobs, and "in this way, human intelligence, or a human touch, is given to the machines"

(Ohno, 1988, p. 6). The TPS reflects a dual concern for automation and autonomy, where workers are tasked with stopping production when abnormalities are identified during the course of work. The TPS is expected to increase efficiency above and beyond traditional mechanistic work design systems by reducing waste. Managers working in organizations using the TPS are believed to be especially cognizant of errors that arise during production because of the systematic focus on errors and continuous improvement (Monden, 2012) alongside increased managerial monitoring and surveillance (Delbridge et al., 1992). Although not formally theorized, these systems can have significant implications for improving opportunities for feedback from the job and from others.

Over decades of using TPS principles in organizations, many other work design advancements emerged as organizational design subsystems within organizations using the TPS. One important subsystem in the TPS is the Just-in-Time approach (JIT) (Monden, 2012). JIT is a production strategy that strives to improve performance by producing the right items in the right quantity at the right time, minimizing waste. These practices have been associated with increased autonomy, task variety, knowledge demands, and interdependence (Brown & Mitchell, 1991), but the exact work characteristics in practice have been characterized as "elusive" and "amorphous" (Dean & Snell, 1991). The small amount of empirical research that has been performed on these JIT practices has shown that work characteristics have a minimal effect on outcomes for workers (Jackson & Martin, 1996), or that outcomes are contingent upon other organizational practices (e.g., individual versus team rewards; Snell & Dean, 1994).

Lean production. Lean production (LP) (Krafcik, 1988; Shah & Ward, 2003, 2007) is the most modern formalization of the TPS, with a specific set of practices that are "lean" in nature (Womack et al., 1990). LP, like the TPS, is focused on creating efficiency through waste reduction, and is believed to halve costs (e.g., labor) relative to mass production (Krafcik, 1988). Although the TPS was believed to have had important outcomes for workers as a second-order effect (Dohse et al., 1985), LP considers the worker's role in the production process explicitly and specifies a systematic approach to work design (Shaw & Ward, 2003). There is significant debate over the consequences of LP for workers, with one camp focusing on the motivational aspects of LP and another focusing on the opportunities for work intensification and anxieties about costly mistakes (Landsbergis et al., 1999);the "lean-production system does indeed remove all slack—that's why it's lean. But it also provides workers with the skills they need to control their work environment and the continuing challenge of making the work go more smoothly" (Womack et al., 1990, p. 101).

LP is said to have two critical components: first, continuous task improvement (reflecting high autonomy, task variety, identity, and feedback from the

78 TRANSFORMATIVE WORK DESIGN

job), and second, a system for identifying the cause of production errors (Womack et al., 1990). To achieve these two goals, work characteristics are identified that highlight the importance of skilled workers (MacDuffie, 1995; Snell et al., 2000). Skill variety is especially critical under LP, as worker control over a varied task domain requires workers to use many skills to accomplish the breadth of potential tasks. Information processing is associated with LP as demands to respond to production errors require monitoring complex data. Additionally, some scholars have pointed to interdependence as a critical aspect of LP as teams rely on one another to complete tasks sequentially.

In contrast to earlier studies of the TPS, LP has received significant attention from work design researchers. LP has been suggested to be a particular challenge for work design theories that are focused on predicting the consequence of individual work characteristics. The LP context is believed to change the nature of the relationships between work characteristics and many outcomes. Indeed, scholars that have focused on certain individual LP practices (e.g., assembly lines) have identified negative outcomes of LP for workers (Parker, 2003; Sprigg & Jackson, 2006) whereas other researchers have found positive outcomes contingent upon different LP practices (e.g., increased boundary-control; Anderson-Connolly et al., 2002; Conti et al., 2006).

Several researchers have posited that LP as an integrated system may have unexpected positive outcomes for workers because of the highly motivating work environment (Adler, 1993; Womack et al., 1990) or because of the specific configuration of work characteristics associated with it (De Treville & Antonakis, 2006). A growing body of research has suggested that the systematic deployment of work characteristics associated with LP can jointly optimize efficiency and motivational outcomes (Cullinane et al., 2013, 2014; Jackson & Mullarkey, 2000; Jackson et al., 1993). Sarah-Jane Cullinane and colleagues (2012, p. 56) conclude that LP has the "potential to enhance both organizational performance (e.g., waste reduction, quality improvements, etc.) and the quality of working life for employees through simple job redesign."

Socio-technical system approaches

Socio-technical systems theory. STS theory (Cherns, 1976; Cummings, 1978; Trist & Bamforth, 1951) is a systematic approach to work design that focuses on the joint optimization of social and technical work systems (Emery, 1959; Trist, 1981). Although often associated with autonomous work groups and the team level of analysis, STS is concerned with entire organizations (Emery & Trist, 1965; Hackman, 1980; Pasmore, 1988; Trist, 1981). The attention placed on teams reflects the assumption that organizations are too large and complex to be centrally managed. Therefore, STS theory suggests that organizations should be designed such that teams close to disturbances can manage any issues that arise (de Sitter et al., 1997).

Coordination between workers, autonomous work groups, and the workers largely engaged with the external environment is a cohesive work system (Cummings, 1978). This systems level approach to work design has important implications for the deployment of work characteristics throughout the entire organization (Ingvaldsen & Rolfsen, 2012). The joint interest in social and technical work systems is reflected in a broad set of work characteristics that are believed to jointly optimize efficiency and satisfaction outcomes. In contrast to the potential for work intensification associated with more mechanistic systems, STS theory's focus on specific characteristics suggests a consciousness of the potential for overload. Conventionally, complete, easily identified pieces of work are most often designated to be completed by an autonomous team, providing high team task identity. The closeness and boundaries of the task should provide feedback (i.e., feedback from the job) and be performed interdependently by the team (Hackman, 1987). Chapter 12 discusses case examples of STS-based interventions for work redesign.

Self-managing organizations. Recently, the concept of implementing self-management throughout an entire organization has gained significant traction in industry under the organizational design practice called "Holacracy" (Robertson, 2015) and in research under the guise of "self-managing organizations" (SMOs) (Lee & Edmonson, 2017). Research on SMOs builds upon STS theory (Trist & Bamforth, 1951), Theory X and Theory Y (McGregor, 1960), and other worker empowerment approaches to work design (Morgeson & Campion, 2003). SMOs systematically remove hierarchical relations between work units, deploying autonomy over team design, task design, and objectives, as well as implementing peer feedback processes (Robertson, 2015). SMOs are expected to empower workers to design their own work, and to behave flexibly and innovatively by removing bureaucratic hurdles from decision-making (Roberston, 2015). SMOs embody the most extreme version of William A. Pasmore and colleagues' (1982, p. 1186) assertion that "the behavior of sociotechnical systems should not be bound by rules, regulations, and procedures except when absolutely necessary."

The Balance Theory of Job Design. The Balance Theory of Job Design (Smith & Sainfort, 1989) examines work design from an organizational lens, analyzing the relationship between sets of organizationally contextualized work characteristics and health factors (Carayon, 2006, 2009; Carayon & Smith, 2000). The Balance Theory of Job Design is closely associated with other systems approaches to work safety and the "macroergonomics" approaches to organizational design (Hendrick, 1991; Kleiner, 2006, 2008) which are themselves closely related to STS theory. The Balance Theory of Job Design suggests that health and safety at work must be approached through organizational level work design and in consideration of a comprehensive set of work design factors (i.e., task, knowledge, social, and contextual characteristics; Carayon et al., 2015).

This theory posits that the design of safety protocols at work does not reflect actual safety practices (Carayon et al., 2015). Safety concerns are conceptualized as unpredictable, emergent situations that must be approached by autonomous workers and teams in the local work environment. Moreover, safety behavior is posited to be sensitive to personal and organizational priorities (Nahrgang et al., 2011), and must therefore be approached with multiple considerations beyond task design. Built on STS theory (Trist & Bamforth, 1951), the Balance Theory of Job Design emphasizes that organizations should grant autonomy as close to the safety behavior as possible (i.e., variance control; Clegg, 2000). Additionally, it emphasizes continuous adaptation to feedback from errors at work (Clegg, 2000; Leveson, 2016). The theory ultimately suggests that the entire system of work characteristics to be deployed must be considered in combination because the environmental context as a whole will have a profound impact on safety practice, regardless of the intended design of work (Carayon et al., 2015).

Strategic human resources approaches

High-performance work systems. Work design has been identified as an important component of high-performance work systems (HPWS) (Huselid, 1995). Early discussions of HPWS suggested that organizations should implement principles of STS theory (Batt & Applebaum, 1995), a proposal that was largely abandoned by later researchers that focused on more specific sets of HR practices. Other early HPWS research suggested that work design is one facet of a "bundle" of HR management practices that should be used in conjunction as "best practices" (Arthur, 1994; Becker & Huselid, 2006; Huselid, 1995; MacDuffie, 1995). Practices outside of work design include incentives, training, selection, and flexible work arrangements, among many others (Huselid, 1995). HPWS focuses on complementarities and synergies between a set of HR management practices, including work design.

Some HPWS research suggests that increasing autonomy, significance, and interdependence alongside other HR practices will help achieve desirable organizational outcomes (Becker & Huselid, 2010). That said, Mark A. Huselid (1995) was clear that job design should be tailored to individual workers such that they can best leverage their unique KSAs. HPWS are expected to generate worker outcomes including higher job satisfaction, lower turnover, and increased productivity (Jiang et al., 2012). Importantly, this literature has focused on how HPWS can influence organizational outcomes relating to firm performance (Combs et al., 2006).

In contrast to the theorized synergistic combination of work design and HR practices found in HPWS, Morgeson and colleagues (2006) found that increasing autonomy in teams was important for improving performance only when other HR practices were not motivating. This disconnect provides evidence for the view that work design may substitute for poor HR practices rather than complementing them as proposed by the HPWS literature. Moreover, Barrick and colleagues (2015) tested the effects of the full set of task characteristics and feedback from others on firm performance, finding that they did not significantly predict firm performance on their own, but did so when combined with other HR practices and transformational leadership. Taken together, these studies suggest that work design and HR decisions should be considered in conjunction, emphasizing that they interact, but are not always synergistic in combination.

Discussions around HPWS suggest that the research is split on the effectiveness of the universal best practice bundles prescribed by earlier HPWS research (Delery & Doty, 1996). Alternative perspectives identify contingencies where certain HR practices may be more effective than others (Youndt et al., 1996; Lepak et al., 2005). One model suggests that bundles of HR practices, including work design, should be differentiated by the human capital they serve, with unique HR configurations for different types of human capital (Lepak & Snell, 1999). Indeed, many HR researchers have debated the merits of using best practice HR policies, pointing to the benefits of policies that are differentiated by job types and organizational levels (Campion et al., 2005; Kang & Snell, 2009; Tsui et al., 1997).

Discussion

The history of work design research has in large part been the history of individual work design and the examination of work characteristics at the individual level of analysis. This attention has led many scholars to imply that we know everything that there is to know about work design. But this assertion is premature given the far smaller bodies of work design research at the team and organizational levels of analysis. We highlighted the uneven amounts of research on each work characteristic at the team level, showing gaps in our knowledge across the task, knowledge, social, and especially the contextual domains. Moreover, we offered a new avenue for examining work design at the organizational level.

Work design research at the organizational level of analysis is in its infancy. We contributed a definition of organizational work design in the hopes of sparking a debate about how organizations can deploy sets of work characteristics to achieve desired outcomes. Although the extant organizational level research we reviewed in this chapter has been performed outside the domain of work design, much of it not even invoking the term, we believe that it provides a substantive foundation for future research. Moreover, work characteristic approaches to work design have more to contribute to organizational research than is implied by their historic treatment in micro-oriented empirical tests. The individual work characteristics have already had a large impact on team and team design research and have the potential to have a large impact on higher level organizational and organizational design research.

Implications and Future Research Directions for Team and Organizational Work Design

Although the 18 individual work characteristics examined by the WDQ reflect a comprehensive approach to analyzing job and work characteristics at the individual level of analysis (Morgeson & Humphrey, 2006), there are some deficiencies in these characteristics for analyzing all work characteristics that emerge at the team level. Future research should consider a broader scope of work characteristics that arise at the team level of analysis. Moreover, level of analysis remains another clear challenge in the multi-level work design literature. Theory is often at the team level of analysis, but work characteristics are measured at the individual level. As our review of the literature has shown, many researchers have used conceptually different meanings for many work characteristics at the individual versus team level of analysis.

Team level

A far more extensive review of the team autonomy literature is warranted than what is provided in this chapter. The differences between team autonomy as a theoretical construct (as defined in this chapter) and the multiple measurements used across studies at the team level merit their own review. At a minimum, identifying studies that use idiosyncratic measures of autonomy could offer insights into the meaning behind subtle differences in measurement. Further, our examination of interdependence at the team level revealed qualitative research that suggests interdependence in autonomous teams can lead to difficulty coordinating with other teams (Ingvaldsen & Rolfsen, 2012). There may be significant costs to autonomy and decentralization relating to coordination when considering the interdependence between teams in multi-team systems and other parts of the organization (Ancona & Caldwell, 1988, 1992). These studies suggest that interdependence between teams is an important future direction for work design scholarship. Many other areas deserve more attention as the world of work changes. For example, how might collaborating with AI as a teammate change the task, knowledge, social, and contextual characteristics of work differently than collaborating with human workers?

Organizational level

Future research on work design at the organizational level is particularly important because it can shape the meaning of work at the lower levels, aligning individual and team behavior with organizational strategy (Campion et al., 2005; Pasmore et al., 1982). Yet, organizational level work design initiatives are infrequently found to predict the design of individual jobs and teams (Arthur, 1994). Future research should consider work design alongside other organizational design considerations to see which decisions take precedence.

An integrative review of the literature on HR constructs that interact with work design is needed to simultaneously advance multi-level work design and HR research. Many studies have approached work design from an HR systems lens, yet, to our knowledge, there is no review of the two subjects together. This is unfortunate because these are both topic domains that managers have significant control over and are likely to have underexamined tradeoffs between them (Morgeson & Campion, 2002, 2003). When managers focus on one domain, they are likely to have to make concessions in the other (e.g., increasing knowledge characteristics increases compensation requirements; Campion & Berger, 1990; Morgeson & Humphrey, 2006).

Organizational design scholars have pointed to the importance of work design as a mechanism through which organizations can achieve their strategic goals. For example, Jeffrey B. Arthur (1994) articulates two bundles of HR practices that are expected to mutually reinforce one another to generate specific outcomes (i.e., commitment and control), but presumably, other bundles are possible. This research on HR bundles offers many HR practices, including work design, as the predictors of desired outcomes like reduced turnover in the commitment bundle, and increased productivity in the control bundle (Arthur, 1994; MacDuffie, 1995). Future research should consider how other aspects of work design might be able to influence a broader set of organizational goals.

Conclusion

Multi-level work design is an important research domain that still has many important research opportunities. We hope that this chapter sparks a larger debate about organizational work design and the ways in which work design research can be further integrated across levels of analysis and with a broader array of organizational research.

References

Adler, P. S. (1993). The "learning bureaucracy": New United Motor Manufacturing, Inc. In B. M. Staw & L. L. Cummings (Eds.), *Research in organizational behavior* (Vol. 15, pp. 111–194). JAI Press.

Adler, P. S., Goldoftas, B., & Levine, D. I. (1999). Flexibility versus efficiency? A case study of model changeovers in the Toyota Production System. *Organization Science 10*(1), 43–68.

Altman, I. (1975). *The environment and social behavior: Privacy, personal space, territory, and crowding.* Brooks/Cole Publishing Company.

Ancona, D. G., & Caldwell, D. F. (1988). Beyond task and maintenance: Defining external functions in groups. *Group and Organization Studies 13*(4), 468–494.

Ancona, D. G., & Caldwell, D. F. (1992). Bridging the boundary: External activity and performance in organizational teams. *Administrative Science Quarterly 37*(4), 634–665.

Anderson-Connolly, R., Grunberg, L., Greenberg, E. S., & Moore, S. (2002). Is lean mean? Workplace transformation and employee well-being. *Work, Employment and Society 16*(3), 389–413.

Arthur, J. B. (1994). Effects of human resource systems on manufacturing performance and turnover. *Academy of Management Journal 37*(3), 670–687.

Babbage, C. (1835). *On the economy of machinery and manufactures.* Knight.

Bakker, A. B., & Demerouti, E. (2007). The job demands-resources model: State of the art. *Journal of Managerial Psychology 22*(3), 309–328.

Barrick, M. R., Thurgood, G. R.,Smith, T. A., & Courtright, S. H. (2015). Collective organizational engagement: Linking motivational antecedents, strategic implementation, and firm performance. *Academy of Management Journal 58*(1), 111–135.

Batt, R., & Applebaum, E. (1995). Worker participation in diverse settings: Does the form affect the outcome, and if so, who benefits? *British Journal of Industrial Relations 33*(3), 7–108.

Becker, B. E., & Huselid, M. A. (2006). Strategic human resources management: Where do we go from here? *Journal of Management 32*(6), 898–925.

Becker, B. E., & Huselid, M. A. (2010). SHRM and job design: Narrowing the divide. *Journal of Organizational Behavior 31*(2), 379–388.

Bligh, M. C., Pearce, C. L., & Kohles, J. C. (2006). The importance of self- and shared leadership in team based knowledge work: A meso-level model of leadership dynamics. *Journal of Managerial Psychology 21*(4), 296–318.

Brown, K. A., & Mitchell, T. R. (1991). A comparison of just-in-time and batch manufacturing: The role of performance obstacles. *Academy of Management Journal 34*(4), 906–917.

Burns, T., & Stalker, G. M. (1961). *The management of innovation.* Tavistock Publications.

Byron, K., Keem, S., Darden, T., Shalley, C. E., & Zhou, J. (2023). Building blocks of idea generation and implementation in teams: A meta-analysis of team design and team creativity and innovation. *Personnel Psychology 76*(1), 249–278.

Campion, M. A. (1988). Interdisciplinary approaches to job design: A constructive replication with extensions. *Journal of Applied Psychology 73*(3), 467–481.

Campion, M. A., & Berger, C. J. (1990). Conceptual integration and empirical test of job design and compensation relationships. *Personnel Psychology 43*(3), 525–553.

Campion, M. A., & McClelland, C. L. (1993). Follow-up and extension of the interdisciplinary costs and benefits of enlarged jobs. *Journal of Applied Psychology 78*(3), 339–351.

Campion, M. A., Medsker, G. J., & Higgs, A. C. (1993). Relations between work group characteristics and effectiveness: Implications for designing effective work groups. *Personnel Psychology 46*(4), 823–847.

Campion, M. A., Mumford, T. V., Morgeson, F. P., & Nahrgang, J. D. (2005). Work redesign: Eight obstacles and opportunities. *Human Resource Management 44*(4), 367–390.

Campion, M. A., Papper, E. M., & Medsker, G. J. (1996). Relations between work team characteristics and effectiveness: A replication and extension. *Personnel Psychology 49*(2), 429–452.

Campion, M. A., & Thayer, P. W. (1985). Development and field evaluation of an interdisciplinary measure of job design. *Journal of Applied Psychology 70*(1), 29–43.

Carayon, P. (2006). Human factors of complex sociotechnical systems. *Applied Ergonomics 37*(4), 525–535.

Carayon, P. (2009). The balance theory and the work system model: Twenty years later. *International Journal of Human–Computer Interaction 25*(5), 313–327.

Carayon, P., Hancock, P., Leveson, N., Noy, I., Sznelwar, L., & van Hootegem, G. (2015). Advancing a sociotechnical systems approach to workplace safety—developing the conceptual framework. *Ergonomics 58*(4), 548–564.

Carayon, P., & Smith, M. J. (2000). Work organization and ergonomics. *Applied Ergonomics 31*, 649–662.

Carter, K. M., Hetrick, A. L., Chen, M., Humphrey, S. E., Morgeson, F. P., & Hoffman, B. J. (2024). How culture shapes the influence of work design characteristics: A narrative and meta-analytic review. *Journal of Management 50*(1), 122–157.

Cherns, A. (1976). The principles of sociotechnical design. *Human Relations 29*(8), 783–792.

Choi, J. N. (2002). External activities and team effectiveness: Review and theoretical development. *Small Group Research 33*(2), 181–208.

Clegg, C. (2000). Sociotechnical principles for system design. *Applied Ergonomics 31*, 463–477.

Cohen, S. G., & Bailey, D. E. (1997). What makes teams work: Group effectiveness research from the shop floor to the executive suite. *Journal of Management 23*(3), 239–290.

Combs, J., Liu, Y., Hall, A., & Ketchen, D. (2006). How much do high-performance work practices matter? A meta-analysis of their effects on organizational performance. *Personnel Psychology 59*(3), 501–528.

Conti, R., Angelis, J., Cooper, C., Faragher, B., & Gill, C. (2006). The effects of lean production on worker job stress. *International Journal of Operations and Production Management 26*(9), 1013–1038.

Cordery, J. L., Morrison, D., Wright, B. M., & Wall, T. D. (2010). The impact of autonomy and task uncertainty on team performance: A longitudinal field study. *Journal of Organizational Behavior 31*(2–3), 240–258.

Courtright, S. H., Thurgood, G. R., Stewart, G. L., & Pierotti, A. J. (2015). Structural interdependence in teams: An integrative framework and meta-analysis. *Journal of Applied Psychology 100*(6), 1825–1846.

Cullinane, S. J., Bosak, J., Flood, P. C., & Demerouti, E. (2013). Job design under lean manufacturing and its impact on employee outcomes. *Organizational Psychology Review 3*(1), 41–61.

Cullinane, S. J., Bosak, J., Flood, P. C., & Demerouti, E. (2014). Job design under lean manufacturing and the quality of working life: A job demands and resources perspective. *International Journal of Human Resource Management 25*(21), 2996–3015.

Cummings, T. G. (1978). Self-regulating work groups: A socio-technical synthesis. *Academy of Management Review 3*(3), 625–634.

Dean, J. W., & Snell, S. A. (1991). Integrated manufacturing and job design: Moderating effects of organizational inertia. *Academy of Management Journal 34*(4), 776–804.

De Dreu, C. K. W., Nijstad, B. A., & van Knippenberg, D. (2008). Motivated information processing in group judgment and decision making. *Personality and Social Psychology Review 12*(1), 22–49.

De Dreu, C. K. W., & Weingart, L. R. (2003). Task versus relationship conflict, team performance, and team member satisfaction: A meta-analysis. *Journal of Applied Psychology 88*(4), 741–749.

Delbridge, R., Turnbull, P., & Wilkinson, B. (1992). Pushing back the frontiers: Management control and work intensification under JIT/TQM factory regimes. *New Technology, Work and Employment 7*(2), 97–106.

De Jong, B. A., Dirks, K. T., & Gillespie, N. (2016). Trust and team performance: A meta-analysis of main effects, moderators, and covariates. *Journal of Applied Psychology 101*(8), 1134–1150.

Delery, J. E., & Doty, D. H. (1996). Modes of theorizing in strategic human resource management: Tests of universalistic, contingency, and configurational performance predictions. *Academy of Management Journal 39*(4), 802–835.

de Sitter, L. U., den Hertog, J. F., & Dankbaar, B. (1997). From complex organizations with simple jobs to simple organizations with complex jobs. *Human Relations 50*(5), 497–534.

De Treville, S., & Antonakis, J. (2006). Could lean production job design be intrinsically motivating? Contextual, configurational, and levels-of-analysis issues. *Journal of Operations Management 24*(2), 99–123.

D'Innocenzo, L., Mathieu, J. E., & Kukenberger, M. R. (2016). A meta-analysis of different forms of shared leadership–team performance relations. *Journal of Management 42*(7), 1964–1991.

Dohse, K., Jürgens, U., & Malsch, T. (1985). From "Fordism" to "Toyotism"? The social organization of the labor process in the Japanese automobile industry. *Politics & Society 14*(2), 115–146.

Donaldson, L. (2001). *The contingency theory of organizations.* SAGE.

Emery, F. E. (1959). *Characteristics of sociotechnical systems.* (Document 529). Tavistock Institute of Human Relations, Human Resources Centre.

Emery, F. E., & Trist, E. L. (1965). The causal texture of organizational environments. *Human Relations 18*(1), 21–32.

Englund, R. K. (1991). Hard work-where will it get you? Labor management in Ur III Mesopotamia. *Journal of Near Eastern Studies 50*(4), 255–280.

Evans, N. J., & Jarvis, P. A. (1980). Group cohesion: A review and reevaluation. *Small Group Behavior, 11*(4), 359–370.

Frazier, M. L., Fainshmidt, S., Klinger, R. L., Pezeshkan, A., & Vracheva, V. (2017). Psychological safety: A meta-analytic review and extension. *Personnel Psychology 70*(1), 113–165.

Fried, Y., & Ferris, G. R. (1987). The validity of the job characteristics model: A review and meta-analysis. *Personnel Psychology 40*(2), 287–322.

Fritzsche, L., Wegge, J., Schmauder, M., Kliegel, M., & Schmidt, K. H. (2014). Good ergonomics and team diversity reduce absenteeism and errors in car manufacturing. *Ergonomics 57*(2), 148–161.

Galbraith, J. R. (1973). *Designing complex organizations.* Addison-Wesley.

Galbraith, J. R. (1974). Organization design: An information processing view. *Interfaces 4*(3), 28–36.

Gibson, C. B., & Birkinshaw, J. (2004). The antecedents, consequences, and mediating role of organizational ambidexterity. *Academy of Management Journal 47*(2), 209–226.

Gilbreth, F. B. (1911). *Motion study.* Constable and Company.

Gladstein, D. L. (1984). Groups in context: A model of task group effectiveness. *Administrative Science Quarterly 29*(4), 499–517.

Gully, S. M., Devine, D. J., & Whitney, D. J. (1995). A meta-analysis of cohesion and performance: Effects of level of analysis and task interdependence. *Small Group Research 26*(4), 497–520.

Gully, S. M., Incalcaterra, K. A., Joshi, A., & Beaubien, J. M. (2002). A meta-analysis of team-efficacy, potency, and performance: Interdependence and level of analysis as moderators of observed relationships. *Journal of Applied Psychology 87*(5), 819–832.

Guzzo, R. A., & Shea, G. P. (1992). Group performance and intergroup relations in organizations. In M. D. Dunnette & L. M. Hough (Eds.), *Handbook of industrial and organizational psychology* (pp. 269–313). Consulting Psychologists Press.

Hackman, J. R. (1976). *The design of self-managing work groups* (Technical Report No. 2). Yale University.

Hackman, J. R. (1983). *A normative model of work team effectiveness* (Technical Report No. 11). Yale University.

Hackman, J. R. (1987). The design of work teams. In J. W. Lorsch (Ed.), *Handbook of organizational behavior* (pp. 315–342). Prentice-Hall.

Hackman, J. R., & Oldham, G. R. (1975). Development of the Job Diagnostic Survey. *Journal of Applied Psychology 60*(2), 159–170.

Hackman, J. R., & Oldham, G. R. (1976). Motivation through the design of work: Test of a theory. *Organizational Behavior and Human Performance 16*, 250–279.

Hackman, J. R., & Oldham, G. R. (1980). *Work redesign.* Addison-Wesley.

Harrison, D. A., & Humphrey, S. E. (2010). Designing for diversity or diversity for design? Tasks, interdependence, and within-unit differences at work. *Journal of Organizational Behavior 31*(2), 328–337.

Hendrick, H. W. (1991). Ergonomics in organizational design and management. *Ergonomics 34*(6), 743–756.

Henningsen, D. D., & Henningsen, M. L. M. (2003). Examining social influence in information-sharing contexts. *Small Group Research 34*(4), 391–412.

Herzberg, F., Mausner, B., & Snyderman, B. B. (1959). *The motivation to work.* Wiley.

Hinsz, V. B., Vollrath, D. A., & Tindale, R. S. (1997). The emerging conceptualization of groups as information processors. *Psychological Bulletin 121*(1), 43–64.

Hofmann, D. A., Burke, M. J., & Zohar, D. (2017). 100 years of occupational safety research: From basic protections and work analysis to a multilevel view of workplace safety and risk. *Journal of Applied Psychology 102*(3), 375–388.

House, R., Rousseau, D. M., & Thomas-Hunt, M. (1995). The meso paradigm: A framework for the integration of micro and macro organizational behavior. In L. L. Cummings & B. M. Staw (Eds.), *Research in organizational behavior* (Vol. 17, pp. 71–114). JAI Press.

Hülsheger, U. R., Anderson, N., & Salgado, J. F. (2009). Team-level predictors of innovation at work: A comprehensive meta-analysis spanning three decades of research. *Journal of Applied Psychology 94*(5), 1128–1145.

Humphrey, S. E., & Aime, F. (2014). Team microdynamics: Toward an organizing approach to teamwork. *Academy of Management Annals 8*(1), 443–503.

Humphrey, S. E., Nahrgang, J. D., & Morgeson, F. P. (2007). Integrating motivational, social, and contextual work design features: A meta-analytic summary and theoretical extension of the work design literature. *Journal of Applied Psychology 92*(5), 1332–1356.

Huselid, M. A. (1995). The impact of human resource management practices on turnover, productivity, and corporate financial performance. *Academy of Management Journal 38*(3), 635–672.

Ingvaldsen, J. A., & Rolfsen, M. (2012). Autonomous work groups and the challenge of inter-group coordination. *Human Relations 65*(7), 861–881.

Jackson, P. R., & Martin, R. (1996). Impact of just-in-time on job content, employee attitudes and well-being: A longitudinal study. *Ergonomics 39*(1), 1–16.

Jackson, P. R., & Mullarkey, S. (2000). Lean production teams and health in garment manufacture. *Journal of Occupational Health Psychology 5*(2), 231–245.

Jackson, P. R., Wall, T. D., Martin, R., & Davids, K. (1993). New measures of job control, cognitive demand, and production responsibility. *Journal of Applied Psychology 78*(5), 753–762.

James, L. R., & Jones, A. P. (1976). Organizational structure: A review of structural dimensions and their conceptual relationships with individual attitudes and behavior. *Organizational Behavior and Human Performance 16*(1), 74–113.

Jiang, K., Lepak, D. P., Hu, J., & Baer, J. C. (2012). How does human resource management influence organizational outcomes? A meta-analytic investigation of mediating mechanisms. *Academy of Management Journal 55*(6), 1264–1294.

Johns, G. (2006). The essential impact of context on organizational behavior. *Academy of Management Review 31*(2), 386–408.

Johns, G. (2018). Advances in the treatment of context in organizational research. *Annual Review of Organizational Psychology and Organizational Behavior 5*, 21–46.

Kang, S. C., & Snell, S. A. (2009). Intellectual capital architectures and ambidextrous learning: A framework for human resource management. *Journal of Management Studies 46*(1), 65–92.

Katz, D., & Kahn, R. L. (1966). *The social psychology of organizations.* Wiley.

Kiggundu, M. N. (1981). Task interdependence and the theory of job design. *Academy of Management Review 6*(3), 499–508.

Kiggundu, M. N. (1983). Task interdependence and job design: Test of a theory. *Organizational Behavior and Human Performance 31*(2), 145–172.

Kirkman, B. L., & Rosen, B. (1999). Beyond self-management: Antecedents and consequences of team empowerment. *Academy of Management Journal 42*(1), 58–74.

Kirkman, B. L., & Rosen, B. (2000). Powering up teams. *Organizational Dynamics 28*(3), 48–66.

Kirkman, B. L., Rosen, B., Tesluk, P. E., & Gibson, C. B. (2004). The impact of team empowerment on virtual team performance: The moderating role of face-to-face interaction. *Academy of Management Journal 47*(2), 175–192.

Kirkman, B. L., Tesluk, P. E., & Rosen, B. (2004). The impact of demographic heterogeneity and team leader-team member demographic fit on team empowerment and effectiveness. *Group and Organization Management 29*(3), 334–368.

Kleiner, B. M. (2006). Macroergonomics: Analysis and design of work systems. *Applied Ergonomics 37*, 81–89.

Kleiner, B. M. (2008). Macroergonomics: Work system analysis and design. *Human Factors 50*(3), 461–467.

Komaki, J. L., Desselles, M. L., & Bowman, E. D. (1989). Definitely not a breeze: Extending an operant model of effective supervision to teams. *Journal of Applied Psychology 74*(3), 522–529.

Kozlowski, S. W. J., & Bell, B. S. (2003). Work groups and teams in organizations: Review update. In W. C. Borman, D. R. Ilgen, & R. J. Klimoski (Eds.), *Handbook of psychology: Industrial and organizational psychology* (Vol. 12, pp. 333–375). Wiley.

Kozlowski, S. W. J., & Ilgen, D. R. (2006). Enhancing the effectiveness of work groups and teams. *Psychological Science in the Public Interest 7*(3), 77–124.

Krafcik, J. F. (1988). Triumph of the lean production system. *Sloan Management Review 30*(1), 41–52.

Landsbergis, P. A., Cahill, J., & Schnall, P. (1999). The impact of lean production and related new systems of work organization on worker health. *Journal of Occupational Health Psychology 4*(2), 108–130.

Langfred, C. W. (2000). The paradox of self-management: Individual and group autonomy in work groups. *Journal of Organizational Behavior 21*(5), 563–585.

Langfred, C. W. (2005). Autonomy and performance in teams: The multilevel moderating effect of task interdependence. *Journal of Management 31*(4), 513–529.

Langfred, C. W. (2007). The downside of self-management: A longitudinal study of the effects of conflict on trust, autonomy, and task interdependence in self-managing teams. *Academy of Management Journal 50*(4), 885–900.

Langfred, C. W., & Moye, N. A. (2004). Effects of task autonomy on performance: An extended model considering motivational, informational, and structural mechanisms. *Journal of Applied Psychology 89*(6), 934–945.

Larson, L., & DeChurch, L. A. (2020). Leading teams in the digital age: Four perspectives on technology and what they mean for leading teams. *Leadership Quarterly 31*(1), 1–18.

Laughlin, P. R. (1980). Social combination processes of cooperative problem-solving groups on verbal intellective tasks. In M. Fishbein (Ed.), *Progress in social psychology* (Vol. 1, pp. 127–155). Erlbaum.

Lawler, E. E. (1981). Pay and organization development. Addison-Wesley.

Leach, D. J., Wall, T. D., Rogelberg, S. G., & Jackson, P. R. (2005). Team autonomy, performance, and member job strain: Uncovering the teamwork KSA link. *Applied Psychology: An International Review 54*(1), 1–24.

Lee, M. Y., & Edmondson, A. C. (2017). Self-managing organizations: Exploring the limits of less-hierarchical organizing. *Research in Organizational Behavior 37*, 35–58.

Lepak, D. P., Bartol, K. M., & Erhardt, N. L. (2005). A contingency framework for the delivery of HR practices. *Human Resource Management Review 15*(2), 139–159.

Lepak, D. P., & Snell, S. A. (1999). The human resource architecture: Toward a theory of human capital allocation and development. *Academy of Management Review 24*(1), 31–48.

Leveson, N. G. (2016). *Engineering a safer world.* MIT Press.

Likert, R. (1961). *New patterns of management.* McGraw-Hill.

MacDuffie, J. P. (1995). Human resource bundles and manufacturing performance: Organizational logic and flexible production systems in the world auto industry. *Industrial and Labor Relations Review 48*(2), 197–221.

March, J. G., & Simon, H. A. (1958). *Organizations.* Wiley.

Marks, M. A., Mathieu, J. E., & Zaccaro, S. I. (2001). A temporally based framework and taxonomy of team processes. *Management Review 26*(3), 356–376.

Martins, L. L., & Sohn, W. (2022). How does diversity affect team cognitive processes? Understanding the cognitive pathways underlying the diversity dividend in teams. *Academy of Management Annals 16*(1), 134–178.

Mathieu, J. E., Gallagher, P. T., Domingo, M. A., & Klock, E. A. (2019). Embracing complexity: Reviewing the past decade of team effectiveness research. *Annual Review of Organizational Psychology and Organizational Behavior 6*, 17–46.

Maynard, M. T., Gilson, L. L., & Mathieu, J. E. (2012). Empowerment-fad or fab? A multilevel review of the past two decades of research. *Journal of Management 38*(4), 1231–1281.

Mayo, E. (1949). *Hawthorne and the Western Electric Company: The social problems of an industrial civilisation.* Routledge.

McGregor, D. (1960). *The human side of enterprise.* McGraw-Hill.

Mesmer-Magnus, J. R., & DeChurch, L. A. (2009). Information sharing and team performance: A meta-analysis. *Journal of Applied Psychology 94*(2), 535–546.

Michel, J. G., & Hambrick, D. C. (1992). Diversification posture and top management team characteristics. *Academy of Management Journal 35*(1), 9–37.

Milliken, F. J., & Martins, L. L. (1996). Searching for common threads: Understanding the multiple effects of diversity in organizational groups. *Academy of Management Review 21*(2), 402–433.

Mintzberg, H. (1979). *The structuring of organizations.* Prentice-Hall.

Monden, Y. (2012). *Toyota Production System: An integrated approach to just-in-time.* 4th ed. Taylor & Francis Group.

Morgeson, F. P. (2005). The external leadership of self-managing teams: Intervening in the context of novel and disruptive events. *Journal of Applied Psychology 90*(3), 497–508.

Morgeson, F. P., Brannick, M. T., & Levine, E. L. (2020). *Job and work analysis: Methods, research, and applications for human resource management.* 3rd ed. SAGE.

Morgeson, F. P., & Campion, M. A. (2002). Minimizing tradeoffs when redesigning work: Evidence from a longitudinal quasi-experiment. *Personnel Psychology 55*(3), 589–612.

Morgeson, F. P., & Campion, M. A. (2003). Work design. In W. C. Borman, D. R. Ilgen, & R. J. Klimoski (Eds.), *Handbook of psychology: Industrial and organizational psychology.* 2nd ed. (Vol. 12, pp. 423–452). Wiley.

Morgeson, F. P., Dierdorff, E. C., & Hmurovic, J. L. (2010). Work design in situ: Understanding the role of occupational and organizational context. *Journal of Organizational Behavior 31*(2), 351–360.

Morgeson, F. P., & Hofmann, D. A. (1999). The structure and function of collective constructs: Implications for multilevel research and theory development. *Academy of Management Review 24*(2), 249–265.

Morgeson, F. P., & Humphrey, S. E. (2006). The Work Design Questionnaire (WDQ): Developing and validating a comprehensive measure for assessing job design and the nature of work. *Journal of Applied Psychology 91*(6), 1321–1339.

Morgeson, F. P., & Humphrey, S. E. (2008). Job and team design: Toward a more integrative conceptualization of work design. In J. Martocchio (Ed.), *Research in personnel and human resources management* (Vol. 27, pp. 39–91). Emerald Group Publishing Limited.

Morgeson, F. P., Johnson, M. D., Campion, M. A., Medsker, G. J., & Mumford, T. V. (2006). Understanding reactions to job redesign: A quasi-experimental investigation of the moderating effects of organizational context on perceptions of performance behavior. *Personnel Psychology 59*(2), 333–363.

Nahrgang, J. D., Morgeson, F. P., & Hofmann, D. A. (2011). Safety at work: A meta-analytic investigation of the link between job demands, job resources, burnout, engagement, and safety outcomes. *Journal of Applied Psychology 96*(1), 71–94.

Nohe, C., & Michaelis, B. (2016). Team OCB, leader charisma, and organizational change: A multilevel study. *Leadership Quarterly 27*(6), 883–895.

Ohno, T. (1988). *Toyota production system: Beyond large-scale production.* Productivity Press.

Oldham, G. R., & Hackman, J. R. (1981). Relationships between organizational structure and employee reactions: Comparing alternative frameworks. *Administrative Science Quarterly 26*(1), 66–83.

Parent-Rocheleau, X., & Parker, S. K. (2022). Algorithms as work designers: How algorithmic management influences the design of jobs. *Human Resource Management Review 32*(3), 1-17.

Parker, S. K. (2003). Longitudinal effects of lean production on employee outcomes and the mediating role of work characteristics. *Journal of Applied Psychology 88*(4), 620–634.

Parker, S. K. (2014). Beyond motivation: Job and work design for development, health, ambidexterity, and more. *Annual Review of Psychology 65*, 661–691.

Parker, S. K., & Grote, G. (2022). Automation, algorithms, and beyond: Why work design matters more than ever in a digital world. *Applied Psychology 71*(4), 1171–1204.

Parker, S. K., Morgeson, F. P., & Johns, G. (2017). 100 years of work design research: Looking back and looking forward. *Journal of Applied Psychology 102*, 403–420.

Parker, S. K., & Wall, T. D. (1998). *Job and work design: Organizing work to promote well-being and effectiveness.* SAGE.

Parker, S. K., Wall, T. D., & Cordery, J. L. (2001). Future work design research and practice: Towards an elaborated model of work design. *Journal of Occupational and Organizational Psychology 74*(4), 413–440.

Pasmore, W., Francis, C., Haldeman, J., & Shani, A. (1982). Sociotechnical systems: A North American reflection on empirical studies of the seventies. *Human Relations 34*(12), 1179–1204.

Pasmore, W. A. (1988). *Designing effective organizations: The sociotechnical systems perspective.* Wiley.

Patterson, M. G., West, M. A., Shackleton, V. J., Dawson, J. F., Lawthom, R., Maitlis, S., Robinson, D. L., & Wallace, A. M. (2005). Validating the organizational climate measure: Links to managerial practices, productivity and innovation. *Journal of Organizational Behavior 26*(4), 379–408.

Paulus, P. B., Dzindolet, M., & Kohn, N. W. (2012). Collaborative creativity—Group creativity and team innovation. In M. D. Mumford (Ed.), *Handbook of organizational creativity* (pp. 327–357). Academic Press.

Pearce, C. L., & Manz, C. C. (2005). The new silver bullets of leadership: The importance of self- and shared leadership in knowledge work. *Organizational Dynamics 34*(2), 130–140.

Pelled, L. H. (1996). Demographic diversity, conflict, and work group outcomes: An intervening process theory. *Organization Science 7*(6), 615–631.

Pelled, L. H., Eisenhardt, K. M., & Xin, K. R. (1999). Exploring the black box: An analysis of work group diversity, conflict and performance. *Administrative Science Quarterly 44*(1), 1–28.

Rico, R., Sánchez-Manzanares, M., Gil, F., & Gibson, C. (2008). Team implicit coordination processes: A team knowledge–based approach. *Academy of Management Review 33*(1), 163–184.

Roberts, K. H., Hulin, C. L., & Rousseau, D. M. (1978). *Developing an interdisciplinary science of organizations.* Jossey-Bass.

Robertson, B. J. (2015). *Holacracy: The new management system for a rapidly changing world.* Henry Holt and Company.

Robertson, M. M., Huang, Y. H., O'Neill, M. J., & Schleifer, L. M. (2008). Flexible workspace design and ergonomics training: Impacts on the psychosocial work environment, musculoskeletal health, and work effectiveness among knowledge workers. *Applied Ergonomics 39*(4), 482–494.

Roethlisberger, F. J., & Dickson, W. J. (1939). *Management and the worker.* Harvard University Press.

Rousseau, V., & Aubé, C. (2010). Team self-managing behaviors and team effectiveness: The moderating effect of task routineness. *Group and Organization Management 35*(6), 751–781.

Ryu, J. W., Neubert, E. M., & Gonzalez-Mulé, E. (2022). Putting the team in the driver's seat: A meta-analysis on the what, why, and when of team autonomy's impact on team effectiveness. *Personnel Psychology 75*(2), 411–439.

Salas, E., Bisbey, T. M., Traylor, A. M., & Rosen, M. A. (2020). Can teamwork promote safety in organizations? *Annual Review of Organizational Psychology and Organizational Behavior 7*, 283–313.

Salas, E., DiazGranados, D., Klein, C., Burke, C. S., Stagl, K. C., Goodwin, G. F., & Halpin, S. M. (2008). Does team training improve team performance? A meta-analysis. *Human Factors 50*(6), 903–933.

Salas, E., Dickinson, T. L., Converse, S. A., & Tannenbaum, S. I. (1992). Toward an understanding of team performance and training. In R. W. Swezey & E. Salas (Eds.), *Teams: Their training and performance* (pp. 3–29). Ablex Publishing.

Seibert, S. E., Wang, G., & Courtright, S. H. (2011). Antecedents and consequences of psychological and team empowerment in organizations: A meta-analytic review. *Journal of Applied Psychology 96*(5), 981–1003.

Shah, R., & Ward, P. T. (2003). Lean manufacturing: Context, practice bundles, and performance. *Journal of Operations Management 21*(2), 129–149.

Shah, R., & Ward, P. T. (2007). Defining and developing measures of lean production. *Journal of Operations Management 25*(4), 785–805.

Shea, G. P., & Guzzo, R. A. (1987). Groups as human resources. In K. M. Rowland & G. R. Ferris (Eds.), *Research in personnel and human resources management* (Vol. 5, pp. 323–356). JAI Press.

Simons, T., Pelled, L. H., & Smith, K. A. (1999). Making use of difference: Diversity, debate, and decision comprehensiveness in top management teams. *Academy of Management Journal 42*(6), 662–673.

Smith, A. (1776). *An inquiry into the nature and causes of the wealth of nations*. W. Strahan and T. Cadell.

Smith, M. J., & Sainfort, P. C. (1989). A balance theory of job design for stress reduction. *International Journal of Industrial Ergonomics 4*(1), 67–79.

Snell, S. A., & Dean, J. W. (1994). Strategic compensation for integrated manufacturing: The moderating effects of jobs and organizational inertia. *Academy of Management Journal 37*(5), 1109–1140.

Snell, S. A., Lepak, D. P., Dean, J. W., & Youndt, M. A. (2000). Selection and training for integrated manufacturing: The moderating effects of job characteristics. *Journal of Management Studies 37*(3), 445–466.

Spreitzer, G. M. (2008). Taking stock: A review of more than twenty years of research on empowerment at work. In C. Cooper & J. Barling (Eds.), *The SAGE handbook of organizational behavior* (Vol. 1, pp. 54–72). Sage.

Sprigg, C. A., & Jackson, P. R. (2006). Call centers as lean service environments: Job-related strain and the mediating role of work design. *Journal of Occupational Health Psychology 11*(2), 197–212.

Stasser, G., & Stewart, D. (1992). Discovery of hidden profiles by decision-making groups: Solving a problem versus making a judgment. *Journal of Personality and Social Psychology 63*(3), 426–460.

Stevens, M. J., & Campion, M. A. (1994). The knowledge, skill, and ability requirements for teamwork: Implications for human resource management. *Journal of Management 20*(2), 503–530.

Stevens, M. J., & Campion, M. A. (1999). Staffing work teams: Development and validation of a selection test for teamwork settings. *Journal of Management 25*(2), 207–228.

Stewart, G. L. (2006). A meta-analytic review of relationships between team design features and team performance. *Journal of Management 32*(1), 29–55.

Stewart, G. L., & Barrick, M. R. (2000). Team structure and performance: Assessing the mediating role of intrateam process and the moderating role of task type. *Academy of Management Journal 43*(2), 135–148.

Sundstrom, E., & Altman, I. (1989). Physical environments and work-group effectiveness. In L. L. Cummings & B. M. Staw (Eds.), *Research in organizational behavior* (Vol. 11, pp. 175–209). JAI Press.

Sundstrom, E., Burt, R. E., & Kamp, D. (1980). Privacy at work: Architectural correlates of job satisfaction and job performance. *Academy of Management Journal 23*(1), 101–117.

Sundstrom, E., De Meuse, K. P., & Futrell, D. (1990). Work teams applications and effectiveness. *American Psychologist 45*(2), 120–133.

Sundstrom, E., Town, J. P., Rice, R. W., Osborn, D. P., & Brill, M. (1994). Office noise satisfaction and performance. *Environment and Behavior 26*(2), 195–222.

Taylor, F. W. (1911). *The principles of scientific management.* Norton.

Thompson, J. D. (1967). *Organizations in action: Social science bases of administrative theory.* McGraw-Hill.

Trist, E. L. (1981). The evolution of socio-technical systems. In *Ontario quality of working life centre* (Vol. 2). Ontario Quality of Working Life Center.

Trist, E. L., & Bamforth, K. W. (1951). Some social and psychological consequences of the longwall method of coal-getting. *Human Relations 4,* 3–38.

Trist, E. L., Higgins, G. W., Murray, H., & Pollock, A. B. (1963). *Organizational choice.* Tavistock Publications.

Tsui, A. S., Pearce, J. L., Porter, L. W., & Tripoli, A. M. (1997). Alternative approaches to the employee-organization relationship: Does investment in employees pay off? *Academy of Management Journal 40*(5), 1089–1121.

van Knippenberg, D., De Dreu, C. K. W., & Homan, A. C. (2004). Work group diversity and group performance: An integrative model and research agenda. *Journal of Applied Psychology 89*(6), 1008–1022.

van Knippenberg, D., & Schippers, M. C. (2007). Work group diversity. *Annual Review of Psychology 58,* 515–541.

Vashdi, D. R., Bamberger, P. A., & Erez, M. (2013). Can surgical teams ever learn? The role of coordination, complexity, and transitivity in action team learning. *Academy of Management Journal 56*(4), 945–971.

Wageman, R. (1995). Interdependence and group effectiveness. *Administrative Science Quarterly 40*(1), 145–180.

Wageman, R. (2001). How leaders foster self-managing team effectiveness: Design choices versus hands-on coaching. *Organization Science 12*(5), 559–577.

Wall, T. D., Kemp, N. J., Jackson, P. R., & Clegg, C. W. (1986). Outcomes of autonomous workgroups: A long-term field experiment. *Academy of Management Journal 29*(2), 280–304.

Wang, D., Waldman, D. A., & Zhang, Z. (2014). A meta-analysis of shared leadership and team effectiveness. *Journal of Applied Psychology 99*(2), 181–198.

Williams, H. M., Parker, S. K., & Turner, N. (2010). Proactively performing teams: The role of work design, transformational leadership, and team composition. *Journal of Occupational and Organizational Psychology 83*(2), 301–324.

de Wit, F. R. C., Greer, L. L., & Jehn, K. A. (2012). The paradox of intragroup conflict: A meta-analysis. *Journal of Applied Psychology 97*(2), 360–390.

Womack, J. P., Jones, D. T., & Roos, D. (1990). *The machine that changed the world.* Rawson Associates.

Youndt, M. A., Snell, S. A., Dean, J. W., & Lepak, D. P. (1996). Human resource management, manufacturing strategy, and firm performance. *Academy of Management Journal 39*(4), 36–66.

Zaccaro, S. J., Michelle, A. M., & DeChurch, L. A. (2012). Multiteam systems: An introduction. In S. J. Zaccaro, A. M. Michelle, & L. A. DeChurch (Eds.), *Multiteam systems: An organization form for dynamic and complex environments* (pp. 3–32). Routledge.

PART 2
OUTCOMES OF WORK DESIGN

Job Design and Well-Being

A Review of the Empirical Evidence

Sabine Sonnentag

Work can be a source of drain and misery—and it can be a source of joy, fulfillment, and growth. If work results in exhaustion and poor well-being or if it contributes to happiness and human flourishing depends profoundly on how work is designed (Parker, 2014). This chapter describes in detail how job design contributes to employee well-being. It will illustrate how core features of a job are related to the jobholders' experience of feeling well and engaged, as opposed to fatigued, anxious, tense, and depressed.

I will start by describing the well-being concept, referring both to hedonic and eudaimonic aspects of well-being. I will then introduce the SMART framework of work design that describes five higher-order categories of work characteristics (Stimulating, Mastery, Autonomous, Relational, Tolerable; Parker & Knight, 2024, see also Parker & Boeing, 2023). In the main part of this chapter, I will present empirical evidence about how these five job features relate to well-being. Specifically, I will summarize meta-analyses on correlational and mainly cross-sectional studies, describe longitudinal primary and meta-analytic studies, and will review experiments conducted in the laboratory, and summarize field interventions. I will close this chapter with a discussion of core findings (including major tensions), and suggestions for future research and job-design practice.

Well-Being Concept

Well-being is a broad concept with its descriptions ranging from well-being as the experience of positive emotional states and the absence of negative states (Diener, 2000) to well-being as "optimal functioning" (Tay et al., 2023). Psychological research distinguishes between a hedonic and an eudaimonic perspective on well-being. The hedonic perspective focuses on well-being as pleasure and happiness. The eudaimonic perspective views well-being as the experience of meaning (Oishi & Westgate, 2022). Both the hedonic and the eudaimonic

Sabine Sonnentag, *Job Design and Well-Being*. In: *Transformative Work Design*. Edited by: Sharon K. Parker et al., Oxford University Press. © Society for Industrial and Organizational Psychology (2025).
DOI: 10.1093/oso/9780197692554.003.0004

perspective found their way into organizational research, with the hedonic perspective clearly being the dominant perspective (Sonnentag, 2015). With respect to the hedonic perspective, organizational researchers often refer to the circumplex model of affect (Russell, 1980) and differentiate between valence and arousal as two fundamental dimensions. Thus, work-related well-being cannot only be described along a positive versus negative continuum, but also along a high-activation versus low-activation continuum. For instance, exhaustion (as a core burnout component; Maslach et al., 2001) and fatigue can be described as negatively toned, low-activation experiences whereas work engagement with its components of vigor, dedication, and absorption (Schaufeli & Bakker, 2004) can be described as positively toned, high-activation experiences. In addition, organizational researchers often also refer to somatic symptoms (e.g., headache, backpain) when they study (low) well-being (Nixon et al., 2011).

The experience of meaningfulness is the core aspect of eudaimonic well-being (Oishi & Westgate, 2022). Broader conceptualizations also incorporate other aspects, such as personal growth, self-realization, authenticity, and virtue (Huta & Waterman, 2014). In addition, alienation (Chiaburu et al., 2014) can be seen as an experience of low eudaimonic well-being.

Well-being has stable and variable components (Sonnentag, 2015). When considering well-being as a consequence of job design, researchers assume that well-being can change over time (i.e., as a consequence of job-design efforts). Although the exact duration of change in well-being is rarely explicitly addressed (but see Guthier et al., 2020), it is reasonable to assume that enduring job features may not manifest in day-to-day fluctuations in well-being, but may develop over longer time periods.

The SMART Framework for Work Design

To integrate the accumulated knowledge from multiple theoretical approaches and the empirical evidence, the Centre for Transformative Work Design (https://www.smartworkdesign.com.au) has developed the SMART work design model as an integrative framework that describes how favorable work should look like (Parker & Knight, 2024). This SMART work design model is very useful for characterizing job-design features that are essential for well-being at work. Therefore, I will use this framework as an organizing principle in this chapter.

SMART is the acronym for five core themes that are important to build a healthy workplace: Stimulating, Mastery, Autonomous, Relational, and Tolerable. Stimulating, as the first theme of the SMART framework, refers to skill variety, task variety, and problem-solving requirements, and information-processing requirements as core ingredients for a well-designed job. Jobs that are high on the stimulating dimension offer tasks that are varied and provide an opportunity for problem solving and learning. The second theme mastery includes job features such as role clarity, job feedback, and feedback from others. Jobholders of mastery-oriented jobs know what they are expected to do and how well they are doing it. Knowing one's role and responsibilities and being provided with feedback helps to perform well on the job. Autonomous work as the third theme implies that the job allows control over work methods, over time-related scheduling of one's tasks, and over other decisions. Autonomous jobs provide the jobholder with a high degree of job control and autonomy in deciding how to go about doing one's work. The fourth theme refers to relational aspects of a job. A job is high on the relational dimension when it provides the jobholder with a sense of support and purpose, and when it fosters social contacts. Thus, social support at work is an essential aspect of a highly relational job. At the same time, relational jobs are low on interpersonal stressors (e.g., interpersonal conflict, harassment, incivility) as these stressful experiences undermine the positive aspects of being interpersonally connected at work. Also having a sense of how one's job impacts other people is an important aspect of this relational dimension. Finally, as the fifth theme of the SMART framework, demands should be tolerable. This tolerability feature links the SMART framework to the job-stress literature that emphasized that demands that are too high and too stressful impair jobholders' health and well-being (Bliese et al., 2017).

Meta-Analyses Summarizing Correlational Studies

During the past decades, researchers conducted hundreds of correlational studies that examined how principles of SMART work design relate to indicators of well-being. Findings of this research stream have been summarized in numerous meta-analyses that I review here.

Stimulating work

Stimulating work implies that the job includes a variety of different tasks (task variety), that a broad variety of skills is needed (skill variety), and that the work is cognitively challenging, for instance by providing problem-solving and information-processing requirements. These job features are in stark contrast to attributes of highly simplified jobs and were already introduced as some of the

100 TRANSFORMATIVE WORK DESIGN

core job characteristics in J. Richard Hackman and Greg R. Oldham's (1976) job characteristics model.

Table 4.1 shows meta-analytic findings on the relationship between various aspects of stimulating work and well-being. Convincing meta-analytic evidence demonstrates that stimulating work is associated with work engagement as an important indicator of hedonic well-being. For instance, task variety and problem-solving demands show positive associations with work engagement (Christian et al., 2011). Meta-analytic associations between stimulating work and indicators of impaired well-being (e.g., anxiety, burnout) are rather small (Mlekus & Maier, 2021) and often not significant (Humphrey et al., 2007). Thus, although stimulating work is generally energizing, it needs to be considered that stimulating work can be overtaxing and might therefore compromise well-being. Primary studies, for instance, suggest that high problem-solving demands are associated with fatigue (Schmitt et al., 2017) and exhaustion (Huo & Boxall, 2018) when no personal or job resources are available that can be used to cope with the stimulating work demands.

In terms of eudaimonic well-being, there is strong meta-analytic evidence that stimulating features of one's work are positively associated with the experience of meaning and growth (Humphrey et al., 2007) and negatively associated with the experience of alienation (Chiaburu et al., 2014).

Mastery-oriented work

Mastery-oriented work means that the job incorporates elements that help workers to feel competent, namely role clarity, job feedback, and feedback from others. Role clarity implies that job holders have a good understanding of their responsibilities and of what is expected from them (cf., Rizzo et al., 1970). Feedback means that the job itself provides "direct and clear information" (Hackman & Oldham, 1976, p. 258) about one's performance. Whereas role clarity—or role ambiguity as the lack of role clarity—has its conceptual origin in role theory (Kahn et al., 1964), job feedback is described as a core job characteristic within the job characteristics model (Hackman & Oldham, 1976).

Empirical evidence is in line with the idea that role clarity is important for hedonic well-being. Meta-analyses reported that lack of role clarity (i.e., role ambiguity) is associated with tension and anxiety (Jackson & Schuler, 1985), depression (Schmidt et al., 2014), exhaustion (Alcaron, 2011), and physical symptoms (Nixon et al., 2011), whereas presence of role clarity is related with work engagement (Mazzetti et al., 2023).

Also with respect to other aspects of mastery, meta-analytic findings tend to support their relevance for hedonic well-being (Table 4.2). For instance,

Table 4.1 Exemplary Meta-Analyses Summarizing Relationships between Stimulating Job Features and Well-being

Authors (Year)	Workplace factor	k	N	r	0 outside 95% CI	Outcome variable
Relationship between skill-variety and hedonic well-being						
Humphrey et al., 2007	Skill variety	6	1,673	−.10	No	Stress
Humphrey et al., 2007	Skill variety	5	1,021	.00	No	Anxiety
Humphrey et al., 2007	Skill variety	4	1,789	.06	No	Burnout/exhaustion
Relationship between task-variety constructs and hedonic well-being						
Crawford et al., 2010	Job variety	6	6,739	.42	Yes	Work engagement
Christian et al., 2011	Task variety	9	9,211	.44	Yes	Work engagement
Mazzetti et al., 2023	Task variety	5	29,820	.39	Yes	Work engagement
Mlekus & Maier, 2021	Job and task rotation	5	—	.20	Yes	General psychological health
Mlekus & Maier, 2021	Job and task rotation	10	—	.13	Yes	Stress and burnout
Relationship between constructs referring to problem-solving demands and hedonic well-being						
Humphrey et al., 2007	Job complexity	3	882	.01	No	Anxiety
Christian et al., 2011	Problem solving demands	9	9,578	.23	Yes	Work engagement
Relationship between stimulating job features and eudaimonic well-being						
Fried & Ferris	Skill variety	5	7,861	.45	not reported	Experienced meaningfulness
Fried & Ferris	Skill variety	20	11,356	.45	not reported	Growth satisfaction
Humphrey et al., 2007	Skill variety	23	11,274	.44	Yes	Experienced meaning
Humphrey et al., 2007	Skill variety	31	15,941	.46	Yes	Growth satisfaction
Chiaburu et al., 2014	Task variety	5	3,073	−.12	Yes	Alienation

Table 4.2 Exemplary Meta-Analyses Summarizing Relationships between Mastery-Oriented Job Features and Well-Being

Authors (Year)	Workplace factor	k	N	r	0 outside 95% CI	Outcome variable
Relationship between role-clarity constructs and hedonic well-being						
Jackson & Schuler (1985)	Role ambiguity	43	7,570	.30	not reported	Tension/anxiety
Frone (1990)	Role ambiguity	10	801	.40	not reported	Job tension
Lee & Ashforth, 1996	Role clarity	6	929	−.30	Yes	Emotional exhaustion
Lee & Ashforth, 1996	Role ambiguity	6	1,518	.16	No	Emotional exhaustion
Örtqvist & Wincent, 2006	Role ambiguity	8	1,435	.35	Yes	Tension
Örtqvist & Wincent, 2006	Role ambiguity	9	1,752	.27	Yes	Exhaustion
Alcaron, 2011	Role ambiguity	51	22,145	.26	Yes	Exhaustion
Nixon et al., 2011	Role ambiguity	33	13,556	.15	Yes	Physical symptoms (cross-sectional studies)
Schmidt et al., 2014	Role ambiguity	27	13,703	.28	Yes	Depression
Mazzetti et al., 2023	Role clarity	7	68, 394	.36	Yes	Work engagement
Relationship between feedback and hedonic well-being						
Humphrey et al., 2007	Feedback from job	6	1,212	−.15	Yes	Stress
Humphrey et al., 2007	Feedback from job	6	9,470	−.26	Yes	Anxiety
Humphrey et al., 2007	Feedback from job	3	1,130	−.09	No	Burnout/exhaustion
Humphrey et al., 2007	Feedback from others	7	1,170	−.25	Yes	Stress
Humphrey et al., 2007	Feedback from others	2	322	−.14	Yes	Burnout/exhaustion
Crawford et al., 2010	Feedback	19	12,125	.28	Yes	Work engagement

Katz et al., 2021	Feedback environment	5	2,210	−.49	Yes	Exhaustion
Katz et al., 2021	Feedback environment	11	4,872	.38	Yes	Work engagement
Mazzetti et al., 2023	Feedback	8	76,378	.40	Yes	Work engagement

Relationship between role-clarity constructs and eudaimonic well-being

Chiaburu et al., 2014	Role ambiguity	11	2,356	.42	Yes	Alienation

Relationship between feedback and eudaimonic well-being

Fried & Ferris, 1987	Job feedback	5	7,861	.38	not reported	Experienced meaningfulness
Fried & Ferris, 1987	Job feedback	20	11,356	.40	not reported	Growth satisfaction
Humphrey et al., 2007	Feedback from job	22	11,225	.37	Yes	Experienced meaning
Humphrey et al., 2007	Feedback from job	31	15,941	.41	Yes	Growth satisfaction
Humphrey et al., 2007	Feedback from others	7	8,824	.28	Yes	Experienced meaning
Humphrey et al., 2007	Feedback from others	7	8,824	.08	No	Growth satisfaction
Chiaburu et al., 2014	Job feedback	6	3,400	−.26	Yes	Alienation

feedback from the job is associated with lower levels of anxiety (Humphrey et al., 2007) and stress (Humphrey et al., 2007), and higher levels of work engagement (Mazzetti et al., 2023). Job feedback seems to be unrelated to burnout (Humphrey et al., 2007), but an overall positive feedback environment is associated with low exhaustion (Katz et al., 2021).

Mastery-oriented work relates to eudaimonic well-being as well. For instance, lack of role clarity (i.e., role ambiguity) is related to alienation (Chiaburu et al., 2014). Feedback is associated with experienced meaning (Humphrey et al., 2007), growth satisfaction (Humphrey et al., 2007), and low alienation (Chiaburu et al., 2014).

Autonomous work

Autonomous work implies control over work scheduling, over work methods, and over decision making. This autonomy principle is essential in several job design models, including Hackman and Oldham's (1976) job characteristics model and Robert Karasek's (1979) job-demand-control model. Also job-design principles derived from self-determination theory (Gagné et al., 2022) rely on this principle, as self-determination theory refers to autonomy as a basic human need. The role of autonomy for hedonic well-being has been widely researched. Meta-analyses summarized in Table 4.3 show rather consistent positive relationships with positive well-being indicators such as work engagement (Christian et al., 2011) and negative relationships with indicators of impaired well-being such as emotional distress (Spector, 1986) and exhaustion (Alcaron, 2011). For physical strain indicators, effects are small, particularly in more recent meta-analyses (Gonzalez-Mulé et al., 2021; Nixon et al., 2011).

Within the job-design literature, there is a tradition to regard certain job features (e.g., autonomy) as not only helpful in itself but also as beneficial in reducing the impact of high demands. For instance, when introducing his job-demand-control model, Karasek (1979, p. 287) argued that a high decision latitude (i.e., high job control) should help workers to transform experienced stress into "energy of action." After a long debate (e.g., Wall et al., 1996), several meta-analyses revisited the assumed moderator effect of autonomy on the relationship between demanding job features and impaired well-being. Although using distinct methodological approaches, all three meta-analyses concluded that there is no evidence to assume that autonomy plays such a moderator role (Gonzalez-Mulé et al., 2021; Guthier et al., 2020; Huth & Chung-Yan, 2023). Thus, although autonomy in itself shows a rather consistent positive association with hedonic well-being, it is not effective in reducing the negative impact of high demands.

Table 4.3 Exemplary Meta-Analyses Summarizing Relationships between Autonomous Job Features and Well-Being

Authors, Year	Workplace factor	k	N	r	0 outside 95% CI	Outcome variable studied
Relationship between autonomy constructs and hedonic well-being						
Spector, 1986	Autonomy	4	1,083	−.28	not reported	Emotional distress
Spector, 1986	Autonomy	6	1,228	−.24	not reported	Physical symptoms
Lee & Ashforth, 1996	Autonomy	11	2,177	−.13	No	Emotional exhaustion
Humphrey et al., 2007	Autonomy	13	12,240	−.18	Yes	Stress
Humphrey et al., 2007	Autonomy	14	4,414	−.08	Yes	Anxiety
Humphrey et al., 2007	Autonomy	14	14,825	−.25	Yes	Burnout/exhaustion
Crawford et al., 2010	Autonomy	32	18,344	.31	Yes	Work engagement
Alcaron, 2011	Autonomy	34	17,165	−.20	Yes	Exhaustion
Alcaron, 2011	Control	56	33,297	−.21	Yes	Exhaustion
Christian et al., 2011	Autonomy	43	24,499	.33	Yes	Work engagement
Nahrgang et al., 2011	Autonomy	5	1,556	−.30	Yes	Burnout
Nahrgang et al., 2011	Autonomy	5	616	.24	Yes	Engagement
Nixon et al., 2011	Lack of control	58	32,645	.07	Yes	Physical symptoms (cross-sectional studies)
Park et al., 2014	Job control	71	48,528	−.16	Yes	Exhaustion
Fila et al., 2017	Control	61	63,236	−.16	Yes	Exhaustion
Gonzalez-Mulé et al., 2021	Job control	52	63,027	−.18	Yes	Psychological strain indicators
Gonzalez-Mulé et al., 2021	Job control	32	99,524	.01	No	Physical strain indicators
Mazzetti et al., 2023	Job control	18	82, 153	.34	Yes	Work engagement
Relationship between autonomy constructs and eudaimonic well-being						
Fried & Ferris, 1987	Autonomy	5	7,861	.42	not reported	Experienced meaningfulness
Fried & Ferris, 1987	Autonomy	20	11,426	.50	not reported	Growth satisfaction
Humphrey et al., 2007	Autonomy	22	11,225	.41	Yes	Experienced meaning
Humphrey et al., 2007	Autonomy	32	17,602	.51	Yes	Growth satisfaction
Chiaburu et al., 2014	Autonomy	7	7,555	−.10	Yes	Alienation

106 TRANSFORMATIVE WORK DESIGN

Working in a highly autonomous job is associated with eudaimonic well-being such as high experienced meaning, high growth satisfaction, and low alienation (Chiaburu et al., 2014; Fried & Ferris, 1987; Humphrey et al., 2007). Overall associations between autonomous work and eudaimonic well-being tend to be stronger than associations between autonomous work and hedonic well-being, particularly when looking at experienced meaning and growth satisfaction as indicators of eudaimonic well-being.

Relational work

Relational work characteristics refer to aspects of interpersonal connectedness at work. This includes provision of social support by one's supervisor and coworkers, the experience of purpose of one's work (i.e., task significance), and social appreciation. In addition to these positive features of interpersonal connectedness at work, also the absence of negative interpersonal aspects (i.e., social stressors, interpersonal conflicts, harassment, incivility) can be subsumed under the relational dimension of the SMART framework. Traditional conceptualizations of job design such as the job characteristics model (Hackman & Oldham, 1976), have already incorporated task significance as a core positively framed job characteristic. Adam Grant (2007) explicitly described the relational job architecture (i.e., job impact on beneficiaries and contact with beneficiaries) as important features of a job. Also within self-determination theory (Deci & Ryan, 2012), interpersonal relatedness is conceptualized as a basic human need and, accordingly, the satisfaction of this relatedness need is important for well-being (Gagné et al., 2022).

As Table 4.4 shows, meta-analyses on the relationship between social support and hedonic well-being clearly show that receiving help and support from others at work is negatively related to experienced stress (Humphrey et al., 2007), anxiety (Humphrey et al., 2007), and exhaustion (Halbesleben, 2006), and positively related to work engagement (Christian et al., 2011; Crawford et al., 2010). Meta-analytic evidence on task significance suggests that this job feature is positively related to work engagement (Christian et al., 2011) and negatively related to burnout (Humphrey et al., 2007), but not to anxiety or stress (Humphrey et al., 2007).

With respect to negative relational work characteristics, meta-analyses showed that social stressors in general, and also specific types of social stressors, are associated with impaired hedonic well-being. For instance, social stressors are related to poor mental health and high burnout (Gerhardt et al., 2021). Most types of interpersonal conflict at work are associated with impaired

Table 4.4 Exemplary Meta-Analyses Summarizing Relationships between Relational Job Features and Well-Being

Authors, Year	Workplace factor	k	N	r	0 outside 95% CI	Outcome variable studied
Relationship between social support and hedonic well-being						
Lee & Ashforth, 1996	Supervisor support	13	3,589	−.31	Yes	Emotional exhaustion
Lee & Ashforth, 1996	Coworker support	14	3,552	−.18	Yes	Emotional exhaustion
Lee & Ashforth, 1996	Peer cohesion	5	657	−.08	No	Emotional exhaustion
Lee & Ashforth, 1996	Team cohesion	2	156	−.20	Yes	Emotional exhaustion
Viswesvaran et al., 1999	Social support	41	15,015	−.23	Yes	Burnout
Halbesleben, 2006	Work support	132	22,557	−.22	Yes	Exhaustion
Humphrey et al., 2007	Social support	10	12,676	−.19	Yes	Anxiety
Humphrey et al., 2007	Social support	11	7,946	−.22	Yes	Stress
Humphrey et al., 2007	Social support	18	10,647	−.27	Yes	Burnout/exhaustion
Crawford et al., 2010	Support	33	17,029	.27	Yes	Engagement
Christian et al., 2011	Social support	38	18,226	.27	Yes	Work engagement
Humphrey et al., 2007	Social support	18	10,647	−.27	Yes	Burnout/exhaustion
Crawford et al., 2010	Support	33	17,029	.27	Yes	Engagement
Christian et al., 2011	Support	38	18,226	.27	Yes	Work engagement
Nahrgang et al., 2011	Social support	6	2,168	−.22	Yes	Burnout
Nahrgang et al., 2011	Social support	17	43,935	.51	Yes	Engagement
Fila et al., 2017	Social support	45	40,570	−.25	Yes	Emotional exhaustion
Michel et al., 2022	Interpersonal resources	4	712	−.29	Yes	Physical fatigue
Michel et al., 2022	Interpersonal resources	3	502	−.25	Yes	Cognitive weariness

continued

Table 4.4 *continued*

Authors, Year	Workplace factor	k	N	r	0 outside 95% CI	Outcome variable studied
Michel et al., 2022	Interpersonal resources	5	735	−.28	Yes	Emotional exhaustion
Holman et al., 2023	Social job resources	16	4,286	.30	Yes	Well-being
Holman et al., 2023	Social job resources	7	2,202	−.10	No	Job strain
Mazzetti et al., 2023	Social resources	22	83,566	.36	Yes	Work engagement
Mazzetti et al., 2023	Co-worker support	10	80,886	.27	Yes	Work engagement
Mazzetti et al., 2023	Supervisor support	16	79,632	.36	Yes	Work engagement
Relationship between task significance and hedonic well-being						
Humphrey et al., 2007	Task significance	5	1,021	−.02	No	Anxiety
Humphrey et al., 2007	Task significance	4	1,008	.04	No	Stress
Humphrey et al., 2007	Task significance	2	756	−.24	Yes	Burnout/exhaustion
Christian et al., 2011	Task significance	4	5,870	.42	Yes	Work engagement
Relationship between meaningfulness and hedonic well-being						
Allan et al., 2019	Meaningful work	4	1,085	−.19	Yes	Negative affect
Allan et al., 2019	Meaningful work	18	6,391	.74	Yes	Engagement
Relationship between social stressors and hedonic well-being						
Bowling & Beehr, 2006	Harassment	27	17,663	.29	not reported	Generic Strain
Bowling & Beehr, 2006	Harassment	16	4,918	.25	not reported	Anxiety
Bowling & Beehr, 2006	Harassment	16	5,625	.28	not reported	Depression
Bowling & Beehr, 2006	Harassment	9	5,633	.33	not reported	Burnout
Bowling & Beehr, 2006	Harassment	16	3,613	.30	not reported	Frustration

Bowling & Beehr, 2006	Harassment	4	1,783	−.21	not reported	Positive emotions at work
Bowling & Beehr, 2006	Harassment	7	1,549	.38	not reported	Negative emotions at work
Willness et al., 2007	Sexual harassment	29	45,880	−.18	Yes	Mental health
Crawford et al., 2010	Emotional conflict	4	3,220	−.16	Yes	Engagement
Nixon et al., 2011	Interpersonal conflict	25	10,215	.22	Yes	Physical symptoms (cross-sectional studies)
Nielsen & Einarsen, 2012	Bullying	12	7,863	.27	Yes	Anxiety
Nielsen & Einarsen, 2012	Bullying	17	17,196	.34	Yes	Depression
Nielsen & Einarsen, 2012	Bullying	11	11,733	.28	Yes	Somatization
Nielsen & Einarsen, 2012	Bullying	11	34,941	.23	Yes	Physical health problems
Nielsen & Einarsen, 2012	Bullying	6	1,229	.37	Yes	Post-traumatic stress
Nielsen & Einarsen, 2012	Bullying	10	4,914	.27	Yes	Burnout
Nielsen & Einarsen, 2012	Bullying	7	6,619	.31	Yes	Strain
Pindek et al., 2019	Mistreatment	13	1,366	.29	Yes	Strain
De Wit et al., 2012	Task conflict	5	623	.05	No	Positive affect
De Wit et al., 2012	Relationship conflict	4	387	−.40	Yes	Positive affect
Verkuil et al., 2015	Bullying	19	68,010	.29	Yes	Depression
Verkuil et al., 2015	Bullying	19	68,802	.34	Yes	Anxiety
Verkuil et al., 2015	Bullying	27	47,522	.37	Yes	Stress-related complaints
Sojo et al., 2016	Work harassment	10	not reported	−.37	Yes	Mental health
Sojo et al., 2016	Sexual harassment	36	not reported	−.27	Yes	Mental health
Sojo et al., 2016	Sexism at work	6	not reported	−.29	Yes	Mental health

continued

Table 4.4 *continued*

Authors, Year	Workplace factor	k	N	r	0 outside 95% CI	Outcome variable studied
Bedi, 2021	Ostracism	7	1,756	.43	Yes	Emotional exhaustion
Bedi, 2021	Ostracism	3	1,023	−.40	Yes	Psychological well-being
Bedi, 2021	Ostracism	5	1,455	−.23	Yes	Engagement
Gerhardt et al., 2021	Social stressors	88	-	−.27	Yes	Mental health
Gerhardt et al., 2021	Social stressors	76	-	.34	Yes	Burnout
Gerhardt et al., 2021	Social stressors	44	-	−.25	Yes	General well-being
Chris et al., 2022	Incivility	37	18,643	.39	Yes	Emotional exhaustion
Chris et al., 2022	Incivility	28	14,286	.29	Yes	Somatic symptoms
Han et al., 2022	Incivility	26	6,503	.41	Yes	Negative affect
Han et al., 2022	Incivility	5	821	−.13	Yes	Positive affect
Han et al., 2022	Incivility	31	10,877	.39	Yes	Burnout
Han et al., 2022	Incivility	40	12,182	.38	Yes	Emotional exhaustion
Han et al., 2022	Incivility	33	13,680	.34	Yes	Stress
Han et al., 2022	Incivility	9	2,753	.27	Yes	Depression
Han et al., 2022	Incivility	7	2,423	.29	Yes	Anxiety
Han et al., 2022	Incivility	5	4,840	−.26	Yes	Psychological well-being
Han et al., 2022	Incivility	7	2,986	−.33	Yes	Mental health
Michel et al., 2022	Interpersonal stressors	3	764	.50	Yes	Emotional exhaustion

Relationship between social support and eudaimonic well-being

Humphrey et al., 2007	Social support	3	1,987	.52	Yes	Growth satisfaction

Relationship between task significance and eudaimonic well-being

Chiaburu et al., 2014	Task significance	4	2,721	−.13	Yes	Alienation
Fried & Ferris, 1987	Task significance	5	7,861	.45	not reported	Experienced meaningfulness
Fried & Ferris, 1987	Task significance	19	11,366	.35	not reported	Growth satisfaction
Humphrey et al., 2007	Task significance	24	11,444	.45	Yes	Experienced meaning
Humphrey et al., 2007	Task significance	29	15,395	.34	Yes	Growth satisfaction

hedonic well-being (de Wit et al., 2012; Nixon et al., 2011). Harassment and bullying are related to several indicators of poor hedonic well-being, including burnout (Bowling & Beehr, 2006; Nielsen & Einarsen, 2012), depression (Bowling & Beehr, 2006; Verkuil et al., 2015), and anxiety (Bowling & Beehr, 2006; Nielsen & Einarsen, 2012). For ostracism, significant meta-analytic correlations were reported for emotional exhaustion, low psychological well-being, and low engagement (Bedi, 2021). Also incivility as a comparably "mild" type of social stressor is associated with symptoms such as emotional exhaustion, depression, and anxiety (Chris et al., 2022; Han et al., 2022).

Compared to the association between relational work features and hedonic well-being, the association between relational work features and eudaimonic well-being has been rarely analyzed in meta-analyses. The existing meta-analytic evidence mainly focused on the role of task significance for eudaimonic well-being and reported positive relationships between task significance and low alienation (Chiaburu et al., 2014), experienced meaning (Humphrey et al., 2007), and growth satisfaction (Humphrey et al., 2007).

Tolerable work

In well-designed jobs, demands should be tolerable. This principle acknowledges that it is unrealistic to have demand-free jobs but emphasizes that demands should not be too high. The SMART framework focuses on role overload (i.e., having to deal with a high workload and high responsibilities), role conflict (i.e., facing conflicting requirements), and work–home conflict (i.e., demands from the job domain interfering with demands from the home domain). The broader job-stress literature describes an even larger set of demands and potentially stressful conditions including organizational constraints, daily hassles, and emotional and self-control demands.

One influential taxonomy of job demands differentiates between challenge and hindrance demands (Cavanaugh et al., 2000). Challenge demands are demands that provide opportunities for task accomplishment and personal growth (Podsakoff et al., 2007) and comprise job features, such as a workload, time pressure, and responsibility. Hindrance demands are demands that impede task accomplishment and personal growth (Podsakoff et al., 2007) and include, for instance, organizational constraints, role conflict, and job insecurity.

Empirical evidence about the relevance of tolerable demands for well-being is exhaustive and rather consistent. Meta-analyses (Table 4.5) show that high demands and stressors in general are related to poor hedonic well-being, including general psychological strain indicators (e.g., Gonzalez-Mulé et al., 2021) and burnout (e.g., Lesener et al., 2019). This picture can also be observed for

Table 4.5 Exemplary Meta-Analyses Summarizing Relationships between Tolerable Job Features and Well-Being

Authors (Year)	Workplace factor	k	N	r	0 outside 95% CI	Outcome variable
Relationship between overall demands and hedonic well-being						
Ford et al., 2014	Stressors in general	91	24,844	.29	Yes	Psychological strain (synchronous at Time 1)
Ford et al., 2014	Stressors in general	29	15,678	.11	Yes	Physical strain (synchronous at Time 1)
Fila et al., 2017	Demands in general	60	63,099	.40	Yes	Emotional exhaustion
Sojo et al., 2016	Stressors in general	30	—	−.34	Yes	Mental health
Lesener et al., 2019	Demands in general	37	—	.41	not reported	Burnout (synchronous at Time 1)
Lesener et al., 2019	Demands in general	35	—	.11	not reported	Work engagement (synchronous at Time 1)
Gonzalez-Mulé et al., 2021	Demands in general	65	71,792	.26	Yes	Psychological strain
Gonzalez-Mulé et al., 2021	Demands in general	34	102,295	.08	Yes	Physical strain
A. Li et al., 2021	Work stressors	20	7,079	.07	Yes	Psychological distress
Q. Li et al., 2021	Demands in general	28	7,088	−.18	Yes	Positive indicators of well-being
Q. Li et al., 2021	Demands in general	75	11,807	.26	Yes	Negative indicators of well-being
Michel et al., 2022	Organizational stressors in general	9	3,028	.29	Yes	Emotional exhaustion
Michel et al., 2022	Organizational stressors in general	8	2,023	.43	Yes	Cognitive weariness
Michel et al., 2022	Organizational stressors in general	15	3,937	.43	Yes	Physical fatigue
Relationship between challenge demands in general and hedonic well-being						
Pindek et al., 2019	Challenge stressors	22	2,203	.28	Yes	Strain
Podsakoff et al., 2007	Challenge stressors	25	7,440	.33	Yes	Strain
Crawford et al., 2010	Challenge demands	18	9,794	.14	Yes	Burnout

continued

Table 4.5 *continued*

Authors (Year)	Workplace factor	k	N	r	0 outside 95% CI	Outcome variable
Crawford et al., 2010	Challenge demands	26	12,487	.14	Yes	Work engagement
Mazzola & Disselhorst, 2019	Challenge stressors	10	2,880	.29	Yes	Psychological strain
Mazzola & Disselhorst, 2019	Challenge stressors	15	5,263	.24	Yes	Burnout
Mazzola & Disselhorst, 2019	Challenge stressors	5	1,557	.14	Yes	Physical strain
Mazzola & Disselhorst, 2019	Challenge stressors	3	537	.09	No	Engagement
Downes et al., 2021	Challenge demands	19	2,053	.27	yes	Psychological strain
Downes et al., 2021	Challenge demands	16	1,446	.11	No	Job engagement
Gonzalez-Mulé et al., 2021	Challenge demands	69	136,735	.11	Yes	Strain in general

Relationship between specific challenge demands and hedonic well-being

Lee & Ashforth, 1996	Workload	6	1,450	.52	Yes	Emotional exhaustion
Lee & Ashforth, 1996	Work pressure	5	681	.41	Yes	Emotional exhaustion
Örtqvist & Wincent, 2006	Role overload	2	375	.26	Yes	Tension
Örtqvist & Wincent, 2006	Role overload	5	1,196	.46	Yes	Exhaustion
Alcaron, 2011	Workload	86	51,529	.40	Yes	Emotional Exhaustion
Nixon et al., 2011	Workload	92	36,610	.22	Yes	Physical symptoms (cross-sectional studies)
Bowling et al., 2015	Workload	24	37,130	−.25	Yes	Mental well-being
Bowling et al., 2015	Workload	29	17,960	.27	Yes	Strain
Bowling et al., 2015	Workload	41	32,554	.21	Yes	Distress
Bowling et al., 2015	Workload	27	19,962	.17	Yes	Depression
Bowling et al., 2015	Workload	12	17,397	.10	Yes	Fatigue
Bowling et al., 2015	Workload	53	48,723	.38	Yes	Emotional exhaustion
Bowling et al., 2015	Workload	50	51,651	.24	Yes	Physical symptoms
Bowling et al., 2015	Workload	11	5,083	−.03	No	Engagement

Pindek et al., 2019	Workload	13	1,162	.24	Yes	Strain
Kubicek et al., 2023	Workload	350	242,436	.35	Yes	Strain
Kubicek et al., 2023	Cognitive demands	84	73,493	.18	Yes	Strain
Holman et al., 2023	Challenge demands	18	7,476	.05	No	Well-being
Holman et al., 2023	Challenge demands	16	7205	.27	Yes	Job strain

Relationship between hindrance demands in general and hedonic well-being

Podsakoff et al., 2007	Hindrance stressors	56	12,454	.41	Yes	Strain
Crawford et al., 2010	Hindrance demands	15	9,439	.24	Yes	Burnout
Crawford et al., 2010	Hindrance demands	28	18,540	−.16	Yes	Work engagement
Pindek et al., 2019	Hindrance stressors	39	3,793	.34	Yes	Strain
Mazzola & Disselhorst, 2019	Hindrance stressors	12	3,717	.36	Yes	Psychological strain
Mazzola & Disselhorst, 2019	Hindrance stressors	18	6,700	.38	Yes	Burnout
Mazzola & Disselhorst, 2019	Hindrance stressors	6	1,785	.24	Yes	Physical strain
Mazzola & Disselhorst, 2019	Hindrance stressors	3	537	−.11	No	Engagement
Downes et al., 2021	Hindrance demands	17	2,037	.38	Yes	Psychological strain
Downes et al., 2021	Hindrance demands	7	751	−.12	No	Job engagement
Gonzalez-Mulé et al., 2021	Hindrance demands	27	32,884	.28	Yes	Strain in general
Holman et al., 2023	Hindrance demands	22	8,696	−.05	No	Well-being
Holman et al., 2023	Hindrance demands	10	3,333	.18	Yes	Job strain

Relationship between specific hindrance demands and hedonic well-being

Jackson & Schuler, 1985	Role conflict	23	4,035	.28	not reported	Tension/Anxiety
Lee & Ashforth, 1996	Role conflict	11	2,824	.42	Yes	Emotional exhaustion
Lee & Ashforth, 1996	Role stress	3	703	.50	Yes	Emotional exhaustion
Lee & Ashforth, 1996	Stressful events	4	903	.45	Yes	Emotional exhaustion

continued

Table 4.5 *continued*

Authors (Year)	Workplace factor	k	N	r	0 outside 95% CI	Outcome variable
Örtqvist & Wincent, 2006	Role conflict	7	1,220	.43	Yes	Tension
Örtqvist & Wincent, 2006	Role conflict	8	1,931	.12	Yes	Exhaustion
Alcaron, 2011	Role conflict	37	13,568	.42	Yes	Emotional Exhaustion
Christian et al., 2011	Physical demands	2	2,333	−.19	Yes	Work engagement
Nahrgang et al., 2011	Risks and hazards	8	3,007	.24	Yes	Burnout
Nahrgang et al., 2011	Risks and hazards	18	31,996	−.48	Yes	Engagement
Nahrgang et al., 2011	Physical demands	11	4,890	.01	No	Burnout
Nahrgang et al., 2011	Physical demands	21	11,284	−.12	No	Engagement
Nixon et al., 2011	Organizational constraints	34	8,212	.33	Yes	Physical symptoms (cross-sectional studies)
Nixon et al., 2011	Role conflict	26	4,880	.27	Yes	Physical symptoms (cross-sectional studies)
Schmidt et al., 2014	Role conflict	20	10,538	.29	Yes	Depression
Pindek & Spector, 2016	Organizational constraints	8	2,764	.35	Yes	Stress (self-report of constraints)
Pindek & Spector, 2016	Organizational constraints	5	790	.42	Yes	Anxiety (self-report of constraints)
Pindek & Spector, 2016	Organizational constraints	15	5,133	.40	Yes	Frustration (self-report of constraints)
Pindek & Spector, 2016	Organizational constraints	7	1,786	.35	Yes	Emotional Exhaustion (self-report of constraints)
Pindek & Spector, 2016	Organizational constraints	42	10,321	.33	Yes	Physical symptoms (self-report of constraints)
Jiang & Lavaysse, 2018	Job insecurity	86	67,119	−.24	Yes	Psychological health
Jiang & Lavaysse, 2018	Job insecurity	64	45,467	.21	Yes	Strain
Jiang & Lavaysse, 2018	Job insecurity	16	7,994	.21	Yes	Anxiety
Jiang & Lavaysse, 2018	Job insecurity	27	22,077	.25	Yes	Depression
Jiang & Lavaysse, 2018	Job insecurity	21	22,840	.20	Yes	Burnout

Jiang & Lavaysse, 2018	Job insecurity	65	50,308	.26	Yes	Emotional exhaustion
Jiang & Lavaysse, 2018	Job insecurity	101	91,563	−.18	Yes	Physical health
Jiang & Lavaysse, 2018	Job insecurity	26	15,387	−.17	Yes	Work engagement
Relationship between other specific demands and hedonic well-being						
Allen et al., 2000	Work-family conflict	13	4,481	.34	not reported	General psychological strain
Allen et al., 2000	Work-family conflict	10	3,582	.40	not reported	Burnout
Allen et al., 2000	Work-family conflict	11	4,304	.34	not reported	Depression
Allen et al., 2000	Work-family conflict	17	7,780	.30	not reported	Somatic/Physical symptoms
Amstad et al., 2011	Work-family interference	15	9,177	.38	Yes	Burnout/Exhaustion
Amstad et al., 2011	Work-family interference	18	8,039	.35	Yes	Psychological Strain
Amstad et al., 2011	Work-family interference	14	9,869	.23	Yes	Depression
Amstad et al., 2011	Work-family interference	6	5,347	.54	Yes	Stress
Amstad et al., 2011	Work-family interference	3	4,804	.14	Yes	Anxiety
Amstad et al., 2011	Work-family interference	18	8,665	.29	Yes	Somatic/Physical symptoms
Nohe et al., 2015	Work-family interference	32	12,906	.32	Yes	Strain (all types; synchronous at Time 1)
Nohe et al., 2015	Work-family interference	20	9,130	.39	Yes	Work-specific strain (synchronous at Time 1)
Reichl et al., 2014	Work-nonwork conflict	96	43,135	.51	Yes	Exhaustion (cross-sectional)
A. Li et al., 2021	Work-family conflict	24	6,344	.12	Yes	Psychological distress
Relationship between demands and eudaimonic well-being						
Chiaburu et al., 2014	Role conflict	12	5,748	.22	Yes	Alienation

challenge (e.g., Downes et al., 2021; Mazzola & Disselhorst, 2019) and hindrance demands (e.g., Crawford et al., 2010; Pindek et al., 2019). However, typically the relationship between hindrance stressors and impaired hedonic well-being is stronger than the relationship between challenge stressors and impaired hedonic well-being (however, see Alcaron, 2011). Of note, associations between various demands and physical strain symptoms tend to be lower than associations between various demands and psychological strain symptoms (e.g., Gonzalez-Mulé et al., 2021; Mazzola & Disselhorst, 2019). Interestingly, demands in general and challenge demands in particular tend to be positively related to work engagement, although the correlations are small (e.g., Crawford et al., 2010) in size and partly not significant (Downes et al., 2021). Hindrance demands, however, are negatively related to work engagement (e.g., Crawford et al., 2010; Nahrgang et al., 2011). In addition, there is clear evidence that work–family conflict is related to poor well-being (e.g., Allen et al., 2000; Nohe et al., 2015).

Taken together, empirical research clearly shows that people who face high demands at work experience poor psychological well-being. Particularly hindrance demands but also challenge demands contribute to these associations. Associations with physical symptoms are less strong, possibly because physical symptoms may not manifest immediately, but only after some time.

Compared to the huge research efforts on the association between demands and hedonic well-being there is relatively little meta-analytical research on the association between demands and eudaimonic well-being. Noteworthy is the meta-analysis by Dan Chiaburu and colleagues (2014) that reported a positive correlation between role conflict and alienation. Although it is highly plausible that demands must be reasonable to stimulate eudaimonic well-being at work, David Blustein and colleagues (2013) cite several primary studies that people can experience their work as meaningful even when they work under rather adverse conditions. Moreover, Winnie Yun Jiang (2021) reported in a qualitative study that during times of extremely high workload, employees may even shift their definition on what makes their work meaningful from a qualitative to a quantitative focus.

Conclusion on correlational studies

In summary, there is convincing meta-analytic evidence that people who work in jobs that are designed according to the SMART framework enjoy a better psychological and partly also a better physical well-being. Because most primary studies used a cross-sectional study design and assessed job-design features and well-being synchronously, the meta-analytic findings reported so far do not imply that working in a job that implements the SMART job features *causes* better well-being. It could be that low well-being influences a drift into poorly designed jobs or third variables (e.g., socioeconomic status) could have an impact on both a person's job features and their well-being, resulting in a spurious correlation.

To move toward a conclusion about causality, stronger study designs are needed. In the next sections, I will report findings from longitudinal field studies, experimental studies conducted in the laboratory, and intervention studies conducted in the field.

Longitudinal Research

Longitudinal studies that assess job-design features and well-being at several points in time are better suited to inform about the directions of the causal processes than are cross-sectional studies. Typically, longitudinal studies assess the momentary level of the outcome variable (e.g., well-being) at baseline and then analyze if the initial level of various job-design aspects (also assessed at baseline) predict the future level of the outcome variable (i.e., well-being at a later time point). In other words, this kind of longitudinal research provides information about whether job-design aspects can explain a change in well-being over time. Moreover, this study design also allows to examine whether initial well-being can explain job-design features at a later point in time (given that job-design features are also assessed at baseline and at a later time point).

Longitudinal studies on job design have been summarized in meta-analyses (Ford et al., 2014; Guthier et al., 2020; Lesener et al., 2019), mainly with a focus on job demands. These meta-analyses converge in the finding that high job demands indeed predict an increase in psychological and physical strain in general (Ford et al., 2014) and in an increase in exhaustion (Guthier et al., 2020) and burnout (Lesener et al., 2019), respectively. Tino Lesener and colleagues (2019) also tested if demands predict change in work engagement but did not find evidence for a significant effect. In addition, they examined if resources predict change in burnout and engagement over time. Resources is a broad category of job features, mainly referring to autonomy and social support. Lesener and colleagues' meta-analytic procedure indeed showed that a high degree of resources is associated with a decrease in burnout and an increase in work engagement over time. Taken together, these meta-analyses show that job-design features can explain change in hedonic well-being over time. It must be noted that the meta-analytic evidence is available mainly for the tolerability aspect of the SMART framework and—to a lesser degree—for the autonomous and relational aspect.

120 TRANSFORMATIVE WORK DESIGN

Longitudinal primary studies focusing on the stimulating and mastery-oriented aspects are rare (Diestel, 2022; Hakanen et al., 2011) and do not always meet the methodological requirements for examining *change* in well-being outcomes because they do not control for baseline levels of well-being. Several studies that addressed the negative end of the relational aspect (e.g., workplace bullying) found that unfavorable relational features of a job can reduce some aspects of well-being over time (Rodríguez-Muñoz et al., 2015; Trépanier et al., 2015). But findings were inconsistent regarding the specific well-being outcomes that were predicted by negative relational job features. As a meta-analytic integration of these diverse findings is missing, it is difficult to arrive at a final conclusion.

Importantly, three meta-analyses that examined lagged relationships between job features and well-being (Ford et al., 2014; Guthier et al., 2020; Lesener et al., 2019) also tested for reverse causation, examining if initial well-being predicts change in job features. All three meta-analyses reported evidence for reverse causation, with poor well-being (high psychological and physical strain, high exhaustion, high burnout) predicting an increase in demands over time, for instance, because exhausted employees may drift to more stressful jobs over time or because they might perceive the demands to be increasingly intense. Lesener and colleagues (2019), who additionally included resources and work engagement in their analysis, reported that high work engagement predicts an increase in resources over time, but no change in demands. Possibly, engaged employees are more able to build new resources (e.g., grow their social network or negotiate more job control) as conservation of resources theory (Hobfoll, 1998) and an extended version of the job-demands-resources model suggest (Bakker et al., 2023).

In conclusion, there is evidence that unfavorable job features are associated with a decrease well-being over time, and that also impaired well-being predicts a deterioration in job features over time. The pattern is most obvious for the tolerability aspect of the SMART model and for job features that have been investigated as resources. Detailed results for stimulating, mastery-oriented, and some of the relational job features are still missing.

Experimental Lab Studies

To bring more light into the causality between job-design features and well-being, researchers have also used experimental designs, often within a laboratory setting. Typically, in these experiments, study participants are invited into a laboratory in which they must work on a task for a predetermined period of time. Researchers manipulate certain features of the task or the circumstances under which the task needs to be completed and randomly assign participants to the various task features or circumstances. This experimental approach of manipulating task features or circumstances and randomly assigning study participants to the various conditions allows strong inference about causality. Ideally, participants report their well-being before starting to work on the task and after task completion. Change in well-being scores is seen as evidence for an effect of manipulated job features on well-being. Some studies, however, use less robust designs and only measure post-task well-being, assuming that randomization was successful and that study participants' well-being in the several experimental groups did not differ before the manipulation. Often, laboratory experiments rely on student participants with little or no work experience, which might make it difficult to generalize findings to employees who work in their jobs for many years.

In this section, I will review experimental studies that tested if the five features of SMART job design result in better well-being. In these studies, well-being was operationalized as a momentary or short-term affective (e.g., experiencing positive affect) and energetic state (e.g., experiencing low fatigue).

Stimulating task features

Experimental evidence suggests that working on stimulating tasks leads to better well-being than working on less stimulating (i.e., repetitive and boring) tasks. For instance, when comparing a stimulating learning task with a repetitive data-entry task, researchers found higher levels of alertness and lower levels of boredom, irritation, and unpleasantness for the stimulating task (Lundberg et al., 1993). Similarly, low task repetitiveness led to lower mental-strain scores than high task repetitiveness (Häusser et al., 2014). Also two vignette experiments on task rotation support the idea that stimulating work is positively related to well-being as participants reading vignettes of a job with high versus low variety reported higher levels of positive affect (Mlekus et al., 2022).

Mastery-oriented task features

Research on feedback is helpful for drawing conclusions about the role of mastery for well-being. Although studies on the impact of feedback mainly rely on experimentally provided feedback—as opposed to feedback implemented within the design of a job—findings clearly show that when people are given information that they perform well (i.e., positive feedback), they feel generally better than when this information is lacking or when even receiving information that they perform poorly (i.e., negative feedback).

For instance, in a within-person experimental study, Remus Ilies and Timothy A. Judge (2005) reported that more favorable feedback—compared to the average level of feedback a study participant received—resulted in higher levels of positive affect and lower levels of negative affect. Similarly, another within-person experiment showed that positive performance feedback had a positive impact on positive affect and a negative impact on negative affect (Ilies et al., 2007). A between-person experiment points into a similar direction. Positive feedback resulted in higher positive and lower negative affect and negative feedback resulted in lower positive and higher negative affect (Belschak & Den Hartog, 2009). Differences between success versus failure feedback were also observed for specific mood states (i.e., energetic arousal, tense arousal, hedonic tone) as well-being indicators (Venables & Fairclough, 2009).

Autonomous task features

Many experiments have examined if autonomy influences well-being. Typically, experimental groups are compared with a control group, with the participants in the experimental groups having more autonomy over how they can proceed while working on the experimental task than participants in the control group. Overall, evidence from experiments that manipulated autonomy is mixed. Some studies found positive effects of autonomy on well-being outcomes such as positive mood (Jimmieson & Terry, 1998), low subjective stress (Searle et al., 2001, Experiment 1), low fatigue (Hockey & Earle, 2006), and low mental strain (Häusser et al., 2014). Other studies, however, did not find such effects (Häusser et al., 2011; Jimmieson & Terry, 1999; Perrewé & Ganster, 1989). When zooming in on specific indicators of poor well-being, it seems safe to say that low autonomy has no main effect on anxiety (Hockey & Earle, 2006; Parker et al., 2013; Perrewé & Ganster, 1989). Interestingly, being granted autonomy over *which* tasks to accomplish—as opposed to autonomy over *how* to accomplish tasks— had a negative effect on exhaustion (Biron & Bamberger, 2010). Michal Biron and Peter A. Bamberger (2010) discussed this effect as structural empowerment and empirically showed that self-efficacy mediated the effect of autonomy on exhaustion.

Often, autonomy has been manipulated in studies in which also demands were manipulated. These studies allow to test the assumption of Karasek's (1979) job-demands-control model that autonomy buffers the negative impact of high demands on well-being, so that high demands are less harmful when autonomy is high. Experimental evidence for such a moderator effect of autonomy is limited, with G. Robert J. Hockey and Fiona Earle (2006, Experiment 2) reporting such a moderator effect, but many more studies not finding such a moderator effect (e.g., Jimmieson & Terry, 1998; Perrewe & Ganster, 1989; Searle et al., 2001). These experimental findings mirror findings from field studies previously summarized (Gonzalez-Mulé et al., 2021; Guthier et al., 2020; Huth & Chung-Yan, 2023) that show that both autonomy and tolerable demands in itself are powerful predictors of well-being, so that the amount of variance that could be explained by the interplay of autonomy and demands is very small (Sonnentag, 2022).

Relational task features

Findings from experimental research on the effects of relational job features on well-being states are mixed as well. For instance, one study that manipulated social support (along with the manipulation of job demands and job control) showed that under the high-support condition study participants experienced less stress (Searle et al., 1999). In other studies, however, social support had no effect on experienced stress level (Hauck et al., 2008; Searle et al., 2001). With respect to task significance as another relational job feature, initial evidence suggests that experiencing task significance indeed leads to increased levels of meaningfulness (Allan et al., 2018). Moreover, being aware of the meaningfulness of one's work has an effect on momentary work engagement (Cantarero et al., 2022).

Tolerable task features

Several studies addressing the tolerability aspect manipulated demand levels and found that completing tasks under high-demand conditions (e.g., high workload) reduced subjective well-being. For instance, study participants experienced higher stress levels when working under high-demand conditions than under low-demand conditions (Flynn & James, 2009; Glaser et al., 1999; Searle et al., 2001; Searle et al., 1999). In addition, negative affect increased, and positive affect decreased (Flynn & Janes, 2009). Also, increased levels of fatigue and arousal were observed in high-workload situations (Hockey & Earle, 2006). It must be noted that this picture is not fully consistent with a number of studies not finding any effect on subjective measures under high-demand conditions

(Häusser et al., 2011; Jimmieson & Terry, 1997, 1998; Perrewé & Ganster, 1989; van As et al., 2022), particularly when the duration of the experiment was relatively short (Jimmieson & Terry, 1998; Perrewe & Ganster 1989; but see Häusser et al., 2011).

Conclusions about experimental laboratory research

Taken together, experimental studies testing core features of the SMART framework suggest that some of these features may indeed have a causal impact on well-being. More specifically, experiments targeting stimulation, mastery, and tolerability provided rather convincing evidence that these features lead to positive short-term well-being outcomes. Findings for autonomy and relational aspects, however, are mixed, with findings on autonomy being particularly scattered, maybe because it is difficult—if not impossible—to grant impactful autonomy in a highly structured laboratory setting.

Moreover, when interpreting the findings from experimental laboratory research, one must keep in mind that most experimental tasks were relatively simple, and outcome measures only covered short-term experiences. These rather short-term affective and fatigue reactions might not be good enough proxies for long-term impairments of well-being. Short-term affective and fatigue reactions might simply demonstrate that effort has been mobilized to accomplish the experimental task. As, in general, short-term affective and fatigue reactions are reversible and develop into longer-term impairments of health and well-being only when recovery processes are deficient (McEwen, 1998; Meijman & Mulder, 1998), short-term reactions are not sufficiently informative to draw conclusions about longer-term implications of well-designed versus poorly designed jobs. To overcome some of these limitations, intervention studies conducted in the field can be helpful.

Field Intervention Studies

Over the decades, researchers conducted numerous field intervention studies in which they tested if changing aspects of a person's work environment results in improved well-being. Similar to experimental laboratory studies, these intervention studies often try to implement an experimental approach; however, because of constraints in the field (e.g., difficulties with random assignment), strong experimental designs are rare and quasi-experimental designs are more common. In this section, I will first review research on relatively broad intervention studies targeting job design. Subsequently, I will zoom in on studies that specifically address several features of the SMART framework. As most studies focused on indicators capturing hedonic well-being, I will focus on hedonic well-being as the outcome measure.

Broad job-design interventions

How to improve employees' jobs so that their well-being stabilizes or improves is on researchers' and practitioners' agenda for a long time (Parker et al., 2017). These interventions took different approaches, with earlier approaches most exclusively focusing on top-down strategies (i.e., implementing job-design changes based on job-design theories, often with the help of change agents) and more recent approaches including bottom-up elements, such as letting employees decide themselves how they might want to adjust their jobs (i.e., job crafting). Both top-down and bottom-up approaches often do not focus on single features of a job as specified within the SMART framework but strive to improve several aspects of a job at the same time (Holman & Axtell, 2016).

These diverse aspects of a job are often summarized as job resources (Knight et al., 2017). Interventions sometimes combine an increase in job resources with measures to reduce stressful conditions (Burgess et al., 2020). Such job-design interventions are often termed organizational (Richardson & Rothstein, 2008) or organization-directed (Dreison et al., 2018) interventions and are contrasted with interventions that aim at influencing processes within the individual such as stress appraisals or communication skills.

Although successful job-design interventions are reported in primary studies (Busch et al., 2017; Holman & Axtell, 2016), meta-analyses paint a less optimistic picture. J. J. Van der Klink (2001) reported a non-significant mean effect size (referring to the difference between intervention and control group) of $d = 0.08$ ($k = 5$, $N = 1,463$, 95% CI [−0.03, 0.19] for organizational interventions. A similar pattern emerged for the organizational interventions summarized by Katherine Richardson and Hannah Rothstein (2008) with an effect size of $d = 0.14$ ($k = 5$, $N = 221$, 95% CI [−0.123, 0.411]. In a more recent meta-analysis, Kimberly Dreison and colleagues (2018) reported that organization-directed interventions significantly reduced emotional exhaustion, but this finding was largely attributable to studies that focused on training and other educational approaches (also subsumed under the category of organization-directed interventions). The remaining organization-directed interventions (including clinical supervision, job redesign, and coworker support groups) had no significant effect on emotional exhaustion (Hedge's $g = .07$, $k = 6$, 95% CI [−.05, .19]). An exception from this pattern of non-significant effects is a meta-analysis by Stefania De Simone and colleagues (2021) that focused on burnout reductions in

126   TRANSFORMATIVE WORK DESIGN

physicians. This meta-analysis found that organization-directed interventions (including workload reductions, improvement in teamwork and leadership, structural changes, but also communication skills training, and mindfulness) resulted in reduced burnout with a standardized mean difference of SMD = −0.446 (k = 8; 95% CI [−0.619, −0.274]. However, because this specific category of interventions also included skill training and mindfulness, it remains unclear if job-design changes alone would be responsible for the promising intervention effects for physicians.

When it comes to job-crafting interventions, meta-analytic findings are mixed as well. While Bogdan Oprea and colleagues (2019) reported a significant effect of job-crafting interventions on work engagement (Hedge's g = .31, k = 9, N = 381, 95% CI [0.14, 0.50]), Janina Björk and colleagues (2021) did not, with a standardized mean difference SDM = 0.14 (k = 9, N = 394, 95% CI [−0.08, 0.36].

Job-design interventions addressing specific features within the SMART framework

As just described, meta-analyses summarizing overall findings of intervention studies resulted in a mixed picture. More information can be gained from studies that assessed which job features are actually changed during job-design interventions and that then examined how changes in specific job features relate to well-being or changes in well-being.

Stimulating job features

With respect to stimulating work characteristics, one could assume that well-being will increase when work becomes more stimulating after a job-redesign intervention. Importantly, to conclude that an increase in stimulating job features is indeed the underlying cause for improved well-being, stimulating job features should be the mediator between the intervention and well-being outcomes (Holman et al., 2010). However, stimulating job features were rarely explicitly studied when examining the well-being implications of job redesign. One exception is a classical study by David Holman and colleagues (2010) that examined a job-redesign intervention in a company specialized in health insurance and health care. This study tested various potential mediators linking the intervention to well-being, with skill utilization (e.g., the experience to use a variety of skills in the job) being the workplace factor referring to stimulating work. Holman and colleagues (2010) found that well-being increased after the intervention in the intervention group but remained stable in the quasi-experimental control group. Importantly, the effect was mediated by increases in skill utilization in the intervention group, suggesting that increases in stimulating work (operationalized as skill utilization) after the intervention can indeed explain why well-being increases.

Mastery-oriented job features

Findings on mastery as a mechanism that potentially links job-design interventions to changes in well-being are mixed. The previously mentioned study by Holman and colleagues (2010) showed that feedback increased after the intervention in the intervention group and served as a mediator between the intervention and increases in well-being. Also in a study by Holman and Carolyn Axtell (2016), feedback mediated the effect of a job redesign intervention on changes in well-being in the experimental intervention group. A study by John Schaubroeck and colleagues (1993) addressed role clarity as an aspect of mastery and did not find an effect of a role-clarification intervention on psychological and physical well-being outcomes. Overall, the number of intervention studies that address mastery features is very limited and conclusions are difficult to draw. The evidence that is available suggests that feedback— but not role clarification—could be a powerful mechanism that contributes to well-being.

Autonomous job features

Research that examined increases in job control or autonomy as an explanatory mechanism for why job redesign can improve well-being resulted in encouraging findings. For instance, Frank Bond and David Bunce (2001) identified job control as a mediator between a work-reorganization intervention and mental health. Similarly, Bond and colleagues (2008) found that job control mediated the association between the work-reorganization intervention and low psychological distress. Moreover, studies of Holman and colleagues (2010) and Holman and Axtell (2016), previously mentioned, showed that job control mediated the effect of the job redesign interventions on well-being.

Other studies point in a similar direction. For instance, Karina Nielsen and Raymond Randall (2012) reported that increases in perceived autonomy co-occurring with perceived changes in working procedures during a teamwork intervention were related to an increase in well-being from before to after the intervention. However, there are also studies that failed to find an effect of job-control interventions on well-being. For instance, Mary Logan and Daniel Ganster (2005) reported that a job control intervention had a positive effect on job satisfaction when supervisor support was high. But neither a main effect of job control nor an interaction effect between job control and supervisor support on mental health measures was found.

Relational job features

Intervention studies addressing relational job features mostly addressed social support, resulting in mixed findings. A classical study examined the effects of team-based interventions using monthly support-group meetings within oncology wards (Le Blanc et al., 2007). Analysis showed that in the intervention group emotional exhaustion decreased during the intervention period and remained reduced at the six-month follow-up, compared to a quasi-experimental control group. Differences in depersonalization between intervention and control group were significant immediately after the intervention, but not at follow-up. Experienced social support, along with other perceived work characteristics, explained low exhaustion and low depersonalization levels during and after the intervention period.

An intervention study with low-skilled workers used a peer-mentoring approach to increase social support (Busch et al., 2017). This intervention resulted in some well-being differences between intervention and a quasi-experimental control group. Blood pressure decreased in the intervention group over time and psychosomatic complaints increased in the control group over time but remained stable in the intervention group.

Other intervention studies, however, suggest that social support targeted during an intervention does not always result in better well-being. For instance, Nielsen and Randall (2012) reported that increased social support occurring after a teamwork intervention was unrelated to changes in well-being from before to after the intervention. Caroline Knight and colleagues (2017) conducted a participatory action intervention to increase work engagement in nursing wards. This research observed that relatedness decreased slightly in the intervention group, while it increased in the control group. No effects on work engagement as well-being outcome were observed.

Overall, intervention studies that targeted social support as relational feature of work again suggest that the processes initiated during an intervention are extremely complex and that the success of interventions depends on many factors. For instance, a classical study by Catherine Heaney and colleagues (1995) demonstrated that interventions may not be equally effective for all study participants in the intervention group. The specific intervention in this study resulted in increased levels of perceived supervisor support only for those members of the intervention group who actually took part in the intervention activities. Moreover, beneficial effects on well-being in terms of reduced depressive symptoms and reduced somatization were observed only for members of the intervention group who had a high likelihood of leaving their job (i.e., who were highly vulnerable).

Task significance as another relational job feature has received little attention in intervention research in relation to well-being. An initial study with professionals working with intellectually disabled individuals shows that exhaustion decreased after an intervention that emphasized task significance (Martínez-Tur et al., 2021). The study design, however, makes it difficult to draw strong conclusions as it could not be tested whether increased task significance was actually the driver of reduced exhaustion.

Tolerable job features

Intervention studies that aim at making work demands more tolerable often do not address the demanding situation itself, but address workers' cognitive, emotional, and behavioral approaches to the demanding situation (Lambert et al., 2022). Although such approaches can be effective in increasing well-being (Richardson & Rothstein, 2008), they are not a job-design intervention in the strict sense. Studies that actually targeted job demands resulted in mixed findings. A classical intervention study with bus drivers by Leif Rydstedt and colleagues (1998) reported a reduction in perceived workload and self-reported hassles in the intervention group, along with an improvement of cardiovascular indicators and reduced distress after work. No effects of the intervention on strain at work, fatigue after work, and psychosomatic complaints were observed. Another intervention study on bus drivers that aimed at reducing demands found a reduction in pressure/tension, but only a marginally significant effect on reduced distress (Cendales-Ayala et al., 2017).

Other intervention studies, however, were even less successful. For instance, intervention studies that used problem-solving committees to identify stressors (Landsbergis & Vivona-Vaughan, 1995) and other participative approaches to improve the work situation (Arapovic-Johansson et al., 2018) failed to find any reduction in job demands. Similarly, other job-design interventions have also failed to result in any improvements with respect to workload (DeJoy et al., 2010), time demands (Moen et al., 2013) or task obstacles (Holman et al., 2010). Taken together, job-design interventions rarely resulted in a reduction of work demands. Those interventions that did successfully reduce demands, however, observed improvements for at least some of the well-being indicators (Rydstedt et al., 1998).

Conclusions about field intervention studies

Overall, findings on the well-being benefits of job-design interventions are mixed. While meta-analyses summarizing overall well-being benefits of job-design interventions reported non-significant findings, primary studies that addressed specific job features often reported benefits of job-design interventions, particularly when interventions included an increase in feedback (as an aspect of a mastery) and an increase in job control. Importantly, job-design interventions seem to be relatively ineffective unless they result in workers' experience that their job has improved (Holman et al., 2010). It might not be surprising that job-design interventions lack positive outcomes when the targeted groups feel that participation in the intervention increases their job demands (Biron et al., 2016) and when they therefore do not participate in meetings or trainings that would make the intervention effective (Heaney et al., 1995). In terms of the organizational embeddedness of job-design interventions, trainings coupled with job design can have benefits and often might be a prerequisite to make job design successful (Daniels et al., 2017).

To conclude, job-design interventions enhancing SMART job features can have a positive impact on hedonic well-being, although the effects are not overwhelming in most cases. Underpowered study designs and arbitrarily chosen time lags for the evaluative assessments (Dormann & Griffin, 2015) may contribute to the inconclusive pattern of findings.

Summary of the Empirical Evidence and Major Tensions in the Research Area

Meta-analyses of correlational (i.e., mainly cross-sectional) studies provide rather convincing evidence that the job features specified in the SMART framework are related to hedonic and eudaimonic well-being. Particularly task variety (as an aspect of stimulating work), role clarity and feedback (as aspects of a mastery-oriented work), job control and autonomy (as instantiations of autonomous work), social support and low social stressors (as relational job features), and tolerable demands are positively related to positive indicators of well-being and negatively related to negative indicators. Interestingly, skill variety (as an aspect of stimulating work) is unrelated to hedonic well-being, and findings for task significance (as a relational job feature) and hedonic well-being are mixed. Particularly with respect to demands, there is some variability in effect sizes depending on the type of demand and the type of outcome. Overall, effect sizes are larger for eudaimonic than for hedonic well-being.

While cross-sectional designs make any conclusions about causality impossible, longitudinal studies are more informative in this respect. Meta-analyses that summarized longitudinal studies suggest that high demands, as well as low autonomy and a lack of supportive relationships, are associated with a decrease in well-being over time. An integrative, longitudinal perspective on stimulating, mastery-oriented, and unfavorable relational job features is still missing.

Considering experimental laboratory studies conducted on features of the SMART framework, it appears that certain features indeed play a causal role in influencing short-term well-being. Stimulating tasks, positive feedback, and tolerable demands have a favorable impact on well-being. Findings for autonomous and relational features, however, are mixed. Although the experimental evidence suggests that certain aspects of stimulating, mastery-oriented, and tolerable job features may have a causal impact, it is too early for a final conclusion to be drawn because experimental research focused on some instantiations of the respective job features and neglected others. For instance, experiments implemented aspects of task variety, positive feedback, and workload, but paid less attention to problem-solving demands, feedback from the task environment (i.e., the "job"), role clarity, and other demanding aspects of work situations (e.g., emotional demands). Thus, we should be careful not to overgeneralize the findings from the experimental laboratory studies.

Meta-analyses on field interventions did not provide evidence for the well-being benefits of job-design interventions, neither for top-down nor for bottom-up (i.e., job crafting) approaches. Although these meta-analytic findings are disappointing, primary studies provide some information about which specific job features addressed in an intervention might lead to improved well-being. For instance, increase in skill utilization as an aspect of stimulating work was associated with improved well-being after an intervention. Findings with respect to mastery were mixed. While better feedback improved well-being, role clarification did not. There is some—although not equivocal—evidence that increase in autonomy implemented in job-design interventions is associated with increased well-being. With respect to the relational aspect of job design, findings on social support are mixed, but findings on task significance are encouraging. When it comes to demands, job-design interventions failed to lead to convincing results, often because the interventions did not result in a reduction of demands. Overall, it is premature to draw final conclusions on the benefits of specific job features specified in the SMART framework because for some features the number of intervention studies is very limited. Nevertheless, findings from field interventions illustrate that improving job-design features in real-world jobs is a very complex endeavor and that it is often difficult to isolate the effect of a specific job feature.

When summarizing research findings across the diverse methodological approaches, it becomes evident that job features included in the SMART framework are empirically related to favorable hedonic and particularly eudaimonic well-being. Moreover, some of the job features also seem to foster aspects of hedonic well-being in a causal way. Particularly with respect to the stronger methodological approaches (i.e., experimental laboratory studies, field interventions), findings, however, remain somewhat mixed. Overall, we see a striking imbalance with respect to the use of purely correlational cross-sectional designs versus more robust research designs. Adding more correlational studies (and meta-analyses of these studies) will not contribute to a better understanding of how job design *influences* well-being.

132 TRANSFORMATIVE WORK DESIGN

In terms of theory, we have relatively general and broad theories that specify which job characteristics should be important for well-being (e.g., Bakker et al., 2023; Hackman & Oldham, 1976; Karasek, 1979), but the theoretical descriptions are relatively limited when it comes to describing in detail *why* the specific job characteristics contribute to well-being. Admittedly, more detail is provided with respect to stressful and demanding situations (Ganster & Rosen, 2013). However, we would need more in-depth theoretical accounts of the mechanisms that link various work characteristics to employee well-being.

A large portion of job-design research takes a "one-size-fits-all" approach, assuming that all job-design features are equally important for everyone and for all situations. Of course, many moderators of effects of job design have been proposed and studied (de Rijk et al., 1998; Hackman & Oldham, 1976). However, what we still miss is an integrative approach that synthesizes the various possible individual and situational factors that act as moderators in the relationship between job-design and well-being. Similar to the overall SMART work design approach (Parker & Knight, 2024) that specifies crucial higher-order work characteristics, the field would benefit from a conceptual and empirical integration of job-design moderators into an overall framework.

Suggestions for Future Research

Although decades of research on job design and well-being provided important insights on how job design relates to well-being, important questions remain unanswered. In this section, six possible directions for future research are proposed—in addition to the general suggestions sketched in the previous section. First, more integrative research is needed. Although there are numerous meta-analyses summarizing cross-sectional evidence on the relationship between job-design features and well-being (e.g., Gonzalez-Mulé et al., 2021; Humphrey et al., 2007) and although several meta-analyses integrated broad studies on interventions (e.g., Dreison et al., 2018; Oprea et al., 2019), meta-analyses that focus on specific job-design features implemented in field interventions or manipulated in experimental laboratory studies are still missing. Such meta-analyses, however, are highly needed to arrive at a summary conclusion about the multitude of findings that still seem to be "mixed" and "inconsistent."

Second, with respect to correlational field research, more studies are needed that use strong longitudinal designs, particularly with respect to some rather neglected features of the SMART framework. With respect to job demands and job resources, numerous longitudinal studies have been conducted during the past decades, with their findings now summarized in insightful meta-analyses (e.g., Guthier et al., 2020). However, much less is known, about if and how, for instance, stimulating features of a job and the opportunity for mastery translate into well-being over time. Before meta-analyses using sophisticated statistical methods are possible, we need more high-quality primary studies, particularly on the neglected features of the SMART framework. These studies should use validated scales for assessing job features and well-being, need to implement at least two to three measurement points, and apply state-of-the-art approaches to data analysis, taking into account, for instance, stable between-person differences (Hamaker et al., 2015).

Third, a more holistic perspective on job design can offer new insights. This chapter mainly focused on the several job features in isolation. However, specific combinations of job features might be particularly beneficial for well-being, whereas others might be particularly detrimental. In specific instances, beneficial and detrimental job features might have contradictory effects resulting overall in a zero effect on well-being. Thus, future research might want to assess and analyze job-design features in a more holistic way. With respect to statistical analysis, latent class or latent profile analyses (Mäkikangas et al., 2018; Wang et al., 2013) would be more suitable than the traditional variable-centered approaches that quickly reach their limits when a large number of several job-design features need to be considered in combination.

Fourth, researchers may want to extend the initial research trend of incorporating time more explicitly in research on job design. During the past decade, researchers paid increasing attention to temporal aspects of the association between job features and well-being, particularly with respect to the demand aspect of work settings (Guthier et al., 2020; Ritter et al., 2016). Such approaches address the question of how long it takes until favorable job-design features translate into an improvement of well-being and how quickly unfavorable job-design features are reflected in impaired well-being. Moreover, they can take into account that individuals are not passive victims of changes occurring in their environment but are able to adapt to such changes (Ritter et al., 2016). It would be interesting to now extend this research line beyond the demand feature. For instance, researchers could examine how long it takes to take full advantage of, for instance, stimulating features of one's job and what is needed to adapt in an optimal way to a highly autonomous job.

Fifth, more research attention needs to be devoted to eudaimonic well-being. Organizational research on job design and well-being has been dominated by a hedonic focus on well-being. After its early implicit inclusion in Hackman and Oldham's (1976) job characteristics model, eudaimonic well-being has been largely neglected, particularly in longitudinal research, field interventions, and experimental research. Findings from cross-sectional research, however, suggest

134   TRANSFORMATIVE WORK DESIGN

that job-design features show stronger empirical associations with indicators of eudaimonic well-being (e.g., experienced meaning, growth satisfaction) than with indicators of hedonic well-being. Therefore, it might be very fruitful to re-introduce eudaimonic well-being into job-design research.

Finally, as meta-analyses of longitudinal studies showed that not only job-design features predict future well-being but that also well-being predicts future job-design features, researchers might want to identify the mechanisms underlying the process by which a person's well-being influences features of their future jobs. In the past, researchers have referred to (self-)selection processes, creation of specific job features (e.g., stressor generation), and perceptual processes when trying to explain why poor well-being has a reverse effect on unfavorable job conditions (De Lange et al., 2004; Guthier et al., 2020). These accounts, however, might be too general to explain what is going on and they may not apply to all job features in the same way.

Practical Implications

In terms of job-design practice, the literature reviewed in this chapter suggests that principles of SMART work design should be implemented in organizations when targeting employee well-being. First, work should be stimulating. It is particularly important that a job comprises a variety of different tasks and that employees can use their skills. A certain level of problem-solving demands most likely is desirable as well—although empirical evidence is relatively limited. Second, work should provide mastery experiences. This can be achieved by feedback, for instance by developing a supportive feedback culture (London & Smither, 2002). Although no benefits of an explicit role-clarification intervention could be observed (Schaubroeck et al., 1993), managers should avoid role ambiguity. Third, providing autonomous work should be an important goal for any job-design practice. Although particularly experimental findings on autonomy were mixed, there is no evidence that autonomous work hinders well-being (as long as role clarity is provided). Often, increased autonomy is the pathway by which interventions result in better employee well-being (e.g., Holman et al., 2010). Fourth, relational job features are important for employee well-being. Organizations can emphasize this job feature by encouraging mutual social support and particularly by putting policies and management practices into place that reduce the likelihood of harmful relational behaviors. Finally, organizations should strive to create tolerable work settings in which demands are manageable. It is particularly important to keep an eye on this tolerability aspect because job-design interventions often do not result in a reduction of job demands.

References

Alcaron, G. M. (2011). A meta-analysis of burnout with job demands, resources, and attitudes. *Journal of Vocational Behavior 79*(2), 549–562. https://doi.org/10.1016/j.jvb.2011.03.007

Allan, B. A., Batz-Barbarich, C., Sterling, H. M., & Tay, L. (2019). Outcomes of meaningful work: A meta-analysis. *Journal of Management Studies 56*(3), 500–528. https://doi.org/10.1111/joms.12406

Allan, B. A., Duffy, R. D., & Collisson, B. (2018). Helping others increases meaningful work: Evidence from three experiments. *Journal of Counseling Psychology 65*(2), 155–165. https://doi.org/10.1037/cou0000228

Allen, T. D., Herst, D. E. L., Bruck, C. S., & Sutton, M. (2000). Consequences associated with work-to-family conflict: A review and agenda for future research. *Journal of Occupational Health Psychology 5*(2), 278–308. https://doi.org/10.1037//1076-899B.5.2.278

Amstad, F. T., Meier, L. L., Fasel, U., Elfering, A., & Semmer, N. K. (2011). A meta-analysis of work-family conflict and various outcomes with a special emphasis on cross-domain versus matching-domain relations. *Journal of Occupational Health Psychology 16*(2), 151–169. https://doi.org/10.1037/a0022170

Arapovic-Johansson, B., Wåhlin, C., Hagberg, J., Kwak, L., Björklund, C., & Jensen, I. (2018). Participatory work place intervention for stress prevention in primary health care. A randomized controlled trial. *European Journal of Work and Organizational Psychology 27*(2), 219–234. https://doi.org/10.1080/1359432X.2018.1431883

Bakker, A. B., Demerouti, E., & Sanz-Vergel, A. (2023). Job demands–resources theory: Ten years later. *Annual Review of Organizational Psychology and Organizational Behavior 10*, 25–53. https://doi.org/10.1146/annurev-orgpsych-120920-053933

Bedi, A. (2021). No herd for black sheep: A meta-analytic review of the predictors and outcomes of workplace ostracism. *Applied Psychology 70*(2), 861–904. https://doi.org/10.1111/apps.12238

Belschak, F. D., & Den Hartog, D. N. (2009). Consequences of positive and negative feedback: The impact on emotions and extra-role behaviors. *Applied Psychology 58*(2), 274–303. https://doi.org/10.1111/j.1464-0597.2008.00336.x

Biron, C., Ivers, H., & Brun, J. P. (2016). Capturing the active ingredients of multicomponent participatory organizational stress interventions using an adapted study design. *Stress and Health 32*(4), 275–284. https://doi.org/10.1002/smi.2700

Biron, M., & Bamberger, P. (2010). The impact of structural empowerment on individual well-being and performance: Taking agent preferences, self-efficacy and operational constraints into account. *Human Relations 63*(2), 163–191. https://doi.org/10.1177/0018726709337039

Björk, J. M., Bolander, P., & Forsman, A. K. (2021). Bottom-up interventions effective in promoting work engagement: A systematic review and meta-analysis. *Frontiers in Psychology 12*, 730421. https://doi.org/10.3389/fpsyg.2021.730421

Bliese, P. D., Edwards, J. R., & Sonnentag, S. (2017). Stress and well-being at work: A century of empirical trends reflecting theoretical and societal influences. *Journal of Applied Psychology 102*(3), 389–402. https://doi.org/10.1037/apl0000109

Blustein, D. L., Lysova, E. I., & Duffy, R. D. (2023). Understanding decent work and meaningful work. *Annual Review of Organizational Psychology and Organizational Behavior 10*(1), 289–314. https://doi.org/10.1146/annurev-orgpsych-031921-024847

Bond, F. W., & Bunce, D. (2001). Job control mediates change in a work reorganizational intervention for stress reduction. *Journal of Occupational Health Psychology* 6(4), 290–302. https://doi.org/10.1037//1076-8998.6.4.290

Bond, F. W., Flaxman, P. E., & Bunce, D. (2008). The influence of psychological flexibility on work redesign: mediated moderation of a work reorganization intervention. *Journal of Applied Psychology* 93(3), 645–654. https://doi.org/10.1037/0021-9010.93. 3.645

Bowling, N. A., Alcaron, G. M., Bragg, C. B., & Hartman, M. J. (2015). A meta-analytic examination of the potential correlates and consequences of workload. *Work & Stress* 29(2), 95–113. https://doi.org/10.1080/02678373.2015.1033037

Bowling, N. A., & Beehr, T. A. (2006). Workplace harassment from the victim's perspective: A theoretical model and meta-analysis. *Journal of Applied Psychology* 91(5), 998–1012. https://doi.org/10.1037/0021-9010.91.5.998

Burgess, M. G., Brough, P., Biggs, A., & Hawkes, A. J. (2020). Why interventions fail: A systematic review of occupational health psychology interventions. *International Journal of Stress Management* 27(2), 195–207. https://doi.org/10.1037/str0000144

Busch, C., Koch, T., Clasen, J., Winkler, E., & Vowinkel, J. (2017). Evaluation of an organizational health intervention for low-skilled workers and immigrants. *Human Relations* 70(8), 994–1016. https://doi.org/10r.g1/107.171/0770/ 10807182762761761668822308

Cantarero, K., van Tilburg, W. A. P., & Smoktunowicz, E. (2022). Other-(vs. self-) oriented meaning interventions enhance momentary work engagement through changes in work meaningfulness. *Journal of Counseling Psychology* 69(4), 443–451. https://doi. org/10.1037/cou0000594

Cavanaugh, M. A., Boswell, W. R., Roehling, M. V., & Boudreau, J. W. (2000). An empirical examination of self-reported work stress among U.S. managers. *Journal of Applied Psychology* 85(1), 65–74. https://doi.org/10.1037//0021-9C10.85.1.65

Cendales-Ayala, B., Useche, S. A., Gómez-Ortiz, V., & Bocarejo, J. P. (2017). Bus operators' responses to job strain: An experimental test of the job demand–control model. *Journal of Occupational Health Psychology* 22(4), 518–527. https://doi.org/10.1037/ ocp0000040

Chiaburu, D. S., Thundiyil, T., & Wang, J. (2014). Alienation and its correlates: A meta-analysis. *European Management Journal* 32(1), 24–36. https://doi.org/10.1016/j.emj. 2013.06.003

Chris, A. C., Provencher, Y., Fogg, C., Thompson, S. C., Cole, A. L., Okaka, O., Bosco, F. A., & González-Morales, M. G. (2022). A meta-analysis of experienced incivility and its correlates: Exploring the dual path model of experienced workplace incivility. *Journal of Occupational Health Psychology* 27(3), 317–338. https://doi.org/10.1037/ ocp0000326

Christian, M. S., Garza, A. S., & Slaughter, J. E. (2011). Work engagement: A quantitative review and test of its relations with task and contextual performance. *Personnel Psychology* 64(1), 89–136. https://doi.org/10.1111/j.1744-6570.2010.01203.x

Crawford, E. R., LePine, J. A., & Rich, B. L. (2010). Linking job demands and resources to employee engagement and burnout: A theoretical extension and meta-analytic test. *Journal of Applied Psychology* 95(5), 834–848. https://doi.org/10.1037/a00 19364

Daniels, K., Gedikli, C., Watson, D., Semkina, A., & Vaughn, O. (2017). Job design, employment practices and well-being: A systematic review of intervention studies. *Ergonomics* 60(9), 1177–1196. https://doi.org/10.1080/00140139.2017.1303085

De Lange, A., Taris, T. W., Kompier, M. A. J., Houtman, I. L. D., & Bongers, P. M. (2004). The relationships between work characteristics and mental health: Examining normal, reversed and reciprocal relationships in a 4-wave study. *Work & Stress 18*(2), 149–166. https://doi.org/10.1080/02678370412331270860

de Rijk, A. E., Le Blanc, P. M., Schaufeli, W. B., & de Jonge, J. (1998). Active coping and need for control as moderators of the job demand-control model: Effects on burnout. *Journal of Occupational and Organizational Psychology 71*(1), 1–18. https://doi.org/10.1111/j.2044-8325.1998.tb00658.x

De Simone, S., Vargas, M., & Servillo, G. (2021). Organizational strategies to reduce physician burnout: A systematic review and meta-analysis. *Aging Clinical and Experimental Research 33*, 883–894. https://doi.org/10.1007/s40520-019-01368-3

de Wit, F. R. C., Greer, L. L., & Jehn, K. A. (2012). The paradox of intragroup conflict: A meta-analysis. *Journal of Applied Psychology 97*(2), 360–390. https://doi.org/10.1037/a0024844

Deci, E. L., & Ryan, R. M. (2012). Motivation, personality, and development within embedded social contexts: An overview of self-determination theory. In R. M. Ryan (Ed.), *Oxford handbook of human motivation* (pp. 85–107). Oxford University Press.

DeJoy, D. M., Wilson, M. G., Vandenberg, R. J., McGrath-Higgins, A. L., & Griffin-Blake, C. S. (2010). Assessing the impact of health work organization intervention. *Journal of Occupational and Organizational Psychology 83*(1), 139–165. https://doi.org/10.1348/096317908X398773

Diener, E. (2000). Subjective well-being: The science of happiness and a proposal for a national index. *American Psychologist 55*(1), 34–43. https://doi.org/10.1037//0003-066X.55.1.34

Diestel, S. (2022). How strategies of selective optimization with compensation and role clarity prevent future increases in affective strain when demands on self-control increase: Results from two longitudinal studies. *Journal of Occupational Health Psychology 27*(4), 426–440. https://doi.org/10.1037/ocp0000328

Dormann, C., & Griffin, M. A. (2015). Optimal time lags in panel studies. *Psychological Methods 20*(4), 489–505. https://doi.org/10.1037/met0000041

Downes, P. E., Reeves, C. J., McCormick, B. W., Boswell, W. R., & Butts, M. M. (2021). Incorporating job demand variability into job demands theory: A meta-analysis. *Journal of Management 47*(6), 1630–1656. https://doi.org/10.1177/0149206320916767

Dreison, K. C., Luther, L., Bonfils, K. A., Sliter, M. T., McGrew, J. H., & Salyers, M. P. (2018). Job burnout in mental health providers: A meta-analysis of 35 years of intervention research. *Journal of Occupational Health Psychology 23*(1), 18–30. https://doi.org/10.1037/ocp0000047

Fila, M. J., Purl, J., & Griffeth, R. W. (2017). Job demands, control and support: Meta-analyzing moderator effects of gender, nationality, and occupation. *Human Resource Management Review 27*, 39–60. https://doi.org/10.1016/j.hrmr.2016.09.004

Flynn, N., & James, J. E. (2009). Relative effects of demand and control on task-related cardiovascular reactivity, task perceptions, performance accuracy, and mood. *International Journal of Psychophysiology 72*(2), 217–227. https://doi.org/10.1016/j.ijpsycho.2008.12.006

Ford, M. T., Matthews, R. A., Wooldridge, J. D., Mishra, V., Kakar, U. M., & Strahan, S. R. (2014). How do occupational stressor-strain effects vary with time? A review and meta-analysis of the relevance of time lags in longitudinal studies. *Work & Stress 28*(1), 9–30. https://doi.org/10.1080/02678373.2013.877096

Fried, Y., & Ferris, G. R. (1987). The validity of the job characteristics model: A review and meta-analysis. *Personnel Psychology 40*(2), 287–322. https://doi.org/10.1111/j.1744-6570.1987.tb00605.x

Frone, M. R. (1990). Intolerance of ambiguity as a moderator of the occupational role stress—strain relationship: A meta-analysis. *Journal of Organizational Behavior 11*(4), 309–320. https://doi.org/10.1002/job.4030110406

Gagné, M., Parker, S. K., Griffin, M. A., Dunlop, P. D., Knight, C., Klonek, F. E., & Parent-Rocheleau, X. (2022). Understanding and shaping the future of work with self-determination theory. *Nature Reviews Psychology 1*(7), 378–392. https://doi.org/10.1038/s44159-022-00056-w

Ganster, D. C., & Rosen, C. C. (2013). Work stress and employee health: A multidisciplinary review. *Journal of Management 39*(5), 1085–1122. https://doi.org/10.1177/0149206313475815

Gerhardt, C., Semmer, N. K., Sauter, S., Walker, A., de Wijn, N., Kälin, W., Kottwitz, M. U., Kersten, B., Ulrich, B., & Elfering, A. (2021). How are social stressors at work related to well-being and health? A systematic review and meta-analysis. *BMC Public Health 21*(1), 890. https://doi.org/10.1186/s12889-021-10894-7

Glaser, D. M., Tatum, B. C., Nebeker, D. M., Sorenson, R. C., & Aiello, J. R. (1999). Workload and social support: Effects on performance and stress. *Human Performance 12*(2), 155–176. https://doi.org/10.1080/08959289909539865

Gonzalez-Mulé, E., Kim, M. M., & Ryu, J. W. (2021). A meta-analytic test of multiplicative and additive models of job demands, resources, and stress. *Journal of Applied Psychology 106*(9), 1391–1411. https://doi.org/10.1037/apl0000840

Grant, A. M. (2007). Relational job design and the motivation to make a prosocial difference. *Academy of Management Review 32*(2), 393–417. https://doi.org/10.5465/AMR.2007.24351328

Guthier, C., Dormann, C., & Voelkle, M. C. (2020). Reciprocal effects between job stressors and burnout: A continuous time meta-analysis of longitudinal studies. *Psychological Bulletin 146*(12), 1146–1173. https://doi.org/10.1037/bul0000304

Hackman, J. R., & Oldham, G. R. (1976). Motivation through the design of work: Test of a theory. *Organizational Behavior and Human Performance 16*(2), 250–279. https://doi.org/10.1016/0030-5073(76)90016-7

Hakanen, J. J., Bakker, A. B., & Jokisaari, M. (2011). A 35-year follow-up study on burnout among Finnish employees. *Journal of Occupational Health Psychology 16*(3), 345–360. https://doi.org/10.1037/a0022903

Halbesleben, J. R. B. (2006). Sources of social support and burnout: A meta-analytic test of the conservation of resources model. *Journal of Applied Psychology 91*(5), 1134–1145. https://doi.org/10.1037/0021-9010.91.5.1134

Hamaker, E. L., Kuiper, R. M., & Grasman, R. P. P. (2015). A critique of the cross-lagged panel model. *Psychological Methods 20*(1), 102. https://doi.org/10.1037/a0038889

Han, S., Harold, C. M., Oh, I. S., Kim, J. K., & Agolli, A. (2022). A meta-analysis integrating 20 years of workplace incivility research: Antecedents, consequences, and boundary conditions. *Journal of Organizational Behavior 43*(3), 497–523. https://doi.org/10.1002/job.2568

Hauck, E. L., Snyder, L. A., & Cox-Fuenzalida, L.-E. (2008). Workload variability and social support: Effects on stress and performance. *Current Psychology 27*, 112–125. https://doi.org/10.1007/s12144-008-9026-x

Häusser, J. A., Mojzisch, A., & Schulz-Hardt, S. (2011). Endocrinological and psychological responses to job stressors: An experimental test of the Job Demand–Control Model. *Psychoneuroendocrinology 36*(7), 1021–1031. https://doi.org/10.1016/j.psyneuen.2010.12.016

Häusser, J. A., Schulz-Hardt, S., Schultze, T., Tomaschek, A., & Mojzisch, A. (2014). Experimental evidence for the effects of task repetitiveness on mental strain and objective work performance. *Journal of Organizational Behavior 35*(5), 705–721. https://doi.org/10.1002/job.1920

Heaney, C. A., Price, R. H., & Rafferty, J. (1995). Increasing coping resources at work: A field experiment to increase social support, improve work team functioning, and enhance employee mental health. *Journal of Organizational Behavior 16*(4), 335–352. https://doi.org/10.1002/job.4030160405

Hobfoll, S. E. (1998). *Stress, culture, and community: The psychology and physiology of stress.* Plenum.

Hockey, G. R. J., & Earle, F. (2006). Control over the scheduling of simulated office work reduces the impact of workload on mental fatigue and task performance. *Journal of Experimental Psychology: Applied 12*(1), 50–65. https://doi.org/10.1037/1076-898X.12.1.50

Holman, D., & Axtell, C. (2016). Can job redesign interventions influence a broad range of employee outcomes by changing multiple job characteristics? A quasi-experimental study. *Journal of Occupational Health Psychology 21*(3), 284–295. https://doi.org/10.1037/a0039962

Holman, D. J., Axtell, C. M., Sprigg, C. A., Totterdell, P., & Wall, T. D. (2010). The mediating role of job characteristics in job design interventions: A serendipitous quasi-experiment. *Journal of Organizational Behavior 31*(1), 84–105. https://doi.org/10.1002/job.631

Holman, D., Escaffi-Schwarz, M., Vasquez, C. A., Irmer, J. P., & Zapf, D. (2023). Does job crafting affect employee outcomes via job characteristics? A meta-analytic test of a key job crafting mechanism. *Journal of Occupational and Organizational Psychology.* https://doi.org/10.1111/joop.12450

Humphrey, S. E., Nahrgang, J. D., & Morgeson, F. P. (2007). Integrating motivational, social, and contextual work design features: A meta-analytic summary and theoretical extension of the work design literature. *Journal of Applied Psychology 92*(5), 1332–1356. https://doi.org/10.1037/0021-9010.92.5.1332

Huo, M. L., & Boxall, P. (2018). Are all aspects of lean production bad for workers? An analysis of how problem-solving demands affect employee well-being. *Human Resource Management Journal 28*(4), 569–584. https://doi.org/10.1111/1748-8583.12204

Huta, V., & Waterman, A. S. (2014). Eudaimonia and its distinction from hedonia: Developing a classification and terminology for understanding conceptual and operational definitions. *Journal of Happiness Studies 15*, 1425–1456. https://doi.org/10.1007/s10902-013-9485-0

Huth, K., & Chung-Yan, G. A. (2023). Quantifying the evidence for the absence of the job demands and job control interaction on workers' well-being: A Bayesian meta-analysis. *Journal of Applied Psychology 108*(6), 1060–1072. https://doi.org/10.1037/apl0001066

Ilies, R., de Pater, I. E., & Judge, T. A. (2007). Differential affective reactions to negative and positive feedback, and the role of self-esteem. *Journal of Managerial Psychology 22*, 590–609. https://doi.org/10.1108/02683940710778459

Ilies, R., & Judge, T. A. (2005). Goal regulations across time: The effects of feedback and affect. *Journal of Applied Psychology 90*, 453–467. https://doi.org/10.1037/0021-9010.90.3.453

Jackson, S. E., & Schuler, R. S. (1985). A meta-analysis and conceptual critique of research on role ambiguity and role conflict in work settings. *Organizational Behavior and Human Performance 33*(1), 16–78. https://doi.org/10.1016/0749-5978(85)90020-2

Jiang, L., & Lavaysse, L. M. (2018). Cognitive and affective job insecurity: A meta-analysis and a primary study. *Journal of Management 44*(5), 2307–2342. https://doi.org/tt0ps.:1//d1o7i.7or/g0/110.4119727/01643921086371787378383553

Jiang, W. Y. (2021). Sustaining meaningful work in a crisis: Adopting and conveying a situational purpose. *Administrative Science Quarterly 66*(3), 806–853. https://doi.org/10.1177/0001839221994049

Jimmieson, N. L., & Terry, D. J. (1997). Responses to an in-basket activity: The role of work stress, behavioral control, and informational control. *Journal of Occupational Health Psychology 2*, 72–83. https://doi.org/10.1037/1076-8998.2.1.72

Jimmieson, N. L., & Terry, D. J. (1998). An experimental study of the effects of work stress, work control, and task information on adjustment. *Applied Psychology: An International Review 47*, 343–369. https://doi.org/10.1111/j.1464-0597.1998.tb00033.x

Jimmieson, N. L., & Terry, D. J. (1999). The moderating role of task characteristics in determining responses to a stressful work simulation. *Journal of Organizational Behavior 20*, 709–736. https://doi.org/10.1002/(SICI)1099-1379(199909)20:5<709: :AID-JOB954>3.0.CO;2-7

Kahn, R. L., Wolfe, D. M., Quinn, R. P., Snoek, J. D., & Rosenthal, R. A. (1964). *Organizational stress: Studies in role conflict and ambiguity*. Wiley.

Karasek, R. (1979). Job demands, job decision latitude, and mental strain: Implications for job redesign. *Administrative Science Quarterly 24*(2), 285–306. https://doi.org/10.2307/2392498

Katz, I. M., Rauvola, R. S., & Rudolph, C. W. (2021). Feedback environment: A meta-analysis. *International Journal of Selection and Assessment 29*(3–4), 305–325. https://doi.org/10.1111/ijsa.12350

Knight, C., Patterson, M., Dawson, J., & Brown, J. (2017). Building and sustaining work engagement–a participatory action intervention to increase work engagement in nursing staff. *European Journal of Work and Organizational Psychology 26*(5), 634–649.

Kubicek, B., Uhlig, L., Hülsheger, U. R., Korunka, C., & Prem, R. (2023). Are all challenge stressors beneficial for learning? A meta-analytical assessment of differential effects of workload and cognitive demands. *Work & Stress 37*(3), 269–298. https://doi.org/10.1080/02678373.2022.2142986

Lambert, B., Caza, B. B., Trinh, E., & Ashford, S. (2022). Individual-centered interventions: Identifying what, how, and why interventions work in organizational contexts. *Academy of Management Annals 16*(2), 508–546. https://doi.org/10.5465/annals.2020.0351

Landsbergis, P. A., & Vivona-Vaughan, E. (1995). Evaluation of an occupational stress intervention in a public agency. *Journal of Organizational Behavior 16*(1), 29–48. https://doi.org/10.1002/job.4030160106

Le Blanc, P. M., Hox, J. J., Schaufeli, W. B., Taris, T. W., & Peeters, M. C. W. (2007). Take care! The evaluation of a team-based burnout intervention program for oncology care providers. *Journal of Applied Psychology 92*(1), 213–227. https://doi.org/10.1037/0021-9010.92.1.213

Lee, R. T., & Ashforth, B. E. (1996). A meta-analytic examination of the correlates of the three dimensions of job burnout. *Journal of Applied Psychology 81*(2), 123–133. https://doi.org/10.1037/0021-9010.81.2.123

Lesener, T., Gusy, B., & Wolter, C. (2019). The job demands-resources model: A meta-analytic review of longitudinal studies. *Work & Stress 33*(1), 76–103. https://doi.org/10.1080/02678373.2018.1529065

Li, A., Cropanzano, R., Butler, A., Shao, P., & Westman, M. (2021). Work–family crossover: A meta-analytic review. *International Journal of Stress Management 28*(2), 89–104. https://doi.org/10.1037/str0000225

Li, Q., Du, H., & Chi, P. (2021). Job stress and well-being among internal migrant workers in China: A review and meta-analysis. *Applied Psychology: Health and Well-Being 13*(3), 537–558. https://doi.org/10.1111/aphw.12266

Logan, M. S., & Ganster, D. C. (2005). An experimental evaluation of a control intervention to alleviate job-related stress. *Journal of Management 31*, 90–107. https://doi.org/0.1177/0149206304271383

London, M., & Smither, J. W. (2002). Feedback orientation, feedback culture, and the longitudinal performance management process. *Human Resource Management Review 12*(1), 81–100. https://doi.org/10.1016/S1053-4822(01)00043-2

Lundberg, U., Melin, B., Evans, G. W., & Holmberg, L. (1993). Physiological deactivation after two contrasting tasks at a video display terminal: Learning vs repetitive data entry. *Ergonomics 36*(6), 601–611. https://doi.org/10.1080/00140139308967923

Mäkikangas, A., Tolvanen, A., Aunola, K., Feldt, T., Mauno, S., & Kinnunen, U. (2018). Multilevel latent profile analysis with covariates: Identifying job characteristics profiles in hierarchical data as an example. *Organizational Research Methods 21*(4), 931–954. https://doi.org/10.1177/1094428118760690

Martínez-Tur, V., Estreder, Y., Tomás, I., Gracia, E., & Moliner, C. (2021). Coping with burnout symptoms through task significance in professionals working with individuals with intellectual disability. *Journal of Work and Organizational Psychology 37*(1), 50–57. https://doi.org/10.5093/jwop2021a2

Maslach, C., Schaufeli, W. B., & Leiter, M. P. (2001). Job burnout. *Annual Review of Psychology 52*, 397–422. https://doi.org/10.1146/annurev.psych.52.1.397

Mazzetti, G., Robledo, E., Vignoli, M., Topa, G., Guglielmi, D., & Schaufeli, W. B. (2023). Work engagement: A meta-analysis using the job demands-resources model. *Psychological Reports 126*(3), 1069–1107. https://doi.org/10.1177/00332941211051988

Mazzola, J. J., & Disselhorst, R. (2019). Should we be "challenging" employees? A critical review and meta-analysis of the challenge-hindrance model of stress. *Journal of Organizational Behavior 40*(8), 949–961. https://doi.org/10.1002/job.2412

McEwen, B. S. (1998). Protective and damaging effects of stress mediators. *New England Journal of Medicine 338*, 171–179. https://doi.org/10.1056/NEJM199801153380307

Meijman, T. F., & Mulder, G. (1998). Psychological aspects of workload. In P. J. D. Drenth & H. Thierry (Eds.), *Handbook of work and organizational psychology, Vol. 2: Work psychology* (pp. 5–33). Psychology Press.

Michel, J. S., Shifrin, N. V., Postier, L. E., Rotch, M. A., & McGoey, K. M. (2022). A meta-analytic validation study of the Shirom–Melamed burnout measure: Examining variable relationships from a job demands–resources perspective. *Journal of Occupational Health Psychology* 27(6), 566–584. https://doi.org/10.1037/ocp0000334

Mlekus, L., Lehmann, J., & Maier, G. W. (2022). New work situations call for familiar work design methods: Effects of task rotation and how they are mediated in a technology-supported workplace. *Frontiers in Psychology 13*, 935952. https://doi.org/10.3389/fpsyg.2022.935952

Mlekus, L., & Maier, G. W. (2021). More hype than substance? A Meta-analysis on job and task rotation [Systematic Review]. *Frontiers in Psychology 12*. https://doi.org/10.3389/fpsyg.2021.633530

Moen, P., Kelly, E. L., & Lam, J. (2013). Healthy work revisited: Do changes in time strain predict well-being? *Journal of Occupational Health Psychology 18*(2), 157–172. https://doi.org/10.1037/a0031804

Nahrgang, J. D., Morgeson, F. P., & Hofmann, D. A. (2011). Safety at work: A meta-analytic investigation of the link between job demands, job resources, burnout, engagement, and safety outcomes. *Journal of Applied Psychology 96*(1), 71–96. https://doi.org/10.1037/a0021484

Nielsen, K., & Randall, R. (2012). The importance of employee participation and perceptions of changes in procedures in a teamworking intervention. *Work & Stress 26*(2), 91–111. https://doi.org/10.1080/02678373.2012.682721

Nielsen, M. B., & Einarsen, S. (2012). Outcomes of exposure to workplace bullying: A meta-analytic review. *Work & Stress 26*(4), 309–332. https://doi.org/10.1080/02678373.2012.734709

Nixon, A. E., Mazzola, J. J., Bauer, J., Krueger, J. R., & Spector, P. E. (2011). Can work make you sick? A meta-analysis of the relationships between job stressors and physical symptoms. *Work & Stress 25*(1), 1–22. https://doi.org/10.1080/02678373.2011.569175

Nohe, C., Meier, L. L., Sonntag, K., & Michel, A. (2015). The chicken or the egg? A meta-analysis of panel studies of the relationship between work-family conflict and strain. *Journal of Applied Psychology 100*(2), 522–536. https://doi.org/10.1037/a0038012

Oishi, S., & Westgate, E. C. (2022). A psychologically rich life: Beyond happiness and meaning. *Psychological Review 129*(4), 790–811. https://doi.org/10.1037/rev0000317

Oprea, B. T., Barzin, L., Vîrgă, D., Iliescu, D., & Rusu, A. (2019). Effectiveness of job crafting interventions: A meta-analysis and utility analysis. *European Journal of Work and Organizational Psychology 28*(6), 723–741. https://doi.org/10.1080/1359432X.2019.1646728

Örtqvist, D., & Wincent, J. (2006). Prominent consequences of role stress: A meta-analytic review. *International Journal of Stress Management 13*(4), 399–422. https://doi.org/10.1037/1072-5245.13.4.399

Park, H. I., Jacob, A. C., Wagner, S. H., & Baiden, M. (2014). Job control and burnout: A meta-analytic test of the Conservation of Resources model. *Applied Psychology 63*(4), 607–642. https://doi.org/10.1111/apps.12008

Parker, S. K. (2014). Beyond motivation: Job and work design for development, health, ambidexterity, and more. *Annual Review of Psychology 65*, 661–691. https://doi.org/10.1146/annurev-psych-010213-115208

Parker, S. K., & Boeing, A. A. (2023). Workplace innovation in the digital era: A role for SMART work design. In P. R. A. Oeij, S. Dondt, & A. J. McMurray (Eds.), *A research agenda for workplace innovation: The challenge of disruptive transitions* (pp. 91–112). Edward Elgar.

Parker, S. K., & Knight, C. (2024). The SMART model of work design: A higher order structure to help see the wood from the trees. *Human Resource Management 63*(2), 265–291. https://doi.org/10.1002/hrm.22200

Parker, S. K., Morgeson, F. P., & Johns, G. (2017). One hundred years of work design research: Looking back and looking forward. *Journal of Applied Psychology 102*(3), 403–420. https://doi.org/10.1037/apl0000106

Parker, S. L., Jimmieson, N. L., & Amiot, C. E. (2013). Self-determination, control, and reactions to changes in workload: A work simulation. *Journal of Occupational Health Psychology 18*, 173–190. https://doi.org/10.1037/a0031803

Perrewé, P. L., & Ganster, D. C. (1989). The impact of job demands and behavioral control on experienced job stress. *Journal of Organizational Behavior 10*(3), 213–229. https://doi.org/10.1002/job.4030100303

Pindek, S., Arvan, M. L., & Spector, P. E. (2019). The stressor–strain relationship in diary studies: A meta-analysis of the within and between levels. *Work & Stress 33*(1), 1–21. https://doi.org/10.1080/02678373.2018.1445672

Pindek, S., & Spector, P. E. (2016). Organizational constraints: A meta-analysis of a major stressor. *Work & Stress 30*(1), 7–25. https://doi.org/10.1080/02678373.2015.1137376

Podsakoff, N. P., LePine, J. A., & LePine, M. A. (2007). Differential challenge stressor-hindrance stressor relationships with job attitudes, turnover intention, turnover, and withdrawal behavior: A meta-analysis. *Journal of Applied Psychology 92*(2), 438–454. https://doi.org/10.1037/0021-9010.92.2.438

Reichl, C., Leiter, M. P., & Spinath, F. M. (2014). Work-nonwork conflict and burnout: A meta-analysis. *Human Relations 67*(8), 979–1005. https://doi.org/10.1177/0018726713509857

Richardson, K. M., & Rothstein, H. R. (2008). Effects of occupational stress management intervention programs: A meta-analysis. *Journal of Occupational Health Psychology 13*(1), 69–93. https://doi.org/10.1037/1076-8998.13.1.69

Ritter, K.-J., Matthews, R. A., Ford, M. T., & Henderson, A. A. (2016). Understanding role stressors and job satisfaction over time using adaptation theory. *Journal of Applied Psychology 101*(12), 1655–1669. https://doi.org/10.1037/apl0000152

Rizzo, J. R., House, R. J., & Lirtzman, S. I. (1970). Role conflict and ambiguity in complex organizations. *Administrative Science Quarterly 15*(2), 150–163. https://doi.org/10.2307/2391486

Rodríguez-Muñoz, A., Moreno-Jiménez, B., & Sanz-Vergel, A. I. (2015). Reciprocal relations between workplace bullying, anxiety, and vigor: A two-wave longitudinal study. *Anxiety, Stress, & Coping 28*(5), 514–530. https://doi.org/10.1080/10615806.2015.1016003

Russell, J. A. (1980). A circumplex model of affect. *Journal of Personality and Social Psychology 39*(6), 1161–1178. https://doi.org/10.1037/h0077714

Rydstedt, L. W., Johansson, G., & Evans, G. W. (1998). The human side of the road: Improving the working conditions of urban bus drivers. *Journal of Occupational Health Psychology 3*(2), 161–171. https://doi.org/10.1037/1076-8998.3.2.161

Schaubroeck, J., Ganster, D. C., Sime, W. E., & Ditman, D. (1993). A field experiment testing supervisory role clarification. *Personnel Psychology 46*(1), 1–25. https://doi.org/10.1111/j.1744-6570.1993.tb00865.x

Schaufeli, W. B., & Bakker, A. B. (2004). Job demands, job resources, and their relationship with burnout and engagement: a multi-sample study. *Journal of Organizational Behavior 25*(3), 293–315. https://doi.org/10.1002/job.248

Schmidt, S., Roesler, U., Kusserow, T., & Rau, R. (2014). Uncertainty in the workplace: Examining role ambiguity and role conflict, and their link to depression—a meta-analysis. *European Journal of Work and Organizational Psychology 23*(1), 91–106. https://doi.org/10.1080/1359432X.2012.711523

Schmitt, A., Belschak, F. D., & Den Hartog, D. N. (2017). Feeling vital after a good night's sleep: The interplay of energetic resources and self-efficacy for daily proactivity. *Journal of Occupational Health Psychology 22*(4), 443–454. https://doi.org/10.1037/ocp0000041

Searle, B., Bright, J. E. H., & Bochner, S. (2001). Helping people to sort it out: The role of social support in the job strain model. *Work & Stress 15*(4), 328–346. https://doi.org/10.1080/02678370110086768

Searle, B. J., Bright, J. E. H., & Bochner, S. (1999). Testing the 3-factor model of occupational stress: the impact of demands, control and social support on a mail sorting task. *Work and Stress 13*, 268–279.

Sojo, V. E., Wood, R. E., & Genat, A. E. (2016). Harmful workplace experiences and women's occupational well-being: A meta-analysis. *Psychology of Women Quarterly 40*(1), 10–40. https://doi.org/10.1177/0361684315599346

Sonnentag, S. (2015). Dynamics of well-being. *Annual Review of Organizational Psychology and Organizational Behavior 2*, 261–293. https://doi.org/10.1146/annurev-orgpsych-032414-111347

Sonnentag, S. (2022). Job stress: Revisiting Karasek's job demand-job control studies. In N. K. Steffens, F. Rink, & M. K. Ryans (Eds.). *Organisational psychology: Revisiting the classical studies* (pp. 111–125). Sage.

Spector, P. E. (1986). Perceived control by employees: A meta-analysis of studies concerning autonomy and participation at work. *Human Relations 39*(11), 1005–1016. https://doi.org/10.1177/001872678603901

Tay, L., Batz-Barbarich, C., Yang, L.-Q., & Wiese, C. W. (2023). Well-being: The ultimate criterion for organizational sciences. *Journal of Business and Psychology 38*, 1141–1157. https://doi.org/10.1007/s10869-023-09908-5

Trépanier, S.-G., Fernet, C., & Austin, S. (2015). A longitudinal investigation of workplace bullying, basic need satisfaction, and employee functioning. *Journal of Occupational Health Psychology 20*(1), 105–116. https://doi.org/10.1037/a0037726

van As, S., Veling, H., Beckers, D. G. J., Earle, F., McMaster, S., Kompier, M. A. J., & Geurts, S. A. E. (2022). The impact of cognitive work demands on subsequent physical activity behavior. *Journal of Experimental Psychology: Applied 28*(3), 629–634. https://doi.org/10.1037/xap0000390

Van der Klink, J. J. L., Blonk, R. W. B., Schene, A. H., & Van Dijk, F. J. H. (2001). The benefits of interventions for work-related stress. *American Journal of Public Health 91*(2), 270–276.

Venables, L., & Fairclough, S. H. (2009). The influence of performance feedback on goal-setting and mental effort regulation. *Motivation and Emotion 33*, 63–74. https://doi.org/10.1007/s11031-008-9116-y

Verkuil, B., Atasayi, S., & Molendijk, M. L. (2015). Workplace bullying and mental health: a meta-analysis on cross-sectional and longitudinal data. *PLoS ONE 10*(8), e0135225. https://doi.org/10.1371/journal.pone.0135225

Viswesvaran, C., Sanchez, J. I., & Fisher, J. (1999). The role of social support in the process of work stress: A meta-analysis. *Journal of Vocational Behavior 54*(2), 314–334. https://doi.org/10.1006/jvbe.1998.1661

Wall, T. D., Jackson, P. R., Mullarkey, S., & Parker, S. K. (1996). The demands-control model of job strain: A more specific test. *Journal of Occupational and Organizational Psychology 69*(2), 153–166. https://doi.org/10.1111/j.2044-8325.1996.tb00607.x

Wang, M., Sinclair, R. R., Zhou, L., & Sears, L. E. (2013). Person-centered analysis: Methods, applications, and implications for occupational health psychology. In R. R. Sinclair, M. Wang, & L. E. Tetrick (Eds.), *Research methods in occupational health psychology: Measurement, design, and data analysis* (pp. 349–373). Routledge.

Willness, C. R., Steel, P., & Lee, K. (2007). A meta-analysis of the antecedents and consequences of workplace sexual harassment. *Personnel Psychology 60*(1), 127–162. https://doi.org/10.1111/j.1744-6570.2007.00067.x

Work Design and Performance

Sandra Ohly and Laura Venz

Introduction

Work design refers to "the content and organization of one's work tasks, activities, relationships, and responsibilities" (Parker, 2014, p. 662), oftentimes expressed in terms of job or work characteristics. Going beyond the core motivational job characteristics (Hackman & Oldham, 1976), social and cognitive characteristics can be identified to describe the content and organization of work tasks and responsibilities. Following John Campbell and Brenton Wiernik (2015), performance refers to behaviors that contribute to organizational goals. Although various similar taxonomies of relevant workplace behaviors exist, we will draw mainly on Mark Griffin, Andrew Neal, and Sharon K. Parker's model (2007), which defines work performance as behavior in formalized and emergent work roles that contributes to organizational effectiveness, and distinguishes proficiency, adaptivity, and proactivity as three types of performance. Compared to other outcomes of work design, performance does not feature prominently in the literature, as identified in a recent review (Parker, Morgeson, & Johns, 2017). Instead, work design research building on the job characteristics model, the job demands-resources model, role theory, or socio-technical systems design seem to have focused on job satisfaction, exhaustion, or innovation (cf. Parker et al., 2017, fig. 5.1). Moreover, when relating work design and performance, the focus was merely on proficiency (i.e., task performance) and other types of performance were often neglected.

This chapter will provide an overview of current research on the topic of work design and performance. Starting with the seminal meta-analysis by Stephen E. Humphrey and colleagues (2007), which linked job characteristics, such as autonomy, task identity, task feedback, and task significance to proficiency, we discuss more recent findings related to (1) a broader set of work characteristics including, for example, cognitive characteristics; (2) a broader set of underlying mechanisms beyond motivation; and (3) a broader range of performance outcomes including proactivity, creativity, adaptivity, and safety. Due to changes in the nature of work (see Wegman et al., 2018), which has seen increasing

---

Sandra Ohly and Laura Venz, *Work Design and Performance*. In: *Transformative Work Design*. Edited by: Sharon K. Parker et al., Oxford University Press. © Society for Industrial and Organizational Psychology (2025). DOI: 10.1093/oso/9780197692554.003.0005

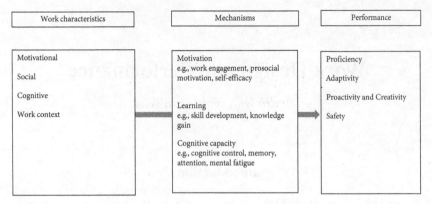

Figure 5.1 Organizing Framework

automation, agile and flexible work practices, and more uncertainty and interdependency, it is important to understand how to promote performance. This chapter will explore how work design can improve different types of performance and identify multiple pathways of how this can be achieved in a changing world of work.

A Model of Job Performance

Going beyond the previously established differentiation of in-role and extra-role performance, Griffin and colleagues (2007) have suggested a new perspective on relevant performance dimensions. Specifically, they argued that in light of increasing uncertainties and interdependencies in modern workplaces, and in addition to fulfilling the core tasks, individuals need to adapt to and initiate changes in their immediate workplace, in their team, and in their organization, resulting in nine different performance dimensions, namely proficiency, adaptivity, and proactivity on the individual, team, and organizational level. The review of recent literature will be organized according to these dimensions with a focus on the individual level.

Proficiency (or task performance) refers to the performance on core work tasks (Campbell & Wiernik, 2015) or primary tasks (Rice, 1958) for which a job was created; that is, to "the extent to which the individual meets role requirements that can be formalized" (Griffin et al., 2007, p. 329). Proficiency was traditionally the focal outcome of work design research. Because of uncertainty, not all aspects of the work role can be formalized, and adapting to or proactively initiating changes becomes important for organizational effectiveness. Therefore, adaptivity and proactivity have been suggested as additional types of performance. Adaptivity refers to "the extent to which an individual adapts to changes in work systems or work roles" (Griffin et al., 2007, p. 329). For example, an individual coping well and supporting changes to work procedures is adaptive. Proactivity refers to the extent to which individuals "take self-directing action to anticipate or initiate change in the work system or work role" (p. 329), such as taking charge of an issue, voicing ideas to supervisors, or initiating changes to working procedures. Beyond adaptivity and proactivity, we also consider creativity as a type of performance related to but different from proactivity. Indeed, work design has long been linked to creativity; that is, the generation of novel and useful ideas (e.g., Oldham & Cummings, 1996). As noted, uncertainty is inherent in many contemporary changes to workplaces and is created by designing autonomous and complex jobs in which the way to accomplish work tasks is often not fully predetermined, increasing the need for novel and useful ideas related to processes and work procedures. Although creativity and proactivity can be distinguished (e.g., in terms of novelty of changes or behavioral manifestations), they share similar antecedents in terms of work design, and we will thus review the relevant literature related to both outcomes in a combined fashion.

According to Griffin and Gudela Grote's (2020) uncertainty regulation model, effective performance depends on the alignment of the requirement and preference related to uncertainty. Individuals are thought to regulate their experienced uncertainty based on the appraisal of the uncertain situation by engaging in different behaviors which, in turn, results in proficiency, adaptivity and proactivity/creativity. Rather than following scripted sequences of behavior to accomplish tasks, individuals need to find new ways to solve problems and pursue work-related goals, for example, in the form of creative behaviors. At the same time, however, there are also situations when creative reactions to uncertainty can be detrimental (see Grote, 2020), namely when it comes to safety performance, behaviors that individuals exhibit "to promote the health and safety of workers, clients, the public, and the environment" (Burke et al., 2002, p. 432). Safety behaviors are relevant performance behaviors because they help prevent accidents and injuries (Griffin & Neal, 2000). As such, examining safety performance as an outcome of work design is important (Hofmann et al., 2017) and this is why we include safety performance in addition to proficiency, adaptivity, proactivity, and creativity.

Although not in the focus, we will also refer to findings related to work design and organizational citizenship behaviors (extra-role behaviors that go beyond formalized task requirements), which might represent proficiency, adaptivity, and proactivity to some degree (Carpini & Parker, 2018). For example, helping and cooperating can be considered part of any work role requiring interdependent action and thus indicates proficiency. Moreover, sportsmanship indicates

150 TRANSFORMATIVE WORK DESIGN

that individuals get on board when changes occur and indicate adaptivity. To link work design to job performance in the form of proficiency, adaptivity, proactivity, and creativity, as well as safety, we will discuss three linking mechanisms (motivation, learning, and cognitive capacity).

Linking Work Design and Job Performance

The model guiding our review and depicting the underlying processes linking work design (i.e., work characteristics) to performance is shown in Figure 5.1.

Work characteristics

We focus our review of work design and performance on research conducted after Humphrey and colleagues' (2007) seminal meta-analysis on the topic. In this meta-analysis, of the core "motivational" job characteristics (Hackman & Oldham, 1976), autonomy, task identity, task significance, and feedback from the job had non-zero correlations with subjective performance (i.e., ratings of performance), whereas only autonomy showed significant relationships with objective performance (i.e., performance outcomes such as piece counts) (Humphrey et al., 2007). In the chapter, for consistency, we will use the label job autonomy also when referring to job control. Beyond the core job characteristics, newer research identified contact with beneficiaries as relevant predictor of performance, for example, in call center employees (Grant, 2008). This led to a raising interest in relational aspects of work design (Grant, 2007), which coincides with increase in interdependence of work roles (Wegman et al., 2018) and higher number of customer service roles in Western economies (Zapf et al., 2021). Humphrey and colleagues' (2007) meta-analytic results support that social work characteristics, especially interdependence and feedback by others, incrementally predict subjective performance. Social support as a job resource can, besides the core job characteristics of autonomy, task variety, task significance and feedback, be linked to higher levels of work engagement, which in turn relates to proficiency (Christian et al., 2011).

In addition to the core and social work characteristics, which mostly reflect job resources, job demands have extensively been studied in relation to performance, often based on the job demands-resources model (Bakker & Demerouti, 2017). In this conjunction, cognitive demands, such as job complexity (i.e., the degree to which a job is multi-faceted and difficult to perform; Nahrgang et al., 2011), have also been examined as work characteristics in relation to job performance. Finally, physical demands, work conditions, and ergonomics—coined work context characteristics by Humphrey and colleagues (2007)—have been studied in terms of work design, mainly in relation to safety performance. In sum, studied work characteristics as predictors of job performance include motivational, social, and cognitive, as well as physical job demands and resources (see Figure 5.1). All these different work characteristics are thought to relate to the different types of job performance via comparable mechanisms, which we will review.

Mechanisms linking work design to performance

Based on the general observation that performance is based on knowledge, skills, and motivation (Campbell & Wiernik, 2015), the effect of work design (i.e., work characteristics) on performance might be due to different mechanisms. In this chapter, we argue that in addition to the perspective dominating work and organizational psychology that work design enhances intrinsic motivation (Hackman & Oldham, 1976), work design might also foster learning (Parker, 2014, 2017), and thus increase performance-relevant skill and knowledge in employees (Alvesson & Kärreman, 2001), as well as optimize demands on human cognitive processing capacity (Kruglanski & Webster, 1996), also benefiting performance.

Motivation

According to the motivational approach (Hackman & Oldham, 1976), enriching work by providing a variety of tasks, and autonomy in accomplishing them, will enhance intrinsic motivation, which in turn benefits performance. Following this initial proposal, research has largely focused on the motivational effects of work design considering various forms of motivation such as job satisfaction (Judge et al., 2001), work engagement (Demerouti et al., 2010), and choice (Seo et al., 2004; Seo et al., 2010). In Humphrey and colleagues' (2007) meta-analysis, experienced meaningfulness was the key critical psychological state linking work design to performance outcomes, which is consistent with the relational perspective on work design, and the key role of prosocial motivation (Grant & Berg, 2012). Meaningfulness is oftentimes experienced in relation to others who benefit from one's work (Barrick et al., 2013). Recent research has also examined forms of motivation based on self-determination theory (Gagné & Deci, 2005). Interestingly, identified motivation, compared to intrinsic motivation, is a better predictor of performance outcomes, including proficiency and proactive performance (Van den Broeck et al., 2021). The effects of well-being on performance (Wright & Cropanzano, 2004) can also in part be attributed to motivational effects (Sonnentag, 2015). We propose that the motivational perspective needs to be supplemented with a stronger focus on learning and cognitive capacity as two additional mechanisms.

Learning, knowledge, and skill

We concur with suggestions that work design can foster learning and, in turn, knowledge and skill, thereby enhancing performance (Parker, 2014). This perspective is in line with Campbell's focus on knowledge and skill as predictors of performance and informed by German action regulation theory (Frese & Zapf, 1994) and the active learning hypothesis (Karasek, 1979). According to the former perspective, learning at work is fostered when employees engage in complete action cycles, comprising goal setting, planning, decision making, monitoring and feedback, and regulating their action on different levels, including the intellectual and more automatic level. Based on this theory, work characteristics, such as job complexity and autonomy, can be linked to learning because the former indicates a need to learn and the latter allows for experimentation in methods and procedures. Moreover, learning occurs in the form of acquiring new knowledge and action patterns (e.g., problem solving; Daniels et al., 2009) as well as by developing more automaticity in task behaviors (see skill development or task routines; Kanfer & Ackerman, 1989; Ohly et al., 2006). Skill development is a focus of the mechanistic approach to work design (see Campion, 1988), which suggests that enhanced skill results from the specialization and simplification of work; in turn, this enhances efficiency in performance. Learning in the broader sense is not only fostered by a simplified work design that allows repeated execution of task behavior, but also by work design that allows contact to a diverse set of perspectives (e.g., customers, colleagues) and knowledge sharing (e.g., by designing interdependent work tasks and offering opportunities for mutual social support; Daniels et al., 2009). In essence, work that allows individual thriving, which includes learning (Spreitzer et al., 2005), can be linked to performance outcomes (Kleine et al., 2019). Research on work design and learning suggests that autonomy predicts learning (Bond & Flaxman, 2006; Decius et al., 2023) in customer service representatives and in white-collar workers (but not blue-collar workers; Decius et al., 2023).

Cognitive capacity

According to a cognitive capacity perspective (Kruglanski & Webster, 1996; see also Parker et al., 2021), performance depends on the amount of cognitive resources (e.g., attentional control, working memory capacity) devoted to the task at hand (Beal et al., 2005). Focusing on the dynamics of performance during the working day, Beal and colleagues proposed that, at any given moment, distractions might occur that hinder focus on the task at hand; that is, on the primary task. For example, interruptions by incoming messages create an attentional pull away from the task. Moreover, thoughts might center around issues unrelated to the task at hand, such as work–family issues or secondary tasks interfering with attention (Oberauer et al., 2016). Secondary tasks might also include tasks that are peripheral to the work role, such as performing certain management functions or collaborating with others. If individuals are required to perform these secondary tasks at the same time, issues with multitasking emerge (e.g., dual task performance; see Leroy et al., 2020; Wang et al., 2020).

This perspective suggests that work design enhances performance when work tasks are allocated in a way that allows employees to fully focus on their primary tasks, which is experienced as flow, or absorption (Bakker, 2008). Experiencing exhaustion or mental fatigue, on the other hand, is a sign that cognitive resources are depleted and cannot be invested in work tasks, resulting in cognitive failures (Daniels et al., 2013), which, for example, impair safety performance (Clarke, 2012). Mental effort is required in many work tasks, including complex tasks or those when dominant impulses need to be overridden (Shenhav et al., 2017), such as when emotion regulation is needed (Zapf et al., 2021) or when formal procedures and safety rules need compliance (Hu et al., 2022), resulting in feelings of fatigue, depletion, and exhaustion. Thus, parts of the effects of well-being on performance (Wright & Cropanzano, 2004) can be explained by a (lack of) cognitive capacity. It follows that work design fosters performance as long as job demands allow for sufficient recovery during the workday and in leisure time so that cognitive resources, such as memory capacity and attention, are replenished (Sonnentag, 2015), and by allowing autonomous determination of when breaks are needed. Moreover, work design that requires physical activity might foster cognitive resources (Calderwood et al., 2021; Ten Brummelhuis et al., 2022).

The cognitive capacity perspective allows additional explanations of the link of "hindering" job demands to lower performance (LePine, 2022). Hindrances distracting attention from the task at hand require extra effort and deplete cognitive resources, which are then not available for primary tasks. The cognitive capacity perspective is in part consistent with a perceptual approach to work design (Campion, 1988) which suggests that reducing work-related information-processing requirements results in a lower likelihood of errors and accidents, effectively enhancing (safety) performance.

Cognitive processes, such as flexible thinking (e.g., broader, inclusive knowledge categorization and deliberation of more potentially relevant concepts), result from employees experiencing positive affect (Amabile et al., 2005), which benefits the performance on complex tasks without standardized solutions (Zhang & Bartol, 2010). Work design fostering the experience of positive affect by providing job resources (autonomy, social support, feedback; Bakker & Demerouti, 2017) is thus particularly beneficial in work environments where

154 TRANSFORMATIVE WORK DESIGN

flexible thinking and problem solving is required (Parke & Seo, 2017) or in highly complex jobs (Judge et al., 2001).

Review of Recent Research

Proficiency and task performance

Supporting a motivational perspective of how work characteristics lead to higher proficiency, work characteristics (e.g., autonomy, feedback, social support, task significance, problem-solving demands and job complexity) (Christian et al., 2011) were positively linked to proficiency via work engagement (a positive affective-motivational state). Possibly individuals who feel positive about work in general are more motivated to exert effort in their primary work tasks. Physical work demands were negatively linked to work engagement. A differentiation of demands into hindrances (requiring additional effort without positive consequences) and challenges (demands requiring effort but likely leading to personal growth) reveals that hindrances decrease whereas challenges increase work engagement (Crawford et al., 2010), leading to effort investment in primary tasks and thereby benefiting proficient performance (see also LePine et al., 2005).

In terms of learning, feedback from the job has been proposed to lead to knowledge of results, which benefits performance (Hackman & Oldham, 1976) but empirical support for this notion is sparse. Active learning, or learning new skills while working, has been linked to high demands and simultaneously high autonomy, but empirical support for this assumption is mixed, which might be due to the operationalization of learning (Häusser et al., 2014). The learning component of thriving (relying on perceptual measures) has been linked to higher task performance (Kleine et al., 2019).

Demanding and stressful conditions (including challenge and hinderance demands) can have a negative impact on performance by reducing the cognitive resources available for individuals to perform work tasks effectively (see also Barnes & Van Dyne, 2009). Attention residue (thinking about unfinished tasks) prohibits the full concentration on the primary task when interruptions occur (Leroy, 2009). However, under high demands, individuals might also concentrate on what they see as the main part of their job, implying that cognitive resources are invested in primary tasks, benefiting task performance.

Adaptive performance

Limited research has examined work design in relation to adaptive performance (Jundt et al., 2015). Sohee Park and Sunyoung Park (2019) reviewed empirical evidence showing that job autonomy, job demands, job resources, and uncertainty link to adaptive performance. Moreover, work engagement before change predicted supervisor-rated adaptive performance after a company changed to flexible offices, and this relationship was explained by the attitude toward the change (Van den Heuvel et al., 2020). These findings suggest that work characteristics that relate to work engagement (Christian et al., 2011) might also be beneficial in fostering adaptive performance through a motivational mechanism. As task-relevant knowledge and skills enable employees to adapt (Park & Park, 2019) work design fostering learning seems relevant (e.g., high job autonomy).

Adaptive behavior is necessarily a secondary task for employees, which poses additional demands and draws on limited cognitive resources. While adapting to changes in the work environment, in team composition, or in work tasks, employees will still need to fulfill their primary tasks, albeit to a lesser degree of proficiency. Dealing with change comes with uncertainty and negative emotions, which requires extra effort in self-regulation and emotion regulation (Keith & Frese, 2005). Supporting the view that adaptive performance might be overtaxing, job demands were negatively related to ratings of adaptive performance when autonomy was low (Van den Heuvel et al., 2020). This indicates that without sufficient opportunity to control the situation, employees might not be able to adapt. Job resources such as job autonomy and social support might help in dealing with high levels of demands (Bakker & Demerouti, 2017).

Proactivity and creativity

In relation to proactive performance, different forms of motivation have been distinguished (Parker et al., 2010), including can-do motivation (e.g., self-efficacy, control appraisal), reason-to motivation (intrinsic and identified motivation), and energized to motivation (e.g., positive affect). Indeed, these motivational mechanisms have received empirical support as underlying the effects of work characteristics, such as job autonomy and social support (Tornau & Frese, 2013), as well as job complexity (Ohly et al., 2006) on proactive performance (Frese et al., 2007; Parker et al., 2006; Van den Broeck et al., 2021; Williams et al., 2010). For creativity as an outcome, motivation was often assumed to be the dominant mechanism as well (Amabile, 1996). In terms of work design, autonomy, job complexity, and the requirement to be creative predict creative results (Hammond et al., 2011). Employees who perform challenging tasks and have high freedom are expected to be more intrinsically motivated (Amabile et al., 1996), which benefits their creative performance because of higher task engagement. However, this effect seems less consistent than expected (Grant &

Berry, 2011), and meta-analytic evidence suggests that, in addition to intrinsic motivation, extrinsic motivation and self-efficacy, as well as positive affect, contribute to creativity (Hammond et al., 2011; Lyubormirsky et al., 2005). Self-efficacy is the appraisal that one's own skills are sufficient to deal with the requirements of the job or to be creative, and as a personal resource is fostered by work characteristics such as job autonomy and social support (Xanthopoulou et al., 2007) and job complexity (Frese et al., 2007).

Going beyond the motivational perspective, given that creativity is dependent on the available knowledge (Amabile, 1996), work design that enhances knowledge sharing and learning is conducive to creativity (Zhou & Hoever, 2014), stressing the role of relational work design (interdependence, social support and feedback from others). For example, creativity is enhanced when employees seek help (Mueller & Kamdar, 2011), suggesting that social support and other resources (Hammond et al., 2011) related to increased knowledge sharing (Witherspoon et al., 2013) are important, arguably because they enhance learning. Although learning has been treated as an outcome of proactivity (Ashforth et al., 2007) or a boundary condition of positive outcomes of proactivity (Parker et al., 2019), there is also reason to believe that learning contributes to proactive behavior. For example, education and job experience are both positively linked to proactivity (Tornau & Frese, 2013).

Cognitive work characteristics, such as job complexity, can be linked to higher creativity through motivation and the requirement to be creative (Unsworth et al., 2005), but also via cognitive mechanisms. When creative requirements are high, generating novel ideas becomes the primary task, whereas creativity represents a secondary task when creative requirements or job complexity are low (Unsworth, 2001). This distinction might help explain the inconsistent effect of job demands on creativity (Byron et al., 2010). Under stressful conditions, when cognitive resources are limited and need to be allocated strategically, employees might concentrate on their primary tasks, which might not involve the generation of novel ideas. Creativity benefits from automaticity in primary work tasks, possibly because more cognitive resources are available (Ohly et al., 2006). Because limited resources are more likely to be invested in core tasks that are part of formal job descriptions and that are rewarded, performance on secondary tasks might suffer under high stress, resulting in lower creativity (Mueller & Kamdar, 2011). Higher cognitive resources (e.g., working memory capacity) can also be linked to voice—in particular voice quality (Wolsink, et al., 2019)—as a form of proactive behavior.

Safety performance

Safety performance reflects work behaviors that "promote the health and safety of workers, clients, the public, and the environment" (Burke et al., 2002, p. 432). Safety behaviors can be subsumed under the two broader safety performance categories of compliance and participation (Neal et al., 2000) with safety compliance relating to in-role behaviors, such as adhering to safety rules and procedures, and safety participation relating to extra-role behaviors, such as promoting safety compliance in coworkers and making safety suggestions.

Work design is an important aspect in ensuring safety performance (Hofmann et al., 2017); nevertheless, research rarely actually examined work design in relation to occupational safety. Extant findings from neighboring research, however, suggest that for safety performance as an outcome, all the different theoretical mechanisms underlying the effects of work design on performance in general also apply to understand the emergence of safety performance (see Beus et al., 2016). Respective research largely focused on safety motivation and safety knowledge and skill as the two core mechanisms relating distal predictors to safety performance (e.g., Christian et al., 2009; Lyubykh et al., 2022; Neal et al., 2000). For example, work pressure and supervisor support were meta-analytically found to predict safety knowledge and safety motivation and, via those, arguably, safety behavior (Beus et al., 2015; Christian et al., 2009). Social work characteristics, in particular leadership (Clarke, 2013) and teamwork (Salas et al., 2020), were shown to play a significant role in safety performance via various cognitive and motivational mechanims. Additionally, belongingness need satisfaction was found to mediate the effects of leadership on safety performance (Yang et al., 2020). This points to both learning and motivational mechanisms underlying work design for safety performance.

Work design includes structuring work, and structural attributes of work are important in informing employees about which role behaviors, including safety behaviors, are expected of them and should be prioritized (Hofmann et al., 2017). This points to the special role of work context characteristics in safety performance. In this regard, for example, the organization-level standardization of work procedures, the use of monitoring equipment, and safety policies are important to consider. Organizations where safety is key, such as power plants or hospitals, often rely on bureaucratic structures following Tayloristic work-design approaches with a division of labor, specialized job roles, a clear hierarchy of positions and responsibilities, and formalized rules and procedures to ensure safety (Dekker, 2014; Parker, 2014). On the other hand, Tayloristic approaches to work design have been found to bring about monotony, which has been discussed as a source of accidents (e.g., McBain, 1970). This indicates a potential friction between stability and flexibility when it comes to safety performance (see Grote, 2020).

Whereas safety design classically includes equipment design and human factors, or ergonomics (Fadier & De la Garza, 2006), changes in the nature of work activities, tasks, and responsibilities, such as from rather physical to mental work, from rigidly set procedures to autonomy, and from division of labor to interdependence (Wegman et al., 2018), bring work characteristics (e.g. job demands and resources) into focus (Beus et al., 2016). This allows us to draw inferences on the role of work design (as we define it) and its underlying mechanisms for safety performance. In this regard, meta-analytic evidence suggests that, for example, physical demands, such as risks and hazards, as well as cognitive demands, such as complexity, are negatively linked to safety behaviors via mental exhaustion and burnout (Nahrgang et al., 2011). Additionally, Sharon Clarke (2012) found in her meta-analysis that hindrances, such as role ambiguity, competing goals, and situational constraints, are negatively related to safety performance behaviors, whereas challenging demands, such as time pressure and workload, are largely unrelated to safety performance behaviors and outcomes. This points to cognitive capacity and mental fatigue playing an important role in impaired safety performance (see Beus et al., 2016). This perspective is supported by notions that cognitive failure is a core mechanism underlying low safety performance (Wallace & Chen, 2005). Regarding job resources, on the other hand, meta-analytic evidence indicates that the core work characteristic of autonomy, as well as social work characteristics such as a supportive environment, are positively related to safety behaviors via motivation and engagement (Nahrgang et al., 2011). As work engagement entails cognitive and motivational facets, this finding supports the cognitive and the motivational mechanisms of work design in predicting high safety performance.

Going beyond the individual level: Team-level and organizational level performance

Whereas work design research is often focused on the individual level (e.g., Humphrey et al., 2007), Griffin and colleagues' (2007) model of work role performance suggests team-level and organization-level proficiency, adaptivity, and proactivity as important performance dimensions as well. Therefore, we provide a short overview of how work design affects team-level and organizational level performance.

Granting a high degree of team-level autonomy (e.g., in self-management work teams) is beneficial for performance in team tasks characterized by high interdependence, non-standardized processes, and uncertainty (Magpili & Pazos, 2018), possibly because the benefits of higher levels of skill play out under these conditions. On the organizational level of analysis, enriched job design (e.g., higher variety and autonomy) was linked to a higher quality of organizational financial performance through higher job satisfaction (Wood et al., 2012) and indirectly to higher productivity. Although this relationship might point to a motivational mechanism, employee skill is important to consider as an alternative explanation (Peccei & Van De Voorde, 2019). Focusing on organizational outcomes, Kamal Birdi and colleagues (2008) showed that empowerment, which implies higher autonomy, and the introduction of teamwork enhanced company performance in manufacturing. They also argued that the effectiveness of teamwork depends on how well individuals are able to work together, pointing to the importance of teamwork processes (Marks et al., 2001). For example, knowledge sharing in teams relates to team creativity (Dong et al., 2017), suggesting that task interdependence in teams is relevant, because more knowledge is shared when interdependent actions are required (Gong et al., 2013; Li et al., 2016). Nevertheless, although teamwork is often used as a way to enrich jobs and motivate individuals, it also creates additional demands (Ogbonnaya, 2019) possibly because of additional performance requirements, such as the necessity to monitor team members' action (Langfred, 2004). In this sense, teamwork processes might be regarded as secondary tasks. Maintaining a good team atmosphere and managing negative emotion in teams might also be considered a secondary task (Zapf et al., 2021), which limits the potential of performance-enhancing effects.

Performance in the Changing World of Work—How Work Design Can Contribute

Recent trends in workplaces contribute to changes in work settings and ways of working, which in turn shape work design (e.g., Schwarzmüller et al., 2018; see chapters on automation, remote work in this volume, and see the section about future work in this chapter). For example, with a rise in volatility, uncertainty, complexity, and ambiguity, agile ways of working find their way into a broad number of organizations and industries beyond information technology and software development where they have originally been developed (Junker et al., 2023). Other examples are the implementation of remote and distributed

160 TRANSFORMATIVE WORK DESIGN

work and increased automation and technology use. We will elaborate on how related changes in work design might affect job performance.

Changes in work design and job performance

Distributed work means that individuals are working together from different places (remote work, telework, working from home). While such new ways of working have been related to higher performance, mainly because of positive effects on job autonomy (Gajendran & Harrison, 2007), they also increase cognitive demands, such as complexity, which require efficient self-regulation to sustain high performance (e.g., Troll et al., 2022). Accordingly, the effect of distributed work on performance seems to depend on the way the work is designed. For example, in jobs with very low interdependence (patent officers), working from anywhere increased objective performance (count of completed cases; Choudhury et al., 2021). Conversely, when interdependence is high, frequent interactions and meetings are required (Nurmi & Hinds, 2020). Possibly because of the higher amount of time spent on coordination activities and less uninterrupted working time, the average output of IT professionals declined slightly, and employee productivity fell 8 percent to 19 percent (Gibbs et al., 2021). This may be explained by detrimental effects on both motivation (see also Ozcelik & Barsade, 2018) and reduced cognitive capacity. Moreover, in distributed work, knowledge sharing becomes more effortful, which suggests that learning is hindered (Allen et al., 2015; Wang & Noe, 2010; Yang et al., 2022), which could also explain lower performance.

Like distributed work, also automation—the reliance on technologies like robots, algorithms, and artificial intelligence (AI)—can influence autonomy, job complexity, social interaction, and other work characteristics, ultimately impacting how motivating (Knight et al., 2021) jobs are, how much they stimulate learning, and how much they tax human capacity. Currently, the predictions on how job performance is going to be affected is difficult because there is evidence of multiple contradictory effects (Parker & Grote, 2022). It is thus important to consider how the labor is divided. Automation implies a certain distribution of work, with technology, including generative AI, fulfilling more standardized procedures and humans being left with more complex, nonstandard demands. For example, in call centers, chat bots are responsible for reaching a sales lead (customer showing interest in a product) and human operators are responsible for providing individualized information and convincing the customer (Jia et al., 2023), with benefits for objective performance outcomes (number of purchases). From a cognitive capacity and learning perspective, technology might serve as a tool to spare memory capacity (Belletier et al., 2021) and alleviate the load of accomplishing secondary tasks (collaboration, knowledge sharing), thereby enhancing proficiency, particularly when it's easy to use. For example, shared networks help monitor team members' contribution to joint projects, and videoconference systems help connect to potential collaborators around the world, enhancing knowledge sharing and learning.

Collaborative work in particular also sees a rise in the adoption of agile work practices (see Junker et al., 2023; Petermann & Zacher, 2020). Besides its primary effects on social work characteristics (Sherehiy & Karwowski, 2014), agile work implies changes in core work characteristics, being positively related to task variety (Petermann & Zacher, 2020) as well as autonomy, feedback from the task and social support, and via these to work engagement (Rietze & Zacher, 2022). Also, agile work is negatively related to the job demands of workload, time pressure, and work interruptions (Rietze & Zacher, 2022). Via these changes in social, cognitive, and motivational work characteristics, agile work is thought to shape motivational processes and ultimately enhance proficiency, adaptivity, and proactivity (e.g., Junker et al., 2022; Peeters et al., 2022). Because cooperation and knowledge sharing are central aspects of agile work (Petermann & Zacher, 2021), agile work likely also stimulates learning, and via this performance. A meta-analysis on agile project management indeed shows medium to large positive effects on performance (Koch et al., 2023). Interestingly, the effect sizes were stronger in occupations such as manufacturing, logistics, and health care than software developers. But agile work might also have downsides because it may increase instead of decrease uncertainties and demands. For example, agile work is suggested to involve high complexity, which places cognitive demands on employees, and the high level of self-organization involved in agile work likely implies high self-regulation demands (Petermann & Zacher, 2022). However, research so far has not examined the role of cognitive demands and mental effort involved in agile work which could be detrimental for performance. This suggests a need for more research on how and why work design affects job performance in a changing world of work.

Future directions

Analyzing how the changing world of work affects work design opens up new perspectives. The selected changes we have described in this chapter suggest that work might become more motivating and might foster learning in terms of providing higher job autonomy, social support, and feedback, but also place higher cognitive demands on employees and impose secondary tasks which might be overtaxing. Also, changes in ways of working and related work design require continuous adaptivity and this can infer with proficiency, proactivity, creativity, and safety. To be able to analyze these, at times conflicting, outcomes of work design, and to be able to analyze potential trade-offs between approaches to work design (Campion, 1988), a more comprehensive assessment of work design is needed, going beyond previous approaches focusing only on job resources and demands or motivational features (see also Schmitt et al., 2003), which are a-priori defined as being either beneficial or detrimental for performance (e.g., Bakker & Demerouti, 2017).

Job complexity is particularly interesting in this regard because it might be motivating and cognitively exhausting at the same time (Humphrey et al., 2007), and it can be expected to increase in many contemporary jobs. Because of the additional demands posed on employees in terms of secondary tasks and dealing with uncertainty, role clarity is essential. Role clarity refers to the knowledge of what part of the job is important, essentially detailing what is the primary task which should be given priority when resources are sparse (e.g., Venz et al., 2018), and what are secondary tasks. As an example of role clarity, creative requirements are a way to clarify that creativity is an expected part of the job. Moreover, role clarity might entail knowledge on why secondary tasks, such as providing support and knowledge, learning new skills, and ensuring safety, are important. In line with Campbell and Wiernik's (2015) argument that behavior can only contribute to organizational goals and, thus, be considered performance when the behavior is aligned with organization goals, results by Andreas Wihler and colleagues (2017) suggest that employees need to use skills and abilities to leverage personal initiative in ways that promote positive perceptions and evaluations of job performance from supervisors. Lack of role clarity might also explain why job crafting does not always lead to high performance (Dierdorff & Jensen, 2018), or why job autonomy is sometimes overtaxing (Stiglbauer & Kovacs, 2018). Feedback from the job and from others is essential to role clarity (Humphrey et al., 2007), and interventions might be tailored to specific ambiguities (Heissler et al., 2023) ensuring the preservation and restoration of cognitive resources.

In this sense, greater precision in theorizing on how the antecedents affect performance will help to design more effective interventions (Knight et al., 2017). The distinction of primary and secondary tasks (see also Zapf et al., 2021) and the cognitive capacity perspective might help in this regard. For some work characteristics, inconsistent and contradictory effects might be explained when focusing on the different mechanisms (e.g., in the case of job complexity). Moreover, disentangling the mechanisms might help theorizing on the role of work engagement, which comprises affective, motivational, and cognitive facets. Examining these mechanisms necessitates the assessment of short-term and long-term effects, taking the dynamics of performance into account (Dalal et al., 2020).

In terms of outcomes, our review revealed that some performance dimensions have received more attention than others. For example, research on task performance or proficiency, creativity, and proactive performance have been summarized in multiple meta-analyses over the last couple of years, whereas research of work design on adaptive and safety performance has been relatively sparse—at least under a concrete work design perspective. In terms of safety performance, we see a promising avenue to consider a broader range of safety behaviors, including behaviors in terms of IT safety and security. Although workplace training seems common and users are motivated to practice IT security, they often do not, and they prioritize other work tasks instead. This points to the role of IT security as a secondary task that is abandoned under high workload. For example, if distracted, employees will be more likely to click on harmful links (e.g., phishing scams) without thinking, suggesting that hindering job demands can lower IT safety performance because of less attention to secondary tasks. For future research, it seems valuable to consider safe internet use as a secondary task. It seems also important to study performance behaviors that target goals that go beyond the individual, team, and organizational levels to include society, such as employee green behavior (Zacher et al., 2023). Finally, future research might benefit from considering several performance dimensions in parallel. For example, adhering to safety policies might contradict proficiency or proactivity (Clarke, 2012). This indicates that one and the same work design measure could have opposite effects on different performance types.

More research is also needed on mechanisms underlying the effects of work design on performance. Especially in terms of adaptive performance, research might benefit from going beyond the dominating motivational perspective and considering work characteristics that help dealing with dual-task performance. Moreover, as learning and knowledge sharing can be seen as important mechanisms of how work design affects performance, a better understanding of relevant work characteristics is needed, also including those that hinder knowledge exchange and learning. The only core work characteristic included in a recent meta-analysis (Arain et al., 2022)—autonomy—was not significantly related to knowledge hiding, whereas time pressure and high workload were found positively related to knowledge hiding. Relational perspectives and social exchange theories are often used as a theoretical framework in knowledge hiding research (Offergelt & Venz, 2023); however, the role of social work characteristics, especially job resources like feedback from others or social support, needs more exploration.

Finally, changes in work settings and new work demands pose a need for continuous research on how new work characteristics affect job performance. For example, AI is likely to occur in many jobs, including healthcare and human resource management, where it has the potential to enhance problem-solving

164 TRANSFORMATIVE WORK DESIGN

and thereby performance in AI–human collaboration by using a sequential division of labor (Jia et al., 2023; Puranam, 2021), with AI conducting initial screening and humans performing the more complex interactions with patients or applicants. However, more complex ways of organizing the division of labor are possible (see Jia et al., 2023), which raises the question how work design will be affected in terms of enrichment and variability. Furthermore, because AI enters many workplaces, it would be interesting to study how decisions on work design and division of labor are made (see Parker et al., 2017). As another example, human–robot collaboration can increase complexity and other cognitive demands, making research on cognitive ergonomics (e.g., Gualtieri et al., 2022) necessary, especially for but not restricted to safety performance.

Conclusion

"Work design matters more than ever" (Parker & Grote, 2022, p. 1171). We concur with this view and hope that by providing a differentiated review of how work design affects different forms of performance and by detailing the mechanisms how this might occur, we can stimulate research for the years to come. When designing work, choices on how to allocate tasks need to be proactively considered during technology implementation, consistent with the socio-technical systems principle of joint optimization (Parker & Grote, 2022). Given that principles of socio-technical design have received support in the past when computer-aided manufacturing was introduced, it seems recommendable to consider these principles again.

References

Allen, T. D., Golden, T. D., & Shockley, K. M. (2015). How effective is telecommuting? Assessing the status of our scientific findings. *Psychological Science in the Public Interest 16*(2), 40–68.

Alvesson, M., & Kärreman, D. (2001). Odd couple: Making sense of the curious concept of knowledge management. *Journal of Management Studies 38*(7), 995–1018.

Amabile, T. M. (1996). *Creativity in context: Update to "The social psychology of creativity."* Boulder, CO: Westview Press.

Amabile, T. M., Barsade, S. G., Mueller, J. S., & Staw, B. M. (2005). Affect and creativity at work. *Administrative Science Quarterly 50*(3), 367–403.

Amabile, T. M., Conti, R., Coon, H., Lazenby, J., & Herron, M. (1996). Assessing the work environment for creativity. *Academy of Management Journal 39*(5), 1154–1184.

Arain, G. A., Bhatti, Z. A., Hameed, I., Khan, A. K., & Rudolph, C. W. (2022). A meta-analysis of the nomological network of knowledge hiding in organizations. *Personnel Psychology 77*(2), 651–682.

Ashforth, B. E., Sluss, D. M., & Saks, A. M. (2007). Socialization tactics, proactive behavior, and newcomer learning: Integrating socialization models. *Journal of Vocational Behavior 70*(3), 447–462.

Bakker, A. B. (2008). The work-related flow inventory: Construction and initial validation of the WOLF. *Journal of Vocational Behavior 72*(3), 400–414.

Bakker, A. B., & Demerouti, E. (2017). Job demands–resources theory: Taking stock and looking forward. *Journal of Occupational Health Psychology 22*(3), 273–285. https://doi.org/10.1037/ocp0000056

Barnes, C. M., & Van Dyne, L. (2009). I'm tired': Differential effects of physical and emotional fatigue on workload management strategies. *Human Relations, 62*(1), 59–92.

Barrick, M. R., Mount, M. K., & Li, N. (2013). The theory of purposeful work behavior: The role of personality, job characteristics, and experienced meaningfulness. *Academy of Management Review 38*(1), 132–153.

Beal, D. J., Weiss, H. M., Barros, E., & MacDermid, S. M. (2005). An episodic process model of affective influences on performance. *Journal of Applied Psychology 90*(6), 1054–1068. https://doi.org/10.1037/0021-9010.90.6.1054

Belletier, C., Charkhabi, M., Pires de Andrade Silva, G., Ametepe, K., Lutz, M., & Izaute, M. (2021). Wearable cognitive assistants in a factory setting: A critical review of a promising way of enhancing cognitive performance and well-being. *Cognition, Technology & Work 23*, 103–116.

Beus, J. M., Dhanani, L. Y., & McCord, M. A. (2015). A meta-analysis of personality and workplace safety: Addressing unanswered questions. *Journal of Applied Psychology 100*(2), 481–498. https://doi.org/10.1037/a0037916

Beus, J. M., McCord, M. A., & Zohar, D. (2016). Workplace safety: A review and research synthesis. *Organizational Psychology Review 6*(4), 352–381.

Birdi, K., Clegg, C., Patterson, M., Robinson, A., Stride, C. B., Wall, T. D., & Wood, S. J. (2008). The impact of human resource and operational management practices on company productivity: A longitudinal study. *Personnel Psychology 61*(3), 467–501.

Bond, F. W., & Flaxman, P. E. (2006). The ability of psychological flexibility and job control to predict learning, job performance, and mental health. *Journal of Organizational Behavior Management 26*(1–2), 113–130.

Van den Broeck, A., Howard, J. L., Van Vaerenbergh, Y., Leroy, H., & Gagné, M. (2021). Beyond intrinsic and extrinsic motivation: A meta-analysis on self-determination theory's multidimensional conceptualization of work motivation. *Organizational Psychology Review 11*(3), 240–273.

Burke, M. J., Sarpy, S. A., Tesluk, P. E., & Smith-Crowe, K. (2002). General safety performance: A test of a grounded theoretical model. *Personnel Psychology 55*(2), 429–457.

Byron, K., Khazanchi, S., & Nazarian, D. (2010). The relationship between stressors and creativity: A meta-analysis examining competing theoretical models. *Journal of Applied Psychology 95*(1), 201–212. https://doi.org/10.1037/a0017868

Calderwood, C., ten Brummelhuis, L. L., Patel, A. S., Watkins, T., Gabriel, A. S., & Rosen, C. C. (2021). Employee physical activity: A multidisciplinary integrative review. *Journal of Management 47*(1), 144–170.

Campbell, J. P., & Wiernik, B. M. (2015). The modeling and assessment of work performance. *Annual Review of Organizational Psychology and Organizational Behavior 2*, 47–74. https://doi.org/10.1146/annurev-orgpsych-032414-111427

Campion, M. A. (1988). Interdisciplinary approaches to job design: A constructive replication with extensions. *Journal of Applied Psychology 73*(3), 467–481. https://doi.org/10.1037/0021-9010.73.3.467

Carpini, J. A., & Parker, S. K. (2018). The bigger picture: How organizational citizenship behaviors fit within a broader conceptualization of work performance. In P. M. Podsakoff, S. B. MacKezie, N. P. Podsakoff (Eds.), *The Oxford handbook of organizational citizenship behavior* (pp. 19–42). Oxford Press.

Choudhury, P., Foroughi, C., & Larson, B. (2021). Work-from-anywhere: The productivity effects of geographic flexibility. *Strategic Management Journal 42*(4), 655–683.

Christian, M. S., Bradley, J. C., Wallace, J. C., & Burke, M. J. (2009). Workplace safety: A meta-analysis of the roles of person and situation factors. *Journal of Applied Psychology 94*(5), 1103–1127. https://doi.org/10.1037/a0016172

Christian, M. S., Garza, A. S., & Slaughter, J. E. (2011). Work engagement: A quantitative review and test of its relations with task and contextual performance. *Personnel Psychology 64*(1), 89–136. https://doi.org/10.1111/j.1744-6570.2010.01203.x

Clarke, S. (2012). The effect of challenge and hindrance stressors on safety behavior and safety outcomes: A meta-analysis. *Journal of Occupational Health Psychology 17*(4), 387–397. https://doi.org/10.1037/a0029817

Clarke, S. (2013). Safety leadership: A meta-analytic review of transformational and transactional leadership styles as antecedents of safety behaviours. *Journal of Occupational and Organizational Psychology 86*(1), 22–49. https://doi.org/10.1111/j.2044-8325.2012.02064.x

Crawford, E. R., LePine, J. A., & Rich, B. L. (2010). Linking job demands and resources to employee engagement and burnout: a theoretical extension and meta-analytic test. *Journal of applied psychology, 95*(5), 834.

Dalal, R. S., Alaybek, B., & Lievens, F. (2020). Within-person job performance variability over short timeframes: Theory, empirical research, and practice. *Annual Review of Organizational Psychology and Organizational Behavior 7*, 421–449.

Daniels, K., Beesley, N., Wimalasiri, V., & Cheyne, A. (2013). Problem solving and well-being: Exploring the instrumental role of job control and social support. *Journal of Management 39*(4), 1016–1043.

Daniels, K., Boocock, G., Glover, J., Hartley, R., & Holland, J. (2009). An experience sampling study of learning, affect, and the demands control support model. *Journal of Applied Psychology 94*(4), 1003–1017. https://doi.org/10.1037/a0015517

Decius, J., Schaper, N., Klug, K., & Seifert, A. (2023). Active learning, active shaping, or both? A cross-lagged panel analysis of reciprocal effects between work design and informal workplace learning, and the mediating role of job crafting. *Journal of Vocational Behavior 144*, 103893.

Dekker, S. W. (2014). The bureaucratization of safety. *Safety Science 70*, 348–357.

Demerouti, E., Cropanzano, R., Bakker, A., & Leiter, M. (2010). From thought to action: Employee work engagement and job performance. In A. B. Bakker and M. P. Leiter (Eds.), Work engagement: A handbook of essential theory and research (pp. 147–163). Psychology Press.

Dierdorff, E. C., & Jensen, J. M. (2018). Crafting in context: Exploring when job crafting is dysfunctional for performance effectiveness. *Journal of Applied Psychology 103*(5), 463–477.

Dong, Y., Bartol, K. M., Zhang, Z.-X., & Li, C. (2017). Enhancing employee creativity via individual skill development and team knowledge sharing: Influences of dual-focused transformational leadership. *Journal of Organizational Behavior 38*(3), 439–458. https://doi.org/10.1002/job.2134

Fadier, E., & De la Garza, C. (2006). Safety design: Towards a new philosophy. *Safety Science 44*(1), 55–73.

Frese, M., & Zapf, D. (1994). Action as the core of work psychology: A German approach. *Handbook of industrial and organizational psychology, 4*(2), 271–340.

Frese, M., Garst, H., & Fay, D. (2007). Making things happen: Reciprocal relationships between work characteristics and personal initiative in a four-wave longitudinal structural equation model. *Journal of Applied Psychology 92*(4), 1084–1102.

Gagné, M., & Deci, E. L. (2005). Self-determination theory and work motivation. *Journal of Organizational Behavior 26*(4), 331–362.

Gajendran, R. S., & Harrison, D. A. (2007). The good, the bad, and the unknown about telecommuting: Meta-analysis of psychological mediators and individual consequences. *Journal of Applied Psychology 92*(6), 1524–1541. https://doi.org/10.1037/0021-9010.92.6.1524

Gibbs, M., Mengel, F., & Siemroth, C. (2021, 19 November). Work from home & productivity: Evidence from personnel & analytics data on IT professionals. University of Chicago, Becker Friedman Institute for Economics Working Paper No. 2021-56. https://ssrn.com/abstract=3843197

Golden, T. D., & Gajendran, R. S. (2019). Unpacking the role of a telecommuter's job in their performance: Examining job complexity, problem solving, interdependence, and social support. *Journal of Business and Psychology 34*(1), 55–69.

Gong, Y., Kim, T., Lee, D., & Zhu, J. (2013). A multilevel model of team goal orientation, information change, and creativity. *Academy of Management Journal 56*, 827–851.

Grant, A. M. (2007). Relational job design and the motivation to make a prosocial difference. *Academy of Management Review 32*(2), 393–417. https://doi.org/10.2307/20159308

Grant, A. M. (2008). The significance of task significance: Job performance effects, relational mechanisms, and boundary conditions. *Journal of Applied Psychology 93*, 108–124.

Grant, A. M., & Berg, J. M. (2012). Prosocial motivation. In K. S. Cameron & G. M. Spreitzer (Eds.), *The Oxford handbook of positive organizational scholarship* (pp. 28–44). Oxford University Press.

Grant, A. M., & Berry, J. W. (2011). The necessity of others is the mother of invention: Intrinsic and prosocial motivations, perspective taking, and creativity. *Academy of Management Journal 54*(1), 73–96. https://doi.org/10.5465/AMJ.2011.59215085

Griffin, M. A., & Grote, G. (2020). When is more uncertainty better? A model of uncertainty regulation and effectiveness. *Academy of Management Review 45*(4), 745–765. https://doi.org/10.5465/amr.2018.0271

Griffin, M. A., & Neal, A. (2000). Perceptions of safety at work: A framework for linking safety climate to safety performance, knowledge, and motivation. *Journal of Occupational Health Psychology 5*, 347–358. http://dx.doi.org/10.1037/1076-8998.5.3.347

Griffin, M. A., Neal, A., & Parker, S. K. (2007). A new model of work role performance: Positive behavior in uncertain and interdependent contexts. *Academy of Management Journal 50*(2), 327–347.

Grote, G. (2020). Safety and autonomy: A contradiction forever? *Safety Science 127*, 104709.

Gualtieri, L., Fraboni, F., De Marchi, M., & Rauch, E. (2022). Development and evaluation of design guidelines for cognitive ergonomics in human-robot collaborative assembly systems. *Applied Ergonomics 104*, 103807.

Hackman, J. R., & Oldham, G. R. (1976). Motivation through the design of work: Test of a theory. *Organizational Behavior and Human Performance 16*(2), 250–279.

Hammond, M. M., Neff, N. L., Farr, J. L., Schwall, A. R., & Zhao, X. (2011). Predictors of individual-level innovation at work: A meta-analysis. *Psychology of Aesthetics, Creativity, and the Arts 5*(1), 90.

Häusser, J. A., Schulz-Hardt, S., & Mojzisch, A. (2014). The active learning hypothesis of the job–demand–control model: An experimental examination. *Ergonomics 57*(1), 23–33.

Heissler, C., Kern, M., & Ohly, S. (2023). *"Dear manager, now I know what you expect": An intervention study on setting clear availability expectations.* Manuscript under review.

Van den Heuvel, M., Demerouti, E., Bakker, A. B., Hetland, J., & Schaufeli, W. B. (2020). How do employees adapt to organizational change? The role of meaning-making and work engagement. *Spanish Journal of Psychology 23*, e56.

Hofmann, D. A., Burke, M. J., & Zohar, D. (2017). 100 years of occupational safety research: From basic protections and work analysis to a multilevel view of workplace safety and risk. *Journal of Applied Psychology 102*(3), 375–388. https://doi.org/10.1037/apl0000114

Hu, X., Jimmieson, N. L., & White, K. M. (2022). Understanding compliance with safe work practices: The role of "can-do" and "reason-to" factors. *Journal of Occupational and Organizational Psychology 95*(2), 405–430.

Humphrey, S. E., Nahrgang, J. D., & Morgeson, F. P. (2007). Integrating motivational, social, and contextual work design features: A meta-analytic summary and theoretical extension of the work design literature. *Journal of Applied Psychology 92*(5), 1332–1356. https://doi.org/10.1037/0021-9010.92.5.1332

Jia, N., Luo, X., Fang, Z., & Liao, C. (2023). When and how artificial intelligence augments employee creativity. *Academy of Management Journal 67* (1).

Judge, T. A., Thoresen, C. J., Bono, J. E., & Patton, G. K. (2001). The job satisfaction–job performance relationship: A qualitative and quantitative review. *Psychological Bulletin 127*(3), 376–407. https://doi.org/10.1037/0033-2909.127.3.376

Jundt, D. K., Shoss, M. K., & Huang, J. L. (2015). Individual adaptive performance in organizations: A review. *Journal of Organizational Behavior 36*(Suppl 1), S53–S71. https://doi.org/10.1002/job.1955

Junker, T. L., Bakker, A. B., Derks, D., & Molenaar, D. (2023). Agile work practices: Measurement and mechanisms. *European Journal of Work and Organizational Psychology 32*(1), 1–22.

Junker, T. L., Bakker, A. B., Gorgievski, M. J., & Derks, D. (2022). Agile work practices and employee proactivity: A multilevel study. *Human Relations 75*(12), 2189–2217.

Kanfer, R., & Ackerman, P. L. (1989). Motivation and cognitive abilities: An integrative/aptitude-treatment interaction approach to skill acquisition. *Journal of Applied Psychology 74*(4), 657–690.

Karasek Jr., R. A. (1979). Job demands, job decision latitude, and mental strain: Implications for job redesign. *Administrative Science Quarterly 24*(2), 285–308.

Keith, N., & Frese, M. (2005). Self-regulation in error management training: Emotion control and metacognition as mediators of performance effects. *Journal of Applied Psychology 90*(4), 677–691. https://doi.org/10.1037/0021-9010.90.4.677

Kleine, A. K., Rudolph, C. W., & Zacher, H. (2019). Thriving at work: A meta-analysis. *Journal of Organizational Behavior 40*(9–10), 973–999.

Knight, C., Kaur, S., & Parker, S. K. (2021, 22 December). Work design in the contemporary era. In *Oxford research encyclopedia of business and management.* https://oxfordre.com/business/view/10.1093/acrefore/9780190224851.001.0001/acrefore-9780190224851-e-353

Knight, C., Patterson, M., & Dawson, J. (2017). Building work engagement: A systematic review and meta-analysis investigating the effectiveness of work engagement interventions. *Journal of Organizational Behavior 38*(6), 792–812.

Koch, J., Drazic, I., & Schermuly, C. C. (2023). The affective, behavioural and cognitive outcomes of agile project management: A preliminary meta-analysis. *Journal of Occupational and Organizational Psychology 96* (3), 678–706.

Kruglanski, A. W., & Webster, D. M. (1996). Motivated closing of the mind: "Seizing" and "freezing." *Psychological Review 103*, 263–283.

Langfred, C. W. (2004). Too much of a good thing? Negative effects of high trust and individual autonomy in self-managing teams. *Academy of Management Journal 47*(3), 385–399.

LePine, J. A., Podsakoff, N. P., & LePine, M. A. (2005). A meta-analytic test of the challenge stressor-hindrance stressor framework: An explanation for inconsistent relationships among stressors and performance. *Academy of Management Journal 48*(5), 764–775. https://doi.org/10.5465/AMJ.2005.18803921

LePine, M. A. (2022). The challenge-hindrance stressor framework: An integrative conceptual review and path forward. *Group & Organization Management 47*(2), 223–254.

Leroy, S. (2009). Why is it so hard to do my work? The challenge of attention residue when switching between work tasks. *Organizational Behavior and Human Decision Processes 109*(2), 168–181.

Leroy, S., Schmidt, A. M., & Madjar, N. (2020). Interruptions and task transitions: Understanding their characteristics, processes, and consequences. *Academy of Management Annals 14*(2), 661–694.

Li, V., Mitchell, R., & Boyle, B. (2016). The divergent effects of transformational leadership on individual and team innovation. *Group & Organization Management 41*, 66–97.

Lyubomirsky, S., King, L., & Diener, E. (2005). The benefits of frequent positive affect: Does happiness lead to success? *Psychological Bulletin 131*(6), 803–855.

Lyubykh, Z., Turner, N., Hershcovis, M. S., & Deng, C. (2022). A meta-analysis of leadership and workplace safety: Examining relative importance, contextual contingencies, and methodological moderators. *Journal of Applied Psychology, 107*(12), 2149–2175. https://doi.org/10.1037/apl0000557

Magpili, N. C., & Pazos, P. (2018). Self-managing team performance: A systematic review of multilevel input factors. *Small Group Research 49*(1), 3–33.

Marks, M. A., Mathieu, J. E., & Zaccaro, S. J. (2001). A temporally based framework and taxonomy of team processes. *Academy of Management Review 26*(3), 356–376.

McBain, W. N. (1970). Arousal, monotony, and accidents in line driving. *Journal of Applied Psychology 54*(6), 509–519. https://doi.org/10.1037/h0030144

Mueller, J. S., & Kamdar, D. (2011). Why seeking help from teammates is a blessing and a curse: A theory of help seeking and individual creativity in team contexts. *Journal of Applied Psychology 96*(2), 263–276. https://doi.org/10.1037/a0021574

Nahrgang, J. D., Morgeson, F. P., & Hofmann, D. A. (2011). Safety at work: A meta-analytic investigation of the link between job demands, job resources, burnout, engagement, and safety outcomes. *Journal of Applied Psychology 96*(1), 71–94. https://doi.org/10.1037/a0021484

Neal, A., Griffin, M. A., & Hart, P. M. (2000). The impact of organizational climate on safety climate and individual behavior. *Safety Science 34*(1–3), 99–109. https://doi.org/10.1016/S0925-7535(00)00008-4

Nurmi, N., & Hinds, P. J. (2020). Work design for global professionals: Connectivity demands, connectivity behaviors, and their effects on psychological and behavioral outcomes. *Organization Studies 41*(12), 1697–1724.

Oberauer, K., Farrell, S., Jarrold, C., & Lewandowsky, S. (2016). What limits working memory capacity? *Psychological Bulletin 142*(7), 758–799. https://doi.org/10.1037/bul0000046

Offergelt, F., & Venz, L. (2023). The joint effects of supervisor knowledge hiding, abusive supervision, and employee political skill on employee knowledge hiding behaviors. *Journal of Knowledge Management 27*(5), 1209–1227.

Ogbonnaya, C. (2019). Exploring possible trade-offs between organisational performance and employee well-being: The role of teamwork practices. *Human Resource Management Journal 29*(3), 451–468.

Ohly, S., Sonnentag, S., & Pluntke, F. (2006). Routinization, work characteristics and their relationships with creative and proactive behaviors. *Journal of Organizational Behavior 27*(3), 257–279. https://doi.org/10.1002/job.376

Oldham, G. R., & Cummings, A. (1996). Employee creativity: Personal and contextual factors at work. *Academy of management journal, 39*(3), 607–634.

Ozcelik, H., & Barsade, S. (2018). No employee an island: Workplace loneliness and employee performance. *Academy of Management Journal 61*, 2343–2366.

Park, S., & Park, S. (2019). Employee adaptive performance and its antecedents: Review and synthesis. *Human Resource Development Review 18*(3), 294–324.

Parke, M. R., & Seo, M. G. (2017). The role of affect climate in organizational effectiveness. *Academy of Management Review 42*(2), 334–360.

Parker, S. K. (2014). Beyond motivation: Job and work design for development, health, ambidexterity, and more. *Annual Review of Psychology 65*, 661–691.

Parker, S. K. (2017). Work design growth model: How work characteristics promote learning and development. In *Autonomous learning in the workplace* (pp. 137–161). Routledge.

Parker, S. K., & Grote, G. (2022). Automation, algorithms, and beyond: Why work design matters more than ever in a digital world. *Applied Psychology 71*(4), 1171–1204.

Parker, S. K., Bindl, U. K., & Strauss, K. (2010). Making things happen: A model of proactive motivation. *Journal of Management 36*(4), 827–856.

Parker, S. K., Van den Broeck, A., & Holman, D. (2017). Work design influences: A synthesis of multilevel factors that affect the design of jobs. *Academy of Management Annals 11*(1), 267–308.

Parker, S. K., Morgeson, F. P., & Johns, G. (2017). One hundred years of work design research: Looking back and looking forward. *Journal of Applied Psychology 102*(3), 403–420. https://doi.org/10.1037/apl0000106

Parker, S. K., Wang, Y., & Liao, J. (2019). When is proactivity wise? A review of factors that influence the individual outcomes of proactive behavior. *Annual Review of Organizational Psychology and Organizational Behavior 6*, 221–248.

Parker, S. K., Ward, M. K., & Fisher, G. G. (2021). Can high-quality jobs help workers learn new tricks? A multidisciplinary review of work design for cognition. *Academy of Management Annals 15*(2), 406–454.

Parker, S. K., Williams, H. M., & Turner, N. (2006). Modeling the antecedents of proactive behavior at work. *Journal of Applied Psychology 91*(3), 636–652. https://doi.org/10.1037/0021-9010.91.3.636

Peccei, R., & Van De Voorde, K. (2019). Human resource management–well-being–performance research revisited: Past, present, and future. *Human Resource Management Journal 29*(4), 539–563.

Peeters, T., Van De Voorde, K., & Paauwe, J. (2022). The effects of working agile on team performance and engagement. *Team Performance Management: An International Journal 28*(1/2), 61–78.

Petermann, M. K., & Zacher, H. (2020). Agility in the workplace: Conceptual analysis, contributing factors, and practical examples. *Industrial and Organizational Psychology 13*(4), 599–609.

Petermann, M. K., & Zacher, H. (2021). Development of a behavioral taxonomy of agility in the workplace. *International Journal of Managing Projects in Business 14*(6), 1383–1405.

Petermann, M. K., & Zacher, H. (2022). Workforce agility: Development and validation of a multidimensional measure. *Frontiers in Psychology 13*, 908.

Puranam, P. (2021). Human–AI collaborative decision-making as an organization design problem. *Journal of Organization Design 10*(2), 75–80.

Rice, A. K. (1958). *Productivity and social organization: The Ahmedabad experiment.* Tavistock.

Rietze, S., & Zacher, H. (2022). Relationships between agile work practices and occupational well-being: The role of job demands and resources. *International Journal of Environmental Research and Public Health 19*(3), 1258.

Salas, E., Bisbey, T. M., Traylor, A. M., & Rosen, M. A. (2020). Can teamwork promote safety in organizations? *Annual Review of Organizational Psychology and Organizational Behavior 7*, 283–313.

Schmitt, N., Cortina, J. M., Ingerick, M. J., & Wiechmann, D. (2003). Personnel selection and employee performance. In I. B. Weiner, N. W. Schmitt, & S. Highhouse (Eds.), Handbook of psychology: Industrial and organizational psychology, (Vol. 12, pp. 77–105). Wiley.

Schwarzmüller, T., Brosi, P., Duman, D., & Welpe, I. M. (2018). How does the digital transformation affect organizations? Key themes of change in work design and leadership. *Management Revue 29*(2), 114–138.

Seo, M. G., Barrett, L. F., & Bartunek, J. M. (2004). The role of affective experience in work motivation. *Academy of Management Review 29*(3), 423–439.

Seo, M. G., Bartunek, J. M., & Barrett, L. F. (2010). The role of affective experience in work motivation: Test of a conceptual model. *Journal of Organizational Behavior 31*(7), 951–968.

Shenhav, A., Musslick, S., Lieder, F., Kool, W., Griffiths, T. L., Cohen, J. D., & Botvinick, M. M. (2017). Toward a rational and mechanistic account of mental effort. *Annual Review of Neuroscience 40*, 99–124.

Sherehiy, B., & Karwowski, W. (2014). The relationship between work organization and workforce agility in small manufacturing enterprises. *International Journal of Industrial Ergonomics 44*(3), 466–473. https://doi.org/10.1016/j.ergon.2014.01.002

Sonnentag, S. (2015). Dynamics of well-being. *Annual Review of Organizational Psychology and Organizational Behavior 2*, 261–293.

Spreitzer, G., Sutcliffe, K., Dutton, J., Sonenshein, S., & Grant, A. M. (2005). A socially embedded model of thriving at work. *Organization Science 16*(5), 537–549. https://doi.org/10.1287/orsc.1050.0153

Stiglbauer, B., & Kovacs, C. (2018). The more, the better? Curvilinear effects of job autonomy on well-being from vitamin model and PE-fit theory perspectives. *Journal of Occupational Health Psychology 23*(4), 520–536.

ten Brummelhuis, L. L., Calderwood, C., Rosen, C. C., & Gabriel, A. S. (2022). Is physical activity before the end of the workday a drain or a gain? Daily implications on work focus in regular exercisers. *Journal of Applied Psychology 107*(10), 1864–1877. https://doi.org/10.1037/apl0000976

Tornau, K., & Frese, M. (2013). Construct clean-up in proactivity research: A meta-analysis on the nomological net of work-related proactivity concepts and their incremental validities. *Applied Psychology: An International Review 62*(1), 44–96. https://doi.org/10.1111/j.1464-0597.2012.00514.x

Troll, E. S., Venz, L., Weitzenegger, F., & Loschelder, D. D. (2022). Working from home during the COVID-19 crisis: How self-control strategies elucidate employees' job performance. *Applied Psychology: An International Review 71*(3), 853–880. https://doi.org/10.1111/apps.12352

Unsworth, K. (2001). Unpacking creativity. *Academy of Management Review 26*(2), 289–297.

Unsworth, K. L., Wall, T. D., & Carter, A. (2005). Creative requirement: A neglected construct in the study of employee creativity? *Group & Organization Management 30*(5), 541–560.

Venz, L., Pundt, A., & Sonnentag, S. (2018). What matters for work engagement? A diary study on resources and the benefits of selective optimization with compensation for state work engagement. *Journal of Organizational Behavior 39*(1), 26–38.

Wallace, J. C., & Chen, G. (2005). Development and validation of a work-specific measure of cognitive failure: Implications for occupational safety. *Journal of Occupational and Organizational Psychology 78*(4), 615–632.

Wang, B., Liu, Y., & Parker, S. K. (2020). How does the use of information communication technology affect individuals? A work design perspective. *Academy of Management Annals 14*(2), 695–725.

Wang, S., & Noe, R. A. (2010). Knowledge sharing: A review and directions for future research. *Human Resource Management Review 20*, 115–131.

Wegman, L. A., Hoffman, B. J., Carter, N. T., Twenge, J. M., & Guenole, N. (2018). Placing job characteristics in context: Cross-temporal meta-analysis of changes in job characteristics since 1975. *Journal of Management 44*(1), 352–386. https://doi.org/10.1177/0149206316654545

Wihler, A., Blickle, G., Ellen III, B. P., Hochwarter, W. A., & Ferris, G. R. (2017). Personal initiative and job performance evaluations: Role of political skill in opportunity recognition and capitalization. *Journal of Management 43*(5), 1388–1420.

Williams, H. M., Parker, S. K., & Turner, N. (2010). Proactively performing teams: The role of work design, transformational leadership, and team composition. *Journal of Occupational and Organizational Psychology 83*(2), 301–324. https://doi.org/10.1348/096317910X502494

Witherspoon, C. L., Bergner, J., Cockrell, C., & Stone, D. N. (2013). Antecedents of organizational knowledge sharing: A meta-analysis and critique. *Journal of Knowledge Management 17*(2), 250–277.

Wolsink, I., Den Hartog, D. N., Belschak, F. D., & Sligte, I. G. (2019). Dual cognitive pathways to voice quality: Frequent voicers improvise, infrequent voicers elaborate. *PLoS One 14*(2), e0212608.

Wood, S., Van Veldhoven, M., Croon, M., & de Menezes, L. M. (2012). Enriched job design, high involvement management and organizational performance: The mediating roles of job satisfaction and well-being. *Human Relations 65*(4), 419–445.

Wright, T. A., & Cropanzano, R. (2004). The role of psychological well-being in job performance: A fresh look at an age-old quest. *Organizational Dynamics 33*(4), 338–351. https://doi.org/10.1016/j.orgdyn.2004.09.002

Xanthopoulou, D., Bakker, A. B., Demerouti, E., & Schaufeli, W. B. (2007). The role of personal resources in the job demands-resources model. *International Journal of Stress Management 14*(2), 121–141. https://doi.org/10.1037/1072-5245.14.2.121

Yang, L., Holtz, D., Jaffe, S., Suri, S., Sinha, S., Weston, J., Joyce, C., Shah, N., Sherman, K., Hecht, B., & Teevan, J. (2022). The effects of remote work on collaboration among information workers. *Nature Human Behaviour 6*(1), 43–54.

Yang, L.-Q., Zheng, X., Liu, X., Lu, C.-Q., & Schaubroeck, J. M. (2020). Abusive supervision, thwarted belongingness, and workplace safety: A group engagement perspective. *Journal of Applied Psychology 105*(3), 230–244. https://doi.org/10.1037/apl0000436

Zacher, H., Rudolph, C. W., & Katz, I. M. (2023). Employee green behavior as the core of environmentally sustainable organizations. *Annual Review of Organizational Psychology and Organizational Behavior 10*, 465–494.

Zapf, D., Kern, M., Tschan, F., Holman, D., & Semmer, N. K. (2021). Emotion work: A work psychology perspective. *Annual Review of Organizational Psychology and Organizational Behavior 8*, 139–172.

Zhang, X., & Bartol, K. M. (2010). The influence of creative process engagement on employee creative performance and overall job performance: A curvilinear assessment. *Journal of Applied Psychology 95*(5), 862–873. https://doi.org/10.1037/a0020173

Zhou, J., & Hoever, I. J. (2014). Research on workplace creativity: A review and redirection. *Annual Review of Organizational Psychology and Organizational Behavior 1*, 333–359. https://doi.org/10.1146/annurev-orgpsych-031413-091226

Work Design and Identity

Taking Stock of What We Know and Charting Pathways for Future Research

Giverny De Boeck, Maïlys M. George, and Aušrinė Vyšniauskaite

Work design, defined as "the content and organization of one's work tasks, activities, relationships, and responsibilities," is a central construct in organizational sciences (Parker, 2014, p. 662). Scholars have studied it for its impact on important organizational and individual outcomes (e.g., performance). While researchers have explored the relationship between work design and many other important organizational constructs, to date one area that remains under-researched and that cuts across fragmented segments of the literature is the relationship between work design and workers' identities. Identities are individuals' answers to the question "Who am I" and are premised on a person's unique characteristics, their social roles and relationships, and their membership in collectives (Caza et al., 2018). As Parker (2014) noted, work design likely affects individuals' identities because it provides the context for a person's work experiences, including identity-related needs fulfilment and identity exploration at work (see Michaelson et al., 2014).

To better integrate scattered insights and pave the way for more studies into this relationship, this chapter reviews existing research on work design and identity. To date, the Job Characteristics Model (JCM) (Hackman & Oldham, 1976) has been the dominant theoretical framework in the work design literature (Parker et al., 2017). Unsurprisingly, when studying the relationship between work design and identity, scholars often use this as a theoretical foundation. Yet, the papers we have reviewed actually use a broader set of characteristics than the initial set put forward in the JCM. Therefore, we chose Frederick P. Morgeson and Stephen E. Humphrey's (2006) Work Design Model (WDM), an expansion of the JCM, to structure our review findings.

Our review covers both theoretical and empirical research. To identify papers for inclusion, we conducted a literature search in Web of Science using a wide selection of keywords (see Appendix). This initial search yielded a total of 69 articles. We complemented this list with results from two cited reference

---

Giverny De Boeck et al., *Work Design and Identity*. In: *Transformative Work Design*. Edited by: Sharon K. Parker et al., Oxford University Press. © Society for Industrial and Organizational Psychology (2025).
DOI: 10.1093/oso/9780197692554.003.0006

searches in Web of Science and Google Scholar in which we traced papers discussing "identity" and citing Parker's (2014) review of the work design literature, for a total of 45 additional papers. Combined, these searches resulted in 114 articles. After excluding papers that did not discuss the relationship between work design and identity and that did not concern workers' own identities, we retained 28 papers that were relevant to our review. Each of the co-authors then read and coded a portion of the papers with a focus on the link between identity processes and work design. Below, we begin by providing a bird's-eye view of the types of identities that have been examined so far in relation to work design. We then use Morgeson and Humphrey's (2006) framework to organize our review findings into task (e.g., task variety), knowledge (e.g., information processing), social (e.g., interdependence), and work-context (e.g., ergonomics) aspects of work design. We supplement our observations with recommendations for future research.

Types of Identities Studied in Relation to Work Design

Individuals hold multiple identities that develop within different aspects of social life, including work and non-work life domains (Ramarajan & Reid, 2013). Examples of work-related identities include occupational identity, organizational identity, and work team identity (Dutton et al., 2010). Non-work identities encompass family-related identities (e.g., identity as a parent) and demographic identities (e.g., gender identity; Ramarajan & Reid, 2013). As noted in our introduction to this chapter, work design mainly affects (and is affected by) individuals' work-related identities. Nevertheless, and perhaps more surprisingly, work design can also influence other aspects of the self that pertain to the non-work domain or aspects of the self that are deemed more stable such as self-evaluations (Parker, 2014).

In addition to the distinction between work- and non-work identities, another useful distinction is that between different types of identities. Scholars have highlighted that different types of identities are often studied using different theories and different processes (Caza et al., 2018). Therefore, in the next section, we delineate which types of work and non-work identities have been studied alongside job design. This overview provides the building blocks for our discussion of future directions and where research is currently lacking.

Work and Non-Work Identities Studied in Relation to Work Design. Firstly, looking at the papers that we have reviewed, scholars have mainly studied *organizational identity*—individuals' perceived oneness with an organization—alongside work design. Work design tends to strengthen organizational identification (e.g., Slattery et al., 2010), but employees, too, can take an active role in shaping their jobs to develop perceptions of oneness with their organization (e.g., Wang et al., 2018).

Secondly, researchers have also investigated the link between work design and *occupational identity* (i.e., individuals' perceived oneness with their occupation). Well-designed jobs seem to boost occupational identity (e.g., Elovainio & Kivimäki, 2001). Conversely, inadequate job design or job design that violates workers' expectations can trigger occupational identity threats (e.g., Mattarelli & Tagliaventi, 2015; Pratt et al., 2006).

Thirdly, work design also impacts (and is impacted by) other work-related identities, including *career identity* (e.g., Sweet et al., 2016), *entrepreneurial identity* (e.g., Feng et al., 2022; Hsu et al., 2021), and *volunteer identity* (e.g., Grant, 2012; van Schie et al., 2019). In short, scholars have studied a relatively wide array of work-related identities in relation to work design.

Finally, while most of the reviewed papers focus on work-related identities, we uncovered a few papers that discuss the nexus of work and non-work identities and the self broadly speaking. In relation to non-work identities, scholars have explored how job characteristics can alleviate conflict between career and *family identities* (Russo & van Hooft, 2011). With regard to the self broadly speaking, Sharon K. Parker (2014) noted that exposure to work design over the long run can affect people's aspirations for who they want to become. Relatedly, work design can affect a person's ability to express their identity (Bankins et al., 2021).

Review Findings: Task, Knowledge, Social, and Contextual Characteristics and Identity Processes

As outlined in the introduction, we use Morgeson and Humphrey's (2006) WDM and specifically their distinction between task, knowledge, social, and contextual characteristics to structure our review findings. Within each section, we indicate if the characteristics are studied as predictors, outcomes, or moderators of identity processes, and discuss some examples. A comprehensive overview of the articles included in the review and how we categorized these can be found in Table 6.1.

Task characteristics concern the range and nature of tasks in a specific job and how that job is accomplished (e.g., task variety, job autonomy). Researchers have explored task characteristics as predictors of identity development and threat. For example, task characteristics explained gender differences in career centrality (the importance of a career to one's identity). Lower task variety, job autonomy, and scheduling flexibility explained why careers were less impor-

Table 6.1 Overview of Review Articles

Work characteristics

	Predictors	Outcomes	Moderators
Task characteristics (k = 18)	Currie & Spyridonidis, 2022; De Boeck et al., 2019; Galperin, 2017; Grant, 2012; Hsu et al., 2021; Jurek & Besta, 2021; Semmer et al., 2015; Medici et al., 2020; Michaelson et al., 2014; Slattery et al., 2010; Sweet et al., 2016; van Schie et al., 2019	Baker & Goodall, 2020; Campion, 1996; Jumelet et al., 2022; Russo & van Hooft, 2011	Feng et al., 2022; Kipfelsberger & Kark, 2018
Knowledge characteristics (k = 4)	De Boeck et al., 2019; Grant, 2012; Slattery et al., 2010	—	Feng et al., 2022
Social characteristics (k = 12)	Galperin, 2017; Grant, 2012; Jurek & Besta, 2021; Sweet et al., 2016; van Schie et al., 2019	Baker & Goodall, 2020; Campion, 1996; Russo & van Hooft, 2011; Singh et al., 2019	Biron, & Bamberger, 2012; Kipfelsberger & Kark, 2018; Rapp et al., 2015.
Contextual characteristics (k = 3)	Stanton et al., 2003	Jumelet et al., 2022	Biron, & Bamberger, 2012
Other characteristics (k = 13)	Bankins et al., 2021; Elovainio & Kivimaki, 2001; Galperin, 2017; Jurek & Besta, 2021; Lazazzara et al., 2020; Medici et al., 2020; Sweet et al., 2016; Wang et al., 2018	Baker & Goodall, 2020; Hsu et al., 2021; Jumelet et al., 2022; Lazazzara et al., 2020; Mattarelli & Tagliaventi, 2015; Russo & van Hooft, 2011	Lazazzara et al., 2020

Note: The final set of articles included in our review (k = 28) is categorized according to type of work characteristics and their relation to identity processes. Some articles belong to multiple categories.

tant to women's sense of self as compared to men's—although this was partially compensated for by women's stronger work relationships (Sweet et al., 2016). Similarly, Giverny De Boeck and colleagues (2019) found that autonomy and job feedback enabled workers to realize their future work selves, which, in turn, increased perceived work meaningfulness. Interestingly, task characteristics can also pose a threat to workers' identities. For example, illegitimate tasks (tasks perceived as unnecessary and unreasonable) threatened organizational members' professional identities and negatively affected their well-being (Semmer et al., 2015).

Researchers have also examined how identity processes influence people's satisfaction with task characteristics. For example, when academics perceived an alignment between their department chairs' identity as distinguished researchers and their own identity, they also reported higher task significance (Baker & Goodall, 2020). Similarly, Jacqueline Jumelet and colleagues (2022) found that employees' role identities influenced their appraisal of job characteristics: Business owners viewed task variety as a challenge rather than a hindrance, because they perceived it as an investment in their role identity.

Two studies have examined task characteristics as moderators of identity processes. Petra Kipfelsberger and Ronit Kark (2018) proposed that supervisors' provision of ever-changing and non-achievable tasks moderates the relationship between supervisors' contributions to employees' identity development and perceived work meaningfulness, such that the more supervisors assign such tasks to employees, the weaker the impact of their identity development contributions will be on perceived work meaningfulness. Jie Feng and colleagues (2022) found that task characteristics moderated the relationship between employees' lingering identities (identities that persist beyond role change) and turnover decisions. For example, employees who still identified as entrepreneurs were less likely to leave paid employment when their jobs offered high decision-making autonomy, supporting their lingering identities.

Knowledge characteristics concern the knowledge, skills, and abilities that are demanded from an individual to perform the job (e.g., skill variety, job complexity). Jeffrey P. Slattery and colleagues (2010) argued that well-designed jobs make employees feel valued and promote organizational identification. They found that temporary workers whose jobs demanded skill variety showed greater commitment to their organization. Similarly, Adam Grant's (2012) Volunteer Work Model emphasizes the role of knowledge characteristics in shaping identity. The model proposes that employees facing poor work design in their regular jobs can seek fulfilment elsewhere such as through volunteering.

When volunteer projects offer enriched task, social, and knowledge opportunities, this can contribute to employees' internalization of a volunteer identity via sustained volunteering participation. However, when scholars tested this model against a self-determination theory (SDT) alternative, they found weak support for Grant's (2012) model as compared to the SDT-based model according to which the quality of motivation employees experience while volunteering (i.e., intrinsic versus extrinsic motivation) plays a more important role than sustained volunteering participation (van Schie et al., 2019). Last, one study examined knowledge characteristics as moderators of identity processes. Feng and colleagues (2022) found that former entrepreneurs were less likely to leave paid employment when their work involved job complexity and new project opportunities, supporting their lingering entrepreneurial identities.

Social characteristics concern the relational design of work (Grant, 2007; Grant & Parker, 2009), and include the various ways in which employees interact with and are influenced by others inside and outside of work (e.g., supervisor support, quality of work relationships, interdependence). Researchers have explored social characteristics as predictors of identity development and threat. For instance, Paweł Jurek and Thomasz Besta (2021) showed that over and above the effect of attractive tasks, attractive work relationships also fostered employees' self-expansion (i.e., self-growth and identity development), resulting in higher employee engagement. Lack of appreciation for employees' work, however, undermined the positive effects of attractive tasks and work relationships on self-expansion. Similarly, Roman Galperin (2017) discovered that interactions with clients helped workers to develop and maintain an expert identity. Such interactions compensated for the negative effect of poor task conditions, such as minimal job discretion and routine performance of low-status tasks on workers' identity development.

Researchers have also examined how identity influences the importance of social characteristics. For example, in a study of 1,828 Dutch workers, scholars found that individuals who valued non-work identities and experienced conflict between work and non-work identities placed greater importance on building good relationships with those colleagues and supervisors that could alleviate this conflict (Russo & van Hooft, 2011). Conversely, individuals for whom work was more central to their identity prioritized characteristics that supported their work identities (e.g., career opportunities). Similarly, researchers studying 41 teams in India found that team members who identified strongly with their profession were more likely to help and share their knowledge with others to fulfil their need for self-expression than teams in which members identified less strongly with their profession (Singh et al., 2019).

Three studies focused on the moderating role of social characteristics in identity processes and their outcomes. For instance, managerial recognition enhanced the positive effect of organizational identification on role performance. Employees who identified strongly with the organization performed even better when they experienced higher managerial recognition (Rapp et al., 2015). Conversely, supervisor support attenuated the negative effect of peer absence norms on workers' absenteeism; for example, workers whose peers were permissive of absenteeism were less absent from work when they perceived their supervisors to be more supportive than workers who did not perceive this support from supervisors (Biron & Bamberger, 2012).

Contextual characteristics concern the physical environment of work (e.g., work conditions, physical demands, and technology use). For instance, researchers have deployed an experimental study to explore the effect of remoteness on human supervisory control in a simulation where teams were in charge of an energy distribution network. The authors manipulated participants' physical proximity to one another (i.e., proximal versus distal condition) and discovered that group identity was higher in the proximal condition than in the distal condition, arguably because being physically close in the same location encouraged greater communication among participants (Stanton et al., 2003). Jumelet and colleagues (2022), on the other hand, studied contextual characteristics as an outcome. Specifically, they found that business owners tended to appraise physical load as a hindrance because it conflicted with their role identities. Finally, Michal Biron and Peter Bamberger (2012) investigated the impact of aversive work conditions, including perceived job hazards and exposure to aversive events, on employees' absenteeism. They discovered that employees with poor work conditions were more likely to be absent from work than employees with better work conditions, an effect which was stronger in the presence of permissive peer absence norms.

Other characteristics concern work characteristics that did not clearly fit within the categories of the WDM (e.g., role ambiguity, pay, favorable hours, workspace). Additionally, this category also includes job crafting (i.e., employees' proactive bottom-up work redesign). Several studies looked at other characteristics as predictors of identity processes. For instance, Marko Elovainio and Mika Kivimäki (2001) showed that role ambiguity (having unclear expectations about work performance) hindered the development of a strong occupational identity in employees, ultimately increasing their strain. Findings from a study investigating the impact of workspace on identity expression revealed that employees who transitioned from closed to open workspaces perceived fewer opportunities to express themselves (e.g., by personalizing the workspace)

(Bankins et al., 2021). Additionally, other studies highlighted the role of job crafting as a predictor, outcome, and moderator of identity processes. For instance, Elisa Mattarelli and Maria Rita Tagliaventi (2015) interviewed offshore professionals and discovered that a misfit between their professional identity and their work triggered professionals' engagement in job crafting to improve their work–identity fit and job satisfaction. Similarly, another study found that Taiwanese entrepreneurs designed jobs for themselves and others such that these would fit their own values and identities (Hsu et al., 2021). Finally, in their review of the job crafting literature, Alessandra Lazazzara and colleagues (2020) also described the role of shared organizational identity in supporting employees' job crafting efforts.

Future Research Directions

Through our review, we have identified several theoretical and methodological directions for future research related to: (1) types of work characteristics, (2) work design mechanisms, (3) types of identity, (4) identity processes, and (5) study design. Table 6.2 provides a summary of the key observations from our review as well as our proposed future research questions.

Table 6.2 Observations and Future Research Questions on the Relationship Between Work Design and Identity

	Research Observations	Future Research Questions
Theoretical		
Types of Work Characteristics	Researchers have mostly studied the relationship between task or social characteristics and identity. Researchers often do not differentiate between different types of work characteristics when studying their effects on identity.	• How do knowledge and contextual characteristics affect work-related identities? (RQ1) • Do different work characteristics vary in their effects on identity? How can we explain these differential effects? (RQ2)
Work Design Mechanisms	Scholars have mostly investigated work characteristics as predictors rather than as outcomes or moderators of identity. The mechanisms explaining the relationship between work design and identity remain undertheorized.	• How do supervisors' identities affect work design decisions? How do workers' identities affect job crafting? How does work design moderate identity processes? (RQ3) • How do psychological states, needs satisfaction, or status, mediate the relationship between work design and identity? (RQ4)

	Research Observations	Future Research Questions
Types of Identity	Researchers have focused on the relationship between work-related identities and work design. Within work-related identities, scholars have mostly investigated organizational and occupational identity.	• How does work design affect non-work identities? How do non-work identities affect job crafting? (RQ5) • How does work design affect other work-related identities such as team identity, role identity, and leader identity? How do such work-related identities affect job crafting and work design? (RQ6)
Identity Processes	Work design can support a person's current and lingering identities. Work (re)design can trigger identity threats. Work characteristics may alleviate identity conflict.	• How does work design affect a person's future and alternative selves? (RQ7) • When does work (re)design trigger identity opportunities? (RQ8) • How does work design relate to identity conflict? (RQ9)

Methodological

	Scholars who use identity theories (e.g., social identity theory) often implicitly assume identity plays a role and do not test it. Most studies on work design and identity are quantitative. There is a dearth of longitudinal research on the relationship between work design and identity. Researchers tend to explore work design and identity in samples of knowledge workers in Western countries.	• Which identity processes can be theorized in relation to work design? Which roles do identity processes play, empirically (e.g., mediation, moderation, antecedent)? (RQ10) • Which processes can be unpacked through qualitative studies? Which new theories can be built? (RQ11) • How does the relationship between work design and identity evolve over time? (RQ12) • What is the impact of work design on identity in other samples? How do dire working conditions affect identity and vice-versa? (RQ13)

Theoretical directions

An important extension of existing work is to study the impact of knowledge and contextual characteristics on identity (RQ1). Specifically, new technological developments such as artificial intelligence and virtual workplaces are shaping job complexity and information processing, which will ultimately affect workers' identities (Mirbabaie et al., 2022; Parker & Grote, 2022). Furthermore, we would recommend studying work characteristics separately rather than by aggregating these into general measures. This would allow scholars to theorize on and test the different mechanisms that can explain the relationship between work characteristics and identity (RQ2; RQ4). Next to studying work characteristics as predictors of identity, researchers should further investigate how identity affects work characteristics (RQ3), answering calls for more research on antecedents to work design (Parker et al., 2017).

In relation to types of identity, we would encourage researchers to further investigate how work design affects (and is affected by) more stable elements of the self and non-work identities (RQ5). Further, scholars could explore a broader array of work-related identities, including leader identity, team identity, and role identity, and how these identities shape top-down work design by supervisors and bottom-up job crafting by employees (RQ6). In terms of identity processes, our review findings reveal that work design can support a person's current and lingering identities. Scholars can further enrich our temporal understanding of the relationship between work design and identity by studying future selves (Strauss et al., 2012) and alternative selves (Obodaru, 2012) (RQ7). Moreover, several papers describe how work characteristics trigger identity threat but there seems to be little research on work characteristics as triggers of identity opportunities (i.e., opportunities for growth in the value, meanings, and/or enactment of an identity; Bataille & Vough, 2022) (RQ8). Finally, more research is needed to uncover how work design affects the experience of identity conflict and vice versa (RQ9).

Methodological directions

To move research forward methodologically, we would urge scholars who use identity in their theorizing about work design to explicitly test the role of identity processes (RQ10). Our observations also showed that most studies were quantitative in nature, using cross-sectional surveys instead of longitudinal designs. In addition to longitudinal designs, we believe that more qualitative research could help research unpack the processes at play in the relationship between work design and identity (RQ11). Moreover, a better understanding of how work design and identity co-evolve over time would yield great insights relevant to companies and individuals alike (RQ12). Finally, most research focuses on knowledge workers in relatively rich, Western countries. Yet, looking beyond these geographies and samples would enrich our theories (RQ13). Taking up our suggestions will ultimately allow scholars to provide guidance for organizations to design work that enables positive self-evaluations and helps people establish harmonious identity networks (Bataille & Vough, 2022).

Implications for Practice

This chapter highlights the importance of paying attention to both work design and identity in tandem in organizations. Specifically, managers should look out for both the consequences work design has for workers' identities and for how workers' identities influence their perceptions of and reactions to work (re-)design. One important finding of our review is that it pays off for organizations to invest in good work design (e.g., by offering workers the chance to use various skills in their jobs, making sure they feel supported by their supervisors, and creating workspaces that they can personalize) as this promotes organizational identification and allows workers to express themselves at work which, in turn, generates positive outcomes such as higher well-being and lower turnover intentions. Moreover, work design can also help organizations attract and retain talent by designing work that matches the identity of potential recruits with desirable profiles. For instance, organizations can offer high job autonomy and complexity to former entrepreneurs such that they can hold onto valuable aspects of their past identities. At the same time, organizations should try to avoid designing work that creates a misfit between how workers perceive themselves and the work that they do (e.g., when managers ask workers to conduct low-status or illegitimate tasks as part of their jobs) as this can threaten workers' identities and can cause negative work outcomes. If it is difficult to prevent work–identity misfit resulting from work redesign (e.g., due to the implementation of technological change), organizations should include other valued work characteristics (e.g., job autonomy) that can help workers craft their jobs to better fit their current or desired identities.

Organizations would also benefit from paying more attention to workers' identities to better understand their reactions to work (re-)design and related work outcomes. That is, identity influences the extent to which workers find work characteristics important. For instance, people who place greater value on their non-work identities attach more importance to social aspects of work compared to people who prioritize their work identities. For those workers, it is therefore important to focus on relational job design. Moreover, people's identities also impact how they appraise specific work characteristics. For instance, while workers can appraise one characteristic (e.g., task variety) positively as a challenge, they can simultaneously appraise another characteristic (e.g., physical load) as a hindrance depending on whether the work

TRANSFORMATIVE WORK DESIGN

characteristic conflicts with their role identities. Finally, we discovered that the identities of important stakeholders in the network of a given employee (e.g., supervisors, peers) also have an influence on how this employee perceives work design and its outcomes. For example, when workers experience a strong alignment between their own identity and that of their direct supervisor, this can improve their perceptions of work design. In other words, to design good work, organizations need to develop a thorough understanding of multiple stakeholders' identities. Heeding this advice will ultimately allow organizational members to realize their potential at work and feel accepted for who they are.

References

*These articles are included in our systematic review of work design and identity.

*Baker, A., & Goodall, A. H. (2020). Feline followers and "umbrella carriers": Department Chairs' influence on faculty job satisfaction and quit intentions. *Research Policy* 49(4), 103955.

*Bankins, S., Tomprou, M. & Kim, B. (2021). Workspace transitions: Conceptualizing and measuring person-space fit and examining its role in workplace outcomes and social network activity. *Journal of Managerial Psychology* 36(4), 344–365.

Bataille, C. D., & Vough, H. C. (2022). More than the sum of my parts: An intrapersonal network approach to identity work in response to identity opportunities and threats. *Academy of Management Review* 47(1), 93–115.

*Biron, M., & Bamberger, P. (2012). Aversive workplace conditions and absenteeism: Taking referent group norms and supervisor support into account. *Journal of Applied Psychology* 97(4), 901.

*Campion, M. A., Papper, E. M., & Medsker, G. J. (1996). Relations between work team characteristics and effectiveness: A replication and extension. *Personnel Psychology*, 49(2), 429–452.

Caza, B. B., Vough, H. C., & Puranik, H. (2018). Identity work in organizations and occupations: Definitions, theories, and pathways forward. *Journal of Organizational Behavior* 39(7), 889–910.

*Currie, G., & Spyridonidis, D. (2022). From what we know to what we do: Human resource management intervention to support mode 2 healthcare research. *Human Resource Management Journal* 34 (2), 504–522.

*De Boeck, G., Dries, N., & Tierens, H. (2019). The experience of untapped potential: Towards a subjective temporal understanding of work meaningfulness. *Journal of Management Studies* 56(3), 529–557.

Dutton, J. E., Roberts, L. M., & Bednar, J. (2010). Pathways for positive identity construction at work: Four types of positive identity and the building of social resources. *Academy of Management Review* 35(2), 265–293.

*Elovainio, M., & Kivimäki, M. (2001). The effects of personal need for structure and occupational identity in the role stress process. *Journal of Social Psychology* 141(3), 365–378.

*Feng, J., Seibert, S., & Allen, D. (2022). Once an entrepreneur, always an entrepreneur? Entrepreneurial identity, job characteristics, and voluntary turnover of former entrepreneurs in paid employment. *Personnel Psychology 75*(1), 179–213.

*Galperin, R. V. (2017). Mass-production of professional services and pseudo-professional identity in tax preparation work. *Academy of Management Discoveries 3*(2), 208–229.

Grant, A. M. (2007). Relational job design and the motivation to make a prosocial difference. *Academy of Management Review 32*(2), 393–417.

*Grant, A. M. (2012). Giving time, time after time: Work design and sustained employee participation in corporate volunteering. *Academy of Management Review 37*(4), 589–615.

Grant, A. M., & Parker, S. K. (2009). 7 redesigning work design theories: The rise of relational and proactive perspectives. *Academy of Management Annals 3*(1), 317–375.

Hackman, J. R., & Oldham, G. R. (1976). Motivation through the design of work: Test of a theory. *Organizational Behavior and Human Performance 16*(2), 250–279.

*Hsu, R. S., Chuang, A., & Wang, A.-C. (2021). Business founders' work design and new venture development. *Journal of Business Venturing 36*(1), 106000.

*Jumelet, J. M., Gorgievski, M. J., & Bakker, A. B. (2022). Understanding business owners' challenge and hindrance appraisals. *Journal of Managerial Psychology 37*(5), 404–424.

*Jurek, P., & Besta, T. (2021). Employees' self-expansion as a mediator between perceived work conditions and work engagement and productive behaviors. *Current Psychology 40*(6), 3048–3057.

*Parker, S. K. (2014). Beyond motivation: Job and work design for development, health, ambidexterity, and more. *Annual Review of Psychology 65*(1), 661–691.

*Kipfelsberger, P., & Kark, R. (2018). "Killing me softly with his/her song": How leaders dismantle followers' sense of work meaningfulness. *Frontiers in Psychology 9*: 654.

*Lazazzara, A., Tims, M., & de Gennaro, D. (2020). The process of reinventing a job: A meta-synthesis of qualitative job crafting research. *Journal of Vocational Behavior 116*, 103267.

*Mattarelli, E., & Tagliaventi, M. R. (2015). How offshore professionals' job dissatisfaction can promote further offshoring: Organizational outcomes of job crafting. *Journal of Management Studies 52*(5), 585–620.

Medici, G., Tschopp, C., Grote, G., & Hirschi, A. (2020). Grass roots of occupational change: Understanding mobility in vocational careers. *Journal of Vocational Behavior 122*, 103480.

*Michaelson, C., Pratt, M. G., Grant, A. M., & Dunn, C. P. (2014). Meaningful work: Connecting business ethics and organization studies. *Journal of Business Ethics 121*(1), 77–90.

Mirbabaie, M., Brünker, F., Möllmann Frick, N. R. J., & Stieglitz, S. (2022). The rise of artificial intelligence—Understanding the AI identity threat at the workplace. *Electronic Markets 32*(1), 73–99.

Morgeson, F. P., & Humphrey, S. E. (2006). The Work Design Questionnaire (WDQ): Developing and validating a comprehensive measure for assessing job design and the nature of work. *Journal of Applied Psychology 91*(6), 1321–1339.

Obodaru, O. (2012). The self not taken: How alternative selves develop and how they influence our professional lives. *Academy of Management Review 37*(1), 34–57.

Parker, S. K., & Grote, G. (2022). Automation, algorithms, and beyond: Why work design matters more than ever in a digital world. *Applied Psychology: An International Review 71*(4), 1171–1204.

Parker, S. K., Morgeson, F. P., & Johns, G. (2017). One hundred years of work design research: Looking back and looking forward. *Journal of Applied Psychology 102*(3), 403–420.

Pratt, M. G., Rockmann, K. W., & Kaufmann, J. B. (2006). Constructing professional identity: The role of work and identity learning cycles in the customization of identity among medical residents. *Academy of Management Journal 49*(2), 235–262.

Ramarajan, L., & Reid, E. (2013). Shattering the myth of separate worlds: Negotiating nonwork identities at work. *Academy of Management Review 38*(4), 621–644.

*Rapp, A., Agnihotri, R., Baker, T. L., & Andzulis, J. M. (2015). Competitive intelligence collection and use by sales and service representatives: How managers' recognition and autonomy moderate individual performance. *Journal of the Academy of Marketing Science 43*(3), 357–374.

*Russo, G., & van Hooft, E. (2011). Identities, conflicting behavioral norms, and the importance of job attributes. *Journal of Economic Psychology 32*(1), 103–119.

*van Schie, S., Gautier, A., Pache, A.-C., & Güntert, S. T. (2019). What keeps corporate volunteers engaged: Extending the volunteer work design model with self-determination theory insights. *Journal of Business Ethics 160*(3), 693–712.

*Semmer, N. K., Jacobshagen, N., Meier, L. L., Elfering, A., Beehr, T. A., Kälin, W., & Tschan, F. (2015). Illegitimate tasks as a source of work stress. *Work and Stress 29*(1), 32–56.

* Singh, S. K., Mittal, S., Sengupta, A., & Pradhan, R. K. (2019). A dual-pathway model of knowledge exchange: Linking human and psychosocial capital with prosocial knowledge effectiveness. *Journal of Knowledge Management 23*(5), 889–914.

*Slattery, J. P., Selvarajan, T. T., Anderson, J. E., & Sardessai, R. (2010), Relationship between job characteristics and attitudes: A study of temporary employees. *Journal of Applied Social Psychology 40*(6), 1539–1565.

*Stanton, N. A., Ashleigh, M. J., Roberts, A. D., & Xu, F. (2003). Virtuality in human supervisory control: Assessing the effects of psychological and social remoteness. *Ergonomics 46*(12), 1215–1232.

Strauss, K., Griffin, M. A., & Parker, S. K. (2012). Future work selves: How salient hoped-for identities motivate proactive career behaviors. *Journal of Applied Psychology 97*(3), 580–598.

*Sweet, S., Sarkisian, N., Matz-Costa, C., & Pitt-Catsouphes, M. (2016). Are women less career centric than men? Structure, culture, and identity investments. *Community, Work & Family 19*(4), 481–500.

*Wang, H.-J., Demerouti, E., Blanc, P. L., & Lu, C.-Q. (2018), Crafting a job in "tough times": When being proactive is positively related to work attachment. *Journal of Occupational and Organizational Psychology 91*(3), 569–590.

Appendix

For the Web of Science search, we searched for the following words in the title, abstract, and/or key words: ("job design" OR "job characteristics" OR "work design" OR "work conditions") AND ("identity theory" OR "source of identity" OR "role identit*" OR "team identit*" OR "family identit*" OR "identity fit" OR "identity-based" OR "volunteer identit*" OR "identity structure*" OR "social identit*" OR "entrepreneurial identit*" OR "professional identit*" OR "occupational identit*" OR "work identit*" OR "organizational identit*" OR "group identit*" OR "worker identit*" OR "age identit*" OR "gender identit*" OR "parent identit*" OR "ethnic identit*" OR "identity work" OR "identity construction" OR "identity threat" OR "identity harm" OR "identity loss" OR "present sel*" OR "past sel*" OR "future sel*" OR "feared sel*" OR "desired sel*" OR "possible sel*" OR "personal identit*" "identity process*" OR "identity management" OR "identity development" OR "self-concept" OR "sense of self").

What You Do Makes Who You Are

The Role of Work Design in Personality Change

Chia-Huei Wu and Ying Wang

Personality, which describes the unique patterns of thoughts, feelings, and behaviors in distinguishing one person from another, is traditionally considered as a set of stable and endurable individual characteristics. William James (1890, p. 126) said that "in most of us, by the age of thirty, the character has set like plaster, and will never soften again." Robert McCrae and Paul Costa (2003, p. 3) defined traits as "the basic dispositions that . . . endure through adulthood." Due to its stability, personality has been drawn on to understand and explain a wide range of individual attitudes and behaviors at work (see Tasselli et al., 2018, for a review). Nevertheless, personality is not unchangeable. Longitudinal studies have shown that personality traits can change throughout an individual's lifespan (see Bleidorn et al., 2022, for a meta-analysis of longitudinal studies). Hence, challenging the static view, personality psychologists now view personality as "sufficiently broad and stable to predict a wide range of important life outcomes, but also malleable enough to potentially serve as powerful yet largely ignored targets for interventions" (Bleidorn et al., 2021, p. 4). Research over the past several decades has provided accumulating evidence that personality changes across the lifespan due to individuals' various life events and circumstances (see Bleidorn et al., 2018; Caspi et al., 2005; McAdams & Olson, 2010). Importantly, as people spend a significant amount of their lifetime engaging in work and employment-related activities, experiences in this domain provide salient drivers for personality change (Wang & Wu, 2021).

In this chapter, we focus on the role of work design in shaping personality change. We aim to show that work design not only shapes one's immediate motivations and behaviors at work, but it can also drive personality change in the long run. The following sections first review the theoretical foundations of work design and personality change to unpack the mechanisms of personality change. Next, we summarize evidence from existing research to empirically demonstrate why and how work design facilitates personality change. Finally, we offer several reflections to help direct future research.

Chia-Huei Wu and Ying Wang, *What You Do Makes Who You Are*. In: *Transformative Work Design*.
Edited by: Sharon K. Parker et al., Oxford University Press. © Society for Industrial and Organizational
Psychology (2025). DOI: 10.1093/oso/9780197692554.003.0007

Theoretical Foundations of Work Design and Personality Change

The role of the work environment in shaping personality change has been well-recognized and discussed in psychology (see Brousseau, 1983; Frese, 1982; Roberts, 2006) and sociology (see House, 1981; Jokela, 2017; McLeod & Lively, 2006; Ryff, 1987). In organizational psychology, scholars studying work design have argued that work characteristics can change personal characteristics via one's work roles and associated daily activities (e.g., Brousseau, 1983; Frese, 1982). For example, Michael Frese and his colleagues (1982; Frese & Zapf, 1994) argued that different jobs impose different cognitive, emotional, and behavioral requirements and stimulation, which shape one's social roles and activities on a daily basis when employees engage in those work activities. In turn, these shape and consolidate one's patterns of thoughts, feelings, and behaviors over time. This notion was further elaborated in recent theoretical frameworks which emphasize that investment in social roles drives personality change (Roberts, 2006; Roberts et al., 2005; Woods et al., 2019; Wrzus & Roberts, 2017). According to these theories, acquiring a job evokes a process of role taking whereby an individual's personality gradually shifts to better respond to the expectancies and requirements that come with the specific role. Such role demands usually tie to a reward structure that not only shapes an individual's role expectations but also introduces feedback mechanisms, such as performance appraisal in organizations, both of which regulate an individual's thoughts, feelings, and behaviors in a certain way and could lead to changes in personality traits over time.

In sociology, scholars studying social structure and personality traditionally viewed individuals as embedded in different layers of social structure (e.g., Kohn, 1989) and sought to understand "the relationship between macro-social systems or processes and individual feelings, attitudes and behaviors" (McLeod & Lively, 2006, p. 76). They recognized that social structure, defined as "a *persisting* and bounded *pattern* of social relationships (or pattern of behavioral intention) among the units (persons or positions) in a social system" (House, 1981, p. 542), can shape individuals' "stable and persisting psychological attributes" (House, 1981, p. 527), which includes personality. As elaborated by Jane McLeod and Kathryn Lively (2006, p. 77), social structure "encompasses features of the macro-social order such as the structure of the labor market and systems of social stratification as well as processes such as industrialization." Because social structure is a broader term that can be operationalized differently, James House (1981) suggested that researchers need to identify specific components of the social system to study phenomenon of interest (the components principle), pay attention to proximal social experiences through which the focused macro-social structures can shape individuals' lives (the proximity principle), and, finally, explain the psychological mechanisms at the individual level to depict how the focused macro-social structures and their elicited proximal social experiences are processed at the individual level (the psychological principle). In line with these principles, scholars used occupational choice and work characteristics as a proxy for social stratification (categorization of people in a society into groups based on socioeconomic background) to capture social structures in a society. First, people at different levels of social classes hold jobs with different occupational and work characteristics (e.g., occupational prestige and job qualities). Second, specific occupational and work characteristics give rise to situational demands and requirements that elicit proximal social—specifically work-rated—experiences which affect individuals' lives. Third, the psychological mechanisms of occupational and work characteristics at the individual level can be drawn from work psychology research. The reasons set out above explain why sociological scholars used occupational choice and work characteristics as a proxy to examine how social structures can affect individual lives and experiences and thus personality (see Spenner, 1988).

Despite coming from different perspectives, the central idea behind the two traditions is that the work environment brings situational demands to evoke personality development by consolidating and reinforcing specific patterns of thoughts, feelings, and behaviors.

Work Design Characteristics and Personality Change

In the endeavor to understand how personality changes as a result of a wide range of contextual factors (see Wang & Wu, 2021; Wood et al., 2019 for reviews), researchers have focused on individuals' immediate work and employment environment to illuminate how different aspects of work design shape individuals' personality. These aspects can be broadly categorized as vocational, task, and relational characteristics. Below we briefly review studies and findings in each of these three domains by focusing on the characteristics that can be influenced by work design.

Vocational characteristics

Vocational characteristics "describe work characteristics in ways that are not specific to individual jobs, but are rather representative of the environment at a higher level of abstraction capturing complex blends of tasks, goals, values, norms and behavioral expectations concerning a vocation"

(Woods et al., 2019, p. 265). They capture distinctive features that differentiate occupations. Although personality has traditionally been used to explain individuals' vocational choice, several studies have investigated the reverse effect and found a long-term impact of vocational characteristics on personality development.

Bart Wille and colleagues (2012) investigated the reciprocal relationships between the Big Five personality traits and the six career roles (i.e., maker, expert, presenter, guide, inspirer, director). Using personality data from 260 participants collected in 1994 and 2009, as well as participants' personal overview of their careers between the two time points, they reported that engagement in a specific role or occupation facilitated change in the relevant trait. For example, engagement in the presenter role was associated with an increase in extraversion.

Wille and Filip De Fruyt (2014) examined the reciprocal relationships between the Big Five personality and occupational characteristics based on John Holland's (1959) taxonomy of occupations and interests—realistic, investigative, artistic, social, enterprising, conventional (RIASEC)—among 266 participants over 15 years, and similarly found associations between career interests and relevant personality traits. For instance, they reported that realistic characteristics were associated with a decrease of neuroticism, an increase of agreeableness, and an increase of conscientiousness.

Also using Holland's taxonomy, Stephen Woods and colleagues (2020) examined the associations between personality in childhood measured in 1965 or 1967, occupational characteristics in 2005, and personality in adulthood in 2013, using a sample of 596 participants from the Hawaii Personality and Health Cohort. Their findings included that artistic and investigative characteristics were associated with an increase in trait openness, and that social characteristics were associated with higher extraversion and agreeableness and lower neuroticism.

Although not all findings in these studies come with straightforward interpretations, collectively they provide evidence that vocational engagement generally promotes normative personality trait development, such as a decrease in neuroticism and an increase of conscientiousness and agreeableness over time.

Instead of including a broad classifications of vocational characteristics, Ravenna Helson and colleagues (1995) focused on occupational creativity, a specific occupational characteristic reflecting work activities involving "complex symbolic constructions, along with the degree of originality, energy, and success" (p. 1175). Using data collected from a cohort of women (n = 103) at age 21 and 52, they found that women engaging in higher occupational creativity increased their intellectual autonomy, ambition, and openness. Recently, Fien Heyde and colleagues (2023) examined the associations of agentic work activities (or those that require assertive interaction) and communal activities (or those that require friendliness and warmth) with changes in trait narcissism over time. Using four-wave data from 1,513 college alumni across six years, they found that communal work activities contribute to a decrease in trait narcissism.

Task characteristics

Task characteristics describe features of tasks that individuals are requested to do in their specific jobs. The job demands-resources model (e.g., Bakker et al., 2023; Karasek, 1979) is a particularly useful framework because it categorizes task characteristics into resources or demands. Job resources are aspects of the job that motivate individuals and stimulate learning and personal growth, whereas job demands are aspects of the job that require sustained effort and involve physiological and/or psychological costs (Bakker et al., 2023). Findings from various longitudinal studies have shown that task characteristics reflecting job resources or demands are associated with personality change.

As for job resources, task characteristics, such as autonomy and complexity, which allow individuals to use their discretion to deal with a wide range of data, tasks, and people, enable individuals to effectively influence their environment. These characteristics bring mastery to experiences at work that foster and strengthen self-determination beliefs (Parker, 2014). Empirically, job autonomy or job complexity has been found to directly and positively associate with changes in the personality traits that reflect self-determination, such as internal locus of control (Wu, Griffin, et al., 2015; three-wave survey data from 3,045 participants over four years), proactive personality (Li et al., 2014, three-wave survey data from 458 participants over four years), self-directedness (Kohn & Schooler, 1982, two-wave survey data from around 770 male participants over a year) and self-competence (Mortimer & Lorence, 1979, two-wave survey data from around 435 male participants over 10 years).

In contrast, demanding jobs tend to be associated with personality change in an undesirable direction, such as by increasing emotional irritation and undermining ambitions (e.g., Kohn & Schooler, 1982; Sutin & Costa, 2010; Wu, 2016). Using data from 1,814 employees over a five-year period, Chia-Huei Wu (2016) reported that increased time demands led to increased job stress over time, which in turn was associated with increased neuroticism and decreased extraversion. Using data from 541 employees, collected annually over five years, Wen-Dong Li and colleagues (2019) found that higher job insecurity was associated with decreased dispositional optimism. Using annual survey data from 1,046 employees over nine years, Wu and colleagues (2020) reported that chronic job insecurity, or continuously experiencing job insecurity over a long time, was associated with an increase in neuroticism and a decrease in conscientiousness and agreeableness—the three traits that respectively relate to one's emotional, social, and motivational stability.

However, researchers also suggested that job demands can sometimes motivate individuals to actively master their environment, facilitating personality change in a positive direction. Angelina Sutin and Costa's (2010) study over 10 years found that while hazardous work (i.e., exposure to dangerous work methods) was associated with a decrease in agreeableness, psychological demands were associated with increased extraversion. Li and colleagues (2014) reported that high job demands in prior years were associated with growth in proactive personality over time. David Holman and David Hughes (2021) noted that a higher workload was associated with increased extraversion, openness, and agreeableness. Overall, the links between job demands and personality change are not yet conclusive, and it is possible that important moderators exist which could help explain this relationship in finer-grained detail.

Relational characteristics

Jobs involve not only tasks but also people, or those who we work with, including supervisors, co-workers in the same or different work units, subordinates, customers, and others. Interactions with these stakeholders can influence one's behavior, attitudes, and beliefs at work, contributing to personality development as individuals enact their social roles embedded in those interactions. Among the different stakeholders, supervisors and co-workers in the same work units may play a more influential role because they are the people with whom we interact, and hence are influenced by, most often. Supervisors not only influence employees via a structural process, such as task assignment, but also via a social influence process through interpersonal interactions. For example, supervisors can influence and enact short-term changes in employees' possible selves (Lord et al., 1999; Shamir, 1991), which could then lead to enduring changes in how employees view themselves. Such an influence on employees' self-concept is also discussed in transformational leadership research (Bass, 1990; Bass & Avolio, 1990) such that transformational leaders could shape followers' self-concept in the long run via a Pygmalion mechanism by enabling them to internalize leaders' expectations (Duan et al., 2017). Co-workers also constitute an important part of the work environment because people learn expected behaviors and performance in their work contexts, and regulate their behaviors accordingly, by observing their peers (Bandura, 1971). The social influence of supervisors and co-workers can facilitate personality change via an Attraction-Selection-Attrition (ASA) mechanism (Schneider, 1987) through which individuals work toward achieving a better fit with their social environment at work (or else they can leave the organization).

To date, only two empirical studies have examined the role of supervisors and co-workers in shaping employees' personality change, which focused on support from these two parties (Li et al., 2014, 2019). Interestingly, neither supervisor support nor co-worker support was found to be associated with changes in proactive personality (Li et al., 2014) or dispositional optimism (Li et al., 2019). It is possible that supervisor support and co-worker support do not convey specific role expectations and thus do not have a salient role in shaping employees' personality change. Future studies could focus on specific behaviors from supervisors and co-workers that can act as stronger situational demands in developing employees' personality. In general, compared to studies on vocational characteristics and task characteristics, less attention has been paid to the link between relational characteristics and personality development, indicating a gap area that needs to be enriched in future research.

Reflections and Future Research Directions

Significant progress has been made over the last several decades in shifting our understanding about personality, enabling us to recognize that it is not as set in stone as we once thought, and instead can be continuously changed by our environment. Nevertheless, given this is still a relatively new area, significant knowledge gaps remain. In this section we provide some reflections with the hope of directing work design research toward positively shaping personality change.

Work design and process of personality change

Traditionally, work design has been discussed from a top-down approach, wherein individuals in positions of formal authority, such as chief executives or managers, design jobs with specific task structures and features aimed at regulating job holders' performance to achieve organizational goals (Parker et al., 2017). This top-down approach is aligned with the perspective undertaken by the previously discussed studies in investigating personality change wherein researchers assumed that work designed by others had the dominant power in enabling personality change of employees, as employees unintentionally develop identities associated with their roles and allow external forces (e.g., work demands) to shape their personality.

However, individuals do not merely passively accept demands in the work environment. Instead, they can actively engage in activities to design or shape their work roles, duties, and relational boundaries, embodied in the concept of job crafting (Tims et al., 2012; Wrzesniewski & Dutton, 2001), and this constitutes a bottom-up work design approach. This approach enables a top-down process of personality change, wherein individuals actively participate in specific roles and intentionally develop their identities. This active social investment can lead to personality development driven by an individual's aspirations to acquire specific characteristics (e.g., becoming more extroverted), either as an end goal or to achieve another purpose (e.g., becoming a top salesperson). Such a top-down process of personality change reflects volitional personality change (e.g., Hudson & Fraley, 2015), and manifests as a self-regulation process for personality change when an individual desires change, perceives it as feasible, and consistently enacts change to make new behaviors habitual (Hennecke et al., 2014). Consequently, when individuals actively engage in job crafting, volitional personality change can occur due to new behaviors becoming habitual within new work configurations. Recognizing this top-down process of personality change can broaden the research scope on how a bottom-up approach of work design can facilitate volitional personality change.

Researchers can take the job crafting perspective to explore various interesting research questions. For instance, different job crafting approaches (e.g., Kooij et al., 2017) can steer personality change differently, as individuals who craft jobs to use their strengths may experience a sense of competence, which could increase achievement orientation and contribute to a broad rise in conscientiousness. In contrast, individuals who craft jobs to suit their career interests might reinforce their existing personality traits as they self-select into specific experiences—a principle articulated in the correspondive principle of personality development (Caspi et al., 2005, p. 470). As another possible idea, while it has been suggested that role demands shape personality change from a stress perspective (Smallfield & Kluemper, 2022), and reinforced by empirical studies showing that demanding work characteristics are associated with stress and anxiety, leading to increase in neuroticism (Li et al., 2023; Wu, 2016; Wu et al., 2020), the job crafting perspective can help identify if and how individuals protect themselves from being affected by work demands, and thus avoid becoming more neurotic over time.

In brief, the flourishing of job crafting research (Lazazzara et al., 2020; Zhang & Parker, 2019) renders the possibility to study the novel question of whether, how, and when individuals can actively shape their work environment to make active social investment and enact personality change.

Methodological challenges

As we indicated earlier in this chapter, several inconsistencies remain concerning the effects of specific work characteristics on personality change. This is not unexpected because each empirical study has used different research designs, such as different time spans and different research variables, and they collected data from different countries which have unique social systems and cultures. Understandably, the endeavor of studying how work design factors drive personality change is methodologically challenging to implement.

As personality change can be a slow process, we need large, longitudinal studies in which personality and work design factors are measured multiple times. This design helps investigate non-linear effects, validating continuity and change patterns, and examining directionality in the reciprocal effects (e.g., Caspi et al., 2005; Ployhart & Vandenberg, 2010). In meeting this stringent requirement, most empirical studies have relied on secondary databases, including large panel data collected at regional or national levels and covering a longer timespan (typically ranging from four to 10 years, with a few spanning over 20 years). However, it should be noted that we still do not know what the appropriate interval is in measuring personality change as a result of work activities, as some evidence has shown that change may take place more quickly when triggered by significant career-related events (e.g., Bleidorn, 2012) or when actively facilitated by professional training and development (e.g., Wang et al., 2018). It is thus useful to complement the existing approach of relying on secondary data by purposefully designing studies in which more frequent assessments can be incorporated. Such a design can offer "sufficiently high temporal resolution" (Bleidorn et al., 2019, p. 22) while yielding opportunities to understand the process of personality change, such as by identifying meaningful mediators.

To understand the effects of work experiences on personality changes from a lifespan perspective, it is ideal to assess individuals' personalities before they enter the labor market, and then track their work experiences and personality change trajectories over time. This design offers several advantages. First, it establishes individuals' baseline level of personality before they gain work experience. Studies focusing on vocational characteristics and personality change have successfully employed this approach (e.g., Heyde et al., 2023; Wille & De Fruyt, 2014). Second, by tracking individuals longitudinally, researchers can gather information not only on their work experiences but also the duration of jobs or work roles they hold. This enables us to examine the effects of work experiences on personality change throughout an employment cycle, a novel approach in the field. Third, tracking individuals' work experiences over multiple job changes, coupled with personality measures, helps address novel research questions, such as understanding the contribution of each job in shaping one's personality and identifying how similarities and differences between previous and current job experiences drive personality changes.

Furthermore, expanding the sources of samples is another critical aspect that future research should consider. Current studies on this topic have predominantly used samples from Western countries, including the United Kingdom, the United States, Australia, and Germany, where nationally representative, household-level data are readily available. It remains unclear whether specific work characteristics play similar roles in shaping personality change for individuals from diverse industrial, economic, or cultural contexts. As studies have shown, people in different contexts demonstrate different attitudes and behaviors to the same work design factors (e.g., Daniels et al., 2007; Erez, 2010; Wu, Luksyte, et al., 2015). Therefore, taking a cross-cultural approach to understand how work design drives personality change trajectories is vital. Such insights are crucial for tailoring work environments and promoting positive personality development across diverse settings globally.

In summary, acknowledging the intricacies of research design, data collection, and diversifying sample sources for studying personality change, we advocate for initiatives focused on deliberately constructing datasets to address unexplored research inquiries.

Implications for Practice

By recognizing the long-term effects of work design in facilitating personality change and development, we would like to highlight three implications for organizations and managers. First, work design can have profound, long-term effects on personality maturation, a process in which an individual becomes "more planful, deliberate, and decisive, but also more considerate and charitable" (Caspi et al., 2005, p. 469), which reflects an increase in emotional stability, conscientiousness, and agreeableness (Hogan & Roberts, 2004; Roberts et al., 2006; Schwaba et al., 2022). As we reviewed earlier in this chapter, work design factors, such as job control and job stressors, can facilitate or undermine personality maturation in driving changes in those traits. Organizations and managers thus indirectly affect personality development in society in the long run by designing and offering good quality work to their employees. Second, while the effects of work design on employees' work motivation and performance can be observed in the short term, the effects of work design on employees' personality changes can take longer to be detected. This means that organizations and managers may not observe such a change if employees do not stay in the organizations or with the same managers over time. However, it does not mean that the efforts of organizations and managers in delivering work design for employees' personality development is worthless. Instead, we encourage organizations and managers to adopt a corporate social responsibility perspective to see work design as a way to contribute to society by facilitating workers' personality development and thus developing productive and involved contributors to society. Third, based on the studies we reviewed earlier, work design factors relevant to personality development, such as job control and demands, are also those used to shape employees' work motivation, performance, and well-being. This observation means that work design for personality development is not unlike work design for motivation, performance, and well-being (see Knight & Klonek, this volume). As such, practically speaking, organizations and managers can continue their focus using good work design practices to foster employees' work motivation, boost their performance, and protect their well-being while aiming to use these practices to facilitate employees' performance development in the long run.

References

Bakker, A. B., Demerouti, E., & Sanz-Vergel, A. (2023). Job demands–resources theory: Ten years later. *Annual Review of Organizational Psychology and Organizational Behavior 10*, 25–53.

Bandura, A. (1971). *Social learning theory.* New York General Learning Press.

Bass, B. M. (1990). From transactional to transformational leadership: Learning to share the vision. *Organizational Dynamics 18*, 19–31.

Bass, B. M., & Avolio, B. J. (1990). The implications of transactional and transformational leadership for individual, team, organizational development. *Research in Organizational Change and Development 4*, 231–272.

Bleidorn, W. (2012). Hitting the road to adulthood: Short-term personality development during a major life transition. *Personality and Social Psychology Bulletin 38*, 1594–1608.

Bleidorn, W., Hill, P. L., Back, M. D., Denissen, J. J. A., Hennecke, M., Hopwood, C. J., Jokela, M., Kandler, C., Lucas, R. E., Luhmann, M., Orth, U., Wagner, J., Wrzus, C., Zimmermann, J., & Roberts, B. (2019). The policy relevance of personality traits. *American Psychologist 74*, 1056–1067.

Bleidorn, W., Hopwood, C. J., Back, M. D., Denissen, J. J. A., Hennecke, M., Hill, P. L., Jokela, M., Kandler, C., Lucas, R. E., Luhmann, M., Orth, U., Roberts, B. W., Wagner, J., Wrzus, C., & Zimmermann, J. (2021). Personality trait stability and change. *Personality Science 2*, 1–20.

Bleidorn, W., Hopwood, C. J., & Luca, R. E. (2018). Life events and personality trait change. *Journal of Personality 86*, 83–96.

Bleidorn, W., Schwaba, T., Zheng, A., Hopwood, C. J., Sosa, S. S., Roberts, B. W., & Briley, D. A. (2022). Personality stability and change: A meta-analysis of longitudinal studies. *Psychological Bulletin 148*, 588–619.

Brousseau, K. R. (1983). Toward a dynamic model of job-person relationships: Findings, research questions, and implications for work system design. *Academy of Management Review 8*, 33–45.

Caspi, A., Roberts, B., & Shiner, R. L. (2005). Personality development: Stability and change. *Annual Review of Psychology 56*, 453–484.

Daniels, K., Tregaskis, O., & Seaton, J. S. (2007). Job control and occupational health: The moderating role of national R&D activity. *Journal of Organizational Behavior 28*, 1–19.

Duan, J., Li, C., Xu, Y., & Wu, C.-H. (2017). Transformational leadership and employee voice behavior: A Pygmalion mechanism. *Journal of Organizational Behavior 38*, 650–670.

Erez, M. (2010). Culture and job design. *Journal of Organizational Behavior 31*, 389–400.

Frese, M. (1982). Occupational socialization and psychological development: An under-emphasized research perspective in industrial psychology. *Journal of Occupational Psychology 55*, 209–224.

Frese, M., & Zapf, D. (1994). Action as the core of work psychology: A German approach. In H. C. Triandis, M. D. Dunnette, & L. M. Hough (Eds.), *Handbook of industrial and organizational psychology*, 2nd ed. (Vol. 4, pp. 271–340). Consulting Psychologists Press.

Helson, R., Roberts, B., & Agronick, G. (1995). Enduringness and change in creative personality and the prediction of occupational creativity. *Journal of Personality and Social Psychology 69*, 1173–1183.

Hennecke, M., Bleidorn, W., Denissen, J. J. A., & Wood, D. (2014). A three-part framework for self-regulated personality development across adulthood. *European Journal of Personality 28*, 289–299.

Heyde, F., Wille, B., Vergauwe, J., Hofmans, J., & Fruyt, F. D. (2023). Reciprocal relationships between narcissism and agentic versus communal work activities across the first six years of the career. *Journal of Applied Psychology 109*(5), 650–667.

Hogan, R., & Roberts, B. W. (2004). A socioanalytic model of maturity. *Journal of Career Assessment 12*, 207–217.

Holland, J. L. (1959). A theory of vocational choice. *Journal of Counseling Psychology 6*, 35–45.

Holman, D. J., & Hughes, D. J. (2021). Transactions between Big-5 personality traits and job characteristics across 20 years. *Journal of Occupational and Organizational Psychology 94*, 762–788.

House, J. S. (1981). Social structure and personality. In M. Rosenberg & R. H. Turner (Eds.), *Social psychology: Sociological perspectives* (pp. 525–561). Basic Books.

Hudson, N. W., & Fraley, R. C. (2015). Volitional personality trait change: Can people choose to change their personality traits? *Journal of Personality and Social Psychology 109*, 490–507.

James, W. (1890). *The principles of psychology: Vol. 1.* New York Henry Holt and Co.

Jokela, M. (2017). Personality and social structure. *European Journal of Personality 31*, 205–207.

Karasek, R. A. (1979). Job demands, job decision latitude and mental strain: Implications for job redesign. *Administrative Science Quarterly 24*, 285–306.

Kohn, M. L. (1989). Social structure and personality: A quintessentially sociological approach to social psychology. *Social Forces 68*, 26–33.

Kohn, M. L., & Schooler, C. (1982). Job conditions and personality: A longitudinal assessment of their reciprocal effects. *American Journal of Sociology 87*, 1257–1286.

Kooij, D. T. A. M., van Woerkom, M., Wilkenloh, J., Dorenbosch, L., & Denissen, J. J. A. (2017). Job crafting towards strengths and interests: The effects of a job crafting intervention on person–job fit and the role of age. *Journal of Applied Psychology 102*, 971–981.

Lazazzara, A., Tims, M., & de Gennaro, D. (2020). The process of reinventing a job: A meta–synthesis of qualitative job crafting research. *Journal of Vocational Behavior 116*, 103267.

Li, W.-D., Fay, D., Frese, M., Harms, P. D., & Gao, X. Y. (2014). Reciprocal relationship between proactive personality and work characteristics: A latent change score approach. *Journal of Applied Psychology 99*, 948–965.

Li, W.-D., Li, S., Fay, D., & Frese, M. (2019). Reciprocal relationships between dispositional optimism and work experiences: A five wave longitudinal investigation. *Journal of Applied Psychology 104*, 1471–1486.

Li, W.-D., Wang, J., Allen, T., Zhang, X., Yu, K., Zhang, H., Huang, J. L., Liu, M., & Li, A. (2023). Getting under the skin? Influences of work–family experiences on personality trait adaptation and reciprocal relationships. *Journal of Personality and Social Psychology 126*(4), 694–718.

Lord, R. G., Brown, D. J., & Freiberg, S. J. (1999). Understanding the dynamics of leadership: The role of follower self-concepts in the leader/follower relationship. *Organizational Behavior and Human Decision Processes 78*, 167–203.

McAdams, D. P., & Olson, B. D. (2010). Personality development: Continuity and change over the life course. *Annual Review of Psychology 61*, 517–542.

McCrae, R. R., & Costa, P. T., Jr. (2003). *Personality in adulthood: A five-factor theory perspective.* 2nd ed. Guilford.

McLeod, J. D., & Lively, K. J. (2006). Social structure and personality. In J. Delamater (Ed.), *Handbook of social psychology* (pp. 77–102). Springer US.

Mortimer, J. T., & Lorence, J. (1979). Occupational experience and the self-concept: A longitudinal study. *Social Psychology Quarterly 42*, 307–323.

Parker, S. K. (2014). Beyond motivation: Job and work design for development, health, ambidexterity, and more. *Annual Review of Psychology 65*, 661–691.

Parker, S. K., Van den Broeck, A., & Holman, D. (2017). Work design influences: A synthesis of multilevel factors that affect the design of jobs. *Academy of Management Annals 11*, 267–308.

Ployhart, R. E., & Vandenberg, R. J. (2010). Longitudinal research: The theory, design, and analysis of change. *Journal of Management 36*, 94–120.

Roberts, B. W. (2006). Personality development and organizational behavior In B. M. Staw (Ed.), *Research on organizational behavior* (pp. 1–41). Elsevier Science/JAI Press.

Roberts, B. W., Walton, K. E., & Viechtbauer, W. (2006). Patterns of mean-level change in personality traits across the life course: A meta-analysis of longitudinal studies. *Psychological Bulletin 132*, 1–25.

Roberts, B. W., Wood, D., & Smith, J. L. (2005). Evaluating five factor theory and social investment perspectives on personality trait development. *Journal of Research in Personality 39*, 166–184.

Ryff, C. D. (1987). The place of personality and social structure research in social psychology. *Journal of Personality and Social Psychology 53*, 1192–1202.

Schneider, B. (1987). The people make the place. *Personnel Psychology 40*, 437–453.

Schwaba, T., Bleidorn, W., Hopwood, C. J., Manuck, S. B., & Wright, A. G. C. (2022). Refining the maturity principle of personality development by examining facets, close others, and comaturation. *Journal of Personality and Social Psychology 122*, 942–

Shamir, B. (1991). Meaning, self and motivation in organizations. *Organization Studies 12*, 405–424.

Smallfield, J., & Kluemper, D. H. (2022). An explanation of personality change in organizational science: Personality as an outcome of workplace stress. *Journal of Management 48*, 851–877.

Spenner, K. I. (1988). Social stratification, work, and personality. *Annual Review of Sociology 14*, 69–97.

Sutin, A. R., & Costa, P. T., Jr. (2010). Reciprocal influences of personality and job characteristics across middle adulthood. *Journal of Personality 78*, 257–288.

Tasselli, S., Kilduff, M., & Landis, B. (2018). Personality change: Implications for organizational behavior. *Academy of Management Annals 12*, 467–493.

Tims, M., Bakker, A. B., & Derks, D. (2012). Development and validation of the job crafting scale. *Journal of Vocational Behavior 80*, 173–186.

Wang, Y., & Wu, C.-H. (2021). *Work and personality change: What we do makes who we are*. Bristol University Press.

Wang, Y., Wu, C.-H., Parker, S. K., & Griffin, M. A. (2018). Developing goal orientations conducive to learning and performance: An intervention study. *Journal of Occupational and Organizational Psychology 91*, 875–895.

Wille, B., Beyers, W., & De Fruyt, F. (2012). A transactional approach to person-environment fit: Reciprocal relations between personality development and career role growth across young to middle adulthood. *Journal of Vocational Behavior 81*, 307–321.

Wille, B., & De Fruyt, F. (2014). Vocations as a source of identity: Reciprocal relations between Big Five personality traits and RIASEC characteristics. *Journal of Applied Psychology 99*, 262–281.

Woods, S. A., Edmonds, G. W., Hampson, S. E., & Lievens, F. (2020). How our work influences who we are: Testing a theory of vocational and personality development over fifty years. *Journal of Research in Personality 85*, 103930.

Woods, S. A., Wille, B., Wu, C.-h., Lievens, F., & De Fruyt, F. (2019). The influence of work on personality trait development: The demands-affordances TrAnsactional (DATA) model, an integrative review, and research agenda. *Journal of Vocational Behavior 110*, 258–271.

Wrzesniewski, A., & Dutton, J. E. (2001). Crafting a job: Revisioning employees as active crafters of their work. *Academy of Management Review 26*(2), 179–201.

Wrzus, C., & Roberts, B. W. (2017). Processes of personality development in adulthood: The TESSERA framework. *Personality and Social Psychology Review 21*, 253–277.

Wu, C.-H. (2016). Personality change via work: A job demand–control model of Big Five personality changes. *Journal of Vocational Behavior 92*, 157–166.

Wu, C.-H., Griffin, M. A., & Parker, S. K. (2015). Developing agency through good work: Longitudinal effects of job autonomy and skill utilization on locus of control. *Journal of Vocational Behavior 89*, 102–108.

Wu, C.-H., Luksyte, A., & Parker, S. K. (2015). Overqualification and subjective well-being at work: The moderating role of job autonomy and culture. *Social Indicators Research 121*, 917–937.

Wu, C.-H., Wang, Y., Parker, S. K., & Griffin, M. A. (2020). Effects of chronic job insecurity on Big Five personality change. *Journal of Applied Psychology 105*, 1308–1326.

Zhang, F., & Parker, S. K. (2019). Reorienting job crafting research: A hierarchical structure of job crafting concepts and integrative review. *Journal of Organizational Behavior 40*, 126–146.

Methodology in Work Design Research
The Past, Present, and (Longitudinal) Future

Anita C. Keller and Iustina C. Armasu

Extensive research and theoretical work (e.g., Fried et al., 2007; Humphrey et al., 2007; Parker et al., 2021) has recognized the significance of work design in shaping individuals' experiences within organizations. The field appears to be reenergized as illustrated by work design reviews spanning more than 100 years of research on the topic (Parker et al., 2017) and theoretical work exploring novel processes and outcomes of work design (e.g., Fried et al., 2007; Parker et al., 2021). At the same time, workplaces are increasingly characterized by numerous change processes initiated by various factors, such as technological advancements or new forms of organizational structures. These developments make workplaces and their influences on employees complex to grasp; however, advances in research methods, particularly in longitudinal research, make it possible to shed light on the complex and dynamic ways work design has implications for employees, organizations, and society. The field has also been criticized for the predominately employed methodologies and research designs (e.g., Oldham & Hackman, 2010; Parker et al., 2017). Hence, this chapter examines the methodologies used in work design research as they form the foundation for establishing the validity of empirical findings. To this end, we systematically analyze the literature published over the last 10 years in leading work design journals. From there, we discuss the strengths of experimental and longitudinal research in more detail before we offer a discussion on different measurement approaches covering various alternatives to self-report assessments. We explore the raised criticisms and how they apply to the current body of literature by considering how the methodological choices help establish or threaten testing of causal relationships and their suitability to test core theoretical assumptions. Last, we provide methodological recommendations for answering pressing work design research questions in the future. As workplaces become more dynamic and uncertain, requiring employees and workplaces to adapt to various crises

---

Anita C. Keller and Iustina C. Armasu, *Methodology in Work Design Research*. In: *Transformative Work Design*. Edited by: Sharon K. Parker et al., Oxford University Press. © Society for Industrial and Organizational Psychology (2025). DOI: 10.1093/oso/9780197692554.003.0008

208   TRANSFORMATIVE WORK DESIGN

and market changes, we highlight methodologies that hold promise for addressing these challenges whilst maintaining methodological rigor.

Where Are We—Past and Current Methodological Choices in Work Design Research

Work design scholars have built a rich and broad body of knowledge using various types of research methodologies. To understand how the field currently conducts work design research (i.e., what methods and designs are used), we searched for published work design articles in six of the leading journals in the field over the last 10 years (i.e., *Academy of Management Journal, Journal of Applied Psychology, Journal of Occupational Health Psychology, Journal of Management, Journal of Organizational Behavior,* and *Journal of Vocational Psychology*). We used a combination of general (e.g., work design, job design) and specific search terms (e.g., job control, autonomy, skill variety, task variety) to identify research focusing on work design and yielded 1,025 articles. To identify research that substantially studied work design (i.e., including some measure of work design; see also exclusion criteria in appendix), we first screened the title (exclusion of 446 papers), then the abstract (exclusion of 136 papers), and finally the full paper (exclusion of 63 papers), resulting in 380 papers. These 380 papers reported on 436 studies (i.e., approximately 11 percent of papers included two to four studies in their paper). Of note, two-thirds of the papers including multiple studies have been published in the last five years, hence the inclusion of multiple, complementary studies appears to be a more recent trend. In Table 8.1, we provide an overview of definitions of methodologies used in the work design literature.

Of the 436 studies, 42 percent (n = 182) used cross-sectional designs,[1] 34 percent (n = 148) longitudinal designs, 13 percent (n = 56) used a dyadic or team design, 9 percent (n = 40) used experimental designs, and 2 percent (n = 10) used a qualitative approach. Within longitudinal research designs, more than half of the studies are intensive longitudinal studies (e.g., experience sampling study, daily diary study) focusing, for example, on daily variations in work design features. Notably, approximately one-quarter of the cross-sectional studies (n = 43) included an other-report, such as supervisor ratings of performance. Over the last 10 years, two trends are noticeable—cross-sectional research designs are becoming slightly less frequent and longitudinal designs slightly

---

[1] This includes time-lagged studies that have not repeated their measures across waves (see Ployhart & Vandenberg [2010] and the section on longitudinal research designs in this chapter).

METHODOLOGY IN WORK DESIGN RESEARCH 209

Table 8.1 Definitions of Research Designs and Measurement Approaches.

Term	Definition
Laboratory study	A study performed in a laboratory that maximizes researcher control over the environment. It can be used in conjunction with experimental designs (testing cause-and-effect relationships) by exposing participants to different conditions or manipulations
Field study	A study performed in a real-world setting that allows for a holistic investigation that considers the complexity and nuances of real-life situations
Research Design	
Qualitative	Collecting non-numeric data from participants (e.g., interviews, observations, text) to gain insights into the subjective experience, attitudes, and behaviors of the participants
Cross-sectional	Collecting data from participants at a single point in time, providing a snapshot of the sample's characteristics or behaviors and a pattern of associations between variables of interest
Simulation	Involves recreating work and social environments in a realistic manner, especially when investigators cannot easily access them; used to study how individuals behave and function in these environments
(Field-) Experiment	Involves the manipulation of one or more variables to determine their (causal) effect on an outcome; includes random assignment to conditions (otherwise called quasi-experiment)
Intervention	Tests the effects of implemented programs, trainings or treatments and assesses its impact on relevant outcomes
Time-lagged	Examines the linkage of two or more variables by temporally separating the measurements across time without repeating them; design can help reduce common method bias
Longitudinal	Assesses the change and stability in variables of interest by repeatedly measuring the same constructs within the same units (e.g., employees, teams, organizations) for at least three times
Panel and cohort study	A longitudinal design used to investigate changes and trajectories over time among a panel (i.e., individuals, households, organizations, etc.) or cohorts (i.e., individuals that share some characteristics such as entering an organization at the same time, birthyear)

continued

210 TRANSFORMATIVE WORK DESIGN

Table 8.1 *continued*

Term	Definition
Intensive longitudinal	A longitudinal design that involves the frequent and repeated collection of data from individuals over a short period of time (e.g., hours, days, weeks), used to capture short-term within-person fluctuations in behaviors, experiences, or physiological responses
Measurement	
Self-report	Participants provide information about their thoughts, feelings, behaviors, or attitudes by answering questions about themselves on questionnaires
Other report	Information about a focal participant is gathered from someone else (e.g., supervisor, coworker, partner) who provides their observations or assessments on the focal participant through questionnaires
Observation	Systematic recording of conditions, behavior, or events in a structured and objective manner by a third-party (e.g., researcher, safety officer)
Biomarkers	A measurable and quantifiable biological characteristic or substance that serves as an indicator of a particular physiological or pathological process, condition, or disease
Cognitive assessment	Used to assess an individual's cognitive abilities and processes, including memory, attention, problem-solving, language skills, and overall cognitive functioning, by means of standardized tests or tasks
Occupational classifications (occupational codes)	Occupational codes (e.g., O*NET) are standardized alphanumeric identifiers assigned to specific job roles or occupations within a structured classification system that are used for the purpose of categorizing and organizing various occupations based on their common characteristics, tasks, skills, education requirements, and other relevant attributes
Tracking data	Systematic collection and analysis of continuous or real-time data generated through the monitoring of various activities or behaviors (e.g., hygiene monitoring, electronic performance monitoring)

more frequent (see Figure 8.1). This is further supported by Figure 8.2, which shows the cumulative numbers of publications per research design per year illustrating that longitudinal research designs start to pick up.

In terms of measurement, most studies included at least some self-report measurements (i.e., 96 percent of studies). Slightly more than half of the studies (i.e., 54 percent) used self-report assessments only, but most studies had multiple assessments across time. The 17 studies that have not used

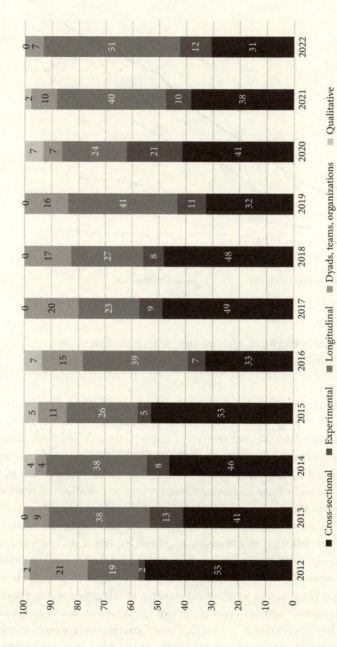

Figure 8.1 Trend in Employed Research Designs Over the Last 10 Years (2012–2022) in Selected Journals (percentage per year)

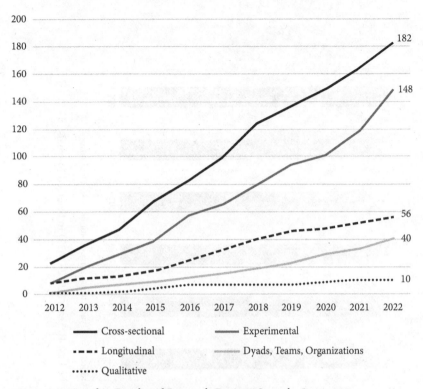

Figure 8.2 Trend in Employed Research Designs Over the Last 10 years (2012–2022) in Selected Journals (cumulative numbers)

any self-report measures used occupational codes (e.g., O*NET), observation, cognitive and knowledge assessment, and data obtained from human resources (HR) (e.g., payroll data). Besides self-report assessments, a considerable number of studies also used other reports, such as a focal employee's performance assessments rated by the supervisor (n = 105). As can be expected for this study context, most of these studies asked supervisors or coworkers to provide insights, however some studies also included partners and parents.

These studies on work design haves led to valuable insights; however, some of these methods fall short of addressing important aspects that are necessary to draw valid and reliable conclusions. Some of the core criticisms that have been raised repeatedly are (1) a lack of intervention studies to test effects of work redesign; (2) a lack of longitudinal research to test processes, temporal order, and dynamics; and (3) exclusive use of self-report measures to assess work design features (Parker et al., 2017). These shortcomings are problematic because they limit the ability to separate cause and effect between work design and outcomes.

Causality refers to the establishment of a specific relationship between variables, in that (changes in) one variable lead(s) to changes in another variable

(Hanges & Wang, 2012). Three conditions must be met to establish a causal relationship between a hypothesized cause and a dependent variable. First, the hypothesized causal and dependent variable need to correlate with each other. Second, changes in the hypothesized causal variable must occur before the predicted changes in the dependent variable, also known as temporal precedence. For example, when investigating the effects of work design on employee outcomes, researchers would expect that an increase in employee autonomy at one point in time would lead to positive changes in well-being at a later point in time. Third, the causal variable-dependent variable relationship must be isolated from other potential causal factors (i.e., alternative explanations need to be ruled out). This is one of the most challenging conditions to fulfill in work design research, as various confounding variables can influence the dependent variable and create difficulty in isolating the effect of the independent variable. For instance, without employing a control group and/or repeated measures when designing interventions, causality cannot be established because various other aspects, such as individual differences (e.g., personality traits, skills) or other environmental factors (e.g., leadership style, industry-specific trends), could lead to the same effect on the dependent variable.

An obstacle to establishing causal relationships in work design research may be due to the large number of cross-sectional studies and self-report data sources. Because cross-sectional studies only measure variables of interest at one timepoint, one cannot fulfill the temporal precedence condition of causality. Further, while cross-sectional studies allow for the establishment of a correlation between two variables, this relationship does not necessarily translate into a causal one because other directions cannot be tested and ruled out (i.e., if work design affects outcomes or if outcomes affect work design). Studies using only self-report assessments may suffer from validity threats because responses may be biased (e.g., common method bias, recall bias, social desirability). In particular, field studies that do not repeat their measures and only use self-report assessments cannot meet the criteria to establish causality because they cannot establish temporal order and rule out alternative explanations. In the following, we examine longitudinal and experimental research designs, which provide potential remedies for some of the concerns outlined above. We illustrate how these research designs are used by (for the most part) providing examples of studies included in our review.

Longitudinal Research Designs

Longitudinal research designs fulfill two of the criteria to establish causality: they can assess whether (1) two variables are associated with each other, and (2) they allow to test whether the predictor variable precedes the dependent variable. Typically, it is difficult to establish the third criterion—being able to

214 TRANSFORMATIVE WORK DESIGN

rule out alternative explanations—because longitudinal studies are often conducted in the field. Nevertheless, longitudinal research designs are becoming more common as establishing the temporal order of a set of variables is critical to advance the field and they allow the testing of elements of temporal change.

A particularly interesting design feature of longitudinal research is that they can answer research questions that focus on change. Longitudinal research designs assess the same constructs among the same participants or units (e.g., dyads, teams, organizations) at least three times to study change over time (Ployhart & Vandenberg, 2010).[2] We distinguish longitudinal studies from time-lagged studies because the latter lacks repeated measures of both predictor and outcome variables, thus preventing researchers from linking intraindividual change in the outcome to intraindividual change in the predictor. Designs with fewer than three measurements also come with limitations that inhibit the ability to analyze change patterns. For example, two assessments cannot distinguish true change from measurement error and can only provide information on linear change but not non-linear changes, such as u-shaped change patterns (Singer & Willett, 2003). Common types of longitudinal designs are panel/cohort studies and intensive longitudinal studies (e.g., experience sampling study, daily diary study). The main difference between the two types is the intensity of assessment and overall observation period. Panel or cohort studies can cover weeks to years (see Table 8.1) while intensive longitudinal studies typically cover days to weeks (see Table 8.1).

Longitudinal designs are a suitable design choice because many theories imply a within-person process—if work design aspects change (e.g., increase in autonomy), outcomes also change (e.g., increase in motivation). Therefore, longitudinal designs are not only used to establish temporal order (i.e., whether X precedes Y or Y precedes X), but also to address research questions that test core assumptions of work design theories and focus on dynamics and change patterns specifically. In a dynamic model, a variable or set of variables moves from a defined state at t to another state at $t+1$; that is, the system evolves over time (Wang et al., 2016). Generally, researchers can use longitudinal designs to test (1) if and how variables change over time (intraindividual change and stability); (2) if there are differences between units (e.g., employees, teams) in these intraindividual change patterns; (3) if change in one variable is associated with change in another variable, either simultaneously or sequentially; (4) what the causes of the intraindividual change are; and (5) what the causes of the

---

[2] This definition explicitly acknowledges change, which is a core aspect of longitudinal research; however, the requirement of three repeated assessments of all constructs may be overly restrictive for some research questions. For example, for questions that include role change (e.g., turnover, transition to supervisory role), two assessments of role status may be sufficient. Hence, in our review of the current work design literature, we classified designs as longitudinal if core constructs were repeated three times (e.g., Li et al., 2017).

interindividual differences in intraindividual change are (Nesselroade & Baltes, 1979).

In the following, we organize the discussion of previous longitudinal work design research and examples into two different, but not mutually exclusive, types to illustrate how longitudinal research designs can be used to address a multitude of work design questions. The first type focuses on identifying and describing changes in one or more variable(s) over time, such as describing the job autonomy trajectory as job newcomers familiarize themselves with their new roles. The second type focuses less on describing the pattern of change (i.e., trajectory) and more on testing reciprocal relationships between stable and fluctuating components of variables of interest, such as testing if increases in job autonomy will lead to subsequent increases in job complexity and vice versa.

Describe and explain change trajectories

Research questions that focus on *change* consider the shape of a trajectory of one or multiple variables over time (e.g., growth in job motivation). Researchers may be interested in understanding if a construct of interest changes quickly or slowly (i.e., speed of change) and what form the change process takes (e.g., gradual, plateau). For example, researchers may wonder how autonomy develops over the career or if a job crafting intervention gradually or abruptly increases work design features such as task complexity. Such descriptive research questions can be expanded by predicting the change trajectory (e.g., differences in speed or shape) or using it to establish a link to (change in) another variable. Longitudinal designs often require analytical approaches such as latent growth curve models, which are models that estimate the average initial status, the average growth rate over the observation period, and variation across individuals for initial status and growth rate (Grimm et al., 2017). For example, Wen-Dong Li and colleagues (2018) used latent growth curve models to showcase that job control and demands increase for most employees early in their career. By predicting the intercepts and slopes through leadership status, they were further able to show that these increases in autonomy are especially pronounced for leaders compared to non-leaders. Similarly, using latent growth curve modeling in a sample of nurses, Florian E. Klonek and colleagues (2023) showed that growth trajectories in skill utilization depend on nurses' individual goal orientations.

These two examples focus on change processes that are considered slow (e.g., changes over years), but research questions can also focus on short-term change processes such as weekly trajectories. For example, Shani Pindek and colleagues (2021) analyzed daily diary data using growth modeling to test the Monday Blues hypothesis, meaning that employees experience work characteristics differently on Mondays than on other weekdays. They found

216   TRANSFORMATIVE WORK DESIGN

that employees perceived more adverse work characteristics (e.g., performance constraints, incivility) early in the week which gradually declined across the workweek. The authors also found that employees are more sensitive (i.e., react stronger) to adverse conditions early in the week than later. So far, these studies mostly reported linear trends; however, with increasing use of longitudinal studies with more measurement points, research could also explore non-linear patterns using growth models (e.g., by testing linear and quadratic slopes or use of discontinuous growth models).

Focus on reciprocal processes

Research questions that focus on reciprocal and dynamic processes test the interplay between changes (and lack thereof) in different constructs of interest. Studies investigate a wide range of topics, such as whether daily task setbacks lead to more exhaustion among employees who work in highly interdependent teams (Chong et al., 2020) or the dynamics of task and relationship conflicts at work and workload within and across days (Somaraju et al., 2022). Besides investigating the effects of change in one construct on other constructs, work design researchers may also be interested in theorizing dynamic processes with different attributes such as feedback loops and asymmetric influences (Cronin & Vancouver, 2019).

Feedback loops consider that changes in construct X lead to changes in other constructs that ultimately further influence and change construct X in the future. For example, researchers may be interested in investigating whether increases in autonomy predict subsequent increases in proactive behavior, whether increases in proactive behavior predict subsequent increases in autonomy, or whether both apply (i.e., reciprocal relationships). Several analytical models are available to test such dynamic relations over time. Two of the more prominent models in work design research are the random intercept cross-lagged panel model (RI-CLPM) (Hamaker et al., 2015) and the latent change score model (McArdle, 2009).[3] For example, Katrien Vangrieken and colleagues (2023) tested the reciprocal interplay between autonomy, workload, and self-efficacy using RI-CLPM. The authors found that increases in workload predict subsequent increases in self-efficacy when autonomy also increases. They also tested for reversed relations and found that increases in self-efficacy predicted subsequent increases in workload but not autonomy. Hence, this study provides information on the temporal order and direction of the effects of work design.

Asymmetric effects are another area of interest for work design researchers. Typically, we assume that as construct A goes up, construct B goes up, and as

---

[3] Alternatively, experience-sampling designs can be used to test reciprocal relationships between constructs that change over shorter time periods (e.g., see Nesher Shoshan and colleagues [2023] for an investigation into reciprocal effects between daily emotional labor demands and exhaustion).

construct A goes down, construct B goes down. However, it can be argued that what leads to an increase in one construct is not the same as what leads to a decrease (Cronin & Vancouver, 2019). Taking this idea of potential asymmetry, Laurenz Meier and colleagues (2023) tested if gaining more favorable work characteristics (e.g., increase in autonomy) equally affects well-being as losing in favorable work characteristics (e.g., decrease in autonomy). Based on the results of three longitudinal studies spanning different time lags, the authors concluded that there is evidence for asymmetric effects in that losing work design quality has a stronger (negative) impact on well-being than gaining does. Some studies also account for specific attributes of the temporal pattern. Christopher Rosen and colleagues (2020) tested if the generally assumed positive effects of challenge demands (e.g., workload) depend on how stable or fluctuating employees experience these demands. Indeed, the authors found that across two longitudinal studies challenge demands have positive effects on performance and well-being, as long as these are stable. If employees experience fluctuation in challenge demands, they are appraised as hindering and consequently affect performance and well-being negatively. These studies illustrate that not only aspects such as time and intensity of exposure to certain work design features matter, but also how people experience the passage through time (i.e., specific temporal patterns such as losing versus gaining and stability versus fluctuation).

Summary

Longitudinal research is a valuable design choice for studying change over time and establishing temporal precedence. It allows researchers to analyze change patterns and test complex reciprocal relationships between variables, providing insights into the dynamics of work design and its effects on individuals and organizations. However, longitudinal designs are costly, and they come with specific challenges that can threaten the validity of the findings.

Experimental and Intervention Research

Experimental designs aim to establish cause and effect relationships by manipulating independent variables to assess their impact on dependent variables. However, they are relatively rare in work design research, with only 9 percent of studies in our review using this design (see Figure 8.1). Well-designed experimental studies aim to understand the direction of hypothesized effects and explain how changes in one construct will lead to changes in another. Experiments are exceptionally well suited to test causal relationships (as previously

218 TRANSFORMATIVE WORK DESIGN

discussed) because they implement an experimental condition (e.g., manipulation of task complexity) and a control condition, and use random assignment of participants to fulfill all three conditions of causality (Eden, 2017). Experimental designs are commonly conducted in laboratory settings that control the environment and help eliminate or minimize confounding factors. However, researchers in the field of work design are often also interested in replicating the complexity of real organizational settings (i.e., external validity). They achieve this through simulation designs, field experiments, and intervention designs (see Table 8.1).

Simulation studies

One approach to address external validity concerns are simulation studies.[4] These designs simulate realistic work environments replicating the challenges faced by employees in specific occupations (e.g., aviation). By observing and manipulating variables of interest, researchers can record the reactions of the target group (i.e., employees instead of students) (Brown et al., 2020). For example, Boris Cendales-Ayala (2017) used a driving simulator to investigate the effects of workload and decision-making latitude on bus drivers' strain. They manipulated workload by varying the number of stops in the driving tasks and decision-making latitude by imposing or removing constraints regarding the time limit participants had to perform the task. They found that decision-latitude buffered the negative effect of workload on strain. Similarly, simulation studies can be used to investigate social aspects of work design and increase experimental realism (i.e., external validity). For example, Julija Mell and colleagues (2020) created a computer strategy game to simulate team informational interdependence. In the study, teams had to collaborate and share information to achieve a system-level goal which was to direct help a humanitarian aid convoy safely to its destination through a war-torn region. The study revealed that information sharing across teams increased performance and that team-focused teams shared less information with system-focused teams.

Quasi- and field experimental studies

It is important to distinguish between quasi- and field experimental studies because these two designs are often mislabeled despite some key differences from one another. Quasi-experiments allow researchers to test differences in the

---

[4] Simulation studies can involve experimental and control conditions (Cendales-Ayala et al., 2017) but they can also be designed without (e.g., Loft et al., 2015). Here we discuss simulation studies using experimental conditions.

dependent variable(s) between two or more naturally occurring groups (Hanges & Wang, 2012). The key difference between a quasi-experiment and a "true" experiment is that researchers conducting an experimental design can *randomly* assign participants to different manipulated conditions. For instance, Steffen Giessner and colleagues (2023) examined the varying impact of leader support on job satisfaction and absenteeism, comparing the effects between employees in merging and non-merging organizations in a quasi-experiment (i.e., employees were not randomly allocated to a [non-] merging organization). Employees in merging organizations experienced a decline in job satisfaction and increased absenteeism during the merger process, but increased supportive leadership helped alleviate these negative effects.

Another way to balance the need for experimental realism and internal validity is through field experiments (Eden, 2017). These designs allow researchers to manipulate variables in naturalistic settings, while preserving some experimental control. They differ from quasi-experimental designs because they involve random allocation of participants to groups. For instance, Jegar Pitchforth and colleagues (2020) investigated the effect of various office designs on employee satisfaction, enjoyment, flow, and productivity. They randomly assigned participants to different office design conditions (e.g., open plan, zoned open plan, activity based, and team-offices). Contrary to popular belief, they found that the open plan office design exerted the most negative effects on employee outcomes while the zoned open plan and team office had positive effects on employee work outcomes in comparison to open and activity-based office designs.

Intervention studies

Intervention studies are a special type of field experiment that is of interest to work design researchers because they aim to systematically examine the effect of training programs or changes in the workplace on employee outcomes. Although there are many approaches to designing interventions, if researchers aim to make causal conclusions about the effects of the intervention, they ought to design interventions that include at least two measurement points (pre- and post-intervention), as well as random assignment to at least one experimental and one control group (Eden, 2017). By ensuring that these conditions are met, researchers can establish temporal precedence and internal validity—essential components of causality.

Two types of interventions can be distinguished: bottom-up and top-down. Bottom-up work design interventions are proactively initiated and led by employees themselves, either individually or in small groups (e.g., job crafting; for more on bottom-up interventions see the relevant chapters in

220 TRANSFORMATIVE WORK DESIGN

this book). Top-down work redesign interventions are typically led by managers and examine how changing the work environment can impact individual and organizational outcomes. For example, Leslie Hammer and colleagues (2011) showed that organizations that trained supervisors to be more supportive of employees' work–life balance saw well-being improvements among their grocery store employees compared to stores who did not train their supervisors. However, this effect was only observed for those employees who had difficulty balancing their family and work lives. In fact, for employees with low family-to-work conflict, effects on well-being were even detrimental.

Summary

Experimental designs are useful for testing causal relationships between work design and outcome variables. However, they may face challenges in terms of external validity which is important for understanding the implications of work design. Experimental and intervention studies often include longitudinal elements by repeating measurements. In experimental designs, the outcome is measured after the manipulation or intervention has been implemented, allowing researchers to establish temporal precedence.

Methodological Considerations for Repeated Measures

Over the last few years, scholars have published insightful reviews of methodologies that include best practices and recommendations for various methods such as experiments (Lonati et al., 2018), longitudinal studies (Ployhart & Ward, 2011; Wang et al., 2017), including specific to intensive longitudinal designs such as diary studies (Gabriel et al., 2019) and team studies (Brown et al., 2020; Maynard et al., 2021). As experiments typically also include repeated measures, we focus the methodological considerations on issues specific to the repeated measurement of variables.

One of the major difficulties of longitudinal research is the decision about the *time lags* between assessments. For some research questions, it might be straightforward to determine whether the process unfolds over shorter (e.g., hours or days) or longer (e.g., months or years) time periods based on theoretical assumptions, prior meta-analytic evidence or simulation (Dormann & van de Ven, 2014; Ford et al., 2014). However, it may be more difficult to decide whether the time lag should be, for example, two weeks, four weeks, or eight weeks.

When the shape and speed of a temporal process is not yet known, more frequent measures are recommended as longer time lags can still be tested through statistical analysis. Given the growing body of longitudinal research, researchers can consult prior work to decide if they want to adopt similar or alternative time lags. To build empirical knowledge in the field, it is crucial that scholarly papers explicitly outline the decision-making process behind design choices in the method section, along with some descriptive analyses about time trends. For example, daily diary studies often control for time trends, but the effects of these control variables are not always reported. Similarly, describing the general change patterns (e.g., results from a latent growth curve model) over the study period would help other researchers to understand what kind of change to expect (e.g., speed and shape of change).

Another major challenge is *dropout*, which threatens the power of a study and can lead to biased samples (e.g., overrepresentation of women or workers with predominantly favorable work design conditions). Study dropout increases with longer time lags and observation periods. One reason for this is that participants often no longer feel connected to the research. For studies that run over longer periods of time, community building strategies may be helpful. For example, researchers can provide participants with study updates in between assessments (e.g., newsletter about study progress and findings) and personal feedback. It is crucial to refrain from offering insights that could change participants' perception or behavior related to the study research questions. Studies often also use monetary incentives to minimize dropout. To encourage commitment, a staggered scheme can be implemented in studies that require more time and effort. In such a scheme, participants get higher incentives for questionnaires earlier in the study compared to later stages in order to build commitment (Ribisl et al., 1996). Related to this, studies focusing on change processes should assess and manage *potential job, status* (e.g., reduction of work hours), and *work design changes* (e.g., change in leadership).

Many research questions focus on how individuals and teams in an organization adapt to work design changes (e.g., introduction of new technology, mergers that change team design). To draw clear conclusions about such questions, *pre-event or intervention data collection* would be needed. Having data available before an event or intervention takes place allows researchers to put the temporal process after the event or intervention into the context of the larger change processes (Bliese et al., 2017). For example, researchers can test if workers' performance fluctuates during the process of introducing new technology and if their performance returns to a prior level after an adaptation period. Many intervention designs which introduce a planned change to work design already employ such designs.

How Can Researchers Measure Work Design?

We discuss self- and other-report, occupational codes, and tracking/monitoring data as common assessment methods for work designs. These approaches come with benefits and disadvantages and we ultimately advocate for combined approaches to leverage the different benefits and overcome some disadvantages.

Surveys (self-report, other-report, and third-party observers)

Most commonly, researchers ask study participants to provide their impression of the conditions under which they work. A widely used example for such an instrument is the Work Design Questionnaire (Morgeson & Humphrey, 2006), which covers task, knowledge, and social characteristics along with the work context. The questionnaire asks employees to indicate the extent of their (dis)agreement with a number of statements that describe conditions at work.

Using self-reports to assess work design aligns with the theoretical assumption that it is the employee's perception of their work conditions that has an impact on their motivation, well-being, and performance. Nevertheless, there are methodological concerns associated with it, especially if all constructs of interest are measured via self-report (e.g., common method bias, Podsakoff et al., 2003). Other concerns include that self-report assessments are influenced by response styles (e.g., social desirability), cognitive biases (e.g., recall bias), and individual dispositions to process the environment, such as neuroticism (Semmer et al., 2004).

Alternatives to self-reports are observations or other reports. For observations, a researcher observes the worker and rates the activities and conditions using checklists and standardized questionnaires (Tomaschek et al., 2018). Such observations tend to be time-consuming and therefore not well suited for dynamic research questions (i.e., repeated observations). Early research comparing self-report with other sources concluded relative good alignment (Fried & Ferris, 1987); however, newer studies show that convergence between two sources may only be low to moderate and may depend on additional factors, such as the specific type of work design (e.g., better alignment for demands than control; Grebner et al., 2005) or individual differences (e.g., gender differences; Waldenström & Härenstam, 2008). Reasons for the limited overlap between employee assessments and observer ratings also relate to the ability to observe the work characteristic either due to the frequency of occurrence or the characteristic leads to an internal state and less observable behavior (e.g., mental states) (Semmer et al., 2004). Other parties in the organization, such as peers and supervisors, can also assess the work design of a focal employee.

However, as supervisors are typically in the position to shape the work design of their employees and therefore are also responsible for those conditions, they may have a more positive view on the conditions under which their employees have to perform the tasks than the focal employees do (Meier & Semmer, 2018).

Occupational codes

Researchers also use occupational dictionaries to code the work design features predominant in a specific occupation. For example, the Dictionary of Occupational Titles (O*NET) offers information on work design features, such as job complexity or emotional demands, and the International Standard Classification of Occupations (ISCO-88) clusters occupations according to skill level and specialization (e.g., range and complexity of tasks). These occupational classification systems offer a more objective assessment of work design and can be used to investigate research questions that focus on differences in exposure. For example, Susan Reh and colleagues (2021) investigated if employees in occupations with considerable emotional work demands (e.g., as in caring or social control professions), experience diminished or strengthened well-being across their working life. Although occupations explain a meaningful amount of variance in work design features (i.e., 16 percent of variance at the between-occupation level; Dierdorff & Morgeson, 2013), substantial variation remains within occupations. Occupation explains more variance in contextual characteristics, such as physical demands, than task and social characteristics, hence the usefulness of such occupational classification systems depends on the specific work design feature in question.

Tracking data and data originally collected for non-research purposes

Some researchers have used tracking data, labor statistics data, or publicly available data to assess work design features and their implications. Hengchen Dai and colleagues (2015) used data from a hand hygiene activity monitoring system to investigate the impact of shift duration on handwashing compliance in hospitals. The system tracked nurses' location and handwashing behavior using wristband-badges recognized by control units at soap dispensers. Additionally, the authors were able to calculate hours at work, hours off work, and safety compliance through this data. In another study by Paola Yam and colleagues (2023), labor statistics data and data from social media were used to investigate the relationship between increased use of robots in the workplace and employees' job insecurity. The authors analyzed robot prevalence data across the United States from the International Federation of Robotics and linked it to the frequency of people searching on job-recruiting webpages (e.g., Glassdoor) per year. These examples illustrate how data collected for legal and/or performance monitoring purposes can be used to assess work design features. However, they do not capture the individual workers' perception of their conditions and the associated psychological experiences.

Summary

Every assessment method has its own limitations. For example, although self-report measures are excellent to provide information about perceptions, meaning, and inner states, there are concerns regarding biased reporting and spurious findings. To mitigate these limitations, researchers may *mix different assessment methods* in a study. For example, our reviewed studies used monitoring, tracking, and HR systems in innovative ways to assess work design and reactions to it. However, these studies often overlook employee perception of work design, preventing them from explaining the reasons behind the outcomes. To bridge this gap, self-report assessments can be used to gain insight into employee perspectives.

Linking Work Design with Physiological Markers and Cognitive Processes

Much research is dedicated to what explains work design and how work design affects various outcomes. Some of these variables are best assessed using self-report measures, particularly variables related to inner states (e.g., motivation) and psychological processes. However, researchers also use other assessment techniques, especially when physiology, health, and cognition are of interest. We now discuss biomarkers and cognitive assessments.

Biomarkers

Biomarkers are indicators that are objectively measured to indicate biological or pathogenic processes (e.g., blood pressure, cortisol). Biomarkers can capture processes outside of consciousness and therefore may or may not overlap with someone's conscious experience. Nevertheless, biomarkers can help to better understand underlying biological mechanisms and outcomes of experiences at work. The majority of researchers using biomarkers focus on how work is best designed so that employees' well-being and health flourishes or at least is not impaired. Various indicators can be differentiated, and we discuss electrodermal, cardiovascular, endocrinological, metabolic, and genetic ones here.

Electrodermal indicators measure sympathetic nervous system activity through skin conductance and can indicate immediate strain responses (e.g., Cendales-Ayala et al., 2017). *Cardiovascular indicators,* such as blood pressure, heart rate, and heart rate variability, reflect the body's response to stress after repeated exposure to stressful work design. For example, recent studies linked cardiovascular indicators to social work characteristics (e.g., Baethge et al., 2020). *Endocrinological indicators,* of which salivary cortisol is most commonly used, indicate immediate or chronic physiological activation in response to stress (e.g., Dettmers et al., 2016). *Metabolic indicators,* including glucose, waist-to-hip ratio, insulin, or cholesterol, can be used to identify adjustment points following prolonged exposure to unfavorable work design (e.g., Fried et al., 2013) *Genetic indicators* can be used to investigate how individuals play a role in shaping work characteristics and ultimately employee outcomes (e.g., well-being), speaking to an interaction between the person and their environment to produce relevant outcomes (e.g., Li et al., 2016).

These studies demonstrate that research using biomarkers align with findings from self-report studies on well-being and health. However, it is of note that such objective measures come with unique challenges and threats to accuracy. One factor is the correct handling of the equipment, which can be difficult to ensure when participants are asked to do it themselves. In addition, indicators may be influenced by socio-demographic variables (e.g., skin conductance changes with age and during the menstrual cycle), patterns across the day (e.g., cortisol), and changes in lifestyle when assessed over longer time periods (e.g., change in workout routine).

Cognition

One of the main outcomes of work design is performance and cognitive processes are relevant to explaining that linkage. However, researchers are also interested in how work design may have an impact on cognition and cognitive processes in itself as the implications go far beyond work performance (Parker et al., 2021).

In the context of work design, cognitive processes can be of interest in the form of learning and knowledge acquisition. For example, in some intervention studies, researchers use knowledge tests at the end of a training to ensure participants acquired the knowledge relevant for the intervention. In one of the earliest studies on work design and cognition, Melvin Kohn and Carmi Schooler (1978) investigated the relation between job complexity and intellectual flexibility over 10 years. To assess intellectual flexibility, they used several indicators ranging from problem-solving tasks to perceptual tests. Their analyses revealed that job complexity had a positive lagged effect on intellectual flexibility, as did flexibility on job complexity. Erik Gonzalez-Mulé and Bethany Cockburn (2020) investigated if job control and cognitive ability would buffer the detrimental effects of unfavorable work design on health and mortality. In the study, cognitive abilities were assessed through five different subtests (i.e., word list recall, digit span, category verbal fluency, number series, backward counting) assessing indicators of episodic memory, working memory, cognitive flexibility, and fluid intelligence. The authors found that these cognitive abilities buffered against the detrimental effect of unfavorable work design on mental health but there was no effect on physical health.

These studies showcase that the work design to which people are exposed and general mental capacities interact with each other. However, because these studies use general measures or averages across different subtests, it is unclear which cognitive processes actually drive these effects. In a different example, Christopher Rosen and colleagues (2016) used the Stroop test in a daily diary setting to assess diminished regulatory resources (e.g., reduced cognitive attention). When completing the Stroop test, participants are confronted with a discrepancy between a word that describes a color (e.g., red) and the word that is printed in a color (e.g., yellow). Participants then must report the color that is spelled out as fast as possible. The authors used reaction time to represent depletion of cognitive resources and showed that experiencing incivility at work lowers the reaction time on the Stroop test which instigated incivility later in the day. Hence, using assessments to capture more specific cognitive processes seems promising. However, researchers have also warned against using task-based assessments that were originally not designed to capture individual differences and that have been developed in the lab. For example, Kyra Göbel and colleagues (2022) presented meta-analytical evidence that task-based and self-report measures of thought control do not correlate with each other, calling into question what kind of psychological processes the two types of assessments represent.

Summary

Biomarkers and cognitive assessments are useful to assess outcomes that are of increasing importance in work design research and offer an objective assessment of these processes. As previously discussed, there are benefits and disadvantages to subjective and (more) objective assessment modes as both come with their distinct sources for error. For biomarkers and cognitive assessments, the handling of the instruments can further influence the accuracy of the assessment. In addition, including biomarkers and cognitive testing in studies can increase the burden on participants and create feelings of intrusiveness. For example, assessment of biomarkers can negatively influence participation in the assessment wave that follows (although no longer-term effects on participation were found) (Pashazadeh et al., 2021).

The Future is Longitudinal—Future Directions for Methods in Work Design Research

The reviewed literature implies that, moving forward, the foundation of research on work design is likely to be longitudinal given that experimental and intervention studies also advocate for incorporation of repeated measurements to be able to test processes and draw firm conclusions. This makes sense as, at the core, work design research questions involve individual change processes that happen over time. Not only do core work design theories imply that work design triggers change in outcomes, work design itself also changes over time. The last few years were a powerful illustration of how work changes gradually (e.g., through accommodation of the aging workforce and migrant workers or rise of project-based and team-based work), but also suddenly (e.g., working-from-home mandates across the world due to COVID-19), and how these changes have implications for workers and organizations. It would be unreasonable to assume that this trend is slowing down as many experts expect that work will change in the next few years for the majority of workers due to the rise and implementation of automation and artificial intelligence. By collecting data at multiple time points over a meaningful period of time, researchers can capture how work and employees are changing, and how these changes dynamically interact with other. A particular strength of longitudinal designs is the establishment of temporal precedence; however, controlling for alternative explanations is much more challenging. We noted that more and more researchers make clever use of existing data (e.g., email exchanges, monitoring data). They also combine different studies that methodologically complement each other into one paper. These strategies have the potential to rigorously test research models and truly advance our body of knowledge. Before closing, we highlight two exciting methodological areas, namely how the social context can be incorporated in study designs and how new technologies such as virtual reality can be used to simulate work environments.

The social context as part of the study design: Dyads, teams, and networks

Given the shift from production to knowledge and service industries, the majority of employees now face work conditions characterized by interdependence and teamwork. Work design scholars are interested in how the social context shapes the work design of employees and teams, but also how the social dynamics influence work design. Studies can be designed to capture the social dynamics directly by sampling dyads, teams, and social networks. *Dyadic* studies can be used to investigate relationships between two people (e.g., supervisor and a focal employee, two co-workers). For example, dyadic data could be used to investigate whether the job crafting behavior of one employee, aimed at gaining high-quality feedback, positively influences their own performance and negatively impacts the performance of their co-worker who provides the feedback. That is because the employee would need to invest some of their work time into providing the feedback. To gather *team* data, researchers typically approach organizations and collect data from multiple teams within one or multiple organizations. Because individual employees are then clustered within teams, researchers typically use multi-level analysis to account for the nested data structure (Maynard et al., 2021). Team research questions can focus on the individual or team level. For example, Erik Gonzalez-Mulé and colleagues (2016) focused on work design at the team level and investigated under what conditions autonomous teams can be high performing teams.

Another approach to capture social dynamics at work is to focus on *social networks*. People not only have relationships with their leaders and direct co-workers but with multiple actors in their professional environment and these relationships can span across hierarchies, units or departments, and even organizations. Social network analysis can provide information on more quantitative (e.g., size) or qualitative (e.g., centrality which refers to the influence of a node in a network) indicators of the network (Zappa & Lomi, 2015). For example, Meredith Woehler and colleagues (2021) focused on network widening versus narrowing during an organizational change process and the role of job insecurity in these processes. To assess network widening and narrowing, the authors analyzed 15 million emails exchanged between the employees in the two organizations over two years.

Simulate the work environment: Virtual and augmented reality

Augmented reality (AR) and virtual reality (VR) are immersive technologies that can provide researchers with unique opportunities to conduct high-fidelity simulations and study different work environments in a controlled setting. These tools can also be applied using simulation experiments and intervention designs, thus increasing methodological rigor and test causality. For example, virtual reality can be used to improve employee compliance with safety routines or use gamification to improve employee learning (Howard & Gutworth, 2020). Other areas of inquiry where AR or VR may be helpful in providing insight are hybrid work arrangements, ergonomic designs, and virtual workspaces. For example, researchers can design simulation studies using VR to explore patterns of communication, office design for optimal productivity, and work satisfaction.

References

Baethge, A., Vahle-Hinz, T., & Rigotti, T. (2020). Coworker support and its relationship to allostasis during a workday: A diary study on trajectories of heart rate variability during work. *Journal of Applied Psychology 105*(5), 506–526. https://doi.org/10.1037/apl0000445

Bliese, P. D., Adler, A. B., & Flynn, P. J. (2017). Transition processes: A review and synthesis integrating methods and theory. *Annual Review of Organizational Psychology and Organizational Behavior 4*, 263–286. https://doi.org/10.1146/annurev-orgpsych-032516-113213

Brown, O., Power, N., & Conchie, S. M. (2020). Immersive simulations with extreme teams. *Organizational Psychology Review 10*(3–4), 115–135. https://doi.org/10.1177/2041386620926037

Cendales-Ayala, B., Useche, S. A., Gómez-Ortiz, V., & Bocarejo, J. P. (2017). Bus operators' responses to job strain: An experimental test of the job demand-control model. *Journal of Occupational Health Psychology 22*(4), 518–527. https://doi.org/10.1037/ocp0000040

Chong, S., Huang, Y., & Chang, C.-H. D. (2020). Supporting interdependent telework employees: A moderated-mediation model linking daily COVID-19 task setbacks to next-day work withdrawal. *Journal of Applied Psychology 105*(12), 1408.

Cronin, M. A., & Vancouver, J. B. (2019). The only constant is change: Expanding theory by incorporating dynamic propoerties into one's models. In S. E. Humphrey & J. M. LeBreton (Eds.), *The handbook of multilevel theory, measurement, and analysis* (pp. 89–114). American Psychological Association. http://ebookcentral.proquest.com/lib/rug/detail.action?docID=5606613

Dai, H., Milkman, K. L., Hofmann, D. A., & Staats, B. R. (2015). The impact of time at work and time off from work on rule compliance: The case of hand hygiene in health care. *Journal of Applied Psychology 100*(3), 846–862. https://doi.org/10.1037/a0038067

Dettmers, J., Vahle-Hinz, T., Bamberg, E., Friedrich, N., & Keller, M. (2016). Extended work availability and its relation with start-of-day mood and cortisol. *Journal of Occupational Health Psychology 21*(1), 105–118. https://doi.org/10.1037/a0039602

Dierdorff, E. C., & Morgeson, F. P. (2013). Getting what the occupation gives: Exploring multilevel links between work design and occupational values. *Personnel Psychology 66*(3), 687–721. https://doi.org/10.1111/peps.12023

Dormann, C., & van de Ven, B. (2014). Timing in methods for studying psychosocial factors at work. In M. F. Dollard, A. Shimazu, R. B. Nordin, P. Brough, & M. R. Tuckey (Eds.), *Psychosocial factors at work in the Asia Pacific* (pp. 89–116). Springer.

Eden, D. (2017). Field experiments in organizations. *Annual Review of Organizational Psychology and Organizational Behavior 4*, 91–122. https://doi.org/10.1146/annurev-orgpsych-041015-062400

Ford, M. T., Matthews, R. A., Wooldridge, J. D., Mishra, V., Kakar, U. M., & Strahan, S. R. (2014). How do occupational stressor-strain effects vary with time? A review and meta-analysis of the relevance of time lags in longitudinal studies. *Work & Stress 28*(1), 9–30. https://doi.org/10.1080/02678373.2013.877096

Fried, Y., & Ferris, G. R. (1987). The validity of the job characteristics model: A review and meta-analysis. *Personnel Psychology 40*(2), 287–322. https://doi.org/https://doi.org/10.1111/j.1744-6570.1987.tb00605.x

Fried, Y., Grant, A. M., Levi, A. S., Hadani, M., & Slowik, L. H. (2007). Job design in temporal context: A career dynamics perspective. *Journal of Organizational Behavior 28*(7), 911–927. https://doi.org/10.1002/job.486

Fried, Y., Laurence, G. A., Shirom, A., Melamed, S., Toker, S., Berliner, S., & Shapira, I. (2013). The relationship between job enrichment and abdominal obesity: A longitudinal field study of apparently healthy individuals. *Journal of Occupational Health Psychology 18*(4), 458–468. https://doi.org/10.1037/a0033730

Gabriel, A. S., Podsakoff, N. P., Beal, D. J., Scott, B. A., Sonnentag, S., Trougakos, J. P., & Butts, M. M. (2019). Experience sampling methods: A discussion of critical trends and considerations for scholarly advancement. *Organizational Research Methods 22*(4), 969–1006. https://doi.org/10.1177/1094428118802626

Giessner, S. R., Dawson, J. F., Horton, K. E., & West, M. (2023). The impact of supportive leadership on employee outcomes during organizational mergers: An organizational-level field study. *Journal of Applied Psychology 108*(4), 686–697. https://doi.org/10.1037/apl0001042

Göbel, K., Hensel, L., Schultheiss, O. C., & Niessen, C. (2022). Meta-analytic evidence shows no relationship between task-based and self-report measures of thought control. *Applied Cognitive Psychology 36*(3), 659–672.

Gonzalez-Mulé, E., & Cockburn, B. S. (2020). This job is (literally) killing me: A moderated-mediated model linking work characteristics to mortality. *Journal of Applied Psychology 106*(1), 140–151. https://doi.org/10.1037/apl0000501

Gonzalez-Mulé, E., Courtright, S. H., DeGeest, D., Seong, J. Y., & Hong, D. S. (2016). Channeled autonomy: The joint effects of autonomy and feedback on team performance through organizational goal clarity. *Journal of Management 42*(7), 2018–2033. https://doi.org/10.1177/0149206314535443

Grebner, S., Semmer, N. K., & Elfering, A. (2005). Working conditions and three types of well-being: A longitudinal study with self-report and rating data. *Journal of Occupational Health Psychology 10*(1), 31–43.

Grimm, K. J., Ram, N., & Estabrook, R. (2017). *Growth modeling: Structural equation and multilevel modeling approaches.* Guilford Press.

Hamaker, E. L., Kuiper, R. M., & Grasman, R. P. (2015). A critique of the cross-lagged panel model. *Psychological Methods 20*(1), 102–116. https://doi.org/10.1037/a0038889

Hammer, L. B., Kossek, E. E., Anger, W. K., Bodner, T., & Zimmerman, K. L. (2011). Clarifying work-family intervention processes: The roles of work–family conflict and family-supportive supervisor behaviors. *Journal of Applied Psychology 96*(1), 134–150. https://doi.org/10.1037/a0020927

Hanges, P. J., & Wang, M. (2012). Seeking the holy grail in organizational science: Uncovering causality through research design. In S. W. J. Kozlowski (Ed.), *The Oxford handbook of organizational psychology* (Vol. *1*, pp. 79–116). Oxford University Press.

Howard, M. C., & Gutworth, M. B. (2020). A meta-analysis of virtual reality training programs for social skill development. *Computers & Education 144*, 103707. https://doi.org/10.1016/j.compedu.2019.103707

Humphrey, S. E., Nahrgang, J. D., & Morgeson, F. P. (2007). Integrating motivational, social, and contextual work design features: A meta-analytic summary and theoretical extension of the work design literature. *Journal of Applied Psychology 92*(5), 1332–1356. https://doi.org/10.1037/0021-9010.92.5.1332

Klonek, F., Zhang, F., Nguyen, H., Johnson, A., Liu, Y., & Parker, S. (2023). The role of individual goal orientations in shaping skill utilization over time: A four-year longitudinal study. *European Journal of Work and Organizational Psychology 32*(3), 346–359. https://doi.org/10.1080/1359432X.2022.2160325

Kohn, M. L., & Schooler, C. (1978). The reciprocal effects of the substantive complexity of work and intellectual flexibility: A longitudinal assessment. *American Journal of Sociology 84*(1), 24–52.

Li, W. D., Schaubroeck, J. M., Xie, J. L., & Keller, A. C. (2018). Is being a leader a mixed blessing? A dual-pathway model linking leadership role occupancy to well-being. *Journal of Organizational Behavior 39*(8), 971–989. https://doi.org/10.1002/job.2273

Li, W. D., Zhang, Z., Song, Z. L., & Arvey, R. D. (2016). It is also in our nature: Genetic influences on work characteristics and in explaining their relationships with well-being. *Journal of Organizational Behavior 37*(6), 868–888. https://doi.org/10.1002/job.2079

Loft, S., Pearcy, B., & Remington, R. W. (2015). Varying the complexity of the prospective memory decision process in an air traffic control simulation. *Zeitschrift für Psychologie, 219*(2), 77–84. https://doi.org/10.1027/2151-2604/a000051

Lonati, S., Quiroga, B. F., Zehnder, C., & Antonakis, J. (2018). On doing relevant and rigorous experiments: Review and recommendations. *Journal of Operations Management 64*, 19–40. https://doi.org/10.1016/j.jom.2018.10.003

Maynard, M. T., Conroy, S., Lacerenza, C. N., & Barnes, L. Y. (2021). Teams in the wild are not extinct, but challenging to research: A guide for conducting impactful team field research with 10 recommendations and 10 best practices. *Organizational Psychology Review 11*(3), 274–318. https://doi.org/10.1177/2041386620986597

McArdle, J. J. (2009). Latent variable modeling of differences and changes with longitudinal data. *Annual Review of Psychology 60*, 577–605. https://doi.org/10.1146/annurev.psych.60.110707.163612

Meier, L. L., Keller, A. C., Reis, D., & Nohe, C. (2023). On the asymmetry of losses and gains: Implications of changing work conditions for well-being. *Journal of Applied Psychology 108* (8), 1408–1424. https://doi.org/10.1037/apl0001080

Meier, L. L., & Semmer, N. K. (2018). Illegitimate tasks as assessed by incumbents and supervisors: Converging only modestly but predicting strain as assessed by incumbents, supervisors, and partners. *European Journal of Work and Organizational Psychology 27*(6), 764–776. https://doi.org/10.1080/1359432X.2018.1526785

Mell, J. N., DeChurch, L. A., Leenders, R. T. A. J., & Contractor, N. (2020). Identity asymmetries: An experimental investigation of social identity and information exchange in multiteam systems. *Academy of Management Journal 63*(5), 1561–1590. https://doi.org/10.5465/amj.2018.0325

Morgeson, F. P., & Humphrey, S. E. (2006). The work design questionnaire (WDQ): Developing and validating a comprehensive measure for assessing job design and the nature of work. *Journal of Applied Psychology 91*(6), 1321–1339. https://doi.org/10.1037/0021-9010.91.6.1321

Nesselroade, J. R., & Baltes, P. B. (1979). *Longitudinal research in the study of behavior and development.* Academic Press.

Oldham, G. R., & Hackman, J. R. (2010). Not what it was and not what it will be: The future of job design research. *Journal of Organizational Behavior 31*(2–3), 463–479. https://doi.org/10.1002/job.678

Parker, S. K., Morgeson, F. P., & Johns, G. (2017). One hundred years of work design research: Looking back and looking forward. *Journal of Applied Psychology 102*(3), 403–420. https://doi.org/10.1037/apl0000106

Parker, S. K., Ward, M. K., & Fisher, G. (2021). Can high-quality jobs help adults learn new tricks? A multi-disciplinary review of work design for cognition. *Academy of Management Annals 15*(2), 406–454. https://doi.org/10.5465/annals.2019.0057

Pashazadeh, F., Cernat, A., & Sakshaug, J. W. (2021). The effects of biological data collection in longitudinal surveys on subsequent wave cooperation. In P. Lynn (Ed.), *Advances in longitudinal survey methodology* (pp. 100–121). Wiley. https://doi.org/10.1002/9781119376965.ch5

Pindek, S., Zhou, Z. E., Kessler, S. R., Krajcevska, A., & Spector, P. E. (2021). Workdays are not created equal: Job satisfaction and job stressors across the workweek. *Human Relations 74*(9), 1447–1472. https://doi.org/10.1177/0018726720924444

Pitchforth, J., Nelson, E. C., van den Helder, M., & Oosting, W. (2020). The work environment pilot: An experiment to determine the optimal office design for a technology company. *PLoS ONE 15*(5), e0232943. https://doi.org/10.1371/journal.pone.0232943

Ployhart, R. E., & Vandenberg, R. J. (2010). Longitudinal research: The theory, design, and analysis of change. *Journal of Management 36*(1), 94–120.

Ployhart, R. E., & Ward, A.-K. (2011). The "quick start guide" for conducting and publishing longitudinal research. *Journal of Business and Psychology 26*(4), 413–422. https://doi.org/10.1007/s10869-011-9209-6

Podsakoff, P. M., MacKenzie, S. B., Lee, J.-Y., & Podsakoff, N. P. (2003). Common method biases in behavioral research: A critical review of the literature and recommended remedies. *Journal of Applied Psychology 88*(5), 879. https://doi.org/10.1037/0021-9010.88.5.879

Reh, S., Wieck, C., & Scheibe, S. (2021). Experience, vulnerability, or overload? Emotional job demands as moderator in trajectories of emotional well-being and job satisfaction across the working lifespan. *Journal of Applied Psychology 106*(11), 1734–1749. https://doi.org/10.1037/apl0000859

Ribisl, K. M., Walton, M. A., Mowbray, C. T., Luke, D. A., Davidson II, W. S., & Bootsmiller, B. J. (1996). Minimizing participant attrition in panel studies through the use of effective retention and tracking strategies: Review and recommendations. *Evaluation and Program Planning 19*(1), 1–25. https://doi.org/10.1016/0149-7189(95)00037-2

Rosen, C. C., Dimotakis, N., Cole, M. S., Taylor, S. G., Simon, L. S., Smith, T. A., & Reina, C. S. (2020). When challenges hinder: An investigation of when and how challenge stressors impact employee outcomes. *Journal of Applied Psychology 105*(10), 1181–1206. https://doi.org/10.1037/apl0000483

Rosen, C. C., Koopman, J., Gabriel, A. S., & Johnson, R. E. (2016). Who strikes back? A daily investigation of when and why incivility begets incivility. *Journal of Applied Psychology 101*(11), 1620–1634. https://doi.org/10.1037/apl0000140

Semmer, N. K., Grebner, S., & Elfering, A. (2004). Beyond self-report: Using observational, physiological, and siutation-based measures in research on occupational stress. In P. L. Perrewé & D. C. Ganster (Eds.), *Research in occupational stress and well-being. Emotional and physiological processes and positive intervention strategies* (Vol. 3, pp. 205–263). Elsevier.

Singer, J. D., & Willett, J. B. (2003). *Applied longitudinal data analysis: Modeling change and event occurrence.* Oxford University Press.

Somaraju, A. V., Griffin, D. J., Olenick, J., Chang, C.-H. D., & Kozlowski, S. W. J. (2022). The dynamic nature of interpersonal conflict and psychological strain in extreme work settings. *Journal of Occupational Health Psychology 27*(1), 53–73. https://doi.org/10.1037/ocp0000290

Tomaschek, A., Lanfer, S. S. L., Melzer, M., Debitz, U., & Buruck, G. (2018). Measuring work-related psychosocial and physical risk factors using workplace observations: A validation study of the "healthy workplace screening." *Safety Science 101*, 197–208. https://doi.org/10.1016/j.ssci.2017.09.006

Vangrieken, K., De Cuyper, N., & De Witte, H. (2023). Karasek's activation hypothesis: A longitudinal test of within-person relationships. *Journal of Organizational Behavior 44*(3), 495–518. https://doi.org/10.1002/job.2669

Waldenström, K., & Härenstam, A. (2008). Does the job demand–control model correspond to externally assessed demands and control for both women and men? *Scandinavian Journal of Public Health 36*(3), 242–249. https://doi.org/10.1177/1403494807085079

Wang, M., Beal, D. J., Chan, D., Newman, D. A., Vancouver, J. B., & Vandenberg, R. J. (2017). Longitudinal research: A panel discussion on conceptual issues, research design, and statistical techniques. *Work, Aging and Retirement 3*(1), 1–24. https://doi.org/10.1093/workar/waw033

Wang, M., Zhou, L., & Zhang, Z. (2016). Dynamic modeling. *Annual Review of Organizational Psychology and Organizational Behavior 3*(1), 241–266. https://doi.org/10.1146/annurev-orgpsych-041015-062553

Woehler, M., Floyd, T. M., Shah, N., Marineau, J. E., Sung, W., Grosser, T. J., Fagan, J., & Labianca, G. J. (2021). Turnover during a corporate merger: How workplace network change influences staying. *Journal of Applied Psychology 106*(12), 1939–1949. https://doi.org/10.1037/apl0000864

Yam, K. C., Tang, P. M., Jackson, J. C., Su, R., & Gray, K. (2023). The rise of robots increases job insecurity and maladaptive workplace behaviors: Multimethod evidence. *Journal of Applied Psychology 108*(5), 850–870. https://doi.org/10.1037/apl0001045

Zappa, P., & Lomi, A. (2015). The analysis of multilevel networks in organizations: Models and empirical tests. *Organizational Research Methods 18*(3), 542–569. https://doi.org/10.1177/1094428115579225

Appendix

Approach for Literature Review

Search terms (to be listed in abstract)

work design or job design or job control or autonomy or skill variety or task variety or task significance or feedback from job or feedback from others or task identity or workload or time pressure or social support or job complexity or task interdependence or information processing or problem solving or ergonomics or physical demands or work conditions or performance constraints or job insecurity

Inclusion criteria

Published between 2012 to 2022 and in one of the following journals: *Academy of Management Journal, Journal of Applied Psychology, Journal of Occupational Health Psychology, Journal of Management, Journal of Organizational Behavior,* and *Journal of Vocational Psychology*

Exclusion criteria

Editorials, reviews, or meta-analysis; student sample; studies focusing on work-family interface only (considered here as a consequence of work design); studies focusing on leadership behavior without measuring any leader behavior that has an impact on others (e.g., papers that focus on leader personality or behavioral tendencies); studies focusing on bottom-up work design behaviors (e.g., job crafting, I-deals) without including top-down work design as these are considered proactive behaviors with the goal to change the work design, not work design itself

PART 3

ANTECEDENTS OF WORK DESIGN

Global and National Factors Shaping Work Design

David Holman and Anthony Rafferty

Introduction

Based on an evolving body of research, there is now a greater appreciation of how work design is shaped by the individual, organizational, national, transnational, and global contexts within which it is embedded. This chapter focuses on the more "distal" national and global factors that influence work design. These include national institutions (e.g., trade unions, employment regulation, safety regulation), national institutional regimes (i.e., national configurations of institutions), as well as other national and global influences relating to the economy (e.g., GDP, employment rates), migration, supply chains, and climate change. A key assumption is that these distal factors affect work design by shaping the decisions made about organizing work by job holders, managers, and other key organizational stakeholders (Parker et al., 2017).

The chapter provides an overview of current and emerging research on the national, international, and global influences on work design (see Table 9.1). Specifically, we focus on the role of institutions is shaping work design, not only because the evidence is perhaps more extensive in relation to institutional factors, but also because the influences of other distal factors (e.g., climate change) are likely to be "filtered" by institutions. This chapter also focuses on national factors, especially national economy, as well as cross-national factors such as migration and climate change, which are two significant global factors with the capacity to shape work design but whose influence is somewhat understudied by work design scholars. Understanding these distal influences on work design is important because they provide the broad context in which individuals and organizations are embedded and hence deepen our understanding of how decisions about organizing work design are made, and therefore about the factors shaping individual, as well as organizational, performance, and well-being.

David Holman and Anthony Rafferty, *Global and National Factors Shaping Work Design*. In: *Transformative Work Design*. Edited by: Sharon K. Parker et al., Oxford University Press. © Society for Industrial and Organizational Psychology (2025). DOI: 10.1093/oso/9780197692554.003.0009

238 TRANSFORMATIVE WORK DESIGN

Table 9.1 Summary of National and Global Influences on Work Design

Factor Type	Examples	Proposed Mechanisms	Extent of Evidence
National *Institution*			
Trade Union	Collective bargaining structure, works councils, workplace representatives	Increase power of worker to secure better quality work designs	Moderate
Employment Policies	Employment protection legislation, welfare provision, active labor market policies (e.g., welfare to work programs)	Mixed effects. May tighten labor market, increase power of the worker to secure better quality work designs, managers improve work design quality to retain/attract workers; however, work first rather than human capital focused active labor market policies may increase the supply of low skilled labor, providing disincentives to upskilling, innovation or technological adoption	Low
Training Systems	On-job/off-job vocational and general skills training, formal education systems	Increases in skills enable organizations to provide better quality work designs	Low
Health & Safety	Hard laws, soft laws (e.g., codes of conduct) and enforcement	Laws and enforcement force reorganization of work	Very low
Institutional Regime	National systems of institutions (e.g., social democratic, Coordinated, Liberal)	As above	Moderate
Economy	Unemployment level, GDP	Tightens labor market (see above)	Low to Moderate
Global			
Supply chain	Supplier contracts	Foster reorganization of work but effects on work design quality depend on contract; high supply chain pressures on cost may lead to deterioration of employment practices	Very low

Factor Type	Examples	Proposed Mechanisms	Extent of Evidence
National Institution			
Migration	Movement of high-skill and low-skill labor	Increases/decreases employment in sectors with high/low quality work designs; emigration labor market effects on origin countries (e.g., skills shortages and brain drain)	Very low
Climate Change	Increasing temperatures, extreme weather events	Direct effects on job demands, greening of economy	Very low

National Institutions and Institutional Regimes

Cross-national comparative organizational research has long highlighted the role of national institutions in shaping organizational strategies and practices (Mueller, 1994). Institutions can be broadly defined as "codifiable systems of social structures" consisting of norms, rules, beliefs, and organizations that enable, guide, and motivate specific behaviors (Gräbner & Ghorbani, 2019; Greif, 2006). At the national level, institutions relevant to work design include trade unions, employment policies, training and education systems, and health and safety regulations. In the following section, we will discuss the research that has examined how these national institutions may influence work design. Following the discussion of national institutional factors, we focus on research that has examined how work design is shaped by national institutional regimes, which can be defined as national systems or conglomerations of institutions. In particular, institutional theories, such as varieties of capitalism (Hall & Soskice, 2001) and employment regime theory (Gallie, 2007), propose that national institutional regimes systematically vary between countries and that this variation results in cross-national variation in organizational features such as work design.

National institutions

A key element of the national institutional context within which organizations operate is the nature of trade union arrangements. Trade unions exert influence on organizational decision-making through involvement in sectoral and national collective bargaining, national coordination bodies, as well as works councils and workplace representatives. When these forms of worker involvement are extensive, and backed by high union membership, trade unions are likely to exert influence on organizational decision-making about work design and other areas that may indirectly affect work design (e.g., securing improvements in skill then enables more complex jobs to be crafted) (Culpepper & Thelen, 2007).

Evidence for the influence of trade unions on work design comes from cross-national surveys (Dollard & Neser, 2013, Eurofound, 2013; cf., Piasana, 2023) and case studies (Hoque, 2017). For example, based on survey data from 19 EU countries, Ingrid Esser and Karen Olsen (2012) found union membership density and collective bargaining coverage to be positively associated with job autonomy, and Francis Green and colleagues (2022) found that union recognition in the United Kingdom workplaces was associated with lower workload. A case study by Maxime Bellego and colleagues (2023) illuminated how Trade unions in a French telecommunications organization used firm and workplace institutions (e.g., works councils, trade union reps) to shape a work reorganization initiative in ways that protected worker interests (i.e., well-being, reduced psychosocial risks) by enhancing job autonomy and employee skills. This case study and others show that the ability of trade unions to shape work design not only depends on the extent of involvement in workplace decision making, but also on union aims, employer behavior, and the role of regulation and the state in supporting collective bargaining institutions and trade union membership (Hoque, 2017, Simms, 2022). Indeed, this might explain the negative relationship between trade union representation and job autonomy in the United Kingdom (Eisele & Schneider, 2020; Gallie et al., 2004). This negative relationship could occur because UK trade unions are prevalent in sectors with low pay and simplified work designs but struggle to improve work design (for exceptions, see Simms, 2017; Hoque, 2017) due to organizational and government strategies and weak regulation that seeks to limit union power and institutional involvement (Simms, 2022).

National employment policies include employment protection legislation (e.g., hiring and firing laws), welfare provision (e.g., unemployment and sickness benefits), and full employment and active labor market policies (e.g., subsidized employment, welfare-to-work programs). Strict employment protection guards against unfair dismissal, welfare provision can reduce the risks of job loss, and active labor market policies that foster worker skills (as opposed to "work-first" programs that increase the supply of unskilled labor) can tighten the labor market. For workers, these conditions may increase their capability to resist work design practices deleterious to well-being (e.g., job simplification) and to avoid taking jobs with low quality work designs (e.g., low autonomy, high demands, standardized tasks). In contrast, an increased focus on "work-first" active labor market policy can lead to increased mandatory requirements for people outside employment to take on any form of paid work and hence decrease the capability of workers to avoid jobs with low quality work designs (Rafferty & Wiggan, 2011). For managers, employment protections may encourage investment in high quality work designs as a means of retaining and attracting employees. (Gustavsen, 2007) or may increase labor hoarding rather than layoffs during economic downturns, thereby reducing the loss of firm specific skills (Burda & Hunt, 2011). Evidence for the effects of national employment policies is limited but supportive. For example, relative to other countries, European countries with strict employment protection legislation have a higher proportion of high quality work designs (Lorenz & Valeyre, 2005) and are less susceptible to declines in cognitive demand (Eurofound, 2015).

National training systems concern the practices through which vocational and general skills are developed, such as on-the-job training, formal training within firms, and formal education systems. Extensive national training systems are characterized by high levels of vocational and general training, both on-the-job and off-the-job, that seek to develop general, vocational and, in particular, job specific skills. One perspective is that extensive national training systems help to foster higher quality work designs because they produce a skilled workforce that allows organizations to provide jobs with higher quality work designs (e.g., higher autonomy, more challenging and complex demands) (Prais et al., 1989) and because highly skilled workers have more power to demand high quality jobs. There is evidence to suggest such effects. National economies with more skilled workers tend to have better quality work designs (Aspøy, 2020; Eurofound, 2017; Stier, 2015) and a study by Esser and Olsen (2012) using data from 19 European countries found that on-the-job training, but not general vocational training, was associated with higher job discretion. However, Tove Mogstad Aspøy (2020, p. 231) has argued that evidence such as this does not necessarily indicate that having more highly skilled employees leads to better quality work design, largely because worker skills are typically a relatively minor factor in decisions about work organization within firms (Ashton et al., 2017). Rather, it is technological change, firm strategy, and other institutional influences that drive improvements in skilled work and high quality work designs (Osterman, 1995), which national training systems respond to by seeking to supply the skills required by these changes. Extensive national training systems do not, therefore, cause high quality work design but play a vital role in supplying the higher-level skills needed for high quality work designs. This process of upskilling also helps workers to obtain high-skill jobs (which typically have higher quality work design), as high-level skills signal to employers during selection processes that the worker has the correct competences and abilities to do the job. Katharina Dengler (2019) illustrated this process in a study that compared the effects of different initiatives that sought to help the unemployed back to work in Germany. The study revealed that initiatives which upskilled participants with job relevant skills (e.g., firm training, vocational training) increased the likelihood of obtaining jobs with high quality work designs and avoiding jobs with low quality work designs (e.g., excessive work demands) compared to initiatives that didn't involve training (subsidized work) or focused on developing general skills (classroom training).

National workplace safety institutions have three key characteristics: (1) the extent to which safety is regulated by "hard law" (i.e., legally binding agreements that precisely specify legal safety thresholds) and "soft" law (i.e., non-binding agreements, voluntary codes of conduct, and national safety standards) (Leka & Jain, 2022); (2) the extent to which state and non-state actors are responsible for formulating regulation, and; (3) the nature and effectiveness of the instruments used to ensure compliance (e.g., insurance incentives, legal sanction, and enforcement agencies) (Rothstein et al., 2020). These institutional structures vary by country. For example, in Germany, safety regulation is based largely on soft law formulated by social mutual insurance bodies (Berufsgenossenschaften [BG]) that are funded by employers and governed with social partners, with compliance enforced through risk-based premiums, fines, and sanctions issued by BG inspectorates. The state supports this through legislation and inspectorates that aid BG self-regulation and deter non-compliance. In contrast, in the United Kingdom, safety regulation is based largely on hard laws devised by the state (as well as some soft regulatory frameworks; Mackay et al., 2004) that are enforced through a state-funded inspectorate.

Although national safety institutions are primarily orientated toward the prevention of employee injury and sickness, they may directly affect work design because, for example, regulations proscribing limits to physical activity (e.g., lifting), working time or work tasks may affect job demands (e.g., physical demands, workload), and job resources (e.g., job autonomy, task variety) (ILO, 1990). National safety institutions may also indirectly shape work design by requiring or encouraging organizations to engage in workplace safety initiatives that focus on the reorganization of work. However, there is a lack of systematic evidence for the effects of national safety institutions on work design. Rather, research has tended to focus on whether national safety institutions (Arocena & Nunez, 2009; Teufer et al., 2019; Toffel et al., 2015), workplace safety initiatives (Cornelissen et al., 2017; Robson et al., 2007; Simard & Marchand, 1997; Teufer et al., 2019), and work design affect safety outcomes (Nahrgang et al., 2011). One exception is a study by Aditya Jain and colleagues (2022) that examined whether national legislation on psychosocial risk across 35 European countries was associated with work design characteristics. Although the amount of variance explained was relatively small, they found that national legislation on psychosocial risk was positively associated with organizational stress-related action plans, which in turn was positively related to job demands (workload, emotional demands) and negatively related to job resources (social support, job discretion, participation). The results for job demands were against expectation and might occur because organizations with demanding work environments are more likely to instigate stress-related action plans. But Jain and colleagues (2022) also point out that this relationship could occur because organizations implement safety and stress-related initiatives that inadvertently increase job demands. Indeed, studies of the introduction of the EU working time directive found that its implementation increased doctors' work demands, as they were expected to do the same amount of work in less time (Duncan & Haslam, 2015; Richter et al., 2014). This suggests the effects of national safety institutions on work might depend on organizational context and change capabilities (Ancona & Nunez, 2009; Rothstein et al., 2020).

National institutional regimes

Understanding how national institutions shape organizational practices is a central concern of institutional theories such as varieties of capitalism (Hall & Soskice, 2001) and employment regime theory (Gallie, 2007). Varieties of capitalism theory emphasize the role of employers in developing institutions to coordinate their actions to address industrial relations, vocational training, and employee cooperation (Hall & Soskice, 2001), whereas employment regime theory focuses on how institutions emerge from the relative power of employers and employees and the role of the state in mediating this relationship (Gallie, 2007). Institutional theories also describe how institutional regimes, (i.e., configurations of institutions) differ across countries. An important corollary of this is that national differences in institutional regimes should result in cross-national variation in work design (Holman et al., 2009).

Employment regime theory is particularly useful because it distinguishes social democratic regimes (the Nordic countries, such as Denmark and Sweden) from continental regimes (e.g., France, Germany) and liberal regimes (e.g., the United Kingdom, Ireland). Social democratic regimes have many institutional characteristics that foster better work design,[1] such as highly influential trade unions (due to involvement in organizational and governmental

---

[1] Higher quality work designs typically have high job resources (e.g., autonomy, social support) moderate to high challenge demands (e.g., workload, problem-solving demands), and low hindrance demands (e.g., task obstacles, technological constraints) (Holman, 2013).

decision-making), high union membership, extensive welfare benefits, active labor market policies, and national training policies. Continental regimes have influential trade unions and strong employment protection, but union influence is weaker than in social democratic regimes as they have a more consultative role. Liberal regimes have limited trade union participation in decision-making (Hyman, 2001), weak employment protection legislation, and limited welfare provision or active labor market policies (Gallie, 2007).

Consistent with the presence of these national institutions, studies indicate that countries with social democratic regimes typically have higher quality work design, particularly regarding job discretion and cognitive demands (Gallie, 2009; Greenan, et al., 2013; Holman, 2013; Holman et al., 2009; Lorenz & Valeyre, 2005). Further, over the past 20 years, job discretion and cognitive demand have remained high in social democratic regimes but declined in continental and liberal regimes (Eurofound, 2015). A similar "Nordic advantage" has been found when comparing job discretion in social democratic regimes to that in other non-European liberal regimes such as the United States, Canada, and Australia (Dobbin & Boychuk, 1999). Work design differences between continental and liberal regimes are less consistently demonstrated (Holman, 2013; Holman et al., 2009). For example, continental regimes countries, such as the Netherlands and Austria, often have better quality work designs than liberal regime countries, while other continental regime countries, such as Germany, do not (Gallie, 2009).

Although evidence indicates that social democratic regimes have higher quality work designs, what is less clear is whether this "Nordic advantage" is due to the relative strength of their institutions (i.e., more influential trade unions, stronger employment policies) or whether it arises from the distinctive features of institutions in these regimes. For instance, compared to trade unions in other European regimes, trade unions in social democratic regimes have typically sought to promote better work design through collective agreements, policy initiatives, and collaborations with government and employer organizations (Gallie, 2007; Sørensen et al., 2014; Sørensen & Weinkopf, 2009). This suggests that trade unions may only affect work design when they explicitly use their influence to improve work design. Indeed, this might help to explain why the influence of trade unions in some continental regime countries does not always lead to better quality work design when compared to liberal regimes with less influential trade unions.

To summarize, research suggests that work design can be shaped by national institutions and institutional regimes. In particular, better quality work design appears more prevalent in countries with trade unions that are able to exert influence on organizational decision-making and in countries with institutional regimes (e.g., social democratic) characterized by regimes that combine highly influential trade unions and active labor market policies. However, the evidence is much more limited regarding the influence on work design from national safety institutions and national training systems. Indeed, there are persuasive arguments to suggest that national training systems do not shape work design but, for example, supply the skills needed for better quality work designs.

National Economic and International Influences

Organizations are embedded within a wider economic context and the health of the national economy can have profound effects on how organizations operate and the decisions managers and workers make about workplace practices (Budhwar & Sparrow, 2002). Another important feature of national economies over the past 40 to 50 years is their transformation by market liberalizations that have reduced governmental regulation and trade barriers (Gupta & Govindarajan, 2004). Global consequences of these changes have included an increase in the movement of goods and services through international supply chains, and an increase in the movement and migration of workers. We therefore consider how work design might be shaped by the health of the national economy and two key changes in the economic and social landscape: international supply chains, and migration. In addition, we consider the role of climate change, arguably the most pressing global issue that society is facing, and which is likely to profoundly affect how organizations operate.

National economy

The health of a nation's economy is indicated by its gross domestic product (GDP) and unemployment level. In economies with relatively high GDP and low unemployment, organizations may have greater capacity to invest in human resource practices, such as training and development, with the resulting increase in employee skills giving managers the opportunity to provide more enriched jobs with higher levels of responsibility (Prais et al., 1989). Low unemployment should also boost employees' individual and collective capacity to secure better working conditions and reduce the likelihood of employees agreeing to increases in workload due to a fear of unemployment (Akerlof, 1982). Although the relationship between variables such as unemployment and job quality may vary between regulatory contexts, for these reasons, work designs in "healthier" economies generally are expected to have lower workloads and be more enriched (e.g., higher job resources such as autonomy, skill variety, and challenge).

With regard to unemployment levels, European countries with high unemployment experienced greater increases in workload from 1995 to 2010 (Eurofound, 2015), while job insecurity, which increases as unemployment rises (Nätti et al., 2005), has been shown to be associated with high job demands and low job discretion (Barling & Kelloway, 1996; Burchell et al., 2005). Turning to GDP, European countries with low GDP experienced greater increases in workload and reductions in cognitive demand from 1995 to 2010 (Eurofound, 2015), while a study of European counties from 2005 to 2015 by Egidio Riva and colleagues (2022) found that countries with a high GDP had more jobs with high quality work designs and fewer jobs with low quality work designs. Furthermore, for low GDP countries, increases in GDP were associated with a larger increase in the prevalence of jobs with high quality work designs and a larger decrease in jobs with low quality work designs when compared to high GDP countries (Riva et al., 2022). Although these studies indicate that the health of the national economy can affect work design, others have failed to find similar relationships between work design and unemployment (Greenan et al., 2013; Piasana, 2023) or GDP (Green & McIntosh, 2001; Greenan et al., 2013). Nathalie Greenan and colleagues (2013), for example, found that high unemployment was related to high job complexity (a combined measure of discretion, job demands and learning opportunities), which they suggested could occur if economic downturns result in the loss of routine jobs.

International supply chains

International supply chains increase the potential for client organizations to influence work design within suppliers. For example, when client organizations select suppliers based on price, suppliers can be "forced" into adopting a cost minimization strategy involving low pay, low skilled work (Arnold & Hartman, 2005; Marchington et al., 2005; Weller et al., 2022), and low quality work designs (e.g., Brown et al., 2005; Verité, 2004). In contrast, client organizations can use their market position to improve suppliers' human resource practices and working conditions in the belief that this will ensure better quality products and protect the client organization's image. This can be achieved by contractually obliging suppliers to comply with codes of conduct that set out minimum standards for work and employment conditions (e.g., health and safety, working time, pay), through long-term collaboration with suppliers, and by encouraging the implementation of specific forms of work organization, (e.g., longer task cycle times) (Holman et al., 2012; Locke et al., 2007). Case studies further indicate that such initiatives are more likely to gain compliance from suppliers when accompanied by a supportive institutional context, such as national labor laws, national labor inspectorates, and trade union representation (Brown, 2015; Locke, et al., 2007; Toffel et al., 2015). Managers and executives within supplier organizations can also vary their strategic responses to client demands, with consequent implications for work design (Kinnie et al., 1999). Richard Locke and Monica Romis (2007) presented a case in which two similar suppliers responded differently to an overseas client's demands to reduce task cycle times. Specifically, one implemented a cell-based production system with job rotation, multiple tasks, and participation in decision making, while the other introduced assembly lines in which employees worked on a single task and had no participation in decision making.

In sum, research suggests that the influence of international supply chains on the quality of work design depends on choices made by clients and suppliers, and the wider institutional context. When client organizations structure supply chains so that competition is more fiercely based on price, which is often the case when suppliers are in developing countries, and suppliers do not operate in a supportive institutional context (e.g., national labor laws, strong trade unions), then this would appear to have more deleterious effects on work design in suppliers. But systematic evidence for the effects of international supply chains on work design—such as would be demonstrated by assessing how work design varies according to supply chain characteristics—is sparse. A further reason why it is important to understand how production or service systems are globally distributed across supply chains concerns how lower quality employment and work design practices may effectively be offshored or concealed. Consequently, an apparent improvement in job quality within a given organization or national context does not necessarily mean a global net improvement if simply reflecting that lower job quality activities are transitioned to another organization or country.

Migration

The movement of people across borders, whether for work, study, or other reasons, has significant implications for economies and societies (e.g., labor and skill supply, demographic change, cultural diversity) (OECD, 2014). However, there is limited research on the effects of migration on work design with most studies instead focusing on economic outcomes such as wage and employment effects (Borjas, 2003). The estimated number of international migrants has grown over the last 50 years. In 2020, there was an estimated 281 million migrants in the world constituting around 3.6 percent of the global population (UN DESA, 2020). This was around three times the number of international migrants in 1970 (McAuliffe & Triandafyllidou, 2021). Migration is driven by various "push" and "pull" factors. Pull factors include economic opportunities and technological change (e.g., advanced communication technology) whereas push factors may include political instability, war, and environmental disaster. Although Europe and Asia, as global regions, receive more immigration than Northern America, in terms of countries, the United States remains the primary destination for migrants followed by Germany, Saudi Arabia, Russia, and the United Kingdom. In terms of emigration, India, Mexico, Russia, and China have the largest emigrant populations in the world (UN DESA, 2021).

In many countries the public debate on the economic and societal effects of immigration remains highly polarized, such as in terms of the positive and negative effects of migration on the labor market, whereas research findings remain mixed. Some research for example suggests that low-skilled migration through increased labor supply may have a marginal downward effect on wages (Dustmann et al., 2013; Quak, 2019). At the same time, other studies find negligible effects on wages or suggest that the impact on outcomes such as wages are more confined to specific sectors, with higher skilled migration even potentially increasing the wages of domestic workers in higher skilled sectors. This may occur through increasing business competitiveness or improving productivity (Battisti et al., 2018; Friedberg & Hunt, 1995; Grossmann & Stadelmann, 2013; Peri et al., 2015). Population growth through migration also increases domestic demand for product and services, meaning accounts that focus solely on labor supply effects or the "lump of labor fallacy" (i.e., the argument that there is a fixed amount of work available in an economy such that an increase in workers decreases the work available to others) may be too simplistic (Portes, 2019). An important question concerns whether migrants' skills substitute or complement existing skills. Higher skilled migration may fill critical skill gaps and help technological innovation and growth in more productive sectors where higher quality work designs are more likely. The social networks of migrants may further increase access to foreign markets and global knowledge networks, increasing learning networks, and contributing to innovation (Lam & Elsayed, 2021).

A further important issue concerns the effects of emigration on economic development and the quality of work within the origin countries of migrants. Remittances sent home by migrants remain a critical source of national income that, in many low- and middle-income countries, exceed foreign direct investment and overseas development assistance in value (Grossman, 2021; ILO, 2018, 2021). At the same time, the emigration of higher skilled workers may lead to "brain drain," contributing to skill shortages, whereas evidence on wage effects remains mixed (Docquier, 2007). Such impacts, however, partly appear dependent on government policy responses. Policy initiatives to improve educational attainment in response to skilled emigration for example could also lead to net upskilling and increase the potential for the development of higher quality work (Lam & Elsayed, 2021).

Global migration also raises equality issues in terms of who has access to high quality work designs. Some research suggests migrants are more likely to be over-qualified, having less access to employment that matches their qualification or skill levels although this can reflect the effects of broader discrimination based upon ethnicity, race, religion or nationality (Rafferty, 2012, 2020). Language barriers or the perceived lower credentials of overseas qualifications from some countries may further contribute to this (Brell et al., 2020). Such factors may contribute to a higher representation of migrant workers within sectors and roles with lower job autonomy (Beyer, 2019). Undocumented work and the high representation of migrant workers within the informal economy further means migrants are exposed to some of the poorest or most abusive working conditions, including conditions of forced labor or modern slavery, or are outside of the purview of employment protections or collective arrangements in the formal economy (O'Connell Davidson, 2013). In such contexts, a concern for higher quality work designs may be secondary to the need for the enforcement of basic labor and health and safety standards underwritten by principles of human dignity. Consequently, a broader view that considers the role of migrants within global production raises normative questions regarding what quality work design means and inequalities in both access to and the global distribution of such work.

Climate change

The impact of climate change is manifest in many ways—such as increases in air temperature and extreme weather events—and is having, and will continue to have, profound effects on society, organizations, and workers (IPCC, 2023). Regarding work design, climate change is likely to have direct effects on work characteristics, and indirect effects through the "greening" of the economy.

One of the most direct impacts of climate change will be to alter the environmental demands of work tasks, particularly the ambient air temperature in which work is performed (Schulte & Chun, 2009). Working in high temperatures increases fatigue and heat stress (which can cause heatstroke and death) and has been shown to reduce labor productivity and safety (Dillender, 2019; Fatima et al., 2021; Kjellstrom et al., 2008). A report by the ILO (2019) estimated that 3.8 percent of working hours will be lost by 2030 due to the increase in global temperature of 1.5°C. Moreover, it is estimated that losses in working hours will be approximately 5 percent in hotter regions, such as Southern Asia and Africa, which is in part due to the greater proportion of jobs in these regions being located in sectors such as construction, manufacturing, forestry, and agriculture. There is also some evidence that higher temperatures can increase the perception of workload (Lan et al., 2010), which suggests that increasing temperatures may also negatively affect the perception of other work demands. One direct effect of climate change may therefore be to increase objective job demands and how they are perceived, although this may depend on the ability of organizations and workers to mitigate the effects of rising temperatures through changes in technology or working practices (e.g., shift patterns).

Climate change may also affect work design indirectly through the "greening" of the economy as governments and organizations seek to halt and mitigate climate change. Organizations may respond to the challenge of climate change by greening organizational practices by, for example, increasing the energy efficiency of buildings and processes, altering supply chains to reduce their environmental impact, and introducing "green" human resource practices, such as hybrid working that enables reductions in commuting. But, as with other organizational changes, how this greening of organizational practices affects work design is likely to depend on how the change is implemented. For example, attempts to improve energy efficiency of manufacturing processes could result in lower task discretion depending on how managers redesign new processes and technology. Governments and organizations may also seek to develop green jobs that are directly concerned with information, technology, and materials that preserve or restore environmental quality. These jobs are often located in sectors (e.g., construction, transportation, waste management, tourism, and agriculture) that tend to offer low-pay/low-skill jobs (Jaeger et al., 2021). As such, the expansion of green jobs may increase the proportion of jobs with lower quality work design, although one compensatory factor may be an increase in the perception of task meaningfulness, as employees are able to work on tasks that contribute positively to restoring the environment (Lysova et al., 2019). However, evidence for the direct and indirect effects of climate change on work design is lacking and thus the arguments offered here are largely speculative in nature.

Discussion

The aim of this chapter was to review the literature on national and global influences on work design. The strongest evidence from this literature indicates that institutional regimes and specific institutions, such as trade unions, do play a role in shaping work design (see Table 9.1). For example, countries with social democratic regimes, which are characterized by highly influential trade unions, tend to have more enriched job designs, and the findings from surveys and case studies also suggests that trade unions can positively affect work design. In addition, there is indicative evidence that the health of the national economy can shape the quality of work design in some countries. However, our review also shows that the literature on national and global influences on work design is relatively small, mainly derived from studies within Europe and somewhat fragmented across the multiplicity of influences. In addition, many key areas lack systematic study. These include important national influences, such as national labor market policies, training systems, and safety institutions, but particularly the influence on work design of transnational factors such as migration, environmental change, and supply chains. In the following section, we discuss directions for future research.

Future research directions

First, the fragmented nature of the field means that it would benefit from a comprehensive framework or model that draws together key institutional and national/transnational influences on work design. Existing findings suggest that employment regime theory could provide a firm theoretical foundation for such a framework. One advantage of developing such a framework would be to assist and guide the development and testing of models that enable the realization of a more accurate account of unique and relative effects. For example, a more comprehensive account of the relative effects of national institutions would include national health and safety institutions, in addition to those types of national institutions typically identified by institutional regime theories, such as collective bargaining arrangements, active employment policies and training systems. Indeed, such an analysis seems imperative given the lack of research on health and safety institutions and work design and the likelihood that such institutions may have an important effect on work design (Leka & Jain, 2022; Rothstein et al., 2020).

Second, we lack detailed accounts of the mechanisms through which national and global factors shape work design. Developing a comprehensive framework for national and global effects on work design would be a first step in setting out the range of these mechanisms. These include changes in the power of trade unions and employees to secure better work design, the supply of skills and labor that affects managerial ability to implement better work designs, and the adoption of workplace initiatives (such as health and safety practices). Methodologically, the limitations of national surveys (such as a lack appropriate measures) means that case studies may be the most productive means of providing insight into these mechanisms. A good example of such a study is provided by Bellego and colleagues (2023), who provide an account of how trade unions in France shaped work design through participation in organizational decision-making processes. Other good examples are by Gabrielle Meagher and colleagues (2016), who compared care work in Australia and Sweden, and Philippe Askenazy and colleagues (2012), who compared retail work in France and the United States. In these studies, through comparative case studies (using a mixture of surveys, interviews with managers, employees and trade unions, analysis of company records) the authors were able to tease out how institutional and organizational factors influenced work and employment conditions in a particular sector, and the role of managers in shaping responses to the broader institutional and operational context of the organization.

Third, the heterogeneity of findings found in survey-based studies suggests that the effects of different national and global factors play out in complex ways in specific contexts. Again, a comprehensive framework would help to guide research on how factors might interact. For example, the involvement of trade unions in many institutional structures suggests that, in certain countries, a fruitful avenue may be to examine complementarities (Hall & Soskice, 2001) between national institutions. Indeed, in some contexts, the nature of trade union involvement in health and safety institutions (such as previously described in Germany) may be critical in determining the effectiveness health and safety institutions. Little is also known about the extent to which the effects of national economic and transnational factors (e.g., migration, climate change, supply chains) are shaped by national institutions. One possibility is that the effects of national economic and transnational factors are filtered by national institutions. For example, the effects of migration on work design might depend on the extent to which active labor market policies identify and develop migrant skills, which may enable managers to sustain enriched work designs, or whether governments adopt a work-first agenda that forces migrants to take low-skilled work and thereby encourages employers to supply jobs with low quality work designs.

Fourth, there are significant empirical gaps regarding key factors (e.g., climate change, migration, supply chains) and geography. In particular, most studies are based on European samples largely due to the availability of suitable data. There is a clear need for studies in other continents, such as Asia, Africa, and South and Central America, where dominant institutional frameworks, such as employment regime theory, may not apply due to different or weaker institutional configurations. Furthermore, issues such as climate change may have a much more significant impact in, for example, African and South-East Asian countries where the effects of increased temperature may be particularly severe. The question of supply chain effects further highlights some limitations regarding organizational level analysis or single country studies given factors producing variation in job design may be inter-organizational or transnational.

Lastly, and before we conclude, it is worth briefly highlighting the practical and policy implications of research in this area. Developing knowledge of the global, transnational, and national factors that shape work design can help managers gain a more thorough understanding of the context in which their organization is embedded and how these might constrain or enable attempts to implement particular forms of work organization and human resource management strategies. For example, knowing that the institutional context is not supportive of a "high-involvement" human resource management approach that requires high quality work designs can alert managers to the need to consider remedial actions to ensure their success if implemented, particularly if organizations operate cross-nationally in countries with different institutional settings. Knowledge of the global and national factors that shape work design can also aid policy makers identify the levers for developing better work designs, and the potential threats to better quality work designs associated with climate change and low-skilled migration.

To conclude, our chapter has reviewed the literature on national and global influences on work design. We have shown that there is evidence for the effects on work design of national institutional regimes, specific institutional factors such as trade unions, and other national factors, such as national economic health. However, more research is needed to better understand how these factors combine in specific contexts to influence work design, the mechanisms through which they shape work design, and to extend our knowledge to cover a broader range of factors (e.g., migration, supply chains, climate change, health and safety institutions) and countries.

References

Akerlof, G. A. (1982). Labor contracts as partial gift exchange. *Quarterly Journal of Economics 97*, 543–569.

Arnold, D. G., & Hartman, L. P. (2005). Beyond sweatshops: Positive deviancy and global labor practice. *Business Ethics 14*, 206–222.

Arocena, P., & Nunez, I. (2009). The effect of occupational safety legislation in preventing accidents at work: Traditional versus advanced manufacturing industries. *Environment and Planning C: Government and Policy 27*, 159–174.

Ashton, D., Lloyd, C., & Warhurst, C. 2017. Business strategies and skills. In C. Warhurst, K. Mayhew, D. Finegold, & J. Buchanan (Eds.), *The Oxford handbook of skills and training* (pp. 301–320). Oxford University Press.

Askenazy, P., Berry, J. B., Carré, F., Prunier-Poulmaire, S., & Tilly, C. (2012). Working in large food retailers in France and the USA: The key role of institutions. *Work, Employment and Society 26*, 588–605.

Aspøy, T. M. (2020). Job quality through upskilling? The case of the cleaning industry in the collective system of Norway. *Journal of Education and Work 33*, 229–241.

Barling, J., & Kelloway, E. K. (1996). Job insecurity and health: The moderating role of workplace control. *Stress Medicine 12*, 253–259.

Battisti, M., Felbermayr, G., Peri, G., & Poutvaara, P. (2018). Immigration, search and redistribution: A quantitative assessment of native welfare. *Journal of the European Economic Association 16*, 1137–1188.

Bellego, M., Doellgast, V., & Pannini, E. (2023). From Taylorism to teams: Organisational and institutional experimentation at France Télécom. *Transfer: European Review of Labour and Research 29* (3), 355–370. https://doi.org/10.1177/10242589231179169

Beyer, R. C. (2019). Job autonomy and education-skill matches of immigrant workers in Germany. *Applied Economics Letters 26*, 1328–1332.

Borjas, G. J. (2003). The labor demand curve is downward sloping: Re-examining the impact of immigration on the labor market. *Quarterly Journal of Economics 118*, 1335–1374.

Brell, C., Dustmann C., & Preston I. (2020). The labor market integration of refugee migrants in high-income countries. *Journal of Economic Perspectives 34*, 94–121.

Brown, G. D. (2015). Effective protection of workers' health and safety in global supply chains. *International Journal of Labour Research 7*, 39–54.

Brown, J. R., Dant, R. P., Ingene, C. A., & Kaufmann, P. J. (2005). Supply chain management and the evolution of the "big middle." *Journal of Retailing 81*, 97–105.

Budhwar, P. S., & Sparrow, P. R. (2002). An integrative framework for understanding cross-national human resource management practices. *Human Resource Management Review 12*, 377–403.

Burchell, B., Ladipo, D., & Wilkinson, F. (Eds.). (2005). *Job insecurity and work intensification*. Routledge.

Burda, M. C., & Hunt, J. (2011). What explains the German labor market miracle in the Great Recession? National Bureau of Economic Research, Working Paper 17187.

Cornelissen, P. A., Van Hoof, J. J., & De Jong, M. D. (2017). Determinants of safety outcomes and performance: A systematic literature review of research in four high-risk industries. *Journal of Safety Research 62*, 127–141.

Culpepper, P. D., & Thelen, K. (2007). Institutions and collective actors in the provision of training: Historical and cross-national comparisons. In K. U. Mayer & H. Solga (Eds.), *Skill formation—Interdisciplinary and cross-national perspectives* (pp. 21–49). Cambridge University Press.

Dengler, K. (2019). Effectiveness of active labour market programmes on the job quality of welfare recipients in Germany. *Journal of Social Policy 48*, 807–838.

Dillender, M. (2019). Climate change and occupational health: Are there limits to our ability to adapt? Upjohn Institute Working Paper, No. 19-299. W. E. Upjohn Institute for Employment Research.

Dobbin, F., & Boychuk, T. (1999). National employment systems and job autonomy: Why job autonomy is high in the Nordic countries and low in the United States, Canada, and Australia. *Organization Studies 20*, 257–291.

Docquier, F., Lohest, O., & Marfouk, A. (2007). Brain drain in developing countries. *World Bank Economic Review 21*, 193–218.

Dollard, M. F., & Neser, D. Y. (2013). Worker health is good for the economy: Union density and psychosocial safety climate as determinants of country differences in worker health and productivity in 31 European countries. *Social Science & Medicine 92*, 114–123.

Duncan, M., & Haslam, C. (2015). A qualitative investigation of foundation year 2 doctors' views on the European working time directive. *Journal of Health Organization and Management 29*, 367–380.

Dustmann, C., Frattini, T., & Preston, I. P. (2013). The effect of immigration along the distribution of wages. *Review of Economic Studies, 80*(1), 145–173.

Eisele, S., & Schneider, M. R. (2020). What do unions do to work design? Computer use, union presence, and Tayloristic jobs in Britain. *Industrial Relations 59*, 604–626.

Esser, I., & Olsen, K. M. (2012). Perceived job quality: Autonomy and job security within a multi-level framework. *European Sociological Review 28*, 443–454.

Eurofound. (2013). *Work organisation and employee involvement in Europe.* Publications Office of the European Union.

Eurofound. (2015). *Convergence and divergence of job quality in Europe from 1995 to 2010.* Publications Office of the European Union.

Eurofound. (2017). *Sixth European working conditions survey—Overview report (2017 update).* Publications Office of the European Union.

Fatima, S. H., Rothmore, P., Giles, L. C., Varghese, B. M., & Bi, P. (2021). Extreme heat and occupational injuries in different climate zones: A systematic review and meta-analysis of epidemiological evidence. *Environment International 148*, 106384.

Friedberg, R. M., & Hunt, J. (1995). The Impact of Immigrants on Host Country Wages, Employment and Growth. *Journal of Economic Perspectives, 9*(2), 23–44.

Gallie, D. (Ed.). (2007). *Employment regimes and the quality of work.* Oxford University Press.

Gallie, D. (2009). Institutional regimes and employee influence at work: A European comparison. *Cambridge Journal of Regions, Economy and Society 2*, 379–393.

Gallie, D., Felstead, A., & Green, F. (2004). Changing patterns of task discretion in Britain. *Work, Employment and Society 18*, 243–266.

Gräbner, C., & Ghorbani, A. (2019). Defining institutions—A review and a synthesis. ICAE Working Paper Series, No. 89, Johannes Kepler University Linz, Institute for Comprehensive Analysis of the Economy (ICAE).

Green, F., Felstead, A., Gallie, D., & Henseke, G. (2022). Working still harder. *ILR Review 75*, 458–487.

Green, F., & McIntosh, S. (2001). The intensification of work in Europe. *Labour Economics 8*, 291–308.

Greenan, N., Kalugina, E., & Walkowiak, E. (2013). Has the quality of working life improved in the EU-15 between 1995 and 2005? *Industrial and Corporate Change 22*, 1–30.

Greif, A. (2006). *Institutions and the path to the modern economy.* Cambridge University Press.

Grossmann, V. (2021). How immigration affects investment and productivity in host and home countries. *IZA World of Labor 292.* https://doi.org/10.15185/izawol.292.v2

Grossmann, V., & Stadelmann, D. (2013). Wage effects of high-skilled migration: International evidence. *World Bank Economic Review 27*, 297–319.

Gupta, A. K., & Govindarajan, V. (2004). *Global strategy and organization.* Wiley.

Gustavsen, B. (2007). Work organization and "the Scandinavian model." *Economic and Industrial Democracy 28*, 650–671.

Hall, P. A., & Soskice, D. (2001). An introduction to varieties of capitalism. In D. Soskice (Ed.), *Varieties of capitalism: The institutional foundation of comparative advantage* (pp. 1–70). Oxford University Press.

Holman, D. (2013). Job types and job quality in Europe. *Human Relations 66*, 475–502.

Holman, D., Frenkel, S., Sørensen, O., & Wood, S. (2009). Work design variation and outcomes in call centers: Strategic choice and institutional explanations. *Industrial & Labor Relations Review 62*, 510–532.

Holman, D., Lamare, R., Grimshaw, D., Holdsworth, L., & Marchington, M. (2012). *The diffusion of "good" HR practices across the supply chain*. Advisory, Conciliation & Arbitration Service.

Hoque, K., Earls, J., Conway, N., & Bacon, N. (2017). Union representation, collective voice and job quality: An analysis of a survey of union members in the UK finance sector. *Economic and Industrial Democracy 38*, 27–50.

Hyman, R. (2001). *Understanding European trade unionism: Between market class and society*. SAGE.

International Labour Organisation. (1990). *The hours we work: New work schedules in policy and practice*. ILO.

International Labour Organisation. (2018). *Global estimates on international migrant workers—results and methodology*. 2nd ed. ILO.

International Labour Organisation. (2019). *Working on a warmer planet: The impact of heat stress on labour productivity and decent work ILO*. ILO.

International Labour Organisation. (2021). *Global estimates on international migrant workers—results and methodology*. 3rd ed. ILO.

IPCC. (2023). *Climate change 2023: Synthesis report*. Contribution of Working Groups I, II and III to the Sixth Assessment Report of the Intergovernmental Panel on Climate Change [Core Writing Team, H. Lee and J. Romero (eds.)]. IPCC.

Jaeger, J., Walls, G., Clarke, E., Altamirano, J., Harsono, A., Mountford, A., Burrow, S., Smith, S., & Tate, A. (2021). *The green jobs advantage: How climate-friendly investments are better job creators*. Working Paper. World Resources Institute.

Jain, A., Torres, L. D., Teoh, K., & Leka, S. (2022). The impact of national legislation on psychosocial risks on organisational action plans, psychosocial working conditions, and employee work-related stress in Europe. *Social Science & Medicine 302*, 114987.

Kinnie, N., Purcell, J., Hutchinson, S., Terry, M., Collinson, M., & Scarbrough, H. (1999). Employment relations in SMEs: Market-driven or customer-shaped? *Employee Relations 21*, 218–235.

Kjellstrom, T., Kovats, S., Lloyd, S., Holt, T., & Tol, R., (2008). The direct impact of climate change on regional labour productivity. ESRI Working Paper, No. 260. The Economic and Social Research Institute (ESRI).

Lam, D., & Elsayed, M. (2021). *Labour markets in low-income countries: Challenges and opportunities*. Oxford University Press.

Lan, L., Lian, Z., & Pan, L. (2010). The effects of air temperature on office workers' well-being, workload and productivity-evaluated with subjective ratings. *Applied Ergonomics 42*, 29–36.

Leka, S., & Jain, A. (2022). Managing health, safety, and well-being at work within changing legal and policy frameworks. In K. Brough, E. Garginer, & K. Daniels (Eds.), *Handbook on management and employment practices* (pp. 809–825). Springer International Publishing.

Locke, R. M., Qin, F., & Brause, A. 2007. Does monitoring improve labor standards? Lessons from Nike. *Industrial & Labor Relations Review 61*, 3–31.

Locke, R. M., & Romis, M. (2007). Improving work conditions in a global supply chain. *MIT Sloan Management Review 48*, 54.

Lorenz, E., & Valeyre, A. (2005). Organisational innovation, human resource management and labour market structure: A comparison of the EU-15. *Journal of Industrial Relations 47*, 424–442.

Lysova, E. I., Allan, B. A., Dik, B. J., Duffy, R. D., & Steger, M. F. (2019). Fostering meaningful work in organizations: A multi-level review and integration. *Journal of Vocational Behavior 110*, 374–389.

MacKay*, C. J., Cousins, R., Kelly, P. J., Lee, S., & McCaig, R. H. (2004). 'Management Standards' and work-related stress in the UK: policy background and science. *Work & Stress, 18*(2), 91–112.

Marchington, M., Grimshaw, D., Rubery, J., & Wilmott, H. (Eds.). (2005). *Fragmenting work: Blurring organisational boundaries and disordering hierarchies.* Oxford University Press.

McAuliffe, M., & Triandafyllidou, M. (2021). *World migration report 2022.* International Organization for Migration (IOM).

Meagher, G., Szebehely, M., & Mears, J. (2016). How institutions matter for job characteristics, quality and experiences: A comparison of home care work for older people in Australia and Sweden. *Work, Employment and Society 30*, 731–749.

Mueller, F. (1994). Societal effect, organizational effect and globalization. *Organization Studies 15*, 407–428.

Nahrgang, J. D., Morgeson, F. P., & Hofmann, D. A. (2011). Safety at work: A meta-analytic investigation of the link between job demands, job resources, burnout, engagement, and safety outcomes. *Journal of Applied Psychology 96*, 71–94.

Nätti, J., Happonen, M., Kinnunen, U., & Mauno, S. (2005). Job insecurity, temporary work and trade union membership in Finland 1977–2003. In H. De Witte (Ed.), *Job insecurity, union involvement and union activism* (pp. 11–48). Ashgate.

O'Connell Davidson, J. (2013). Troubling freedom: Migration, debt, and modern slavery. *Migration Studies 1*, 176–195.

OECD. (2014). *Migration policy debates.* OECD Publishing.

Osterman, P. (1995). Skill, training, and work organization in American establishments. *Industrial Relations 34*, 125–146.

Parker, S. K., Van den Broeck, A., & Holman, D. (2017). Work design influences: A synthesis of multilevel factors that affect the design of jobs. *Academy of Management Annals 11*, 267–308.

Peri, G., Shih, K., & Sparber, C. (2015). STEM workers, H-1B visas, and productivity in US cities. *Journal of Labor Economics 33*(S1), S225–S255.

Piasana, A. (2023). Job quality in turbulent times: An update of the European Job Quality Index. ETUI Research Paper–Working Paper.

Portes J. (2019). The economics of migration. *Contexts 18*, 12–17.

Prais, S. J., Jarvis, V., & Wagner, K. (1989). Productivity and vocational skills in services in Britain and Germany: Hotels. *National Institute Economic Review 130*, 52–74.

Quak, E. (2019). *The effects economic integration of migrants have on the economy of host countries.* Institute of Development Studies.

Rafferty, A. L. (2012). Ethnic penalties in graduate level over-education, unemployment and wages: Evidence from Britain. *Work, Employment and Society 26*, 987–1006.

Rafferty, A. L. (2020). Skill underutilization and under-skilling in Europe: The role of workplace discrimination. *Work, Employment and Society 34*, 317–335.

Rafferty, A. L., & Wiggan, J. (2011). Choice and welfare reform: Lone parents' decision making around paid work and family life. *Journal of Social Policy 40*, 275–293.

Richter, A., Kostova, P., Baur, X., & Wegner, R. (2014). Less work: More burnout? A comparison of working conditions and the risk of burnout by German physicians before and after the implementation of the EU working time directive. *International Archives of Occupational and Environmental Health 87*, 205–215.

Riva, E., Lucchini, M., & Vandekerckhove, S. (2022). Space-time variations in job types: A tale of "three Europes." *International Journal of Sociology 52*, 420–447.

Robson, L. S., Clarke, J. A., Cullen, K., Bielecky, A., Severin, C., Bigelow, P. L., & Mahood, Q. (2007). The effectiveness of occupational health and safety management system interventions: A systematic review. *Safety Science 45*, 329–353.

Rothstein, H., Paul, R., & Demeritt, D. (2020). The boundary conditions for regulation: Welfare systems, state traditions, and the varied governance of work safety in Europe. *Governance 33*, 21–39.

Schulte, P., & Chun, H. (2009). Climate change and occupational safety and health: Establishing a preliminary framework. *Journal of Occupational and Environmental Hygiene 6*, 542–554.

Simard, M., & Marchand, A. (1997). Workgroups' propensity to comply with safety rules: The influence of micro-macro organisational factors. *Ergonomics 40*, 172–188.

Simms, M. (2017). Unions and job quality in the UK: Extending interest representation within regulation institutions. *Work and Occupations 44*, 47–67.

Simms, M. (2022). Trade unions and job quality. In C. Warhust, C. Mathiey, & R. Dwyer (Eds.), *The Oxford handbook of job quality* (pp. 542–558). Oxford Academic Press.

Sørensen, O. H., Doellgast, V., & Bojesen, A. (2014). Intermediary cooperative associations and the institutionalization of participative work practices: A case study in the Danish public sector. *Economic and Industrial Democracy 36*, 701–725.

Sørensen, O. H., & Weinkopf, C. 2009. Pay and working conditions in finance and utility call centres in Denmark and Germany. *European Journal of Industrial Relations 15*, 395–416.

Stier, H. (2015). The skill-divide in job quality: A cross-national analysis of 28 countries. *Social Science Research 49*, 70–80.

Teufer, B., Ebenberger, A., Affengruber, L., Kien, C., Klerings, I., Szelag, M., Grillich, L., & Griebler, U. (2019). Evidence-based occupational health and safety interventions: A comprehensive overview of reviews. *BMJ Open 9*(12), e032528.

Toffel, M. W., Short, J. L., & Ouellet, M. (2015). Codes in context: How states, markets, and civil society shape adherence to global labor standards. *Regulation & Governance 9*, 205–223.

United Nations Department of Economic and Social Affairs (UN DESA). (2021). International Migration 2020 Highlights (ST/ESA/SER.A/452). UN DESA.

Verité. (2004). Excessive overtime in Chinese supplier factories: Causes, impacts, and recommendations for action. http://www.verite.org/news/Excessiveovertime

Weller, S., Barnes, T., & Kimberley, N. (2022). Geographies of job quality. In C. Warhust, C. Mathiey, & R. Dwyer (Eds.), *The Oxford handbook of job quality* (pp. 203–218). Oxford Academic Press.

Shaping Work Design

The Influence of Occupational, Organizational, and Work Group Factors

Daniela M. Andrei, Amy Wei Tian, Florian E. Klonek, and Lander J. G. Vermeerbergen

Introduction

Over the past two decades, researchers have called for a more comprehensive understanding of workplace contextual features that play a powerful role in constraining or enabling various work characteristics of contemporary workplaces (Morgeson et al., 2010; Oldham & Hackman, 2010). Such contextual antecedents of work design have been shown to reside at different levels, ranging from individual, work group, organizational, and higher-level external influences (Parker et al., 2017). To date, most of the emerging research on the antecedents of work design has focused on the role of individual-level factors. However, a better understanding of the factors that go beyond the individual-level antecedents is needed, not only to advance research on work design but also to identify the most effective and impactful ways in which better work can be achieved through more strategic and systemic approaches. This chapter will provide an overview of the occupational, organizational, managerial, and work group antecedents of work design. Occupational factors include both the objective boundaries (i.e., the type of work performed) and subjective boundaries (i.e., occupational values, professional identity) that characterize occupational contexts (Dierdorff, 2019). Organizational antecedents include formal properties of the organization (e.g., size and organizational structure) and as well as its cultural features (e.g., organizational culture and climate) (de Sitter et al., 1997; Oldham & Hackman, 2010). Local workgroup factors refer to features of a department, a working unit, or a team and include leadership influences (Parker et al., 2017).

By adopting a multi-level and multifaceted perspective, we point toward ways in which better work can be achieved through more strategic and systemic approaches to work design. Moreover, we aim to identify promising directions

---

Daniela M. Andrei, et al. *Shaping Work Design*. In: *Transformative Work Design*.
Edited by: Sharon K. Parker et al., Oxford University Press. © Society for Industrial and Organizational Psychology (2025). DOI: 10.1093/oso/9780197692554.003.0010

Occupational Factors

Amongst the higher-level factors that are beyond the influence of organizations (Parker et al., 2017), occupations have been indicated as closely linked to work roles and, therefore, to work design (Dierdorff & Morgeson, 2007, 2013). Given the nature of today's work environment, characterized by increased workforce mobility and shorter tenure with a single employer, occupations are expected to have a stronger impact on employees' work experience than the employing organization (Dierdorff, 2019). For example, analyzing data from a sample of 230 occupations, Dierdorff and Morgeson (2013) found that approximately 16 percent of observed variance in individual-level work characteristics can be explained by occupational values.

Occupations are defined as "collections of work roles with similar goals that require the performance of distinctive activities as well as the application of specialized skills or knowledge to accomplish these goals" (Dierdorff et al., 2009, p. 974). These collections emerge from a process of negotiated and socially constructed consensus over time (Trice, 1993) and span across different organizations while sharing the same purpose and similar employee expectations (Dierdorff & Morgeson, 2007). Consequently, occupations generate both objective boundaries (i.e., task requirements) and subjective boundaries (i.e., occupational values or identity). These boundaries influence the structuring of work, giving rise to specific contextual features including "social or interpersonal elements, physical or psychological demands, values, norms, regulations, interests, etc.,"—all of which affect work design (Dierdorff, 2019, p. 399).

Emerging theory and research suggest that the relationship between occupations and work design can be multifaceted, ranging from direct to indirect and to even reverse effects, where changes in work design can subsequently influence occupational roles (Dierdorff & Morgeson, 2013; Parker et al., 2017). First, occupations can directly influence work design through objective boundaries created around tasks and responsibilities which further shape employees' experience of work characteristics (Morgeson et al., 2010). By constraining the emergence and distribution of formal and informal tasks and responsibilities across roles, and by regulating the knowledge, skills, and abilities that are required to complete these tasks, occupations can dictate the salience of work characteristics. Indeed, professional occupations, as well as occupations with high level of cognitive demands, were shown to foster work designs that are higher in knowledge characteristics, such as problem solving, information processing, and task complexity (Dierdorff & Morgeson, 2013, Morgeson & Humphrey, 2006). Similarly, occupations high in interdependence and responsibility for others, such as healthcare or protective services, typically result in work designs with greater task significance (Morgeson & Humphrey, 2006), but also increased work–family conflict due to their demands (Dierdorff & Ellington, 2008). Occupational factors were shown to dictate the salience of work characteristics even when the same type of role is considered. Focusing only on managerial roles across 58 different occupations, Dierdorff and colleagues (2009) found that up to 39 percent of the variance in role requirements related to managing logistics and technology can be explained by occupation. This means that even though all the tasks and responsibilities of a managerial role are similar in nature, their importance, and the frequency with which they are required or enacted may vary significantly depending on the occupational context. Similar effects have been observed in a study conducted across several blue-collar occupations, with the occupational context shown to be the only significant predictor of employees' desire to alternate between mental and physical tasks even when other factors such as gender, age, task experience, and perceived job control were accounted for (Jahncke et al., 2017).

Second, occupations can influence work design in more insidious or indirect ways. Dierdorff and colleagues (2009) argued that over time, occupations can evolve into very distinctive contexts in which work roles are performed, resulting in distinct "cultural" features. These distinct features, much like those seen in organizational cultures, are expected to reinforce and maintain structures through which interactions and roles are ordered (Dierdorff, 2019). Through the process of occupational socialization, these structures can exert a strong influence not only over what and how employees learn or prioritize at work, but also over the way they might define and chose to enact and/or expand their roles (Dierdorff, 2019). The theory of work adjustment describes these structures in terms of occupational reinforcer patterns because they favor the selection and reinforcement of particular activities, tasks, and behaviors that individuals value differently (Dawis & Lofquist, 1984). These reinforcer patterns signal to employees what an occupation has to offer, and work designs emerge or are adjusted to enable employees to gain the occupational reinforcers available (Dierdorff & Morgeson, 2013). Two such reinforcer patterns that have received research attention are occupational values and occupational identity. Dierdorff and Morgeson (2013) found that in occupations high in values of independence (such as private investigators or civil engineers) task-related characteristics, such as task complexity, problem solving, or autonomy, are more likely to emerge due to consistent reinforcement of personal initiative. Similarly, occupations high in altruistic values, such as healthcare nurses or aged care workers, facilitate the emergence of work designs high in relational work design characteristics due to the constant reinforcement of service to others. However, as service to others is predominantly a singular and unidirectional type of interaction, they were also found to constrain the emergence of interdependent work designs (Dierdorff & Morgeson, 2013). In a similar way, occupational identities were shown to influence the way employees respond to implementation of large-scale work redesign interventions in higher education (Hay et al., 2021) as well as public services (Chen & Reay, 2021). Interestingly, the study conducted by Chen and Reay (2021) provides insights into a more complex process by which initial reactions to work redesign are aimed to protect occupational identities, either by refusing to enact the changes, or sometimes even by leaving the organization. However, as the work redesign continues to be enforced, and workers engage with the new tasks, they end up modifying their identity in a way that affirms the new ways of working. Further support for the importance of occupational identity is provided by studies investigating how employees who failed to pursue their desired occupation or calling approach work. Such employees were shown to respond to unanswered callings or forgone professional identities by thoroughly revising their current work roles and using job crafting and vicarious enactment (Berg et al., 2010; Obodaru, 2017) to maintain the self-concept associated with the desired occupation.

While the impact of occupations on work design continues to be an understudied area, the literature that is emerging on this topic appears to point toward a few directions with potential to strengthen the field. One such direction is provided by studies actively incorporating social theories, such as social identity theory or social categorization theory, into their approach to occupational influences on work design. Focusing on occupational identity, work by Hay (2020) indicates that people who are in positions to make decisions about the work design of others (such as members of a steering committee) use occupations as salient lenses through which they interpret the situation and arrive to a set of work redesign solutions. In this instance, members of the steering committee were shown to draw both on their own occupational identity, as well as on occupational prototypes of other members to articulate and gain support for proposed redesign solutions (Hay, 2020). This work complements studies showing that during the actual implementation of work redesign solutions employees might aim to protect or shape work designs that are congruent with their occupational identity (Chen & Reay, 2021; Hay et al., 2021). While further empirical (quantitative) work is needed to provide further insights into these processes, we concur with Parker and colleagues (2017) that a closer consideration of occupational identity represents a fruitful avenue for advancing work on the role of occupations for work re/design.

Furthermore, there is an increased acknowledgment in the literature that processes by which occupational factors affect work design are extremely dynamic, contributing to the reinforcer patterns previously described. While the empirical evidence is very limited, some of the studies already discussed shed light on how work design can feed back into occupational factors via its dynamic interplay with occupational identity (Chen & Reay, 2021). Additionally, some research points to work design as a potentially strong driver for cultivating occupational commitment, with core job characteristics, such as variety, identity, significance, autonomy, and feedback, shown to shape employee's attitudes toward their profession in a multi sample study (Jiang et al., 2022). Building on the research reviewed so far in this section, it can be argued that by strengthening occupational commitment, work design inherently contributes to a stronger occupational context, which in turn has greater potential to shape work design. Continuing along this path of addressing the intricate and complex interplay between occupations and work design opens exciting new opportunities for scientific inquiry. Furthermore, it provides avenues for a better understanding of how work design characteristics and occupational factors can reinforce each other over time and guide targeted organizational interventions.

Organizational Factors

Several properties of the broader organizational context have been theorized to constrain or enhance the emergence of particular work designs (Morgeson et al., 2010; Parker et al., 2017). These properties encompass both formal properties of the organization (e.g., size, centralization, formalization, technological systems, management, and control systems), and its cultural features (e.g., organizational culture and climate) (Oldham & Hackman, 2010). In this section, the primary focus will be on discussing how the organizational structure and human resource management (HRM) strategies, policies, and practices play important roles in shaping work design.

Organizational structure and design

Organizational structure is an umbrella term that refers to a set of formal organizational characteristics determined by key organizational decisions, including how units in departments are grouped, the level of centralization of decision making, and the formalization of processes and procedures (Morgeson et al., 2010). In general, these characteristics explain the division of work across organizational units (i.e., teams and departments) and how these units work together to deliver products or services to clients (Thompson, 1969; Vriens et al., 2018). The socio-technical systems theory (Trist & Bamforth, 1951) has long theorized complex interactions between organizational structure, tasks, technology, and people in organizations. From this perspective, individual level work structure (i.e., work design) is inherently linked to the organizational structure of an organization. The modern iterations of the socio-technical systems theory (Benders et al., 2000; Van Eijnatten, 1993) highlight the need for work design that balance technical performance while also enhancing employees' work life quality. The aim is to shift away from designing "simple jobs in complex organizations" to "complex jobs in simple organizations" (de Sitter et al., 1997).

There are two approaches when studying the impact of organizational structures on work design. First, research on how organizational structure affects work often focuses on specific organizational characteristics, such as unit grouping (e.g., Bidwell, 2010; Melé, 2005; Victor et al., 2000), centralization of decision-making (e.g., Aubé et al., 2018; Germov, 2005; Harley, 1999), the formalization of organizational processes and procedures (e.g., Huising, 2015; Knight et al., 2018), and job specialization (e.g., Hodgson & Briand, 2013; Peci et al., 2019). Second, some studies also look at the overall configurational impact of these features combined, by investigating bureaucracies (e.g., Adler & Borys, 1996), socio-technical structures (e.g., Ingvaldsen & Rolfsen, 2012; Rousseau, 1977), or agile organizations (Hodgson & Briand, 2013). Another example of configurational impact are studies examining organizational redesign initiatives aimed at introducing lean production methods, which found reduced employees' job autonomy, skill utilization, and participation in decision making (Parker, 2003).

Largely, both these approaches agree that high levels of formalization, specialization, and centralization tend to negatively impact work design by facilitating the emergence of roles that are narrowly defined and highly specialized with low autonomy and reduced opportunities for development (Morgeson et al., 2010; Oldham & Hackman, 1981; Parker et al., 2017). For example, organizational centralization, by creating distinct line divisions for staff, limits the development of enriched work designs for production workers in manufacturing (Dhondt & Benders, 1998). This happens because centralization facilitates roles that are either focused on production (within production units), or on indirect supervisory, administrative, or managerial tasks (within specialized units) (de Sitter et al., 1997; Huys et al., 1999). As a result, workers in production units will inherently end up with lower levels of autonomy, variety, and opportunities for skill development. Similar results were found also in the service sector where, for example, having separate divisions for staff and frontline care workers led to frontline care jobs having lower autonomy and task variety (Vermeerbergen et al., 2021). In contrast, highly decentralized organizations are more likely to facilitate the emergence of jobs that combine both operational and control responsibilities. This is because the responsibilities usually handled by supervisory, administrative, or managerial departments are delegated to production units (Huys et al., 1999).

However, the relationship between organizational structure and work design is not necessarily straightforward with some studies pointing toward potential beneficial effects. For example, formalization has been shown to reduce role ambiguity and role conflict for professional workers (Organ & Greene, 1981). Furthermore, it can facilitate better coordination among primary care physicians, enabling them to delegate cases and contributing to increased autonomy over work schedules (Nemeth et al., 2006). These findings point toward complex processes by which characteristics of organizations can shape the quality and experience of work for employees depending on other contextual factors.

Additionally, studies on the effect of organizational restructuring further inform our understanding of how changes in organizational design and structure affect work design. One notable example of organizational restructuring is downsizing. Because downsizing is a process that typically aims to reduce the number of staff while maintaining the same level of outputs, it is generally expected to have negative consequences for work design mainly due to increased demands. Indeed, downsizing is often found to lead to increased effort, time pressure, and workload (Quinlan & Bohle, 2009), but also other demanding aspects of jobs such as job insecurity and physical or emotional demands (Boyd et al., 2014; Ferrie et al., 2007). These effects are not limited to demands, with research also showing that downsizing tends to reduce job autonomy and employees' opportunities to use their skills effectively (Ferrie et al., 2007; Knudsen et al., 2003). However, reinforcing the earlier point on the complexity of these relationships, research suggests that these negative effects can be prevented if interventions such as downsizing are accompanied by purposeful work redesign efforts aimed at preserving the quality of work (Parker, 2003).

While more bridge-building across the organizational-level structures and employee-level work design is necessary, it is encouraging to note that emerging work design models incorporate more explicit theorizing about the links between system-level organizing conditions and work design. In their recent model, Parker and Knight (2024) argue that horizontal division and allocation of labor will be more relevant for stimulating work characteristics, such as task variety, skills variety, information processing requirements, while the vertical division of labor and allocation of authority is more likely to shape employees autonomous work characteristics, such as work methods autonomy, scheduling autonomy, or decision-making autonomy. Additionally, organizational decisions around the integration of effort across units via information are expected to shape mastery related work characteristics, such as role clarity and job feedback, while integration mechanisms based on social processes will shape relational work characteristics, such as task significance and social support. Finally, the degree of effort required to achieve shared organizational goals will shape the type and level of demands experienced by employees (Parker & Knight, 2024). This new model offers clear insights into how organizational structuring principles might be related to work design. We hope it will stimulate more empirical research on how organizational and employee level work structures connect, especially focusing on the integration mechanisms and their links with work design.

HRM strategies, policies, and practices

Strategic HRM theory (SHRM) posits direct links between organizational strategy; HRM policies and practices, including work design; and organizational performance. Specifically, SHRM theory asserts that optimal organizational performance is achieved when there is a congruence between organizational strategy and HRM practices (Jackson et al., 2014; Wood et al., 2006). In this regard, work design is identified as a key component of the broader HRM system (Boon et al., 2019; Boselie et al., 2005; Posthuma et al., 2013).

Central to SHRM theory are the concepts of vertical and horizontal alignment. Vertical alignment ensures that HRM practices are directly linked to and support the strategic goals of the organization, while horizontal alignment ensures consistency and complementarity among HRM practices (Guest, 1997). This dual alignment is not only crucial for fostering a coherent and synergistic HRM system that supports organizational strategic goals, but it also presents direct implications for work design. From a vertical alignment perspective, it has been posited that organizations aiming for competitive advantages through cost minimization are inclined to develop an operational context oriented toward standardization of processes and efficiency to enable mass production at lower costs. Consequently, this approach is more likely to motivate an HRM approach that prioritizes more Tayloristic work designs due to their reduced training, induction, and replacement costs (Parker et al., 2017). Concurrently, from a horizontal alignment perspective, it is anticipated that other HRM practices, like the use of less secure, contingent employment contracts or reduced employment benefits (Lawler, 1986), are expected to further compound the impact on work design. Conversely, organizations that are aiming for competitive advantage through differentiation are more inclined to facilitate the adoption of "high-involvement" HRM practices that emphasize employee empowerment, skill development, and participation, favoring the emergence of work designs that are challenging, and allow for increased employee autonomy and skill use. The coherence of HRM practices, such as training and development, high rewards and recognition, and secure employment contracts, further support these enriched work designs (Parker et al., 2017).

Limited but growing empirical evidence provides some support for the propositions of SHRM regarding the impact of organizational strategy and work design. Analyses drawing on large datasets indicate that organizations tend to opt for a particular work design approach (e.g., Tayloristic vs. enriched) and implement it coherently across the entire establishment (Gibbs et al., 2010). This is in line with research focusing on specific industries, such as call centers, where a differentiation strategy was shown to be associated with higher levels of job autonomy compared to organizations focusing on cost minimization (Holman et al., 2009; Wood et al., 2006). In a similar vein, organizations that employ more control-oriented HRM strategies are shown to foster the emergence of more constrained work designs, compared to organizations that prioritize commitment-oriented HRM strategies, which encourage work design that support collective goals and increase commitment (Walton, 1985).

Going beyond strategic orientation, the literature on horizontal alignment among HRM practices—such as reward systems, training systems, and work systems—has predominantly neglected implications for work design and redesign (Christina et al., 2017). An exception is Susanne Tafvelin and colleagues' (2019) quasi-experimental study, which shows the positive outcomes of synchronizing a job redesign initiative with training and development effort. Their findings suggest that such alignment not only results in better work design for employees (increased support), but also improves the overall climate for innovation. They argue that the redesign of leader roles to reduce administrative tasks creates opportunities for providing better support. However, this redesign needs to be combined with targeted training to provide supervisors with specific guidance on how to better support employees. The study asserts that the use of any of these strategies alone would not have been able to deliver a tangible improvement in employee support and climate for innovation. Furthermore, the experimental study conducted by Christina and colleagues (2017) illustrates both vertical and horizontal HRM alignment, and sheds light on how a shift toward more pro-environmental organizational goals necessitate—and are facilitated by—horizontal HRM alignment encompassing training and development, performance management, and work (re)design. In this case, alignment processes resulted in changes in the workload model as well as increased autonomy and responsibility at the individual employee level.

In terms of the exact mechanisms by which HRM alignment can affect work design, recent developments in the literature suggest direct effects of both HRM systems and more granular HRM practices on the structuring and restructuring of work design. For example, the adaptation of flexible work arrangements has been shown to increase autonomy regarding work scheduling and location (Allen et al., 2021; Berber et al., 2023). Implementing job rotation has been found to directly increase skill use (Kampkötter et al., 2018). However, it is worth noting that the impact of specific HRM practices on work design is not unequivocally beneficial. For example, while flexible work arrangements and working from home can increase autonomy and work–life balance, they may also induce a sense of work intensification (Kelliher & Anderson, 2010) and increased emotional demands (Shirmohammadi et al., 2022). These mixed effects point toward the inherent complexity of HRM effects on work design and the need to adopt a more contextualized approach when examining these relationships, with a more careful consideration of the specific job roles and work tasks (Macky & Boxall, 2008).

Going beyond direct effects, HRM practices can also affect work design through indirect pathways, by influencing managers' approach to work (re)design, and/or by influencing the way employees engage in job crafting activities to alter their work tasks (Tafvelin et al., 2019). More specifically, the implementation of certain HRM practices at the organizational level can indirectly affect work design at both team and individual levels by providing the necessary skills, motivation, and opportunities for managers and employees to design and redesign work for themselves or for others. Additionally, HRM practices often serve as signals to employees about what the organization values, and the extent to which the organization cares about them as individuals (Snell & Morris, 2021). These perceived signals, in turn, are likely to alter how employees organize, perform, and modify their jobs and work tasks. For example, HRM practices, such as training and development, provide signals either for employees to develop better quality jobs themselves (e.g., van den Heuvel et al., 2015) or encourage managers to actively improve job design for their subordinates (Odle-Dusseau et al., 2016). Similarly, implementation of pay-for-performance schemes can signal that the organization values individual performance, and therefore facilitates the emergence of work designs that enable greater responsibility and proactive job crafting (Lazear, 2000). From the standpoint of motivation and opportunity, HRM practices such as job rotation can indirectly catalyze job crafting behaviors by increasing one's structural and social resources and one's sense of self-competence to engage in designing more complex and enriched jobs and work tasks (e.g., Berdicchia et al., 2016).

The HRM landscape, as well as that of work, is changing significantly, driven by various forces such as rapid technological advancements, demographic changes, and major large-scale stressors such as the COVID-19 pandemic. Therefore, topics related to gig workers, remote/hybrid workforce management, algorithmic workforce management, agile HRM, and employee well-being are gaining traction over more traditional HRM practices. Despite significant changes in HRM trends and work dynamics, research focusing on the interplay between these HRM trends and work design remains extremely limited. However, emerging evidence points again to potential interrelationships. For example, recent research has started to explore the flexibility of employee–employer relationships, particularly in the context of non-standard work arrangements, such as gig economy workers and temporary or precarious work (Ashford et al., 2018; Cropanzano et al., 2023; Spreitzer et al., 2017) (see also Chapter 20, this volume). It has been argued that to adapt and thrive in the gig economy, organizations need to reconsider how jobs and work tasks should be diversified, structured, and conducted to effectively leverage a digital workforce characterized by diverse competencies and needs (Schroeder et al., 2021). Additionally, with these trends, we also see an increased adoption and reliance on algorithmic management, which is creating a complex set of potential implications for work design. Interestingly, algorithmic management—irrespective of the specific HR function (e.g., scheduling, performance management, compensation)—appears to mostly affect work design negatively, reducing autonomy, task complexity and variety, while increasing job demands and insecurity (Parent-Rocheleau & Parker, 2022). Nevertheless, the same authors point toward the idea that these negative effects might be mitigated through thoughtful decisions made at the design and implementation stages. With the rapid development of technology in contemporary organizations, there is a pressing need for more research to focus on the role of these emerging HR trends and their potential interplay with work design. A better understanding of their impact is critical for optimizing employee well-being and performance, as well as overall organizational effectiveness.

Local Work Group Factors

Parker and colleagues' (2017) framework identified four work group-level factors in the literature that are critical antecedents of individual job design: work group composition (e.g., group diversity and/or heterogeneity), work group interdependence (i.e., the degree to which members are required to interact with one another to complete tasks), work group autonomy (i.e., the extent to which autonomy is present at the team-level), and work group leadership (i.e.,

270 TRANSFORMATIVE WORK DESIGN

the extent to which leaders engage in decision-making about dividing labor and influencing individual jobs). This section will explicitly build on and extend this work by reviewing key studies emphasizing this multi-level perspective and with a particular focus on the role of group autonomy and the role of group leadership.

Group/team factors

Group-level factors are more local antecedents than organizational factors and describe features of a department, a working unit, or a team (Parker et al., 2017). Teams and work groups are often seen as distinct concepts due to their varying levels of interdependence and shared goals. However, in this section, for reasons of simplicity, we will bundle these concepts together and discuss the role of "local work group factors" and their impact on individual work design. We take a multi-level perspective (Kozlowski & Klein, 2000) and consider how group factors at the collective level trickle down and impact individual experiences of job design.

Team work design refers to the nature and organization of tasks, activities, and responsibilities applied to the team level (Morgeson & Campion, 2021; Parker, 2014). When examining how team-level factors relate to individual job design, researchers have predominantly looked at the impact of team autonomy as a higher-level context factor on individual autonomy and job demands (Chen et al., 2007; Cruz & Pil, 2011; van Mierlo et al., 2007). In other words, this research is investigating whether and how more autonomy for the overall team translates into individual level perceptions of job autonomy. Therefore, it is not surprising that this literature has mostly focused on the concept of self-managing teams. As self-managing teams are discussed in detail in Chapter 12, we will only highlight a couple of main implications for individual work design here.

Self-managing teams (SMTs) are given elevated levels of autonomy in how the group, as a whole, can get their work done, and multi-level research suggests that implications for individual work design can be more complex than initially theorized. Despite the implementation of SMTs often being underpinned by key work characteristics (e.g., the idea that entire work groups should have high levels of autonomy, elevated levels of task variety, task significance, task identity, and feedback) a review by van Mierlo and colleagues (2005) highlighted that these underlying work design dimensions and implications are rarely assessed and/or tested as mediating the effects of SMTs on individual and team-level well-being. An exception is the study conducted by van Mierlo and colleagues (2007) who tested the (often implicit) assumption that elevated levels of team autonomy benefit individual well-being via increased individual task autonomy and task variety, as well as reduced individual demands (i.e., reduced pace and quantity of work, time pressure under which individuals are working). Expected effects on job demands were based on the argument that autonomous teams have more discretion in distributing tasks among members. The authors tested their model in a sample of 80 self-managing teams from care and nursing organizations and largely found support for their hypotheses, except for the mediating role of task variety between team autonomy and individual well-being, which was not supported.

In a similar vein, Cruz and Pil (2011) also argued that team autonomy benefits individual job autonomy. Of note, Cruz and Pil (2011) used a more fine-grained approach with respect to team autonomy and distinguished between different types of autonomy, including the extent to which teams can make decisions, the team's responsibility for products, and the ability of team members to appoint their own team leader. Furthermore, and in contrast to van Mierlo and colleagues (2005), Cruz and Pil (2011) argued that team autonomy, and particularly increased levels of team-decision making, should increase individual demands (i.e., workload and time pressure) because it requires individuals to have more consensus-driven discussions when it comes to scheduling tasks or discussing quality of products. The authors tested their hypotheses in a relatively large sample (292 team-based departments) using the 2004 UK Workplace Employment Relations Survey. Similar to the results obtained by van Mierlo and colleagues (2005), Cruz and Pil (2011) found that team decision-making autonomy is associated with an increase in individual autonomy (although no support was found for team leader appointment and team responsibility for products and services being associated with individual autonomy). However, and in contrast to results by van Mierlo and colleagues (2005), both team decision-making and team responsibility were associated with an increase in individual demands, suggesting that in some cases, group-level factors can improve some dimensions of individual job design (e.g., autonomy), but worsen others (e.g., increasing demands).

Finally, Chen and colleagues (2007) looked at the concept of team empowerment, which shares considerable overlap with the idea of SMT—the main difference is that empowerment focuses on psychological aspects of experiencing autonomy, impact, and meaning, whereas the concept of SMTs is rooted more in structural changes that elevate levels of team control. Team empowerment encapsulates the idea that a team collectively believes that they have the autonomy and capability to perform meaningful work that can impact their organization. Chen and colleagues (2007) tested the hypothesis that team empowerment increases individual empowerment, which is conducive to individual performance. However, in their study of 62 teams from the United States (responsible for ordering and maintaining merchandise products), they found no support for this hypothesis.

As well as group autonomy, there is some evidence that team emergent psychological states, such as team conflict, can impact individuals' work design. For example, Langfred (2004) showed that members in teams that have a high level of conflict experience low levels of job autonomy which may be because team members monitor each other's work closely and do not leave much discretion to individuals.

One key insight from these three multi-level studies is that team autonomy (and related concepts like team empowerment) has more nuanced and complex implications (including negative effects) for individual work design than academics have traditionally assumed. For example, individual work demands, and particularly individual workload and time pressure, can be affected both positively and negatively by higher levels of team autonomy (Cruz & Pil, 2011; van Mierlo et al., 2007). Much of the existing research provides a snapshot and static perspective into how group-level factors trickle down to individual job design. The reality is that group-level factors may unfold differently over the short versus longer timeframe. For example, increasing team autonomy may at first create more coordination demands, thus increasing individual workload perceptions based on the need to discuss role clarity, scheduling, and discussion of "who does what." However, over the longer-term, once teams with high levels of autonomy have developed a shared mental model of how they accomplish work, the elevated control may be of help when it comes to managing workload demands. Future research is required to better understand the multi-level effects of how team work design affects individual job design over time. However, this type of research is complex and very costly as it requires not only large number of teams (for statistical power), but also repeated measurements of groups or teams (Maynard et al., 2021). For example, the null findings from Chen and colleagues' (2007) impressive multi-level study could be attributed to a lack of statistical power. Yet access to surveying large number of teams is often considerably challenging for researchers interested in group-level and team-level questions. Further, team membership can be fluid, and many employees work in multiple teams and/or change team membership which creates additional research complexities.

Leadership Factors

Emerging theory regarding the antecedents of work design has long pointed toward managers and leaders in organizations being at the center of the top-down influences of work design (Morgeson et al., 2010; Parker et al., 2017). Research suggests that leaders can influence work design by either altering objective or structural characteristics of jobs and/or by shaping the way employees make sense of and perceive their tasks, responsibilities, and the work environment (Parker et al., 2017, 2019). This is in line with leadership theory and research that has long positioned work design as one of the main mechanisms by which leaders can influence important employee outcomes such as performance and well-being (Inceoglu et al., 2018; Piccolo & Colquitt, 2006; Yukl, 2008).

First, regarding the structural pathway, evidence provides support for the idea that leaders can directly alter the structural or objective characteristics of the work, for example by allowing employees high levels of autonomy (e.g., Offerman & Hellmann, 1996), by allocating tasks in a way that ensures more variety or social interactions (Parker et al., 2019), or by implementing systems that provide increased levels of feedback (Korek et al., 2010). Focusing on more specific types of leadership, transformational leadership was shown to support work characteristics such as autonomy, variety, and role clarity (Korek et al., 2010; Nielsen et al., 2008; Piccolo & Colquitt, 2006). Similar positive effects have been evidenced for authentic and ethical leadership (Read & Laschinger, 2015). However, more passive or directive forms of leadership have been shown to have opposite effects on work design, leading to increased role ambiguity or reduced social support (Skogstad et al., 2014). Leaders' influence on the structural characteristics of work can also manifest more indirectly through the impact that their behaviors and attitudes can have in either supporting or thwarting employees' motivation and attempts at (re)designing their own work via proactive behaviors, such as job crafting (Tang et al., 2020; Thun & Bakker, 2018) or negotiating I-deals (Liao et al., 2016). For example, leaders have been shown to play an important role in encouraging employees to proactively craft their jobs to achieve higher levels of challenge or support (Wang et al., 2017). These more indirect processes have the potential to lead to positive spirals in which support for employee crafting can lead to better performance and well-being via a stronger person environment fit, which in turn can trigger leaders to allocate even more opportunities for crafting or other types of resources (e.g., Khan et al., 2022; Wang et al., 2017).

Second, the perceptual pathway for leadership influence on work design is rooted in arguments that work characteristics are only partially grounded in the objective characteristics of ones' job and should be conceptualized as perceptual terms that involve a certain degree of subjectivity (Judge et al., 2000). Leadership has been argued to influence the perceptual aspects of work design through its sense-making function. Theories focused on sense-making, meaning, and social information processing in organizations (Salancik & Pfeffer, 1978; Smircich & Morgan, 1982) suggest that leaders' attitudes and behaviors serve as an important and salient sources of social information that can direct employees' attention to certain work aspects and influence the way they might judge their tasks, responsibilities, and the work environment (Bass & Avolio, 1993). In line with these arguments, a study by Griffin (1991) showed

274 TRANSFORMATIVE WORK DESIGN

that leadership behaviors aimed at changing job perceptions were associated with changes in perceived work characteristics three months later, even though no tangible (or structural) changes were observed in the actual jobs. These results support the idea that even when leaders have little to no opportunities to influence or change actual work designs, they can still influence employees' subjective interpretations of the work environment (Purvanova et al., 2006).

While most of the literature covered in this section tends to focus on the associations between leadership behaviors and work design characteristics, some more in-depth approaches on the role of leadership in shaping work design are also emerging. First, research is starting to not only move toward comparing several types of leader behaviors with each other, but also provide some attention to the way different types of leadership explain variance in work design at both between-person (stable differences between different employees) and within-person (fluctuations within an individual over time) levels of analysis. Sarmah and colleagues (2022) for example, found negative effects for controlling leadership via demands, but only at the between-person level, while autonomy supportive leadership had a positive effect on work engagement via increased job resources both at the within- and between-person levels of analysis. Their study calls for more attention to be given to potentially asymmetric effects of different types of leadership, as well as when different levels of work design are considered.

Second, a body of research is emerging that examines how people in general, as well as those in managerial or leadership positions, are making decisions about the work design of others (Parker et al., 2019). Interestingly, this line of research is showing that people are more likely to make decisions that lead to more simplified and narrow work designs, but also that their own work design heavily informs their approach to designing work for others. This finding provides interesting insights into possible cyclic processes through which both good and bad work designs can be perpetuated as they become implicit forms of knowledge about how work should be organized, which can then influence approaches to work (re)design. We thoroughly believe that the expansion of both these directions of research into more fine-grained influences of leadership on work design has the potential to significantly advance scholarship in this space and better inform managerial practice.

Directions for Future Research

While we have already identified some emerging and future directions for each of the antecedents discussed in the present chapter, this section focuses on several broader directions that can apply across all or most of these factors.

First, the antecedents of work design reviewed and discussed in the present chapter represent an inherently multi-level structure. But despite repeated calls for more rigorous multi-level research (Parker et al., 2017), the existing literature continues to be dominated by single-level approaches. We therefore echo existing calls for more cross-level research that focuses not only on the interplay of each of these higher-level factors and individual work design, but more importantly, also addresses the interplay between these factors themselves. As an example, occupational factors have been theorized to interact with organizational structure factors. Dierdorff and Morgeson (2013) argued that the association between occupational values such as achievement and job autonomy can be expected to be stronger in more decentralized organizational structures, while occupations high in values of independence might reduce the association between mechanistic structures and increased specialization. Greater attention to such interaction effects should be extended to the interplay between higher-level contextual factors and individual-level antecedents of work design, especially considering existing evidence that work characteristics, such as job autonomy, are shaped by regulatory structures in the work environment (such as instructions, rules, procedures, standards) as well as individuals' own motivational tendencies and/or preferences (Hamstra et al., 2024). However, research should not stop at interactions, as the research reviewed in this chapter and emerging theory points to dynamic and often circular processes linking occupational, organizational, and work group level factors to work design.

In particular, we call for a better understanding of the "trickle-up" effects of work design (Oldham & Hackman, 2010; Parker et al., 2017), as empirical research in this space continues to adopt mainly a traditional, top-down perspective focusing on how higher-level factors can facilitate or constrain the emergence of particular work design characteristics. While emerging theory on the antecedents of work design does theorize bottom-up processes (Parker et al., 2017), the focus is mainly on employee led work design via job crafting, with little consideration for further flow-on effects on factors at higher levels. However, in the contemporary context, in which we see swift changes to work design being implemented, such as the almost instant transition from office work to remote and virtual work during the COVID-19 pandemic, the consideration of how properties at higher levels are impacted by work (re)design changes becomes critical. As seen with the accelerated transition to remote and virtual work, the implications for higher level factors are numerous, ranging from new technologies being implemented, changes in leadership and management practices, dismantling and reorganizing of teams, offices, and departments, adoption of new organizational designs and strategies. Furthermore, it has been argued that these impacts are even wider than the organization, affecting the mix of occupations required as well as the key knowledge and skills required within occupations. Such changes in work design, even when they are not spurred by large-scale stressors but by incremental improvements via work redesign and management solutions, have the potential of loosening constraints that exist at higher levels. When this happens, it can lead to virtuous cycles in which, for example, autonomous work designs prompt further decentralization of organizational structures that reinforce autonomy (Clegg & Spencer, 2007). Therefore, an increased research focus on these trickle-up processes has the potential to significantly advance our understanding of how work design emerges and is sustained over time via dynamic, top-down, and bottom-up, processes.

Finally, we call for more research that goes beyond the traditional focus on chronic work design to facilitate a better understanding of how work design changes for individual employees over time, and the way various multi-level antecedents contribute, or not, to these changes. This is especially important given emerging evidence that the effects of higher-level antecedents such as leadership on work design are not identical at different levels of analysis (Sarmah et al., 2022). Similar asymmetric relationships across the different levels of work design could exist for other antecedents of work design. While most research in this field focuses on how higher level contextual factors contribute to stable, between-person differences in work design, incorporating a focus on within individual levels of analysis would support a better understanding of the processes by which work design is shaped and changes over time, which becomes ever more critical given the fast-changing nature of contemporary jobs (Fraccaroli et al., 2024).

Beyond the theoretical advancement of work design research, there are practical implications that justify a greater interest in the contextual factors that shape work design. We concur with Parker and colleagues (2017) in pointing out that applied work redesign interventions would particularly benefit from a better understanding of these influencing factors that can often act as barriers to successful implementation. Furthermore, a better understanding of the higher-level influences on work design can better inform broader policies and measures aimed at increasing the quality of work across organizations, industries, and sectors. This is especially important given the profound shifts in contemporary work due to factors such as large-scale stressors, technological advancements, demographic changes, and increased uncertainty.

References

Adler, P. S., & Borys, B. (1996). Two types of bureaucracy: Enabling and coercive. *Administrative Science Quarterly 41*(1), 61–89.

Allen, J., Alpass, F. M., Szabó, Á., & Stephens, C. V. (2021). Impact of flexible work arrangements on key challenges to work engagement among older workers. *Work, Aging and Retirement 7*(4), 404–417.

Ashford, S. J., Caza, B. B., & Reid, E. M. (2018). From surviving to thriving in the gig economy: A research agenda for individuals in the new world of work. *Research in Organizational Behavior 38*, 23–41.

Aubé, C., Rousseau, V., & Brunelle, E. (2018). Flow experience in teams: The role of shared leadership. *Journal of Occupational Health Psychology 23*(2), 198–206.

Bass, B. M., & Avolio, B. J. (1993). Transformational leadership and organizational culture. *Public Administration Quarterly 17*(1), 112–121.

Benders, J., Doorewaard, H., & Poutsma, E. (2000). Modern socio-technology. In M. M. Beyerlein (Ed.), *Work teams: Past, present and future* (pp. 169–180). Kluwer.

Berber, A., Findikli, M. A., Marescaux, E., Rofcanin, Y., Mughal, F., & Swart, J. (2023). Exploring the effects of reduced load work arrangements (RLWAs): The role of individual autonomy and workplace level justice perceptions. *European Management Journal 41*(5), 720–729.

Berdicchia, D., Nicolli, F., & Masino, G. (2016). Job enlargement, job crafting and the moderating role of self-competence. *Journal of Managerial Psychology 31*(2), 318–330.

Berg, J. M., Grant, A. M., & Johnson, V. (2010). When callings are calling: Crafting work and leisure in pursuit of unanswered occupational callings. *Organization Science 21*(5), 973–994.

Bidwell, M. (2010). Problems deciding: how the structure of make-or-buy decisions leads to transaction misalignment. *Organization Science 21*(2), 362–379.

Boon, C., Den Hartog, D. N., & Lepak, D. P. (2019). A systematic review of human resource management systems and their measurement. *Journal of Management 45*(6), 2498–2537.

Boselie, P., Dietz, G., & Boon, C. (2005). Commonalities and contradictions in HRM and performance research. *Human Resource Management Journal 15*(3), 67–94.

Boyd, C. M., Tuckey, M. R., & Winefield, A. H. (2014). Perceived effects of organizational downsizing and staff cuts on the stress experience: The role of resources. *Stress and Health 30*(1), 53–64.

Chen, G., Kirkman, B. L., Kanfer, R., Allen, D., & Rosen, B. (2007). A multilevel study of leadership, empowerment, and performance in teams. *Journal of Applied Psychology 92*(2), 331.

Chen, Y., & Reay, T. (2021). Responding to imposed job redesign: The evolving dynamics of work and identity in restructuring professional identity. *Human Relations 74*(10), 1541–1571.

Christina, S., Dainty, A., Daniels, K., Tregaskis, O., & Waterson, P. (2017). Shut the fridge door! HRM alignment, job redesign and energy performance. *Human Resource Management Journal 27*(3), 382–402.

Clegg, C., & Spencer, C. (2007). A circular and dynamic model of the process of job design. *Journal of Occupational and Organizational Psychology 80*(2), 321–339.

Cropanzano, R., Keplinger, K., Lambert, B. K., Caza, B., & Ashford, S. J. (2023). The organizational psychology of gig work: An integrative conceptual review. *Journal of Applied Psychology 108*(3), 492–519.

Cruz, K. S., & Pil, F. K. (2011). Team design and stress: A multilevel analysis. *Human Relations 64*(10), 1265–1289.

Dhondt, S., & Benders, J. (1998). Missing links: Production structures and quality of working life in the clothing industry. *International Journal of Operations & Production Management 18*(12), 1189–1204.

Dierdorff, E. C. (2019). Toward reviving an occupation with occupations. *Annual Review of Organizational Psychology and Organizational Behavior 6*, 397–419.

278 TRANSFORMATIVE WORK DESIGN

Dierdorff, E. C., & Ellington, J. K. (2008). It's the nature of the work: examining behavior-based sources of work-family conflict across occupations. *Journal of Applied Psychology* 93(4), 883.

Dierdorff, E. C., & Morgeson, F. P. (2007). Consensus in work role requirements: The influence of discrete occupational context on role expectations. *Journal of Applied Psychology* 92(5), 1228–1241.

Dierdorff, E. C., & Morgeson, F. P. (2013). Getting what the occupation gives: Exploring multilevel links between work design and occupational values. *Personnel Psychology* 66(3), 687–721.

Dierdorff, E. C., Rubin, R. S., & Morgeson, F. P. (2009). The milieu of managerial work: An integrative framework linking work context to role requirements. *Journal of Applied Psychology* 94(4), 972–988.

Ferrie, J. E., Westerlund, H., Oxenstierna, G., & Theorell, T. (2007). The impact of moderate and major workplace expansion and downsizing on the psychosocial and physical work environment and income in Sweden. *Scandinavian Journal of Public Health* 35(1), 62–69.

Fraccaroli, F., Zaniboni, S., & Truxillo, D. M. (2024). Challenges in the new economy: A new era for work design. *Annual Review of Organizational Psychology and Organizational Behavior* 11, 307–335.

Germov, J. (2005). Managerialism in the Australian public health sector: Towards the hyper-rationalization of professional bureaucracies. *Sociology of Health & Illness* 27(6), 738–758.

Gibbs, M., Levenson, A., & Zoghi, C. (2010). Why are jobs designed the way they are? In S. W. Polachek & K. Tatsiramos (Eds.), *Jobs, training, and worker well-being* (pp. 107–154). Emerald Group Publishing Limited.

Griffin, R. W. (1991). Effects of work redesign on employee perceptions, attitudes, and behaviors: A long-term investigation. *Academy of Management Journal* 34(2), 425–435.

Guest, D. E. (1997). Human resource management and performance: A review and research agenda. *International Journal of Human Resource Management* 8(3), 263–276.

Hamstra, M. R., Laurijssen, L. M., & Schreurs, B. (2024). The impact of regulatory fit on experienced autonomy. *Social Psychological and Personality Science* 15(3), 340–350.

Harley, B. (1999). The myth of empowerment: Work organization, hierarchy, and employee autonomy in contemporary Australian workplaces. *Work, Employment and Society* 13(1), 41–66.

Hay, G. J. (2020). *The embeddedness of work design in occupational context* [Doctoral dissertation, The University of Western Australia]. https://research-repository.uwa.edu.au/en/publications/the-embeddedness-of-work-design-in-occupational-context

Hay, G. J., Parker, S. K., & Luksyte, A. (2021). Making sense of organisational change failure: An identity lens. *Human Relations* 74(2), 180–207.

Hodgson, D., & Briand, L. (2013). Controlling the uncontrollable: "Agile" teams and illusions of autonomy in creative work. *Work, Employment and Society* 27(2), 308–325.

Holman, D., Frenkel, S., Sørensen, O., & Wood, S. (2009). Work design variation and outcomes in call centers: Strategic choice and institutional explanations. *Industrial and Labor Relations Review* 62(4), 510–532.

Huising, R. (2015). To hive or to hold? Producing professional authority through scut work. *Administrative Science Quarterly* 60(2), 263–299.

Huys, R., Sels, L., Van Hootegem, G., Bundervoet, J., & Henderickx, E. (1999). Toward less division of labor? New production concepts in the automotive, chemical, clothing, and machine tool industries. *Human Relations 52*(1), 67–93.

Inceoglu, I., Thomas, G., Chu, C., Plans, D., & Gerbasi, A. (2018). Leadership behavior and employee well-being: An integrated review and a future research agenda. *Leadership Quarterly 29*(1), 179–202.

Ingvaldsen, J. A., & Rolfsen, M. (2012). Autonomous work groups and the challenge of inter-group coordination. *Human Relations 65*(7), 861–881.

Jackson, S. E., Schuler, R. S., & Jiang, K. (2014). An aspirational framework for strategic human resource management. *Academy of Management Annals 8*(1), 1–56.

Jahncke, H., Hygge, S., Mathiassen, S. E., Hallman, D., Mixter, S., & Lyskov, E. (2017). Variation at work: Alternations between physically and mentally demanding tasks in blue-collar occupations. *Ergonomics 60*(9), 1218–1227.

Jiang, Y., Wang, Q., & Weng, Q. (2022). Job characteristics as drivers of occupational commitment: the mediating mechanisms. *Current Psychology, 41*(1), 18–28.

Judge, T. A., Bono, J. E., & Locke, E. A. (2000). Personality and job satisfaction: The mediating role of job characteristics. *Journal of Applied Psychology 85*(2), 237.

Kampkötter, P., Harbring, C., & Sliwka, D. (2018). Job rotation and employee performance: Evidence from a longitudinal study in the financial services industry. *International Journal of Human Resource Management 29*(10), 1709–1735.

Kelliher, C., & Anderson, D. (2010). Doing more with less? Flexible working practices and the intensification of work. *Human Relations 63*(1), 83–106.

Khan, M. M., Mubarik, M. S., Islam, T., Rehman, A., Ahmed, S. S., Khan, E., & Sohail, F. (2022). How servant leadership triggers innovative work behavior: Exploring the sequential mediating role of psychological empowerment and job crafting. *European Journal of Innovation Management 25*(4), 1037–1055.

Knight, A. P., Menges, J. I., & Bruch, H. (2018). Organizational affective tone: A meso perspective on the origins and effects of consistent affect in organizations. *Academy of Management Journal 61*(1), 191–219.

Knudsen, H. K., Aaron Johnson, J., Martin, J. K., & Roman, P. M. (2003). Downsizing survival: The experience of work and organizational commitment. *Sociological Inquiry 73*(2), 265–283.

Korek, S., Felfe, J., & Zaepernick-Rothe, U. (2010). Transformational leadership and commitment: A multilevel analysis of group-level influences and mediating processes. *European Journal of Work and Organizational Psychology 19*(3), 364–387.

Kozlowski, S. W. J., & Klein, K. J. (2000). Multilevel approach to theory and research in organizations—Contextual, temporal, and emergent processes. In K. J. Klein & S. W. J. Kozlowski (Eds.), *Multilevel theory, research and methods in organizations: Foundations, extensions, and new directions* (pp. 3–90). Jossey-Bass.

Langfred, C. W. (2004). Too much of a good thing? Negative effects of high trust and individual autonomy in self-managing teams. *Academy of Management Journal 47*(3), 385–399.

Lawler III, E. E. (1986). *High-involvement management: Participative strategies for improving organizational performance*. Jossey-Bass Publishers.

Lazear, E. P. 2000. The power of incentives. *American Economic Review 90*(2), 410–414.

Liao, C., Wayne, S. J., & Rousseau, D. M. (2016). Idiosyncratic deals in contemporary organizations: A qualitative and meta-analytical review. *Journal of Organizational Behavior 37*, S9–S29.

280 TRANSFORMATIVE WORK DESIGN

Lofquist, L. H., & Dawis, R. V. (1984). Research on work adjustment and satisfaction: Implications for career counseling. In S. D. Brown & R. W. Lent (Eds.), Handbook of counseling psychology (pp. 216–237). Wiley.

Macky, K., & Boxall, P. (2008). High-involvement work processes, work intensification and employee well-being: A study of New Zealand worker experiences. *Asia Pacific Journal of Human Resources 46*(1), 38–55.

Maynard, M. T., Conroy, S., Lacerenza, C. N., & Barnes, L. Y. (2021). Teams in the wild are not extinct, but challenging to research: A guide for conducting impactful team field research with 10 recommendations and 10 best practices. *Organizational Psychology Review 11*(3), 274–318.

Melé, D. (2005). Exploring the principle of subsidiarity in organizational forms. *Journal of Business Ethics 60*, 293–305.

Morgeson, F. P., & Campion, M. A. (2021). Job and team design. In G. Salvendy (Ed.), Handbook of human factors and ergonomics (pp. 383–413). Wiley.

Morgeson, F. P., Dierdorff, E. C., & Hmurovic, J. L. (2010). Work design in situ: Understanding the role of occupational and organizational context. *Journal of Organizational Behavior 31*(2–3), 351–360.

Morgeson, F. P., & Humphrey, S. E. (2006). The Work Design Questionnaire (WDQ): Developing and validating a comprehensive measure for assessing job design and the nature of work. *Journal of Applied Psychology 91*(6), 1321.

Nemeth, C., O'Connor, M., Klock, P. A., & Cook, R. (2006). Discovering healthcare cognition: The use of cognitive artifacts to reveal cognitive work. *Organization Studies 27*(7), 1011–1035.

Nielsen, K., Randall, R., Yarker, J., & Brenner, S. O. (2008). The effects of transformational leadership on followers' perceived work characteristics and psychological well-being: A longitudinal study. *Work & Stress 22*(1), 16–32.

Obodaru, O. (2017). Forgone, but not forgotten: Toward a theory of forgone professional identities. *Academy of Management Journal 60*(2), 523–553.

Odle-Dusseau, H. N., Hammer, L. B., Crain, T. L., & Bodner, T. E. (2016). The influence of family-supportive supervisor training on employee job performance and attitudes: An organizational work–family intervention. *Journal of Occupational Health Psychology 21*(3), 296–308.

Offermann, L. R., & Hellmann, P. S. (1996). Leadership behavior and subordinate stress: A 360° view. *Journal of Occupational Health Psychology 1*(4), 382.

Oldham, G. R., & Hackman, J. R. (1981). Relationships between organizational structure and employee reactions: Comparing alternative frameworks. *Administrative Science Quarterly 26*, 66–83.

Oldham, G. R., & Hackman, J. R. (2010). Not what it was and not what it will be: The future of job design research. *Journal of Organizational Behavior 31*(2–3), 463–479.

Organ, D. W., & Greene, C. N. (1981). The effects of formalization on professional involvement: A compensatory process approach. *Administrative Science Quarterly 26*, 237–252.

Parent-Rocheleau, X., & Parker, S. K. (2022). Algorithms as work designers: How algorithmic management influences the design of jobs. *Human Resource Management Review 32*(3), 100838.

Parker, S. K. (2003). Longitudinal effects of lean production on employee outcomes and the mediating role of work characteristics. *Journal of Applied Psychology 88*(4), 620–634.

Parker, S. K. (2014). Going beyond motivation: Work design for development, health, ambidexterity, and more. *Annual Review of Psychology 65*, 661–691.

Parker, S. K., Andrei, D. M., & Van den Broeck, A. (2019). Poor work design begets poor work design: Capacity and willingness antecedents of individual work design behavior. *Journal of Applied Psychology 104*(7), 907.

Parker, S. K., Van den Broeck, A., & Holman, D. (2017). Work design influences: A synthesis of multilevel factors that affect the design of jobs. *Academy of Management Annals 11*(1), 267–308.

Parker, S. K., & Knight, C. (2024). The SMART model of work design: A higher order structure to help see the wood from the trees. *Human Resource Management 63*(2), 265–291.

Peci, A., & Rudloff Pulgar, O. C. (2019). Autonomous bureaucrats in independent bureaucracies? Loyalty perceptions within supreme audit institutions. *Public Management Review 21*(1), 47–68.

Piccolo, R. F., & Colquitt, J. A. (2006). Transformational leadership and job behaviors: The mediating role of core job characteristics. *Academy of Management Journal 49*(2), 327–340.

Posthuma, R. A., Campion, M. C., Masimova, M., & Campion, M. A. (2013). A high performance work practices taxonomy: Integrating the literature and directing future research. *Journal of Management 39*(5), 1184–1220.

Purvanova, R. K., Bono, J. E., & Dzieweczynski, J. (2006). Transformational leadership, job characteristics, and organizational citizenship performance. *Human Performance 19*(1), 1–22.

Quinlan, M., & Bohle, P. (2009). Overstretched and unreciprocated commitment: Reviewing research on the occupational health and safety effects of downsizing and job insecurity. *International Journal of Health Services 39*(1), 1–44.

Read, E. A., & Laschinger, H. K. (2015). The influence of authentic leadership and empowerment on nurses' relational social capital, mental health and job satisfaction over the first year of practice. *Journal of Advanced Nursing 71*(7), 1611–1623.

Rousseau, D.vM. (1977). Technological differences in job characteristics, employee satisfaction, and motivation: A synthesis of job design research and sociotechnical systems theory. *Organizational Behavior and Human Performance 19*(1), 18–42.

Salancik, G. R., & Pfeffer, J. (1978). A social information processing approach to job attitudes and task design. *Administrative Science Quarterly 23*, 224–253.

Sarmah, P., Van den Broeck, A., Schreurs, B., Proost, K., & Germeys, F. (2022). Autonomy supportive and controlling leadership as antecedents of work design and employee well-being. *BRQ Business Research Quarterly 25*(1), 44–61.

Schroeder, A. N., Bricka, T. M., & Whitaker, J. H. (2021). Work design in a digitized gig economy. *Human Resource Management Review 31*(1), https://doi.org/10.1016/j.hrmr.2019.100692

Shirmohammadi, M., Chan Au, W., & Beigi, M. (2022). Antecedents and outcomes of work-life balance while working from home: A review of the research conducted during the COVID-19 pandemic. *Human Resource Development Review 21*(4), 473–516.

de Sitter, L. U., Den Hertog, J. F., & Dankbaarl, B. 1997. From complex organizations with simple jobs to simple organizations with complex jobs. *Human Relations 50*(5), 497–534.

Skogstad, A., Hetland, J., Glasø, L., & Einarsen, S. (2014). Is avoidant leadership a root cause of subordinate stress? Longitudinal relationships between laissez-faire leadership and role ambiguity. *Work & Stress 28*(4), 323–341.

Smircich, L., & Morgan, G. (1982). Leadership: The management of meaning. *Journal of Applied Behavioral Science 18*(3), 257–273.

Snell, S. A., & Morris, S. S. (2021). Time for realignment: The HR ecosystem. *Academy of Management Perspectives 35*(2), 219–236.

Spreitzer, G. M., Cameron, L., & Garrett, L. (2017). Alternative work arrangements: Two images of the new world of work. *Annual Review of Organizational Psychology and Organizational Behavior 4*, 473–499.

Tafvelin, S., Stenling, A., Lundmark, R., & Westerberg, K. (2019). Aligning job redesign with leadership training to improve supervisor support: A quasi-experimental study of the integration of HR practices. *European Journal of Work and Organizational Psychology 28*(1), 74–84.

Tang, S., Zhang, G., & Wang, H. J. (2020). Daily empowering leadership and job crafting: Examining moderators. *International Journal of Environmental Research and Public Health 17*(16), 5756.

Thompson, V. A. (1969). *Bureaucracy and innovation.* University of Alabama Press.

Thun, S., & Bakker, A. B. (2018). Empowering leadership and job crafting: The role of employee optimism. *Stress and Health 34*(4), 573–581.

Trist, E. L., & Bamforth, K.W. (1951). Some social and psychological consequences of the longwall method of coal-getting: An examination of the psychological situation and defenses of a work group in relation to the social structure and technological content of the work system. *Human Relations 4*(1), 3–38.

van den Heuvel, M., Demerouti, E., & Peeters, M. C. W. (2015). The job crafting intervention: Effects on job resources, self-efficacy, and affective well-being. *Journal of Occupational and Organizational Psychology 88*(3), 511–532.

Van Eijnatten, F. (1993). *The paradigm that changed the work place.* Swedish Centre for Working Life/Van Gorcum.

van Mierlo, H., Rutte, C. G., Kompier, M. A., & Doorewaard, H. A. (2005). Self-managing teamwork and psychological well-being: Review of a multilevel research domain. *Group & Organization Management 30*(2), 211–235.

van Mierlo, H., Rutte, C. G., Vermunt, J. K., Kompier, M. A. J., & Doorewaard, J. A.C. M. (2007). A multi-level mediation model of the relationships between team autonomy, individual task design and psychological well-being. *Journal of Occupational and Organizational Psychology 80*(4), 647–664.

Vermeerbergen, L., McDermott, A. M., & Benders, J. (2021). Managers shaping the service triangle: Navigating resident and worker interests through work design in nursing homes. *Work and Occupations 48*(1), 70–98.

Victor, B., Boynton, A., & Stephens-Jahng, T. (2000). The effective design of work under total quality management. *Organization Science 11*(1), 102–117.

Vriens, D. J., Achterbergh, J. M. I. M., & Gulpers, L. 2018. Virtuous structures. *Journal of Business Ethics 150*(3), 671–690.

Walton, R. E. (1985). *From control to commitment in the workplace: In factory after factory, there is a revolution under way in the management of work.* US Department of Labor, Bureau of Labor-Management Relations and Cooperative Programs.

Wang, H. J., Demerouti, E., & Le Blanc, P. (2017). Transformational leadership, adaptability, and job crafting: The moderating role of organizational identification. *Journal of Vocational Behavior 100*, 185–195.

Wood, S., Holman, D., & Stride, C. (2006). Human resource management and performance in UK call centres. *British Journal of Industrial Relations 44*(1), 99–124.

Yukl, G. (2008). How leaders influence organizational effectiveness. *Leadership Quarterly 19*(6), 708–722.

On the Creation of Developmental Jobs

Irene de Pater

> *The strongest principle of growth lies in human choice.*
> —George Eliot (Pseudonym of Mary Ann Evans), 1876

Frederick Herzberg (1965) suggested that "more emphasis is needed on the challenge and interest of the job that workers are required to do" (p. 373). Not only because the content of one's job (e.g., responsibility, interesting work, achievement) is a strong driver of positive job attitudes and work motivation but also because "it is the challenge of the task that is the means for unleashing [one's] talent" (p. 371). Indeed, challenging work experiences or *developmental challenge*,[1] defined as "work activities for which existing tactics and routines are inadequate and that require new ways of dealing with work situations" (de Pater, Van Vianen, Bechtoldt, et al., 2009, p. 299) are critical for an employee's effective functioning and growth (e.g., Noe et al., 2014; Parker et al., 2021). This chapter provides an overview of research on the creation of developmental jobs to date and identifies avenues for future research on this topic.

Developmental challenge

The most commonly used framework to study developmental challenge is Cynthia McCauley and colleagues' (1999) Job Challenge Profile. The Job Challenge Profile distinguishes five categories of developmental challenges: creating change (inherited problems, new directions, problems with employees), dealing with diversity (work group diversity, working across cultures), experiencing a job transition (unfamiliar responsibilities), managing at high levels of responsibility (high stakes, scope, and scale), and managing boundaries (external pressure, influencing without authority). These developmental challenges provide "the motivation and opportunity to learn" (McCauley et al., 1994, p. 544) and

---

[1] Researchers have used various labels to refer to challenging work experiences, such as, among others, challenging assignments (Preenen et al., 2011, 2014), developmental job components (McCauley et al., 1994), and developmental job experiences (Kim, 2021; Matsuo, 2019, 2022).

Irene de Pater, *On the Creation of Developmental Jobs*. In: *Transformative Work Design*. Edited by: Sharon K. Parker et al., Oxford University Press. © Society for Industrial and Organizational Psychology (2025). DOI: 10.1093/oso/9780197692554.003.0011

result in the development of abilities, insights, knowledge, norms, and values that increase one's capacities for effective functioning (de Pater, Van Vianen, Bechtoldt, et al., 2009; London, 2002).

Although research on developmental challenge initially focused on its impact on learning managerial skills (e.g., Brutus et al., 2000; McCauley et al., 1994) and the career development of employees working in managerial roles (e.g., Kirchmeyer, 1995; Lyness & Thompson, 1997, 2000), research has shown that developmental challenge is also pivotal for the learning (e.g., Preenen et al., 2011; Preenen et al., 2015) and career development (e.g., Aryee & Chu, 2012; de Pater, Van Vianen, Bechtoldt, et al., 2009) of employees in non-managerial roles. More recently, research has branched out and examined a wider range of outcomes of developmental challenge. This research has shown, among other findings, that challenging work experiences are important for attracting, motivating, and retaining employees (e.g., Dimitrova, 2020; Konrad et al., 2000; Piccolo & Colquitt, 2006); relate to increased psychological capital (Kim et al., 2021), well-being (Preenen et al., 2019), and psychological empowerment (Matsuo, 2019, 2022); and result in increased creativity and innovative work behaviors (Battistelli et al., 2019; Kim et al., 2021; Matsuo, 2022).

These research findings suggest that the benefits of challenging work experiences are paramount and that developmental challenge could be useful in enhancing the quality of employees' work, work life, and work-related outcomes (Preenen et al., 2019). Notwithstanding the above, research also suggests that employees differ in the extent to which they have access to and engage in developmental challenges (e.g., de Pater, Van Vianen, Bechtoldt, et al., 2009; DeRue & Wellman, 2009). However, research has, so far, largely ignored antecedents of engagement in developmental challenges (Battistelli et al., 2019; Parker et al., 2017). It is important to address this issue both theoretically and empirically to gain insight into factors that stimulate access to and engagement in developmental challenges. Especially relevant in this regard are theories related to learning motivation, career development, and diversity and inclusion. From a practical perspective, insight into antecedents of developmental challenge may inform employees, supervisors, and human resource managers on how to stimulate employee learning and career development.

The remainder of the chapter starts with a review of research that has examined antecedents of developmental challenge. Next, it will address factors that affect employees' choice for engaging in developmental challenge, factors the affect the division of developmental challenges among team members, and factors that affect supervisors' assignment of developmental challenges.

Antecedents of developmental challenge

The sparse research that has examined individual differences in developmental challenge has, to date, been especially focused on gender, with the aim to uncover gendered processes (i.e., processes where individuals' gender affect their outcomes) that could explain the gap in career success. Some studies have shown that women have fewer developmental challenges than men (Benschop et al., 2001; de Pater et al., 2010; de Pater, Van Vianen, Fischer, et al., 2009). Other studies did not find gender differences in the extent to which employees engage in developmental challenges but uncovered that it is more difficult for women than for men to obtain them (Lyness & Thompson, 2000) and that men engage in different developmental challenges then women. Men were found to engage in developmental challenges that were qualitatively more challenging (King et al., 2012), whereas women had more developmental challenges related to obstacles (e.g., working with a difficult boss, lack of support from top management; Ohlott et al., 1994) and challenges that involved non-authority relationships (Lyness & Thompson, 2000).

Gender differences in developmental challenges

Research aimed at developing a better understanding of the origins of gender differences in developmental challenge has taken various, complementary, perspectives. Drawing on, among others, social cognitive theory (Bandura, 1997; Bandura & Locke, 2003) and goal orientation theory (Dweck, 1986; Elliott & Dweck, 1988) researchers examined gender differences in *preferences* for and *choices* to engage in developmental challenge. Research in a laboratory setting has shown that men and women did not differ in their preferences for or tendencies to choose challenging tasks (de Pater, Van Vianen, Fischer, et al., 2009; King et al., 2012), but that in an achievement setting where their performance would be evaluated, women chose to engage in fewer challenging tasks than men (de Pater, Van Vianen, Fischer, et al., 2009). Drawing on social cognitive theory (Bandura, 1997; Bandura & Locke, 2003) and social role theory (Eagly, 1987), Irene de Pater, Annelies Van Vianen, Ronald Humphrey, and colleagues (2009) conducted a laboratory study to examine the impact of *task division among team members*. This study showed that when men and women who initially chose to perform similar tasks had to divide challenging and non-challenging tasks among them, men ended up conducting more of the challenging tasks, whereas women ended up conducting more of the non-challenging tasks. Finally, drawing on, among others, ambivalent sexism theory (Glick & Fiske, 1996), lack-of-fit theory (Heilman, 2001), and role congruity theory (Eagly & Karau, 2002), others examined the impact of *task assignment by supervisors* on the extent to which men and women have developmental challenges in their work. A field study showed that supervisors are more inclined to assign challenging tasks to men than to women (de Pater et al., 2010), whereas studies in a laboratory setting showed that female "employees" were only disadvantaged when tasks were assigned by a male "supervisor" (Mai-Dalton & Sullivan, 1981) who scored high on benevolent sexism (King et al., 2012).

The above shows that employees not only have developmental challenges assigned to them but also choose to engage in developmental challenges and negotiate with their peers to obtain developmental challenge. This aligns with the assumption that one's job content tends to be the outcome of mutual influence and negotiation (Graen et al., 1973). Building on this notion, we next explore factors that make it more likely for employees to choose for developmental challenges, to negotiate for developmental challenges, and that increase the likelihood supervisors will assign them developmental challenges.

Choosing developmental challenges

Research on job crafting—"the changes to a job that workers make with the intention of improving the job for themselves" (Bruning & Campion, 2018, p. 499)—has shown that employees themselves decide on a considerable proportion of the work activities they engage in at work (e.g., Tims et al., 2012; Wrzesniewski & Dutton, 2001). For instance, management trainees and recent university graduates working at junior job levels indicated to have initiated on average 30.24 percent to 32.42 percent of their work activities themselves, respectively, rising to 49.51 percent for employees working in middle-level jobs (de Pater, Van Vianen, Bechtoldt, et al., 2009). Whether or not employees choose challenging work experiences is likely to depend on their individual characteristics and their work environment.

Individual characteristics related to choosing developmental challenges. Employees are most likely to seek out developmental challenges when they believe they can successfully perform challenging tasks or when they want to learn and further develop themselves (Preenen et al., 2014). Hence, individual characteristics that may predispose employees to choose challenging work experiences are proactive personality, learning goal orientation, and self-efficacy.

Proactive personality. Employees who have a proactive personality are predisposed to engage in behaviors that alter their environment. They tend to be relatively unconstrained by forces in their work environment. They show initiative and "select, create, and influence situations in which they work" (Seibert et al., 1999, p. 417) to bring about meaningful change for themselves and their organization. Proactive personality relates to both objective and subjective career success because people with a proactive personality identify and create opportunities to engage in activities that result in learning and development

(Fuller & Marler, 2009). Hence, it is likely that proactive employees will more often choose to engage in developmental challenges than their more reactive counterparts. Although research has not addressed the relationship between proactive personality and the choice to engage in developmental challenge, a positive relationship has been identified between proactive personality and approach crafting (i.e., "effortful and directed actions to seek positive aspects of work"; Zhang & Parker, 2019, p. 130), creating challenge demands (i.e., workload, time pressure, cognitive demands; Tims et al., 2012; Van den Broeck et al., 2010), and engagement in challenging work experiences (de Pater, Van Vianen, Fischer, et al., 2009).

Learning goal orientation. Theory on achievement motivation distinguishes two types of goals that people may pursue in achievement-oriented settings: learning goals and performance goals (e.g., Dweck, 1986; Elliott & Dweck, 1988). Individuals holding a performance goal seek to gain or maintain favorable—and avoid unfavorable—judgments of their abilities and competence. Because engagement in developmental challenges involves increased risk of failure (de Pater, Van Vianen, Bechtoldt, et al., 2009; Earley et al., 1989), employees holding a performance goal may prefer to choose fewer challenging tasks and assignments. Those holding a learning goal seek to increase their abilities and competence or learn something new. To develop their abilities and competence, they choose to learn while taking the risk to display errors, mistakes, and failure (e.g., Dweck, 1986; Elliott & Dweck, 1988). Because engagement in developmental challenges results in learning and development, it is likely that employees holding learning goals will choose developmental challenges. This aligns with the finding that employee learning orientation positively relates to the extent to which they have challenging work experiences (Aryee & Chu, 2012; Matsuo, 2019) and suggests that through eliciting a learning orientation, managers may be able to stimulate their employees to choose challenge, which future research could explore.

Self-efficacy. Self-efficacy, which refers to an individual's perceived capabilities to learn or successfully perform a given task or activity (Bandura, 1997; Bandura & Locke, 2003), results in motivational outcomes, such as interest in, preferences for, and choices to engage with specific tasks and activities (Bandura, 1997; Schunk & Dibenedetto, 2021). Research has consistently shown that people tend to pursue tasks for which their self-efficacy is high but shun tasks for which their self-efficacy is low (Bandura & Locke, 2003). In line with this finding, de Pater (2005) found a strong correlation between individuals' perceived competence and preferences for challenging tasks and Irene de Pater, Annelies Van Vianen, Agneta Fischer, and colleagues (2009) and Irene de Pater, Annelies Van Vianen, Ronald Humphrey, and colleagues (2009) found a positive relationship between generalized self-efficacy and the choice to perform challenging tasks. This suggests that increasing employees' self-efficacy may be a fruitful approach to increase their choosing to engage in developmental challenges.

Situational factors related to choosing developmental challenges. Individuals tend to adapt their beliefs, attitudes, and behaviors to their social environment (Salancik & Pfeffer, 1978) and employees' work environment is likely to affect the tasks they choose to engage in (Thomas & Griffin, 1983). Given that engagement in developmental challenge entails an increased risk of failure and, potentially, decreased performance (de Pater, Van Vianen, Bechtoldt, et al., 2009), empowering leadership and the organization's learning culture may provide important cues that guide employees' task choices.

Empowering leadership. Empowering leadership refers to "the process of implementing conditions that increase employees' feelings of self-efficacy and control (e.g., participative decision making), removing conditions that foster a sense of powerlessness (e.g., bureaucracy), and allowing them the freedom to be as flexible as circumstances warrant" (Ahearne et al., 2005, p. 946). Empowering leaders share power with and delegate authority and responsibilities to their subordinates. They motivate their employees to work autonomously, foster their self-efficacy, and stimulate their learning and development (e.g., Amundsen & Martinsen, 2014; Sharma & Kirkman, 2015). Given that self-efficacy relates to one's preferences for and choice to engage in developmental challenge (de Pater, Van Vianen, Fischer, et al., 2009; de Pater, Van Vianen, Humphrey, et al., 2009) and that developmental challenges typically involve higher levels of responsibility and autonomy (McCauley et al., 1999; McCauley et al., 1994), it is likely that empowering leaders stimulate their employees to choose developmental challenges to learn and develop themselves.

Organization learning culture. The learning culture of an organization reflects the extent to which the organization stimulates and facilitates employee learning and knowledge sharing (Egan et al., 2004; Li et al., 2009). Organizations with strong learning cultures embrace learning as one of their core-values and "focus on people, concern for all stakeholders, stimulation of experimentation, encouraging an attitude of responsible risk, readiness to recognize errors and learn from them, and promotion of open and intense communication, as well as promotion of cooperation, interdependence and share of knowledge" (Rebelo & Duarte Gomes, 2011, p. 174). Given that developmental challenges require one to discover solutions to novel problems, to develop new strategies for task completion (e.g., McCauley et al., 1999; McCauley et al., 1994), and involve learning from mistakes (de Pater, Van Vianen, Bechtoldt, et al., 2009), strong learning cultures may stimulate employees' to choose developmental challenge.

Negotiating for developmental challenges

Employees often work in teams, where roles and tasks are divided and assigned among team members who interdependently work toward a common goal (Salas et al., 2000). Hence, the type of tasks employees perform also results from an allocation process during which team members agree on and decide who will perform what tasks (de Pater, Van Vianen, Humphrey, et al., 2009). Of note is that the allocation of tasks among team members should, ideally, maximize team effectiveness and achievement (Ilgen et al., 2005; Owens & Hekman, 2016). This implies that it is important to assign tasks to employees who are best equipped to successfully complete them (Owens & Hekman, 2016; Rego et al., 2019). Yet, it is also important that team members learn and expand their knowledge and skills and foster team learning (Ilgen et al., 2005), thus less experienced team members should have challenging work experiences. Whether or not employees will negotiate for developmental challenge is likely to depend both on individual characteristics and characteristics of the team. It is likely that individual characteristics that predispose employees to choose to engage in developmental challenges (i.e., proactive personality, learning goal orientation, and self-efficacy) also affect the likelihood that they will negotiate for them. Yet, in team settings, other factors, such as one's status in the group or stereotypes and biases may also influence the extent to which employees negotiate with their colleagues to obtain developmental challenge.

Team factors related to negotiating for developmental challenges. Organizations and work teams comprise employees from different cultural backgrounds and age groups, with different sexual orientations, norms and values, experiences and workstyles, skills and abilities, and motivational orientations (Roberson et al., 2017). Diversity may support team performance because it broadens the types of experiences, insights, and perspectives available to the team. Yet, if not well managed, diversity may also result in social comparisons, intergroup biases, and perceived status differentials that affect the decisions and behaviors of the members of a team (Van Knippenberg et al., 2020; Weiss et al., 2017). And although research has, so far, not addressed this issue, it may be that such social comparisons, biases, and perceived status differentials affect one's inclination to negotiate for developmental challenge.

For instance, a study on task allocation decisions in male–female dyads showed that although the men and women in the sample did not differ in their self-reported self-efficacy, their initial choice to perform challenging tasks, or the negotiation tactics they used during the task allocation process, men were allocated an increasing number of the challenging tasks, whereas women ended up with an increasing number of non-challenging tasks (de Pater, Van Vianen, Humphrey, et al., 2009). The authors suggested that because the dyads had to work together to complete a set of tasks (three challenging tasks and three non-challenging tasks) in an achievement context, they may have assessed their competence relative to each other (Foschi, 2000). And because they had no actual information about each other's performance, participants may have used gender—a diffuse status characteristic—as basis for their relative competence evaluations (Abele et al., 2021; Meyer et al., 2022). Men tend to be stereotyped as more competent than women (Fiske et al., 2002; Heilman & Welle, 2006), so women may believe that men would be more capable to conduct the challenging tasks than they are and give men the space to excel (Meyer et al., 2022) rather than to negotiate for the developmental challenges they intended to perform. Interpersonal differences among team members in other individual characteristics, such as age, experience, cultural background, and education may impact one's willingness to negotiate for developmental challenge in a similar way. Future research could usefully address the impact of team diversity on employee learning and development through negotiation for and engagement in developmental challenge.

Supervisor assignment of developmental challenges

The assignment of tasks and responsibilities to subordinates and providing them the autonomy to carry them out is critical for managerial success (Akinola et al., 2018). What tasks and responsibilities supervisors assign to whom may have a profound impact on the opportunities for learning and development, and ultimately, the career success of their subordinates (de Pater et al., 2010; Ohlott et al., 1994). To what extent a supervisor will assign developmental challenges to specific subordinates is likely to depend on both their own and their subordinates' characteristics.

Subordinate characteristics related to assignment of developmental challenges. Social information processing theory (Salancik & Pfeffer, 1978) suggests that supervisors are likely to look for and process cues in their work environment before deciding what tasks to delegate to which of their employees. Research has shown that supervisors' perceptions of an employee's job performance, self-efficacy, and the quality of the supervisor–employee relationship are likely to affect their willingness to assign an employee developmental challenges (de Pater et al., 2010; Parker et al., 2017).

Employee job performance. Delegating challenging tasks and activities is risky because employees may make mistakes or fail to successfully complete the challenges assigned to them. Hence, it is likely that supervisors will assign developmental challenges to subordinates they trust to perform well. Indeed, research has shown that employee job performance positively relates to supervisor willingness to empower employees (Wang et al., 2022) and assign them challenging tasks (de Pater et al., 2010).

Employee self-efficacy. Another cue supervisors may rely on is an employee's self-efficacy. Employees who believe that they are able to learn and complete challenging tasks may also show that they are interested in having developmental challenges assigned to them and signal that they will persevere when they encounter setbacks (Bandura & Locke, 2003; de Pater et al., 2010). As such, supervisors may be inclined to assign them developmental challenges, especially when they have no access to actual performance indicators.

High quality supervisor-subordinate relationships. Both employee task performance and their self-efficacy provide cues related to their competence to successfully (learn to) complete developmental challenges. Yet, supervisors also must trust the employees to whom they assign developmental challenges to not abuse the power and autonomy awarded to them. Hence, the quality of the supervisor–subordinate relationship may provide an important cue that affects supervisors' willingness to assign developmental challenges to a subordinate. Of interest is that although Irene de Pater and colleagues (2010) found that employee performance and the quality of the supervisor–subordinate relationship both predicted supervisor willingness to assign a subordinate challenging tasks, Shenghui Wang and colleagues (2022) found an interaction between these cues. That is, supervisors empowered high-performing employees with whom they had a high-quality relationship but did not empower high-performing employees with whom they had a low-quality relationship.

Supervisor characteristics related to assignment of developmental challenges. The above shows that supervisors take relevant subordinate characteristics into consideration when making task allocation decisions. However, irrelevant subordinate characteristics, such as gender, age, and cultural background, that may trigger stereotypical thoughts and behaviors (King et al., 2012; Parker et al., 2017) and supervisor traits, such as learning goal orientation and self-confidence (Bechtoldt, 2015; Preenen et al., 2014), also affect whom supervisors assign developmental challenges.

Stereotypes. The lack-of-fit model (e.g., Heilman, 2001) suggests that decisions supervisors make related to the assignment of roles and tasks depend, among others, on stereotypical believes they hold about subordinates' interests, skills, and attributes. Supervisors may for instance assign fewer developmental challenges to women because they hold the stereotypical believe that women would be less capable or willing than men to effectively perform them (de Pater et al., 2010). In a similar vein, they may not assign developmental challenges to relatively older employees because they may assume that older employees are less willing to engage in developmental activities (Van Vianen et al., 2011). Future research could usefully explore biases that affect supervisor task allocation and actions that could be taken to minimize their impact.

294 TRANSFORMATIVE WORK DESIGN

Learning goal orientation. Implicit self-theories refer to the beliefs people have about how fixed or malleable their personal characteristics are. These beliefs drive their attributions, goals, and actions (Dweck, 1999). Those who believe that their capacities, skills, and competencies are fixed are likely to have a performance goal orientation, whereas those who assume their capacities, skills, and competencies can be developed are more likely to have a learning goal orientation. Hence an individual's learning goal orientation may not only relate to seeking to increase one's own abilities and competence (e.g., Dweck, 1986; Elliott & Dweck, 1988), but may also affect the extent to which they enable others to develop their abilities and competence through developmental challenges (Preenen et al., 2014; Van Vianen et al., 2011). Convincing managers that an individual's capacities are flexible might, therefore, increase the likelihood that they assign more developmental challenges—even to less well performing subordinates.

Supervisor self-confidence. Although it seems likely that supervisors would assign developmental challenges to employees who exhibit self-confidence and signal their interest in developmental challenges (de Pater et al., 2010), research suggests that may not always be the case. For instance, Myriam Bechtoldt (2015) showed that supervisors who score high on impostorism—which is characterized by self-doubt about one's abilities and competencies, discounting one's performance and achievements, and attributing success to external factors (e.g., Clance, 1986)—were more inclined to assign challenging tasks to employees who were insecure rather than secure about their own abilities. This suggests that the reasons why supervisors assign their subordinates developmental challenges and to whom they assign such challenges are not as straightforward as would be expected. This opens interesting avenues for future research exploring the impact of supervisor–subordinate compatibility on the developmental challenges they allocate their employees.

Avenues for Future Research

The previous discussion shows that although the benefits of challenging work experiences are paramount and that developmental challenge could be useful in enhancing the quality of employees' work, work life, and work-related outcomes (Preenen et al., 2019), little is known about the antecedents of employees' engagement in developmental challenges. Even less is known about factors that may stimulate employees to choose and negotiate for developmental challenges and that will increase the extent to which supervisors—equally—assign developmental challenges to their subordinates. There are several avenues to address these gaps the literature.

First, research should examine leadership behaviors that stimulate their employees to choose and negotiate for developmental challenges through, for instance, increasing their self-efficacy and eliciting a learning goal orientation. Studying empowering leadership behaviors could be especially relevant in this regard because such behaviors include granting employees autonomy, expressing confidence in employees' abilities to perform well, and providing support for learning and development (Ahearne et al., 2005; Amundsen & Martinsen, 2014). It may also be worthwhile to explore whether inclusive leadership behaviors would stimulate employees to choose and negotiate for developmental challenges. Inclusive leadership aims to—simultaneously—satisfy employees' need to belong and to be unique (Shore et al., 2011) and has been found to relate to employee self-efficacy and taking charge behaviors (Veli Korkmaz et al., 2022), which may increase their self-initiated engagement in developmental challenges. At the team level, inclusive leadership stimulates the development of a common identity and reduces perceived status differentials (Mitchell et al., 2015) and may thus decrease the prevalence of social comparison and intergroup biases that affect the task related choices, decisions, and behaviors of the members of a team.

Second, research should explore factors that relate to supervisors' inclination to assign their subordinates challenging tasks. Previous research has shown that employees who have high task discretion engage in more developmental challenges than those with low task discretion (de Pater, Van Vianen, Bechtoldt, et al., 2009), suggesting that employees may want to engage in more developmental challenges than supervisors assign them. Indeed, Sharon K. Parker and colleagues (2019) showed that managers tend to design more deskilled rather than enriched work for others and Jie Cao and Monika Hamori (2020) found that 73 percent of the employees in their sample received fewer developmental challenges than they needed. These research findings underline the need to examine supervisors' task allocation decisions. At the individual level, examining supervisor awareness of the impact of developmental challenge may be especially relevant. From a theoretical perspective, research suggests that those familiar with theories on psychosocial work design or have experience working in enriched jobs are more inclined to design enriched jobs for others (Parker et al., 2019). From a practical perspective, supervisors can develop insight into the importance and impact of developmental challenges through experiential and more formal learning. At the organizational level, it may be especially relevant to examine the impact of organizational culture on supervisors' task allocation decisions. For instance, supervisors working in organizations with a strong learning culture, where learning is one of the core-values (Rebelo & Duarte Gomes, 2011), may be more inclined to assign their employees developmental challenge. In a similar vein, working in an error management culture where errors are not punished but that, instead, focus on positive consequences of errors (van Dyck et al., 2005) may allow supervisors to assign their employees more developmental challenges because of lower perceived costs of potential failure.

Other issues related to developmental challenge that warrant attention are boundary conditions and potential negative effects. For instance, Jie Cao and Monika Hamori (2020) showed that an individual's need for developmental challenge played an important role in the relationship between developmental challenge and affective commitment and turnover intention. Stephen H. Courtright and colleagues (2014) showed that developmental challenge not only results in work engagement but could also result in emotional exhaustion for those low on leadership self-efficacy, whereas Yuntao Dong and colleagues (2014) found that developmental challenge may not only elicit positive but also negative feelings. Hence, it is important to further explore boundary conditions for the positive consequences of developmental challenge.

References

Abele, A. E., Ellemers, N., Fiske, S. T., Koch, A., & Yzerbyt, V. (2021). Navigating the social world: Toward an integrated framework for evaluating self, individuals, and groups. *Psychological Review 128*(2), 290–314. https://doi.org/10.1037/rev0000262

Ahearne, M., Mathieu, J., & Rapp, A. (2005). To empower or not to empower your sales force? An empirical examination of the influence of leadership empowerment behavior on customer satisfaction and performance. *Journal of Applied Psychology 90*(5), 945–955. https://doi.org/10.1037/0021-9010.90.5.945

Akinola, M., Martin, A. E., & Phillips, K. W. (2018). To delegate or not to delegate: Gender differences in affective associations and behavioral responses to delegation. *Academy of Management Journal 61*(4), 1467–1491. https://doi.org/10.5465/amj. 2016.0662

Amundsen, S., & Martinsen, Ø. L. (2014). Empowering leadership: Construct clarification, conceptualization, and validation of a new scale. *Leadership Quarterly 25*(3), 487–511. https://doi.org/10.1016/j.leaqua.2013.11.009

Aryee, S., & Chu, C. W. L. (2012). Antecedents and outcomes of challenging job experiences: A social cognitive perspective. *Human Performance 25*(3), 215–234. https://doi.org/10.1080/08959285.2012.684082

Bandura, A. (1997). *Self-efficacy: The exercise of control*. Freeman.

Bandura, A., & Locke, E. A. (2003). Negative self-efficacy and goal effects revisited. *Journal of Applied Psychology 88*, 87–99. https://doi.org/10.1037/0021-9010.88.1.87

Battistelli, A., Odoardi, C., Vandenberghe, C., Di Napoli, G., & Piccione, L. (2019). Information sharing and innovative work behavior: The role of work-based learning, challenging tasks, and organizational commitment. *Human Resource Development Quarterly 30*(3), 361–381. https://doi.org/10.1002/hrdq.21344

Bechtoldt, M. N. (2015). Wanted: Self-doubting employees—Managers scoring positively on impostorism favor insecure employees in task delegation. *Personality and Individual Differences 86*, 482–486. https://doi.org/10.1016/j.paid.2015.07.002

Benschop, Y., Halsema, L., & Schreurs, P. (2001). The division of labour and inequalities between the sexes: An ideological dilemma. *Gender, Work & Organization 8*(1), 1–18. https://doi.org/10.1111/1468-0432.00119

Bruning, P. F., & Campion, M. A. (2018). A role-resource approach–avoidance model of job crafting: A multimethod integration and extension of job crafting theory. *Academy of Management Journal 61*(2), 499–522. https://doi.org/10.5465/amj.2015.0604

Brutus, S., Ruderman, M. N., Ohlott, P. J., & McCauley, C. D. (2000). Developing from job experiences: The role of organization-based self-esteem. *Human Resource Development Quarterly 11*(4), 367–380. https://doi.org/10.1002/1532-1096(200024)11:4<367::AID-HRDQ4>3.0.CO;2-6

Cao, J., & Hamori, M. (2020). How can employers benefit most from developmental job experiences? The needs–supplies fit perspective. *Journal of Applied Psychology 105*(4), 422–432. https://doi.org/10.1037/apl0000449

Clance, P. R. (1986). *The impostor phenomenon: When success makes you feel like a fake.* Bantam Books.

Courtright, S. H., Colbert, A. E., & Choi, D. (2014). Fired up or burned out? How developmental challenge differentially impacts leader behavior. *Journal of Applied Psychology 99*, 681–696. https://doi.org/10.1037/a0035790

de Pater, I. E. (2005). *Doing things right or doing the right thing: A new perspective on the gender gap in career success* [Unpublished dissertation, University of Amsterdam].

de Pater, I. E., Van Vianen, A. E. M., & Bechtoldt, M. N. (2010). Gender differences in job challenge: A matter of task allocation. *Gender, Work & Organization 17*(4), 433–453. https://doi.org/10.1111/j.1468-0432.2009.00477.x

de Pater, I. E., Van Vianen, A. E. M., Bechtoldt, M. N., & Klehe, U. C. (2009). Employees' challenging job experiences and supervisors' evaluations of promotability. *Personnel Psychology 62*, 297–325. https://doi.org/10.1111/j.1744-6570.2009.01139.x

de Pater, I. E., Van Vianen, A. E. M., Fischer, A. H., & Van Ginkel, W. P. (2009). Challenging experiences: Gender differences in task choice. *Journal of Managerial Psychology 24*(1), 4–28. https://doi.org/10.1108/02683940910922519

de Pater, I. E., Van Vianen, A. E. M., Humphrey, R. H., Sleeth, R. G., Hartman, N. S., & Fischer, A. H. (2009). Individual task choice and the division of challenging tasks between men and women. *Group & Organization Management 34*(5), 563–589. https://doi.org/10.1177/1059601108331240

DeRue, D. S., & Wellman, N. (2009). Developing leaders via experience: The role of developmental challenge, learning orientation, and feedback availability. *Journal of Applied Psychology 94*, 859–875. https://doi.org/10.1037/a0015317

Dimitrova, M. (2020). Of discovery and dread: The importance of work challenges for international business travelers' thriving and global role turnover intentions. *Journal of Organizational Behavior 41*(4), 369–383. https://doi.org/10.1002/job.2430

Dong, Y., Seo, M.-G., & Bartol, K. M. (2014). No pain, no gain: An affect-based model of developmental job experience and the buffering effects of emotional intelligence. *Academy of Management Journal 57*, 1056–1077. https://doi.org/10.5465/amj.2011.0687

Dweck, C. S. (1986). Motivational processes affecting learning. *American Psychologist 41*(10), 1040–1048. https://doi.org/10.1037/0003-066X.41.10.1040

Dweck, C. S. (1999). *Self-theories: their role in motivation, personality, and development.* Psychology Press.

Eagly, A. H. (1987). *Sex differences in social behavior: A social-role interpretation.* Lawrence Erlbaum Associates.

Eagly, A. H., & Karau, S. J. (2002). Role congruity theory of prejudice toward female leaders. *Psychological Review 109*(3), 573–598. https://doi.org/10.1037/0033-295X.109.3.573

Earley, P. C., Connolly, T., & Ekegren, G. (1989). Goals, strategy development, and task performance: Some limits on the efficacy of goal setting. *Journal of Applied Psychology 74*(1), 24–33. https://doi.org/10.1037/0021-9010.74.1.24

Egan, T. M., Yang, B., & Bartlett, K. R. (2004). The effects of organizational learning culture and job satisfaction on motivation to transfer learning and turnover intention. *Human Resource Development Quarterly 15*(3), 279–301. https://doi.org/10.1002/hrdq.1104

Elliott, E. S., & Dweck, C. S. (1988). Goals: An approach to motivation and achievement. *Journal of Personality and Social Psychology 54*(1), 5–12. https://doi.org/10.1037//0022-3514.54.1.5

Fiske, S. T., Cuddy, A. J. C., Glick, P., & Xu, J. (2002). A model of (often mixed) stereotype content: Competence and warmth respectively follow from perceived status and competition. *Journal of Personality and Social Psychology 82*(6), 878–902. https://doi.org/10.1037/0022-3514.82.6.878

Foschi, M. (2000). Double standards for competence: Theory and research. *Annual Review of Sociology 26*, 21–42. http://www.jstor.org/stable/223435

Fuller, B., & Marler, L. E. (2009). Change driven by nature: A meta-analytic review of the proactive personality literature. *Journal of Vocational Behavior 75*(3), 329–345. https://doi.org/10.1016/j.jvb.2009.05.008

Glick, P., & Fiske, S. T. (1996). The ambivalent sexism inventory: Differentiating hostile and benevolent sexism. *Journal of Personality and Social Psychology 70*(3), 491–512. https://doi.org/10.1037/0022-3514.70.3.491

Graen, G. B., Orris, J. B., & Johnson, T. W. (1973). Role assimilation processes in a complex organization. *Journal of Vocational Behavior 3*(4), 395–420. https://doi.org/10.1016/0001-8791(73)90053-5

Heilman, M. E. (2001). Description and prescription: How gender stereotypes prevent women's ascent up the organizational ladder. *Journal of Social Issues 57*(4), 657–674. https://doi.org/10.1111/0022-4537.00234

Heilman, M. E., & Welle, B. (2006). Disadvantaged by diversity? The effects of diversity goals on competence perceptions. *Journal of Applied Social Psychology 36*(5), 1291–1319. https://doi.org/10.1111/j.0021-9029.2006.00043.x

Herzberg, F. (1965). The new industrial psychology. *Industrial and Labor Relations Review, 18*(3), 364–376. https://doi.org/10.2307/2520909

Ilgen, D. R., Hollenbeck, J. R., Johnson, M., & Jundt, D. (2005). Teams in organizations: from input-process-output models to IMOI models. *Annual Review of Psychology 56*, 517–543. https://doi.org/10.1146/annurev.psych.56.091103.070250

Kim, D., Shin, J., Seo, M.-G., & Sung, M.-J. (2021). Enjoy the pain that you cannot avoid: Investigation on the relationship between developmental job experience and employees' innovative behavior. *Journal of Business Research 126*, 363–375. https://doi.org/10.1016/j.jbusres.2020.12.064

King, E. B., Botsford, W., Hebl, M. R., Kazama, S., Perkins, A., & Dawson, J. F. (2012). Benevolent sexism at work: Gender differences in the distribution of challenging developmental experiences. *Journal of Management 38*(6), 1835–1866. https://doi.org/10.1177/0149206310365902

Kirchmeyer, C. (1995). Demographic similarity to the work group: A longitudinal study of managers at the early career stage. *Journal of Organizational Behavior 16*(1), 67–83. https://doi.org/10.1002/job.4030160109

Konrad, A. M., Ritchie, J. E., Jr., Lieb, P., & Corrigall, E. (2000). Sex differences and similarities in job attribute preferences: A meta-analysis. *Psychological Bulletin 126*, 593–641. https://doi.org/10.1037/0033-2909.126.4.593

Li, J., Brake, G., Champion, A., Fuller, T., Gabel, S., & Hatcher-Busch, L. (2009). Workplace learning: The roles of knowledge accessibility and management. *Journal of Workplace Learning 21*(4), 347–364. https://doi.org/10.1108/13665620910954238

London, M. (2002). Organizational assistance in career development. In D. C. Feldman (Ed.), *Work careers: A developmental perspective* (pp. 323–345). Jossey-Bass.

Lyness, K. S., & Thompson, D. E. (1997). Above the glass ceiling? A comparison of matched samples of female and male executives. *Journal of Applied Psychology 82*(3), 359–375. https://doi.org/10.1037/0021-9010.82.3.359

Lyness, K. S., & Thompson, D. E. (2000). Climbing the corporate ladder: Do female and male executives follow the same route? *Journal of Applied Psychology 85*(1), 86–101. https://doi.org/10.1037/0021-9010.85.1.86

Mai-Dalton, R. R., & Sullivan, J. J. (1981). The effects of manager's sex on the assignment to a challenging or a dull task and reasons for the choice. *Academy of Management Journal 24*, 603–612. https://doi.org/10.2307/255578

Matsuo, M. (2019). Empowerment through self-improvement skills: The role of learning goals and personal growth initiative. *Journal of Vocational Behavior 115*, 103311. https://doi.org/10.1016/j.jvb.2019.05.008

Matsuo, M. (2022). Influences of developmental job experience and learning goal orientation on employee creativity: mediating role of psychological empowerment. *Human Resource Development International 25*(1), 4–18. https://doi.org/10.1080/13678868.2020.1824449

McCauley, C. D., Ohlott, P. J., & Ruderman, M. N. (1999). *Job challenge profile.* Jossey-Bass/Pfeiffer.

McCauley, C. D., Ruderman, M. N., Ohlott, P. J., & Morrow, J. E. (1994). Assessing the developmental components of managerial jobs. *Journal of Applied Psychology 79*, 544–560. https://doi.org/10.1037/0021-9010.79.4.544

Meyer, B., van Dijk, H., & van Engen, M. (2022). (Mitigating) the self-fulfillment of gender stereotypes in teams: The interplay of competence attributions, behavioral dominance, individual performance, and diversity beliefs. *Journal of Applied Psychology 107*(11), 1907–1925. https://doi.org/10.1037/apl0000995

Mitchell, R., Boyle, B., Parker, V., Giles, M., Chiang, V., & Joyce, P. (2015). Managing inclusiveness and diversity in teams: How leader inclusiveness affects performance through status and team Identity. *Human Resource Management 54*(2), 217–239. https://doi.org/doi.org/10.1002/hrm.21658

Noe, R. A., Clarke, A. D. M., & Klein, H. J. (2014). Learning in the twenty-first-century workplace. *Annual Review of Organizational Psychology and Organizational Behavior 1*, 245–275. https://doi.org/10.1146/annurev-orgpsych-031413-091321

Ohlott, P. J., Ruderman, M. N., & McCauley, C. D. (1994). Gender differences in managers' developmental job experiences. *Academy of Management Journal 37*, 46–67. https://doi.org/10.2307/256769

Owens, B. P., & Hekman, D. R. (2016). How does leader humility influence team performance? Exploring the mechanisms of contagion and collective promotion focus. *Academy of Management Journal 59*(3), 1088–1111. https://doi.org/10.5465/amj.2013.0660

Parker, S., Van den Broeck, A., & Holman, D. (2017). Work design influences: A synthesis of multilevel factors that affect the design of jobs. *Academy of Management Annals 11*, 267–308. https://doi.org/10.5465/annals.2014.0054

Parker, S. K., Andrei, D. M., & Van den Broeck, A. (2019). Poor work design begets poor work design: Capacity and willingness antecedents of individual work design behavior. *Journal of Applied Psychology 104*(7), 907–928. https://doi.org/10.1037/apl0000383

Parker, S. K., Ward, M. K., & Fisher, G. G. (2021). Can high-quality jobs help workers learn new tricks? A multidisciplinary review of work design for cognition. *Academy of Management Annals 15*(2), 406–454. https://doi.org/10.5465/annals.2019.0057

Piccolo, R. F., & Colquitt, J. A. (2006). Transformational leadership and job behaviors: The mediating role of core job characteristics. *Academy of Management Journal 49*(2), 327–340. https://doi.org/10.5465/AMJ.2006.20786079

Preenen, P. T., Dorenbosch, L., Plantinga, E., & Dhondt, S. (2019). The influence of task challenge on skill utilization, affective wellbeing and intrapreneurial behaviour. *Economic and Industrial Democracy 40*(4), 954–975. https://doi.org/10.1177/0143831x16677367

Preenen, P. T. Y., de Pater, I. E., Van Vianen, A. E. M., & Keijzer, L. (2011). Managing voluntary turnover through challenging assignments. *Group & Organization Management 36*, 308–344. https://doi.org/10.1177/1059601111402067

Preenen, P. T. Y., Van Vianen, A. E. M., & de Pater, I. E. (2014). Challenging tasks: The role of employees' and supervisors' goal orientations. *European Journal of Work and Organizational Psychology 23*(1), 48–61. https://doi.org/10.1080/1359432X.2012.702420

Preenen, P. T. Y., Verbiest, S., Van Vianen, A. E. M., & Van Wijk, E. (2015). Informal learning of temporary agency workers in low-skill jobs: The role of self-profiling, career control, and job challenge. *Career Development International 20*(4), 339–362. https://doi.org/10.1108/CDI-12-2013-01

Rebelo, T. M., & Duarte Gomes, A. (2011). Conditioning factors of an organizational learning culture. *Journal of Workplace Learning 23*(3), 173–194. https://doi.org/10.1108/13665621111117215

Rego, A., Owens, B., Yam, K. C., Bluhm, D., Cunha, M. P. e., Silard, A., Gonçalves, L., Martins, M., Simpson, A. V., & Liu, W. (2019). Leader humility and team performance: Exploring the mediating mechanisms of team PsyCap and task allocation effectiveness. *Journal of Management 45*(3), 1009–1033. https://doi.org/10.1177/0149206316688941

Roberson, Q., Holmes IV, O., & Perry, J. L. (2017). Transforming research on diversity and firm performance: A dynamic capabilities perspective. *Academy of Management Annals 11*(1), 189–216. https://doi.org/10.5465/annals.2014.0019

Salancik, G. R., & Pfeffer, J. (1978). A social information processing approach to job attitudes and task design. *Administrative Science Quarterly 23*(2), 224–253. https://doi.org/10.2307/2392563

Salas, E., Burke, C. S., & Cannon-Bowers, J. A. (2000). Teamwork: Emerging principles. *International Journal of Management Reviews 2*(4), 339–356. https://doi.org/https://doi.org/10.1111/1468-2370.00046

Schunk, D., & Dibenedetto, M. (2021). Self-efficacy and human motivation. In A. J. Elliot (Ed.), *Advances in motivation science* (Vol. 8, pp. 153–179). Science Direct. https://doi.org/10.1016/bs.adms.2020.10.001

Seibert, S. E., Crant, J. M., & Kraimer, M. L. (1999). Proactive personality and career success. *Journal of Applied Psychology, 84*(3), 416–427. https://doi.org/10.1037/0021-9010.84.3.416

Sharma, P. N., & Kirkman, B. L. (2015). Leveraging leaders: A literature review and future lines of inquiry for empowering leadership research. *Group & Organization Management 40*(2), 193–237. https://doi.org/10.1177/1059601115574906

Shore, L. M., Randel, A. E., Chung, B. G., Dean, M. A., Holcombe Ehrhart, K., & Singh, G. (2011). Inclusion and diversity in work groups: A review and model for future research. *Journal of Management 37*(4), 1262–1289. https://doi.org/10.1177/0149206310385943

Thomas, J., & Griffin, R. (1983). The social information processing model of task design: A review of the literature. *Academy of Management Review 8*(4), 672–682. https://doi.org/10.5465/amr.1983.4284679

Tims, M., Bakker, A. B., & Derks, D. (2012). Development and validation of the job crafting scale. *Journal of Vocational Behavior 80*(1), 173–186. https://doi.org/10.1016/j.jvb.2011.05.009

Van den Broeck, A., De Cuyper, N., De Witte, H., & Vansteenkiste, M. (2010). Not all job demands are equal: Differentiating job hindrances and job challenges in the Job Demands-Resources model. *European Journal of Work and Organizational Psychology 19*, 735–760. https://doi.org/10.1080/13594320903223839

van Dyck, C., Frese, M., Baer, M., & Sonnentag, S. (2005). Organizational error management culture and its impact on performance: A two-study replication. *Journal of Applied Psychology 90*(6), 1228–1240. https://doi.org/10.1037/0021-9010.90.6.1228

Van Knippenberg, D., Nishii, L., & Dwertmann, D. (2020). Synergy from diversity: Managing team diversity to enhance performance. *Behavioral Science & Policy 6*, 75–92. https://doi.org/10.1353/bsp.2020.0007

Van Vianen, A. E. M., Dalhoeven, B. A. G. W., & de Pater, I. E. (2011). Aging and training and development willingness: Employee and supervisor mindsets. *Journal of Organizational Behavior 32*(2), 226–247. https://doi.org/10.1002/job.685

Veli Korkmaz, A., van Engen, M. L., Knappert, L., & Schalk, R. (2022). About and beyond leading uniqueness and belongingness: A systematic review of inclusive leadership research. *Human Resource Management Review 32*(4), 100894. https://doi.org/10.1016/j.hrmr.2022.100894

Wang, S., de Pater, I. E., Yi, M., Zhang, Y., & Yang, T.-P. (2022). Empowering leadership: Employee-related antecedents and consequences. *Asia Pacific Journal of Management 39*(2), 457–481. https://doi.org/10.1007/s10490-020-09734-w

Weiss, M., Kolbe, M., Grote, G., Spahn, D. R., & Grande, B. (2017). Why didn't you say something? Effects of after-event reviews on voice behaviour and hierarchy beliefs in multi-professional action teams. *European Journal of Work and Organizational Psychology 26*(1), 66–80. https://doi.org/10.1080/1359432X.2016.1208652

Wrzesniewski, A., & Dutton, D. (2001). Crafting a job: Revisioning employees as active crafters of their work. *Academy of Management Review 26*, 179–201. https://doi.org/10.5465/AMR.2001.4378011

Zhang, F., & Parker, S. K. (2019). Reorienting job crafting research: A hierarchical structure of job crafting concepts and integrative review. *Journal of Organizational Behavior 40*(2), 126–146. https://doi.org/10.1002/job.2332

PART 4

TOP-DOWN WORK REDESIGN

How and Why Do Top-Down Work Redesign Interventions Impact Well-Being and Performance?

Caroline Knight and Florian E. Klonek

Work redesign interventions refer to strategies which change the structure, content, activities, roles, and/or responsibilities of the work that people do (Knight et al., 2019)[1]. The term, "top-down" specifically refers to those interventions which are led by senior management and applied across whole organizations or large parts of them (Hornung et al., 2010). Work redesign interventions may also be bottom-up; that is, self-initiated and led by individuals themselves (Hornung et al., 2010), however, these types of interventions are a focus of other chapters in this volume and will not be covered here.

Managers and organizations are typically responsible for designing work. Yet poor quality work continues to exist (Parker et al., 2019). A key factor driving this phenomenon is the decisions managers make about how to design work. Managers allocate, organize, and structure the work within teams, units, and departments. They are also instrumental in developing employee capability through providing development opportunities and feedback, and they play a core role in recruitment, where they may develop job descriptions and selection criteria for new roles. This suggests that managers are "work designers" with a powerful role in shaping employees' work design. However, these work designers often do not have knowledge about how to design good quality work, and may tend to create simplified, routinized jobs which focus more on getting a task done than on how enriching, motivating, and stimulating the work is (Parker et al., 2019).

Therefore, it is important for both theory and practice to understand how managers and organizations can effectively re-design work. In other words, what is it that organizations and managers can do to improve work design for individual workers, an entire team, or even a whole organization? The goal of this

---

[1] Both authors contributed equally to this chapter.

Caroline Knight and Florian E. Klonek, *How and Why Do Top-Down Work Redesign Interventions Impact Well-Being and Performance?*. In: *Transformative Work Design*. Edited by: Sharon K. Parker et al., Oxford University Press.
© Society for Industrial and Organizational Psychology (2025). DOI: 10.1093/oso/9780197692554.003.0012

chapter is to provide an overview of how managers can redesign work for optimal well-being and performance. Different types of top-down work redesign interventions across different industries and organizational levels will be presented, their effectiveness discussed, and underlying theoretical mechanisms that explain their effectiveness considered.

Top-down work redesign interventions have a long heritage (for reviews, see Daniels et al., 2017; Knight & Parker, 2021), however, surprisingly little attention has been paid to interventions in books covering work design (for an exception, see Hackman & Oldham, 1980). Yet, one of the fundamental reasons for unpacking the theory, mechanisms, and processes underlying the impact of work design on outcomes is so that we can understand how to change work to make it optimally healthy and productive for all workers. Often, research which has focused on top-down interventions has taken a macro-level approach, for example, investigating the impact of human resource practices and policies (e.g., Black et al., 2004; Workman & Bommer, 2004), or the restructuring of departments and work groups (e.g., Boning et al., 2007; Workman & Bommer, 2004), on organizational outcomes. While some exceptions exist (e.g., see Camuffo et al., 2017), this research often fails to consider the impact that such changes have on how individuals experience their work (i.e., their job characteristics). This is particularly surprising given that it is theoretically well established that changes at a macro, organizational level need to be aligned with changes at a micro, individual level to be effective for improving well-being and performance (Oreg et al., 2011). Dissonance between the two can lead to resistance, low morale and work motivation, increasing levels of turnover, and, ultimately, poorer performance. Despite this theory around the cross-level effects between macro and micro factors, the research base is not extensive. However, there have been two systematic reviews of note which address these issues, which are discussed next (Daniels et al., 2017; Knight et al., 2021).

A systematic review conducted by Caroline Knight and Sharon K. Parker (2021) explores the impact of top-down interventions on work design and performance. In their sample of 55 studies, they observed five types of interventions, with individual level interventions, namely relational, and both participative and non-participative job enrichment and enlargement interventions, demonstrating the strongest evidence of impact on performance via changes in individual's work design. Evidence was also observed for the effectiveness of creating self-managing teams (team-level) and implementing system-wide interventions (organizational level).

Another systematic review by Kevin Daniels and colleagues (2017) explores how changes to employment practices impacts work design, with follow-up effects for well-being. From 33 studies, they found that training workers to shape their own jobs and system-wide changes (such as implementing new technological systems or health and safety policies) were able to positively improve work design and impact well-being and performance. In accordance with Knight and colleagues (2021), they also found that employee participation was important for success, as well as managerial commitment and alignment between different systems and components of organizations. While it is not new that employee participation, managerial commitment, and alignment of systems and processes across different organizational levels is critical for the success of organizations, these factors continue to be overlooked in the planning and implementation phases of work redesign interventions (for more on this, see Nielsen, and Daniels et al., this volume).

Taken together, the evidence shows that work re-design plays a central role in positively affecting both performance and well-being, two of the most important outcomes for the success of all organizations. Yet, we have noted that poor quality work continues to exist. In this chapter, we aim to address this problem by providing theoretical and practical knowledge to help managers and organizations redesign work. In so doing, we go beyond previous top-down intervention research and make three unique contributions. First, we integrate previous reviews to provide an overview of the current state of the field, highlighting what is known and not known. We organize our discussion around a framework of the different types of top-down work redesign interventions that have been tested and elaborate on the mechanisms underlying these work redesigns. This integration is important to make sense of the findings to date, provide a coherent narrative around how and why top-down interventions work, and identify important avenues for future research. Failing to integrate literature can hinder progress, leading to "reinvention of the wheel," and a lack of research direction. Our goal is to create a resource which provides a solid grounding in the theoretical knowledge required to move top-down work redesign intervention research forward.

Second, we provide a multi-level focus, which is missing from most previous reviews, by providing an in-depth exploration of self-managing teams to shed light on the intricate multi-level relationships inherent in work redesign. This is important because employees are almost always socially and structurally embedded in teams and units within organizations such that work redesign must consider implications for the team, as well as individual team members (Grant & Parker, 2009). Effectively redesigning the work of teams is likely to become an increasingly important issue as we adopt different technologies and work patterns (e.g., remote and hybrid work) and grapple with managing the challenges that are faced by these factors, such as effectively collaborating and communicating with team members who share limited time in the office together, or indeed, are located in different geographical regions and time zones.

308　TRANSFORMATIVE WORK DESIGN

Third, we offer practical suggestions for implementing top-down work redesign interventions to help practitioners apply theory to practice. These complement the strategies found in the other intervention chapters in this volume. We hope that, together, these practical suggestions can help redirect the trend for poorly designed work toward work which is optimally healthy and productive for all.

After providing a brief history of top-down work design interventions, we draw on Knight and Parker's organizing framework and present four key types of intervention (see also Table 12.1): (1) job enrichment and

Table 12.1 Overview of Top-down Work Redesign Intervention Types

Intervention type	Purpose	Example work redesign strategies	Example studies
Job enrichment and enlargement	To increase work motivation by improving perceptions of job characteristics (e.g., autonomy, variety, feedback)	Job rotation Increasing employee responsibilities and decision-making control Employee participation in redesign opportunities (e.g., problem-solving, brainstorming solutions)	Campion & McClelland, 1993; Griffin, 1991; Holman & Axtell, 2016; Locke et al., 1976
Relational interventions	To develop task significance, meaning in work, and increase connection and a sense of belonging with others	Increase beneficiary contact (e.g., solicit feedback from or meet clients, customers, patients) Increase structural support (e.g., more staff)	Bellé, 2014; Grant, 2008; Parker et al., 2013
Self-managing teams	To devolve autonomy and responsibilities from senior managers to teams and work groups	Restructuring so that teams are responsible for work and team members together organize what, when and how work is done	Cordery et al., 1991; Morgeson et al., 2006; Wall & Clegg, 1981
Organizational and system-wide changes	To change policy, practices, and systems to increase efficiency, productivity and performance	High performance work practices Involving employees in decision-making Alignment of reward, information and communication systems	Christina et al., 2017; Robertson et al., 2008; Tregaski et al., 2013

enlargement interventions, (2) relational interventions, (3) self-managing teams, and (4) organizational and system-wide interventions. To elaborate on the complex multi-level nature of top-down work redesign interventions, we provide an in-depth discussion of self-managing teams (SMTs). That is, with respect to SMTs, we highlight when (i.e., in what contexts), how (i.e., through what mechanisms), and for whom (i.e., which groups of people), these interventions work well. We then discuss some common mechanisms underlying all four intervention types generally, and we conclude the chapter with future research directions as well as practical implications. Figure 12.1 provides an overview of the different intervention types, underlying mechanisms, and outcomes.

We acknowledge that the four types of top-down work redesign intervention presented here are not mutually exclusive; it is possible that an intervention to create self-managing teams, for example, not only increases team autonomy but also enriches jobs by providing individuals with more autonomy, increased responsibility for tasks, and feedback from their team members. Nor are these intervention types exhaustive; instead, they merely reflect the themes observed in the current body of literature. In addition, we acknowledge that some interventions are multimodal, that is, they involve two or more different types of intervention, such as a job enrichment intervention (e.g., increasing employee decision-making ability) coupled with system-wide changes (e.g., technology implementation). It is beyond the scope of this chapter to explore these in depth. Further, we do not focus on implementing, sustaining, or evaluating top-down interventions; while extremely important to consider when assessing intervention effectiveness, we are delighted that these topics are the focus of other chapters in this book.

A Brief History of Top-Down Work Redesign Interventions

Top-down work redesign interventions have a long history. Even as early as the 1950s, there are articles detailing work redesign interventions. For example, Nancy Morse and Everett Reimer (1956) observed how training clerical workers to take more control over decision making resulted in higher perceptions of autonomy in an experimental group compared to a control group. From the 1970s, more work redesign interventions emerged, which also tended to focus on enriching jobs by increasing autonomy (e.g., Cohen & Turney, 1978; Gomez & Mussio, 1975; Locke et al., 1976; Powell & Schlacter, 1971), in keeping with the dominant work design theories of the time (e.g., job characteristics model, Hackman & Oldham, 1976).

At the same time as job enrichment interventions emerged, socio-technical interventions also emerged. These were predicated on socio-technical systems

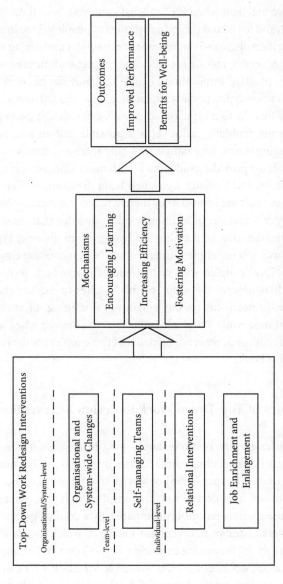

Figure 12.1 Overview of Top-down Work Redesign Interventions, Underlying Mechanisms, and Outcomes

Note: This is a simplified diagram. Multi-level effects are more complicated than depicted here. Cross-level relationships have been omitted for clarity.

(STS) theory, another dominant work design theory with a long heritage, which considers the organization as a system comprising social and technical elements which need to align and work in synergy to be effective (Cherns, 1976). In STS interventions, the focus is on groups of employees and the tasks they perform, the relationships between these different groups, and the technology with which they interact, with a view to improving the fit between the technology and the social system (for an early example, see Pasmore & King, 1978). STS thinking led to interventions which experimented with the creation of self-managing teams, or autonomous work groups, in an effort to empower groups/teams of workers to take responsibility for their work tasks without the need for a senior leader (Cummings, 1978).

A parallel stream of research approached organization-wide interventions from a human resource management perspective, viewing employees as human capital in need of development and training to encourage motivation and performance (Batt, 2002). According to this perspective, high performance work practices (HPWPs), such as performance management, reward and pay systems, and directly involving employees in decision-making and consultation processes (Wood et al., 2012), are critical for organizational performance. These practices are aligned with each other (horizontally) and with high-level organizational strategic goals (vertically) for maximum impact (Guest, 1997). Although often not directly acknowledged in this literature, these practices change work design primarily by increasing autonomy, with training and development also potentially increasing variety and job complexity if a role is expanded and enriched as a result.

With the arrival of the 21st century, relational interventions gained traction. These took an individual level perspective and evolved from increasing research demonstrating the importance of social aspects of jobs for well-being and performance (for a review, see Grant & Parker, 2009). These interventions focus on the relationships and connections that individuals make with others in their organization, with a focus on developing the purpose and meaning of jobs. Jobs which individuals perceive to be significant in the grander scheme of things, which they believe really have a positive impact on others within and beyond their organization (e.g., clients, customers, patients), provide a sense of meaning, help meet the basic human need for relatedness (Deci & Ryan, 2000), are prosocially motivating, and lead to better well-being and performance (Grant, 2007, 2008).

Having provided a brief overview and history of top-down work redesign interventions, we now turn to focus on the different types of intervention more specifically. First, we consider two types of individual level intervention (job

312   TRANSFORMATIVE WORK DESIGN

enrichment and enlargement, and relational interventions), before providing a deeper dive of team level interventions (i.e., SMTs), and finally discussing organizational and system-wide interventions.

Job enrichment and enlargement interventions

Job enlargement refers to increasing the scope of a job by increasing the number and variety of tasks a worker is responsible for. This serves to make the job less monotonous and dull, with the aim of improving job satisfaction and performance (Parker, 2014). Job enrichment goes a step further, by not only increasing the number and types of job tasks a worker engages in, but also increasing the amount of autonomy, complexity and responsibility offered by the job (Parker, 2014). Job enrichment may also include opportunities for skill development and learning. These types of changes are theorized to make deeper, more profound changes than job enlargement alone, by making jobs more meaningful and motivating, ultimately improving worker engagement and performance. Often, job enrichment and enlargement occur together, for example, when new tasks introduced increase variety but are also more complex in nature, require training to complete, or naturally involve more responsibility. Job enrichment and enlargement may also be participative or non-participative, depending on whether workers themselves are involved in deciding what and how jobs should be redesigned. Both types have been found to be successful for improving job attitudes such as job satisfaction (e.g., Cohen & Turney, 1978) and performance (Knight & Parker, 2021).

We noted earlier that job enrichment and enlargement interventions have a long heritage. For example, Edwin Locke and colleagues (1976) conducted an experiment with clerical workers in a federal agency, involving intervention groups and matched control groups. They found that when individuals were put into teams, given autonomy to decide between themselves which tasks members would work on, and tasks were rotated, productivity improved, and work absences decreased. In another example, Stanley Cohen and John Turney (1978) used a participative approach with army communications personnel to develop solutions to problems highlighted by a diagnostic work design survey. Training to develop managers' skills in conjunction with increasing worker responsibilities and control over when and how work tasks were completed was aimed at increasing intrinsic work motivation. Success was observed in the form of increased job satisfaction and performance.

In more contemporary times, job enrichment and enlargement remain important strategies for changing the nature of work. For example, David Holman and Carolyn Axtell (2016) found that increasing job autonomy and feedback in call center employees improved both well-being and supervisor-rated job performance. In this intervention, employees worked together to brainstorm solutions to work design issues, highlighting how involving employees in the intervention design phase can prove advantageous.

Despite evidence for the success of job enrichment and enlargement interventions for increasing perceptions of work characteristics, leading to improved well-being, job attitudes, and performance, a number of studies demonstrate mixed effects, or no effects (Knight & Parker, 2021). For example, Rodger Griffeth (1985) conducted an experiment in which desk receptionists underwent work redesign which was either participative or non-participative, and were compared to a control group. They observed an increase in skill variety, task significance, job feedback, and feedback from others in the intervention condition, but no significant increases in autonomy or task identity. In addition, the redesign improved general and growth satisfaction, and turnover reduced. However, participation in the redesign was only associated with general satisfaction, which the authors note may have been due to the relatively restricted opportunity of workers to participate (one 90-minute meeting).

Even though studies appear to have had effects on different work characteristics following work redesign, what is common amongst these studies is that work has still been enriched in some way, whether by increasing autonomy, feedback, skill variety, or some other work characteristic. This is important because it suggests a robust effect of job enrichment and enlargement interventions for improving perceptions of work characteristics, and outcomes such as well-being, job attitudes, and performance. However, it also suggests that we still do not know under exactly what conditions these interventions are effective, which is a key direction for future research.

Relational Interventions

Individuals are embedded within social systems at work; that is, social networks, groups, and hierarchies. The social nature of work is commonly referred to as relational work design. Relational work design interventions aim to positively change these social systems and the interactions and relationships that characterize a job. These interventions are based on theory and evidence which shows that when workers are able to develop meaningful connections with others at work, understand the benefit of their work on others, and build their networks, they experience a deeper sense of purpose, fulfillment, and social worth, a greater sense of belonging to their team, department, and organization, and greater work motivation (Grant & Parker, 2009). All of this translates into better well-being and performance.

314 TRANSFORMATIVE WORK DESIGN

In a series of experiments, Adam Grant (2008) demonstrated the importance of a core aspect of relational work design, task significance, on performance. Understanding the significance of one's work on others necessitates a strong connection to the people who benefit from the work, whether that be customers, clients, patients, or colleagues. In one experiment, Grant (2008) found that university fundraisers who read stories from students who had benefited from scholarship donations performed better (i.e., raised more money) than a comparison or control group. Grant (2008) also empirically demonstrated that improving task significance increases social impact and social worth, which refer to the degree to which employees feel their actions benefit others, and are valued by others, respectively. Social impact and social worth could act as psychological mechanisms through which task significance improves performance, though this relationship needs to be explored in future research.

Taking a different approach, Parker and colleagues (2013) evaluated an intervention which aimed to increase the emotional and structural support of junior doctors based in an Australian hospital by providing an advanced practice nurse to work alongside them on overtime shifts. These practice nurses offered coaching, advice, knowledge, and general emotional support. Parker and colleagues (2013) found that during shifts when the doctors had access to an advanced practice nurse, performance was higher than during shifts when the practice nurse was not present. Further, this effect was stronger for those who had greater clarity about others' roles. Affect also played a moderating role, with lower negative affect being related to higher skill use and proactivity, and higher negative affect being related to lower perceptions of role overload.

Taken together, these two examples of relational work design interventions demonstrate the wide scope of such interventions, with unique relational aspects being targeted in each one. They also demonstrate the complex nature of the relationships between different relational work components, moderators (or "boundary conditions"), and various outcomes.

Self-Managing Teams

The key conceptual feature of SMTs is that the team—as a whole—is given autonomy over when and how their work is done (Cummings, 1978). Further, team members carry out a whole task and use a range of skills. Team members also have high levels of interdependence, which is seen as a key characteristic of teamwork (Kozlowski & Ilgen, 2006). It is important to note that there is a variety of terms for SMTs that exist in the literature (for an excellent overview, see van Mierlo et al., 2005). These include *autonomous work groups*, *self-directed work group/team, self-organizing work group/team, self-regulating work group/team, empowered work group/team, autonomous work group/team,* and/or *semiautonomous work group/team.* For the remainder of this chapter and for consistency, we use SMTs. Because the implementation of SMTs involves managers providing the entire team with autonomy (i.e., moving control that usually sits with a manager to team members), it can be conceived as a top-down intervention. However, SMTs equally involve bottom-up processes; that is, team members can use their autonomy to be more proactive in terms of organizing work and various tasks, and initiating changes in how work is accomplished.

Redesigning work at the team-level requires a multi-level perspective (Klein et al., 2000) because concepts like job autonomy reside at the level of the individual and they are conceptually different to a group-level construct like team autonomy (they also require different measurement approaches). It is important to acknowledge that there is significantly more research focusing on individual job characteristics (e.g., job autonomy, task variety) than research on group-level work design concepts—and sometimes, researchers do not clearly specify at which level the constructs operate or were manipulated (see van Mierlo et al., 2005). Some studies also use measures or designs that are not well aligned with the level of theory. In what follows, we review some of the key literature highlighting the role of SMTs, pointing out why they are important and how and when they affect team performance.

SMTs are important for collective performance as well as for workers' individual well-being. Historically, the use of SMTs were introduced as an alternative to explore more self-managed ways in which coal miners could complete their work (Trist et al., 1977). A prominent approach in underground mining was the "longwall approach" that allowed efficient extraction of large volumes of coal or minerals, requiring fewer miners to accomplish the same amount of work compared to other methods. However, the longwall approach also was physically demanding for miners and required long periods of standing, bending, and operating heavy machinery. The introduction of SMTs helped to better deal with the unpredictable conditions underground (Trist et al., 1977) and to alleviate the physical demands of the work by distributing tasks among team members and rotating job duties.

To-date, there is a rich empirical literature focusing on the impact of SMTs on both team-level performance outcomes as well as individual-level outcomes (Campion et al., 1993; Stewart, 2006; van Mierlo et al., 2005). For example, research from Michael Campion and colleagues (1993) showed that self-management in teams had a positive impact on various group-level outcomes, including productivity, employee satisfaction, and manager judgements of effectiveness.

316   TRANSFORMATIVE WORK DESIGN

The implementation of SMTs is not only beneficial for productivity, but for the psychological well-being of employees who work within these teams. In a review focusing on the benefits of SMTs for psychological well-being, Hans van Mierlo and colleagues (2005) identified four key psychological well-being outcomes, including job satisfaction, organizational commitment, work motivation, and reduced absenteeism. The authors summarized results across 18 quasi-experimental studies and showed that SMTs are most consistently associated with an increase in job satisfaction. The authors also analyzed correlational studies (noting that these studies have a less rigorous research design) to investigate the effect of specific work subdimensions characterizing SMTs (i.e., the five core characteristics of the job characteristics model; Hackman & Oldham, 1976: job autonomy, task variety, task significance, task identity, job feedback) across a broader set of psychological well-being outcomes. Overall, the five job dimensions showed positive relationships with numerous indicators of psychological well-being (quality of life, work motivation, reduced absenteeism). It is noteworthy that the authors pointed out some key problems with existing research on SMTs, including problems with the level of theory, measurement, and analysis (team vs. individual-level constructs, team vs. individual-level data collection and analyses) within the studies that they reviewed. For example, by applying concepts like job autonomy from the job characteristic model from the individual-level to the team-level, it is important to acknowledge that the meaning of the construct changes. To illustrate, a concept like individual job autonomy (i.e., the extent to which a job allows freedom, independence, and discretion to schedule work, make decisions, and choose the methods used to perform tasks for an individual) is different to a concept like team autonomy (i.e., the extent to which a team has freedom in making these decisions). Further, it requires investigating whether the relationship between this construct at the higher (i.e., team) level changes its relationships with other constructs. Although some efforts have been made to better understand the complex trickle-down and multi-level effects of team-level work redesign on individual job characteristics and well-being outcomes (van Mierlo et al., 2007), it also highlights that we still have some incomplete understanding of the multi-level effects of SMTs.

Most meta-analytic reviews following the review by van Mierlo and colleagues (2005) focused on the key dimensions of SMTs (i.e., autonomy, significance, interdependence) and they showed similar positive results with team performance (e.g., Carter et al., 2019; Stewart, 2006). The meta-analyses by Greg Stewart (2006) showed moderate positive relationships between the key dimensions of SMTs task design, including autonomy, interdependence (which they called intra-team coordination) and meaningfulness (i.e., teams perceiving their work to be worthwhile and important), and team performance (for autonomy, $\rho = .25$, including a wide credibility interval of $-.01$ to $.51$, which suggests contextual moderators; for interdependence, ρ = .16, for meaningfulness, ρ = .25). Similarly, a more recent meta-analysis from Kameron M. Carter and colleagues (2018) showed that SMT autonomy, interdependence, and meaningfulness were all positively related to team performance (r = .15 to .30).

Although the evidence suggests that SMTs are beneficial for team and individual performance, in particular job satisfaction, there is a longstanding acknowledgement that the successful implementation of self-managing teams depends on certain boundary conditions. That is, next, we highlight the important role of the context in which these teams are embedded. Context is defined here as situational opportunities and constraints that affect the occurrence and meaning of organizational behavior as well as functional relationships between variables (i.e., the magnitude and direction of a relationship between two variables) (Johns, 2006).

Following the key context dimensions from Gary Johns (2006), it is important to explore *where* SMTs are implemented (e.g., for which industry or in which culture), *when* to implement SMTs (e.g., as a response to deal better with uncertainty), *for whom* SMTs are implemented (e.g., for what occupation or particular demographics), and also *why* SMTs are implemented (e.g., to deal with productivity problems or low job satisfaction). Below, we provide some answers to these questions.

Where is it best to implement SMTs?

Regarding the "where are SMTs implemented?" question, empirical evidence suggests that industry as a critical context does indeed matter (Carter et al., 2019). Carter and colleagues analyzed the effect of team autonomy on team outcomes across different industries (including high-tech, manufacturing, service, and student teams) using meta-analytic techniques (k = 14 studies). They showed highest associations for team autonomy on team performance in high-tech industries (i.e., industries focusing on innovation, research, and development) (r = .42) and only moderate association for service teams (i.e., teams with predominantly customer-oriented interactions) (r = .15). The key advantage of implementing SMTs in high-tech industries is that teams often must react to environmental uncertainties to a higher degree than teams working in more stable environments (e.g., manufacturing or service industries), where tasks are more constant and/or have more predictable cycles. In these high-tech environments, giving teams some latitude in decision-making and allowing them to complete a variety of different tasks seems particularly beneficial to deal with the complexities of the high-tech industry, such as when teams work

318 TRANSFORMATIVE WORK DESIGN

in knowledge-generating R&D departments. The factor of dealing with uncertainty also seems to play a role with respect to the question of when SMTs should be implemented which we answer next.

When is it best to implement SMTs?

Research suggests that SMTs and the role of team autonomy are particularly beneficial when teams must deal with uncertainty, which is defined as having a lack of predictability associated with inputs, outputs of the broader technical system within which the work was performed (Cordery et al., 2010). In a longitudinal field study, John Cordery and colleagues (2010) analyzed teams who had to deal with wastewater treatment. These teams had to work under increasing levels of task uncertainty with wastewater technology that generated instability in the wastewater treatment processes. For example, some plants had a technical design that required either a low (or high) level of biological methods for the overall treatment processes. The use of biological methods is inherently more complex and involves several interrelated subprocesses. That is, teams operating with these (more uncertain) biological methods were less able to know in advance how treatment process would work on a day-to-day basis. With increased uncertainty, teams initially showed reduced performance (lower quality of treated effluent produced by the teams)—although this negative effect of task uncertainty on team performances was not significant. What is more important is that after an intervention focused on increasing team autonomy, the teams showed improvements in team performance (i.e., lower variability in wastewater production). The SMT intervention that targeted increasing their autonomy involved some significant changes in the organization of wastewater treatment plants by redesigned production operatives into plant-level production teams and eliminating the roles of supervisors and plant superintendent. Each team became self-directed in determining how and when their work was performed (within the boundaries of agreed deadlines, production targets, and quality standards). The intervention involved changes in individual job descriptions which were adjusted into team-level role descriptions that outlined the responsibilities ofo the team overall in managing all aspects of the plant's performance. These SMTs received responsibilities for tasks that were previously performed by higher-level managers which meant that they had substantial discretion in choosing work methods, scheduling their tasks, deciding which team members were allocated to different tasks, scheduling/approving their leave, managing work covers when someone was absent from work, having responsibilities for their own operational/development budget, and ordering goods/services. In summary, SMTs (i.e., teams with high levels of autonomy) were particularly effective (i.e., producing less variability in wastewater production) when working under high levels of task uncertainty (i.e., dealing with a lack of predictability in the broader technical work system).

Another important contingency factor shown to impact the performance of self-managing teams is the level of task interdependence; that is, the degree to which the interaction and coordination of team members is required to complete work (Langfred, 2005). Teams that have high task interdependence, meaning they work closely together and rely on each other to complete their tasks, are more likely to benefit from team autonomy without incurring extra coordination costs. However, teams with low task interdependence may experience significant performance loss from having to coordinate and interact to take advantage of team autonomy. Field studies have shown that teams with higher levels of task interdependence showed better performance and motivation when they were given more autonomy, while teams with lower levels of task interdependence often experienced performance deficits when given autonomy (Janz et al., 1977; Langfred, 2000, 2005). In summary, team autonomy works best when there is high task interdependence, and this is consistent with the findings of existing field studies.

For whom is it best to implement SMTs?

Another important question relating to the boundary conditions is "for whom is it best to implement SMTs?" The "who" question relates to understanding the demographics of a team. Thus, one important factor is the level of team diversity which considers whether there are differences in personal attributes (e.g., age, gender, race [i.e., differences between team members that are visible from the "surface"]). These surface-level differences can lead to perceived differences within the team that can create so-called faultlines. Faultlines are dividing lines that indicate a split of subgroups based on the alignment of personal attributes between team members (Rico et al., 2007). An example of a faultline (looking at the two attributes "age" and "gender") could be a team that has a few team members who are young and female, but also another subgroup of team members who are male and older. If this team can be clearly divided into these two subgroups and these subgroups do not interact well with one another, this is indicative of a strong faultline. That is, the younger women tend to collaborate and work more closely with each other, while the older men may collaborate within their own subgroup. This division can lead to a lack of communication and collaboration between these two subgroups and thus result in a less effective team overall.

320 TRANSFORMATIVE WORK DESIGN

Experimental research indicates that the implementation of SMTs is less advisable when team faultlines are very strong (i.e., when strong subgroups exist within the same team) because autonomy intensifies team members' awareness of interpersonal differences (Rico et al., 2007). The reason for this is that team autonomy requires stronger internal coordination between team members (rather than structuring a task from the outside). However, collective decision making makes team members more vulnerable to conflicts arising out of dissimilarities between these subgroups. In their experimental study, Rámon Rico and colleagues (2007) showed that an experimental manipulation to increase team autonomy decreased both the decision-making quality and levels of social integration (i.e., the degree to which team members feel satisfied with and committed to team interactions and their willingness to stay in the team) for teams that had strong faultlines. In contrast, for teams with weak faultlines (i.e., no subgroups), providing autonomy showed positive effects on decision-making quality and social integration. That is, in these teams, autonomy helped to make the most of their diversity. By working together and communicating, they could combine their different skills and ideas to come up with better solutions.

How do SMTs improve performance?

Next, we focus on some of the underlying theoretical processes that help to better understand the mechanisms through which self-management in teams improves team effectiveness. A key mechanism proposed in the literature is the concept of team empowerment. There is a distinction between structural empowerment versus psychological empowerment (Kirkman & Rosen, 1999). Structural empowerment refers to the design of work or task characteristics that promote team autonomy and shared decision-making. On the other hand, psychological empowerment is a motivational concept which describes the extent to which teams perceive that they are in control of their work (Maynard et al., 2012). In other words, while structural empowerment is concerned with organizational conditions (i.e., the implementation of self-managing teams), psychological empowerment focuses on perceptions or cognitive states regarding empowerment—along with the collective perception that the team is in control of their work.

There are several studies suggesting that work design (i.e., key features of self-managing teams) is an antecedent of psychological team empowerment. Furthermore, team empowerment is associated with team effectiveness (Maynard et al., 2012; Seibert et al., 2011), including variables like performance, productivity, customer satisfaction, innovation, and decision making.

As well as team empowerment, SMTs might also impact team effectiveness outcomes via other team-level (e.g., group cohesion) or individual mechanisms (i.e., reduced work demands). For example, the introduction of self-management might also increase group cohesion which is an important emergent state in teams (Langfred, 2000). Furthermore, the increase in team autonomy could also improve individually experienced work characteristics, such as a reduction in individual demands and/or increases in individual autonomy which can improve psychological well-being and active learning (van Mierlo et al., 2007).

Finally, other mechanisms hypothesized to be affected by SMTs are improved intra-team processes, improved learning and development, and quicker responses at the source (Parker et al., 2001). For example, the implementation of SMTs tends to improve task interdependence which is associated with improved problem-solving strategies between team members (Tesluk & Mathieu, 1999). An SMT approach can also benefit by providing learning opportunities because team members are self-organized and, thus, benefit from transferring their skills (i.e., learning from each other). These team learning processes provide more flexibility and help the team in achieving its goals (Yli-Kauhaluoma, 2021). Finally, one mechanism that SMTs share with STS approaches is the idea that variances should be controlled at the source (Wall & Martin, 1987). In other words, when there are disruptions in the daily workflow (e.g., machines not working properly or ordering specific parts for their work), SMTs have enough discretion to quickly respond to these disruptions and fix them themselves rather than asking central support staff for help (which tends to slow down work processes and is not conducive to developing tacit knowledge). In the next section, we will further expand on principles from sociotechnical systems theory as they often involve more organizational-wide changes.

Organizational and System-Wide Interventions

Work design interventions can also focus on larger units, including the entire organization. In the context of organizational-level work design interventions, interventions might draw on principles from STS theory (Cherns, 1976). When using STS approaches, work systems are considered as a combination of technological components and social components (Clegg, 2000). The technology aspect encompasses equipment and operational methods employed to convert raw materials into products or services. Social aspects include the work structure that establishes the connections between individuals, technology, and other workers. The main idea in STS system thinking is to consider both technical and social factors in relation to work design. In other words, when designing (or redesigning) work systems, it is necessary to consider the linkages between individuals and the technology that is employed (Cherns, 1976). This approach takes into consideration that technology shapes work practices and social systems, for example, the introduction of new production systems can change job roles and specific work practices. At the same time, social components shape if and how technology is used. Overall, an STS perspective advocates toward analyzing the complex interconnections between the social and technical components that we can observe in a given work system. In a case study, Georgia Hay and colleagues (2020) applied STS thinking to better understand the improved redesign of the healthcare system in Western Australia, in particular, with respect to dealing with complex patients who suffer from rare diseases. In their longitudinal qualitative study, the authors highlight how the improved management and diagnoses of these patients adopted some of the principles from STS in the redesign of their work system. That is, the redesigned system allowed better collaboration and integration between different specialists who work with rare diseases patients (i.e., improving the social work system). The redesign involved adoption of regular expert panel meetings, which allowed clinicians to expand their skills and knowledge with respect to technological developments in genetic testing. This redesign shows how technology (i.e., new developments in genetic testing) shapes social systems, but also how social systems need autonomy and teamwork to make best use of technological developments.

As noted earlier in this chapter, organization-wide interventions may also take a human resource management (HRM) approach by implementing HPWPs, which can impact work design at the level of departments, teams, and individuals. For example, Sian Christina and colleagues (2017) evaluated an intervention to improve energy efficiency behaviors in a multinational retail organizations. They found that assigning energy tasks to departmental managers, rather than separate "energy champions," and aligning these tasks with individual performance goals as well as organizational energy goals served to improve compliance with the completion of energy tasks at the individual level as well as reduce energy consumption at the organizational level. In doing so, the work of the departmental managers was redesigned to incorporate training and performance measures to support the integration of these energy tasks. This is an example of how both vertically and horizontally aligning HRM practices with each other can impact an individual's work design. In this case, vertical alignment involved integrating organizational systems and goals with departmental managers' job roles and responsibilities, while horizontal alignment involved aligning these managers' job roles and tasks with their own performance goals. Vertical alignment is one way in which cross-level effects can occur, with the work design of individuals or teams being altered in line with changes at organizational levels.

Common Mechanisms Underlying Work Redesign Interventions

A common theme amongst all four types of work design intervention discussed in this chapter is their ability to improve well-being and performance outcomes. Knight and Parker (2021) identified three common underlying mechanisms through which this occurs: (1) by fostering work motivation, (2) by encouraging learning, and (3) by increasing efficiency.

Fostering work motivation

It is well established that work which is characterized by high levels of resources such as autonomy, variety, feedback, and support is intrinsically motivating and leads to positive outcomes (Humphrey et al., 2007). Such work enables individuals to satisfy basic human needs for autonomy, competence and relatedness (a sense of belonging and connection to others) (Deci & Ryan, 2000), leading to higher job satisfaction, engagement, and commitment, and lower turnover (for a meta-analysis, see van den Broeck et al., 2016). Jobs rich in these characteristics also stimulate proactive motivation, which is defined as a sense that an individual "can do," has a "reason to" and is "energized to" invest effort in work tasks (Parker et al., 2010). Resource theories such as the job demands-control-support (Karasek & Theorell, 1990), and job demands-resource (JD-R; Demerouti et al., 2001) theories also suggest that high levels of work characteristics ("resources") help individuals cope with high levels of demands, and thus protect them from strain, burnout, and decreased work motivation. Indeed, conservation of resources (COR; Hobfoll, 2002) theory suggests that when resources are low, or demands are high, individuals are motivated to conserve the resources they have and build them up where possible, with increasing resources leading to increasing work motivation in an upward spiral. While the four types of intervention discussed in this chapter may focus on changing different work characteristics (e.g., autonomy vs relational characteristics), and impact different outcomes, they will all do so by increasing fostering work motivation.

Encouraging learning

Work which offers opportunities for feedback on how one is doing, sharing knowledge, and developing skills and abilities, enables individuals to learn and grow (Parker et al., 2021). Desmond Leach and colleagues (2003) observed how empowering workers to take responsibility for machine faults in a paper manufacture organization in the UK allowed them to develop their knowledge

324 TRANSFORMATIVE WORK DESIGN

about fixing faults. In particular, these workers were provided timely feed-back about faults, and they had access to technical support systems (engineers and operators), enabling the social transfer of knowledge to aid fault rectification. This demonstrates how interventions can have a multi-pronged work design approach by focusing on improving a number of work characteristics—in this case, autonomy, variety, feedback, and support—which together encourage learning and development, with associated performance benefits. Although it has long been theorized that enriched work promotes learning (e.g., Karasek, 1979), research is still at a nascent stage of development, with some empirical work supporting these links emerging (Taris et al., 2003, Wielenga-Beijer et al., 2010).

Increasing efficiency

Efficiency refers to improving organizational processes so that performance and productivity is improved. Toby Wall and colleagues (1992) noted how giving workers autonomy on a production line enabled a "quick-response" mechanism that improved efficiency by increasing the speed at which workers could deal with problems and machine faults. Additionally, encouraging specialization may improve efficiency by allowing highly technical tasks to be completed more quickly by highly trained workers (Humphrey at al., 2007). At an organizational level, improving systems can improve performance measures such as revenue and profit margins. For example, using a randomized controlled trial design, Christina and colleagues (2017) found that the energy behaviors and consumption of retail stores in the UK were improved when workers' energy tasks were aligned with training and performance management systems and goals. This demonstrates how work design changes at the system level can have wide reaching outcomes, not only for the organization, but also for the environment (in this case potentially reducing carbon emissions).

These three mechanisms (i.e., fostering motivation, encouraging motivation, increasing efficiency) provide a broad foundation for understanding how work redesign interventions impact outcomes. It is important to note that they are not mutually exclusive; just as a single intervention is likely to change more than one work characteristic, so is it likely that this intervention will operate through multiple mechanisms to impact outcomes. If we revisit the example by Leach and colleagues (2003), a myriad of work characteristics (e.g., autonomy, variety feedback, support) were improved which would likely not only have increased on the job learning, but also improved efficiency and work motivation due to the increased variety and challenge offered to workers by the expansion of their role.

Future Directions

Reviews and meta-analyses show that a growing body of research has explored the impact of work redesign interventions on well-being and performance, with the bulk of this research at the individual level (Daniels et al., 2017; Knight & Parker, 2021) with limited research at the team level, and virtually no research which has looked at organizational outcomes from work redesign interventions across several different organizations. This is likely to be due to the practicalities associated with negotiating, designing, running, and evaluating large-scale interventions of this nature (see Nielsen et al. and Daniels et al., this volume). Nevertheless, we observe that there are a number of ways in which work redesign intervention research can move forward and have real impact.

First, there is virtually no research which has attempted to change the work design of whole industries by engaging with policymakers, industry bodies, and multiple organizations simultaneously (Parker & Jorritsma, 2021). Yet doing so, if successful, will have wide-reaching effects which are more likely to make a real difference and be sustained. As an example, Parker and colleagues (2018) worked with the mining industry in Western Australia alongside representatives from multiple industry bodies and stakeholders to understand the impact of fly-in-fly-out (FIFO) work arrangements on the mental health and well-being of workers. FIFO workers typically fly to another part of the state to work for a period of two to four weeks doing, 12-hour shifts, before returning home for one to two weeks. They found that mental health was poorer amongst these workers than in the general population, with a greater likelihood of suicide. They also found that changes to work design were one way that these risks could be alleviated, and proposed recommendations which informed wider industry developments (e.g., a FIFO Code of Practice). We suggest that researchers could take a broader view of intervention impact, look above the parapet, and consider focusing on multi-organizational, industry-wide research to inform policy and practice at industry and national levels. Tracking work design and outcomes before and after the implementation of such policies would offer a means of evaluating the effectiveness of this sort of intervention. We do not suggest that interventions at industry or national level are easy but something to aspire to.

Second, we encourage future research to explore in more depth how work design interventions like the implementation of SMTs affect performance-relevant team processes; that is, interactions between team members that transform inputs into outcomes through cognitive, verbal, and behavioral activities directed toward organizing work tasks to achieve collective goals (Marks et al., 2001) as well as other team emergent psychological states (i.e., team confidence or team efficacy). Team processes encompass various aspects, including how well team members coordinate with each other and synchronize their work, how much they plan for future work and or think about contingency plans when things go wrong, as well as how well teams manage emotions and develop motivation (Mathieu et al., 2020). Because SMTs increase the autonomy of the entire team as well as interdependencies between team members, we would expect improvements in how well teams engage in planning processes and team coordination. These team-level processes are critically relevant for teams to be effective (LePine et al., 2008). However, research focusing on how SMT interventions affect both long-term and short-term changes and adaptations in team processes are needed to understand the interplay between team-level work design interventions and team functioning over time (Klonek et al., 2019). We also encourage researchers to use novel methods that allow the exploration of these team-level mechanisms in more depth, including live observations or video-recordings of critical performance episodes (Klonek et al., 2020). These methods enable us to better understand time-sensitive processes as they unfold and can substantially contribute to theory development (Twemlow et al., 2022).

Third, echoing previous calls for multi-level research (e.g., Martin et al., 2016; Parker, 2014), we suggest conducting cross-level research which investigates the complex interplay between changes at organizational, team, department, and individual levels. Little is known about how work design changes at one level impacts another level, or the mechanisms by which this occurs (Knight & Parker, 2021). Yet employees are typically embedded in multiple layers of organization and hierarchy in their workplaces. Understanding better how people are affected by work design changes at different levels could help managers in designing and executing organizational change. This type of research would also help to answer whether effects of SMTs are different if they represent a top-down intervention or if they are initiated by the team members (i.e., bottom-up).

Fourth, work redesign intervention research should consider a person-centered approach. Individuals are embedded in their jobs, and thus experience "whole" jobs, rather than discrete aspects of jobs. In this chapter, we have noted how interventions aimed at changing one characteristic, such as autonomy, are likely to impact other characteristics, such as variety and feedback (e.g., Leach et al., 2003; Wall et al., 1992). It therefore makes sense to consider the patterns, or constellations, of work characteristics that individuals experience as a whole, and how these are changed following a work redesign. Work design profile research has explored the different profile groups that emerge (e.g., Igic et al., 2017; Keller et al., 2017; Knight et al., 2022) but has not investigated whether and how individuals could transition from a "poorer" work design profile (e.g., high strain profile of the JD-R) to a more enriched profile (e.g., active profile of the JD-R). Doing so would help pinpoint targets for intervention at a broader level than variable centered research might allow.

Implications for Practice

It is important that theoretical advances in our understanding of how top-down work redesigns work are translated into practice to generate meaningful impact on work quality. For maximum impact, the suggestions provided here should be considered alongside those in the other intervention chapters in this volume.

First, a comprehensive assessment of employees' work design is required to understand what the issues are that need redesigning (Briner & Walshe, 2015). It is important to consider work design at different levels at this point, and organizational factors which may be contributing to the status quo, such as policies, feedback and reward structures, and leadership behaviors. The results of this assessment can be used to identify where problems lie, and therefore potential targets for work redesign. The ideal approach is to assess work design before and after a redesign intervention. This allows the assessment of whether an intervention resulted in any changes in work design, and particularly, which specific work characteristics have been affected (van Mierlo et al., 2005). This is a critical step to understand whether an intervention had any unintended consequences that might reduce its effectiveness. For example, the implementation of self-managing teams can be associated with a bundle of changes in autonomy, task interdependence, and identity, but may potentially also initially increase workload within a team due to increased coordination demands.

Second, it is important to remember that there is no perfect redesign or single solution, and that employee participation in the redesign process is particularly important. Different solutions will work with varying degrees of success depending on the organizational context and goals and perseverance may be necessary to arrive at an optimal solution. Research suggests that focusing on developing meaningful work and connections with others is likely to be important, alongside the opportunity to participate in decision-making around work redesign. Thus, organizations should refrain from mandating work redesign without the consultation of staff. Managers could provide open forums to solicit ideas and discussion from employees, as well as providing opportunities for individuals to understand the importance of their work (e.g., by sharing feedback from clients, customers, or patients).

Third, it is critical that organizational factors are aligned with work redesigns to be successful (Daniels et al., 2017; Knight & Parker, 2021). For example, if sharing feedback from beneficiaries of the work employees do is not aligned with workers' goals, it may not have the intended consequence of improving work meaning and sense of purpose.

Fourth, evaluating the effectiveness of interventions on a continuing basis is important to assess whether the changes are working or other changes need to be implemented. This means assessing work design and associated outcomes, such as engagement, work meaning, and performance, on a repeated basis to assess trends over time. This type of data can be used to pinpoint factors which are really driving the outcomes desired, enabling resources to be invested in appropriate channels.

In summary, top-down work redesigns are inherently messy and complex. They should only be attempted with strong managerial and organizational support, in the full knowledge that the road ahead is likely to be challenging. However, with perseverance, the rewards reaped are likely to be great, promoting high quality work which is optimal for both well-being and performance. Finally, implementing and evaluating the effectiveness of work redesign interventions is critically important for our discipline as they provide the best evidence that our research insights can be translated into practice and make real impact that benefits workers. Because research on work redesign interventions is inherently complex and difficult, we also encourage journal editors and reviewers to be more open toward research studies and designs rather than focusing on specific designs (e.g., experimental manipulation of conditions) that can be extremely difficult to achieve in practice and may not consider organizational and employee needs.

References

Batt, R. (2002). Managing customer services: Human resource practices, quit rates, and sales growth. *Academy of Management Journal 45*(3), 587–597.

Bellé, N. (2014). Leading to make a difference: A field experiment on the performance effects of transformational leadership perceived social impact and public service motivation. *Journal of Public Administration Research and Theory 24*(1): 109–136.

Black, S. E., Lynch, L. M., & Krivelyova, A. (2004). How workers fare when employers innovate. *Industrial Relations: A Journal of Economy and Society 43*(1), 44–66.

Boning, B., Ichniowski, C., & Shaw, K. (2007). Opportunity counts: Teams and the effectiveness of production incentives. *Journal of Labor Economics 25*(4), 613–650.

Briner, R. B., & Walshe, N. D. (2015). An evidence-based approach to improving the quality of resource-oriented well-being interventions at work. *Journal of Occupational and Organizational Psychology 88*(3), 563–586.

Campion M. A., and McClelland C. L., (1993). Follow-up and extension of the interdisciplinary costs and benefits of enlarged jobs. *Journal of Applied Psychology 78*(3), 339–351.

Campion, M. A., Medsker, G. J., & Higgs, A. C. (1993). Relations between work group characteristics and effectiveness: Implications for designing effective work groups. *Personnel Psychology 46*(4), 823–847.

Camuffo, A., De Stefano, F., & Paolino, C. (2017). Safety reloaded: Lean operations and high involvement work practices for sustainable workplaces. *Journal of Business Ethics 143*, 245–259.

Carter, K. M., Mead, B. A., Stewart, G. L., Nielsen, J. D., & Solimeo, S. L. (2019). Reviewing work team design characteristics across industries: Combining meta-analysis and comprehensive synthesis. *Small Group Research 50*(1), 138–188.

Cherns, A. (1976). The principles of sociotechnical design. *Human Relations 29*, 783–792.

Christina, S., Dainty, A., Daniels, K., Tregaskis, O., & Waterson, P. (2017). Shut the fridge door! HRM alignment, job redesign and energy performance. *Human Resource Management Journal 27*(3), 382–402.

Clegg, C. W. (2000). Sociotechnical principles for system design. *Applied Ergonomics 31*, 463–477. http://dx.doi.org/10.1016/S0003-6870(00)00009-0

Cohen, S. L, & Turney, J. R. (1978). Intervening at the bottom: Organizational development with enlisted personnel in an army work. *Personnel Psychology 31*(4), 715–730.

Cordery, J. L., Mueller W. S., & Smith L. M. (1991). Attitudinal and behavioral effects of autonomous group working: A longitudinal field study. *The Academy of Management Journal 34*, 464–476.

Cordery, J. L., Morrison, D., Wright, B. M., & Wall, T. D. (2010). The impact of autonomy and task uncertainty on team performance: A longitudinal field study. *Journal of Organizational Behavior 31*(2–3), 240–258.

Cummings, T. G. (1978). Self-regulating work groups: A sociotechnical synthesis. *Academy of Management Review 3*, 625–634.

Deci, E. L., & Ryan, R. M. (2000). The "what" and "why" of goal pursuits: Human needs and the self-determination of behavior. *Psychological Inquiry 11*(4), 227–268.

Demerouti, E., Bakker, A. B., Nachreiner, F., & Schaufeli, W. B. (2001). The job demands-resources model of burnout. *Journal of Applied Psychology 86*(3), 499–512. https://doi.org/10.1037/0021-9010.86.3.499

Daniels, K., Gedikli, C., Watson, D., Semkina, A., & Vaughn, O. (2017). Job design, employment practices and well-being: A systematic review of intervention studies. *Ergonomics 60*(9), 1177–1196.

Gomez, L. R., & Mussio, S. J. (1975). An application of job enrichment in a civil service setting: A demonstration study. *Public Personnel Management 4*(1), 49–54.

Grant, A. M. (2007). Relational job design and the motivation to make a prosocial difference. *Academy of Management Review 32*(2), 393–417.

Grant, A. M. (2008). The significance of task significance: Job performance effects, relational mechanisms, and boundary conditions. *Journal of Applied Psychology 93*(1), 108–124.

Grant, A. M., & Parker, S. K. (2009). Redesigning work design theories: The rise of relational and proactive perspectives. *Academy of Management Annals 3*(1), 317–375. https://doi.org/10.1080/19416520903047327

Griffeth, R. W. (1985). Moderation of the effects of job enrichment by participation: A longitudinal field experiment. *Organizational Behavior and Human Decision Processes 35*(1), 73–93.

Griffin R. W. (1991). Effects of work redesign on employee perceptions attitudes and behaviors: A long-term investigation. *The Academy of Management Journal 34*(2): 425–435.

Guest, D. E. (1997). Human resource management and performance: A review and research agenda. *International Journal of Human Resource Management 8*(3), 263–276.

Hackman, J. R., & Oldham, G. R. (1976). Motivation through the design of work: Test of a theory. *Organizational Behavior and Human Performance 16*(2), 250–279. https://doi.org/10.1016/0030-5073(76)90016-7

Hackman, J. R., & Oldham, G. R. (1980). *Work redesign*. Addison-Wesley.

Hay, G. J., Klonek, F. E., & Parker, S. K. (2020). Diagnosing rare diseases: A sociotechnical approach to the design of complex work systems. *Applied Ergonomics 86*, 103095.

Hobfoll, S. E. (2002). Social and psychological resources and adaptation. *Review of General Psychology 6*, 307–324.

Holman, D., & Axtell, C. (2016). Can job redesign interventions influence a broad range of employee outcomes by changing multiple job characteristics? A quasi-experimental study. *Journal of Occupational Health Psychology 21*(3), 284–295.

Hornung, S., Rousseau, D. M., Glaser, J., Angerer, P., & Weigl, M. (2010). Beyond top-down and bottom-up work redesign: Customizing job content through idiosyncratic deals. *Journal of Organizational Behavior 31*(2–3), 187–215.

Humphrey, S. E., Nahrgang, J. D., & Morgeson, F. P. (2007). Integrating motivational, social, and contextual work design features: A meta-analytic summary and theoretical extension of the work design literature. *Journal of Applied Psychology 92*(5), 1332–1356. https://doi.org/10.1037/0021-9010.92.5.1332

Igic, I., Keller, A. C., Elfering, A., Tschan, F., Kälin, W., & Semmer, N. K. (2017). Ten-year trajectories of stressors and resources at work: Cumulative and chronic effects on health and well-being. *Journal of Applied Psychology 102*(9), 1317–1343.

Janz, B. D., Colquitt, J. A., & Noe, R. A. (1997). Knowledge worker team effectiveness: The role of autonomy, interdependence, team development, and contextual support variables. *Personnel Psychology 50*(4), 877–904.

Johns, G. (2006). The essential impact of context on organizational behavior. Academy of management *review 31*(2), 386–408. http://www.jstor.org/stable/20159208

Karasek Jr, R. A. (1979). Job demands, job decision latitude, and mental strain: Implications for job redesign. *Administrative Science Quarterly 24*, 285–308. https://doi.org/10.2307/2392498

Karasek, R., & Theorell, T. (1990). *Healthy work: Stress, productivity, and the reconstruction of working life*. Basic Books.

Keller, A. C., Igic, I., Meier, L. L., Semmer, N. K., Schaubroeck, J. M., Brunner, B., & Elfering, A. (2017). Testing job typologies and identifying at-risk subpopulations using factor mixture models. *Journal of Occupational Health Psychology 22*(4), 503–516.

Kirkman, B. L., & Rosen, B. (1999). Beyond self-management: Antecedents and consequences of team empowerment. *Academy of Management Journal 42*(1), 58–74.

Klein, K. J., & Kozlowski, S. W. J. (2000). From micro to meso: Critical steps in conceptualizing and conducting multilevel research. *Organizational Research Methods 3*, 211–236.

Klonek, F., Gerpott, F. H., Lehmann-Willenbrock, N., & Parker, S. K. (2019). Time to go wild: How to conceptualize and measure process dynamics in real teams with high-resolution. *Organizational Psychology Review 9*(4), 245–275.

Klonek, F. E., Meinecke, A. L., Hay, G., & Parker, S. K. (2020). Capturing team dynamics in the wild: The communication analysis tool. *Small Group Research 51*(3), 303–341.

Knight, C., & Parker, S. K. (2021). How work redesign interventions affect performance: An evidence-based model from a systematic review. *Human Relations 74*(1). https://doi.org/10.1177/0018726719865604

Knight, C., McLarnon, M. J., Wenzel, R., & Parker, S. (2022). The importance of relational work design characteristics: A person-centred approach. *Australian Journal of Management 47*(4), 705–728.

Kozlowski, S. W. J., & Ilgen, D. R. (2006). Enhancing the effectiveness of work groups and teams. *Psychological Science in the Public Interest 7*, 77–124.

Langfred, C. W. (2000). The paradox of self-management: Individual and group autonomy in work groups. *Journal of Organizational Behavior 21*, 563–585.

Langfred, C. W. (2005). Autonomy and performance in teams: The multilevel moderating effect of task interdependence. *Journal of Management 31*(4), 513–529.

Leach, D. J., Wall, T. D., & Jackson, P. R. (2003). The effect of empowerment on job knowledge: An empirical test involving operators of complex technology. *Journal of Occupational and Organizational Psychology 76*(1), 27–52.

LePine, J. A., Piccolo, R. F., Jackson, C. L., Mathieu, J. E., & Saul, J. R. (2008). A meta-analysis of teamwork processes: Tests of a multidimensional model and relationships with team effectiveness criteria. *Personnel Psychology 61*(2), 273–307.

Locke, E. A., Sirota, D., & Wolfson, A. D. (1976). An experimental case study of the successes and failures of job enrichment in a government agency. *Journal of Applied Psychology 61*(6), 701–711.

Marks, M. A., Mathieu, J. E., & Zaccaro, S. J. (2001). A temporally based framework and taxonomy of team processes. *Academy of Management Review 26*(3), 356–376.

Martin, A., Karanika-Murray, M., Biron, C., & Sanderson, K. (2016). The psychosocial work environment, employee mental health and organizational interventions: Improving research and practice by taking a multilevel approach. *Stress and Health 32*(3), 201–215.

Mathieu, J. E., Luciano, M. M., D'Innocenzo, L., Klock, E. A., & LePine, J. A. (2020). The development and construct validity of a team processes survey measure. *Organizational Research Methods 23*(3), 399–431.

Maynard, M. T., Gilson, L. L., & Mathieu, J. E. (2012). Empowerment—fad or fab? A multilevel review of the past two decades of research. *Journal of Management 38*(4), 1231–1281.

Morse, N. C., & Reimer, E. (1956). The experimental change of a major organizational variable. *Journal of Abnormal and Social Psychology 52*(1), 120.

Oreg, S., Vakola, M., & Armenakis, A. (2011). Change recipients' reactions to organizational change: A 60-year review of quantitative studies. *Journal of Applied Behavioral Science 47*(4), 461–524.

Parker, S. K. (2014). Beyond motivation: Job and work design for development, health, ambidexterity, and more. *Annual Review of Psychology 65*(1), 661–691. https://doi.org/10.1146/annurev-psych-010213-115208

Parker, S. K., Andrei, D. M., & Van den Broeck, A. (2019). Poor work design begets poor work design: Capacity and willingness antecedents of individual work design behavior. *Journal of Applied Psychology 104*(7), 907–928. https://doi.org/10.1037/apl0000383

Parker, S. K., Bindl, U. K., & Strauss, K. (2010). Making things happen: A model of proactive motivation. *Journal of Management 36*(4), 827–856.

Parker, S. K., Fruhen, L., Burton, C., McQuade, S., Loveny, J., Griffin, M. A., Page, A., Chikritzhs, T., Crock, S., Jorritsman, K., & Esmond, J. (2018). *Impact of FIFO work arrangements on the mental health and wellbeing of FIFO workers*. WA Mental Health Commission. https://www.mhc.wa.gov.au/media/2547/impact-of-fifo-work-arrangement-on-the-mentalhealth-and-wellbeing-of-fifo-workers-full-report.pdf

Parker, S. K., Johnson, A., Collins, C., & Nguyen, H. (2013). Making the most of structural support: Moderating influence of employees' clarity and negative affect. *Academy of Management Journal 56*(3), 867–892. https://doi.org/10.5465/amj.2010.0927

Parker, S. K., & Jorritsma, K. (2021). Good work design for all: Multiple pathways to making a difference. *European Journal of Work and Organizational Psychology 30*(3), 456–468. https://doi.org/10.1080/1359432X.2020.1860121

Parker, S. K., Ward, M. K., & Fisher, G. G. (2021). Can high-quality jobs help workers learn new tricks? A multidisciplinary review of work design for cognition. *Academy of Management Annals 15*(2), 406–454. https://doi.org/10.5465/annals.2019.0057

Parker, S. K., Wall, T. D., & Cordery, J. L. (2001). Future work design research and practice: Towards an elaborated model of work design. *Journal of Occupational and Organizational Psychology 74*(4), 413–440.

Pasmore, W. A., & King, D. C. (1978). Understanding organizational change: A comparative study of multifaceted interventions. *Journal of Applied Behavioral Science 14*(4), 455–468.

Powell, R. M., & Schlacter, J. L. (1971). Participative management a panacea? *Academy of Management Journal 14*(2), 165–173.

Taris, T. W., Kompier, M. A., De Lange, A. H., Schaufeli, W. B., & Schreurs, P. J. (2003). Learning new behaviour patterns: A longitudinal test of Karasek's active learning hypothesis among Dutch teachers. *Work & Stress 17*(1), 1–20.

Trist, E. L., Susman, G. I., & Brown, G. R. (1977). An experiment in autonomous working in an American underground coal mine. *Human Relations 30*, 201–236. http://dx.doi.org/10.1177/001872677703000301

Rico, R., Molleman, E., Sánchez-Manzanares, M., & Van der Vegt, G. S. (2007). The effects of diversity faultlines and team task autonomy on decision quality and social integration. *Journal of Management 33*(1), 111–132.

Robertson, M. M., Huang, Y. H., O'Neill, M. J., & Schleifer, L. M. (2008). Flexible workspace design and ergonomics training: Impacts on the psychosocial work environment musculoskeletal health and work effectiveness among knowledge workers. *Applied Ergonomics 39*(4), 482–494.

Seibert, S. E., Wang, G., & Courtright, S. H. (2011). Antecedents and consequences of psychological and team empowerment in organizations: A meta-analytic review. *Journal of Applied Psychology 96*(5), 981.

Stewart, G. L. (2006). A meta-analytic review of relationships between team design features and team performance. *Journal of Management 32*(1), 29–55.

Tesluk, P. E., & Mathieu, J. E. (1999). Overcoming roadblocks to effectiveness: Incorporating management of performance barriers into models of work group effectiveness. *Journal of Applied Psychology 84*, 200–217.

Tregaskis O., Daniels K., Glover L., et al. (2013). High performance work practices and firm performance: A longitudinal case study. *British Journal of Management 24*(2), 225–244.

Twemlow, M., Tims, M., & Khapova, S. N. (2022). A process model of peer reactions to team member proactivity. *Human Relations 76*(9), 1317–1351. https://doi.org/10.1177/00187267221094023

Wall, T. D., Jackson, P. R., & Davids, K. (1992). Operator work design and robotics system performance: A serendipitous field study. *Journal of Applied Psychology 77*(3), 353–362. https://doi.org/10.1037/0021-9010.77.3.353

Wall, T. D., & Martin, R. (1987). Job and work design. In C. L. Cooper & I. T. Robertson (Eds.), *International review of industrial and organisational psychology* (pp. 61–91). Wiley.

Van den Broeck, A., Ferris, D. L., Chang, C. H., & Rosen, C. C. (2016). A review of self-determination theory's basic psychological needs at work. *Journal of Management 42*(5), 1195–1229. https://doi.org/10.1177/0149206316632058

Van Mierlo, H., Rutte, C. G., Kompier, M. A., & Doorewaard, H. A. (2005). Self-managing teamwork and psychological well-being: Review of a multilevel research domain. *Group & Organization Management 30*(2), 211–235.

Van Mierlo, H., Rutte, C. G., Vermunt, J. K., Kompier, M. A. J., & Doorewaard, J. A. C. M. (2007). A multi-level mediation model of the relationships between team autonomy, individual task design and psychological well-being. *Journal of Occupational and Organizational Psychology 80*(4), 647–664.

Wielenga-Meijer, E. G., Taris, T. W., Kompier, M. A., & Wigboldus, D. H. (2010). From task characteristics to learning: A systematic review. *Scandinavian Journal of Psychology 51*(5), 363–375. https://doi.org/10.1111/j.1467-9450.2009.00768.x

Wood, S., Van Veldhoven, M., Croon, M., & de Menezes, L. M. (2012). Enriched job design, high involvement management and organizational performance: The mediating roles of job satisfaction and well-being. *Human Relations 65*(4), 419–445.

Workman, M., & Bommer, W. (2004). Redesigning computer call center work: A longitudinal field experiment. *Journal of Organizational Behavior 25*(3), 317–337.

Yli-Kauhaluoma, S. (2021). Self-managing teams in a public library: Learning arrangements at work. In B. Elkjaer (Eds.), *Current practices in workplace and organizational learning: Revisiting the classics and advancing knowledge* (pp. 169–184). Springer.

Implementing and Sustaining Work Redesign

Kevin Daniels, David Watson, Rachel Nayani, and Helen Fitzhugh

Introduction

The purpose of this chapter is to examine how organizationally initiated job redesign interventions come to be sustained. By focusing on job *redesign*, rather than job design, we focus on changes to how work is configured, conducted, coordinated, and scheduled (cf., Morgeson & Humphrey, 2008; Parker & Ohly, 2008). Examples include changes to who makes decisions, changes to working hours, constraining or expanding the number of tasks to be performed by a worker. By examining how job redesign is sustained, we add to the literature on the antecedents of job design (Parker et al., 2017). We focus on organizationally initiated changes to jobs, also known as "top-down" job redesign (Grant & Parker, 2009) because organizations spend considerable resources in efforts focused on "top-down" job redesign. Moreover, "top-down" job redesign may have potential for some of the most extensive changes to how jobs are configured, conducted, coordinated, and scheduled (Daniels et al., 2017). Further, governments could also spend considerable resources informing organizational "top-down" job redesign in the form of regulation and guidance. Therefore, organizationally initiated sanctioned approaches to job redesign merit detailed analysis.

There is robust evidence linking "good" job design (e.g., worker autonomy, skill use) to beneficial health and performance outcomes, and there is also robust evidence linking "bad" job design (e.g., excessive work demands, role conflict) to adverse health and performance outcomes. This evidence is summarized in multiple systematic reviews and meta-analyses (e.g., Kivimäki et al., 2012; Milner et al., 2018; Rugulies et al., 2020; Stansfeld & Candy, 2006; Then et al., 2014).

Much of this evidence, especially in respect of health outcomes, comes from large-scale, longitudinal, epidemiological surveys. Although such epidemiological evidence is capable of attaining very high levels of rigor for causal analysis,

Kevin Daniels et al., *Implementing and Sustaining Work Redesign*. In: *Transformative Work Design*. Edited by: Sharon K. Parker et al., Oxford University Press. © Society for Industrial and Organizational Psychology (2025). DOI: 10.1093/oso/9780197692554.003.0013

this evidence base is limited for two main reasons. First, controlled trials, especially large-scale randomized control trials, provide more robust causal evidence linking discrete and deliberate changes to job design (i.e., job redesign) to performance and health outcomes (Cook et al., 1990), but there are not yet enough long-term trials of this sort to provide a solid base for generalizations on precisely which forms of job redesign work in which circumstances and for whom. Unfortunately, a second source of relevant evidence (i.e., surveys of jobs as they are) is abundant but does not provide any evidence on how job redesign can be managed in a way that brings about and sustains beneficial societal outcomes (in relation to, for example, productivity, health, environmental sustainability).

The purpose of the current chapter is to examine how job redesign can be managed and sustained for beneficial outcomes. There are two elements of how job redesign comes to be managed and sustained. First, implementation of job redesign over the short-term (months) and, second, sustaining those changes over the longer term (many years). In this chapter, we consider both. In relation to implementation over the shorter-term, there is a wealth of research synthesized into systematic reviews upon which to draw, especially in the area of job redesign for protecting and improving worker health and well-being. We will draw on this literature in this chapter. In relation to sustaining job redesign over the longer term, the evidence base is much less well developed, and therefore conclusions are necessarily more tentative. Nevertheless, some conclusions in respect of this evidence base are possible. We will also consider both intra-organizational change efforts and attempts to redesign jobs across multiple organizations in the form of regulation and industry guidance.

First, we examine the current state of the evidence in respect of job redesign and limitations in the overall evidence base. Second, we examine evidence on the implementation of discrete job redesign interventions within organizations and how such interventions may be sustained over the longer term. Third, we examine initiatives that may lead multiple organizations to attempt to effect job redesign. Fourth, before concluding the chapter, we explore the implications of taking a longer-term perspective on sustaining job redesign for future directions in policy, practice, research, and methods.

State of the Evidence

There have been numerous reviews of the effects of job redesign on health and well-being outcomes, but fewer in relation to performance outcomes. In relation to health and well-being outcomes, reviews of the effects of job redesign have contrasting conclusions. For example, two meta-analytic reviews (Richardson & Rothstein, 2008; Van der Klink et al., 2001) reported no effects of job redesign, and other reviews have concluded there are mixed effects (Bhui et al., 2012), and in some case adverse effects (Bambra et al., 2007; Daniels et al., 2017; Fox et al., 2022). Two reviews concluded extensive, system-wide job redesign interventions are more likely to realize beneficial health and well-being outcomes than job redesign focused on changes to a small number of work characteristics (Daniels et al., 2017; Montano et al., 2014). On the other hand, Kimberly Fox and colleagues (2022) concluded interventions targeted at flexible working patterns were more likely than other forms of job redesign to have benefits for health and well-being. In respect of performance, Caroline Knight and Sharon K. Parker (2021) found that 39 out of 46 studies of job redesign evidenced positive impacts on performance, although two studies reported some negative impacts. Of the types of job redesign reviewed by Knight and Parker, the most equivocal findings were for autonomous work group interventions and system-wide interventions. However, even for these forms of job redesign, there was some evidence of the potential for realizing performance benefits. Similarly, in their review of the simultaneous effects of job redesign on employee health/well-being and performance, Kevin Daniels and colleagues (2017) concluded system-wide interventions were most likely to realize benefits for health/well-being and performance compared to other types of job redesign interventions.

Reviews of job redesign studies do indicate the potential for job redesign to realize benefits for both employers and employees, reflecting the mutual gains perspective on the employment relationship (Kochan & Osterman, 1994). However, there are multiple caveats. One caveat relates to how job redesign is implemented. It has long been recognized that implementation matters and can explain why some job redesign interventions fail to deliver benefits (Egan et al., 2009). Implementation has been defined as "the dynamic process of adapting the program [i.e., intervention] to the context of action while maintaining the intervention's core principles" (Herrera-Sánchez et al., 2017, p. 4).

One systematic review (Roodbari et al., 2022) concluded job redesign interventions would be more likely to realize benefits if a range of contextual factors are in place, such as support from senior managers, middle managers, and external consultants. However, other reviews have concluded that although favorable factors of the kind listed by Hamid Roodbari and colleagues (2022) are helpful for implementation, lack of supporting factors can be overcome (Daniels et al., 2021) and even helpful contextual factors, such as high levels of resourcing, do not guarantee success (Newman, 2021). Further, drawing on Mintzberg's (1987) work on strategic change, Paul Fuller and colleagues (2019) argued that factors that adversely influence the implementation of one sort of intervention may make another feasible or more appropriate. If this is the case, a team of researchers focused narrowly on a specific intervention may conclude that job redesign has not been implemented, although another form of job redesign may come to be implemented outside of the awareness of the research team.

Two other caveats are interconnected. One is that models of what constitutes "good" jobs indicate good jobs have many facets (Irvine et al., 2018; MacKay et al., 2004), such as minimum guaranteed hours, safe working conditions, role clarity, and worker autonomy. Another is that job redesign takes place within wider organizational contexts with multiple moving parts, structures, systems, and within the context of an organizational culture and strategy that evolve (and indeed should evolve, Johnson, 1987). The implication of these two caveats is that for shorter-term impacts and longer-term sustainability of job redesign, a job redesign intervention must somehow connect or be integrated with other aspects of job design and the other moving parts of the organization (Knight & Parker, 2021; see also Wall et al., 2002). The extensive system-wide interventions described in the Knight and Parker (2021) and Daniels and colleagues (2017) reviews might be more likely to engage with these other aspects of an organization because of their systemic nature. Further, job design relates to the tasks and duties workers perform; that is, what workers do. If organizational culture is "the way we do things around here" (Deal & Kennedy, 1982), then job redesign arguably can be used as a lever to change organizational cultures or as means of aligning job design to better fit with the prevailing organizational culture. Although job design as an aspect of organizational culture is largely ignored by job design theorists (Erez, 2010), the tasks of workers could be framed as organizational rituals and routines. Organizational rituals and routines are considered by culture theorists as behavioral manifestations of organizational culture (Johnson, 1987). Moreover, jobs are embedded in organizational structures, control systems (e.g., performance management systems), and social relationships between individual and groups of workers, which are also seen as manifestations of organizational culture. Therefore, job redesign could usefully entail consideration of how job redesign connects with aspects of culture, including underpinning assumptions about the organization, the stories workers tell each other about the organization, and its power structures and symbols (see, e.g., Johnson, 1987; Schein, 2016).

In summary, implementation of any specific job redesign intervention matters. However, a narrow focus on one specific job redesign intervention misses many other factors that may play out over a longer period of time and outside of any specific intervention. Correspondingly, there is a need to consider job redesign in its wider and dynamic context, and how job redesign could itself alter the wider context.

Implementing and Evolving Job Redesign

The current literature on the implementation of job redesign can inform us of the factors that can affect the implementation of discrete job redesign efforts in the short to medium term, but rarely over the longer term. The main reason for making this conclusion has less to do with the complexity of tracking the effects of a specific intervention over several years in the context of other changes occurring. Rather, the conclusion is based largely on the relatively short-term nature of most intervention studies. Of studies that included an element of job redesign covered in Daniels and colleagues' review (2021) of implementing workplace health and well-being initiatives (41 studies in total included were solely or partially focused on job redesign and reported follow-ups), some 29 percent had the longest post-intervention follow-up of six months or less, 59 percent had the longest post-intervention follow-up of one year or less, 90 percent had the longest post-intervention follow-up of two years or less, and 98 percent had the longest post-intervention follow-up of three years or less. These figures indicate that any conclusions we can draw on the sustainability of job redesign interventions are based on a majority of studies with follow-ups of less than a year and an overwhelming majority of studies with follow-ups of less than two years. Given the significant investment in time and other resources entailed in many top-down job redesign interventions, we might presume job redesign, and any benefits, would be intended to be sustained for longer than two years.

Notwithstanding short follow-ups, Daniels and colleagues (2021) identified three critical success factors common to the implementation of all workplace health and well-being initiatives, including those focused on job redesign. These three critical success factors are (1) continuity in efforts at implementing, adapting, or otherwise sustaining the intervention; (2) effective learning from implementation so as to enable adaptation; and (3) effective and inclusive governance in the form of, for example, steering or working groups. Although Daniels and colleagues' (2021) conclusions are limited by the follow-ups of studies included in the review, subsequent qualitative fieldwork (Daniels et al., 2022) indicated these success factors may also be applicable for successful implementation over longer periods.

However, missing from current reviews of the evidence base is systematic coverage of how a specific job redesign intervention connects to the wider organizational environment (Daniels et al., 2022; Knight & Parker, 2021). To make these connections, a number of researchers (e.g., Daniels et al., 2022; Fridrich et al., 2015; Nielsen & Randall, 2013) follow Gary Johns (2006) in making the distinction between discrete and omnibus organizational contexts. In the context of job redesign, the discrete context encapsulates the implementation

340 TRANSFORMATIVE WORK DESIGN

of a specific job redesign intervention. The omnibus context captures factors in the organization, as a whole (e.g., overall strategy), and its environment (e.g., relations with suppliers, labor market conditions).

To these two elements of context, Daniels and colleagues (2022) have added the delivery context: The delivery context relates to co-ordination and management of a program of activities with a specific aim. It can be, but need not be, associated with a specific management structure, such as continuous improvement groups or steering committees. Daniels and colleagues (2022) developed the concept of the delivery context in relation to programs of activities related to workplace health and well-being, wherein which best practice and regulatory guidance (e.g., HSE, n.d.; ISO, 2018; NICE, n.d.) prescribe job (re)design as an essential element for the prevention of work-related health conditions. However, equally, the delivery context could be applied in other areas within which job redesign is an element, such as workplace safety or environmental sustainability programs (see Tregaskis et al., 2013 and Christina et al., 2017 as examples). Where job redesign is narrowly focused on a single, one-off intervention, rather than a rolling program of activities, the discrete and delivery contexts are synonymous. The delivery context connects multiple discrete contexts concerned with the implementation of focused and specific interventions with the wider omnibus context. The delivery context therefore can be the locus of how job redesign and related activities become sustained and evolve.

The delivery context is held to have two categories of functions. First, coordinating functions include developing an overall strategy and planning for a program of activities; baseline assessments; securing resources for implementation; communications and information provision; and oversight of implementation through coordinating activities, standardizing activities, or tailoring to specific circumstances as required and monitoring progress. Second, political and symbolic functions relate to consistently signaling the intent and overall importance of the overall program of activities and specific elements of job redesign within that program (Bowen & Ostroff, 2004), conveying what powerful stakeholders consider important (Hardy, 1996) and influencing stakeholders to assist with, or not resist, implementation (Hardy, 1996; Kimura, 2015). This can involve consultation with multiple stakeholders as well as coercion or co-option into program governance to ensure compliance. Both consultation and coercion/co-option are ostensibly political, given their links to power and influence. Consultation and coercion/co-option also have symbolic elements. For example, in relation to a job redesign intervention to improve job autonomy, consultation, as an act of ceding power, has symbolic value in signaling the importance of devolved authority. As another example, where jobs are being redesigned to improve safety outcomes, coercive displays enacted through performance management systems may reinforce compliance with safety protocols, and therefore signal the importance of safety performance in an organization. Other symbolic aspects can be as mundane as reconfiguring display boards and tidying up workstations as part of implementing lean management practices (Newman, 2021).

As the locus of connecting the discrete context of a job redesign intervention to the wider organizational omnibus context, organizational actors in the delivery context need to take decisions that maximize the compatibility of job redesign and other organizational practices/systems/structures to ensure compatibility and alignment (Cherns, 1987; Guest, 1997). This is so that job redesign does not work against other elements of the organization or vice versa. An often cited example of misalignment is jobs that require teamwork for organizational success, but using individualized performance-related pay structures for such jobs (Kerr, 1975). The evidence indicates that job redesign aligned with other organizational elements leads to performance benefits (Knight & Parker, 2021) and potentially health and well-being benefits as well (Daniels et al., 2017). With the delivery context, organizational actors may make three generic decisions for connections between job redesign and other elements of the organizations. These generic choices are labeled grafting, fracturing, and Gestalting by Daniels and colleagues (2022). The choices of grafting, fracturing, and Gestalting are not mutually exclusive, and two or more could occur together or in different sequences.

Grafting relates to adapting job redesign so that it is compatible with existing elements within the organization. To take the example of semi-autonomous teamworking and individualized performance related pay, grafting would mean using another form of job redesign that is compatible with performance related pay. So, if the original intent was to use semi-autonomous teamworking to promote feelings of autonomy and relatedness amongst workers with little task interdependence, the job redesign intervention would need to be modified. In this example, collective decision making would be incompatible with both individualized performance related pay and low task interdependence. Therefore, workers might be authorized to take decisions individually rather than collectively in their own immediate work area (autonomy compatible with existing individualized pay incentives) and relatedness promoted in other ways, such as through social events or team-based training. Modifying the nature of the job redesign intervention so that it is consistent with what already exists in the organization is generally recommended in conceptual and prescriptive frameworks for job redesign to promote health and well-being (see Daniels et al., 2022, for a review of these frameworks). Indeed, grafting is the route of least (political) resistance because very little else in the organization may have to change, especially where the goal of job redesign is to promote a secondary organizational goal (e.g., worker health or environmental sustainability beyond meeting statutory requirements) rather than a primary goal (e.g., profitability).

Fracturing is about questioning whether other elements of the organization that are not compatible with an intended job redesign intervention should also be replaced. Such questioning and creating conflict between other elements of the organization and intended job redesign could be evident where job redesign is an element of organizational culture change (Johnson, 1987, 1990; Reger et al., 1994), such that job redesign is symbolic of the need for wider change. For example, enhancing workers' job autonomy and introducing semi-autonomous work teams necessarily involves transfer of power from middle managers to front line workers, and so can change existing power structures in organizations and thus enable change in other areas. Alternatively, conflict could be created in other ways to enable easier implementation of job redesign. In a system-wide intervention including elements of job redesign targeted at improving safety performance, workers were encouraged to challenge unsafe behaviors through training in communication and regular messaging from senior managers (Tregaskis et al., 2013). Similarly, introducing flexible work scheduling practices may require regular communications to challenge managers who refuse to allow workers to self-schedule working days (Daniels et al., 2022). The necessity and motivation for fracturing may become evident after noticeable organizational shocks precipitated by poor performance or other salient signals, such as fatal accidents and work-related suicides (cf., Johnson, 1987, 1988).

Gestalting concerns bringing job redesign together with other organizational elements under a common purpose. This can entail simultaneous or sequential change in job redesign and other organizational elements, such as seen in system-wide interventions within which training, job redesign, messaging, and performance management practices are altered for a common purpose such as safety (Tregaskis et al., 2013) or environmental sustainability (Christina et al., 2017). However, it can also entail communicating how job redesign practices align with existing practices to meet a common goal, even if such practices had not been connected before. Daniels and colleagues (2022) give the example of an organization that created a workplace well-being steering group comprising corporate social responsibility, facilities, human resources managers, and diversity networks to create a common internal company brand around well-being, of which one element included flexible work scheduling practices.

Earlier we noted shocks can precipitate job redesign. However, shocks can also derail job redesign efforts and organizations may revert to old practices, especially when the intent of job redesign is not to pursue a primary organizational goal, as in the case of job redesign to promote worker health and well-being (Biron & Karanika-Murray, 2015). Shocks may even prompt job redesign that threatens employee health, well-being, and safety through an intensification of work (Cook et al., 2016). Such external shocks point to the fragility of the employment relationship, especially when organizations seek to maximize benefits for the organization (e.g., productivity, profit) and workers (e.g., pay, employee health and well-being) (Dobbins & Dundon, 2017). The simultaneous pursuit of organizational and worker co-benefits is known as the mutual gains or mutuality perspective on the employment relationship (Boxall, 2013; Guest, 2017), of which progressive forms of job design are an essential element (e.g., extensive skill use and variety, job autonomy; Ogbonnaya et al., 2017, as compared to Taylorist approaches). The benefits for organizations from pursuing mutual gains are held to stem principally from social exchange (Blau, 1964), in which employees reciprocate favorable treatment from employers with loyalty and effort.

For organizations wishing to pursue mutual gains through job redesign, several other elements appear to be important for successful and sustained job redesign. One of these may be the authenticity within which job redesign is implemented (Nayani et al., 2022), where employees come to attribute organizational authenticity through organizational and managerial actions that are consistent, visible, and value-congruent (Cording et al., 2014). For example, organizations would be viewed as inauthentic if espoused organizational values were "our people are our greatest asset" and then introduced insecure working practices, requiring longer working hours and introducing electronic performance surveillance systems that curtailed worker autonomy. The requirement for authenticity introduces a temporal aspect to job redesign because of the need for consistent and value-congruent actions, such that multiple actions are required, and actions follow from espoused values.

Both the pursuit of mutual gains and authenticity requires effort on the part of the organization (Bélanger & Edwards, 2007; Peterson, 2005). Partly this effort stems from the potential vulnerability of mutuality in the employment relationship to external shocks (Dobbins & Dundon, 2017) and partly from the need for visible action for authenticity. Given organizational changes also, this may also require continual shifting of working practices, including job design, so that job design evolves to address employee concerns as employee concerns change (Nayani et al., 2022). For example, as a stable workforce ages, there may be a need to redesign jobs so that work can be performed sitting down or standing up and/or with the use of technological aids, so that workers with muscular-skeletal problems are able to perform their work. Proactively altering job design to address worker concerns as they arise, or before they arise, demonstrates authenticity because changes to jobs are consistent with addressing employee needs for their health and well-being. Therefore, authenticity requires processes for organizations to notice shifts in employee concerns, and therefore respond to those shifts. Often, this will involve various forms of formal employee consultation and communication fora embedded in the delivery context (e.g., employee-employer working groups) as well as more informal forms of two-way communication with employees.

Mutual gains may be more likely where there is a good prevailing employment climate, evidenced by job security, mutual trust between workers and management, organizational justice, and fair treatment (Glover et al., 2014). Moreover, hard gains (e.g., increases in organizational headcount, bonuses, safety) may be precursors to softer gains (e.g., personal growth, development, well-being) (Glover et al., 2014). Further, authenticity itself needs to be built over time (Nayani et al., 2022). Therefore, at least within a mutual gains framework, there is a long-term element of job redesign, within which embedding and sustaining job redesign requires continual adaptation and evolution. Further, it appears this adaptation and evolution should be co-produced between workers and managers (and potentially other stakeholders) to meet worker needs.

To conclude this section, in the short term, it appears that job redesign efforts require continuity of efforts in implementation, effective learning to enable adaptation and effective and inclusive governance. Over the longer term, processes for learning and governance are embedded in a delivery context that connects a specific job redesign intervention (discrete context) to the wider organization (omnibus context) so that there is integration and evolution of job redesign efforts with other elements of the organization (e.g., performance management and training systems). Connecting may entail grafting job redesign onto existing practices, fracturing other practices so that job redesign is an element of wider organizational change or bringing job redesign together with other organization elements as a Gestalt. For job redesign focused on providing mutual gains for management and workers, the temporal aspect is important for building a good employment climate and organizational authenticity, so that job redesign efforts evolve to meet employee concerns.

Job Redesign Across Organizations

Cross-national comparisons of job design (Holman, this volume) indicate that different institutional arrangements can influence how jobs are designed. In this section, we examine some of the levers that can be used to influence job design across multiple organizations, and then examine some such initiatives in more detail. However, outside of areas where there are clearly quantifiable thresholds, such as wages, working hours, and dose–response relationships between exposure to a hazardous situation or substance and health and safety outcomes, so-called hard regulation around job design appears to be difficult (Dickinson,

2022; Mishiba, 2020). For example, "hard" regulation is difficult in those areas of job design concerned with the relationships between mental health and work, or around employment relations and conditions. This is because of uncertain dose–response relationships and complex causal relationships between job design and mental health (Rick & Briner, 2000), as well as the multifaceted nature of "good" job design (Irvine et al., 2018). Therefore, many approaches adopted by regulators and professional institutions to influence the design of work are based on "softer" regulation in the form of guidance or charters. One danger with such forms of guidance is that employers may engage with the guidance at a symbolic or surface level only and not engage fully with good practice (Hoque, 2003; Tyers et al., 2009; see points made earlier about authenticity).

A recent review (Daniels, 2023) examined four sets of guidance influential in the United Kingdom around best practice in job design and health. These are the UK's Health and Safety Executive (HSE) Management Standards for Work-Related Stress (HSE, n.d.), the National Institute of Health and Social Care's guidance for mental well-being at work (NICE, n.d.), the International Organization for Standardization's standard for workplace health and safety (ISO, 2018), and Public Health England's Workplace Wellbeing Charter (Hofman et al., 2018). A general conclusion from the review was that the guidance on offer placed too much emphasis on *what* changes need to be made (e.g., improve job autonomy, reduce role ambiguity) but too little emphasis on *how* to make those changes. For example, in their review of HSE's Management Standards, Karina Nielsen and colleagues (2021) concluded the Standards did not provide enough guidance on how to involve workers in the process of job redesign for better health outcomes. Guidance that gives too little attention to implementation may be sub-optimal.

The HSE's Management Standards for Work-Related Stress were subject to an empirical examination (Tyers et al., 2009). From a sample of 100 organizations that volunteered in an initial trial of the implementation of the Standards, Claire Tyers and colleagues (2009), found that 38 had dropped out of the trial and many more had made no changes in respect of job redesign 18 to 24 months after starting the trial. Moreover, the 100 organizations that volunteered to pioneer the Standards had support that would not normally be freely available to organizations to implement the Standards, namely consultancy support from the HSE and another UK government agency (Advisory, Conciliation, and Arbitration Service). Notwithstanding concerns over guidance on implementation included in various forms of guidance, the level of implementation reported by Tyers and colleagues (2009) indicates a startlingly high failure rate of the Standards. Moreover, evidence from the Netherlands (Taris et al., 2010) does suggest the findings may replicate across different forms of guidance. Therefore, it may be the case that initiatives to improve job redesign across multiple organizations would benefit from developing alternatives or supplements to generic national/international standards.

Alternative approaches could entail developing guidance specific to industrial sectors or specific localities (Parker & Jorritsma, 2020). Developing guidance for specific sectors would be a benefit by being able to focus on issues and concerns common to organizations using similar organizational forms and technologies, thus allowing learning to transfer across an industrial sector. This may require "link" organizations, which may offer consultancy or convene industry conferences and workshops. One example is the UK's Rail Safety and Standards Board, which is focused on rail safety through encouraging collaboration between employers operating in this industry (e.g., train operators, construction firms, rail maintenance operators). This approach might be feasible for large employers or where there are industry clusters in a place (such as the City Mental Health Alliance in London that focuses on financial and professional services organizations). However, for smaller employers and where employment is diffuse across multiple sectors, localized approaches may be appropriate. In a review of new approaches of Employment Charters introduced recently in different city regions in England, Peter Dickinson (2022) concluded local, placed-based guidance has the potential to enhance working conditions, but also recommended that guidance should be co-developed with a range of local stakeholders and there should be a mechanism for shared learning across localities. In the following paragraphs, we briefly describe three local initiatives targeted at aspects of job redesign, two from the United Kingdom and one from Finland.

In the Finnish example (Linna et al., 2011), localized interventions were developed for a range of public sector workers in two Finnish towns (Raisio and Nokia) that aimed to improve interactions between workers and managers, workers' opportunities to participate in the development of their work, and decision making over their work. In this quantitative study, the outcome variables reported were perceptions of interactional justice and procedural justice, respectively defined by Linna and colleagues (2011) as equity and fairness in how supervisors treat employees and fairness in the procedures by which resources and rewards are distributed. There were increases in perceptions of interactional justice in intervention towns following the intervention, but not increases in procedural justice. Positive evaluations of the implementation of the intervention were associated with increases in perceptions of both forms of justice assessed. Although Linna and colleagues (2011) do not report on any localized factors that may have influenced implementation, including any shared learning across workplaces within each town, the study does indicate the potential for placed-based job redesign initiatives to have some success.

The "Good Jobs Project" (Fitzhugh et al., 2023) is an initiative that originated in the English cathedral city of Norwich with the support of the city council and a civil society group known as the Norwich Good Economy Commission. Subsequently, the project expanded to cover other local government areas (known as borough councils) around Norwich in the county of Norfolk. High skilled, high paid, and secure work in the county is concentrated in three sectors focused on energy production, bioscience, and public services. However, much of the economy has employment in small businesses in low skilled, low paid, and seasonal work in food production (e.g., fruit pickers), tourism, retail, hospitality, and care. Managers in these businesses rarely have formal training in management. Researchers from one of the county's universities (University of East Anglia) were asked to develop a simple resource for local employers to improve the quality of work in small businesses in food production, tourism, retail, hospitality, and care. The resource includes a simple fact sheet, frequently asked question sheets, and a workbook. The resource was developed using three principles. First, there is a recognition that managers can have significant influence on the design of jobs (Parker & Jorritsma, 2020), especially in smaller businesses that may have fewer formal structures and procedures than larger organizations. Second, that existing guidance, at least in the United Kingdom, can be too time consuming and complex to implement, and is couched in language that is not intuitive for managers. Therefore, and third, that guidance should be developed using workers' and managers' own terms, so that there is a common language and an intuitive set of easy to understand and implement actions to improve work. The resource developed describes "*Four Boosts to Frontline Work*" that are: "*Let me connect*," which is specific to customer facing work but pertains to task identity in the Job Characteristics Model (Hackman & Oldham, 1980); "*Care about me and my life*," which pertains to flexible working and skills development; "*Have my back*," which pertains to management support; and "*Make me part of the conversation*," which pertains to employee involvement. Initial, albeit informal, evaluations are that the resource has been well received both in the localities where it has been developed and in other sectors characterized by highly skilled, professional work (e.g., health).

Monder Ram and colleagues (2022) describe a two-year action research project targeted at improving working practices in small ethnic minority businesses in catering and creative sectors, which entailed the businesses working alongside a university-based research team, formally constituted business and professional groups (e.g., Chartered Institute of Personnel and Development, the United Kingdom's professional institute for human resources professionals) and "local trusted intermediaries." These local trusted intermediaries were respectively a network of groups connected to ethnic minority businesses and a music business with a social mission to promote artists from diverse backgrounds. The research consisted of a series of meetings, interviews, and focus groups that explored more productive ways of organizing work. The research indicated the importance of multi-stakeholder approaches to local initiatives to improve work and a critical role of the local trusted intermediaries in connecting employers with employment experts (professionals and university-based researchers). The local trusted intermediaries had legitimacy with the ethnic minority businesses in their respective sectors that provided a platform through which more productive ways of organizing work could be implemented. Moreover, through enhancing collaboration, the intermediaries were able to provide a conduit to access other resources held by the other actors for mutual benefit. In the case of this particular study, this was evidenced through engaging students from the university to design a training package on product branding through social media use.

To conclude this section, there may be potential to effect job redesign across multiple organizations in a single initiative. Such an initiative needs to supply guidance on how to implement job redesign, as well as guidance on what constitutes a "good" outcome. Moreover, generic guidance offered through national or supra-national agencies may need to be augmented by more specific guidance for specific sectors or specific localities. More specific guidance may need to be co-developed with employers and employees themselves alongside other trusted stakeholders, so that guidance is both intelligible and legitimate for employers and employees. The three examples provided at the end of this section all involved university-based research teams engaging with multiple employers in specific locations to effect change in the design of jobs.

Future Directions: Implications for Policy, Practice, Research, and Methods

In taking a longer-term perspective on job redesign compared to prior job redesign research, we have made a number of observations on how management practice and policy guidance might be improved to support the implementation and sustainability of job redesign interventions. These observations are summarized in Table 13.1 and Table 13.2. In themselves, these observations could inform the development of research questions for future studies that, in turn, could refine the implications for policy and practice. These observations could also be incorporated into pedagogical interventions aimed at enhancing professionals' competences in top-down job redesign, thus adding to existing research on how professionals influence others' job design (Parker et al., 2019).

The specific observations made in Table 13.1 and Table 13.2 highlight wider areas within which to develop lines of research where there are significant gaps in understanding. First, there is an opportunity to develop novel research questions from taking a longer-term perspective on job redesign. Questions

IMPLEMENTING AND SUSTAINING WORK REDESIGN 349

Table 13.1 Good Practice for Implementing and Sustaining Job Redesign

Practice Area	Function	Good Practice
General		Favorable contexts (e.g., resourcing, middle management support) are helpful for implementation but adverse contexts for implementation can be overcome.
Critical success factors for implementing job redesign		Continuity in efforts at implementing, adapting, or otherwise sustaining the change.
		Effective learning from implementation to enable adaptation of the change. Effective and inclusive governance of the change process.
Management of the delivery context for job redesign	Co-ordinating functions: Strategy and planning, assessments, resourcing, communications, oversight and coordination	Sustaining job redesign requires governance of a program of activities. Governance fulfils a number of coordinating functions, including strategy development and planning, baseline assessments, securing resources, communications and information provision, standardizing activities or tailoring to specific circumstances as required, and monitoring progress.
	Political and symbolic functions: Signal intent and importance	Governance has political and symbolic functions relating to consistent of the intent of job redesign and importance of the overall program.
		Authentic organizational action to obtain mutual gains for employees and organizations through job redesign requires evolution to job design as employee concerns change.
		Authentic organizational action to obtain mutual gains requires processes for organizations to notice shifts in employee concerns, so that organizations can respond to those shifts.

continued

350 TRANSFORMATIVE WORK DESIGN

Table 13.1 *continued*

Practice Area	Function	Good Practice
Alignment between delivery context and wider organizational context for job redesign	Reduction of conflict between job redesign and other elements of organization	Consider how planned job redesign fits with other aspects of the organization, and how far does planned job redesign reflect the prevailing organizational culture and other aspects of the organization. Consider three differing approaches to address reduction of conflict: - Adapt the job redesign intervention to other elements of the organization (grafting). - Adapt other elements of the organization to the job re-design (fracturing). - Create a common purpose for the job redesign intervention and these other elements of the organization (Gestalting).

may pertain to how jobs evolve in ways that are congruent (i.e., authentic) with espoused organizational values, or how job redesign may unintentionally undermine organizational values over the longer term. The organizational politics of and cultural elements of job redesign also merit more detailed examination (cf., Erez, 2010). For example, questions may relate to how conflict caused by job redesign is reconciled or how job redesign may act as a catalyst for changes in organizational culture. As well as continuing to examine links between job redesign and other aspects of organizations, we consider there is much to be gained from how job redesign and other initiatives focused on the same goal (e.g., environmental sustainability) are linked together and with the wider organization environment. Questions may relate to how job redesign is introduced simultaneously with other initiatives in a coherent program of changes, how job redesign fits into sequences of changes (including other forms of job redesign) or how job redesign inhibits planned future changes or encourages unplanned changes (cf., Fuller et al., 2019). One major area where there are few extant studies relates to the effects and implementation of coordinated job redesign activities across multiple organizations (either in the same industrial sector or place). Appropriate counterfactuals for such studies would include organizations that do not introduce top-down job redesign and organizations that introduce top-down job redesign outside of a sector- or place-based initiative.

Table 13.2 Good Practice for Policy Makers of Job Redesign

Policy Area		Good Practice
Policy, standards, and guidance	Address the "how" of implementation	Guidance should address how to implement and sustain job redesign as well as what changes to make.
	Standards that accommodate sectoral and locality differences	National level guidance would benefit from supplementary sector or locality specific guidance.
	Consultation	Guidance should be co-developed with workers and managers, so that guidance uses workers' and managers' terms, phrases, and vocabularies for job design.
		Guidance should be co-developed with trusted intermediary organizations that link expert groups (e.g., researchers, professional institutes) with end users (workers, managers).

For future directions for research methods, we maintain that research on discrete job redesign efforts would continue to benefit from appropriately powered, longitudinal controlled designs (e.g., randomized control trial, nonequivalent control group design) alongside analysis of factors that may influence implementation (Knight & Parker, 2021; Nielsen & Miraglia, 2017) and longer-term follow-ups. Such designs can be applied to discrete interventions within organizations, as is normally the case in the literature (cf., Knight & Parker, 2021) or interventions targeted at multiple organizations (Linna et al., 2011).

Daniels and colleagues (2022) have recommended researchers using controlled designs make efforts to capture data on (1) how the intervention was adapted during implementation, (2) how learning was captured during implementation that enabled adaptation, (3) how the intervention was sustained over time, (4) how the intervention was coordinated with other initiatives targeted at the same end goal (e.g., how were job redesign and training coordinated in an environmental sustainability program), (5) whether conflict was resolved or mitigated between implementing the intervention and other elements of organization by adapting the intervention to fit what already exists in the organization, (6) whether conflict was resolved or mitigated between the intervention and other elements of organization by adapting other organizational elements to fit the intervention, (7) whether conflict was resolved or mitigated between the intervention and other elements of organization by creating a common purpose for the job redesign intervention and these other elements, and (8) whether the effects of job redesign (beneficial, adverse, or null) can be attributed to the intervention working as hypothesized, the intervention working in ways that were not anticipated or no meaningful change in the design of jobs. Where researchers are themselves involved in the implementation and evaluation of an intervention, then because of the need to assess adaptation, the evaluation necessarily becomes action research (cf., Ram et al., 2022).

Examining how job redesign evolves in organizations or even across organizations over the longer term may require different methods and different disciplinary expertise. One approach may be to borrow methods from the areas of strategic change and organizational culture change, which use predominantly qualitative and historical/documentary methods (see Patey et al., 2021). However, such research is not able to quantify effects sizes, which is desirable to determine the relative cost-effectiveness of different forms of job redesign as well as job redesign interventions relative to other forms of human resources interventions (e.g., changes to recruitment). Therefore, there may be value in considering using large ("big") data bases and/or simulation studies to forecast the effects of discrete job redesign changes and how job redesign evolves over longer periods of time.

Conclusions

This chapter has examined alternative approaches to classic intervention studies for understanding the impacts of job redesign. We do not advocate for abandoning controlled trials in the study of job redesign. Rather we advocate augmenting existing approaches with alternatives. One alternative, to take a longer term and evolving perspective on job design, entails researchers considering in more detail how job redesign connects with other elements of the organization and, over time, future changes in the design of jobs. Another alternative, examining how job redesign can be effected in multiple organizations simultaneously, entails examining how multiple stakeholders interact, communicate, and co-produce job redesign interventions. In both cases, the alternatives may entail adopting new methodologies and asking new research questions about how job redesign interventions come to be implemented and sustained.

Acknowledgement

This work has been supported by research awards from the Economic and Social Research Council (grant numbers ES/S012648/1 and ES/T001771/1), Norwich City Council/Norwich Good Economy Commission and the Higher Education Innovation Fund.

References

Bambra, C., Egan, M., Thomas, S., Petticrew, M., & Whitehead, M. (2007). The psychosocial and health effects of workplace reorganization. 2: A systematic review of task restructuring interventions. *Journal of Epidemiology and Community Health 61*, 1028–1037.

Bélanger, J., & Edwards, P. (2007). The conditions promoting compromise in the workplace. *British Journal of Industrial Relations 45*, 713–734.

Bhui, K. S., Dinos, S., Stansfeld, S. A., & White, P. D. (2012). A synthesis of the evidence for managing stress at work: A review of the reviews reporting on anxiety, depression, and absenteeism. *Journal of Environmental and Public Health 2012*, 515874.

Biron, C., & Karanika-Murray, M. (Eds.). (2015). *Derailed organizational interventions for stress and wellbeing: Confessions of failure and solutions for success*. Springer.

Blau, P. M. (1964). *Exchange and power in social life*. Wiley.

Bowen, D. E., & Ostroff, C. (2004). Understanding HRM–firm performance linkages: The role of the "strength" of the HRM system. *Academy of Management Review 29*, 203–221.

Boxall, P. (2013). Mutuality in the management of human resources: Assessing the quality of alignment in employment relationships. *Human Resource Management Journal 21*, 3–17.

Cherns, A. (1987). Principles of sociotechnical design revisited. *Human Relations 40*, 153–161.

Christina, S., Dainty, A., Daniels, K., Tregaskis, O., Waterson, P. (2017). Shut the fridge door! HRM alignment, job redesign and energy performance. *Human Resource Management Journal 27*, 382–402.

Cook, T. D., Campbell, D. T., & Peracchio, L. (1990). Quasi experimentation. In M. D. Dunnette & L. M. Hough (Eds.), *Handbook of industrial and organizational psychology* (2nd ed., Vol. 1, pp 491-576). Consulting Psychologists Press.

Cook, H., MacKenzie, R., & Forde, C. (2016). HRM and performance: The vulnerability of soft HRM practices during recession and retrenchment. *Human Resource Management Journal 26*, 557–571.

Cording, M., Harrison, J. S., Hoskisson, R. E., & Jonsen, K. (2014). Walking the talk: A multistakeholder exploration of organizational authenticity, employee productivity, and post-merger performance. *Academy of Management Perspectives 28*, 38–56.

Daniels, K. (2023). *Work, jobs and common mental health problems—what guidance should employers receive. Evidence paper*. ReWAGE—Renewing Work Advisory Group of Experts.

Daniels, K., Gedikli, C., Watson, D., Semkina, A., & Vaughn, O. (2017). Job design, employment practices and well-being: A systematic review of intervention studies. *Ergonomics 60*, 1177–1196.

Daniels, K., Watson, D., Nayani, R., & Tregaskis, O. (2022). *Achieving sustainable workplace wellbeing.* Springer Nature.

Daniels, K., Watson, D., Nayani, R., Tregaskis, O., Hogg, M., Etuknwa, A., & Semkina, A. (2021). Implementing practices focused on workplace health and psychological wellbeing: A systematic review. *Social Science and Medicine 227*, 113888.

Deal, T. E., & Kennedy, A. A. (1982). *Corporate cultures: The rites and rituals of corporate life.* Addison-Wesley.

Dickinson, P. (2022). *Review of employment charters in the English mayoral combined authorities.* Evidence paper. ReWAGE—Renewing Work Advisory Group of Experts.

Dobbins, T., & Dundon, T. (2017). The chimera of sustainable labour–management partnership. *British Journal of Management 28*, 519–533.

Egan, M., Bambra, C., Petticrew, M., & Whitehead, M. (2009). Reviewing evidence on complex social interventions: Appraising implementation in systematic reviews of the health effects of organisational-level workplace interventions. *Journal of Epidemiology & Community Health 63*, 4–11.

Erez, M. (2010). Culture and job design. *Journal of Organizational Behavior 31*, 389–400.

Fitzhugh, H., Woodard, R., & James, A. (2023). *Recognising tensions, barriers and strategies for widening acceptance to public sociology engagement with businesses in the Good Jobs Project.* British Sociological Society Conference.

Fox, K. E., Johnson, S. T., Berkman, L. F., Sianoja, M., Soh, Y., Kubzansky, L. D., & Kelly, E. L. (2022). Organisational-and group-level workplace interventions and their effect on multiple domains of worker well-being: A systematic review. *Work & Stress 36*, 30–59.

Fridrich, A., Jenny, G. J., & Bauer, G. F. (2015). The context, process, and outcome evaluation model for organisational health interventions. *BioMed Research International 2015*, 414832.

Fuller, P., Randall, R., Dainty, A., Haslam, R., & Gibb A. (2019). Applying a longitudinal tracer methodology to evaluate complex interventions in complex settings. *European Journal of Work and Organizational Psychology 28*, 443–452.

Glover, L., Tregaskis, O., & Butler, P. (2014). Mutual gains? The workers' verdict: a longitudinal study. *International Journal of Human Resource Management 25*, 895–914.

Grant, A. M., & Parker, S. K. (2009). 7 redesigning work design theories: The rise of relational and proactive perspectives. *Academy of Management Annals 3*, 317–375.

Guest, D. E. (1997). Human resource management and performance: A review and research agenda. *International Journal of Human Resource Management 8*, 263–276.

Guest, D. E. (2017). Human resource management and employee well-being: Towards a new analytic framework. *Human Resource Management Journal 27*, 22–38.

Hackman, J. R., & Oldham, G. R. (1980). *Work redesign.* Addison-Wesley.

Hardy, C. (1996). Understanding power: Bringing about strategic change. *British Journal of Management 7*, S3–S16.

Herrera-Sánchez, I. M., León-Pérez, J. M., & León-Rubio, J. M. (2017). Steps to ensure a successful implementation of occupational health and safety interventions at an organizational level. *Frontiers in Psychology 8*, 2135.

Hofman, J., Garrod, B., Stewart, K., Stepanek, M., & Van Belle, J. (2018). *Workplace wellbeing charter: Analysis of take-up and impact.* Rand Europe

Hoque, K. (2003). All in all, it's just another plaque on the wall: The incidence and impact of the Investors in People standard. *Journal of Management Studies 40*, 543–571.

HSE (Health & Safety Executive). (n.d.). https://www.hse.gov.uk/stress/standards/

Irvine, G., White, D., & Diffley, M. (2018). *Measuring good work: The final report of the Job Quality Working Group.* Carnegie UK/Royal Society of Arts and Manufactures.

ISO (International Organization for Standardization). (2018). *Occupational health and safety management systems: General guidelines for the application of ISO 45001. Guidance on managing occupational health.* International Organization for Standardization.

Johns, G. (2006). The essential impact of context on organizational behavior. *Academy of Management Review 31*, 386–408.

Johnson, G. (1987). *Strategic change and the management process.* Blackwell.

Johnson, G. (1988). Rethinking incrementalism. *Strategic Management Journal 9*, 75–91.

Johnson, G. (1990). Managing strategic change: The role of symbolic action. *British Journal of Management 1*, 183–200.

Kerr, S. (1975). On the folly of rewarding A, while hoping for B. *Academy of Management Journal 18*, 769–783.

Kimura, T. (2015). A review of political skill: Current research trend and directions for future research. *International Journal of Management Reviews 17*, 312–332.

Kivimäki, M., Nyberg, S. T., Batty, G. D., Fransson, E. I., Heikkilä, K., Alfredsson, L., Bjorner, J. B., Borritz, M., Burr, H., Casini, A., Clays, E., De Bacquer, D., Dragano, N., Ferrie, J. E., Geuskens, G. A., Goldberg, M., Hamer, M., Hooftman, W. E., Houtman, I. L., Joensuu, M., . . . IPD-Work Consortium. (2012). Job strain as a risk factor for coronary heart disease: A collaborative meta-analysis of individual participant data. *Lancet 380*, 1491–1497.

Knight, C., & Parker, S. K. (2021). How work redesign interventions affect performance: An evidence-based model from a systematic review. *Human Relations 74*, 69–104.

Kochan, T., & Osterman, P. (1994). *The mutual gains enterprise: Forging a winning partnership among labor, management and government.* Harvard Business School Press.

Linna, A., Väänänen, A., Elovainio, M., Kivimäki, M., Pentti, J., & Vahtera, J. (2011). Effect of participative intervention on organisational justice perceptions: A quasi-experimental study on Finnish public sector employees. *International Journal of Human Resource Management 22*, 706–721.

MacKay, C. J., Cousins, R., Kelly, P. J., Lee, S., & McCaig, R. H. (2004). "Management Standards" and work-related stress in the UK: Policy background and science. *Work & Stress 18*, 91–112.

Milner, A., Witt, K., LaMontagne, A. D., & Niedhammer, I. (2018). Psychosocial job stressors and suicidality: A meta-analysis and systematic review. *Occupational and Environmental Medicine 75*, 245–253.

Mintzberg, H. (1987). The strategy concept 1: 5 Ps for strategy. *California Management Review 30*, 11–24.

Mishiba, T. (2020). *Workplace mental health law: Comparative perspectives.* Routledge.

Montano, D., Hoven, H., & Siegrist, J. (2014). Effects of organisational-level interventions at work on employees' health: A systematic review. *BMC Public Health 14*, 1–9.

Morgeson, F. P., & Humphrey, S. E. (2008). Job and team design: Toward a more integrative conceptualization of work design. *Research in Personnel and Human Resources Management 27*, 39–91.

Nayani, R., Baric, M., Patey, J., Fitzhugh, H., Watson, D., Tregaskis, O., & Daniels, K. (2022). Authenticity in the pursuit of mutuality during crisis. *British Journal of Management 33*, 1144–1162.

Newman, I. (2021). *Mechanisms for rapid organisational cultural change to support lean implementation.* [Doctoral dissertation, University of East Anglia].

NICE (National Institute for Health and Care Excellence). (n.d.). Mental wellbeing at work. https://www.nice.org.uk/guidance/ng212

Nielsen, K., & Miraglia, M. (2017). What works for whom in which circumstances? On the need to move beyond the "what works?" question in organizational intervention research. *Human Relations 70*, 40–62.

Nielsen, K., & Randall, R. (2013). Opening the black box: Presenting a model for evaluating organizational-level interventions. *European Journal of Work and Organizational Psychology 22*, 601–617.

Nielsen, K., Axtell, C., & Taylor, S. (2021). National approaches to wellbeing interventions: The UK Management Standards as an example. In T. Wall, C. L. Cooper, & P. Brough (Eds.), *The SAGE handbook of organizational wellbeing* (pp. 368-382). SAGE.

Ogbonnaya, C., Daniels, K., Connolly, S., & van Veldhoven, M. (2017). Integrated and isolated impact of high performance work practices on employee health and wellbeing: A comparative study. *Journal of Occupational Health Psychology 22*, 98–114.

Parker, S. K., Andrei, D. M., & Van den Broeck, A. (2019). Poor work design begets poor work design: Capacity and willingness antecedents of individual work design behavior. *Journal of Applied Psychology 104*, 907–928.

Parker, S. K., & Jorritsma, K. (2020). Good work design for all: Multiple pathways to making a difference. *European Journal of Work and Organizational Psychology 30*, 456–468.

Parker, S. K., & Ohly, S. (2008). Designing motivating work. In R. Kanfer, G. Chen, & R. Pritchard (Eds.), *Work motivation: Past, present and future* (pp. 234-286). Routledge.

Parker, S. K., Van den Broeck, A., & Holman, D. (2017). Work design influences: A synthesis of multilevel factors that affect the design of jobs. *Academy of Management Annals 11*, 267–308.

Patey, J., Nasamu, E., Nayani, R., Watson, D., Connolly, S., & Daniels, K. (2021). Evaluating multicomponent wellbeing strategies: Theoretical and methodological insights. In T. Wall, C. L. Cooper, & P. Brough, (Eds.), *The SAGE handbook of organizational wellbeing* (pp. 478-493). SAGE.

Peterson, R. A. (2005). In search of authenticity. *Journal of Management Studies 42*, 1083–1098.

Ram, M., McCarthy, I., Green, A., & Scully, J. (2022). Towards a more inclusive human resource community: Engaging ethnic minority microbusinesses in human resource development programmes targeted at more productive methods of operating. *Human Resource Management Journal 32*, 540–554.

Reger, R. K., Mullane, J. V., Gustafson, L. T., & DeMarie, S. M. (1994). Creating earthquakes to change organizational mindsets. *Academy of Management Perspectives 8*, 31–43.

Richardson K. M., & Rothstein H. R. (2008). Effects of occupational stress management intervention programs: A meta-analysis. *Journal of Occupational Health Psychology 13*, 69–93.

Rick, J., & Briner, R. B. (2000). Psychosocial risk assessment: Problems and prospects. *Occupational Medicine 50*, 310–314.

Roodbari, H., Axtell, C., Nielsen, K., & Sorensen, G. (2022). Organisational interventions to improve employees' health and wellbeing: A realist synthesis. *Applied Psychology 71*, 1058–1081.

Rugulies, R., Aust, B., & Madsen, I. E. (2020). Occupational determinants of affective disorders. In U. Bültmann & J. Siegrist (Eds.), *Handbook of disability, work and health* (pp. 207–304). Springer.

Schein, E. H. (2016). *Organizational culture and leadership*. Wiley.

Stansfeld, S., & Candy, B. (2006). Psychosocial work environment and mental health—A meta-analytic review. *Scandinavian Journal of Work, Environment & Health 32*, 443–462.

Taris, T. W., van der Wal, I., & Kompier, M. A. J. (2010). Large-scale job stress interventions. In J. Houdmont & S. Leka (Eds.), *Contemporary occupational health psychology: Global perspectives on research and practice*, Vol. 1 (pp. 77-97). Wiley-Blackwell.

Then, F. S., Luck, T., Luppa, M., Thinschmidt, M., Deckert, S., Nieuwenhuijsen, K., Seidler, A., & Riedel-Heller, S. G. (2014). Systematic review of the effect of the psychosocial working environment on cognition and dementia. *Occupational and Environmental Medicine 71*, 358–365.

Tregaskis, O., Daniels, K., Glover, L., Butler, P., & Meyer, M. (2013). High performance work practices and firm performance: A longitudinal case study. *British Journal of Management 24*, 225–244.

Tyers, C., Broughton, A., Denvir, A., Wilson, S., & O'Regan, S. (2009). *Organisational responses to the HSE Management Standards for Work-Related Stress. Progress of the sector implementation plan—Phase 1. Research report 693*. HSE Books.

Van der Klink, J. J., Blonk, R. W., Schene, A. H., & Van Dijk, F. J. (2001). The benefits of interventions for work-related stress. *American Journal of Public Health 91*, 270.

Wall, T. D., Cordery, J. L., & Clegg, C. W. (2002). Empowerment, performance, and operational uncertainty: A theoretical integration. *Applied Psychology 51*, 146–169.

Unleashing Magic

A PARRTH to Participatory Work Redesign

Sharon K. Parker

Faced with disengaged call center agents, and at the request of managers and unions, researchers in the United Kingdom conducted a work redesign intervention to improve the quality of work (Holman & Axtell, 2016). In a two-day workshop, call center agents brainstormed ideas and solutions to problems with their current work design, and were then involved in implementing the agreed changes. A rigorous evaluation showed that autonomy and feedback both increased after the work redesign, as did supervisor-rated job performance, employee well-being, and psychological contract fulfilment. One of the critical success factors identified for this intervention was that employees were able to significantly contribute their ideas throughout the redesign process; that is, worker participation in the change process.

In contrast, consider a Finnish intervention intended to improve work and well-being amongst service and health workers (Dahl-Jørgensen & Saksvik, 2005). Despite considerable investment from the researchers, and willingness from at least some of the leaders, the end-result of the process was limited work design and outcome change in one group, and no evidence of change in a second group. Why? According to the research team, a key factor was the lack of participation of workers in the change process. The content of changes in the most unsuccessful group was set by senior managers, with little input from employees, local managers, or others. Even when input was sought, not all workers were given time by their managers to participate in the intervention; a situation compounded by the client-facing work of many participants. Further, some employees opted not to engage in the process even though they had the chance to do so because they believed no real change was likely.

These two contrasting examples highlight the importance of the process of work redesign change, or *how* change is designed and implemented. This is an important issue because many organizational interventions designed to improve work quality fail to succeed (see, e.g., Lamontagne et al., 2007; Nielsen et al., 2010). Implementation can fail due to a lack of commitment from senior managers or other stakeholders, a lack of commitment from workers, time

---

Sharon K. Parker, *Unleashing Magic*. In: *Transformative Work Design*. Edited by: Sharon K. Parker et al., Oxford University Press. © Society for Industrial and Organizational Psychology (2025).
DOI: 10.1093/oso/9780197692554.003.0014

360 TRANSFORMATIVE WORK DESIGN

constraints and other resource deficiencies, and/or co-occurring changes or external events beyond the project. Sometimes a change is not sustained over time or does not spread beyond a pilot, perhaps due to the failure to align wider organizational systems and practices or perhaps due to insufficient investment into continued employee participation. Sometimes one is unsure of the impact of work redesign because it has not been properly evaluated.

These challenges can be minimized with careful attention to the process of change, and especially the effective participation of key stakeholders. In what follows, I unpack the PARRTH process, which I created to help prevent implementation failures of work redesign. But before I do so, I delve into why participation can be so crucial.

The Power of Participation in Work Redesign

Participation involves having workers whose roles are being redesigned, as well as other relevant others, actively involved in the "what" of the intervention (its design) and/or the "how" (its implementation) (Nielsen et al., 2010). Research on organizational interventions shows that work redesigns tend to be more likely to be successful if a participatory approach is adopted (Daniels et al., 2017; Nielsen & Randall, 2012b).

In Figure 14.1, I propose that, when effectively managed, participation of relevant stakeholders in the design and implementation of change creates *better quality solutions that "fit" the context, increased ownership of change, enhanced capacity for future change, strengthened social cohesion, and compliance with legislation*—all of which can contribute to successful work redesign. I further propose these effects can occur directly as well as indirectly through improving work quality, such as how SMART it is (Parker & Knight, 2023). As Figure 14.1 indicates, I also suggest that achieving the positive outcomes of effective participation can cycle back to foster yet more participation. I unpack the key elements of the model further.

Direct processes. First, workers are the experts in their own jobs, and so their engagement can generate *better quality solutions that are more likely to fit the context*. Including other stakeholders, such as managers and relevant others (e.g., health and safety representatives), means that the views of these stakeholders are also included, further ensuring the redesign will be a fit to the specific context from diverse perspectives. In a successful work redesign in which physical demands were reduced to help make the work of aging workers more tolerable (Loch et al., 2010), the importance of involving production workers in the change process was highlighted: "*Managers can articulate the problem and choose amongst solutions, but they are not necessarily a good source*

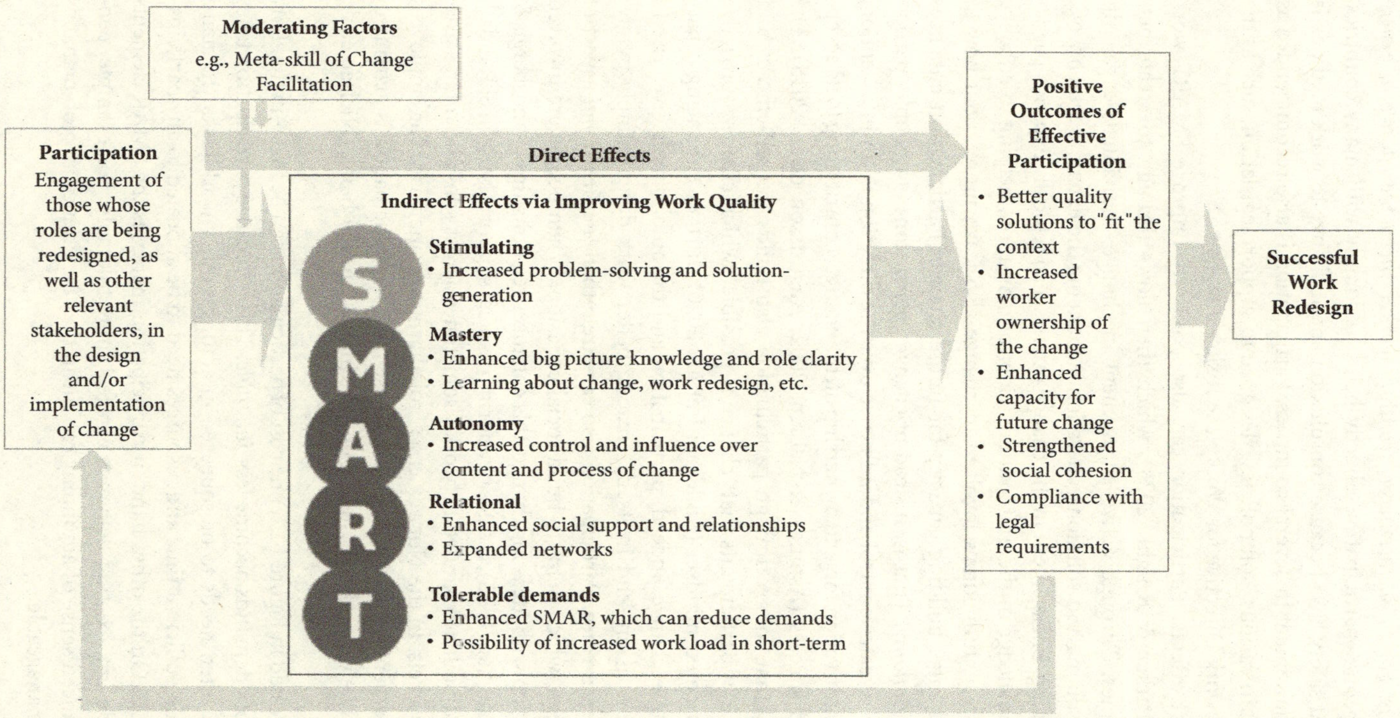

Figure 14.1 How Participation in Work Redesign Can Promote Positive Outcomes Directly and Indirectly through Increasing the Extent to which Work is SMART

362 TRANSFORMATIVE WORK DESIGN

of solutions. For those to emerge, frontline workers need the chance to exper-iment." Second, participation directly helps to comply with many countries' health and safety laws because consultation about change to work methods is a legal requirement in several countries. Participation is also recommended as important in various "soft policies" designed to support legislation, such as the EU Framework Directive for Workplace Risk Management.

Indirect effects. Participation can also positively improve SMART work aspects (Parker & Knight, 2023), which then flows through to create bet-ter outcomes. Through active engagement in change, individuals engage in problem-solving and solution-generation, enhancing the extent to which work is *Stimulating*. Engagement in the change process also typically expands partic-ipants' knowledge of the unit and the wider organization, helping to enhance their *Mastery*. Individuals involved in change also learn more about how to achieve change, building capacity for future change. Participation enhances worker *Autonomy*. That is, instead of change "being done" to people, partici-pants have greater control and influence over the direction of an intervention, fostering motivation for, and ownership of, the change, contributing to its accep-tance and success (Ashmos & Nathan, 2002; Augustsson et al., 2015). The autonomy that comes through participation also builds the self-efficacy and confidence of participants that "change is possible," which creates a proactive change-oriented mindset (Abildgaard et al., 2020), further enhancing capac-ity for future change. Indeed, participation and the autonomy it gives rise to can be seen as an "end in itself," creating better work design simply by giv-ing workers a voice. Participation also can strengthen the *Relational* aspect of work design, which helps to build social cohesion. When people are involved in coming up with ideas for change, this enhances relationships (Landsbergis & Vivona-Vaughan, 1995), creates new forms of social support (Nielsen & Randall, 2012), and builds expanded networks, sometimes across silos and often across roles and levels. In the Norway case, "role harmony" increased for employees in the intervention. The more that a sense of team participation is generated, the more likely that there will be a positive impact on well-being (Nielsen et al., 2012).

As indicated in Figure 14.1, one cost of participation can be that—in the short term—work demands become less *Tolerable*. This is because participation takes time, and often needs to be squeezed in amongst other work tasks. To guard against this, sufficient time and resources need to be allocated to any participa-tive process. On the other hand, if participation increases the SMAR elements of work design, existing demands can feel more tolerable. For example, peo-ple's enhanced sense of autonomy can mean they experience any job demands as more manageable.

As depicted by the positive feedback loop from "outcomes" to participation, a virtuous spiral can be created in which participation engenders yet more participation. In one company that introduced team work (Nielsen & Randall, 2012), those employees with higher job autonomy were more likely to participate at the outset in the redesign process. Then, having been involved in the process, they were more likely to experience greater autonomy (as well as greater social support and well-being) after the implementation of teamwork. Thus, autonomy led to yet more autonomy via participation in a positive dynamic. As another example, a successful participatory work redesign in a very challenging health care environment in Norway led to some important reductions in job stress, more Tolerable work demands, and a more positive learning climate (Mikkelsen et al., 2000). In comparison, things got worse in the same period for employees in a control group. Participation meant that employees worked on problems they felt were important, and when they saw managers were taking their concerns seriously, they became more courageous about putting forward ideas, showing the emergence of a positive cycle in which participation generated further participation.

Moderating factors. Running a participatory process, however, can be challenging and "new territory" for many organizations. As elaborated in the next section, if the process is not effectively managed and facilitated, then participation can fail to achieve the outlined benefits.

The PARRRTH Model: An Overview

To help manage an effective work redesign process, I propose the PARRRTH model of redesign that draws together ideas from participatory organizational interventions (e.g., Abilgaard et al., 2020; Nielsen this volume), action research (Murphy & Hurrell, 1987), design thinking (e.g., Razzouk & Shute, 2012), and appreciative inquiry (e.g., Bushe, 2012). PARRTH is usually a "top down" change process, endorsed and driven by individuals in positions of authority such as the Human Resources (HR) Director, the Health & Safety team, or senior managers. It involves five phases: Prepare, Assess, Reflect, Redesign, Track, and Habituate, each with several steps (see Figure 14.2). PARRTH is not always a simple linear path; sometimes, it is necessary to cycle back and forth between phases. PARRTH is characterized not only by participation, but also a data-based approach to change, which allows the intervention to be fully contextualized to the situation rather than an off-the-shelf approach.

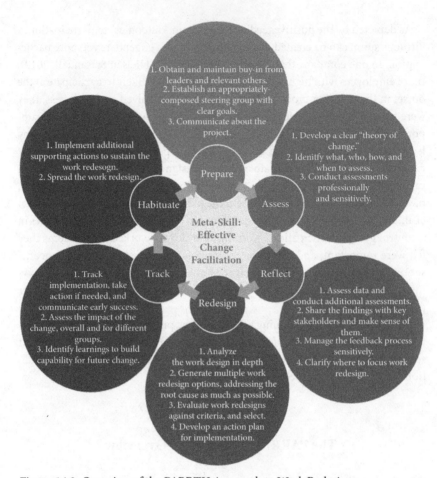

Figure 14.2 Overview of the PARRTH Approach to Work Redesign

In what follows, I describe each of the five phases. I then propose the critical meta-skill of effective change facilitation needed to execute the PARRTH process.

Prepare

The purpose of the Prepare phase is to lay a successful foundation for the work redesign in which there is a shared commitment to the project from relevant stakeholders and especially senior leaders, an appropriate steering group, and a clear communication strategy. Although the specific steps of the Prepare phase can shift according to the situation, common steps include the following:

1. Obtain and maintain buy-in from leaders and relevant others. Support from high-level management is one of the most critical factors influencing the success of organizational change (Oreg & Berson, 2019). Achieving senior-level support might require building a business case, such as by aligning the initiative to the company strategy and/or to problems facing the organization. Importantly, achieving buy-in means going beyond rhetorical statements, and securing resources for the project (e.g., training funds, allocation of time for participation). One challenge is that managers often expect instant results. As I say to those hoping to redesign work in a one-hour workshop, "if it were that easy, you would have already done it."

This step also includes helping leaders to understand the importance of a participatory approach, which can be quite uncomfortable for those who are used to a more directive style. It may be necessary to help reduce the sense of risk for senior management by establishing guard rails for the change. These include, for example, clarifying up front any "no go" changes, setting up a process for the steering group to regularly check in with senior management, and an agreement to carry out the change in a pilot area to begin. Another guard rail is the assurance of a full evaluation of the pilot before any larger scale change.

It is important to identify any constraints on the intervention from senior leaders, as well as a commitment from leaders to support the implementation of reasonable suggestions for change. In one of my early work redesign efforts, after going through a participatory process in which groups developed plans for improving their work, the manager did not allow the intervention because he did not agree with the planned actions. Such "surprises" late in the process are a recipe for cynicism and learned helplessness.

Commitment from other stakeholders, such as unions and/or work councils and middle-level managers (who are often the ones who implement change), are also needed for project success. One way to secure this commitment is to involve representatives from key stakeholder groups in a project steering group.

2. Establish an appropriately composed steering group with clear goals. A steering group is a team that oversees the project. Sometimes the team will oversee the activities of local redesign teams (formed later in the process); however, in small units, the steering group can also be the team who redesigns the work. A steering group spreads the ownership of the redesign process beyond a single champion who might leave the organization and/or lose interest. A diverse composition of the group also ensures that the major voices are included in the decision-making.

As to composition, it is ideal to include representatives of all key stakeholder groups as members. For instance, assuming that frontline work is being redesigned, the steering group might include a facilitator (an internal or external change agent), representatives from relevant functions (e.g., health and safety, human resources, or production), representatives of those whose work is being redesigned (e.g., there might be one line manager from the teams, some front-line members, and a representative of other interdependent roles), a middle- or senior-level manager, and, in the case of unionized groups, a union member. Representing managers in the process is important because their support is needed to drive implementation; yet, at the same time, work redesign often changes managers' roles and generates uncertainty. Managers thus need to be on the journey.

Once the group is set up, ascertain the goals of the project and the criteria for success. For example, is the overarching goal to create work designs that are healthier for workers whilst simultaneously maintaining productivity? Or something else? It is important to build a shared mental model, or collective understanding, of the purpose of the intervention amongst steering group members (Nielsen & Abildgaard, 2013). Usually, if they haven't already, steering group members benefit from some training about work design and organizational change.

An example of a successful project team occurred in a successful participatory redesign within a Danish psychiatric hospital (Pryce et al., 2006). Part of the change focused on improving the shift structure to improve worker well-being, and it involved eight voluntary teams of nurses and healthcare workers, with four teams randomly selected to be intervention groups and four teams included as control groups. A project group was set up to oversee the design and implementation of a new shift structure, including two consultants and five to seven others (frontline staff, health/safety representatives). Each of the four teams involved in the intervention also had its own steering committee. Each steering committee, after training about work schedule interventions, had the goal to develop, implement, and monitor a scheduling intervention appropriate for their team, with support from the overall project team.

3. Communicate about the project. Communication is vital for any change. When people know what is happening, and why, this helps to generate commitment to the change and alleviate anxiety and uncertainty. Aspects that the steering group will need to communicate to others in the organizations include the goals of the project and why it matters, senior managements' commitment, "What's in it for me" for key stakeholders, who is on the steering group, how people can contribute ideas to the group or raise questions, the steps of the project (e.g., surveys, interviews, workshops), and updates on progress. Different methods can be used to communicate, ranging from a video message from the senior leader to online channels to articles in the company newsletter. The existing methods of communication in the organization should be used as much as possible.

Assess

The purpose of the Assess phase is threefold: to diagnose the existing situation, identifying what the work design and associated issues are, for whom;[1] to collect the baseline information against which the impact of the initiative can later be assessed (see Track); and to help lay a strong foundation for widespread participation because Assess involves finding out about the experiences of the workforce. Pertinent steps for Assess include the following:

1. Develop a clear model of the change, sometimes referred to as a "Theory of Change" (Weiss, 1995). A theory of change is often best achieved by starting from the desired end goal: that is, what sort of outcomes is the redesign expected to achieve? Then, tracking backward, what sort of intermediary outcomes are needed to achieve that impact? Tracking even further backward, what activities will generate those intermediary outcomes? Finally, what inputs will enable the activities to be achieved? As well as specifying the expected sequence of inputs through to impact, a theory of change identifies "assumptions" or aspects that are assumed to be in place for success. An example (simple) theory of change is shown in Figure 14.3. While things rarely work out as neatly as any theory of change implies, the process of mapping it out can help the team to develop a shared mental model about the intervention, as well as to lay the foundation for the assessment.

2. Identify what, who, how, and when to assess. "What" is assessed will be guided by the theory of change (or similar). It will almost always be important to assess work design—or the degree to which the work is Stimulating, has Mastery, has Autonomy, is Relational, and has Tolerable demands. This way, the project team can identify the key work design issues to redesign and can later evaluate whether the intervention improves the work quality as intended. It is also important to assess the outcomes of work design, which likely includes outcomes for individuals (e.g., their mental health and well-being) and outcomes for teams and organizations (e.g., performance). Usually, it is also valuable to assess key demographic factors and other individual or team factors. For example, organizations typically want to drill down to understand how work design issues vary for different job roles and work units. Assessing factors like gender, having children, age, and so on, can also help build an understanding of key influences on work design and outcomes.

The Assess phase is also an opportunity to investigate factors that affect the *process* of the change, or the political, social, and organizational aspects that might interfere with or enable a successful change process. Aspects to consider,

---

[1] In some cases, diagnosis might have already occurred and, in fact, have led to the project in the first place

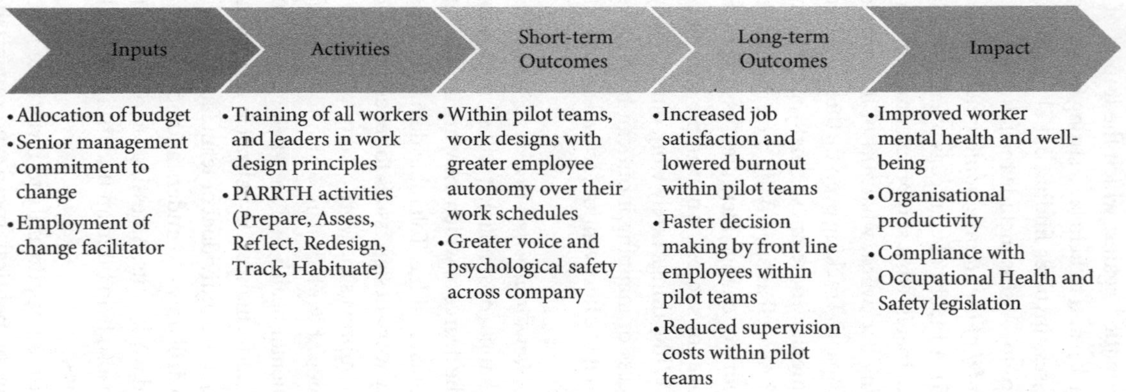

Inputs	Activities	Short-term Outcomes	Long-term Outcomes	Impact
• Allocation of budget • Senior management commitment to change • Employment of change facilitator	• Training of all workers and leaders in work design principles • PARRTH activities (Prepare, Assess, Reflect, Redesign, Track, Habituate)	• Within pilot teams, work designs with greater employee autonomy over their work schedules • Greater voice and psychological safety across company	• Increased job satisfaction and lowered burnout within pilot teams • Faster decision making by front line employees within pilot teams • Reduced supervision costs within pilot teams	• Improved worker mental health and well-being • Organisational productivity • Compliance with Occupational Health and Safety legislation

Figure 14.3 Example of a Simple Theory of Change for a Work Redesign Project.

for example, include: What change projects have been successful in the past, or unsuccessful, and why? Who are key people to get and keep on board? Information from such questions can inform later redesign decisions. For example, if the organization is very hierarchical and senior leadership support is tenuous, radical work designs like self-managing teams will likely fail to get traction.

"Who" is assessed will depend on the focus and scope of the change. It is usually important to assess beyond the target group of interest because there are interdependencies amongst work roles. For example, one might be focused on improving the work of call center agents. But call center agent work is intimately tied to the work of their team leaders, and potentially to other groups. Those whose work affects, and is affected by, call center agents should be assessed. Also, one should seek to include in the assessment a control or comparison group if possible (O'Shea et al., 2016), which is a group of similar workers whose work is *not* being redesigned. Sometimes this group of people are what is referred to as a "staggered" control group, which means their work is not changed at the same time as the intervention group, but it is changed at a later point. This can help address the issue that people often don't want to do a survey if they are not going to be part of an intervention.

As to "how" to assess, confidential surveys are a quantitative way to measure work design, outcomes like job satisfaction and mental health, and some of the key influences on work design (those that can be easily quantified, like which level a person is employed at or leader behavior). As many organizations routinely assess their workers via engagement surveys and the like, it sometimes makes sense to add additional items to existing survey processes than to implement entirely new ones. Interviews with representative individuals (preferably not just with people hand-picked by management) can be a helpful way to get deeper insights into how the work system operates, as well as people's views of very sensitive topics like harassment or mental health. Focus groups (usually with bosses in a separate focus group) can also be useful for gathering many people's ideas relatively quickly, although it is important to be aware that negative processes can emerge such as group think (a situation in which everyone conforms with each other's views), silence (individuals keeping quiet about their views for fear it will affect their careers, or other such reasons), and the challenge of dealing with dominant voices. From an appreciative inquiry perspective, it is considered useful to understand "the best of what is," such as asking service providers about the times when they have delivered outstanding service. Collation of relevant objective data, such as company records of absenteeism, performance or productivity data, customer satisfaction, exit interviews, and turnover, can complement employee perceptions and beliefs. Observation as an assessment tool is a useful but underused approach, with value in both formal observations (e.g., transcribing meetings) and informal observing

370   TRANSFORMATIVE WORK DESIGN

(noticing what feedback is shown on the walls, etc.). Analysis of strategic documents, such as reports from previous assessments, company strategy/vision documents, and the like, also help to build a picture of the organization.

Regarding "when" to assess, at a minimum, one should measure the situation before the intervention and just after the intervention such that, by comparing pre- and post- data, the effects of change are indicated. Ideally, one would also assess the situation quite some months after the intervention—even a year—to evaluate the longer-term impact of change. The latter matters because sometimes positive effects do not always emerge immediately and, on the other hand, sometimes unexpected negative effects emerge.

3. Conduct the assessments professionally and sensitively. Irrespective of what methods you use, it is important to conduct assessments in such a way as to build trust and lay the foundation for continued participation of key stakeholders. Most important is recognizing the sensitivity of some of the information you gather, especially any data that has people's names attached. Ideally, you will use independent researchers or consultants who can assure confidentiality (i.e., not sharing or disclosing any individual data to anyone in the company). Sometimes data is sensitive even if it is at the team or unit level (a leader of a unit, for example, will likely feel defensive if the teams' view of their leadership is negative). Thus, data should be collected, stored, and fed back in ways that protect people and that build trust in the change process. Otherwise, people might also not feel psychologically safe enough to be honest about their experiences and/or they may distrust the next phase of change. Another challenge is that sometimes there has been historically too much assessment and not enough action, creating workers who are cynical about engaging in assessment processes.

Reflect

The purpose of the Reflect phase is to take stock of the data collected in the Assess phase: to collectively agree what "problem is being focused on and for whom." A further purpose is to feed back the results of Assess to key stakeholders because this helps to maintain and build participation, openness, and trust in the process. Steps include:

1. Synthesize the Assess data and conduct additional assessments or analyses. The steering team at this point will likely have multiple sources of information; some of it clear and consistent; other details contradictory or ambiguous. For example, interviews might give depth, but they also can give rise to contrasting viewpoints. Survey data can help in these situations because it synthesizes yet gives equal weight to the views of many individuals. It is important to make sense of the information collected in the Assess phase through analysis, discussion, and debate.

Sometimes further explorations are needed to understand the findings at a deeper level. For example, in a case in BMW, Germany, in which production work was ultimately redesigned to be more physically Tolerable to aging workers (Loch et al., 2010), each of 100 tasks were analyzed according to whether the demands of the task "fit" with the abilities of the workers. The project team observed considerable *variation* in ability–task fit scores, leading the team to realize that some older workers were able to maintain their abilities whereas some are not. This led the team to the insight that productivity declines are not inevitable with aging, such that it might be possible to redesign work to help those older individuals who are struggling to keep up.

2. Share the findings with key stakeholders and collectively make sense of them. A well-designed feedback process involves sharing the findings with those who have provided the data (e.g., workers), as well as other relevant stakeholders (e.g., senior leaders). The feedback should be provided in such a way that there is an opportunity for discussion, allowing the project team to "sense check" their interpretation of the information and to gather ideas for where, or for whom, redesigns might focus.

Feedback discussions are also an opportunity for stakeholders to learn about the perspectives of others. For instance, through an independently gathered feedback process, managers often get an insight into the work design experiences of their staff in a way that has previously been lacking. Opportunities also often emerge for the steering team to gather reactions to their early ideas for change. The value of such a process was highlighted in the Xerox interventions (Bailyn, 2011). As part of their participatory action research, the researchers gave feedback to a "fairly controlling" division head. In contrast to senior managements' belief that a decline in requests for greater schedule flexibility signaled a decline in desire for flexibility, the research team communicated that a "self-defeating negative feedback loop" had arisen. Because supervisors traditionally either ignored or said no to flexibility requests, workers had stopped bothering making the requests, despite a strong desire for greater flexibility. Providing this feedback to senior management, and getting them to accept it, was essential to secure their commitment to a new schedule.

Feedback discussions are also an important opportunity for worker voice. By actively soliciting the views of employees, managers, and others, ownership of the change, and trust in the process, is enhanced. Another value-add of reflection sessions is that—because the feedback is usually structured in terms of insights about work design and outcomes—they are an opportunity to educate more people about work design. Feedback sessions are also a chance to remind people of the goals of the project and advise them on next steps.

372 TRANSFORMATIVE WORK DESIGN

3. Manage the feedback process sensitively. Feedback processes can be challenging. Workers can feel their views are misrepresented, or that they might get into "trouble" with their boss for sharing their views. Supervisors and managers can feel they are being blamed for their workers' poor work design. A sense of competition can emerge if comparative findings from multiple units or teams are presented. Appropriate steps need to be taken to prevent or address such challenges. For instance, it might be important to provide feedback to teams without their managers being present. Likewise, some data might be sensitive, and hence need to be handled differently. For example, perceptions of leaders might be best shared privately with each individual leader, similar to a 360-degree feedback process, rather than in a public forum. Feedback should be presented in a balanced way, without blame and judgment, recognizing that stakeholders will be less likely to "take on" ideas if they feel under attack.

4. Clarify where to focus the work redesign. The Reflect phase usually concludes by identifying where to focus the redesign efforts, such as whether to focus on a particular role (e.g., the role of team leaders) or a particular unit. Sometimes there is an agreement to focus on the most salient work design issue, such as job demands or low autonomy, for all units. Such decisions depend partly on the project goal. For example, if the change is part of a work health and safety activity, the most "at risk groups" (with the poorest mental health and well-being) might be the target. But, when the redesign is an experiment to assess whether change should be considered more broadly in the company, a key factor for selecting where to focus might be where workers and leaders are open to change.

Redesign

The purpose of the Redesign phase is to decide on and plan an appropriate work redesign. There needs to be a divergent sub-phase that involves generating ideas for redesign, followed by a convergent sub-phase in which ideas and solutions are chosen. Often there is some cycling back and forward between divergent and convergent processes. Redesign steps include:

1. Analyze the work design in depth. Although the Assess phase might have indicated a key work design challenge—let us say "low mastery in Team X"— further discussion and analysis will likely be needed to understand *why* mastery is lacking in Team X and exactly what this means. For example, why do team X members experience low role clarity? Is it a lack of clarity about what to do, which tasks or goals are most important, or how well one is doing? Does everyone in the team experience a lack of clarity?

In some cases, those whose work is being redesigned (Team X) are best placed to engage directly in these discussions, facilitated by the change agent, with the steering group maintaining an oversight role. One approach is to provide teams with the opportunity to identify causes of their work design, such as by using problem solving tools like the "why why" approach (in which one repeatedly asks 'why' to try to get to the root cause). This team-led process is effectively a form of "collective team crafting" because the group is working together to understand and change their team's work design. Typically, this approach works well when teams have had little opportunity and/or authority to improve their own work, so there is some "low hanging" fruit. It can also be an effective way to achieve some quick wins to boost teams' self-efficacy for change.

A downside, however, is that teams may take the way things have always been done for granted. They may simply be unable to see the "root" causes of poor work design yet addressing the root cause will result in more powerful and sustainable work designs. More systemic change can be fostered by conducting a deeper analysis of the work system; that is, fully understanding how the work is carried out, what the goals are, what the tasks are, who makes decisions, the flow of activities, how information is shared, and where interdependencies lie. Job analysis tools—typically used when creating or revising job descriptions—can be useful in such an analysis (DuVernet, 2013). These tools involve identifying the core tasks and activities currently being done; identifying which tasks are important into the future; and mapping out the skills, knowledge, and other resources required to do the tasks. This information can later be used to reconfigure tasks and roles and to identify supporting changes, such as additional training requirements. In one case, we created a miniature mockup of a submarine so that alternative potential shift systems could be more readily compared (Boeing et al., 2020). Example job analysis tools include functional job analysis (identifying the data, people, skills and things needed to do the work), task inventories (task are identified and then the importance, time spent, and frequency of each task is analyzed and noted), tracer studies or process mapping (the flow of a product is "traced" through the system), and critical incident techniques (identifying instances when things went either exceptionally well or exceptionally poorly and then identifying why). Other simple ideas include exploring "a day in the life of" the worker, or the identification and analysis of the key pain points—and highlights—that a worker faces in their work. Techniques used in other work improvement programs, such as Kaizen, lean production, or Design Thinking, can also be adapted to understand the work system, so long as they include a focus on improving the quality of work for workers (rather than, for instance, a sole focus on improving customer experiences).

Crucially, the interdependence between individual jobs needs to be understood. For example, in one of our projects to redesign the highly unstimulating

374 TRANSFORMATIVE WORK DESIGN

role of train drivers whose roles had been automated, management decided that considering other roles in the system was "out of scope" for the project, which significantly constrained the opportunities for developing better roles for the (ex)train drivers. Optimally, therefore, a wide perspective should be adopted so that, rather than focusing on tasks or activities within specific individual jobs, the whole set of tasks and activities within the team or unit are considered.

An example of a deep analysis of the work system comes from the work conducted by Professor Fred Zilstra and colleagues to design work that is more inclusive. In this work, the project team sought to redistribute the tasks of overloaded professionals in a way that creates job opportunities for people with disabilities and/or no present professional qualifications. With this goal in mind, the researchers carried out a task analysis in a nursing home in which nurses and carers were significantly overloaded, with staff shortages and difficulties attracting and retaining staff (Mulders et al., 2022). Task analysis identified 72 tasks that did not require a healthcare qualification. Nurses and carers spend about 245 hours per week on these tasks; an astonishing 30 percent of their work time. The 72 tasks were then categorized into four processes: care, nutrition, well-being, and domestic work, with this information then used to create new inclusive roles for intellectually disabled staff.

2. *Generate multiple work redesign options, addressing the root cause as much as possible.* The reason for developing a deep understanding of the work system is to be able to generate ideas for how, beyond the present approach, work might be designed for greater worker mental health, well-being, learning, and performance. For example, are there different and more meaningful ways of dividing and combining tasks, or allocating decisions? Can some tasks be removed altogether or done more efficiently to reduce demands? As far as possible, solutions that address the root causes of poor work design should be generated.

In the case of the previously discussed inclusive work design, after identifying tasks and grouping tasks into four overall processes, participative work redesign sessions were conducted with staff representatives of unit staff to create three new support roles: general assistant, living assistant, and domestic assistant. The process of creating these roles was guided by ensuring both the new roles, and the roles of nurses, were well-designed. For instance, it was important to ensure that the new roles for the intellectually disabled individuals were not overly complex yet still meaningful. The SMART model can be used as criteria to guide the design of new roles, and/or their selection.

One of the challenges when designing new roles is that it can be hard for participants to see beyond traditional ways that the work is conducted. If they do see different ways, they can sometimes dismiss them as too radical or disruptive. Key to this phase, therefore, is trying to encourage more out-of-the-box thinking and challenging taken-for-granted approaches. The facilitator can play an important role here, such as playing devil's advocate to ask, "what if . . . ?." One interesting way to stimulate diverse thinking was adopted by a research team in the UK. Led by Professor David Holman, researchers worked with project teams to come up with ideas for improving call center work. The teams were invited to first come up with work designs for healthy work; second, a work design for productive work; and then third, a work design for both healthy and productive work. This approach led to wide-ranging ideas. An appreciative inquiry approach is to ask participants to "dream"—imagining their group at its very best, representing this symbolically, and then using this vision to create concrete proposals for change (Bushe, 2012).

Making it clear that any ideas will be evaluated using pre-agreed criteria, as discussed next, can provide a guard rail because those involved in redesign understand that the idea-generation phase is not binding and so they feel liberated to explore novel possibilities.

3. *Evaluate work redesigns against criteria and then select.* Once ideas are generated, there then needs to be a process to select from, or prioritize, the different options. One very simple approach uses a matrix with two dimensions: "potential impact on key outcomes" and "effort ratio." Ideas can be mapped onto the matrix. One might then choose from the high-impact, low-effort ratio (quick wins) and high-impact, high-effort ratio (major projects) according to time scales, and taking into account what actions are within the project team's sphere of influence and control. A mixture of quick wins and major projects is optimal: quick wins enable early success and help with momentum, whereas major projects will be slower to implement yet often deal with the root cause of problems.

If several work design options have been generated, another strategy is to systematically assess each new option against a more detailed set of criteria. As an example, a photographic company introduced new technology into its production department and wanted to use the opportunity to create healthier and more productive work roles. My colleagues and I helped to facilitate this process (Nadin et al., 2001). The project team, a representative group of workers (e.g., operators, design specialists) and a facilitator (a member of the research team), generated three diverse work design scenarios. Scenario 1 captured the existing approach to roles, with a high degree of specialization of tasks. Scenario 2 involved partial multiskilling of roles. Scenario 3 involved complete multiskilling of roles across departmental boundaries. Each scenario was then systematically evaluated by the project team against 12 previously agreed upon criteria, including, amongst others, control and ownership (Agency), skill variety (Stimulating), task load (Tolerable), physical security, social contact (Relational), training requirements, impact on efficiency, impact on quality, and overall impact. This process helped to generate a common language, and it stimulated vigorous debate about the tradeoffs of certain designs and their implications. None of the scenarios was an outright perfect model, but Scenario 2 was ultimately chosen as the closest, and was developed further. The key point is that the criteria are agreed on by multiple stakeholders—not just workers or just managers—and they should be linked to the key project goals.

4. Develop an action plan for implementing the work design. Once the work design ideas are selected, flesh out the ideas to identify any additional steps. For example, is additional consultation with key stakeholders required? Is there a need for further sign off from senior leaders? Regarding the latter, even if prior agreement was given, with the frequent turnover of leadership and the constant shifting of priorities, it can't always be assumed that what was agreed at the start of a project will be upheld. Workers, too, might need further consultation. For example, in the successful case of BMW discussed earlier, there was initial resistance to the idea of the pilot new assembly line—both from younger workers who felt they would be slowed down by unproductive older workers and by older workers who preferred to stay in their comfort zone. The team driving the change had many one-on-one conversations with workers to help persuade them to get on board. They promised workers they could return to their original lines after a year if they preferred—providing a "guardrail" to help secure commitment.

To facilitate implementation of the chosen ideas for work redesign, develop an action plan with a clear timeline and clear accountabilities for who will do what. This should include all the steps and activities minimally needed to bring about the role redesign successfully, including additional training required, communication, and so on. For example, will those whose roles are to be redesigned need additional training? Will managers and supervisors need further training? What is the timing for which change? When creating an action plan, as much as possible, accountability should be embedded into existing structures. For example, perhaps there can be regular progress reports at the unit's quarterly meetings? Perhaps responsibility for delivery can be built into relevant stakeholders' goals for the year?

Track

This phase has three purposes. First, early in the change process, it is important to keep track of the "process" of change, allowing an opportunity for early adaptions is needed. Second, the Track phase is when the post-intervention assessment takes place (a repeat of Assess) to investigate what impact the intervention has had, including where and for whom the impact is greatest or weakest. Third, the Track phase is important for learning what has contributed to success or failure to help build future change capability. Track steps include:

1. Soon after implementation, track the process and take action, including communicating early success. The action plan from the previous phase includes who is accountable for what. But action plans can easily be ignored or postponed in the face of pressing organizational demand. When I try to lose weight, it is not enough for me to be clear about why this is important, what my approach is going to be, or what my detailed plans are. I need monitoring! I set up monthly meetings with a dietician, with the main point of these sessions being a "weigh in" because that is the best way I have found to keep me accountable. The facilitator or another stakeholder might need to similarly hold teams to account for their actions. One tactic can be to book in a session in which the team redesigning their work, and/or the steering group, present their progress to senior leaders. Such sessions not only create accountability, but they also provide an opportunity for senior leaders to publicly share successes, help overcome roadblocks, and to reaffirm their commitment. Another tactic is to conduct interviews and focus groups to keep track of the "process" of change. Early, during, or just after implementation is the best time to do this because there is still an opportunity to intervene if the redesign appears to be going haywire. Engage in observation, attend relevant meetings, and schedule check ins, intervening when necessary.

The early days of a new initiative or way of working can be precarious. Unexpected problems can emerge. Sharing stories of success can help to maintain the momentum, be this through newsletters, company blogs, or communications from the senior leaders. Sometimes an internal knowledge-sharing group can evolve—or be consciously created—as a way for different groups to share their learnings and experiences.

2. Assess the impact of the change, overall and for different individuals and groups. If the intervention is intended to improve SMART work design, then SMART work design should be re-assessed after implementation to ensure the intervention has the intended effect, or as its sometimes referred to, has "implementation fidelity" (Steckler & Linnan, 2002). To the extent possible, the same people should be reassessed, such that their pre-intervention data (Assess Phase) and post-intervention data (Track phase) can be statistically linked and the most rigorous analyses conducted. Also, to the extent possible, the Assess data should be obtained for those in the comparison (control) groups who were not subjected to the interventions, with some analysis and checks undertaken to understand whether any co-occurring change has happened (e.g., restructuring) that needs to be taken account. For example, in one study in which people were allowed greater autonomy to work from home (Bloom et al., 2015), the intervention group had a drop in performance. This might have led to the conclusion that the intervention was a failure, except that the project team identified that business in the market had slowed down. In fact, there was a much larger drop in performance for the control group workers who did not have the autonomy to work from home, showing the intervention had a protective effect.

Ideally, as with the Assess phase, data should come from different sources (e.g., surveys, interviews, objective data) to build the most comprehensive picture. This strategy also helps to fill holes when one source of data is weak. In addition, when evaluating impact, it is ideal to go beyond asking "was there an overall change?" to ask, for instance, "for whom is it working best?" and "do different individuals or teams benefit in what way?." As an example of this approach, we implemented a job crafting intervention amongst professionals and managers enrolled in a part-time MBA program (Knight et al., 2021). The impact of the intervention varied. For individuals who had a very high initial workload, the intervention led to an increase in crafting to make work more Tolerable, such as by reducing stressful tasks. But for individuals who started out with a low workload, there was an increase in crafting to improve other aspects of their work, such as efforts to increase Autonomy. Thus, the type or degree of impact might vary for different individuals (e.g., for those with distinct abilities, personalities), demographic groups (e.g., gender, age), role levels or occupational groups (e.g., managers vs. not), and different teams or business units.

The latter point is especially crucial because implementation almost always varies in different teams/units, and it is important to see if and how this shapes the impact of the role redesign. For example, in a Swedish hospital, an intervention involving the use of Kaizen to improve work quality was taken up differently across distinct units, despite all having the same level senior management support (Augustsson et al., 2015). The units that had more success with the intervention were those that were more collaborative at the outset, participated more in the process, and were more positive about integrating Kaizen tools into existing practices.

3. Identify learnings to build capability for future change. The Track phase should ideally include evaluations of the process of change, assessing for example, whether individuals felt they were involved in the change, whether communication was adequate, what factors enabled and supported the change, and what factors inhibited success. The goal here is to help strengthen the organization's capacity for future change through reflection about what worked or did not work. Sometimes, unintended consequences emerge from a change. This is because work roles operate within a complex system. In complex systems, change in one part of the system can have surprising effects in other parts of the system. Identifying if there have been unintended negative or positive consequences, and how these can be prevented or harnessed, respectively, is important to reflect on.

In the case of the redesign of shifts in the Danish psychiatric hospitals, analyses from repeating a survey showed mostly positive change, such as statistically significant increases in job satisfaction, work–life balance, social support, and sense of community, with no such change occurred in the control group. The analysis of the "process" of change identified several learnings, such as that the benefits of the intervention took time to emerge, and that it was important to have independent external facilitators who were able to help navigate complexities and tensions between different staff. Some unintended positive changes also emerged. For instance, because individuals took responsibility for balancing the rota, they came to understand the costs of absence and the rationale behind resource allocation.

Habituate

The purpose of the Habituate phase is to make sure everything is in place to embed and sustain the change, and—if appropriate—to scale the change to other places in the organization. Habituate steps include:

1. Implement additional supporting actions to sustain the work redesign. Wider systems, leader behavior, and individual behaviors are often needed to enable and sustain new work designs. All these elements should align with the work redesign for the change to be sustained. For example, aspects to be considered include identifying what sorts of knowledge, skills, abilities, behaviors, and attitudes are important for workers, leaders, or others in the redesigned roles (and associated issues for training, recruitment, performance assessment/promotion systems, etc.); investigating what information and communication systems need to change; and ascertaining whether any complementary changes in products, services, or technology needed. As an example of the latter, an important enabler of cross-skilling is simplifying the number of products offered in retail stores. Professor Zeynep Ton (2014) argues that simplifying products simplifies operations, which employees can readily learn about each product, and hence operated with cross-skilled.

In the case of the Danish psychiatric hospitals and the revised shift structure, over time, revisions were made to the intervention to enhance its sustainability. For example, some individuals did not like the responsibility of balancing the rota, and it was recognized that these individuals needed additional skills to take on the role. Clear rules and norms were also established to combat the competition for particular shifts that emerged over time.

380 TRANSFORMATIVE WORK DESIGN

2. Spread the change. Aligning systems is an important way in which change is "mainstreamed" and embedded. Building change capability internally is also important, partly from a cost perspective (external change agents tend to be expensive) and partly because change is so frequent these days that it simply makes sense to have in-house capability if possible.

One of the biggest mistakes I have observed when shifting from a successful pilot to a larger-scale "roll out" is neglecting the role of employee participation. These is sometimes a sense "we have shown it works so why do we need to involve everyone again?." Such an attitude misses the fact that participation is likely to have been central to why the role redesign worked in the first place. So, participation is likely to continue to be important even for larger-scale change, either using a similar process as used for the pilot or adopting an indirect model of participation in which representatives of a role or team have the opportunity to participate.

The Meta-Skill of Effective Change Facilitation

Paramount to the success of the PARRTH process is the skill of the facilitator who is able to work through what can be complex emotional and political issues, such as demarcations, threatened identities, and anxiety about change. In some of our earlier intervention research, we concluded that a *"tool alone will not produce the desired results . . . it is essential for the process to be skillfully and sensitively managed"* (Nadin et al., 2001). In our case, two project teams initially opted for minimal change because they wanted to avoid upsetting others or being associated with a change that might be linked to job loss. A highly skilled and trusted facilitator was needed to address these and other such concerns. In conflictual settings, facilitators need to avoid being perceived as favoring one party or the other (e.g., being seen as a "tool of the management") and keep focused on the goals of the project, which usually involve optimizing the synergy between positive outcomes for workers and positive outcomes for productivity. A skilled facilitator also builds the psychological safety necessary for individuals to generate diverse and open-minded ideas.

As an example, in an intervention to improve work schedule flexibility in Xerox, the project team took various steps to increase the palatability of the intervention to a highly risk-averse senior management team. Not only did the project team ensure the pilot intervention was open to everyone (not just women or parents), but they also set up the principle that flexibility could only be made available *"as long as the work gets done."* Flexibility came to be seen as an opportunity for *"rethinking work effectiveness, rather than as a problem for individual employees and their supervisors*" (Bailyn, 2011, p. 102). As this example highlights, effective facilitation is both critical and challenging, showing the importance of a skilled change agent throughout the whole PARRTH process.

Conclusion

As the title of this chapter suggests, an effective participative work redesign process can unleash magic. It can prompt an enormous amount of positive energy from those involved that, in turn, leads to higher quality work. But such a work redesign process is not for the faint hearted, requiring a significant investment of time, combined with skilled facilitation. It is my hope that, by bringing together some of the critical components for success identified across various studies and approaches, the PARRTH model provides useful guidance for those embarking on this journey. I hope, too, that this model stimulates more research into the process of change as we know a great deal about what sorts of work design are needed, yet much less about how to achieve them.

References

Abildgaard, J. S., Hasson, H., von Thiele Schwarz, U., Løvseth, L. T., Ala-Laurinaho, A., & Nielsen, K. (2020). Forms of participation: The development and application of a conceptual model of participation in work environment interventions. *Economic and Industrial Democracy 41*(3), 746–769.

Ashmos, D. P., & Nathan, M. L. (2002). Team sense-making: A mental model for navigating uncharted territories. *Journal of Managerial Issues 14* (2), 198–217.

Augustsson, H., von Thiele Schwarz, U., Stenfors-Hayes, T., & Hasson, H. (2015). Investigating variations in implementation fidelity of an organizational-level occupational health intervention. *International Journal of Behavioral Medicine 22*, 345–355.

Bailyn, L. (2011). Redesigning work for gender equity and work–personal life integration. *Community, Work & Family 14*(1), 97–112.

Bloom, N., Liang, J., Roberts, J., & Ying, Z. J. (2015). Does working from home work? Evidence from a Chinese experiment. *Quarterly Journal of Economics* 130, 165–218.

Boeing, A. A., Jorristma, K., Griffin, M. A., & Parker, S. K. (2020). Surfacing the social factors early: A sociotechnical approach to the design of a future submarine. *Australian Journal of Management 45*(3), 527–545.

Bushe, G. R. (2012). Appreciative inquiry: Theory and critique. In D. M. Boje, B. Burnes, & J. Hassard (Eds.), *The Routledge companion to organizational change* (pp. 87–103). Routledge.

Dahl-Jørgensen, C., & Saksvik, P. Ø. (2005). The impact of two organizational interventions on the health of service sector workers. *International Journal of Health Services 35*(3), 529–549.

Daniels, K., Gedikli, C., Watson, D., Semkina, A., & Vaughn, O. (2017). Job design, employment practices and well-being: A systematic review of intervention studies. *Ergonomics 60*(9), 1177–1196.

DuVernet, A. M. (2013). Using job analytic information to (re) design jobs: Best practices and methods. In M. A. Wilson (Ed.), *The handbook of work analysis* (pp. 356–374). Routledge.

Holman, D., & Axtell, C. (2016). Can job redesign interventions influence a broad range of employee outcomes by changing multiple job characteristics? A quasi-experimental study. *Journal of Occupational Health Psychology 21*(3), 284–295.

Knight, C., Tims, M., Gawke, J., & Parker, S. K. (2021). When do job crafting interventions work? The moderating roles of workload, intervention intensity, and participation. *Journal of Vocational Behavior 124*, 103522.

Lamontagne, A. D., Keegel, T., Louie, A. M., Ostry, A., & Landsbergis, P. A. (2007). A systematic review of the job-stress intervention evaluation literature, 1990–2005. *International Journal of Occupational and Environmental Health 13*(3), 268–280.

Landsbergis, P. A., & Vivona-Vaughan, E. (1995). Evaluation of an occupational stress intervention in a public agency. *Journal of Organizational Behavior 16*(1), 29–48.

Loch, C., Sting, F., Bauer, N., & Mauermann, H. (2010). How BMW is defusing the demographic time bomb. *Harvard Business Review 88*(3), 99–102.

Mikkelsen, A., Saksvik, P. Ø., & Landsbergis, P. (2000). The impact of a participatory organizational intervention on job stress in community health care institutions. *Work & Stress 14*(2), 156–170.

Mulders, H., van Ruitenbeek, G., Wagener, B., & Zijlstra, F. (2022). Toward more inclusive work organizations by redesigning work. *Frontiers in Rehabilitation Sciences 3*, 861561.

Murphy, L. R., & Hurrell Jr, J. J. (1987). Stress management in the process of occupational stress reduction. *Journal of Managerial Psychology 2*(1), 18–23.

Nadin, S. J., Waterson, P. E., & Parker, S. K. (2001). Participation in job redesign: An evaluation of the use of a sociotechnical tool and its impact. *Human Factors and Ergonomics in Manufacturing & Service Industries 11*(1), 53–69.

Nielsen, K., & Abildgaard, J. S. (2013). Organizational interventions: A research-based framework for the evaluation of both process and effects. *Work & Stress 27*(3), 278–297.

Nielsen, K., & Randall, R. (2012). The importance of employee participation and perceptions of changes in procedures in a teamworking intervention. *Work & Stress 26*(2), 91–111.

Nielsen, K., Taris, T. W., & Cox, T. (2010). The future of organizational interventions: Addressing the challenges of today's organizations. *Work & Stress 24*(3), 219–233.

Oreg, S., & Berson, Y. (2019). Leaders' impact on organizational change: Bridging theoretical and methodological chasms. *Academy of Management Annals 13*(1), 272–307.

O'Shea, D., O'Connell, B. H., & Gallagher, S. (2016). Randomised controlled trials in WOHP interventions: A review and guidelines for use. *Applied Psychology 65*(2), 190–222.

Parker, S. K., & Knight, C. (2023). The SMART model of work design: A higher order structure to help see the wood from the trees. *Human Resource Management 63*(2), 265–291.

Pryce, J., Albertsen, K., & Nielsen, K. (2006). Evaluation of an open-rota system in a Danish psychiatric hospital: A mechanism for improving job satisfaction and work–life balance. *Journal of Nursing Management 14*(4), 282–288.

Razzouk, R., & Shute, V. (2012). What is design thinking and why is it important. *Review of Educational Research 82*(3), 330–348.

Steckler, A. E., & Linnan, L. E. (2002). *Process evaluation for public health interventions and research.* Jossey-Bass/Wiley.

Ton, Z. (2014). *The good jobs strategy: How the smartest companies invest in employees to lower costs and boost profits.* Houghton Mifflin Harcourt.

Weiss, C. H. (1995). Nothing as practical as good theory: Exploring theory-based evaluation for comprehensive community initiatives for children and families. In J. Connell, A. Kubisch, L. Schorr, & C. Weiss, (Eds.), *New approaches to evaluating community initiatives* (pp. 65–92). Aspen Institute.

Understanding the Outcomes of Work Transformations

Evaluation of Organizational Interventions

Karina Nielsen

I once ran a workshop on the design, implementation, and evaluation of organizational interventions for a class of PhD students. When putting forward the argument for evaluating the intervention's processes to fully understand the effects of such interventions, I added that, in other fields, the randomized controlled intervention design might be suitable for evaluating intervention effectiveness. One of the PhD students, a former senior nurse manager, raised her hand and gave the perfect example of why we always need to understand intervention processes, regardless of the type of intervention. She had been involved in a double-blind trial, meaning that neither the patients nor the nurses administering the pill knew which was the treatment pill and which was the placebo (a pill containing no treatment such as a sugar or a saltwater pill). One day a patient had come in to get a new batch of pills and had said: "You have changed the pill." The nurse asked: "How do you know?" The patient answered: "Because when I flush the pill down the toilet, it no longer floats." The lesson learned here is that if we deal with human participants, the only thing that is certain is that we can never fully predict their behaviors. A pill can have all the most effective ingredients but will never have an effect if only flushed down the toilet. Translating this into the field of work (re)design and organizational interventions, I argue that if we want to transform work designs, we need to fully understand what works for whom in which circumstances. In the present chapter, I review the traditional approaches to determining the effectiveness of organizational interventions, with a particular emphasis on the limitations on what has been considered the gold standard of evaluation, namely the randomized controlled trial (RCT). I then discuss the implications of acknowledging the limitation of such study designs and what is considered good quality in the design of intervention. Next, I propose that we need to evaluate how the intervention is implemented and how participants' perception and

---

Karina Nielsen, *Understanding the Outcomes of Work Transformations*. In: *Transformative Work Design*. Edited by: Sharon K. Parker et et., Oxford University Press. © Society for Industrial and Organizational Psychology (2025). DOI: 10.1093/oso/9780197692554.003.0015

386   TRANSFORMATIVE WORK DESIGN

actions influence intervention outcomes. Further, we need to consider multiple outcomes that benefit participating organizations in the long term. I synthesize these arguments in a novel framework for reporting and evaluating the quality of intervention studies in the Framework for Reporting and Assessing the Quality of Organizational Interventions (FRAQOI).

What Are Organizational Interventions?

Organizational interventions are aimed at improving employee health and well-being through changing the way work is organized, designed, and managed (Nielsen, 2022). By redesigning work, working conditions may improve (e.g., increasing social support, autonomy and decreasing adverse job demands, conflict and role ambiguity) (Nielsen, 2022). One example of an organizational intervention is a study in the Danish eldercare, where self-managing work teams were implemented to improve employee health and well-being (Nielsen & Randall, 2012). Workers were divided into small teams who would be responsible for planning the rota, task completion, and team meetings to increase autonomy and workers developed a mission statement on good collaboration to promote social support (Nielsen et al., 2010a).

In a large representative survey of Danish workplaces, Sannie Thorsen and colleagues (2017) found that in organizations that engage in efforts to improve the working conditions, employees reported significantly better working conditions one year later. However, a recent review of reviews of the effectiveness of organizational interventions concluded that there is inconsistent evidence that such interventions are effective—sometimes they work and sometimes they do not (Aust et al., 2023)—which calls for a better understanding of why and how such interventions work. Evaluation of organizational interventions is crucial not only to understand the outcomes of the specific intervention but because evaluation should be used to inform future interventions. In the present chapter, I discuss traditional methods to evaluate organizational interventions and review some recent developments in how interventions are evaluated. I propose a new framework for how we may report and review the quality of interventions with a view to accumulating learning from intervention evaluations to extract knowledge on what works for whom in which circumstances.

Organizational interventions are often participatory in nature, meaning that employees, managers, and other key stakeholders jointly agree on the processes of the intervention and what changes need to be made to the way work is organized, designed, and managed (Nielsen, 2023). Participatory interventions typically go through five phases (Nielsen, 2023). First, in the preparation or initiation phase, the methods and structure of the intervention are determined (e.g., a steering group is established, the intervention process is agreed upon), including the identification of what needs to change, and a communication strategy is developed. Second, a screening is conducted to identify what working conditions need to change. Screening is often conducted using a survey; however, in smaller organizations using qualitative methods and interactive workshops may be preferable (Nielsen et al., 2018). Third, in the action planning phase, the results of the screening are translated into feasible and appropriate action plans identifying what transformations to work design, organization, and management need to be made. These action plans should be developed in collaboration between managers, employees, and other key stakeholders. Fourth, action plans are implemented and the progress should be monitored, allowing for flexibility to change should action plans prove to no longer be feasible and appropriate. Finally, interventions should be evaluated. What such an evaluation should look like is the focus of this chapter. I argue that if we want to truly transform workplaces, we need to rethink how we evaluate our organizational interventions.

Evaluating the Effectiveness of Organizational Interventions

Earlier reviews and meta-analyses examining the effectiveness of organizational interventions were characterized by two approaches (Richardson & Rothstein, 2008; van der Klink et al., 2001). First, organizational interventions were pitched against individual interventions to determine which were more effective. Second, they relied on assumptions of evidence-based levels of hierarchy derived from the medical and public health field. These approaches have been criticized for not capturing the complexity of organizational interventions to truly detect the effects of attempts to transform working conditions.

Pitching organizational interventions against individual interventions

The meta-analyses of Jac van der Klink and colleagues (2001) and Katherine Richardson and Hannah Rothstein (2008) compared organizational interventions with individual targeted interventions (i.e., interventions aimed at changing the individual workers' cognitions, emotions, and behaviors) (Nielsen & Shepherd, 2022). Karina Nielsen and Mariella Miraglia (2017) argued that this comparison is like comparing apples and oranges. Individual-level interventions, such as training interventions, follow a pre-planned and pre-defined training protocol of the sessions to be implemented, with clear instructions of what needs to happen when and with little consideration of what happens after the intervention has finished (Nielsen & Shepherd, 2022; WHO, 2004). In organizational interventions it is what happens after the intervention's action planning sessions that is of interest (i.e., what work transformations are implemented). It is not the action planning workshops/sessions in themselves that bring about change but the actual implementation of action plans making changes to work policies, practices, and procedures (Nielsen & Randall, 2012). Furthermore, changes to work policies, practices, and procedures are complex and require many people to change their behaviors, and as many different action plans may be implemented it is difficult to determine the best time for follow-up. Further, funding often restricts lengthy follow-ups (Nielsen, 2013; Nielsen & Randall, 2012).

In medical trials it is often assumed that once the treatment is withdrawn, patients return to pre-treatment levels (Aggarwal & Ranganathan, 2019). Such assumptions are contrary to organizational interventions where the intention is for the intervention to have a lasting outcome beyond the intervention's activities (Nielsen & Abildgaard, 2013).

Arguments have been made that organizations need to develop their capability to continuously work with emerging adverse working conditions rather than simply addressing the adverse working conditions at the time of screening (e.g., low levels of autonomy) to have a sustainable effect (Nielsen, 2022; Nielsen et al., submitted). The COVID-19 pandemic presents an excellent example of how working conditions may change with short notice as people were forced to work from home and frontline workers were at risk of infection (Morawa et al., 2021). Organizations need to have the systems in place to act quickly on such risks; therefore, evaluating whether learning capability is developed is crucial (Nielsen et al., 2023, 2024).

More recently, some have also argued for individual-level interventions aimed at improving mental health and well-being, and so the processes of transferring learning to daily working life must be understood (i.e., understanding the long-term effects). Nielsen and Shepherd (2022) argued that simple post-intervention (measurements immediately after training has been completed) and short-term follow-ups are inadequate to evaluate the long-term effects of individual-level interventions. Training transfer—the extent to which learning is transferred to the workplace and maintained over time—is crucial to the sustainable effects of individual-level interventions (Nielsen & Shepherd, 2022).

Nielsen and Rose Shepherd (2022) suggested that the work context is crucial to training transfer. If, for example, participants try to change their job crafting strategies because of a job crafting intervention, but they are met with resistance from leaders or colleagues and are therefore unable to change their working conditions, they may make fewer attempts to job craft over time. If they return and find they can job craft, they are likely to increase their attempts. Only those participants who successfully job craft after the intervention has finished and apply learning in day-to-day work are likely to report improved well-being. In other words, the impact of intervention processes is important for both organizational and individual interventions but neither are captured in the simple comparisons of the effects of either type of intervention.

In summary, it is not straightforward to compare organizational and individual level interventions, and research should consider what happens once intervention activities have been completed to understand the sustainable effects of both types of intervention.

Evidence-based levels of hierarchy

Earlier reviews have assumed that a hierarchy of evidence exists depending on the quality of the study design (WHO, 2022). One example of such hierarchy of evidence is the Betty Ackley and colleagues (2008) evidence-based guidelines. These guidelines suggest that at the top of the evidence hierarchy, offering the highest level of evidence, are systematic reviews and meta-analyses of all RCTs in the area. At the second level of the hierarchy is the evidence obtained from at least one "well-designed" RCT, suggesting multi-site RCTs as an example of a well-designed study. At the third level of hierarchy is the evidence obtained from "well-designed" controlled trials without randomization (i.e., quasi-experimental studies that have a control group but without randomization). At the fourth level of the hierarchy, evidence is obtained from case-control or cohort studies. At the fifth level of the hierarchy, evidence is obtained from systematic reviews of descriptive and qualitative studies (meta-syntheses). At the sixth level of the hierarchy is the evidence from a single descriptive or qualitative study and, finally, at the seventh level of the hierarchy is the evidence acquired through seeking the opinion of authorities and/or the consideration of reports of expert committees. Assuming evidence based on this hierarchy rests on the assumption that all RCTs are of good quality, which is obviously not always the case, a fundamental flaw of this thinking is that it ignores the crucial design elements of the studies that go into a meta-analysis. For example, a meta-analysis of eight RCTs with only post-intervention data (i.e., data collected immediately after the intervention) will be rated higher quality than a single RCT which showed an effect 12 months after completion of the intervention. The single RCT, however, gives a better indication of the long-term effects of the intervention than the sum of the eight RCTs that do not include a follow-up. In the hierarchy of evidence, there is no mention of interventions without a control group or evaluations that use adapted study designs (i.e., where participants are allocated to the intervention and the control group, based on their actual exposure to the intervention) (Randall et al., 2005). While meta-analyses provide a good understanding of whether there is a link between different factors (e.g., whether job resources are linked to employee health and well-being) (Nielsen et al., 2017), meta-analyses on organizational interventions do not capture the complexity of organizational interventions. The seminal meta-analyses by van der Klink and colleagues (2001) and Richardson and Rothstein (2008) both assumed that the RCT was the most appropriate design for evaluating the effectiveness of organizational interventions, and Richardson and Rothstein (2008) discarded any studies that did not use the RCT design.

In summary, relying on the RCT as the highest level of evidence is not without its challenges because such study designs on their own may not tell us much about the sustainability of interventions. In the following, I will challenge three underlying assumptions of the RCT design, further questioning whether the RCT design on its own is suitable for evaluating organizational interventions.

Challenges of the RCT design in organizational interventions

A key element of intervention quality is internal and external validity (Campbell & Stanley, 1963). Internal validity refers to the extent to which a cause-and-effect relationship between the intervention and its outcomes can be established (Cook & Campbell, 1979; Newcomer et al., 2015). High internal validity is achieved when a study fulfils the three conditions required for causal inference: covariation (the intervention is linked to the outcome); time–order relationship (the intervention occurs before any changes in outcomes); and elimination of plausible alternative causes (there are no alternative explanations for improvements in intervention outcomes; Shaugnessy et al., 2012). It is assumed that RCTs fulfil these three conditions (Cook & Campbell, 1979; Shaugnessy et al., 2012). External validity refers to the extent to which the same outcomes of an intervention can be observed across multiple settings (Cook & Campbell, 1979; Newcomer et al., 2015). If RCTs replicated in different settings produce the same results, external validity is assumed (Nielsen & Miraglia, 2017).

Although the RCT design is regarded as the gold standard for establishing the effectiveness of interventions, and also by many in organizational intervention research (Aust et al., 2023), effect sizes on their own do not provide interventionists with information on whether the intervention's outcomes can be reproduced in other settings (Moore et al., 2015) or how large a proportion of participants benefit from the intervention or why (Burgess et al., 2020). The use of the RCT in participatory organizational interventions is problematic for several reasons. In organizational settings, it is nearly impossible to control the environment.

Events may occur throughout the intervention period and the context plays a key role in facilitating or hindering the successful implementation of the intervention (Nielsen et al., 2010b). Nielsen and Miraglia (2017) argued that RCTs are unsuitable for determining the effects of organizational interventions for three reasons.

First, key to RCTs is the pre-determination of the methods and the content of the intervention (WHO, 2004); however, in organizational interventions, methods and the content of the intervention are developed as part of the intervention through the participatory process (Nielsen, 2023). What happens at one stage of the intervention influences the next (Nielsen & Abildgaard, 2013). This presents a challenge to the first condition of internal validity because RCT designs only enable researchers to determine whether there was a change or not. Organizational intervention outcomes are driven by both the process of how the intervention is implemented and how the intervention activities were perceived by participants and the content of the intervention (the changes made to work design, management, and organization; Nielsen, 2023).

Second, it is challenging to identify equivalent control groups with which to compare the intervention group (Pawson, 2013). Each organization has its own culture, policies, practices, and procedures that make comparisons across organizations difficult. Even at the departmental level within the same organization, identifying control groups is difficult. Often, there is only one department of its kind (e.g., finance department), but even when there are more departments of the same kind, they will vary in size, culture, norms, values, composition, and leadership. Furthermore, Nielsen and Miraglia (2017) argued that it is unethical to identify departments in need of intervention, only to then deny them support. Kirsten Nabe-Nielsen and colleagues (2015) measured readiness for change in the baseline study, after randomization had happened, and found that readiness for change was higher in the intervention group than in the control group. Talking to the steering group, they found that the intervention group felt they had "won the lottery." Furthermore, double blinding is impossible in organizational settings. The participatory method requires that employees and managers engage in decision making about what changes they are active agents in to make work transformations happen (Nielsen, 2013).

Third, in complex interventions, such as organizational interventions, it is near impossible to determine whether any changes in outcomes can be ascribed to the intervention processes or work transformations (Nielsen & Miraglia, 2017). Three studies that exemplify the difficulties of using the RCT design are the studies of Karen Albertsen and colleagues (2014), Nielsen and colleagues (2006) and Nielsen and Raymond Randall (2012). In a study on the implementation of an IT rota system in eldercare, Albertsen and colleagues (2014) found that the same intervention had very different outcomes in three organizations.

In the first organization, no improvements in work–life balance and well-being were observed because the IT system had not been used. In the second organization, work–life balance improved. The IT system supported existing principles of procedures but made the process fairer and easier. In the third organization, work–life balance deteriorated. Interviews revealed that management feared losing power and overrode planning made by the IT system, resulting in more evening work and unpredictable working hours. The same intervention had different outcomes in three organizations depending on the context and the degree of implementation, meaning that the link between intervention and outcomes is not straightforward. The study also provides an excellent example of why multisite interventions are not a quality criterion on their own as proposed by Ackley and colleagues (2008).

In a teamwork intervention, Nielsen and Randall (2012) explored the impact of the participatory process and the extent to which changes in work practices had been implemented. Employees' involvement in the design and implementation of teamwork was related to more changes in work practices and procedures being implemented, but importantly also directly related to higher levels of social support post-intervention. This social support was associated with increased job satisfaction. The actual changes to work practices and procedures were found to be related directly to higher levels of job satisfaction and to well-being through an increase in autonomy.

Nielsen and colleagues (2006) found unexpected results in a study of industrial canteens. Evaluation showed improvements in outcomes in one control group and one intervention group, whereas no deterioration in outcomes could be observed in another intervention group and another control group. Improvements in the one control group were attributed to the leader of the poorly performing intervention group changing jobs and becoming the leader of the successful control group. This leader had resented being in the control group and had brought in the services of the occupational health service that supported the intervention group, effectively replicating the intervention. The poorly performing intervention group had planned but not implemented activities (Nielsen et al., 2006).

In summary, ensuring external and internal validity may not be as straightforward as suggested and these three studies highlight the challenges of relying on the RCT design. Although RCTs can detect what would have happened if no intervention had been implemented, by studying changes in the control groups, it is not feasible to use on its own in organizational interventions because it does not consider the complexity of these interventions and it only tests whether something works and not how and why it worked. Understanding the context and the processes of organizational interventions is crucial to understanding what works for whom in which circumstances.

Understanding intervention processes

Due to the challenges of implementing organizational interventions, calls have been made for evaluation of intervention processes. Process evaluation has been defined as the "individual, collective and management perceptions and actions in implementing any intervention and their influence on the overall result of the intervention" (Nytrø et al., 2000, p. 214). Multiple benefits of process evaluation have been identified. First, by conducting process evaluation, participants are given a voice (French et al., 2022) and conclusions can be drawn on why an intervention succeeded or failed (Armstrong et al., 2008). Second, using information from process evaluation can help improve the intervention under study, making adjustments to ensure the likelihood of a successful outcome (French et al., 2022), but process evaluation may also help draw conclusions about the extent to which an intervention can be transferred to other settings and under what circumstances it may be transferred to other settings (Armstrong et al., 2008) and can thus be used to inform future interventions (von Thiele Schwarz et al., 2021).

What works for whom in which circumstances

In the previous sections, I have argued that the RCT is not suitable on its own for evaluating organizational interventions; however, there has been limited discussion of a suitable alternative. In their critical review, Nielsen and Miraglia (2017) called for a systematic approach to integrating process and effect evaluation and suggested that realist evaluation; that is, an evaluation that seeks to answer the questions of what works for whom in which circumstances (Pawson & Tilley, 1997), may offer an alternative to the RCT evaluation paradigm.

Originating in public health (Pawson, 2013), realist evaluation seeks to answer the question of what works for whom in which circumstances (Pawson & Tilley, 1997). Key to realist evaluation is the development and test of program theories that may further our understanding of why an intervention succeeds or fails to bring about intended outcomes (Pawson, 2013). Program theory refers to the theory of what causes change and the conditions that need to be in place for intervention to work (Greenhalgh et al., 2015). The answers to what works for whom in which circumstances is tested through Context + Mechanism = Outcome (CMO)-configurations (Pawson, 2013; Pawson & Tilley, 1997). Context refers to the conditions in which the intervention finds itself, as described earlier. Mechanisms are what make the intervention work. A CMO-configuration can pertain to either parts of, or the entire, intervention and one CMO-configuration can be embedded in another (Pawson & Tilley, 1997).

394 TRANSFORMATIVE WORK DESIGN

A key tenet is that the intervention itself does not bring about change; interventions work through participants' interpretations, considerations, decisions, and behaviors (Pawson, 2013). In other words, participants actively craft the intervention, which is in line with the participatory approach of organizational interventions (Nielsen, 2013; Nielsen & Miraglia, 2017). Outcomes are akin to the effects of interventions, and in the case of organizational interventions, improvements in the working conditions and in the health and well-being of participants (Nielsen & Miraglia, 2017).

Nielsen and Johan Abildgaard (2013) developed a process evaluation framework of evaluating organizational interventions based on realist evaluation. They suggested that for each phase of the intervention—the preparation, screening, action, planning and implementation phases—the potential mechanisms should be identified and measured. Also in each phase, potential barriers and facilitators in the organizational context should be considered, be they omnibus or discrete contextual factors.

One criticism of the realist evaluation approach is its over-emphasis of participants' interpretations and reflections at the expense of evaluating the implementation of objective intervention components. Also from the public health domain, several implementation frameworks have been developed, such as the RE-AIM model (Glasgow et al., 2019). The R of RE-AIM stands for Reach and refers to the number, proportion, and representativeness of the population who chooses to participate in the intervention. In organizational interventions, whole departments usually participate and, as such, the relevance of reach in this context mostly refers to whether employees elect to participate in intervention process workshops, such as action planning workshops, or participate in activities outlined in action plans, such as training activities (Sorensen et al., 2021). E refers to Effectiveness and concerns the evaluation of the outcomes of interventions. A stands for Adoption and refers to the number of intervention agents (i.e., those who deliver the intervention that are willing to employ the intervention). In organizational interventions, this could be the number of departmental managers agreeing to implement the intervention in their department. I refers to Implementation and the degree to which the intervention protocol is followed. As participatory organizational interventions are organic in nature, developing over time, implementation in organizational intervention may refer to the extent to which action plans are implemented according to plan. M stands for Maintenance and refers to (1) whether changes in behaviors are maintained over time after the intervention is completed, and (2) whether an intervention is integrated into existing policies, practices, and procedures. This is akin to our earlier discussion of sustainability and has equal value in organizational intervention evaluation. Recently, the RE-AIM framework has been extended with the recommendations of employing qualitative methods to understand the how and why of interventions but with little concrete advice on how to employ such qualitative methods (Glasgow et al., 2019).

A limitation of existing realist evaluations of organizational interventions is that they have focused on the reporting on the tests of CMO-configurations, with few examples of how CMO-configurations were developed. One rare example is the study of Hamid Roodbari and colleagues (2021b), who documented how interviews, focus groups, and workplace observations were used to develop CMO-configurations and in a later paper reported how these configurations were tested (Roodbari et al., 2022).

As contextual factors may be needed to trigger the interventions mechanism, interventions cannot simply be transferred from one context to the other because it is assumed that it is the interaction between context and mechanisms that bring about the intended outcomes (Greenhalgh et al., 2015). Thus, organizational interventions work differently in different contexts and through different mechanisms (Nielsen & Miraglia, 2017); however, the in-depth understanding of what works for whom in which circumstances is transferable (Goodridge et al., 2015).

In contrast to the RCT domain, where meta-analysis is used to draw conclusions about their effectiveness, realist synthesis is used in realist evaluation to synthesize evidence of what works for whom in which circumstances in the realist evaluation domain (Nielsen & Miraglia, 2017; Pawson, 2013). Based on the RAMESES standards for reporting realist evaluation (Greenhalgh et al., 2015), Roodbari and colleagues (2021a) synthesized evidence from 18 participatory organizational interventions and identified nine mechanisms, which may bring about well-being outcomes. The nine key process mechanisms identified to make interventions work included interventions implemented according to plan, employing a participatory approach, support for the intervention process from middle and senior managers, communication about the intervention process, content and progress to participants, and the management of the intervention process by external or internal consultants.

Realist evaluation offers a way forward to bridge the gap between the process evaluation and effect evaluation. Literature reviews on the intervention processes of organizational interventions have largely failed to link process and effect evaluation (e.g., Aust et al., 2023; Egan et al., 2009; Havermans et al., 2016), with the exceptions of Roodbari and colleagues (2021a) and Nielsen and colleagues (2022). Indeed, researchers often choose to report the effects in one study and the processes of the interventions in another when reporting the results of their interventions (e.g., Framke et al., 2015, 2016).

Using process evaluation data as input to formative evaluation

One important benefit of process evaluation is its potential to provide ongoing input on how to adjust the implementation of the intervention, increasing the likelihood of a successful outcome (French et al., 2022; Nielsen & Randall, 2013). This line of thinking stems from the literature on formative and summative evaluation. Formative evaluation is conducted during the development or improvement of a program or course while summative evaluation involves making judgments about the efficacy of a program or course at its conclusion (Cizek et al., 2019). Formative evaluation is widely recognized in the learning and education literature (Bin Mubayrik, 2020), but it has received limited attention in the organizational literature (Nielsen et al., 2023).

A key characteristic of formative evaluation is continuous monitoring during the learning process with the aim to observe and improve program performance (i.e., its ability to bring about the intended outcomes). Furthermore, formative evaluation explores the participants' learning capability, thus focusing on meaningful feedback. Formative evaluation data are gathered at multiple time points during the process and evaluation is considered a continuous regular process (Bin Mubayrik, 2020). Nielsen and Randall (2013) suggested the use of ongoing process evaluation to optimize the implementation and suggested it may help organizations take corrective actions if the intervention is not being implemented according to plan. Ongoing process evaluation may thus be used to minimize the risks of negative or unwanted side effects (von Thiele Schwarz et al., 2021).

In summary, process evaluation and realist evaluation may help overcome the challenges of internal and external validity for four reasons. First, it enables us to understand how the intervention components, be it process or content, are related to the intervention's outcomes. Second, it enables us to actively measure whether intervention components are implemented before outcome measures are collected. Third, rather than assuming the confounders or contextual factors can be held constant and controlled for, process evaluation and realist evaluation integrates contextual factors in the outcome analysis and explores the role context has in triggering the mechanisms of the intervention. Finally, realist synthesis enables the transfer of learning from one context to another, increasing the likelihood of successful intervention implementation. The use of process evaluation and realist evaluation, however, requires that we rethink how we report our intervention studies in scientific publications and how we assess the quality of organizational interventions.

Assessing and Reporting Intervention Quality

Inspired by public health, organizational interventions' quality has been rated according to the study's alignment with RCT principles (e.g., Aust et al., 2023). As such, existing frameworks for evaluating the quality of organizational interventions have failed to consider the complex and emergent nature of organizational interventions.

One assessment and reporting framework often used is the Quality Assessment Tool for Quantitative Studies (Thomas et al., 2004), recommended by the *Cochrane Handbook for Systematic Reviews* (Effective Public Health Practice Project, EFPPH, 2020). According to this framework, quantitative studies can be rated on eight dimensions: selection bias, study design, confounders, blinding, data collection methods, withdrawals and dropouts, intervention integrity, and analyses.

These criteria are not directly transferable to organizational interventions. First, selection bias concerns arise when clinicians delivering the intervention select who gets the intervention or when participants select themselves. In organizational interventions, the pool is not from a selected group of patients who have been diagnosed with the same illness, but departments with a particular need are often selected within an organization (Framke et al., 2016). If the scope for development in a department is limited, we may see a ceiling effect and the department will not benefit from the intervention (Nielsen et al., 2006).

Second, I have previously discussed the limitations of the RCT design in terms of internal and external validity.

Third, confounders in the EPHPP concern demographics, such as race, sex, age, socioeconomic status, education, and health outcomes. However, in organizational interventions, confounders, also known as contextual factors (Nielsen & Randall, 2013), may strengthen or dilute the effects of the intervention (Nielsen & Randall, 2015). Nielsen and Randall (2013) distinguished between omnibus and discrete contextual factors. The omnibus context refers to the cultural, systemic, and existing working conditions in the organization (Nielsen & Abildgaard, 2013). For example, in the Nielsen and Randall (2012) study, pre-existing working conditions influenced the extent to which participants engaged in the participatory process and implemented teamwork procedures. The discrete context refers to the specific events happening throughout the intervention period, such as changes in managers (Nielsen et al., 2006) or restructuring (Nielsen et al., 2010b). Organizations and their context are complex, and it is impossible to control for all variables. For example, underlying cultural values may only be exposed during the course of the intervention (Biron et al., 2010), and the discrete context may influence the course of the intervention, the best example possibly being the COVID-19 pandemic that prevented people from meeting in-person during lockdown (Bouziri et al., 2020), thus ruling out face-to-face intervention workshops and activities. Nielsen and colleagues (2021) argued that rather than seeing the context as confounding this should be integrated in the planning of the interventions, for example, if employees report limited readiness for change, more communication is needed to help employees understand how they may benefit from the intervention. A flexible intervention design would enable rapid adjustments to the intervention process, for example, by introducing an online tool that enables working on action plans without meeting face-to-face.

Fourth, blinding is not desirable nor possible in organizational interventions because participants are the crafters of the intervention and work practices and procedures cannot be changed without the conscious efforts of participants (Nielsen, 2013).

Fifth, data collection and methods refer to tools used to evaluate as valid and reliable; however, as participatory organizational interventions may take many forms depending on the national and occupational context (Nielsen & Brough, 2023), quantitative process evaluation measures should be tailored to the intervention in question (Randall et al., 2009) and qualitative methods offer the flexibility to hone in on issues deemed of particular importance in the given context (Nielsen et al., 2023) (e.g., discrete contextual factors such as the impact of the COVID-19 pandemic).

Sixth, the EPHPP does not specify dropout relating to withdrawal from intervention activities, only failure to respond to follow-up questionnaires. Dropout from organizational interventions is common in organizational interventions; for example, as workers move jobs, turnover is high in some occupations, and it is not unusual for employees to move between departments within one organization. Dropout from responding to follow-up surveys, therefore, may not be a good measure of intervention quality because we often do not know if people did not respond to the questionnaire or if they have moved jobs. Although organizational data on turnover may be available, such data are rarely shared with researchers due to confidentiality concerns.

Seventh, intervention integrity is composed of three elements. The first element refers to the extent to which participants received the intervention or were exposed to the intervention. The underlying assumption is that participants are passive recipients and play no role in designing and implementing the intervention, nor do they make any active decisions to be implemented as the content of action plans, which is not the case for organizational interventions as participants actively craft the intervention process (Nielsen, 2013). The second element is consistency in implementation of integrity in the EPHPP. Translating this to organizational interventions, we need to assess whether action plans were implemented according to plan. The third element of integrity is unintended effects, which also holds value in organizational interventions. We need to understand whether wide ranging work transformations bring about unintended effects. Integrity can thus be translated into a quality criterion also for organizational intervention evaluation.

Finally, the quality criterion of appropriate analysis also holds value in organizational interventions. Multi-level analyses are often required to capture the nested nature of organization, and analyses should capture how intervention context and processes are linked to outcomes (Nielsen et al., 2023). Adapted study designs exploring the effects between those who participated in the intervention against those who should have but did not (Randall et al., 2005) are often warranted.

Quality criteria guidelines for organizational interventions

Relating to organizational interventions follow Deirdre O'Shea and colleagues (2016) suggested revised guidelines for assessing and reporting the quality of organizational interventions, adding some elements in addition to those already existing for RCTs (i.e., randomization, blinding). O'Shea and colleagues (2016) suggested also reporting the context and the processes of interventions but did not question whether the RCT is an appropriate study design for organizational interventions.

Matt Egan and colleagues (2009) developed a checklist for reporting the reporting, planning, and implementation of organizational interventions. The key themes included motivation (why did management decide to implement the intervention?), theory of change (were the proposed pathways from implementation to outcomes made explicit?), implementation context (did the study provide any contextual information relevant to implementation?), experience (what previous experience did implementers have in implementing interventions, were managers and employees trained in implementing interventions?), planning and delivery consultation (what, if any, collaboration processes between managers, employees and other key stakeholders are reported in the planning and delivery stages?), manager support (were line managers and supervisors supportive of the intervention?), employee support (were employees supportive of the intervention?), resources (what resources were required as part of the implementation [e.g., time, money, equipment]?), and differential effects and population characteristics (whom did the intervention work for and for whom did it not work?). All these questions are crucial to understand the implementation of interventions and must be answered to enable the transfer of interventions to new settings. However, although these factors are important,

400 TRANSFORMATIVE WORK DESIGN

they focus more on implementation and not on how the degree of implementation may explain intervention outcomes.

Rob Briner and Neil Walshe (2015) made the argument for evidence-based interventions, suggesting that the key to successful interventions to improve well-being is their underpinnings in work psychology theory. They suggested 12 items that should be reported, primarily focused on the why, what, who, where, when, and how much, but failed to consider the role of participants in making or breaking the intervention (Nielsen, 2017) and the emergent nature of participatory interventions. Caroline French and colleagues (2022) argued that process evaluation is often suboptimal, lacking justifications for methodology and areas of enquiry and displaying a scarcity of description of the methods used. They suggested that knowledge provided by process evaluation should be assessed in terms of its credibility, accuracy, and completeness. I argue that if we want to study the true transformation that organizational interventions may enable, we need new criteria for assessing the quality of such interventions that capture the complexity characterizing these interventions. In the following section, I will present a novel Framework for Reporting and Assessing the Quality of Organizational Interventions (FRAQOI).

Framework for Reporting and Assessing the Quality of Organizational Interventions (FRAQOI)

In response to the limitations of current frameworks for assessment, and the quality of organizational interventions, I propose the development of a novel framework for reporting and assessing the quality of organizational interventions. This framework may help researchers detect the true impact of their work transformations and may provide valuable information on how to design, implement, and evaluate such work transformations. I suggest key criteria, some of which are included from existing frameworks (EFFPH, Thomas et al., 2004); the Egan and colleagues (2009) checklist; and the RE-AIM (Glasgow et al., 2019), while others are new and inspired by realist evaluation. Table 15.1 presents an overview of the suggested FRAQOI.

In the pre-implementation phases, the preparation phase, and the screening phase, focus should be on describing the design of the intervention, the implementation strategies, and program theories underlying the design choices, together with a thorough evaluation plan outlining what data will capture the intervention content, process, implementation, and outcomes, and the contextual factors needed to support successful implementation. In the implementation phase, action planning development processes and content should be described, together with the program theories developed about the working

UNDERSTANDING THE OUTCOMES OF WORK TRANSFORMATIONS   401

Table 15.1 The Framework for Reporting and Assessing the Quality of Organizational Interventions (FRAQOI)

Pre-implementation phases (preparation and screening phases)	Assessment criteria
Recruitment	How are organizations selected for participation? How are departments, if any, selected? Is a description given of why these were selected? Is there a description of the recruitment strategy? Have power calculations been conducted to ensure appropriate sample sizes?
Selection bias	How large a proportion of the participants have been offered the opportunity to give their views on the adverse working conditions experienced? If surveys, are response rates representative of the population? Are reasons given for low response rates in surveys? If qualitative, how and who were invited to participate in activities? How many accepted? Why did some employees decline participation?
Intervention process explained	Has the intervention strategy been explained at each phase been outlined: In the preparation phase: Composition and justification of steering group and communication strategy. In the screening phase: Justification for screening method. Strategies in place for high quality screening, such as insurance of high response rates in surveys, time allocated to participate in screening, feedback of results. In the action planning phase: What tools are used to develop action plans? Who is involved in developing action plans? How are action plans developed (e.g., how many workshops are planned)? In the implementation phase: How is monitoring of successful implementation ensured?
Intervention process program theory	Have conditions assumed to be needed for the intervention to work been identified? Have key process and implementation mechanisms been identified? Have proximal and distal outcomes been identified? Has one or more initial CMO-configurations for the intervention process been developed?
Evaluation planning	Has an evaluation plan been developed for what data, qualitative and quantitative, to collect to test program theories? Is the evaluation plan mapped on to initial CMO-configurations? Are validated quantitative process evaluation measures used? Are validated tools tailored to the specific intervention? If tailored measures are used, are the validity and reliability of measures tested? Are qualitive process evaluation measures planned that facilitate the understanding of variations and unexpected effects?

continued

402 TRANSFORMATIVE WORK DESIGN

Table 15.1 *continued*

Pre-implementation phases (preparation and screening phases)	Assessment criteria
Context assessment	Have the contextual factors that need to be in place for the intervention to work been assessed and corrective measures taken?
Implementation phases (action planning and implementation phases)	
Action plan program theory	Have conditions assumed to be needed for the action plans to be implemented been identified? Have mechanisms of the action plans been identified? Have proximal and distal outcomes been identified? Have initial CMO-configurations been identified for all action plans?
Action planning adherence	Are the plans for action plan development followed? Are planned workshops held according to plan? How many participated? How many dropped out from intervention activities (e.g., steering group meetings and workshops)?
Amendment of evaluation plan	Has the evaluation plan been updated to include data collection specific to developed action plans? Is such data collection mapped on to initial action plan CMO-configurations?
Evidence of formative evaluation?	To what extent is process data collected during the intervention fed back to participants? Are results acted upon?
Action plan adherence	Is the plan for implementing action plans adhered to?
Process evaluation adherence	Are the implementation and process evaluation plans adhered to, i.e., are data collected as planned?
Post-implementation	
Drop out of follow-up	Is dropout analyzed? Is dropout due to participants not responding to questionnaires or due to no longer working in the intervention group?
Analysis of data	Are appropriate data analyses conducted? Isnested data considered? For example, are process evaluation quantitative measures validated and integrated into outcome analyses? Are qualitative and quantitative data collection integrated into analyses of what works for whom in which circumstances?
Refinement of CMO-configurations	Are initial CMO-configurations tested and refined? Are confounders/contextual factors integrated into analyses? Are implementation, process, and action plan CMO-configurations tested?

UNDERSTANDING THE OUTCOMES OF WORK TRANSFORMATIONS   403

Pre-implementation phases (preparation and screening phases)	Assessment criteria
Consideration of outcomes	Are multiple outcomes considered: Proximal and distal outcomes? Learning capability and meaning in organizational members? Unintended effects?
Sustainability	Are there reflections or evaluations of the long-term integration into the organization's health and safety systems, policies, practices, and procedures?

mechanisms and the context needed for successful implementation of action plans. Adherence to the implementation and evaluation strategy should be reported, together with reflections on deviations and the role formative evaluation played in making changes to the implementation and evaluation plans. Finally, in the evaluation phase, focus should be on evaluating the interaction between implementation, processes, and content of action plans and how these explain the intervention's proximal and distal outcomes, using appropriate analyses. CMO-configurations should be tested and initial CMO-configurations should be refined. Analyses of the sustainability of interventions should be included, including the long-term effects of learning capability and integration into workplace health and safety management systems.

A challenge of the framework and such comprehensive reporting is the page limits enforced by many scholarly journals, but the FigShare platform (https://figshare.com/) and similar platforms may be used to share such additional information, thus enabling researchers to gain additional insights into the design and implementation of studies, which may increase learning and ensure better quality studies in the future.

Implications for research

The FRAQOI might serve as a useful tool for researchers in their design, implementation, evaluation, and reporting of organizational interventions. Using the FRAQOI has some important implications for how we conduct our interventions.

First, the use of the FRAQOI requires thorough preparation. In the design phase, researchers should not only plan the methods and decide which tools to use but should also develop a thorough program theory for the content and the process of the intervention and how to collect appropriate data at each step to ensure evaluation can answer the question of what works for whom in which circumstances. Roodbari and colleagues (2023) developed the Integrated Realist Evaluation Model for Organizational Interventions to offer researchers guidance on how to go through all phases of realist evaluation from developing CMO-configurations over data collection to evaluation of data, considering both implementation and process factors.

Second, although the main focus of the FRAQOI is on assessing and reporting the quality of organizational interventions, as previously discussed, the data collected may also support researchers implementing interventions that have a greater chance of success. Data collected should not only be used for reporting purposes; it can also feed into the intervention process itself and be used as a formative evaluation. For example, if action plans are not implemented according to plan, then this information can be used as a feedback loop to refine action plans during the intervention itself, which may thus increase the chances of the intervention achieving its intended outcomes (von Thiele Schwarz et al., 2021).

Third, in the FRAQOI, I have suggested that one quality criterion is the integration of quantitative process and effect evaluation; however, I have not suggested how this may be done. In the few existing studies using quantitative data to test CMO-configurations, the focus has been on moderators and mediators; that is, how contextual factors influence process and how these processes influence outcomes (cf., Nielsen & Randall, 2012). I mentioned earlier that current meta-analyses on organizational interventions have not considered the context and processes of organizational interventions; however, as the evidence base grows for which contextual and process factors influence intervention outcomes, meta-analyses may explore these testing mediators and moderators of intervention outcomes. This approach has been applied in the training transfer domain where Brian Blume and colleagues (2010) found that context (individual and work environment factors) and process (quality of training delivery) influenced successful training transfer (i.e., learned skills were applied and maintained in the workplace).

A limitation of the current approach to testing CMO-configurations quantitatively is the limited numbers of variables included in analyses and the inability to determine which factors are the most important for determining the intervention's outcomes (Roczniewska et al., 2023). It may be that there are some contextual and process factors that are necessary, but not sufficient to bring about the intended outcomes, while others may be sufficient, not but necessary. Different combinations of context and process factors may interact to ensure a successful intervention outcome (Roczniewska et al., 2023). Coincidence analysis (Baumgartner & Thiem, 2015) has only received limited attention in organizational intervention evaluation, but it may shed light on difference-makers (i.e., the factors that explain an intervention's outcomes). For example, Marta Roczniewska and colleagues (2023) found that in a large multi-site intervention, participants felt the intervention was relevant to the organizational context if there were no conflicting changes (a context factor) and management was supportive of the intervention (a process factor) *or* if there had been no conflicting change (context) and the team responsible for implementing the intervention felt they understood their role, they had been able to involve other colleagues in the intervention process and they had the chance to learn from their experiences (all process factors). Coincidence analysis may thus present a way forward for testing complex CMO-configurations, determining which factors are the most important in bringing about a successful intervention outcome, while also identifying different pathways to the same result. For example, if management support is low, engaging employee representatives in implementing the intervention may be another way to ensure the intervention achieves its intended outcomes.

Implications for practice

In this chapter, I have discussed evaluation of organizational interventions which aim to transform work policies, practices, and procedures. The focus has been on what researchers need to do differently; however, this shift in intervention evaluation also has important implications for practitioners. First, when planning, developing, and implementing interventions, it is important that practitioners familiarize themselves with the recommendations for intervention design, which have been extracted from process evaluations. Although there is a scarcity of literature that provides specific recommendations, Karina Nielsen and Andrew Noblet (2018) edited a book in which they invited researchers to provide practical examples of the interventions in which they had participated, together with their practical experiences of implementation.

Second, practitioners should consider how interventions can not only lead to improvements in proximal (i.e., working conditions such as autonomy, support, role clarity) and distal outcomes (i.e., well-being outcomes such as psychological well-being job satisfaction, work engagement and burnout; Fox et al., 2021), but also consider participants' perceptions of intervention capability and how to support the development of learning capability. Despite interventions achieving improvements in proximal and distal outcomes, organizational participants may not always perceive the intervention as a success, and vice versa. Sometimes an intervention that failed to show any outcomes can be perceived as a success or meaningful by organizational participants (Briner & Walshe, 2015).

Organizational participants may perceive the intervention to be a success if it changed the culture and the way organizations manage well-being issues in the organization (Nielsen et al., 2014). Practitioners may want to establish reflection

TRANSFORMATIVE WORK DESIGN

groups that meet regularly to discuss and reflect on key learnings from the interventions and how these may be integrated into existing health and safety management policies, processes, and procedures.

Third, relating to the second point, practitioners should consider how to conduct organizational evaluation. Key questions to ask are those that can help integrate learning into health and safety management and human resource policies, processes, and procedures. Key questions to ask are about the activities implemented: what worked well and what did not work so well. Did any changes need to be made underway and why? Do participants at different levels feel the intervention activities support the identification and implementation of activities? Were changes and progress communicated in a way that made sense? Were there any unintended effects of the activities, positive as well as negative? Did the solutions work equally well for all employees? What made some activities work better than others? How was the process? Were timeframes realistic and sufficient to achieve the intended outcomes? Key here is to extract learning that ensures that work transformations to support employee well-being stay on the agenda and become part of daily business.

Conclusion

In this chapter I have argued that if we want to understand whether we truly transform organizations through our interventions, we need to rethink how we evaluate our interventions. We need to rethink what we consider good quality in interventions and move beyond the RCT as the gold standard to ask what works for whom in which circumstances, using realist evaluation as our underlying framework for evaluation. Such reframing allows us to value different intervention designs and data beyond the data collected from quantitative before and after randomized, controlled designs. This offers greater freedom in what data we collect—be it qualitative or qualitative. Collecting data on the context and the processes of interventions is key to answering the question of what works for whom in which circumstances. Such data can not only be used to evaluate the effectiveness of organizational interventions, but it may also be used to support the intervention process itself if fed back to the organization, and adequate supportive activities to ensure the intervention process is on track are available. Evaluation should not only be of benefit to researchers but also to organizations, and the development of the capability to manage adverse working conditions should be evaluated in addition to the evaluation of well-being outcomes. This shift in data collection strategies also requires us to rethink how we assess the quality of organizational interventions and how they are reported.

I have suggested the FRAQOI as a way forward to assessing organizational interventions. It is my hope that this can help us move beyond the debate of whether work transformations work or not.

References

Ackley, B. J., Swan, B. A., Ladwig, G., & Tucker, S. (2008). *Evidence-based nursing care guidelines: Medical-surgical interventions* (p. 7). Mosby Elsevier.

Aggarwal, R., & Ranganathan, P. (2019). Study designs: Part 4–Interventional studies. *Perspectives in Clinical Research 10*(3), 137–139. https://doi.org/10.4103/picr.PICR_91_19

Albertsen, K., Garde, A. H., Nabe-Nielsen, K., Hansen, Å. M., Lund, H., & Hvid, H. (2014). Work–life balance among shift workers: Results from an intervention study about self-rostering. *International Archives of Occupational and Environmental Health 87*, 265–274.

Armstrong, R., Waters, E., Moore, L., Riggs, E., Cuervo, L. G., Lumbiganon, P., & Hawe, P. (2008). Improving the reporting of public health intervention research: Advancing TREND and CONSORT. *Journal of Public Health 30*(1), 103–109. https://doi.org/10.1093/pubmed/fdm082

Aust, B., Møller, J. L., Nordentoft, M., Frydendall, K. B., Bengtsen, E., Jensen, A. B., Garde, A. H., Kompier, M., Semmer, N., Rugulies, R., & Jaspers, S. Ø. (2023). How effective are organizational-level interventions in improving the psychosocial work environment, health, and retention of workers? A systematic overview of systematic reviews. *Scandinavian Journal of Work, Environment & Health 49*(5), 315–329.

Baumgartner, M., & Thiem, A. (2015). Identifying complex causal dependencies in configurational data with coincidence analysis. *The R Journal 7*(1), 176–184. https://doi.org/10.32614/RJ-2015-014

Bin Mubayrik, H. F. (2020). New trends in formative-summative evaluations for adult education. *Sage Open 10*(3), 2158244020941006.

Biron, C., Gatrell, C., & Cooper, C. L. (2010). Autopsy of a failure: Evaluating process and contextual issues in an organizational-level work stress intervention. *International Journal of Stress Management 17*(2), 135–158. https://doi.org/10.1037/a0018772

Bouziri, H., Smith, D. R., Descatha, A., Dab, W., & Jean, K. (2020). Working from home in the time of COVID-19: How to best preserve occupational health? *Occupational and Environmental Medicine 77*(7), 509–510. http://dx.doi.org/10.1136/oemed-2020-106599

Blume, B. D., Ford, J. K., Baldwin, T. T., & Huang, J. L. (2010). Transfer of training: A meta-analytic review. *Journal of Management 36*(4), 1065–1105. https://doi.org/10.1177/0149206309352880

Briner, R. B., & Walshe, N. D. (2015). An evidence-based approach to improving the quality of resource-oriented well-being interventions at work. *Journal of Occupational and Organizational Psychology 88*(3), 563–586. https://doi.org/10.1111/joop.12133

Burgess, M. G., Brough, P., Biggs, A., & Hawkes, A. J. (2020). Why interventions fail: A systematic review of occupational health psychology interventions. *International Journal of Stress Management 27*(2), 195–207. https://doi.org/10.1037/str0000144

408   TRANSFORMATIVE WORK DESIGN

Campbell, D. T., & Stanley, J. C. (1963). *Experimental and quasi-experimental designs for research*. Rand McNally.

Cizek, G. J., Andrade, H. L., & Bennett, R. E. (2019). Formative assessment: History, definition, and progress. In H. L. Andrade, R. E. Bennett, & G. J. Cizek (Eds.), *Handbook of formative assessment in the disciplines* (pp. 3–19). Routledge.

Cook, T. D., & Campbell, D. T. (1979). *Quasi-experimentation: Design and analysis issues for field settings*. Houghton Mifflin Company.

Effective Public Health Practice Project. (2020). *Quality assessment tool for quantitative studies dictionary*. Effective Public Health Practice Project. https://merst.ca/wp-content/uploads/2018/02/quality-assessment-tool_2010.pdf

Egan, M., Bambra, C., Petticrew, M., & Whitehead, M. (2009). Reviewing evidence on complex social interventions: Appraising implementation in systematic reviews of the health effects of organisational-level workplace interventions. *Journal of Epidemiology & Community Health 63*(1), 4–11.

Fox, K. E., Johnson, S. T., Berkman, L. F., Sianoja, M., Soh, Y., Kubzansky, L. D., & Kelly, E. L. (2021). Organisational-and group-level workplace interventions and their effect on multiple domains of worker well-being: A systematic review. *Work & Stress, Work & Stress 33*(1), 30–59. https://doi.org/10.1080/02678373.2021.1969476

Framke, E., & Sørensen, O. H. (2015). Implementation of a participatory organisational-level occupational health intervention-focusing on the primary task. *International Journal of Human Factors and Ergonomics 3*(3–4), 254–270.

Framke, E., Sørensen, O. H., Pedersen, J., & Ruglies, R. (2016). Effect of a participatory organizational-level occupational health intervention on short-term sickness absence: A cluster randomized controlled trial. *Scandinavian Journal of Work, Environment & Health 42*(3), 192–200.

French, C., Dowrick, A., Fudge, N., Pinnock, H., & Taylor, S. J. (2022). What do we want to get out of this? A critical interpretive synthesis of the value of process evaluations, with a practical planning framework. *BMC Medical Research Methodology 22*(1), 1–22.

Glasgow, R. E., Harden, S. M., Gaglio, B., Rabin, B., Smith, M. L., Porter, G. C., Ory, M. G., & Estabrooks, P. A. (2019). RE-AIM planning and evaluation framework: Adapting to new science and practice with a 20-year review. *Frontiers in Public Health 7*, 64.

Greenhalgh, T., Wong, G., Jagosh, J., Greenhalgh, J., Manzano, A., Westhorp, G., & Pawson, R. (2015). Protocol—the RAMESES II study: Developing guidance and reporting standards for realist evaluation. *BMJ Open 5*(8), e008567.

Goodridge, D., Westhorp, G., Rotter, T., Dobson, R., & Bath, B. (2015). Lean and leadership practices: Development of an initial realist program theory. *BMC Health Services Research 15*(1), 1–15. https://doi.org/10.1186/s12913-015-1030-x

Havermans, B. M., Schelvis, R. M., Boot, C. R., Brouwers, E. P., Anema, J. R., & van der Beek, A. J. (2016). Process variables in organizational stress management intervention evaluation research: A systematic review. *Scandinavian Journal of Work, Environment & Health 42*, 371–381.

Moore, G. F., Audrey, S., Barker, M., Bond, L., Bonell, C., Hardeman, W., Moore, L., O'Cathain, A., Tinati, T., Wight, D., & Baird, J. (2015). Process evaluation of complex interventions: Medical Research Council guidance. *British Medical Journal 350*, h1258.

Morawa, E., Schug, C., Geiser, F., Beschoner, P., Jerg-Bretzke, L., Albus, C., Weidner, K., Hiebel, N., Borho, A., & Erim, Y. (2021). Psychosocial burden and working conditions during the COVID-19 pandemic in Germany: The VOICE survey among 3678 health care workers in hospitals. *Journal of Psychosomatic Research 144*, 110415.

Nabe-Nielsen, K., Persson, R., Nielsen, K., Olsen, O., Carneiro, I. G., & Garde, A. H. (2015). Perspectives on randomization and readiness for change in a workplace intervention study. In M. Karanika-Murray & C. Biron (Eds.), *Derailed organizational interventions for stress and well-being: Confessions of failure and solutions for success* (pp. 201–208). Springer.

Newcomer, K. E., Hatry, H. P., & Wholey, J. S. (Eds.). (2015). *Handbook of practical program evaluation* (pp. 5–29) Jossey-Bass & Pfeiffer Imprints, Wiley.

Nielsen, K. (2013). How can we make organizational interventions work? Employees and line managers as actively crafting interventions. *Human Relations 66*(8), 1029–1050. https://doi.org/10.1177/0018726713477164

Nielsen, K. (2017). Leaders can make or break an intervention—but are they the villains of the play? In K. Kelloway, K. Nielsen, & J. Dimoff (Eds.), *Leading to occupational health and safety: How leadership behaviours impact organizational safety and well-being* (pp. 197–210). Wiley.

Nielsen, K. (2022, 21 December). Organizational interventions. In *The Oxford research encyclopedia of psychology.* https://oxfordre.com/psychology/view/10.1093/acrefore/9780190236557.001.0001/acrefore-9780190236557-e-109

Nielsen, K. (2023). Improving employee well-being through improving working conditions: A review on how we can make participatory organizational interventions work. In L. E. Tetrick, G. G. Fisher, M. T. Ford, & J. C. Quick (Eds.), *Handbook of occupational health psychology* (3rd ed., pp. 449-466). APA.

Nielsen, K., & Abildgaard, J. S. (2013). Organizational interventions: A research-based framework for the evaluation of both process and effects. *Work & Stress 27*, 278–297. https://doi.org/10.1080/02678373.2013.812358

Nielsen, K., Axtell, C., & Sorensen, G. (2021). Organizational interventions: Fitting the intervention to the context to ensure the participatory process. In E. K. Kelloway & C. Cooper (Eds.), *A research agenda for workplace stress and wellbeing* (pp. 191–210). Edward Elgar Publishing.

Nielsen, K., & Brough, P. (2023). The tricky issue of worker participation in organizational interventions within occupational health psychology. In N. De Cuyper, E. Selenko, M. Euwema & W. Schaufeli (Eds.), *Facts and fables in work psychology: A critical interrogation and future proofing of job insecurity, precarious employment, and burnout* (pp. 195–215). Edward Elgar Publishing.

Nielsen, K., De Angelis, M., Innstrand, S. T., & Mazzetti, G. (2023). Quantitative process measures in interventions to improve employees' mental health: a systematic literature review and the IPEF framework. *Work & Stress 37*(1), 1–26, https://doi.org/10.1080/02678373.2022.2080775

Nielsen, K., Di Tecco, C., Yarker, J., & Vignoli, M. (2024). An integrated approach to managing wellbeing in the workplace. In P. Brough and G. Kinman (Eds.), *Wellbeing at work in a turbulent era* (pp. 240–259). Edward Elgar.

Nielsen, K., Fredslund, H., Christensen, K. B., & Albertsen, K. (2006). Success or failure? Interpreting and understanding the impact of interventions. *Work & Stress 20*(3), 272–287.

Nielsen, K., Jorgensen, M. B., Milczarek, M., & Munar, L. (2018). *Healthy workers, thriving companies—A practical guide to wellbeing at work tackling psychosocial risks*

410 TRANSFORMATIVE WORK DESIGN

and musculoskeletal disorders in small businesses. European Agency for Occupational Safety and Health at Work.

Nielsen, K., & Miraglia, M. (2017). Critical essay: What works for whom in which circumstances? On the need to move beyond the "what works?" question in organizational intervention. *Human Relations 70*(1), 40–62. https://doi.org/10.1177/0018726716670226

Nielsen, K., Nielsen, M. B., Ogbonnaya, C., Känsälä, M., Saari, E., & Isaksson, K. (2017). Workplace resources to improve both employee well-being and performance: A systematic review and meta-analysis. *Work & Stress 31*(2), 101–120.

Nielsen, K., & Randall, R. (2012). The importance of employee participation and perception of changes in procedures in a teamworking intervention. *Work & Stress 26*, 91–111. https://doi.org/10.1080/02678373.2012.682721

Nielsen, K., & Randall, R. (2015). Addressing the fit of planned interventions to the organizational context. In M. Karanika-Murray & C. Biron (Eds.), *Derailed organizational stress and well-being interventions: Confessions of failure and solutions for success* (pp. 107–118). Springer.

Nielsen, K., Randall, R., & Christensen, K. B. (2010a). Developing new ways of evaluating organizational-level interventions. In J. Houdmont & S. Leka (Eds.), *Contemporary occupational health psychology: Global perspectives on research and practice (2010–2011)* (pp. 21–45). Wiley-Blackwell.

Nielsen, K., Randall, R., & Christensen, K. B. (2010b). Does training managers enhance the effects of implementing team-working? A longitudinal, mixed methods field study. *Human Relations 63*(11), 1719–1741. https://doi.org/10.1177/0018726710365004

Nielsen, K., Abildgaard, J. S., & Daniels, K. (2014). Putting context into organizational intervention design: Using tailored questionnaires to measure initiatives for worker well-being. *Human Relations 67*(12), 1537–1560.

Nielsen, K., & Noblet, A. (2018). Introduction: Organizational interventions: Where we are, where we go from here?. In *Organizational Interventions for Health and Well-being* (pp. 1–21). Routledge.

Nielsen, K., & Shepherd, R. (2022). Understanding the outcomes of training to improve employee mental health: A novel framework for training transfer and effectiveness evaluation. *Work & Stress* 36(4), 377–391. https://doi.org/10.1080/02678373.2022.2028318

Nytrø, K., Saksvik, P. Ø., Mikkelsen, A., Bohle, P., & Quinlan, M. (2000). An appraisal of key factors in the implementation of occupational stress interventions. *Work & Stress 14*, 213225. https://doi.org/10.1080/02678370010024749

O'Shea, D., O'Connell, B. H., & Gallagher, S. (2016). Randomised controlled trials in WOHP interventions: A review and guidelines for use. *Applied Psychology 65*(2), 190–222. https://doi.org/10.1111/apps.12053

Pawson, R. (2013). *The science of evaluation: A realist manifesto.* SAGE.

Pawson, R., & Tilley, N. (1997). *Realistic evaluation.* SAGE.

Randall, R., Griffiths, A., & Cox, T. (2005). Evaluating organizational stress-management interventions using adapted study designs. *European Journal of Work and Organizational Psychology 14*(1), 23–41. doi.org/10.1080/13594320444000209

Randall, R., Nielsen, K., & Tvedt, S. D. (2009). The development of five scales to measure employees' appraisals of organizational-level stress management interventions. *Work & Stress 23*(1), 1–23.

Richardson, K. M., & Rothstein, H. R. (2008). Effects of occupational stress management intervention programs: a meta-analysis. *Journal of Occupational Health Psychology 13*(1), 69–93. https://doi.org/10.1037/1076-8998.13.1.69

Roczniewska, M., Tafvelin, S., Nielsen, K., von Thiele Schwarz, U., Miech, E. J., Hasson, H., Edwards, K., Abildgaard, J. S., & Sørensen, S. H. (2023). Simple roads to failure, complex paths to success: An evaluation of conditions explaining perceived fit of an organizational occupational health intervention. *Applied Psychology: An International Review 73*(3), 1103–1130. https://doi:10.1111/apps.12502

Roodbari, H., Axtell, C., Nielsen, K., & Sorensen, G. (2021a). Organisational interventions to improve employees' health and wellbeing: A realist synthesis. *Applied Psychology 71*(3), 1–24. https://doi.org/10.1111/apps.12346

Roodbari, H., Nielsen, K., Axtell, C., Peters, S., & Sorensen, G. (2021b). Developing initial middle range theories in realist evaluation: A case of an organisational intervention. *International Journal of Environmental Research and Public Health 18*(16), 8360. http://doi.org/10.3390/ijerph18168360.

Roodbari, H., Nielsen, K., & Axtell, C. (2023). What works for whom in which circumstances? An integrated realist evaluation model for organisational interventions. *Scandinavian Journal of Work and Organizational Psychology 8*, article 4.

Roodbari, H., Nielsen, K., Axtell, C., Peters, S. E., & Sorensen, G. (2022). Testing middle range theories in realist evaluation: A case of a participatory organisational intervention. *International Journal of Workplace Health Management 15*(6), 694–710. https://doi.org/10.1108/IJWHM-12-2021-0219.

Shaugnessy, J. J., Zechmeister, E. B., & Zechmeister, J. S. (2012). *Research methods in psychology*. 9th ed. McGraw-Hill.

Sorensen, G., Peters, S., Nielsen, K., Stelson, E., Wallace, L., Burke, L., Nagler, E., Roodbari, H., Karapanos, M., & Wagner, G. (2021). Implementation of an organizational intervention to improve low-wage food service workers' safety, health and wellbeing: Findings from the Workplace Organizational Health Study. *BMC Public Health 21*, 1869. https://doi.org/10.1186/s12889-021-11937-9

Thomas, B. H., Ciliska, D., Dobbins, M., & Micucci, S. (2004). A process for systematically reviewing the literature: Providing the research evidence for public health nursing interventions. *Worldviews on Evidence-Based Nursing 1*(3), 176–184. https://doi.org/10.1111/j.1524-475X.2004.04006.x

Thorsen, S. V., Madsen, I. E. H., Flyvholm, M. A., & Hasle, P. (2017). Associations between the workplace-effort in psychosocial risk management and the employee-rating of the psychosocial work environment–a multilevel study of 7565 employees in 1013 workplaces. *Scandinavian Journal of Public Health 45*(5), 463–467. https://doi.org/10.1177/1403494817696377

Van der Klink, J. J., Blonk, R. W., Schene, A. H., & Van Dijk, F. J. (2001). The benefits of interventions for work-related stress. *American Journal of Public Health*, 91(2), 270–276. doi:10.2105/ajph.91.2.270

von Thiele Schwarz, U., Nielsen, K., Edwards, K., Hasson, H., Ipsen, C., Savage, C., Abildgaard, J. S., Richter, A., Lornudd, C., Mazzocato, P., & Reed, J. E. (2021). How

412 TRANSFORMATIVE WORK DESIGN

to design, implement and evaluate organizational interventions for maximum impact: The Sigtuna Principles. *European Journal of Work and Organizational Psychology* *30*(3), 415–427.

World Health Organization. (2022). *WHO guidelines on mental health at work.* World Health Organization.

World Health Organization. (2004). *A practical guide for health researchers.* World Health Organization Regional Office for the Eastern Mediterranean.

PART 5

BOTTOM-UP WORK REDESIGN

Job Crafting Theory and Perspectives

Maria Tims and Melissa Twemlow

Alongside the continuous focus on top-down work redesign interventions initiated by organizations to improve their employees' motivation and performance (Grant et al., 2010), individuals are also increasingly encouraged to self-improve the design of their jobs (Grant & Parker, 2009). The burgeoning need for employees to consider their tasks and roles more flexibly remains evident in light of ongoing workplace developments, including increased complexity, uncertainty, diversity, and technological advancements. Regarded as a highly effective bottom-up approach to work redesign, these self-initiated behaviors that employees take to actively shape their jobs have been referred to as job crafting (Tims & Bakker, 2010; Wrzesniewski & Dutton, 2001). Besides individually, team members can also collectively, and often spontaneously (Iida et al., 2021), craft their work. Team crafting enables team members to better achieve team goals and objectives (Leana et al., 2009), while at the same time improving their own work engagement (Llorente-Alonso & Topa, 2019). By initiating changes to their tasks and roles, employees and teams can create a better balance between their job demands and resources, thereby making their work more engaging and meaningful, and perform better (Rudolph et al., 2017).

In this chapter, we aim to make three contributions to the (team) job crafting literature. The first is to organize current theories and perspectives on job crafting as multiple attempts have been made to revise job crafting definitions in the past five years. This resulted in diverse terminology, such as promotion and prevention job crafting (Lichtenthaler & Fischbach, 2018), role-based and resource-based approach and avoidance job crafting (Bruning & Campion, 2018), and approach and avoidance crafting (Zhang & Parker, 2019). Building on Amy Wrzesniewski and Jane Dutton's (2001) task, relational, and/or cognitive crafting, and Maria Tims and Arnold B. Bakker's (2010) crafting of job demands and/or resources, these scholars either combined (Lichtenthaler & Fischbach, 2018), reorganized and redefined (Bruning & Campion, 2018), or integrated them into a hierarchical structure (Zhang & Parker, 2019). We also discuss the social perspective that has been recently introduced in job crafting research.

Maria Tims and Melissa Twemlow, *Job Crafting Theory and Perspectives*. In: *Transformative Work Design*. Edited by: Sharon K. Parker et al., Oxford University Press. © Society for Industrial and Organizational Psychology (2025). DOI: 10.1093/oso/9780197692554.003.0016

416   TRANSFORMATIVE WORK DESIGN

The second aim of this chapter is to examine the generalizability of job crafting. The main assumption is that everybody can craft their jobs, irrespective of the type of job, role, and organizational context (Tims & Bakker, 2010; Wrzesniewski & Dutton, 2001) and that its consequences are similarly beneficial to all. In line with this premise, job crafting research has provided evidence for its positive outcomes, with findings covering employees from various sectors, mostly including manufacturing (Solberg & Wong, 2016), healthcare (Renkema et al., 2023), and education (Dubbelt et al., 2019), and from a wide range of professions, ranging from physicians (van Leeuwen et al., 2021) to offshore professionals (Mattarelli & Tagliaventi, 2015). While job crafting has been shown to benefit employees and teams over the world, research has neglected to consider how the work context in each sector impacts these findings. For instance, can we assume that decreasing hindering job demands has negative outcomes for all types of work design or might this mostly be beneficial to those working in healthcare? And can we posit that job crafting is positively related to work engagement for a wide range of workers, or do we need to be more specific for whom this effect might hold? In other words, research thus far has not yet differentiated between the features defining their sample's work context and the motives and/or outcomes of their job crafting efforts. Therefore, in this chapter, we focus on the role that three prominent sectors in the literature (i.e., healthcare, education, and manufacturing) have on job crafting by individuals and teams. Lastly, we also aim to contribute by reviewing which specific job crafting antecedents, mechanisms, and outcomes have been studied in these sectors so far.

Job Crafting Theories and Perspectives

Employees are increasingly encouraged to proactively take control of changing themselves or their workplace (Parker et al., 2010). Proactive behaviors are self-starting, change-oriented, and future-focused within the context of work (Parker et al., 2006). Job crafting is considered a salient type of proactive behavior, whereby the primary focus is on actively changing one's job (Tims et al., 2012; Wrzesniewski & Dutton, 2001). The changes that job crafters make to their work conditions do not require formal negotiations with supervisors. Furthermore, job crafting differentiates itself from other proactive behaviors because it is a standalone behavior that enables individuals to pursue more motivating jobs without necessarily improving the work organization or others. Thus, employees can engage in crafting their jobs without being active participants in a work redesign intervention of their organization (Nadin et al., 2001).

The considerable empirical attention that the job crafting literature has received so far is mostly built on either of the following two different conceptual underpinnings: job crafting as the cognitive, task, and relational alterations to one's job (Wrzesniewski & Dutton, 2001), and Tims and Bakker's (2010) conceptualization of job crafting from the perspective of the Job Demands-Resources (JD-R) theory (Bakker & Demerouti, 2007). We will review these next and then examine the efforts to integrate these different streams of job crafting research.

Wrzesniewski and Dutton (2001) argued that employees undertake actions that shape their work tasks and relationships. These actions can refer to physical and/or cognitive changes that workers make in their tasks (e.g., increasing the number of tasks or thinking differently about a task) and/or the relationships at work (e.g., influencing the number and strength of relationships at work). Job crafting continuously takes place within the defined job, resulting in individuals experiencing a change in the job, the meaning of the job, and their identity (Wrzesniewski & Dutton, 2001). Further studies into physical and cognitive crafting of tasks and relationships have highlighted specific challenges and adaptive moves that surround job crafters (Berg et al., 2010) and have provided evidence that a perceived identity threat could result in individual and team crafting behaviors (Mattarelli & Tagliaventi, 2015). Also, job crafting efforts are associated positively with self-image (Lyons, 2008) and the need for both a positive self-image and human connection predicted job crafting (Niessen et al., 2016). Moreover, these crafting behaviors—assessed with different measures—are associated positively with organizational citizenship behaviors and job satisfaction (Slemp & Vella-Brodrick, 2013), organizational commitment (Leana et al., 2009), and engagement and productivity (Vogel et al., 2016).

Alternatively, Tims and Bakker (2010) have argued that job crafting might be best captured by focusing on the job demands and resources that a worker changes because this is also how work design is generally studied. As suggested by JD-R theory (Bakker et al., 2023; Demerouti et al., 2001), job demands refer to aspects of the work environment that require physical or psychological effort. Prolonged exposure to high job demands has been associated with negative health and performance outcomes (Aronsson et al., 2017). Job resources are aspects of the work environment that help workers achieve their work tasks, develop themselves, and have the ability to reduce or buffer the costs of high job demands (Bakker et al., 2005). Placing job crafting within this theoretical perspective on work design, it has been defined as reducing hindering job demands (e.g., cognitive or emotional job demands), increasing challenging job demands (e.g., job complexity), increasing structural job resources (e.g., autonomy or variety), and increasing social job resources (e.g., social support; Tims et al., 2012).

Meta-analyses (Lichtenthaler & Fischbach, 2019; Rudolph et al., 2017) found that most studies in their dataset used the JD-R job crafting approach and have showcased that, among others, proactive personality (Bakker et al., 2012),

418   TRANSFORMATIVE WORK DESIGN

self-efficacy (Tims et al., 2014), and trait promotion focus (Lichtenthaler & Fischbach, 2016) are associated positively with crafting job resources and challenging job demands, while prevention focus is related positively with decreasing hindering job demands. Often-studied outcomes included work-related well-being, such as work engagement and burnout, in-role and extra-role performance, and turnover intentions, in which increasing job resources and challenging job demands were associated positively with work engagement and in-role and extra-role performance and negatively with burnout and turnover intentions, whereas decreasing hindering job demands associated positively with burnout (Lichtenthaler & Fischbach, 2019) and turnover intentions (Rudolph et al., 2017).

Efforts to integrate job crafting perspectives

Interestingly, several articles emerged that attempted to integrate the two dominant job crafting perspectives advanced by Wrzesniewski and Dutton (2001) and Tims and Bakker (2010). These articles (to be discussed in chronological order: Lichtenthaler & Fischbach, 2016, 2019; Bruning & Campion, 2018; Zhang & Parker, 2019) recognized similarities and differences between the two approaches. Concerning their similarities, job crafting refers to proactive, self-initiated changes at work that are intended to improve the experience of work for the employee; the idea that job crafters can obtain more or fewer work characteristics; and that it takes place within the boundaries of the defined job, thereby not requiring formal approval and excluding those without a predefined job (e.g., entrepreneurs). However, differences are also acknowledged. The most obvious differences are that Wrzesniewski and Dutton (2001) refer to physical and cognitive crafting of tasks and/or relationships, whereas Tims and Bakker (2010) distinguish between crafting job demands and job resources, and that the former authors included a cognitive element in their definition of job crafting, whereas the latter authors did not.

The offered integrative solutions suggested organizing the job crafting dimensions under a higher-level theoretical framework. First, drawing on regulatory focus theory (Higgins, 1997) that distinguishes between promotion (i.e., striving for growth, development, and maximizing positive outcomes) and prevention (i.e., striving for safety, security and aim to minimize negative outcomes) focus, it has been proposed that particularly a promotion focus would spur job crafting behaviors (Tims & Bakker, 2010). A cross-sectional study by Veerle Brenninkmeijer and Marleen Hekkert-Koning (2015) indeed supported that promotion focus was associated with increasing job resources and challenging job demands, although not with decreasing hindering job demands. Instead, a prevention focus related positively to decreasing hindering job demands and was unrelated to the other job crafting dimensions. These different associations for promotion and prevention motivations to different forms of job crafting were also found by Paraskevas Petrou and Evangelia Demerouti (2015).

Building on these studies, and aiming to integrate the two job crafting approaches, Phillipp Lichtenthaler and Andrea Fischbach (2016, 2019) labeled increasing job resources and challenging job demands, and expansion-oriented task, relational, and cognitive crafting as promotion-focused job crafting; and decreasing hindering job demands and contraction-oriented task and relational crafting as prevention-focused job crafting. The authors argued that both dominant conceptualizations consider job crafting predominantly from a promotion perspective, whereas perceiving contraction forms of job crafting as prevention-oriented may help explain the unexpected negative relationships between these job crafting forms and outcomes. Based on a meta-analysis of 149 independent samples including 46,780 employees, Lichtenthaler and Fischbach (2019) concluded that promotion-focused crafting represents a gain spiral that has a positive reciprocal relationship with work engagement and a negative reciprocal relationship with burnout. Prevention-focused crafting follows the pattern of loss cycles: it was positively reciprocally related to burnout and negatively related to work engagement at Time 2 (not reciprocally). Hereby, the authors advanced the motivational perspective that regulatory focus helps to integrate job crafting behaviors and to better predict their associated outcomes.

The other two papers aiming to integrate the job crafting literature draw on approach and avoidance motivation, which is highly similar to regulatory focus. Patrick Bruning and Michael Campion (2018) seem to equate the two theories, whereas Fangfang Zhang and Sharon K. Parker (2019, p. 129) argued that approach-avoidance motivation theory (Elliot, 2006) represents a more "systemic" theory as it can influence one's regulatory focus (Scholer & Higgins, 2008). Bruning and Campion (2018) propose a role-resource approach-avoidance model of job crafting in which the role-based aspect refers to Wrzesniewski and Dutton's (2001) job crafting approach and the resource-based aspect refers to Tims and Bakker's (2010) perspective on job crafting. However, we agree with Zhang and Parker (2019), who argued that the differences between the two job crafting approaches are not as black-and-white as Bruning and Campion (2018) suggested when looking at the shared overlap in motivations and outcomes that are theorized and studied, and even between items proposed to study role or resource crafting.

In their integration effort, Zhang and Parker (2019) propose a hierarchical structure to capture job crafting, with at its highest level approach and avoidance crafting orientations that represent whether employees pursue crafting that moves toward positive end-states or away from negative end-states, respectively.

420   TRANSFORMATIVE WORK DESIGN

The second level focuses on the job crafting form, which includes behavioral and cognitive crafting. Finally, the third level represents the job crafting content, which measures what is being changed, and these authors propose focusing on job resources or job demands here. According to Zhang and Parker (2019), it is at this lowest level, job crafting content, that the differences between the two job crafting approaches become apparent, whereby the hierarchical structure may help to also see their similarities. The hierarchical structure results in eight possible ways to craft one's job (e.g., avoidance behavioral demands crafting) and may be able to capture new job crafting constructs through further distinguishing new job crafting forms (e.g., approach cognitive resources crafting). Throughout this chapter, we refer to these eight distinct job crafting constructs and alternatively use the term "approach-avoidance behavioral crafting" when a composite (and inseparable) score of (team) approach and avoidance crafting was reported.

Placing job crafting within a social perspective

Whereas the discussion so far focused on integrating job crafting at the employee level, an increasing number of scholars have emphasized the role of others when crafting one's job. Moving beyond individual and team crafting, we now see an increasing number of studies that focus on the impact of approach and avoidance crafting on others in their work context (Tims & Parker, 2020). This impact can be direct (e.g., asking a coworker for help to increase one's resources) or indirect (e.g., observing a coworker asking another person for help to increase their resources). Lotta Harju and colleagues (2023), for instance, found that contact with and impact on other people shaped the way jobs are crafted (see also Bizzi, 2017). However, most studies to date have focused on how others react to observing the job crafting of their colleagues. For example, Christine Fong and colleagues (2022) showed that colleague-observed approach behavioral resources and demands crafting was associated with an increase in their willingness to cooperate with the job crafter and a decrease in expected conflict with the job crafter. The opposite results were found when the colleague observed avoidance behavioral demands crafting. Importantly, these reactions were determined by their perceived contribution to the crafted change; if colleagues perceived the change to contribute to their work, they responded with a higher willingness to cooperate and expected less conflict with the job crafter. In another study, Fong and colleagues (2021) focused on supervisor reactions to the observed avoidance behavioral demands crafting of their employees and found that supervisors decreased their support for these crafters because they perceived these job crafting behaviors to be destructive.

Gwendolyn Watson and Robert Sinclair (2022) reported that approach behavioral resource crafting was associated with higher levels of coworker—but not supervisor—support over time. Similarly, Danina Mainka and Stefan Suß (2023) found positive coworker evaluations for approach and negative evaluations for avoidance behavioral resource crafting, while also showing that the relationship between avoidance behavioral resource crafting and a negative coworker evaluation was stronger when resources were perceived to be infinite. Finally, using relative deprivation theory, Yanan Dong and colleagues (2023) found that coworkers' job crafting (a composite job crafting score excluding the focal employee's score) resulted in feelings of relative deprivations compared to similar others, which, in turn, caused them to undermine their coworkers and show less prosocial behaviors to them. To summarize, the impact of job crafting goes further than just the job crafter, so it is important to take into account the social context in which the crafting takes place (Tims & Parker, 2020). Currently, we conclude that approach (avoidance) behavioral crafting is likely to be considered more (less) favorable by coworkers in an interdependent work context. In what follows, we elaborate on how the integrative perspective on job crafting has been studied in specific work contexts.

Job Crafting in Different Work Contexts

To identify the work contexts most often studied, we coded all samples from the reference list of a recent state-of-the-art job crafting paper covering studies from 2017 to 2021 (Tims et al., 2022). Afterward, we extended this coding for publications from an additional search once we identified the top three sectors (i.e., articles published before 2017 and after 2021). As a result, we focus here on three major sectors in which many job crafting studies have taken place: healthcare, education, and manufacturing.

Job crafting in healthcare

The majority of job crafting research has been conducted among employees working in the healthcare sector encompassing a wide range of professions, such as nurses in elderly care (Audenaert et al., 2020) or hospitals (Pan et al., 2021), physicians (Renkema et al., 2023), doctors (Hu et al., 2019), and dentists (Hakanen et al., 2018). While these jobs cannot fully be generalized, some elements characterize working in healthcare. First, healthcare professionals rely on social support, from coworkers, patients, and the organization, as their jobs are considered to be highly emotionally demanding (De Jonge et al.,

2008), generally with inadequate work infrastructures, personal recognition, or decision-making latitude (Evans et al., 2006). This close coordination and shared decision-making between coworkers occurs frequently under severe time pressure (Klainin, 2009). In addition, healthcare professionals often have low control over tasks (e.g., many interruptions; Burnard et al., 2000) and scheduling of their work (e.g., long and rotating shift work; Ganesan et al., 2019), which increases stress and emotional exhaustion (Evans et al., 2006). Nevertheless, healthcare workers have meaningful work and tasks with high significance, which some consider a calling.

To date, many scholars have confirmed that approach job crafting can result in higher levels of work engagement (e.g., Bakker et al., 2016), which is also found among samples of healthcare employees (e.g., Saudi Arabian nurses; Baghdadi et al., 2021). Furthermore, approach job crafting is positively related to quality of care (Yepes-Baldó et al., 2018), whereby especially approach behavioral resources crafting was positively related to person-organization fit (Bakker, 2017) and task and creative performance of healthcare professionals (Gordon et al., 2015). Anne Mäkikangas (2018) studied Finnish rehabilitation employees and revealed that more "active" job crafters—those who simultaneously used multiple crafting strategies—reported higher levels of day-specific work engagement than "passive" crafters. Hereby, avoidance crafting was less detrimental to work engagement when "active" crafters combined it with approach crafting. Possibly the sample's many years of work experience allowed them to better adapt their crafting efforts to their personal work contexts, in which approach crafting compensated for the potentially negative effects of avoidance crafting. Reversing the relationship, following Finnish dentists for four years, work engagement was found to positively predict approach crafting and negatively predict avoidance crafting over time (Hakanen et al., 2018).

In two job crafting interventions, Heather Gordon and colleagues (2018) trained medical specialists and nurses to optimize their work environment. For the medical specialists, the job crafting intervention focused on effective teamwork and the quality of care. The experimental group attended a job crafting workshop and formulated a personal crafting plan after the workshop. Compared with the control group that did not yet receive the workshop, the intervention group scored higher on well-being and (task, adaptive, and contextual) performance after the intervention compared to the control group when they engaged in approach behavioral demands crafting. The intervention for the nurses was different in that it focused on specific personal crafting plans for specific weeks (e.g., approach behavioral resources crafting in weeks 1 and 3; avoidance behavioral demands crafting in week 2). The nurses who participated in the intervention reported more approach behavioral resources crafting compared to the control group at the follow-up. For both professions, avoidance behavioral demands crafting negatively influenced their work engagement and increased exhaustion. In short, for the medical specialists, approach behavioral demands crafting was important for their work engagement and performance, while for the nurses this was approach behavioral resources crafting.

Also, an intervention to boost the job crafting behaviors of Dutch physicians was conducted, whereby the intervention group received a two-hour job crafting group training and an individual coaching call (Van Leeuwen et al., 2021). Eight weeks after the pre-test and compared to the waiting list control group, the intervention group only reported an increase in avoidance behavioral demands crafting, not in approach forms of crafting. The authors proposed that this might be explained by the rationale that physicians already have interesting work, although they are often frustrated with hindering job demands. Renkema and colleagues (2023) also warned that specific work contexts, such as those of physicians, should be considered more seriously when studying job crafting as they can have negative consequences. Specifically, drawing from interviews with Dutch physicians, those authors found that the perceived pressure of being held accountable combined with their personal interests triggered and motivated them to engage in self-serving (approach and avoidance) crafting.

Lastly, leadership plays a substantial role in job crafting studies in the healthcare context. Among medical staff members of a Chinese hospital, He Ding and colleagues (2020) revealed that approach crafting mediated the relationship between humble leadership and organizational citizenship behavior. Also, leaders who empower employees can stimulate approach crafting, as was found by Mieke Audenaert and colleagues (2020) among Belgian elderly care nurses. Especially when empowering leadership was combined with receiving social support from coworkers, employees' approach behavioral demands crafting was stimulated.

As many healthcare employees work in interdependent teams, scholars have also focused on team crafting. In 2013, Tims and colleagues revealed that, at both the individual and team level, approach crafting was related to job performance via work engagement for Dutch teams providing occupational health services. Qiao Hu and colleagues (2019) also demonstrated that both individual and team approach crafting were positively associated with the individual work engagement of medical professionals from a Chinese hospital. Comparably, Tuan Luu (2017) showed that team work engagement mediated the positive relationship between team approach-avoidance behavioral crafting and team service recovery performance. Hereby, service culture moderated this first relationship, highlighting that team crafting encouraged Vietnamese physicians and nurses to better serve their patient's needs. Besides work engagement, team

424 TRANSFORMATIVE WORK DESIGN

approach crafting could also improve hospital wards' job satisfaction, workplace social capital, and reduce psychological distress, as strong correlations were found by Mako Iida and colleagues (2021) among Japanese nurses.

Leaders could play a vital role in keeping healthcare teams satisfied. According to JiaLiang Pan and colleagues (2021), Chinese hospital nurses reported that their leaders provided them access to resources that the team needed to collectively craft their jobs, which in turn, enabled their job satisfaction. In line with this, Mäkikangas and colleagues (2017) revealed that connecting leaders, encouraging interpersonal bonding, could stimulate Finnish rehabilitation teams to engage in team approach-avoidance crafting. Moreover, the authors deemed self-efficacy for teamwork, positive individual affect, and an innovative team climate to be crucial daily antecedents of team crafting (Mäkikangas et al., 2017).

In sum, research reveals that engaging in approach behavioral resources crafting improves person–job fit, performance, and work engagement of healthcare professionals, notably more for active crafters and after interventions. Contrarily, avoidance behavioral demands crafting increased exhaustion and lowered their work engagement, unless healthcare workers received coworker support, empowering leadership, or combined it with approach-oriented crafting.

Job crafting in education

Job crafting research also covers a wide range of teachers, lecturers, and supportive educational staff, ranging from those working at pre-schools (Leana et al., 2009), primary schools (van Wingerden et al., 2017), secondary schools (Alonso et al., 2019), special education schools (Ghitulescu, 2007), and universities (Kooij et al., 2017a). Teaching is a cognitively and emotionally demanding job: teachers reported exceptionally high levels of emotional exhaustion, which arise from frequent negative social interactions with students and parents criticizing or even verbally abusing them, and conflicts with coworkers (Feuerhahn et al., 2013). Moreover, cognitively demanding aspects of their work are the excessive demands under time pressure and classroom disruptions (Hakanen et al., 2006), and the need for broad skill sets and knowledge (Ghitulescu, 2007). Nevertheless, the majority are enthusiastic about their work and find it intrinsically rewarding through the interactions with and achievements of students (Woods, 1999).

Job crafting studies highlight that educational professionals engage in approach resources crafting behaviors (e.g., van Wingerden & Poell, 2019), for example, to acquire new skills or ask coworkers for help (Vangrieken et al., 2015). Yet, the way work in the education sector is organized has a critical impact on the type of job crafting and their motives. For instance, work discretion and task interdependence were positively associated with special education teachers' approach behavioral and cognitive crafting (Ghitulescu, 2007), whereby the former type of crafting was more prominent when work was more collaborative. Furthermore, organizational identification appeared to promote approach behavioral crafting among teachers, which in turn was positively related to their creativity and organizational citizenship behavior (Lin et al., 2017). In particular, a favorable psychosocial school climate for teachers combined with approach-avoidance behavioral crafting positively predicted well-being among German teachers (Dreer, 2022). Lastly, perceived organizational support was a crucial contextual mediating factor in the relationship between approach-avoidance behavioral crafting and job satisfaction among Italian school teachers (Ingusci et al., 2016).

Thus far, scholars have found considerable support for the positive effects of approach-avoidance behavioral crafting on performance and work engagement for educational professionals. For instance, among Chinese school teachers, approach-avoidance behavioral crafting mediated the relationship between satisfying basic psychological needs and cultivating student creativity (Huang et al., 2022). In another comparable sample, Weiwei Shang (2022) found that the positive association between approach-avoidance behavioral crafting and job performance was mediated by both work meaning and engagement.

Alongside performance, approach-avoidance behavioral crafting positively predicted the work engagement and commitment of Nigerian university lecturers, consequently predicting job satisfaction (Ogbuanya & Chukwuedo, 2017). Work engagement was also fostered by approach-avoidance behavioral crafting among South African high school teachers, whereby psychological meaningfulness mediated this relationship (Peral & Geldenhuys, 2016). Similarly, Indonesian preschool and primary school teachers experienced higher work engagement when they engaged in approach-avoidance behavioral crafting, which was stimulated by their demanding, autonomous work environment and perceived organizational support (Saragih et al., 2020). However, adopting a self-regulation perspective, Zhonghao Wang and colleagues (2022) expected that it would be challenging for Chinese university professors and instructors to maintain crafting their jobs over a semester. Indeed, they found a general declining tendency in approach-avoidance behavioral crafting, especially by faculty members with higher job autonomy who received limited career support from family and friends. Interestingly, this inability to maintain crafting when work demands increase contrasts with previous meta-analytical results highlighting the positive association between autonomy and approach crafting (Rudolph et al., 2017).

Furthermore, also among teachers interventions appeared to be successful in fostering job crafting (Dubbelt et al., 2019; van Wingerden et al., 2017). A job crafting workshop among university employees was successful in increasing approach behavioral resources crafting and avoidance behavioral demands crafting compared to the control group. Six weeks after the workshop, the former fostered higher work engagement, task performance, and career satisfaction (Dubbelt et al., 2019). Contrarily, Jessica van Wingerden and colleagues (2017) did not find any changes in work engagement, job demands, and resilience after conducting an approach-avoidance behavioral crafting intervention (i.e., three four-hour job crafting training sessions on proactive goal setting) among Dutch primary school teachers. However, interestingly, one year later, the authors did find an increase in job performance, performance feedback, self-efficacy, and opportunities for professional development when compared to the control group. Relatedly, over one year, Dorien Kooij and colleagues (2017a) found that employees of a Dutch university who had an open-ended future time perspective also approach-behavioral crafted more often, which increased their work engagement and job performance. Alternatively, employees whose limited future time perspective increased that year did not reduce their avoidance behavioral crafting, although there was a relationship between avoidance behavioral crafting and lower levels of work engagement and performance.

Lastly, team crafting has received scholarly attention in this field, albeit limited. Carrie Leana and colleagues' (2009) study was among the first to treat individual and team approach behavioral crafting as two distinct constructs. Especially for less experienced childcare teachers, individual approach crafting was positively associated with their performance. Alternatively, high-performing teachers engaged in more team approach crafting, thereby gaining stronger job attachment. For all teachers, team approach crafting was related to higher levels of job satisfaction, organizational commitment, and quality of care. Relying on the same approach behavioral crafting measurement designed for teachers, team crafting was also found to be positively related to higher job satisfaction in Spain (Alonso et al., 2019). Finally, among Finnish educational employees, scholars have revealed that team approach behavioral resources crafting can enhance team performance (Mäkikangas et al., 2016), via their team members' work engagement.

To conclude, educational professionals mostly engaged in approach crafting, both individually and as a team, which was found to positively impact their (team's) job satisfaction, performance, and work engagement. While many studies in this sector did not distinguish among job crafting types, particularly behaviorally crafting resources was stimulated by job characteristics (i.e., autonomy, task interdependence) and favorable organizational contexts (i.e., school climate, organizational support), and through interventions.

Job crafting in manufacturing

The final noteworthy sector represented job crafting studies conducted in manufacturing. Broadly speaking, manufacturing encompasses fabricating or assembling components of raw materials into final products on a fairly large scale, such as the production of automobiles, food, clothing, electronics, and chemicals. Work design characteristics occurring regularly in this sector are standardization and specialization or task variety and job rotation, flexibility, teamwork, and cross-functional collaboration. Flexible, remote, and virtual teamwork has changed the work for employees responsible for sustaining production (Kitagawa et al., 2021).

Again, work engagement is a central topic. For instance, among manufacturers from South Africa, Leon De Beer and colleagues (2016) found that approach (not avoidance) behavioral crafting positively predicted work engagement and job satisfaction. Similarly, approach-avoidance behavioral crafting by Chinese manufacturing employees strengthened their occupational satisfaction and innovative behavior via work engagement (Ren et al., 2020). Lastly, a job crafting intervention program provided to Japanese managers, of which two-thirds worked in manufacturing, proved to increase work engagement and approach cognitive resources crafting and reduced their psychological distress after a one-month follow-up (Sakuraya et al., 2016).

Furthermore, in manufacturing, researchers examined organizational identification in the job crafting process. For example, Zhang and colleagues (2021) uncovered the positive moderating role of organizational identity on the positive relationship between overqualification and approach behavioral resources crafting among Chinese manufacturing employees. In turn, the crafting was positively related to their psychological well-being and supervisor-rated task performance. Finally, Jipeng Qi and colleagues (2014) found that Chinese manufacturing employees who felt more emotionally attached to the organization (i.e., organizational embeddedness and affective commitment) engaged in more approach behavioral and cognitive crafting. This relationship was weakened in employees with high levels of internal social capital because they acquired the resources to craft their jobs from their interpersonal interactions at work. Particularly, high-quality interactions with team members have been shown to increase approach-avoidance behavioral crafting, specifically for employees with a prevention focus (Hung et al., 2020).

Building on excessive demands, Elizabeth Solberg and Sut Wong (2016) stressed that perceived role overload was detrimental to Norwegian manufacturing employees' crafting efforts. Yet this depended on the interactive fit between employees and their leaders. The combination of having both highly adaptive employees and leaders with a low need for structure allowed for a positive relationship between role overload and approach crafting. Thereby, these findings contribute to the premise that "proactivity requires adaptivity" (cf., Berg et al., 2010) from both employees and leaders to enable approach crafting when excessive job demands hinder initiating changes. Justin Berg and colleagues (2010), who partly drew from a manufacturing sample, found that higher-ranked employees were able to approach craft their jobs with less adaptive effort than lower-raked employees, whereby their adaptive moves were more focused on changing their jobs for themselves than for others.

Furthermore, studies have shed insights into the skills and motivation of job crafting among manufacturing professionals while considering the boundaries of their work. As such, Canan Karabey and Gokhan Kerse (2017) found positive correlations between the psychological capital of employees from a sugar manufacturer and their approach behavioral and cognitive crafting. Studying Swedish car manufacturing employees, Brenda Ghitulescu (2007) showed that task complexity and work discretion predicted more approach behavioral (not cognitive) crafting. Also, when these employees engaged in more approach behavioral crafting, they were found to be more effective at their jobs in terms of quality and efficiency, particularly when they possessed a broader skill set. Instead, approach cognitive crafting had a positive effect on job satisfaction and organizational commitment. Relatedly, Sarah-Jane Cullinane and colleagues (2017) revealed that skill utilization was associated with approach behavioral resources crafting (not demands), especially when employees had high boundary control and low task interdependence. Thus, manufacturing employees who worked more independently and were involved in regular decision-making were more likely to seek advice or learn something new on days when they applied their skills on the job. In turn, on days when employees engaged in approach behavioral crafting, they experienced higher work engagement resulting from high levels of social interactions within the teams. Lorenzo Bizzi (2017) confirmed the importance of others and their work characteristics: the feedback on the job and autonomy of organizational contacts positively affected the approach behavioral crafting of employees engaged in the manufacturing of pharmaceuticals.

To conclude, approach behavioral and cognitive crafting among manufacturing professionals yielded beneficial outcomes for work engagement and job satisfaction. This relationship was strengthened for crafting resources when employees had complex tasks for which they actively used their skills and when they identified or felt more emotionally attached to the organization. Furthermore, increased or too low job demands encouraged approach crafting, also through supervisory support when the high demands were considered hindering.

Discussion

With the focus on individual job redesign, this chapter sought to first present an overview of job crafting theory and particularly efforts to integrate the two dominant perspectives of Wrzesniewski and Dutton (2001) and Tims and Bakker (2010). While each integration has shown its value, our main takeaway is that it is insightful to distinguish between crafting as approach- or avoidance-motivated (Bruning & Campion, 2018; Zhang & Parker, 2019). This distinction might indeed help in formulating better predictions of the antecedents and outcomes of different job crafting orientations. Furthermore, with the continuous increase in new forms of job crafting, it is important to highlight what kind of changes actually occur in the job crafter's work design (i.e., job demands and/or resources). As such, the hierarchical model of Zhang and Parker (2019) may serve this integration best as it also considers cognitive crafting besides the behavioral crafting form. We also discussed the more recent perspective that job crafting should be studied from a wider perspective, including coworkers and supervisors, given that they may be impacted (in)directly by job crafting efforts (cf., Tims & Parker, 2020).

Based on this discussion of job crafting theories and perspectives, we then reviewed the literature to identify whether the findings are generalizable across the most often studied sectors of healthcare, education, and manufacturing. Interestingly, they have focused on different antecedents of job crafting, though similar outcomes. Referring to our introductory questions, we can conclude that, in general, results regarding the outcomes of job crafting hold across all three sectors and thereby hold for a wide range of employees. That is, approach crafting was most likely associated with higher levels of work engagement, satisfaction, and performance, whereas avoidance crafting was mostly negatively associated with these outcomes and positively with exhaustion. However, it is more challenging to generalize job crafting antecedents as differences were present across the three sectors regarding studied work design and work context characteristics. To illustrate, in education and manufacturing, studies focused more on organizational commitment and attachment as predictors for approach behavioral resources crafting, while in healthcare supportive leadership was more central. This could indicate that healthcare employees rely more on supervisory and team empowerment to craft resources. Also, in comparison, less attention was paid to team crafting in manufacturing, and instead more studies focused on approach cognitive resources crafting to manage role overload. Therefore, work design characteristics could stimulate the need for and engagement in more specific types of crafting as well as potentially inform its impact on others. Nevertheless, limited information was available about cognitive crafting

430 TRANSFORMATIVE WORK DESIGN

across these sectors, and in many cases (especially for education samples), a composite score of approach and avoidance crafting was used rather than separating them to examine differential effects. This overview highlights some important considerations for future research.

Suggestions for Future Research

In this section, we discuss three areas of future research that warrant attention to help move the job crafting field forward: i) studying job crafting dimensions; ii) studying job crafting in relation to its sector, work context, and work design; and iii) studying the changes to one's work realized through job crafting.

Studying job crafting dimensions

An important first step for future job crafting research is to focus on the specific job crafting dimensions and to unpack the different antecedents and outcomes of these dimensions. Given that eight job crafting strategies are proposed (Zhang & Parker, 2019), research is now needed that addresses how to best work with these dimensions in practice. We have often received requests on how to shorten our 21-item job crafting scale (Tims et al., 2012), whereas a newer scale measuring these eight dimensions includes even more items (48 items; Lopper et al., 2023). Thus, from both a theoretical and practical standpoint, it will be insightful to examine the unique value of each of the dimensions in relation to each other and to their antecedents and outcomes. So far, little research is available to draw any conclusions, and we look forward to seeing the added value of studying approach cognitive demands crafting and avoidance behavioral resources crafting, for example. We foresee a database emerging that contains crafting items for specific job demands and resources from which researchers can select items that best fit their research context. This way, studying job crafting can remain efficient and fit the work design and social context.

Studying job crafting in relation to its sector, work context, and work design

Another issue we wish to highlight, based on our overview of job crafting in the three most-often studied work contexts, is that limited attention has been paid to unique work design aspects that form the research context. In many studies, the focus was on the outcomes of job crafting with little attention to how the work design (in)directly shapes crafting. Some reference has been made to studying autonomy, task interdependence, and organizational support in the education sector (Ghitulescu, 2007) and to role overload, social interactions, and skills in the manufacturing sector (Cullinane et al., 2017; Solberg & Wong, 2016). Given that the findings related to outcomes are similar across these sectors, it may be concluded that job crafting works for all. However, it remains important to know whether these findings still hold when incorporating information about the specific work design characteristics. In other words, there is a risk of overgeneralizing research findings obtained in different sectors yet among employees with similar work design characteristics. This attention to work design may help to explain inconsistent findings. For example, focusing on avoidance crafting, Audenaert and colleagues (2020) found that coworker support was not associated with avoidance crafting, whereas Tiphaine Huyghebaert-Zouaghi and colleagues (2021) found that coworker support was positively associated with avoidance crafting. A potential explanation may lie in the work context of the specific samples (i.e., convenience versus elderly care).

Studying the changes to one's work realized through job crafting

Another future research suggestion is to be more considerate of the changes that employees actually make in their work. In many studies, work-related well-being or performance are examined as the outcomes of job crafting. Despite their acknowledged importance for employees and organizations alike, we urge researchers to also start unpacking *what* actually changes when employees craft their jobs. Which job demands and resources are most likely to change, why, and under what conditions? Do employees change both job characteristics and cognitions at the same time or is there a specific sequence in these job crafting behaviors? For example, it has been suggested that cognitive crafting may be the result of actually changing a job (Wrzesniewski & Dutton, 2001) or instead when job characteristics cannot be crafted (Tims et al., 2012). With regard to changes in job characteristics, Tims and colleagues (2013) found support for an increase in structural and social job resources, but not for an increase in challenging job demands or a decrease in hindering job demands after job crafting. This finding led them to suggest that it may be more difficult to change demands than to change resources. Interestingly, Harju and colleagues (2021) found that approach crafting predicted an increase in the *demands* job complexity and workload and, similar to Tims and colleagues (2013) that avoidance

432   TRANSFORMATIVE WORK DESIGN

crafting was unrelated to a decrease in hindrance demands. However, avoidance crafting predicted a decrease in job complexity. Thus, approach and avoidance crafting may influence both resources and demands in different ways. Clearly, more research is needed to rigorously test the simultaneous effect of job crafting on job demands and resources.

Studying the social impact of job crafting within interdependent work contexts

Future research may also further examine the social context in which job crafting takes place. One way forward is to focus on the impact that crafting one's own job demands and resources (behaviorally or cognitively) has on the experienced job demands and resources of colleagues. Another potential research area is to focus on how the work context may help to reveal when job crafting is positively or negatively evaluated and reacted to. Knowledge about the high workload or conflicting situation of the job crafter may create more leeway for avoidance crafting than when the job crafter has no such extenuating circumstances. Importantly, examining these ideas with longitudinal research designs may also shed light on the temporariness of job crafting and whether it is possible to maintain specific job crafting strategies for a long time or whether they are more appropriate for a short time only. It is our hope that these research suggestions will help advance job crafting theory so that interventions can become more successful.

Implications for practice

Job crafting is an effective strategy for employees and teams who wish to improve their performance, motivation, and well-being, from which organizations can also benefit. Our chapter indicates that in most types of work contexts, approach behavioral demands and resources crafting can induce favorable (work) outcomes. Employees should be encouraged to take an active role in changing aspects of their jobs when they feel that there is room for improvement. Managers and team leaders could play an invaluable role in stimulating job crafting among their employees, for instance by being a role model, and by facilitating a work context that provides sufficient autonomy to craft jobs. They could also provide job crafting workshops or train their employees and teams about different job crafting strategies, including avoidance strategies, while touching upon the consequences that crafting can have for others in an interdependent work context.

References

Alonso, C., Fernández-Salinero, S., & Topa, G. (2019). The impact of both individual and collaborative job crafting on Spanish teachers' well-being. *Education Sciences 9*, 74–83.

Aronsson, G., Theorell, T., Grape, T., Hammarström, A., Hogstedt, C., Marteinsdottir, I., Skoog, I., Träskman-Bendz, L., & Hall, C. (2017). A systematic review including meta-analysis of work environment and burnout symptoms. *BMC Public Health 17*, 1–13.

Audenaert, M., George, B., Bauwens, R., Decuypere, A., Descamps, A. M., Muylaert, J., Ma, R., & Decramer, A. (2020). Empowering leadership, social support, and job crafting in public organizations: A multilevel study. *Public Personnel Management 49*(3), 367–392.

Baghdadi, N. A., Farghaly Abd-EL Aliem, S. M., & Alsayed, S. K. (2021). The relationship between nurses' job crafting behaviours and their work engagement. *Journal of Nursing Management 29*(2), 214–219.

Bakker, A. B. (2017). Job crafting among health care professionals: The role of work engagement. *Journal of Nursing Management 26*(3), 321–331.

Bakker, A. B., & Demerouti, E. (2007). The job demands-resources model: State of the art. *Journal of Managerial Psychology 22*(3), 309–328.

Bakker, A. B., Demerouti, E., & Euwema, M. C. (2005). Job resources buffer the impact of job demands on burnout. *Journal of Occupational Health Psychology 10*(2), 170–180.

Bakker, A. B., Demerouti, E., & Sanz-Vergel, A. (2023). Job demands–resources theory: Ten years later. *Annual Review of Organizational Psychology and Organizational Behavior 10*, 25–53.

Bakker, A. B., Rodríguez-Muñoz, A., & Sanz Vergel, A. I. (2016). Modelling job crafting behaviours: Implications for work engagement. *Human Relations 69*(1), 169–189.

Bakker, A. B., Tims, M., & Derks, D. (2012). Proactive personality and job performance: The role of job crafting and work engagement. *Human Relations 65*(10), 1359–1378.

Berg, J. M., Wrzesniewski, A., & Dutton, J. E. (2010). Perceiving and responding to challenges in job crafting at different ranks: When proactivity requires adaptivity. *Journal of Organizational Behavior 31*(2–3), 158–186.

Bizzi, L. (2017). Network characteristics: When an individual's job crafting depends on the jobs of others. *Human Relations 70*(4), 436–460.

Brenninkmeijer, V., & Hekkert-Koning, M. (2015). To craft or not to craft: The relationships between regulatory focus, job crafting and work outcomes. *Career Development International 20*, 147–162.

Bruning, P., & Campion, M. (2018). A role-resource approach-avoidance model of job crafting: A multi-method integration and extension of job crafting theory. *Academy of Management Journal 61*(2), 499–522.

Burnard, P., Edwards, D., Fothergill, A., Hannigan, B., & Coyle, D. (2000). Community mental health nurses in Wales: Self-reported stressors and coping strategies. *Journal of Psychiatric and Mental Health Nursing 7*(6), 523–528.

Cullinane, S. J., Bosak, J., Flood, P. C., & Demerouti, E. (2017). Job crafting for lean engagement: The interplay of day and job-level characteristics. *European Journal of Work and Organizational Psychology 26*(4), 541–554.

De Beer, L. T., Tims, M., & Bakker, A. B. (2016). Job crafting and its impact on work engagement and job satisfaction in mining and manufacturing. *South African Journal of Economic and Management Sciences 19*(3), 400–412.

De Jonge, J., Le Blanc, P. M., Peeters, M. C. W., & Noordam, H. (2008). Emotional job demands and the role of matching resources: A cross-sectional survey study among healthcare workers. *International Journal of Nursing Studies 45*, 1460–1469.

Demerouti, E., Bakker, A.B., Nachreiner, F., & Schaufeli, W.B. (2001). The job demands-resources model of burnout. *Journal of Applied Psychology 86*, 499–512.

Ding, H., Yu, E., Chu, X., Li, Y., & Amin, K. (2020). Humble leadership affects organizational citizenship behavior: The sequential mediating effect of strengths use and job crafting. *Frontiers in Psychology 11*, 65.

Dong, Y., Zhang, L., Wang, H-J., & Jiang, J. (2023). Why is crafting the job associated with less prosocial reactions and more social undermining? The role of feelings of relative deprivation and zero-sum mindset. *Journal of Business Ethics 184*, 175–190.

Dreer, B. (2022). Teacher well-being: Investigating the contributions of school climate and job crafting. *Cogent Education 9*(1), 2044583.

Dubbelt, L., Demerouti, E., & Rispens, S. (2019). The value of job crafting for work engagement, task performance, and career satisfaction: Longitudinal and quasi-experimental evidence. *European Journal of Work and Organizational Psychology 28*(3), 300–314.

Elliot, A. J. (2006). The hierarchical model of approach–avoidance motivation. *Motivation and Emotion 30*(2), 111–116.

Evans, S., Huxley, P., Gately, C., Webber, M., Mears, A., Pajak, S., Medina, J., Kendall, T., & Katona, C. (2006). Mental health, burnout and job satisfaction among mental health social workers in England and Wales. *British Journal of Psychiatry 188*(1), 75–80.

Feuerhahn, N., Bellingrath, S., & Kudielka, B. M. (2013). The interplay of matching and non-matching job demands and resources on emotional exhaustion among teachers. *Applied Psychology: Health and Well-Being 5*(2), 171–192.

Fong, C. Y. M., Tims, M., & Khapova, S. N. (2022). Coworker responses to job crafting: Implications for willingness to cooperate and conflict. *Journal of Vocational Behavior 138*, 103781.

Fong, C. Y. M., Tims, M., Khapova, S. N., & Beijer, S. (2021). Supervisor reactions to avoidance job crafting: The role of political skill and approach job crafting. *Applied Psychology: An International Review 70*(3), 1209–1241.

Ganesan, S., Magee, M., Stone, J. E., Mulhall, M. D., Collins, A., Howard, M. E., Lockley, S. W., Rajaratnam, S. M. W., & Sletten, T. L. (2019). The impact of shift work on sleep, alertness and performance in healthcare workers. *Scientific Reports 9*(1), 4635.

Ghitulescu, B. E. (2007). *Shaping tasks and relationships at work: Examining the antecedents and consequences of employee job crafting* [Doctoral dissertation, University of Pittsburgh].

Gordon, H. J., Demerouti, E., Le Blanc, P. M., Bakker, A. B., Bipp, T., & Verhagen, M. A. (2018). Individual job redesign: Job crafting interventions in healthcare. *Journal of Vocational Behavior 104*, 98–114.

Gordon, H., Demerouti, E., Le Blanc, P., & Bipp, T. (2015). Job crafting and performance of Dutch and American health care professionals. *Journal of Personnel Psychology 14*(4), 192–202.

Grant, A. M., Fried, Y., Parker, S. K., & Frese, M. (2010). Putting job design in context: Introduction to the special issue. *Journal of Organizational Behavior 31*, 145–157.

Grant, A. M., & Parker, S. K. (2009). 7 Redesigning work design theories: The rise of relational and proactive perspectives. *Academy of Management Annals 3*(1), 317–375.

Hakanen, J. J., Bakker, A. B., & Schaufeli, W. (2006). Burnout and work engagement among teachers. *Journal of School Psychology 43*, 495–513.

Hakanen, J., Peeters, M., & Schaufeli, W. (2018). Different types of employee well-being across time and their relationships with job crafting. *Journal of Occupational Health Psychology 23*(2), 289–301.

Harju, L. K., Kaltiainen, J., & Hakanen, J. J. (2021). The double-edged sword of job crafting: The effects of job crafting on changes in job demands and employee well-being. *Human Resource Management 60*, 953–968.

Harju, L. K., Tims, M., Hakanen, J. J., & Khapova, S. N. (2023). Crafting for oneself while considering others: How the relational design of work shapes job crafting. *International Journal of Human Resource Management 35*(1), 67–97.

Higgins, E. T. (1997). Beyond pleasure and pain. *American Psychologist 52*(12), 1280–1300.

Hu, Q., Schaufeli, W. B., Taris, T. W., Shimazu, A. & Dollard, M. F. (2019). Resource crafting: Is it really "resource" crafting—or just crafting? *Frontiers in Psychology 10*, 614–625.

Huang, X., Sun, M., & Wang, D. (2022). Work harder and smarter: The critical role of teachers' job crafting in promoting teaching for creativity. *Teaching and Teacher Education 116*, 103758.

Hung, T. K., Wang, C. H., Tian, M., & Yang, Y. J. (2020). A cross-level investigation of team-member exchange on team and individual job crafting with the moderating effect of regulatory focus. *International Journal of Environmental Research and Public Health 17*(6), 2044.

Huyghebaert-Zouaghi, T., Berjot, S., Cougot, B., & Gillet, N. (2021). Psychological and relational conditions for job crafting to occur. *Stress and Health 37*, 516–527.

Iida, M., Watanabe, K., Imamura, K., Sakuraya, A., Asaoka, H., Sato, N., Nozawa, K., & Kawakami, N. (2021). Development and validation of the Japanese version of the team job crafting scale for nurses. *Research in Nursing & Health 44*(2), 329–343.

Ingusci, E., Callea, A., Chirumbolo, A., & Urbini, F. (2016). Job crafting and job satisfaction in a sample of Italian teachers: The mediating role of perceived organizational support. *Journal of Applied Statistical Analysis 9*(4), 675–687.

Karabey, C. N., & Kerse, G. (2017). The relationship between job crafting and psychological capital: A survey in a manufacturing business. *PressAcademia Procedia 3*(1), 909–915.

Kitagawa, R., Kuroda, S., Okudaira, H., & Owan, H. (2021). Working from home and productivity under the COVID-19 pandemic: Using survey data of four manufacturing firms. *PLoS One 16*(12), e0261761.

Klainin, P. (2009). Stress and health outcomes: The mediating role of negative affectivity in female health care workers. *International Journal of Stress Management 16*, 45–64.

Kooij, D. T., Tims, M., & Akkermans, J. (2017a). The influence of future time perspective on work engagement and job performance: The role of job crafting. *European Journal of Work and Organizational Psychology 26*(1), 4–15.

Leana, C., Appelbaum, E., & Shevchuk, I. (2009). Work process and quality of care in early childhood education: The role of job crafting. *Academy of Management Journal 52*(6), 1169–1192.

Lichtenthaler, P. W., & Fischbach, A. (2016, August). Promotion-and prevention-focused job crafting: A theoretical extension and meta-analytical test. Paper presented at the 76th Annual Meeting of Academy of Management, Anaheim, United States.

Lichtenthaler, P. W., & Fischbach, A. (2018). Leadership, job crafting, and employee health and performance. *Leadership and Organization Development Journal 39*(5), 620–632.

Lichtenthaler, P. W., & Fischbach, A. (2019). A meta-analysis on promotion-and prevention-focused job crafting. *European Journal of Work and Organizational Psychology 28*(1), 30–50.

Lin, B., Law, K. S., & Zhou, J. (2017). Why is underemployment related to creativity and OCB? A task-crafting explanation of the curvilinear moderated relations. *Academy of Management Journal 60*(1), 156–177.

Llorente-Alonso, M., & Topa, G. (2019). Individual crafting, collaborative crafting, and job satisfaction: The mediator role of engagement. *Journal of Work and Organizational Psychology 35*(3), 217–226.

Lopper, E., Horstmann, K. T., & Hoppe, A. (2023). The approach-avoidance job crafting scale: Development and validation of a measurement of the hierarchical structure of job crafting. *Applied Psychology: An International Review 73*(1), 93–134.

Luu, T. T. (2017). Collective job crafting and team service recovery performance: A moderated mediation mechanism. *Marketing Intelligence & Planning 35*(5), 641–656.

Lyons, P. (2008). The crafting of jobs and individual differences. *Journal of Business and Psychology 23*, 25–36.

Mainka, D., & Suß, S. (2022). A scenario-based quasi-experimental study of co-workers' cognitive responses to an individual's resource-focused job crafting. *German Journal of Human Resource Management 37*, 1–27.

Mäkikangas, A. (2018). Job crafting profiles and work engagement: A person-centered approach. *Journal of Vocational Behavior 106*, 101–111.

Mäkikangas, A., Aunola, K., Seppälä, P., & Hakanen, J. (2016). Work engagement–team performance relationship: Shared job crafting as a moderator. *Journal of Occupational and Organizational Psychology 89*(4), 772–790.

Mäkikangas, A., Bakker, A. B., & Schaufeli, W. B. (2017). Antecedents of daily team job crafting. *European Journal of Work and Organizational Psychology 26*(3), 421–433.

Mattarelli, E., & Tagliaventi, M. R. (2015). How offshore professionals' job dissatisfaction can promote further offshoring: Organizational outcomes of job crafting. *Journal of Management Studies 52*(5), 585–620.

Nadin, S. J., Waterson, P. E., & Parker, S. K. (2001). Participation in job redesign: An evaluation of the use of a sociotechnical tool and its impact. *Human Factors and Ergonomics in Manufacturing & Service Industries 11*(1), 53–69.

Niessen, C., Weseler, D., & Kostova, P. (2016). When and why do individuals craft their jobs? The role of individual motivation and work characteristics for job crafting. *Human Relations 69*(6), 1287–1313.

Ogbuanya, T. C., & Chukwuedo, S. O. (2017). Job crafting-satisfaction relationship in electrical/electronic technology education programme: Do work engagement and commitment matter? *Revista de Psicología del Trabajo y de las Organizaciones 33*(3), 165–173.

Pan, J., Chiu, C. Y., & Wu, K. S. (2021). Leader-member exchange fosters nurses' job and life satisfaction: The mediating effect of job crafting. *PLoS One 16*(4), e0250789.

Parker, S. K., Bindl, U. K., & Strauss, K. (2010). Making things happen: A model of proactive motivation. *Journal of Management 36*(4), 827–856.

Parker, S. K., Williams, H. M., & Turner, N. (2006). Modeling the antecedents of proactive behavior at work. *Journal of Applied Psychology 91*(3), 636–652.

Peral, S., & Geldenhuys, M. (2016). The effects of job crafting on subjective well-being amongst South African high school teachers. *SA Journal of Industrial Psychology 42*(1), 1–13.

Petrou, P., & Demerouti, E. (2015). Trait-level and week-level regulatory focus as a motivation to craft a job. *Career Development International 20*, 102–118.

Qi, J., Li, J., & Zhang, Q. (2014). How organizational embeddedness and affective commitment influence job crafting. *Social Behavior and Personality: An International Journal 42*(10), 1629–1638.

Ren, T., Cao, L., & Chin, T. (2020). Crafting jobs for occupational satisfaction and innovation among manufacturing workers facing the COVID-19 crisis. *International Journal of Environmental Research and Public Health 17*(11), 3953.

Renkema, E., Broekhuis, M., Tims, M., & Ahaus, K. (2023). Working around: Job crafting in the context of public and professional accountability. Human Relations 76(9), 1352–1381.

Rudolph, C., Katz, I., Lavigne, K., & Zacher, H. (2017). Job crafting: A meta-analysis of relationships with individual differences, job characteristics, and work outcomes. *Journal of Vocational Behavior 102*, 112–138.

Saragih, S., Margaretha, M., & Situmorang, A. P. (2020). Analyzing antecedents and consequence of job crafting. *International Journal of Management, Economics and Social Sciences 9*(2), 76–89.

Sakuraya, A., Shimazu, A., Imamura, K., Namba, K., & Kawakami, N. (2016). Effects of a job crafting intervention program on work engagement among Japanese employees: A pretest-posttest study. *BMC Psychology 4*, 1–9.

Scholer, A. A., & Higgins, E. T. (2008). Distinguishing levels of approach and avoidance: An analysis using regulatory focus theory. In A. J. Elliot (Ed.), *Handbook of approach and avoidance motivation* (pp. 489–503). Psychology Press.

Shang, W. (2022). The effects of job crafting on job performance among ideological and political education teachers: The mediating role of work meaning and work engagement. *Sustainability 14*(14), 8820.

Slemp, G. R., & Vella-Brodrick, D. A. (2013). The Job Crafting Questionnaire: A new scale to measure the extent to which employees engage in job crafting. *International Journal of Wellbeing 3*(2), 126–146.

Solberg, E., & Wong, S. I. (2016). Crafting one's job to take charge of role overload: When proactivity requires adaptivity across levels. *Leadership Quarterly 27*(5), 713–725.

Tims, M., & Bakker, A. B. (2010). Job crafting: Towards a new model of individual job redesign. *SA Journal of Industrial Psychology 36*(2), 1–9.

Tims, M., Bakker, A. B., & Derks, D. (2012). Development and validation of the job crafting scale. *Journal of Vocational Behavior 80*(1), 173–186.

Tims, M., Bakker, A. B., & Derks, D. (2014). Daily job crafting and the self-efficacy-performance relationship. *Journal of Managerial Psychology 29*(5), 490–507.

Tims, M., Bakker, A. B., Derks, D., & Van Rhenen, W. (2013). Job crafting at the team and individual level: Implications for work engagement and performance. *Group & Organization Management 38*(4), 427–454.

Tims, M., & Parker, S. K. (2020). How coworkers attribute, react to, and shape job crafting. *Organizational Psychology Review 10*(1), 29–54.

Tims, M., Twemlow, M., & Fong, C. Y. M. (2022). A state-of-the-art overview of job-crafting research: Current trends and future research directions. *Career Development International 27*, 54–78.

Vangrieken, K., Dochy, F., Raes, E., & Kyndt, E. (2015). Teacher collaboration: A systematic review. *Educational Research Review 15*, 17–40.

Van Leeuwen, E. H., Taris, T. W., Van den Heuvel, M., Knies, E., Van Rensen, E. L., & Lammers, J. W. J. (2021). A career crafting training program: results of an intervention study. *Frontiers in Psychology 12*, 1477.

van Wingerden, J., Bakker, A. B., & Derks, D. (2017). Fostering employee well-being via a job crafting intervention. *Journal of Vocational Behavior 100*, 164–174.

van Wingerden, J., & Poell, R. F. (2019). Meaningful work and resilience among teachers: The mediating role of work engagement and job crafting. *PLoS One 14*(9), e0222518.

Vogel, R. M., Rodell, J. B., & Lynch, J. W. (2016). Engaged and productive misfits: How job crafting and leisure activity mitigate the negative effects of value incongruence. *Academy of Management Journal 59*(5), 1561–1584.

Wang, Z., Huang, J. L., & Xie, B. (2022). Maintaining job crafting over time: Joint effect of autonomy and career support from family and friends. *Career Development International 27*(4), 433–449.

Watson, G. P., & Sinclair, R. R. (2022). Getting crafty: Examining social resource crafting's relationship with work engagement and social support. *Stress and Health 39*, 588–599.

Woods, P. (1999). Intensification and stress in teaching. In R. Vandenberghe & A. M. Huberman (Eds.), *Understanding and preventing teacher burnout* (pp. 115–138). Cambridge University Press.

Wrzesniewski, A., & Dutton, J. E. (2001). Crafting a job: Revisioning employees as active crafters of their work. *Academy of Management Review 26*(2), 179–201.

Yepes-Baldó, M., Romeo, M., Westerberg, K., & Nordin, M. (2018). Job crafting, employee well-being, and quality of care. *Western Journal of Nursing Research 40*, 52–66.

Zhang, F., & Parker, S. K. (2019). Reorienting job crafting research: A hierarchical structure of job crafting concepts and integrative review. *Journal of Organizational Behavior 40*, 126–146.

Zhang, F., Wang, B., Qian, J., & Parker, S. K. (2021). Job crafting towards strengths and job crafting towards interests in overqualified employees: Different outcomes and boundary effects. *Journal of Organizational Behavior 42*(5), 587–603.

Job Crafting Interventions

Evangelia Demerouti, Maria Peeters, and Machteld van den Heuvel

Introduction

In the ever-evolving landscape of work, organizations are increasingly recognizing the importance of creating environments that foster employee engagement, well-being, and performance. However, the complex needs and desires of today's workforce may no longer be met by traditional top-down approaches to job redesign, in which management optimizes job demands and resources to achieve successful organizational outcomes (Briner & Reynolds, 1999; Nielsen, 2013). Such interventions tend to overlook employees' specific needs and preferences and disregard the unique knowledge and expertise of those directly involved in the work, which can lead to resistance, decreased motivation, and suboptimal outcomes of the redesign process. Therefore, job redesign interventions with more participatory approaches are necessary (Nielsen, 2013). Participatory approaches have many advantages because they emphasize active collaboration between employees and management during change processes, give employees more job control, and take into account employees' active role in bringing about changes to their work environment (Nielsen, 2013). Most importantly, they consider employees to be "the experts" of their jobs because they are most familiar with their own work. Along with the demand for increased employee participation in job redesign initiatives, a trend of encouraging employees' proactive behavior has grown in popularity. This so-called proactive viewpoint is a modern method of job redesign that reflects a trend toward individualization (Parker & Zhang, 2016). Proactive perspectives capture the growing significance of workers taking the initiative to anticipate and execute changes in the way work is performed. They put a special emphasis on the anticipatory actions taken by employees to alter the way that roles, tasks, and responsibilities are performed (Frese & Fay, 2001). It is against this background that the concept of "job crafting" has gained significant attention as a powerful tool for contemporary job redesign. Job crafting refers to the proactive behavior of employees who reshape and redefine their own work experiences to better fit with their personal needs, strengths, and preferences (Tims & Bakker, 2010).

Evangelia Demerouti et al., *Job Crafting Interventions*. In: *Transformative Work Design*. Edited by: Sharon K. Parker et al., Oxford University Press. © Society for Industrial and Organizational Psychology (2025).
DOI: 10.1093/oso/9780197692554.003.0017

440 TRANSFORMATIVE WORK DESIGN

By empowering employees to take an active role in shaping their work environments, job crafting offers a promising approach to job redesign that goes beyond traditional top-down methods. The Job Demands-Resources (JD-R) theory (Bakker et al., 2023; Demerouti et al., 2001; Demerouti & Bakker, 2022) offers an effective framework for examining *how* people can actively "fit" their jobs with their personal skills, needs, and abilities because it explicitly takes into account that people are active agents in the constantly changing work context who can be motivated to optimize their job demands (i.e., aspects of the job that require effort) and resources (i.e., aspects of the job that facilitate effective functioning) to achieve their work goals.

The goals of this chapter are (1) to introduce job crafting as a tool for individual job redesign by explaining its meaning and comparing it with other interventions; (2) to describe a blueprint for a job crafting intervention (from now on called "the job crafting intervention") that has been shown to stimulate job crafting behavior, work-related well-being, and employee work performance; (3) to discuss the mechanisms through which the job crafting intervention leads to improvements of favorable distal outcomes for both employees and organizations; (4) to review the existing evidence regarding the effectiveness of the intervention; and (5) to conclude with several suggestions to further improve the effectiveness of the intervention. Taken together, to inspire future research and practical applications of job crafting interventions, this chapter aims to synthesize theorizing and empirical evidence on the topic. This will allow researchers to learn from and build on prior findings which, in the end, will improve the quality of job crafting interventions.

Individual Job Redesign through Job Crafting

Job crafting has been approached from two perspectives. Wrzesniewski and Dutton (2001) defined job crafting as the changes individuals make in their task or relational boundaries, as well as cognitive changes in perceptions of their work, to find more meaning in their job. Accordingly, task crafting refers to one's role by adding or dropping responsibilities. Relational crafting refers to reshaping the nature of interactions by changing up who we work with and how. Cognitive crafting refers to changing the mindsets about the tasks that people do by reframing how one sees the job. Although Wrzesniewski and Dutton (2001) define job crafting as daily behavior rather than long-term changes, only a few studies have studied daily crafting using their approach (e.g., Geldenhuys et al., 2021). On the contrary, job crafting has also been defined based on the Demands-Resources (JD–R) theory (Bakker et al., 2023; Demerouti et al., 2001; Demerouti & Bakker, 2022). Accordingly, job crafting is conceptualized as the changes employees make in their job to balance their job demands (i.e., aspects of the job that require effort and are associated with psychophysiological costs; Demerouti et al., 2001) and job resources (i.e., aspects of the job that facilitate dealing with job demands, goal accomplishment, and growth; Demerouti et al., 2001) with their personal abilities and needs (Tims & Bakker, 2010). According to this approach, job crafting can take the form of *expansion-oriented* crafting which is aimed at accumulating external and internal resources that enable employees to grow and find meaning (i.e., seeking resources, seeking challenges), and *reduction-oriented* job crafting (Demerouti & Peeters, 2018), which refers to behaviors that are targeted toward minimizing or optimizing the emotionally, mentally, or physically demanding aspects of one's job (i.e., reducing or optimizing demands).

More specifically, seeking resources (e.g., performance feedback, advice from colleagues, support from managers, maximizing job autonomy) represents a strategy to achieve goals and to complete tasks, as well as to deal with job demands, whereas *seeking challenges* represents behaviors such as seeking new tasks at work or asking for more responsibilities once assigned tasks have been finished. *Reducing demands* includes behaviors targeted at minimizing the emotionally, mentally, or physically demanding aspects of one's work and reducing one's workload. Evangelia Demerouti and Maria Peeters (2018) introduced *optimizing demands* as another reduction-oriented job crafting strategy that refers to attempts to bypass inefficient processes and eliminate obstacles. Whereas optimizing demands focuses on making work processes more efficient, reducing demands aims at making the job less strenuous (Demerouti et al., 2019). Although other approaches to conceptualizing job crafting have also been suggested (see Zhang & Parker, 2019), these have not been tested for job crafting interventions. As these job crafting strategies are found to fluctuate daily, they are possible behaviors to learn through job crafting training. Taken together, job crafting is considered a possible solution to the challenges of the current job redesign as employees can (1) more flexibly and quickly modify how organizational changes affect their jobs, (2) shape them more effectively, and (3) consider their needs and preferences and thus achieving person–job fit (Roczniewska et al., 2023).

A Blueprint for a Job Crafting Intervention

Underlying most of the job crafting interventions is the intervention developed following the JD-R theory approach to job crafting (e.g., Demerouti et al., 2017, 2021; Dubbelt et al., 2019; Gordon et al., 2018; van den Heuvel et al., 2015). The intervention aimed to increase employees' awareness regarding how they can adapt their job to their own needs to experience more joy, engagement, and meaning in their work via two routes: (1) through promoting the self-directed behavior of employees, and (2) through stimulating reflection. The job crafting intervention consists of several phases (see Figure 17.1): (1) interviews with employees and other relevant stakeholders like supervisors/managers; (2) a job crafting workshop; (3) weekly job crafting assignment in employees' work setting, using a diary or logbook; and (4) a reflection session.

In the first phase and before the intervention is conducted, *interviews* are held with potential participants to make sure the intervention addresses the needs of employees. With structured interviews employees are asked to describe their daily work tasks, the relevant job demands (e.g., "What are hindering aspects in your work contexts?"; "What positive challenges do you perceive at work?"), and job resources (e.g., "What helps you to achieve your work-related goals?"). Using a critical incident technique, during the interviews employees are asked to describe what good performance looks like in their job and what may hinder them from achieving this. Lastly, employees also provide examples of their past job crafting behavior. This information is used to set examples and to customize the intervention to the specific job.

The second phase of the intervention concerns the job crafting *workshop*. Its duration may last from two to eight hours depending on the context/study and is provided in small groups of employees (up to a maximum of 20). The workshop consists of several parts. First, participants receive a brief introduction to the JD-R theory, which they then apply to their own job by conducting a simple job analysis. Specifically, participants create an overview of their most important daily tasks and sub-tasks, which helps them to indicate the job demands and job resources that are relevant for their job. Next, the job crafting strategies are introduced. Consequently, participants are asked to reflect on a personal best practice story from past job crafting behavior, which they then discuss in sub-groups to learn from each other and to help each other find new ways of crafting. The last part of the workshop is dedicated to completing a so-called Personal Crafting Plan (PCP). Participants again focus on their own work environment and identify one or more work characteristics (demands or resources)

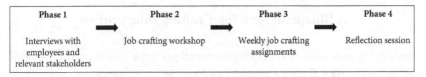

Figure 17.1 Timeline of the Job Crafting Intervention

Table 17.1 Examples of Crafting Assignments

Seeking Resources	Seeking Challenges	Reducing Demands
• Look for feedback • Look for support • Use your autonomy • Participation in the works council • Look for learning opportunities • Decoration of workplace • Map with compliments in Outlook • Invest in relationships	• Use your talent/interests (sports, language knowledge) • Coaching/mentoring • Strategical thinking • New projects	• Simplify tasks • Work more efficiently/plan/time management • Delegate tasks • Let go of perfectionism and idealism • Make clear agreements • Look for a quiet space • Use relationships

or work situations that they would like to change using crafting. The PCP consists of specific crafting actions that the participants undertake after the workshop for a period of three or four weeks depending on the study context (see Table 17.1 for some examples). A small booklet is provided to participants to complete their job crafting goals for the weeks following the workshop and to keep reports of their crafting activities for that week. The job crafting goals must be SMART (Specific, Measurable, Attainable, Realistic, and Timely). Alternatively, Jessica van Wingerden and colleagues (2016) and Caroline Knight and colleagues (2021) used an adapted version of the Job Crafting Exercise (Berg et al., 2013), The Job Crafting Exercise represents a self-developmental paper-and-pencil tool which helps individuals recognize ways in which they could craft their jobs to better fit their motives, strengths, and passions. We describe this intervention in more detail below.

In the third phase, employees practice job crafting in their work setting. Specifically, in the weeks following the training, participants reach their self-set goals specified in the PCP. This was done to create new experiences with the newly acquired knowledge of job crafting, as well as feelings of mastery when goals were achieved (Hulshof et al., 2020). Which job crafting goal participants experimented with each week differs per study. In the job crafting intervention of Machteld van den Heuvel and colleagues (2015), participants performed the self-set job crafting actions in the following order per week: increase resources (i.e., search for feedback and social support), decrease demands (i.e., reduce physical or cognitive demands), seek job challenges (i.e., new tasks and responsibilities), and again increase resources (i.e., search for autonomy,

444   TRANSFORMATIVE WORK DESIGN

participation in decision making, and developmental possibilities). They chose for this order because they expected that boosting the presence of resources may be easier than changing the level of demands. This was confirmed, in the process evaluation as participants found it sometimes difficult to reduce demands, because not all demands are within their span of control. Later intervention studies generally invited participants to practice three job crafting goals and chose a different order for the PCP content to target it to the particular needs of the organization involved. For instance, whereas the intervention of Heather Gordon and colleagues (2018) followed the order of seeking resources (week 1), seeking challenges (week 2), and reducing demands (week 3), the intervention of Demerouti and colleagues (2017) asked participants to seek resources in week 1 and 3 and to seek challenges in week 2. In this way, they started and ended with a simpler assignment, which was more feasible for employees who were undergoing organizational changes. Several of the interventions included sending reminder emails to the participants each week to refresh their goals. No conclusions can be drawn about which sequence of job crafting assignments may work best in a certain context because there is still limited empirical evidence. Whereas most intervention studies asked participants to complete a self-set goal, Knight and colleagues (2021) followed an alternative approach. Specifically, they included weekly encouragement over four weeks to engage in specific job crafting activities, which we call Job Crafting Boosts. Participants were encouraged and reminded to engage in three assignments (called Job Crafting Boosts) per week and job crafting dimension by selecting from a list provided by the researchers.

In the last phase, several of the interventions conclude a reflection session lasting a few hours. During this session, participants discuss their experiences during the weeks of experimenting with job crafting to learn from each other's successes, problems, and solutions. Finally, attention is spent on how employees can overcome potential obstacles that hinder the implementation of job crafting attempts in the future and how they can make a habit out of it.

Next to this job crafting intervention based on the JD-R theory and the job characteristics approach, there are interventions that use the job crafting exercise approach of Justin Berg and colleagues (2013). Their "Job Crafting Exercise (JCE)" is a workbook that assists participants in (1) identifying their work values, strengths and work passions; (2) identifying specific job tasks that participants find challenging or stressful, and the desired changes to those tasks; (3) reflecting on the meaning of tasks and activities at work; and (4) creating an action plan to address the desired changes in their jobs and implementing the plan. This exercise generally consists of a job analysis in which individuals assess their jobs in terms of the types of tasks they complete at work, which tasks they find personally meaningful, and which they find time- and energy-intensive. Reflection followed, in which individuals considered which things they would like more of in their jobs, and those they might like to reduce. Then, individuals are instructed to make an individual job crafting plan or carry out activities aimed at achieving specific job crafting goals.

The JCE can be used for (1) self-development: individuals take the JCE on their own; (2) group workshops: organizations invite employees to participate in professional development workshops to complete the JCE; (3) classroom teaching: instructors use the JCE in the classroom to teach employees about job crafting theory and how employees can redesign their own jobs; and (4) one-on-one coaching: coaches help clients navigate the JCE.

Defining and Categorizing Job Crafting Interventions in the Broader Workplace Interventions Literature

Workplace intervention research has boomed in the last decade (Lambert et al., 2022). The necessity to provide solutions for problems in society and on the work-floor is growing, as seems the interest in contributing to such practically applicable solutions to real-life problems. With this increased attention to interventions in the workplace, numerous studies have been done since 2010, while a clear overarching framework and clear definitions have been lacking. In this regard, intervention research focuses on organizations' and employees' needs integrating various perspectives and foci. This will help to clarify and categorize what interventions aim to change or bring about, using what change mechanisms or working ingredients, and at what level in the organization (Lambert et al., 2022, Nielsen & Miraglia, 2017). Based on their review of 172 intervention studies, Brittany Lambert and colleagues (2022) define individual-centered interventions as *"intended, theory-based actions aimed at improving individual, group or organizational outcomes by interfering with, stopping, or modifying a process, that is deemed ineffective or unhealthy in a workplace setting."* Regarding the pathways that make interventions effective, they further propose that change can be brought about via a behavioral, cognitive, affective, physical, or situational pathway, thereby focusing on the individual as an active agent that channels the intended changes.

Job crafting-based interventions largely fit in this definition; however, from our perspective, it is important to add here that job crafting is a process that not only aims to "fix" ineffective or unhealthy processes in a workplace setting but may also focus on strengthening or optimizing elements that are already working quite well for an individual or a team. In other words: how to preserve the things that work well? Further, the definition states rightly that the actions may focus on improving outcomes at various levels in the organization, which is in line with the IGLOO model (i.e., integration of resources at five levels: the Individual, the Group, the Leader, the Organizational and the Overarching contextual; Nielsen et al., 2018) and the multi-level approach to the psychosocial work environment (Bakker & Demerouti, 2018). However, job crafting-based interventions that actually focus on such outcomes (e.g., team crafting intervention studies) are as of yet scarce and the mechanisms that bring about changes at a group level may be more complex than the proposed mechanisms at the individual level previously discussed. Another gap that we see here is that it is not always clear in the literature what is meant by organization-level or organizational interventions. Some scholars describe such interventions as theory-based actions that change the way work is designed, organized, and managed (Nielsen, 2013), while others focus more on the organization-wide implementation of certain interventions, rather than what is changed by the intervention. Another factor that may impede clarity in the field of workplace interventions is that researchers from diverse fields (occupational health, health promotion, positive psychology, leadership and teams, organizational change and development, management and organizational behavior) have yet to build bridges and are not always aware of developments within each other's line of research.

The definition of individual centered interventions gives rise to various categorizations and we add to those by listing a number of common ways to categorize interventions. First, stemming from health promotion literature, a well-known distinction focuses on *when* in the process of health deterioration one intervenes. Primary interventions aim to prevent employees from falling ill by eliminating stressors or eliminating exposure to harmful influences (e.g., redesigning tasks or changing working schedules). Secondary interventions aim to boost employee resilience (rather than removing the stressor), for example, mindfulness training, stress management training, and recovery interventions, while tertiary interventions focus on treatment after employees have fallen ill or are unable to work (e.g., cognitive-behavioral techniques or EMDR) (Kompier & Cooper, 1999) More focused on the content of the intervention, Knight and colleagues (2017), found four categories of interventions in their systematic review on interventions boosting work engagement, namely (1) personal resource building, (2) job resource building, (3) leadership development, and (4) health promotion.

Where can we place job crafting interventions in this developing structure of various categorizations? Job crafting interventions have contributed significantly to the development of a happy and healthy work-life for employees

(Holman et al., 2023; Mukherjee & Dhar, 2023; Oprea et al., 2019). The outcomes studied in job crafting intervention research focus mainly on well-being-related outcomes (e.g., positive affect and meaningful work), work-related well-being outcomes, (e.g., work engagement and burnout), and performance outcomes (e.g., task performance and contextual performance).

Based on previous work, the definition by Lambert and colleagues (2022), and practical experience, we propose that job crafting interventions aim to support employees, teams, and leaders to initiate proactive behaviors and to develop new ways of perceiving and altering the work-related environment and its tasks, activities and social aspects. Those proactive behaviors and cognitions can manifest themselves in actions with both a primary (e.g., delegating tasks) as well as a secondary focus (asking for support with a certain task) (van den Heuvel et al., 2015). In this regard, and referring to the categories by Knight and colleagues (2017), the job crafting intervention in its form as a training course can be described as both personal resource building (e.g., cognitions about the self that boost resilience) as well as job resource building (e.g., colleague support). Further, the self-set actions may contain elements of health promotion (e.g., taking walks during lunch). Taking everything into account, job crafting interventions in the form of group training or used in one-to-one coaching can be described as secondary, individual-focused interventions. This is because offering the training itself will not alter or eliminate work stressors (i.e., primary prevention focus), but will empower participants to make structural changes in their work environment (i.e., secondary, resilience-building focus). As such, the training may have effects that can be described as primary interventions because participants may make primary changes such as changing their work schedule, working with a different colleague, changing equipment to avoid physical demands, or delegating tasks (i.e., actions to eliminate the stressor).

Depending on the role and the purpose of the training, individuals can craft in their role as team members or in their role as leaders, which may change the content of the actions that are initiated as an outcome of the training.

As a final reflection of the place of job crafting interventions in broader frameworks of interventions, we want to point out the implications of the high level of abstraction of the umbrella term "job crafting." Concepts differ in their level of concreteness, meaning the extent to which a concept has a direct association with events, actions, properties, relations, or objects we can touch, see, feel, hear, smell, or taste (Löhr, 2022). What does the term job crafting practically mean? In job crafting intervention studies, researchers typically give examples, and early studies that have developed scales have come up with examples of behaviors that could be exemplary for a certain type of job crafting (e.g., asking for feedback or support as an example of seeking resources), but given that inherent in the term job crafting is the idea that people initiate

448   TRANSFORMATIVE WORK DESIGN

small, idiosyncratic actions, those attempts to make job crafting concrete can never fully capture all options. Although attempts have been made to further subdivide the concept into role-resource-based crafting and approach-avoidance crafting (Bruning & Campion, 2018; Zhang & Parker, 2019), it is still unclear how these categories translate to actual employee actions following a job crafting intervention, making it difficult to measure job crafting adequately. A further downside of this issue is that it can lead to "jingle-jangle fallacy" type issues (Kelley, 1927; Marsh et al., 2019), where any action can be categorized as job crafting, even actions that are known as different standalone concepts already (e.g., feedback-seeking). A practical advantage of the abstract nature of job crafting is that a job crafting intervention allows employees to fully personalize their action plan to their own situation. We, therefore, recommend adding to existing qualitative work on the job crafting process (e.g., Lazazzara et al., 2020) to generate knowledge on what participants in job crafting interventions actually do and how it relates to the content of the intervention. An important finding in the meta-synthesis by Alessandra Lazazzara and colleagues (2020) is that more focus is needed on either supportive or constraining work context of the employee and how this interacts with motives to craft. Constraining work environments may force employees to craft their jobs with behavior that tends to trigger negative outcomes, such as withdrawal, which seems closer to a reactive coping behavior, rather than a proactive behavior in line with job crafting theory. To build on this work, future qualitative studies may focus on groups of job crafting intervention participants and their varying motives to take part in the course, their levels of energy and motivation, as well as the forms of job crafting they choose in their action plan. The focus could be on how the actions were inspired by what ingredients of the training, the temporal order in which they are carried out, and how the actions impact their work and work experiences after the training in their day-to-day work context. Realist evaluation may be particularly useful to evaluate what forms of job crafting may work best, for which participants, and under which circumstances (Nielsen & Miraglia, 2017). This may help to further tailor interventions (and the measures used to evaluate them) to support employees in varying contexts, including self-employed workers, to reap the benefits of job crafting, and also to recognize when job crafting is not an appropriate intervention.

This last point refers to our recommendation to both job crafting researchers and practitioners, to include a thorough check in the needs assessment phase to see what structural resources/health and well-being facilities an organization has available besides offering job crafting. This is important as job crafting interventions may backfire when participants perceive the intervention as a way by which they are made responsible for their own well-being and motivation, while the organization does not invest enough in structural factors needed for a motivated and healthy workforce (e.g., safe work environments, fair HR practices, rewards, and procedures, as well as investing in high-quality people leadership capacities).

The Theoretical Background of the Job Crafting Interventions

Job crafting interventions, like most interventions, are rooted in theories that specify what behaviors or skills to train and how to train them so that participants acquire these new behaviors or skills. More specifically, the job crafting interventions that follow the JD-R perspective use job crafting behaviors as the means to improve the design and level of job demands, job resources, and personal resources. This perspective suggests that by training people how to effectively craft their jobs, they will be better able to (1) arrange the job resources that they need to deal with job demands; (2) mobilize resources they need to reach their work-related goals; (3) optimize or reduce hindering demands; and (4) create challenges in their work that fit their preferences, strengths, and interests. Thus, job crafting behavior is the vehicle through which the interventions should produce favorable outcomes. The intervention is expected to be effective because it teaches individuals how to adjust their work in small and effective ways such that it fits their preferences. Put differently, job crafting enhances the person–environment fit (Lu et al., 2014). As job crafting concerns changes that individuals make to their tasks, demands, and resources intending to align those elements to their preferences, they can potentially restore their person–environment fit, assuming they are successful in executing their crafting actions. The job crafting interventions based on Wrzesniewski and Dutton's (2001) perspective are suggested to work because they allow employees to align values, strengths, and passions and their link to tasks, relationships, and cognitions regarding the significance of the work. The outcome of both types of job crafting interventions may be similar in terms of behavioral change; however, the theoretical starting point, training methods, and focus are slightly different (Berg et al., 2013; van den Heuvel et al., 2015).

Besides the theoretical background regarding the target of the interventions, the interventions also need a theoretical background to guide the design and the form of the intervention to stimulate learning and behavioral change. The majority of the interventions integrate principles of the goal-setting theory (Latham & Locke, 2007). In line with goal-setting theory, individuals formulate goals that help direct attention and effort toward goal-relevant activities, increasing persistence, and enabling individuals to reach their goals and experience mastery

(Latham & Locke, 2007). Besides using goal-setting theory, several studies (e.g., van den Heuvel et al., 2015) integrate elements of the social cognitive theory in the intervention (Bandura, 1989). The theory suggests that the interaction between person, behavior, and environment is critical for planning behavior change interventions, underscoring that people are not passive recipients of an intervention. The theory also states that learning occurs in a social context (Bandura, 1989) and emphasizes the human ability to self-regulate, via self-monitoring (i.e., observation of one's own behavior), goal-setting, feedback, and the enlistment of social support (Bandura, 1997). Accordingly, successful behavior change is achieved through mastery experiences, triggered by vicarious learning and imagery, verbal persuasion from others, and adjustments to physiological and emotional states. All these elements are integrated into the design of most interventions.

Several studies integrate elements of experiential learning theory to increase job crafting behavior (Kolb et al., 2001). That is, the intervention builds on participants' past experiences with job crafting to facilitate learning and actual behavioral change. According to David Kolb and colleagues (2001), learning starts with concrete experiences with the behavior, followed by reflection on this behavior, which is followed by creating abstract ideas about the new behavior that eventually end up in the last stage where individuals actively test the behavior to create new experiences. To stimulate learning, Gordon and colleagues (2018) added Situated Experiential Learning Narratives (SELN; Benner et al., 2011), which suggests the use of experiential learning in the form of narratives to improve problem understanding, critical thinking, and know-how. The SELN helps to stimulate participants' actualization and understanding of how their work behaviors could be viewed as a form of job crafting. Stimulating reflection can help individuals bridge the gap between positive past behavioral and future goals (i.e., stimulate actualization of job crafting) and increase understanding of what helps them to proactively adjust their jobs (Benner, 1984).

Recently, Arianna Costantini and colleagues (2022) integrated the principles of the theory of planned behavior (Ajzen, 2015) in their intervention. Accordingly and in line with the theory of planned behavior, the intervention focuses on attitudes, social norms, and perceived behavior control to formulate intentions to job craft ultimately should lead to job crafting behaviors (Costantini et al., 2022). To accomplish this, the intervention integrated several behavioral change techniques such as focusing on past successes, listing the pros and cons of job crafting, goal setting, action planning, and self-monitoring.

Taken together, job crafting interventions aim to improve job characteristics (JD-R theory) or professional identity (Wrzesniewski and Dutton's (2001) building on the suggestions of goal-setting theory (Latham & Locke, 2007), social cognitive theory (Bandura, 1989), experiential learning theory (Kolb et al., 2001), situated experiential learning narratives (Benner, 1984), and the theory of planned behavior (Ajzen, 2015). It builds on past experiences, stimulates reflection, learning, and goal setting, and it creates successful experiences by teaching people how they can be co-creators of their own job.

Impact of Job Crafting Interventions on Outcomes

The effectiveness of the job crafting interventions has been evaluated in one meta-analysis by Bogdan Oprea and colleagues (2019) and one recent review by Tulika Mukherjee and Rajib Dhar (2023). The meta-analysis was conducted based on 14 job crafting intervention studies and found positive and significant effects of the job crafting interventions on overall job crafting, as well as on specific job crafting behaviors to increase job challenges and to decrease hindering job demands (Oprea et al., 2019). The findings have additionally shown that job crafting interventions were effective in helping employees achieve better work engagement and increase their higher contextual performance but did not boost task or adaptive performance. Gains in task performance were only found for healthcare employees. However, results from individual intervention studies reveal inconsistent findings across different types of crafting behaviors as Oprea and colleagues' (2019) meta-analysis reported relatively large confidence intervals for the effect of interventions on job crafting and sub-dimensions (overall job crafting, $g = 0.26$, 95%-CI $= 0.09$–0.44; seeking job resources, $g = 0.19$, 95%-CI $= 0.01$–0.38; reducing hindrance demands, $g = 0.57$, 95%-CI $= 0.15$–0.99). These relatively large confidence intervals may be explained by the fact that the studies varied in their effectiveness to improve the specific job crafting dimensions. For instance, whereas Lonneke Dubbelt and colleagues (2019) and van Wingerden and colleagues (2017a) found that their job crafting intervention increased seeking resources and decreasing demands behaviors, but did not increase seeking challenges, the study of van Wingerden and colleagues (2017b) reported that the job crafting intervention increased seeking challenges but did not increase seeking resources, nor did it affect decreasing hindering demands. Oprea and colleagues' (2019) meta-analysis further showed that creating Job Crafting Plans involving both organizational and personal goals boosted the effectiveness of interventions rather than focusing only on individual goals. The occupation was not found to have a moderator effect on the effectiveness of the interventions to improve overall job crafting. These results should be interpreted with caution, however, given the low study numbers ($K = 14$) which reduces robustness, and the limited number of occupations and settings upon which moderator analyses were based (Knight et al., 2021). Moreover, the effects of enhancing job crafting behaviors on performance were fully explained by increases in work engagement. One major limitation of the aforementioned meta-analysis is that the majority of the included studies used relatively short-term follow-ups. Oprea and colleagues (2019) conducted also a utility analysis which indicated substantial benefits of job crafting interventions as they are expected to lead to an increase of $2,310 per three months per employee in revenue from improved performance for the next three months following the intervention.

Knight and colleagues (2021) examined the conditions under which job crafting interventions are effective in changing proactive behaviors by comparing the effectiveness of two job crafting interventions (i.e., a less intense intervention versus one of four weeks long). No significant differences were observed between intervention groups in any job crafting behaviors. Irrespective of the intervention, participants with a high initial workload engaged in more crafting behaviors to decrease their hindering demands, whereas those with a low initial workload engaged in more crafting behaviors aimed at increasing structural resources. Examining the effectiveness of job crafting interventions for specific employee groups is therefore important as those who need the intervention more also profit more from following the intervention.

The most recent systematic review of job crafting interventions was conducted by Mukherjee and Dhar (2023), which included a total of 33 studies. Of these studies, 72 percent were conducted in Europe and employed a quasi-experimental research design, whereas only 15 percent failed to include any control group. In terms of intervention approach, the majority (79 percent) of the interventions were tailored for the population in consideration by conducting interviews or group discussions with people from the participating organization, or by providing tailored job crafting examples and tailored feedback to the participants. The majority (67 percent) of the intervention studies used the JD-R theory as the sole theoretical approach or combined this with the goal-setting theory, experiential learning theory, and the conservation of resources (COR) theory. These interventions focused on empowering employees to alter the physical elements of their job by procuring additional resources or restructuring existing ones in order to minimize job demands and, consequently, strain. The other large group of interventions used Wrzesniewski and Dutton (2001) job crafting theory as a theoretical background and aimed to enable employees to broaden or constrict their work and interpersonal role boundaries, as well as their sense of meaning and purpose at work to effectively utilize strengths and direct efforts toward fulfilling their interests. Compared with the latter interventions, the former interventions have largely been consistent in their impact on job crafting behavior. The majority of studies delivered all or part of the intervention through workshops (61 percent), while another 27 percent was instructor-led training. Only three studies used web-based intervention delivery methods involving e-learning and self-paced coaching.

Approximately 67 percent of the interventions proved to be effective in improving job crafting behaviors. This indicates that job crafting interventions were generally effective in boosting the trained behaviors as a test of manipulation check. Next to job crafting, about 42 percent of the interventions found an improvement in work-related attitudes, particularly improvement of work engagement but also need satisfaction and decrease in disengagement. Also, mental health was improved in 30 percent of the studies including decreased psychological distress, reduced negative affect, reduced emotional exhaustion, and improved positive affect and work–life balance. Although job crafting interventions have been more effective in improving contextual performance (Oprea et al., 2019), they have also been found to improve task performance (Gordon et al., 2018; van Wingerden et al., 2016, 2017a, 2017b) and adaptive performance (Demerouti et al., 2017; Gordon et al., 2018). Similar to the job crafting literature (Petrou et al., 2018), job crafting interventions are found to have a favorable effect on employees' ability to deal with organizational change, such as openness to change (Demerouti et al., 2017), change related-safety behavior and positive attitude to change (Demerouti et al., 2021).

Process Evaluation of Job Crafting Interventions

Next to the effectiveness of the interventions to improve favorable outcomes, several studies have examined how (mediators) and when and for whom (moderators) interventions are effective. Uncovering the proper mechanisms of change, which unfold during the job crafting interventions is not only important to understand these processes (why does the intervention lead to outcomes) but also to exclude alternative explanations. Using a quasi-experimental study design and a control condition rules out the possibility of a Hawthorne effect, as individuals in the experimental condition should show improvements in the distal outcomes due to the trained behaviors (job crafting) instead of the attention that they received from the researchers or due to participation in change per se (Holman et al., 2010).

Mukherjee and Dhar (2023) found in their review that of the 10 studies that tested mediating mechanisms, job crafting behavior was the most prominent mediator, either as an overall job crafting score or specific dimensions of job crafting. However, no conclusions can be drawn that either a specific job crafting dimension or the overall job crafting score are more effective mediators as results differ per study context. Next to job crafting two other mediators have been found to mediate the intervention-outcome relationship. Supporting the role of a motivational pathway, van Wingerden and colleagues (2017a) found that the job crafting intervention leads to work engagement through the mediating function of employees' sense of satisfaction with their basic needs. Representing the role of an affective pathway, Demerouti and colleagues (2017) found that positive affect mediates the association between job crafting intervention and openness to change and adaptive performance.

In their meta-analysis, Oprea and colleagues (2019) found that the job crafting interventions were more effective in improving work engagement when the participants created job crafting plans that involved both organizational and personal goals rather than only personal goals. Occupation did not have a moderator effect on overall job crafting. Moreover, autonomy (Barzin et al., 2021) and workload (Barzin et al., 2021; Knight et al., 2021; Kuijpers et al., 2020) were the most frequently reported moderator variables. Workload moderated the indirect relationship between intervention and work engagement via job crafting such that this effect was found significant only for workers with a heavy workload and not for those facing mild or no workload (Kuijpers et al., 2020). On the contrary, Barzin and colleagues (2021) found that when participants' levels of workload were high, the intervention led to a decrease in strengths use. Moreover, the intervention of Barzin and colleagues (2021) showed that when autonomy levels were high, the intervention decreased seeking social resources job crafting behavior perhaps because the intervention supports employees in feeling more empowered, and feel lower need to seek external help, such as social support, coaching or mentoring. In line with the expectations, participants who reported low levels of autonomy increased their work–life balance more as a result of the intervention compared to those with high levels of autonomy.

Regarding the moderating role of individual demographic characteristics, research by Dorien Kooij and colleagues (2017) found that age significantly moderated the effect of job crafting intervention on crafting toward strengths; however, age failed to act as a moderator between the intervention and crafting toward interests. A strikingly unexpected result was the detrimental effect of job crafting intervention on crafting behaviors and subsequently on person–job fit for younger employees. These results highlight older workers' capability and determination to craft in line with their talents and desires making them more receptive to the intervention and at the same time the difficulty of younger employees to deal with insights that come out during the training (e.g., participant's person–job misfit that comes out during the exercises; Mukherjee & Dhar, 2023).

Taken together, although it is important to empirically test the mediating mechanism through which the intervention increases positive outcomes, less than one-third of the studies seem to conduct such tests. Job crafting behaviors seem to be the most frequently found mediating mechanism although the specific dimensions vary per study. Only a few studies have tested the role of moderators in modifying the effectiveness of the interventions. The results are not consistent across the studies pointing to the necessity to accumulate more evidence.

Future Research on Job Crafting Interventions

Although many questions remain unanswered, given the knowledge base so far and the results that job crafting interventions seem to lead to, it is worthwhile to continue to optimize the design, implementation, and evaluation methodologies of job crafting interventions. Below we suggest a number of avenues that can build and strengthen job crafting intervention research and practice.

Suggestions to increase the effectiveness of job crafting interventions

Needs assessment. Broaden the needs assessment to other stakeholders in the organization. To gain a broader view of what needs to change in the organization to improve well-being and performance, it is important to include other stakeholders and broader data in the pre-intervention interviews. Existing data such as employee satisfaction surveys can also help to assess where change is most needed and to assess whether job crafting is the most appropriate intervention, given other policies and procedures in the organization. When the basic building blocks for safe and healthy work are not in place, we recommend addressing those structural needs first and only later implementing job crafting interventions. This avoids a "blaming the victim" approach, where employees feel made responsible for their own work engagement, while the organization is not doing their fair share to create a healthy workplace.

Multi-level interventions. To sustain and facilitate the positive effects of job crafting interventions on employees, we recommend exploring ways of combining individual-level interventions with interventions focused on other levels in the organization. According to the IGLOO framework of multi-level interventions, chances of systemically improving health and well-being in organizations are greater when interventions are combined at different levels in the organization (De Angelis et al., 2020), such as combining a team job crafting intervention with a focus on leadership development (van den Heuvel et al., 2023).

Job crafting for leaders. Related to the above, and important to improve the transfer of learning from the intervention to the work floor, is to train leaders in the principles of job crafting. Not only to improve their own well-being and performance but also to make them aware that job crafting is a form of self-regulation that can support employees to stay motivated and healthy at work. Haijiang Wang (2017) demonstrated that leaders can support employees to perform well by motivating them to craft their job. Taking this a step further, leaders can be trained to stimulate job crafting behaviors in their followers. A recent example is the intervention for senior leaders in a hospital setting by Evelien van Leeuwen and colleagues (2023). Future studies should further examine how to best include leaders in the process of effective job crafting of employees.

Using technology and AI. Looking ahead, we recommend that job crafting intervention researchers increase the collaboration with digital technology and AI experts. This may be particularly important to help employees to stick to their self-set goals. Action plans could be digitalized with reminders to keep up the motivation of the participants. For example, using "coaching chatbots" may be an effective way to allow for more than a reminder, but such a chatbot may prolong the effects of the intervention, by providing guidance, feedback, and advice after the group training session. We still think that group sessions are an important part of job crafting interventions because the social exchange that takes place between participants from various work environments seems to strengthen the awareness of their own work situation as well as the commitment to the self-set changes. These mechanisms could be empirically studied in future studies and AI-based job crafting interventions could be compared with more traditional group-based sessions. The recent studies by Lorenz Verelst and colleagues (2021) and Demerouti (2023) showed that job crafting can be stimulated with e-learning modules which were shown to not only be effective in stimulating job crafting behavior (see Verelst et al., 2021) but also outcomes, like motivation, through job crafting (see Demerouti, 2023).

Suggestions to improve the methodology of job crafting interventions

Although in the past decades job crafting interventions have acquired a strong theoretical and empirical basis, there are still several issues that need to be addressed in future research and practice in order to further develop the design and methodology of the intervention as well as the study on its efficacy to (1) apply rigorous research designs, (2) use active control groups, (3) consider customized intervention groups and measures, (4) consider a broad range of mediating explanatory mechanisms, (5) expand the choice of moderators, and (6) carefully choose the types of outcomes.

Apply rigorous research designs. Based on their systematic review of job crafting interventions Mukherjee and Dhar (2023) present several recommendations for the advancement of establishing the effectiveness of job crafting interventions. One essential suggestion is to aim to adopt randomized control trials (RCTs) in which participants are randomly assigned to control and experimental groups. However, because RCTs are notoriously challenging to conduct in real-world settings, a quasi-experimental interrupted time series design may be used instead. Longitudinal research designs are advised for assessing the long-term impact of job crafting interventions and are recommended for use. Prior literature and theory can assist researchers in projecting how soon and over what time period changes in employee job crafting behavior will occur. Finally, for interventions to reach universal findings, studies must be repeated and replicated over a broader range of occupational contexts and groups.

Use active control groups. A prerequisite for RCTs is the use of control groups. The review of Mukherjee and Dhar (2023) reveals that hardly any studies make use of active control groups (see amongst others Knight et al., 2021 for a notable exception). Active control groups enable researchers to compare two types of interventions and measure their effectiveness against one another, as well as assure internal validity.

Consider customized intervention groups. Future studies may focus on developing interventions that address the needs of specific groups (van den Heuvel et al., 2019). Burned-out employees, for instance, have different needs and motivations than those who are engaged, satisfied, or workaholics. It would therefore a positive development to create customized versions of job crafting interventions aimed specifically at training employees at high risk of developing burnout and employees returning to work after burnout so that not only their burnout symptoms are reduced but also their functioning and performance at work can be improved. This is also in line with the study of Knight and colleagues (2021) who found that participants with a high initial workload engaged in more crafting behaviors to decrease their hindering demands, whereas those with a low initial workload engaged in more crafting behaviors aimed at increasing structural resources.

In addition, examining the effectiveness of job crafting interventions for specific employee groups might also be a worthwhile endeavor. In addition, most intervention studies have been done in WEIRD contexts (Western, Educated, Industrialized, Rich, and Democratic) and more knowledge is needed on how job crafting interventions work in non-WEIRD contexts (Duan et al., 2022). When using customized intervention designs for various groups and contexts, it is recommended to also customize measures to more precisely measure the impact of interventions (see, e.g., Nielsen & Abildgaard, 2012).

Consider a broad range of mediating, explanatory mechanisms. Current empirical research has only provided a limited understanding of the distinctive mechanisms by which job crafting interventions influence desired outcomes. In this respect, Mukherjee and Dhar (2023) recommend using the JD-R framework and the job characteristics theory to investigate a broad range of job characteristics and personal resources as potential mediating mechanisms in delivering desirable outcomes. Next to this, future research should also consider self-determination theory-based mechanisms and social exchange-based mechanisms as potential explaining processes that underpin the intervention–outcome relationship.

Expand the choice of moderators. Research suggests that there are several contingency factors that are relevant to the occurrence of job crafting (van den Heuvel et al., 2019) and yet moderators of job crafting interventions are still underexplored. In line with Mukherjee and Dhar (2023), we suggest incorporating and carefully exploring the role of relevant moderators on the individual, organizational, and team and leadership levels.

Carefully choose the types of outcomes. It is vital for future research to critically examine the types of outcomes that are relevant to the work content and context of the training participants. Extending the range of outcomes to test if the intervention may also produce undesirable outcomes, like counterproductive work behaviors, is also essential (Demerouti & Bakker, 2022). Furthermore, future research must also keep up with modern workplace issues and trends and avoid ignoring essential contemporary outcomes such as creativity and innovation, customer-service related outcomes, and career-related constructs like sustainable employability.

Conclusions

In recent years, our understanding of job crafting interventions has advanced significantly, revealing a variety of insights, methods, and techniques. In general, this growing knowledge has shed light on the advantages of empowering employees to reshape their own work experiences. The goal of this chapter was to synthesize existing knowledge about the development, theorizing, and effectiveness of job crafting interventions with the hope of inspiring future researchers and practitioners to learn from and build on prior experiences with job crafting interventions. In addition, despite the wealth of knowledge gained, the chapter also addressed some challenges that lie on the horizon in the field of job crafting interventions. One such major challenge is understanding and improving the transfer of learning from the intervention to the work floor to ensure the long-term effects of job crafting on employee well-being and performance. Addressing individual differences and tailoring job crafting approaches to meet diverse employee needs in diverse work contexts (such as non-WEIRD contexts) is also an ongoing challenge. Moreover, considering the influence of leadership in supporting or hindering job crafting initiatives presents yet other additional challenges. In addition, we also need to be mindful of potential unintended consequences that may arise from job crafting interventions, such as increased workload or counterproductive work behavior. By creatively addressing these and other challenges, and hereby embracing new possibilities that emerging technologies can offer, we can harness the full potential of job crafting interventions. Continued collaboration between academia and organizations is pivotal to navigating these challenges and developing evidence-based best practices for effective job crafting interventions that ultimately create more fulfilling work environments.

References

Ajzen, I. (2015). The theory of planned behaviour is alive and well, and not ready to retire: A commentary on Sniehotta, Presseau, and Araújo-Soares. *Health Psychology Review 9*, 131–137.

Bakker, A. B., & Demerouti, E. (2018). Multiple levels in job demands-resources theory: Implications for employee well-being and performance. In E. Diener, S. Oishi, & L. Tay (Eds.), *Handbook of wellbeing* (pp. 1–13). DEF Publishers.

Bakker, A. B., Demerouti, E., & Sanz-Vergel, A. (2023). Job demands–resources theory: Ten years later. *Annual Review of Organizational Psychology and Organizational Behavior 10*, 25–53.

Bandura, A. (1989). Human agency in social cognitive theory. *American Psychologist 44*(9), 1175.

Bandura, A. (1997). *Self-efficacy: The exercise of control*. Freeman.

Barzin, L., Vîrga, D. M., & Rusu, A. (2021). The effectiveness of a job crafting, strengths use, and deficit correction intervention on employee proactive behaviors and well-being: A randomized controlled trial. *Psihologia Resurselor Umane 19*(2), 100–122. https://doi.org/10.24837/pru.v19i2.496

Benner, P. (1984). *From novice to expert*. Addison-Wesley.

Benner, P. E., Benner, P., Hooper-Kyriakidis, P. L., Kyriakidis, P. L. H., & Stannard, D. (2011). *Clinical wisdom and interventions in acute and critical care: A thinking-in-action approach*. Springer Publishing Company.

Berg, J. M., Dutton, J. E., Wrzesniewski, A., & Baker, W. E. (2013). *Job crafting exercise*. University of Michigan.

Briner, R. B., & Reynolds, S. (1999). The costs, benefits, and limitations of organizational level stress interventions. *Journal of Organizational Behavior 20*(5), 647–664.

Bruning, P. F., & Campion, M. A. (2018). A role-resource approach-avoidance model of job crafting: A multimethod integration and extension of job crafting theory. *Academy of Management Journal 61*(2), 499–522. https://doi.org/10.5465/amj.2015.0604

Costantini, A., Demerouti, E., Ceschi, A., & Sartori, R. (2022). Implementing job crafting behaviors: Exploring the effects of a job crafting intervention based on the theory of planned behavior. *Journal of Applied Behavioral Science 58*(3), 477–512. https://doi.org/10.1177/0021886320975913

De Angelis, M., Giusino, D., Nielsen, K., Aboagye, E., Christensen, M., Innstrand, S. T., Mazzetti, G., van den Heuvel, M., Sijbom, R. B. L., Pelzer, V. Chiesa, R., & Pietrantoni, L. (2020). H-WORK project: Multilevel interventions to promote mental health in SMEs and public workplaces. *International Journal of Environmental Research and Public Health 17*, 8035. https://doi.org/10.3390/ijerph17218035

Demerouti, E. (2023). Effective employee strategies for remote working: An online self-training intervention. *Journal of Vocational Behavior 142*, 103857.

Demerouti, E., & Bakker, A. B. (2022). Job demands-resources theory in times of crises: New propositions. *Organizational Psychology Review 13*, 209–236. https://doi.org/10.1177/20413866221135022

Demerouti, E., Bakker, A. B., Nachreiner, F., & Schaufeli, W. B. (2001). The job demands-resources model of burnout. *Journal of Applied Psychology 86*(3), 499.

Demerouti, E., & Peeters, M. C. (2018). Transmission of reduction-oriented crafting among colleagues: A diary study on the moderating role of working conditions. *Journal of Occupational and Organizational Psychology 91*(2), 209–234

Demerouti, E., Soyer, L. M., Vakola, M., & Xanthopoulou, D. (2021). The effects of a job crafting intervention on the success of an organizational change effort in a blue-collar work environment. *Journal of Occupational and Organizational Psychology 94*(2), 374–399.

Demerouti, E. Veldhuis, W., Coombes, C., & Hunter, R. (2019) Burnout among pilots: Psychosocial factors related to happiness and performance at simulator training. *Ergonomics 62*(2), 233–245 https://doi.org/10.1080/00140139.2018.1464667

Demerouti, E., Xanthopoulou, D., Petrou, P., & Karagkounis, C. (2017). Does job crafting assist dealing with organizational changes due to austerity measures? Two studies among Greek employees. *European Journal of Work and Organizational Psychology 26*(4), 574–589.

Duan, W., Klibert, J., Schotanus-Dijkstra, M., Llorens, S., van den Heuvel, M., Mayer, C-H., Tomasulo, D., Liao, Y., & van Zyl, L. E. (2022). Positive psychological interventions: How, when and why they work: Beyond WEIRD contexts. *Frontiers in Psychology 13*, 1–8 https://doi.org/10.3389/fpsyg.2022.1021539

Dubbelt, L., Demerouti, E., & Rispens, S. (2019). The value of job crafting for work engagement, task performance, and career satisfaction: Longitudinal and quasi- experimental evidence. *European Journal of Work and Organizational Psychology 28*(3), 300–314. https://doi.org/10.1080/1359432X.2019.1576632

Frese, M., & Fay, D. (2001). Personal initiative: An active performance concept for work in the 21st century. *Research in Organizational Behavior 23*, 133–187.

Geldenhuys, M., Bakker, A. B., & Demerouti, E. (2021). How task, relational and cognitive crafting relate to job performance: A weekly diary study on the role of meaningfulness. *European Journal of Work and Organizational Psychology 30*(1), 83–94.

Gordon, H. J., Demerouti, E., Le Blanc, P. M., Bakker, A. B., Bipp, T., & Verhagen, M. A. (2018). Individual job redesign: Job crafting interventions in healthcare. *Journal of Vocational Behavior 104*, 98–114.

Holman, D. J., Axtell, C. M., Sprigg, C. A., Totterdell, P., & Wall, T. D. (2010). The mediating role of job characteristics in job redesign interventions: A serendipitous quasi-experiment. *Journal of Organizational Behavior 31*(1), 84–105.

Holman, D., Escaffi-Schwarz, M., Vasquez, C. A., Irmer, J. P., & Zapf, D. (2023). Does job crafting affect employee outcomes via job characteristics? A meta-analytic test of a key job crafting mechanism. *Journal of Occupational and Organizational Psychology 97*, 47–73.

Hulshof, I. L., Demerouti, E., & Le Blanc, P. M. (2020). Providing services during times of change: Can employees maintain their levels of empowerment, work engagement and service quality through a job crafting intervention? *Frontiers in Psychology 11*, 87. https://doi.org/10.3389/fpsyg.2020.00087

Kelley, T. L. (1927). *Interpretation of educational measurements*. World Book Co.

Knight, C., Patterson, M., & Dawson, J. (2017). Building work engagement: A systematic review and meta-analysis investigating the effectiveness of work engagement interventions. *Journal of Organizational Behavior 38*, 792–812.

Knight, C., Tims, M., Gawke, J., & Parker, S. K. (2021). When do job crafting interventions work? The moderating roles of workload, intervention intensity, and participation. *Journal of Vocational Behavior 124*, 103522. https://doi.org/10.1016/j.jvb.2020.103522

Kolb, D. A., Boyatzis, R. E., & Mainemelis, C. (2001). *Experiential learning theory: Previous research and new directions in perspectives on thinking, learning, and cognitive styles*. Taylor & Francis.

Kompier, M. A. J., & Cooper, C. L. (Eds.). (1999). *Preventing stress, improving productivity: European case studies in the workplace*. Routledge.

Kooij, D. T., van Woerkom, M., Wilkenloh, J., Dorenbosch, L., & Denissen, J. J. (2017). Job crafting towards strengths and interests: The effects of a job crafting intervention on person–job fit and the role of age. *Journal of Applied Psychology 102*(6), 971.

Kuijpers, E., Kooij, D. T. A. M., & van Woerkom, M. (2020). Align your job with yourself: The relationship between a job crafting intervention and work engagement, and the role of workload. *Journal of Occupational Health Psychology 25*(1), 1–16. https://doi.org/10.1037/ocp0000175

Lambert, B., Caza, B. B., Trinh, E., & Ashford, S. (2022). Individual-centered interventions: Identifying what, how, and why interventions work in organizational contexts. *Academy of Management Annals 16*, 508–546.

Latham, G. P., & Locke, E. A. (2007). New developments in and directions for goal-setting research. *European Psychologist 12*(4), 290–300. https://doi.org/10.1027/1016-9040.12.4.290

Lazazzara, A., Tims, M., & De Gennaro, D. (2020). The process of reinventing a job: A meta-synthesis of qualitative job crafting research. *Journal of Vocational Behavior 116*, 103267.

Löhr, G. (2022). What are abstract concepts? On lexical ambiguity and concreteness ratings. *Review of Philosophy and Psychology 13*, 549–566. https://doi.org/10.1007/s13164-021-00542-9

Lu, C. Q., Wang, H. J., Lu, J. J., Du, D. Y., & Bakker, A. B. (2014). Does work engagement increase person–job fit? The role of job crafting and job insecurity. *Journal of Vocational Behavior 84*(2), 142–152.

Marsh, H. W., Pekrun, R., Parker, P. D., Murayama, K., Guo, J., Dicke, T., & Arens, A. K. (2019). The murky distinction between self-concept and self-efficacy: Beware of lurking jingle-jangle fallacies. *Journal of Educational Psychology 111*(2), 331.

Mukherjee, T., & Dhar, R. L. (2023). Unraveling the black box of job crafting interventions: A systematic literature review and future prospects. *Applied Psychology 72*, 1270–1323.

Nielsen, K. (2013). How can we make organizational interventions work? Employees and line managers as actively crafting interventions. *Human Relations 66*(8), 1029–1050.

Nielsen, K., & Abildgaard, J. S. (2012). The development and validation of a job crafting measure for use with blue-collar workers. *Work & Stress 26*(4), 365–384.

Nielsen, K., & Miraglia, M. (2017). What works for whom in which circumstances? On the need to move beyond the "what works?" question in organizational intervention research. *Human Relations 70*, 40–62.

Nielsen, K., Yarker, J., Munir, F., & Bültmann, U. (2018). IGLOO: An integrated framework for sustainable return to work in workers with common mental disorders. *Work & Stress 32*, 400–417.

Oprea, B. T., Barzin, L., Vîrgă, D., Iliescu, D., & Rusu, A. (2019). Effectiveness of job crafting interventions: A meta-analysis and utility analysis. *European Journal of Work and Organizational Psychology 28*(6), 723–741.

Parker, S. K., & Zhang, F. (2016). Designing work that works in the contemporary world: Future directions for job design research. In A. Shimazu, R. Nordin, M. Dollard, & J. Oakman (Eds.), *Psychosocial factors at work in the Asia pacific: From theory to practice* (pp. 135–150). Springer.

Petrou, P., Demerouti, E., & Schaufeli, W. B. (2018). Crafting the Change: The Role of Employee Job Crafting Behaviors for Successful Organizational Change. *Journal of Management 44*(5), 1766–1792. https://doi.org/10.1177/0149206315624961

Roczniewska, M., Rogala, A., Marszałek, M., Hasson, H., Bakker, A. B., & von Thiele Schwarz, U. (2023). Job crafting interventions: What works, for whom, why, and in which contexts? Research protocol for a systematic review with coincidence analysis. *Systematic Reviews 12*, 10. https://doi.org/10.1186/s13643-023-02170-z

Tims, M., & Bakker, A. B. (2010). Job crafting: Towards a new model of individual job redesign. *SA Journal of Industrial Psychology 36*(2), 1–9.

van den Heuvel, M., Demerouti, E., & Peeters, M. C. W. (2015). The job crafting intervention: Effects on job resources, self-efficacy, and affective well-being. *Journal of Occupational and Organizational Psychology 88*(3), 511–532.

van den Heuvel, M., Pelzer, V., Sijbom, R, Van Hooft, E. (2023). The strengths-based team crafting intervention for project teams: Development, implementation and initial results [Conference Presentation]. Twenty-first European Association of Work and Organizational Psychology Conference, 24–27 May, Katowice, Poland. https://eawop2023.org/static/sites/tcekd_eawop_2022/DRAFT-book-of-abstract.pdf

van den Heuvel, M., Petrou, P., Demerouti, E., & Peeters, M. C. W. (2019). Job crafting: What do we know, where do we go? In T. Taris, M. Peeters, & H. De Witte (Eds.), *The fun and frustration of modern working life: Contributions from an occupational health psychology perspective* (pp. 198–211). Pelckmans Pro

van Leeuwen, E. H., Knies, E., van Rensen, E. L. J., Taris, T. W., van den Heuvel, M., & Lammers, J.-W. J. (2023). The systematic development of an online career-oriented people management training for line managers of professionals: A pilot field intervention study. *Public Personnel Management 53*(1), 61–84. https://doi.org/10.1177/00910260231176510

van Wingerden, J., Bakker, A. B., & Derks, D. (2016). A test of a job demands-resources intervention. *Journal of Managerial Psychology 31*(3), 686–701.

van Wingerden, J., Bakker, A. B., & Derks, D. (2017a). The longitudinal impact of a job crafting intervention. *European Journal of Work and Organizational Psychology 26*, 107–119.

van Wingerden, J., Bakker, A. B., & Derks, D. (2017b). Fostering employee well-being via a job crafting intervention. *Journal of Vocational Behavior 100*, 164–174.

Verelst, L., De Cooman, R., Verbruggen, M., van Laar, C., & Meeussen, L. (2021). The development and validation of an electronic job crafting intervention: Testing the links with job crafting and person–job fit. *Journal of Occupational and Organizational Psychology 94*(2), 338–373.

Wang, H. H. (2017). *Leadership, job crafting and work outcomes: can leaders cultivate well-performing job crafters?* [Doctoral dissertation, Eindhoven University of Technology].

Wrzesniewski, A., & Dutton, J. E. (2001). Crafting a job: Revisioning employees as active crafters of their work. *Academy of Management Review 26*(2), 179–201.

Zhang, F., & Parker, S. K. (2019). Reorienting job crafting research: A hierarchical structure of job crafting concepts and integrative review. *Journal of Organizational Behavior 40*(2), 126–146.

It Pays to Play

Playful Work Design

Arnold B. Bakker and Yuri S. Scharp

Job design research of the past two decades has clearly shown that individuals can thrive in jobs that are challenging and resourceful (Bakker et al., 2023a). Thus, complex tasks and deadlines are particularly engaging if employees have access to relevant job resources, such as autonomy, skill variety, and opportunities for development. However, it is more difficult to thrive when work is characterized by hindrance job demands, such as bureaucratic hassles and interpersonal conflicts (LePine et al., 2005; Scharp et al., 2021). Even advanced work tasks may eventually be experienced as unfulfilling when these tasks become repetitive or monotonous (e.g., Da Silva Moro et al., 2022). How do employees stay engaged on the days they are confronted with such hindrance demands?

In this chapter, we discuss a new bottom-up approach to job design called playful work design—"the proactive cognitive-behavioral orientation aimed at fostering fun and challenge during work activities through creating, seeking, and resolving surprises and complexities" (Scharp et al., 2023, p. 7). Whereas job crafting is a job design strategy referring to proactively changing the prevailing job demands and job resources (Tims et al., 2016), playful work design takes place at the *task* level and reflects proactively using an alternative approach to work without necessarily changing the nature of the job. After discussing the role of play at work, we introduce the playful work design concept, and review recent research on its predictors, outcomes, and boundaries. We also consider opportunities for future research and outline how organizations may foster playful work design through leadership and training interventions.

Theoretical Background

Play at work may take various forms—an employee may make jokes while helping a customer, play a game of soccer with colleagues as part of an interdepartmental competition, or challenge themselves to deal with forty emails in one hour. According to Meredith Van Vleet and Brooke Feeney (2015, p. 640),

Arnold B. Bakker and Yuri S. Scharp, *It Pays to Play*. In: *Transformative Work Design*. Edited by: Sharon K. Parker et al., Oxford University Press. © Society for Industrial and Organizational Psychology (2025). DOI: 10.1093/oso/9780197692554.003.0018

play is an "activity or behavior that (a) is carried out with the goal of amusement and fun, (b) involves an enthusiastic and in-the-moment attitude or approach, and (c) is highly interactive among play partners or with the activity itself." While play may at times be at odds with work and have social costs (Petelczyc et al., 2018), research has primarily revealed favorable consequences, such as developing instrumental relationships with clients and creating bonding experiences with colleagues (cf., Fisher, 1992). Play activity increases task involvement, encourages divergent thinking, and improves problem solving (Jacobs & Statler, 2006). Moreover, play can reduce job stress and boredom and increase learning and creativity (Celestine & Yeo, 2021; Petelczyc et al., 2018).

In his book, *Homo Ludens* (*Playing Man*), the Dutch philosopher Johan Huizinga (1949) identified two types of play: ludic and agonistic play. Ludic comes from the Latin word *ludus*, which refers to fun things, such as stage shows, games, and jokes (Merriam-Webster, 2022). Ludic play is spontaneous, arbitrary, and irrational, and focuses on the use of humor and fantasy; for example, when joking, using vivid imagination, and improvisational acting (e.g., Barnett, 2007; Martin & Ford, 2018). Agonistic comes from the Greek word *agōn*, which refers to competition and contest. Agonistic play is more serious and rational, and focuses on challenges, rules, and goals, such as in sports, games, and competition (e.g., Csikszentmihalyi, 2014). We discuss below how both forms of play are included in our playful work design approach.

Playful Work Design

When employees practice playful work design, they use play and personal initiative to create fun and competition during work activities (Scharp et al., 2023). This involves proactively changing how the work activity is approached and performed to regulate cognitions and emotions and to stimulate active learning (Celestine & Yeo, 2021). Thus, playful work design is a proactive cognitive-behavioral approach to work activities that aims to make these activities more interesting and meaningful. For example, a retail security guard may try to predict customer behavior, thereby setting a goal and creating a challenge. As another example, a university professor may use a curious word in a boring meeting to invigorate herself and colleagues through an element of surprise (for more examples, see Table 18.1).

The examples highlight several defining characteristics that differentiate playful work design from other forms of play. First, playful work design is self-initiated, whereas play in the form of a soccer match between departments

Table 18.1 Examples of Playful Work Design Aimed at Creating Fun and Competition

Designing Fun	Designing Competition
A call center employee imagines a funny narrative that explains the issue to the customer to make work more amusing.	A cashier makes their work more challenging by scanning articles as fast as possible.
A teacher makes grading more fun by adding small doodles and drawings.	A train operator fosters excitement by striving to finish their announcement exactly when the train comes to a halt at the station.
A healthcare worker integrates jokes into their appointment with a patient.	A delivery worker promotes a sense of triumph by aiming to finish their route faster than their personal record.
An administrative worker enters data into the file to the rhythm of the music.	A programmer creates excitement by approaching coding as a puzzle.
A copyeditor tries to discover amusing incongruities in the text.	A receptionist challenges themselves to greet every person in a different way.

or gamification of employee training is initiated by others. Second, playful work design aims to channel attention toward the task in contrast to play initiatives, such as fantasizing or a game of ping pong, which divert attention away from work. Third, playful work design is embedded in work activities, whereas non-work episodes contextualize other forms of play, such as exchanging jokes during lunch or video gaming. Fourth, playful work design primarily focuses on regulating the personal experience of work, whereas other play initiatives, such as hostile humor, mainly use play to regulate the affective experience of others.

When employees use playful work design, they approach the work activity as an opportunity for play and identify how play can increase their personal interest and meaning. They may achieve this by using two distinguishable strategies: designing fun and designing competition (Scharp et al., 2023). First, employees may *design fun*, amusement, and entertainment during work activities by using humor, fantasy, narratives, music, and creativity. Second, employees may *design competition*, challenge, and drive during work activities by segmenting tasks, keeping score, testing predictions, and striving to outperform past achievements. While designing fun and designing competition differ in the envisioned future and in how this is achieved (see Table 18.1), the two strategies correspond in the proactive use of play to foster activated positive emotions.

468   TRANSFORMATIVE WORK DESIGN

Important here is that individuals are proactive and intentionally change their approach to work so that it becomes more engaging. Proactive individuals challenge the status quo rather than passively adapting to the situation or events (Crant, 2000). Proactive behavior is defined as "anticipatory action that employees take to impact themselves and/or their environments" (Grant & Ashford, 2008, p. 13). The literature has revealed several examples of proactive behavior, including role expansion, feedback-seeking, and job crafting (Parker et al., 2010). Such behaviors may improve the situation or oneself by generating various personal and social resources. Playful work design differentiates itself from these proactive behaviors due to its embedded and dynamic nature at the task-level. In contrast to other proactive behaviors that reflect activities in themselves, playful work design is embedded in existing activities—it improves the *experience* by restructuring cognition and behavior in relation to the activities. Playful work design promotes greater compatibility between the worker and the work activity through proactive changes in the self (i.e., how work is approached) and the situation (i.e., how work is performed).

It should be noted that job crafting has been defined as behaviors through which employees proactively change their (1) own job demands and job resources (Tims et al., 2016), or (2) work tasks, social relationships, or the perception of work (Wrzesniewski & Dutton, 2001). The latter strategy is called *cognitive crafting*, and it involves actively changing the thoughts or beliefs regarding one's job or reframing the purpose of work so that it becomes more meaningful. Cognitive crafting seems partly related to playful work design. However, crafting is not necessarily playful and instead operates at a higher-order level (i.e., considering the job as a whole and in relation to the organization or society; Bindl et al., 2019). In contrast, playful work design involves behaviors and thoughts that directly facilitate task execution (by making specific tasks more interesting, playful, challenging, and entertaining). Research has indeed shown that job crafting and playful work design have unique effects on performance (Bakker et al., 2020).

Employees may bundle, merge, or alternate between play initiatives (see Figure 18.1). When employees bundle play initiatives, they stack play initiatives of similar nature during a task. For instance, when an information and communication technology (ICT) worker fosters fun and entertainment by exchanging jokes with a customer in addition to imagining an amusing narrative that explains how the issue arose, they bundle designing fun initiatives. In contrast, merging play initiatives implies using designing fun in combination with designing competition. For instance, the ICT worker *merges* initiatives when they work to the rhythm of music (designing fun) as well as strives to set a time record (designing competition) to foster fun and drive. Finally, when employees *alternate* between designing fun and designing competition, they switch initiatives between tasks. For instance, the ICT worker may approach each paragraph as a challenge when writing a report (designing competition), but then imagine themselves as a detective while solving coding issues (designing fun).

According to the job demands–resources (JD-R) theory (Bakker et al., 2023a), employees may have various motives to engage in proactive behaviors. When work is stressful, employees have a good reason to use job crafting strategies; for example, they may try to optimize their job demands or increase their job resources. When work is boring, employees may want to use job crafting by taking on new job responsibilities. Playful work design differs from job crafting behaviors in that playful work design focuses on the tasks that are performed during specific work episodes. Instead of changing aspects of the job, employees may playfully approach their existing tasks so that these tasks become more fun and/or more challenging. Indeed, JD-R theory proposes that playful work design can be used to promote work engagement and prevent job stress by designing tasks to be more fun (i.e., more interesting, surprising, meaningful—thus, more resourceful from a psychological perspective) and by designing tasks to be more competitive (more inspiring, difficult, and stimulating—thus more challenging). Challenging but resourceful tasks can pull attention and generate meaning as well as task engagement, and indirectly improve task performance (Hopstaken et al., 2016; Reina-Tamayo et al., 2017).

In a series of studies, Yuri S. Scharp and colleagues (2023) developed a psychometrically sound and valid instrument to measure the two forms of playful work design. The findings indicate that the instrument reliably captures individual differences in prototypical manifestations of designing fun and designing competition. In support of the instrument's validity, we have shown that playful work design is positively associated with constructs related to play and proactivity but unrelated to constructs indicative of withdrawal. Moreover, confirmatory factor analyses indicated that playful work design is distinct from job crafting. In addition, several studies have provided evidence for the validity and reliability of the instrument when the items were reframed to indicate day-level behaviors (e.g., Liu et al., 2023; Scharp et al., 2019). The results showed that the two-dimensional factor structure also accurately represents within-person differences in playful work design. The general and daily versions of the instrument enable systematic research into how differences in playful work design between individuals, as well as fluctuations between situations, relate to antecedents and outcomes.

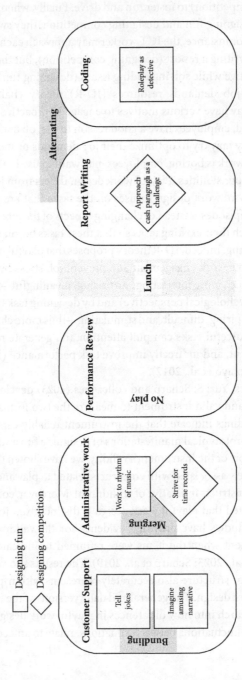

Figure 18.1 Illustration of Bundling, Merging, and Alternating Playful Work Design Initiatives for a Part of the Day of an ICT Worker

Empirical Evidence for Playful Work Design

Some individuals have a natural tendency to be whimsical and seek diversion and entertainment (Proyer, 2012)—a tendency that may convert into playful interactions with work tasks, colleagues, and clients. This raises the question of whether personality is also involved in playful work design. Scharp and colleagues (2023) found that playful work design is more likely among individuals who have a creative personality and who are open to experiences. Individuals with a preference for variety, who are driven by curiosity and have an active imagination are more likely to redesign their work tasks to be more playful. Moreover, Scharp and colleagues (2023, Studies 1 and 3) showed that ludic traits, such as playfulness, humor, and curiosity, were the most important predictors of designing fun, whereas agonistic traits, such as achievement striving, competitiveness, and reward responsiveness, were the most important predictors of designing competition. Similarly, while both playful work design dimensions related to colleague-ratings of work engagement, individuals who designed fun were especially seen as more creative by their colleagues, whereas designing competition mainly predicted their perception of exerted effort.

The predisposition to engage in playful activities and social interactions has been related to stress coping, intrinsic motivation, creativity, and innovative behaviors (Proyer, 2012). This suggests that personality traits may also facilitate or undermine the effectiveness of playful work design. Scharp and colleagues (2019) measured personality traits as well as daily work behaviors for one week and showed that trait playfulness strengthened the positive impact of daily designing competition on work engagement and creativity. Trait openness strengthened the positive impact of daily designing fun on these outcomes. Using a survey design with one month in-between two measurement waves, Miriam Dishon-Berkovits and colleagues (2023) proposed that conscientiousness would moderate the effect of playful work design on work engagement and job performance. Because trait conscientiousness is related to self-discipline, dutifulness, and competence, the authors argued and showed that playful work design particularly facilitated work engagement and performance for individuals *low* in conscientiousness. Apparently, these individuals lacked the perseverance and self-control needed to accomplish things at work—but playful work design helped this group, in particular, to reach their performance goals.

According to Claire Petelczyc and colleagues (2018), individuals use play at work to combat boredom, deal with stress, stimulate flow experiences, or reframe work as a positive experience. Research on playful work design has provided evidence for most of these motives. Arnold B. Bakker and colleagues

(2020) investigated daily playful work design among naval cadets who sailed a large vessel across the Atlantic Ocean. Results showed that playful work design had the strongest positive impact on colleague-ratings of task performance when daily work pressure was low rather than high. This effect was independent of the impact of daily job crafting—and indicated that singing songs during night watches and using humor in interactions with colleagues helped cadets invest effort in their work and stay engaged when work was less challenging.

A later study among another cohort of naval cadets (Bakker, Hetland, et al., 2023) showed that daily designing fun and designing competition had a combined (multiplicative) impact on daily well-being (activated positive affect and reduced exhaustion) and indirectly facilitated performance. Consistent with these findings, Dishon-Berkovits and colleagues (2023) found that playful work design by Israeli employees was most effective in increasing work engagement and job performance when employees experienced boredom during work. Previous research has shown that boredom is more likely when employees are confronted with monotonous and repetitive work, or experience cognitive underload and poor skill utilization (Schaufeli & Salanova, 2014).

Scharp and colleagues (2021) hypothesized that playful work design would be most effective when employees are confronted with daily hindrance job demands—stressors that frustrate important psychological needs. They made a distinction between agency hindrances (repetitive tasks, monotony, and simple tasks) and communion hindrances (interpersonal conflicts, social isolation, emotional job demands), and they predicted that designing competition would help to deal with agency hindrances and that designing fun would help to deal with communion hindrances. The findings supported these specific hypotheses. Daily designing competition moderated (weakened) the negative impact of agency hindrances on work engagement (and indirectly on performance). In contrast, daily designing fun moderated (weakened) the negative impact of communion hindrances on work engagement and performance. Consistent with these findings, Scharp and colleagues (2022b) reasoned that playful work design may especially benefit the well-being of platform workers because they are often confronted with adverse working conditions. They found that platform workers reported lower well-being (lower work engagement, higher exhaustion) than individuals with regular employment arrangements such as a permanent contract, temporary contract, on-demand contract, or self-employment. However, as predicted, particularly platform workers who redesigned their work to be more playful were able to protect their well-being.

In the midst of the COVID-19 pandemic, Bakker and Jessica van Wingerden (2021) investigated how bank employees used playful work design to deal with rumination—repetitively and passively focusing on symptoms of distress caused by COVID-19. Such thoughts impair one's ability to solve problems and can result in a range of negative consequences (Lyubomirsky & Tkach, 2003). Using a repeated measures design, Bakker and van Wingerden (2021) found that playful work design weakened the impact of rumination about COVID-19 on exhaustion and depressive complaints. By playfully redesigning their work tasks, the bank employees distracted themselves from their ruminative thoughts—which helped them to stay vigorous and strong.

In another study, Scharp and colleagues (2022a) investigated basic psychological need satisfaction as an explanatory mechanism. They used self-determination theory to argue and show that daily playful work design would foster daily work engagement through the satisfaction of basic psychological needs. More specifically, on days when employees used playful work design they satisfied their need for autonomy, relatedness, and competence. The satisfaction of the need for autonomy explained why employees felt more engaged on days they designed fun, whereas the satisfaction of the need for competence explained why designing tasks to be more competitive increased work engagement. Similarly, Bakker and colleagues (2023b) found employees performed better on days they designed fun and designed competition because they satisfied their basic needs. These findings show that playful work design can satisfy basic needs, just like job crafting (Bakker & Oerlemans, 2019).

Finally, in an unpublished study among academic staff, Bakker (2023) found that university professors who were confronted with high job demands scored lower on work engagement. However, professors who frequently used playful work design (designing fun and competition) or job crafting in the form of optimizing demands could alleviate the negative impact of daily hassles and emotional demands on work engagement. Taken together, these findings indicate that playful work design promotes work engagement and helps to protect well-being when employees encounter various stressors or hindrance job demands.

Implications for Practice

Organizations may stimulate playful work design through interventions such as trainings and workshops. Such interventions may aim at promoting participants' knowledge and skills in playful work design to realize cognitive and behavioral change. Trainings and workshops may facilitate abstract conceptualization of playful work design, offer concrete experiences (e.g., exercises and knowledge sharing), stimulate reflection on how experiences may change, and facilitate active experimentation with playful work design ideas for future implementation (Kolb & Kolb, 2010). Preliminary support for the effectiveness of a training intervention comes from a small (unpublished) field experiment conducted by Bakker and Scharp in 2020 among a heterogeneous sample of workers. Participants in the intervention group (n = 23) received a lecture about JD-R theory and playful work design. Subsequently, they identified past experiences with playful work design and shared these experiences in subgroups. Finally, they identified opportunities for playful work design in the future. The control group (n = 20) consisted of a waiting list that received no instructions. Results showed that the intervention group increased in playful work design behaviors one month later (Time 2), whereas there was no change in the control group. Furthermore, playful work design was positively associated with work engagement and meaningfulness at Time 2. These findings suggest that stimulating playful work design may be a worthwhile endeavor for organizations.

Organizations may also stimulate playful work design through leadership interventions. Leaders may learn to empower their employees so that they feel comfortable to engage in playful and proactive behaviors. Research has shown that empowering and transformational leadership are positively related to various proactive behaviors, including job crafting (Bakker et al., 2022; Hetland et al., 2018; Thun & Bakker, 2018). This suggests that when leaders trust their followers and provide them with autonomy, followers take personal initiatives to better fit their work with their preferences, interests, and abilities. In the only study linking leadership to playful work design, Muhammad Khan (2023) found that employees' attitude of curiosity especially translated into playful work design behaviors when leaders provided autonomy support.

Discussion

In this chapter, we introduced the concept of playful work design. A series of studies have provided evidence for the two-factor structure of the playful work design instrument, distinguishing between designing fun and designing competition. Playful work design strategies can be reliably assessed, and empirical research shows that many employees naturally engage in these proactive behaviors. Playful work design concerns the interactive involvement with tasks in terms of seeking, finding, and resolving surprises and complexities to garner positive affective states (Scharp et al., 2023). When employees design fun and design competition, they restructure their tasks through cognition and behavior. Hence, active learning seems to be a basic mechanism involved in playful work design as employees engage with the intricacies of their tasks to discover opportunities for play and implement them. Research shows that this process (i.e., playful work design) has important organizational outcomes, including employee well-being (e.g., positive affect, flow, work engagement), creativity, and task performance. People with a playful personality are more likely to engage in playful work design. Creativity, curiosity, openness, achievement orientation, and competitiveness are among the traits that predispose employees to show playful work design. Playful work design is also most effective when needed: when hindrance demands are high, or when challenge demands are low. Moreover, consistent with JD-R theory (Bakker et al., 2023a), we have found that the combination of designing competition and designing fun has the most positive impact on employee well-being and task performance. This is because the combination of the two main playful work design strategies simultaneously fosters challenges and psychological resources during task execution.

Playful work design is defined by its transformative capacity. A bus driver challenging themselves to drive as smoothly as possible and a cashier exchanging jokes with customers while scanning articles promptly shapes the experience of work. By designing fun and designing competition, employees increase their interactivity with the task (and others), and create a sense of progression, potential surprises, and a sense of control. Yet, the imposed experiential qualities of playful work design might be relatively volatile. When the bus driver and cashier seize their efforts to design fun and competition, the imposed reality may quickly dissipate, returning the experience of the task to its ordinary state. Hence, the most sustainable use of playful work design would be to complement this strategy with other JD-R strategies, such as job design and job crafting.

Future Research

We see several opportunities for future research. First, because playful work design has favorable consequences, it is important to further explore how organizations may encourage employees to engage in proactive and playful behaviors when performing their work. Thus far, research suggests that playful work design manifests somewhat independently of the work environment (Bakker et al., 2020; Scharp et al., 2021; Scharp et al., 2023). Indeed, regardless of whether the job provides employees with significant autonomy in decision-making, they may approach and perform their work activities playfully. Nonetheless, the environment may represent an essential predictor of playful work design. Play is traditionally associated with non-work activities. Such beliefs hamper individuals from considering initiating play during work activities. Therefore, signals from the environment that play is permitted and desired may be key predictors (Bateson et al., 2006). The natural inclination to play when the environment signals for it becomes apparent when we consider that most people adopt a playful attitude when interacting with an infant or participating in a game. Similarly, people and objects may stimulate employees to design work playfully.

Leaders and colleagues may both stimulate play. By initiating play themselves, they may signal that play is psychologically safe and welcome. In addition, research has shown that leaders may encourage proactive work behaviors by using empowering or transformational leadership (Hetland et al., 2018; Thun & Bakker, 2018). Empowering leaders provide sufficient job resources and entrust employees with added responsibilities (Ahearne et al., 2005). When employees have the time and latitude to decide for themselves how to perform their tasks, they can create meaning by approaching tasks in proactive ways (Thun & Bakker, 2018). It would be interesting to discover how leaders can stimulate playful work design. Khan (2023) found that leaders who provided autonomy support encouraged employees with a curious attitude to engage in playful work design strategies. Future research may investigate whether leaders can act as role models and influence their employees with playful leadership behaviors. Also, research may reveal whether leaders can learn to facilitate playful work design during (agile) team meetings by creating norms and when actively interacting with their employees (Junker et al., 2022).

Situational characteristics, such as playful objects or real-time progression indicators, may also stimulate playful work design. One option is to signal playfulness in the work environment (e.g., by decorating the wall with pictures of active and playful individuals). A recent study has suggested that in playful work contexts, employees are more open to mood-enhancing, energizing, and uniting behaviors of others and feel more engaged in their work (Fortuin et al., 2023). Similarly, research suggests that introducing playful props in meetings stimulates playfulness and the use of humor (Pham & Bartels, 2021; West et al., 2016). In addition, real-time indicators of progression may stimulate employees to design competition. For instance, employees often use the progression of time as input for developing challenges during work activities. The gamification of other indicators may further stimulate playful work design. For instance, the number of "unread" emails in an email client provides an opportunity to design competition, which may become more apparent when this indicator is designed playfully.

It also seems important for our understanding of playful work design to find out whether there is a tipping point and possible dark side of this behavior. Could playful work design have negative effects on well-being and task performance; for example, when used in an inappropriate social context? Because playfulness is subjective and a matter of interpretation, colleagues or clients could misinterpret the motives of playful actors, which may then backfire and result in impaired social relationships. In addition, designing competition may overextend employees when they work in an already demanding work environment. Future research may reveal the potentially unfavorable consequences of playful work design.

The effects of playful work design may also depend on whether it is (1) habitual, chronic behavior that is consistent across situations (between-person perspective that looks at differences between individuals), or (2) fluctuating behavior that changes from task to task and from day to day (within-person perspective that looks at differences between situations). Most previous studies have investigated short-term fluctuations in playful work design and found favorable effects. However, it is conceivable that chronic forms of playful work design may also have detrimental effects on employee well-being and performance; for example, constantly designing fun and competition during work tasks may not fit with the social norm and may deplete energy (cf., Bakker & Oerlemans, 2019).

It is interesting to note that recent research has revealed that the playful work design concept is generalizable across life domains. Huatian Wang and colleagues (2023) used a weekly diary study to investigate playful study design among university students. They showed that during weeks students proactively used playful study design (e.g., used mind mapping to summarize information, used humor in tutorial meetings), they were more engaged in their study tasks and more likely to reach study goals. Playful study design was most strongly related to goal attainment for students high (vs. low) in proactive personality. Wei Liu and colleagues (2023) used experience sampling to investigate how playful study design during daily study episodes was related to the peak experience of flow, positive affect, and reduced fatigue. Results showed that when students playfully designed their study tasks, they were intrinsically motivated and experienced more flow. Flow, in turn, contributed positively to momentary well-being (activated positive affect, reduced fatigue).

In another series of studies, Sarina Verwijmeren and colleagues (2023) investigated playful sport design among athletes practicing various types of sports (e.g., ball sports, watersports, athletics, cycle sports, gymnastics). They found that playful sport design was most likely among athletes who were characterized by, for example, fantasy proneness, openness to experience, and achievement striving. Athletes who playfully designed their training sessions reported better subjective and objective sports performance (e.g., ran faster on a ten thousand-meter race). Taken together, these early findings provide evidence for the robustness and external validity of the playful work design concept. Future research may further examine how and when playful study and sport design can be effectively used in teaching and training, respectively.

Conclusion

Play is a natural phenomenon that occurs across all domains of life. Research on playful work design shows that the work domain is no exception. Notably, the findings reveal that when individuals approach and conduct their work activities playfully to design fun and competition, they report improved well-being and performance. We conclude it pays to play in an organizational context.

References

Ahearne, M., Mathieu, J., & Rapp, A. (2005). To empower or not to empower your sales force? An empirical examination of the influence of leadership empowerment behavior on customer satisfaction and performance. *Journal of Applied Psychology 90*, 945–955.

Bakker, A. B. (2023). Playful work design among professors. Manuscript in preparation.

Bakker, A. B., Breevaart, K., Scharp, Y. S., & de Vries, J. D. (2023b). Daily self-leadership and playful work design: Proactive approaches of work in times of crisis. *Journal of Applied Behavioral Science 59*(2), 314–336.

Bakker, A. B., Demerouti, E., & Sanz-Vergel, A. (2023a). Job demands–resources theory: Ten years later. *Annual Review of Organizational Psychology and Organizational Behavior 10*, 25–53.

Bakker, A. B., Hetland, J., Kjellevold-Olsen, O., & Espevik, R. (2022). Daily transformational leadership: A source of inspiration for follower performance? *European Management Journal 41*, 700–708.

Bakker, A. B., Hetland, J., Kjellevold-Olsen, O., & Espevik, R. (2023). The duality of playful work design: A diary study of designing fun and competition. Manuscript submitted for publication.

Bakker, A. B., Hetland, J., Kjellevold-Olsen, O., Espevik, R., & De Vries, J. D. (2020). Job crafting and playful work design: Links with performance during busy and quiet days. *Journal of Vocational Behavior 122*, 103478.

Bakker, A. B., & Oerlemans, W. G. (2019). Daily job crafting and momentary work engagement: A self-determination and self-regulation perspective. *Journal of Vocational Behavior 112*, 417–430.

Bakker, A. B., & van Wingerden, J. (2021). Rumination about COVID-19 and employee well-being: The role of playful work design. *Canadian Psychology 62*, 73–79.

Barnett, L. A. (2007). The nature of playfulness in young adults. *Personality and Individual Differences 43*, 949–958.

Bateson, M., Nettle, D., & Roberts, G. (2006). Cues of being watched enhance cooperation in a real-world setting. *Biology Letters 2*, 412–414.

Bindl, U. K., Unsworth, K. L., Gibson, C. B., & Stride, C. B. (2019). Job crafting revisited: Implications of an extended framework for active changes at work. *Journal of Applied Psychology 104*, 605–628.

Celestine, N. A., & Yeo, G. (2021). Having some fun with it: A theoretical review and typology of activity-based play-at-work. *Journal of Organizational Behavior 42*(2), 252–268.

Crant, J. M. (2000). Proactive behavior in organizations. *Journal of Management 26*(3), 435–462.

Csikszentmihalyi, M. (2014). *Flow and the foundations of positive psychology.* Springer.

Da Silva Moro, J., Pezzini Soares, J., Massignan, C., Butini Oliveira, L., Machado Ribeiro, D., Cardoso, M., De Luca Canto, G., & Bolan, M. (2022). Burnout syndrome among dentists: A systematic review and meta-analysis. *Journal of Evidence-Based Dental Practice 22*, 101724.

Dishon-Berkovits, M., Bakker, A. B., & Peters, P. (2023). Playful work design, engagement, and performance: The role of boredom and conscientiousness. *International Journal of Human Resource Management 35*, 256–283.

Fisher, E. P. (1992). The impact of play on development: A meta-analysis. *Play & Culture 5*(2), 159–181.

Fortuin, D., Bakker, A. B., van Mierlo, H., Petrou, P., & Demerouti, E. (2023). How and when do employees energize their team members? The role of team boosting behaviors. *Occupational Health Science 7*, 143–165.

Grant, A. M., & Ashford, S. J. (2008). The dynamics of proactivity at work. *Research in Organizational Behavior 28*, 3–34.

Hetland, J., Hetland, H., Bakker, A. B., & Demerouti, E. (2018). Daily transformational leadership and employee job crafting: The role of promotion focus. *European Management Journal 36*, 746–756.

Hopstaken, J., Van der Linden, D., Bakker, A. B., Kompier, M. A. J., & Leung, Y. K. (2016). Shifts in attention during mental fatigue: Evidence from subjective, behavioral, physiological, and eye-tracking data. *Journal of Experimental Psychology: Human Perception and Performance 42*, 878–889.

Huizinga, J. (1949). *Homo ludens: A study of the play-element in culture.* Routledge & Kegan Paul.

Jacobs, C. D., & Statler, M. (2006). Toward a technology of foolishness: Developing scenarios through serious play. *International Studies of Management & Organization 36*(3), 77–92.

Junker, T. L., Bakker, A. B., Gorgievski, M. J., & Derks, D. (2022). Agile work practices and employee proactivity: A multilevel study. *Human Relations 75*(12), 2189–2217.

Khan, M. A. (2023). From work meaningfulness to playful work design: The role of epistemic curiosity and perceived Leader's autonomous support. *IIM Ranchi Journal of Management Studies 2*, 97–113.

Kolb, A. Y., & Kolb, D. A. (2010). Learning to play, playing to learn: A case study of a ludic learning space. *Journal of Organizational Change Management 23*, 26–50.

LePine, J. A., Podsakoff, N. P., & LePine, M. A. (2005). A meta-analytic test of the challenge stressor-hindrance stressor framework: An explanation for inconsistent relationships among stressors and performance. *Academy of Management Journal 48*, 764–775.

Liu, W., Van der Linden, D., & Bakker, A. B. (2023). *Is proactive behavior a double-edged sword? The link between flow and attentional performance.* Manuscript under review.

Lyubomirsky, S., & Tkach, C. (2003). The consequences of dysphoric rumination. In C. Papageorgiou & A. Wells (Eds.), *Rumination: Nature, theory, and treatment of negative thinking in depression* (pp. 21–41). John Wiley & Sons.

Martin, R. A., & Ford, T. (2018). *The psychology of humor: An integrative approach.* Elsevier.

Merriam-Webster. (2022). Ludic. Merriam-Webster.com dictionary. https://www.merriam-webster.com/dictionary/ludic

Parker, S. K., & Collins, C. G. (2010). Taking stock: Integrating and differentiating multiple proactive behaviors. *Journal of Management 36*, 633–662.

Petelczyc, C. A., Capezio, A., Wang, L., Restubog, S. L. D., & Aquino, K. (2018). Play at work: An integrative review and agenda for future research. *Journal of Management 44*, 161–190.

Pham, T. H., & Bartels, L. K. (2021). Laughing with you or laughing at you: The influence of playfulness and humor on employees' meeting satisfaction and effectiveness. *Journal of Organizational Psychology 21*, 1–18.

Proyer, R. T. (2012). Examining playfulness in adults: Testing its correlates with personality, positive psychological functioning, goal aspirations, and multi-methodically assessed ingenuity. *Psychological Test and Assessment Modeling 54*, 103–127.

Reina-Tamayo, A. M., Bakker, A. B., & Derks, D. (2017). Episodic demands, resources, and engagement: An experience sampling study. *Journal of Personnel Psychology 16*, 125–136.

Scharp, Y., Bakker, A. B., & Breevaart, K. (2022a). Playful work design and employee work engagement: A self-determination perspective. *Journal of Vocational Behavior 134*, 103693.

Scharp, Y. S., Bakker, A. B., Breevaart, K., Kruup, K., & Uusberg, A. (2023). Playful work design: Conceptualization, measurement, and validity. *Human Relations 76*, 509–550.

Scharp, Y. S., Breevaart, K., & Bakker, A. B. (2021). Using playful work design to deal with hindrance job demands: A quantitative diary study. *Journal of Occupational Health Psychology 26*, 175–188.

Scharp, Y. S., Breevaart, K., Bakker, A. B., & Van der Linden, D. (2019). Daily playful work design: A trait activation perspective. *Journal of Research in Personality 82*, 103850.

Scharp, Y. S., ter Hoeven, C., Bakker, A. B., Gorgievski, M., den Dulk, L., & Koster, F. (2022b). Samenhang van platformwerk met werkomstandigheden en welzijn. *Tijdschrift voor Arbeidsvraagstukken 38*(4), 580–600.

Schaufeli, W. B., & Salanova, M. (2014). Burnout, boredom and engagement at the workplace. In M. C. W. Peeters, J. de Jonge, & T. W. Taris (Eds.), *People at work: An introduction to contemporary work psychology* (pp. 293–320). Wiley.

Thun, S., & Bakker, A. B. (2018). Empowering leadership and job crafting: The role of employee optimism. *Stress and Health 34*, 573–581.

Tims, M., Derks, D., & Bakker, A. B. (2016). Job crafting and its relationships with person-job fit and meaningfulness: A three-wave study. *Journal of Vocational Behavior 92*, 44–53.

Van Vleet, M., & Feeney, B. C. (2015). Young at heart: A perspective for advancing research on play in adulthood. *Perspectives on Psychological Science 10*(5), 639–645.

Verwijmeren, S., de Vries, J. D., & Bakker, A. B. (2023). Playful sport design: A game changer? *Journal of Applied Sport Psychology 36*, 45–74.

Wang, H., Ren, Y., & Liu, W. (2023). A weekly diary study on playful study design, study engagement, and goal attainment: The role of proactive personality. *Journal of Happiness Studies 24*, 159–184.

West, S. E., Hoff, E., & Carlsson, I. (2016). Play and productivity: Enhancing the creative climate at workplace meetings with play cues. *American Journal of Play 9*, 71–86.

Wrzesniewski, A., & Dutton, J. E. (2001). Crafting a job: Revisioning employees as active crafters of their work. *Academy of Management Review 26*, 179–201.

PART 6

FUTURE WORK

Artificial Intelligence

How It Changes the Landscape for Work Design Research and Practice

Nadine Bienefeld and Gudela Grote

Introduction

Artificial intelligence (AI)—systems "that build on machine learning, computation, and statistical techniques, as well as rely on large data sets to generate responses, classifications, or dynamic predictions" (Faraj et al., 2018, p. 62)—presents unparalleled opportunities for automating and augmenting human work and for economic growth (World Economic Forum, 2024).[1] As with other technologies, it is likely that, overall, AI will augment rather than replace human work (Eloundou et al., 2023; World Economic Forum, 2024). However, AI-induced transitions on the labor market may also entail massive job losses (Goldman Sachs, 2023). In this chapter, we address these impending changes from the perspective of work design by assessing the influence of AI-induced automation and augmentation on job quality, occupations, and the broader significance of human work. We also look into the working conditions of technology developers themselves to better gauge challenges and opportunities for shaping rapidly evolving AI technologies, especially generative AI[2] like ChatGPT (OpenAI, 2024), in accordance with principles of human-centered design. In the following, we expand on these topics and offer concrete suggestions for future research and practice (see Table 19.1) to support work design researchers, policymakers, and practitioners in their efforts to harness the opportunities of AI to foster workers' competence development, performance, and well-being.

---

[1] Equal contributions, alphabetical order.
[2] Generative AI is a form of AI that is capable of creating new data instances like text, images, video, audio, code, or synthetic data via large pre-trained models.

Nadine Bienefeld and Gudela Grote, *Artificial Intelligence*. In: *Transformative Work Design*.
Edited by: Sharon K. Parker, Florian E. Klonek, Caroline Knight and Fangfang Zhang, Oxford University Press.
© Society for Industrial and Organizational Psychology (2025). DOI: 10.1093/oso/9780197692554.003.0019

Table 19.1 Questions for Future Research and Practice in Work Design

Overarching Concern	General Topic	Specific Research Questions	Possible Research Approaches	Relevance for Future Work Design Practice
Job quality	Job autonomy	How does AI automation/augmentation of work tasks affect job autonomy across various professions? What new design principles apply to enable human control over increasingly capable AI?	Ethnographic studies observing human–AI collaboration across various professions. Studies combining work design assessment with human–system integration methodology applied to AI development processes.	New work design principles and methods for increasing job autonomy and control in new areas including areas outside of work. Guidelines for designing AI in line with work design principles.
		How should accountability for errors be distributed across different stakeholder groups when full human control is no longer possible?	Qualitative research across multiple stakeholder groups (users, developers, managers, regulators).	Guidelines and policies to promote fair distribution of accountability across stakeholder groups.
	Skill variety and use	Which generic and specific skills will be needed in the near, mid-term, and long-term future?	Prospective experimental studies using scenarios of future work tasks and roles to identify necessary future skills (e.g., by use of established assessment center techniques).	Changes to educational curricula and professional development programs to help people develop these skills and to reposition careers as broadly applicable portfolios of skills.
		How can human skills be maintained despite the increasing use of AI automation/augmentation?	Longitudinal field studies comparing skill retention in workplaces using similar AI automation/augmentation technologies but with versus without the possibility to practice manual skills.	Guidelines and policies on how to maintain necessary human skills (cf., ICAO mandates pilots to regularly practice manual flying skills).

		How can work design mitigate reductions in skill variety and use, especially in roles with already narrowly defined tasks?	Qualitative studies exploring job crafting opportunities in narrowly defined and AI automated/augmented roles.	Redesigning job roles to increase motivation and satisfaction (e.g., by expanding task variety or promoting job-crafting beyond narrowly defined roles).
	Social and relational work characteristics	What effects does human–AI collaboration have on interpersonal relations at work, including changes in trust among co-workers?	Longitudinal qualitative and quantitative studies document changes in social and relational work characteristics.	New models of work design considering AI agents as "team members" able to influence social and relational aspects of work.
		How can AI facilitate better communication between humans in a work context?	Experimental studies comparing traditional with AI-facilitated communication at work.	Guidelines and public policies for a meaningful and socially desirable use of AI to facilitate interpersonal communication at work.
		How can the time gained from AI-enabled efficiency gains be invested in strengthening social and relational aspects of work?	Ethnographic studies before, during, and after AI implementation focusing on social and relational aspects at work.	Guidelines regarding the re-distribution of time spent at work toward social and relational work characteristics.
Changing occupations and meaning of work	Occupational identity	How is people's sense of identity affected through occupational changes?	Longitudinal research on identity development during occupational transitions.	Changes to educational curricula and professional development programs to help people move through identity changes.
		How can work design prepare people for occupational transitions?	Comparative studies on the success of occupational transitions in relation to work design characteristics such as learning opportunities and autonomy for job crafting.	Guidelines for individuals and organizations on how to support occupational transitions through top-down and bottom-up work design.

continued

Table 19.1 *continued*

Overarching Concern	General Topic	Specific Research Questions	Possible Research Approaches	Relevance for Future Work Design Practice
	Meaning of work	Can working with advanced technology create a new sense of identity based on feeling engaged in more future-oriented work?	Qualitative and quantitative research on identity changes in relation to technology implementation and use.	Guidelines for technology implementation in organizations that foster workers' ownership and identification.
		How can high levels of productivity be maintained in shortened work weeks without creating unhealthy levels of work intensification?	Experimental designs comparing traditional and reduced work hours.	New models of work design that prioritize work–life balance.
		With reduced hours spent with paid work, what new opportunities arise for meaningful unpaid work (e.g., through volunteering or care work)?	Pilot studies on four-day work weeks to investigate people's emerging activities with the increase in leisure time.	Public policy and organizational strategies that support meaningful unpaid work.
		How can work design principles be applied to unpaid work?	Work analyses of unpaid work (e.g., in volunteering and care work).	Guidelines for volunteer-based organizations to adhere to work design principles and support for individuals to shape their working conditions during unpaid work.
		What job choices do people make when their livelihood is secured by an unconditional basic income and how does that affect their sense of identity?	Longitudinal studies, possibly replicating or extending the Finnish experiment.	Public policy and organizational strategies around compensation and work design.
Understanding and shaping technology developers' work	Effective work practices	How can interdisciplinary collaboration be facilitated during technology development?	Qualitative studies on work practices in technology development, especially in relation to stakeholder participation.	New design methods with broad stakeholder participation; increased emphasis on social skills in engineering education.

	How can technology developers be supported in managing increasing amounts of uncertainty in their work?	Ethnographic and survey studies on the effects of agile development methods on technology developers' performance and well-being.	More effective agile practices and better work design for developers.
Changing work roles	What technical and social support do technology developers need to manage the limits of their own control over the technology they produce, especially regarding ethical implications?	Ethnographic and survey-based studies of work practices in technology development to identify enabling conditions for explainable and responsible AI development.	Methods for explainable and responsible AI development; work redesign and support for transitioning into a new professional identity for technology developers.
	How can technology developers be empowered to become brokers for worker interests?	Comparative case studies on work practices during technology development (e.g., using network analysis).	Changes in job descriptions and the required work design for technology developers.

AI-Induced Changes in Job Quality

For any new technology, the fundamental question has always been whether it is meant to replace or augment human work. In either case, job quality (i.e., a job's match with basic human needs such as autonomy and meaning; Grote & Guest, 2017) is affected as task functions are redistributed between humans and technology. The concept of human-centered design calls for allocating functions in a way that keeps humans in the loop of whatever work processes they are responsible for as part of their overall job (Hollnagel & Woods, 2005). However, as humans become supervisory controllers of automated systems (Sheridan, 2012), a sense of disengagement and loss of meaningfulness in work can result. For example, pathologists who solely oversee an AI system's ability to identify malign tumors might find their role monotonous and repetitive, resulting in diminished attention and motivation and an increased risk of missing erroneous decisions by the AI. Such overreliance on technology is a well-known effect of high levels of automation (Parasuraman & Manzey, 2010).

Socio-technical system design principles emphasize the complementarity of humans and technology and call for a balanced consideration of technical (e.g., AI) and social (e.g., human skills) components to optimize system performance and worker well-being, thereby also ensuring high job quality (Clegg, 2000). Many AI systems currently fall short of these standards, leading to compromised human work and overall performance (Endsley et al., 2022; Johnson & Vera, 2019). Addressing these shortcomings is a priority, to which work design researchers can greatly contribute. For instance, Nadine Bienefeld and colleagues (2024 & 2025) recently demonstrated among Intensive Care Unit (ICU) nurses and physicians that AI-based technologies, when aligned with good work design principles, can improve key work characteristics such as autonomy, skill variety, and flexibility. In high-demand fields like healthcare, where skilled labor shortages are prevalent, such initiatives hold considerable potential to mitigate these challenges.

In the following, we briefly summarize extant research on which such efforts can build, focusing on three work characteristics that are at the core of high-quality jobs: (1) job autonomy, (2) skill variety and use, and (3) social and relational aspects (for a more extensive literature review, see Parker & Grote, 2022). For each of these key work characteristics, we highlight the implications of automation and augmentation by AI systems and suggest questions for work design research that warrant particular attention (see Table 19.1).

Job autonomy is defined by the degree to which employees have the freedom, independence, and discretion to plan and execute their tasks. It helps to alleviate stress (Karasek, 1979), enhances meaning and motivation (Hackman & Oldham, 1976), and supports proactivity in the face of task and situational uncertainty (Parker et al., 2017). AI's role in task automation and augmentation has mixed implications for job autonomy. For blue-collar workers, automating routine tasks has long enhanced job autonomy and satisfaction (Hampel et al., 2022; Walsh & Strano, 2018), and these benefits are now reaching white-collar professionals and knowledge workers, including those in law and medicine, due to AI's evolving capabilities (Felten et al., 2023; Waschull et al., 2022). A recent report by Accenture (2023) predicts that AI could automate or augment up to 40 percent of tasks across professions. For example, customer service tasks can be divided into fully automatable (four tasks), AI-augmented (five tasks), and human-exclusive (four tasks). Such a redistribution of work between humans and AI—if done in line with the criteria of good work design—could lead to higher levels of autonomy and meaning as people may be able to focus on the more interesting aspects of their work. For instance, Mareike Milanez (2023) found that financial service providers using an AI chatbot to automate basic customer queries and simple administrative tasks experienced higher autonomy and meaning because they could focus on more interesting and complex customer interactions. Similarly, junior call center agents with support from AI performed better and reported greater satisfaction, likely due to enhanced autonomy in handling complex cases (Brynjolfsson et al., 2023). Moreover, research commissioned by the Organisation for Economic Co-operation and Development (OECD) indicates that the majority of finance and manufacturing workers reported increased task control from AI, correlating with improved job performance and conditions (Lane et al., 2023). With tools like Microsoft 365 Copilot, knowledge workers may similarly benefit from AI agents writing emails, analyzing spreadsheets, or summarizing meetings (Microsoft, 2024).

However, AI may also reduce autonomy for highly skilled specialists, like radiologists, potentially leading to boredom, disengagement, and misapplication of technology (Lebovitz et al., 2022). Furthermore, the deployment of non-transparent algorithms has sparked concerns about human autonomy in decision-making processes (Hagendorff et al., 2023) and the potential loss of control over the decision-making process (Vaassen, 2022). This is especially problematic for professionals who remain responsible for decision outcomes such as physicians making life or death decisions, bankers commissioning risky financial investments, or managers basing far-reaching decisions on an AI's advice (Meskó & Topol, 2023; Shrestha et al., 2019; van den Broek et al., 2021). The development of explainable AI for users—i.e., AI systems that professionals can make sense of within the context of their work rather than mathematical explanations of the AI model itself—is thus key to using AI safely and effectively (Bienefeld, Boss, et al., 2023).

Lastly, AI can also be used for algorithmic management which poses a threat to autonomy, especially when it replaces managerial decision-making (Kellogg et al., 2020). For example, warehouse workers under algorithmic supervision often have no control over their actions, and call center devices instruct employees on when they should moderate their emotional responses (Briône, 2020). Continuous performance monitoring in various sectors can dehumanize workers and create alienation (Jarrahi et al., 2021; Schmidt, 2015; Wood, 2021).

This leads to critical questions for work design. How do AI automation and augmentation of work tasks affect job autonomy across various professions? What new design principles apply to enable human control over increasingly capable AI? How should accountability for errors be distributed across different stakeholder groups when full control by frontline workers is no longer possible?

Skill variety and use concern the diversity of skills a job requires and their utilization (Parker et al., 2017). Skill variety and usage are expected to change with AI automation and augmentation simply because individuals concentrate on fewer or different tasks. If these tasks are intellectually engaging and meaningful, this focus could positively influence job satisfaction and well-being. Supporting this, 63 percent of AI users in an OECD survey reported increased job satisfaction (Lane et al., 2023), a finding echoed by a Japanese worker survey (Yamamoto, 2019). However, the full impact of AI systems that change entire work processes, particularly those employing generative AI, remains uncertain. These systems' capacity to handle diverse data, including text, code, images, or video, to perform various tasks could automate tasks people prefer to do themselves (Webb et al., 2023). Recent developments show generative AI systems passing complex exams, such as the US medical licensing and attorney examinations, and MBA entry tests for leading US business schools (Katz et al., 2023; Kung et al., 2023; Varanasi, 2023), signaling a potential shift in highly skilled professional roles. This potential shift is signaled by Edward Felten and colleagues (2021, 2023), who identified financial examiners and purchasing agents as needing role reorientation in 2021 and now, in 2023, place higher education teachers of English language, history, and law on the top of their list. Even programmers and data scientists are experiencing significant role transformations, as will be discussed below (Wiec, 2020).

Professionals collaborating with AI must thus develop meta-cognitive abilities like critical thinking, problem-solving, and ethical judgment, along with social skills such as communication and conflict resolution (Frank et al., 2019). Interestingly, social capabilities have surpassed STEM proficiency in IBM's recent future skills report (IBM, 2024). In essence, these developments suggest significant shifts in job characteristics, calling for work design research and practice addressing the following questions: Which generic skills such as critical thinking and specific skills such as programming will be needed in the near, mid-term, and long-term future? How can human skills be maintained despite the increasing use of AI automation and augmentation? How can work design mitigate reductions in skill variety and use, especially in roles with already narrowly defined tasks?

Social and relational work characteristics. Social and relational work characteristics concern the opportunity for social contact and support in the workplace as well as possibilities and demands for cooperation and communication (Grant & Parker, 2009). AI-driven automation or augmentation could impair social and relational work characteristics, with potentially adverse effects on job quality. This scenario might emerge if AI-driven chatbots replace human colleagues or HR advisors in responding to worker inquiries, or if algorithms, rather than supervisors, schedule work shifts (Briône, 2020; Jarrahi et al., 2021; Wood, 2021). Such developments could erode the social dimensions of work, as exemplified by the experiences of AmazonTurk or Uber workers reporting impediments in the formation of social bonds leading to the isolation of individual workers and potentially impacting well-being and productivity (Mateescu & Elish, 2019; Möhlmann & Henfridsson, 2019).

In contrast, other research indicates that AI, including social robots and chatbots, can improve human interactions, creating a more amiable and cooperative environment (Traeger et al., 2020). For instance, AI assistance in intensive care teams has been linked to improved communication dynamics, such as voicing critical information, possibly by diminishing social tensions (Bienefeld, Kolbe, et al., 2023). AI has shown promise also in imitating empathetic responses in interpersonal scenarios like physician-patient dialogues (Ayers et al., 2023), potentially aiding professionals in preparing for sensitive conversations (Lee et al., 2023).

Despite AI's growing presence, human interaction retains its significance, and the efficiencies gained from AI should be reallocated to enhance personal connections with customers, patients, colleagues, or the like. Future research should investigate how AI might bolster relational aspects of workplace communication while considering the ethical implications, such as the authenticity of emotion used in empathic conversation. Further questions include what effects human–AI collaboration has on interpersonal relations at work, including changes in trust among co-workers, between leaders and followers, or with customers and patients. And finally, how can the time gained from AI-enabled efficiency gains be used to strengthen social and relational aspects of work?

To conclude this section, the intricate interplay between AI automation and augmentation and their positive and negative effects on work characteristics such as job autonomy, skill variety, and relational aspects underscores the importance of considering work design in shaping future work practices (Parker & Grote, 2020, 2022). This is especially important considering recent trends like the "grand resignation" and heightened employee dissatisfaction, as underscored by the recent survey by Gallup (2024). Solutions emerge from both top-down and bottom-up strategies. While top-down organizational approaches to work design hold great potential, they remain scarce, primarily because they demand significant strategic organizational shifts (Grote et al., 2000; Knight & Parker, 2021). Their effectiveness warrants additional exploration by work design researchers and practitioners. Conversely, bottom-up approaches, like job crafting, are gaining traction with positive outcomes, especially concerning technology adoption (Knight et al., 2021; Wang et al., 2020, 2021). Work design scholars should explore interventions promoting job crafting, encouraging employees to discover their purpose, and cultivating a growth mindset, combined with methodologies like design thinking (Burnett, 2023). Such endeavors promise to unlock motivating and novel opportunities for workers to thrive in an AI-automated or augmented world of work.

AI-Induced Changes in Occupations and the Meaning of Human Work

AI does not only change the makeup of individuals' jobs but can also make and break whole occupations. The emergence of data scientists is an interesting case in this respect. With the advent of "big data" through the massive growth of digital services and the digitalization of most work processes, new statistical and computational competencies have been sought to derive knowledge from these data. However, as AI systems taught on such large data sets become more capable, they may also learn those skills, eventually making data scientists redundant (Davenport & Patil, 2022). Even innovation itself is changing as human product designers increasingly work alongside machine designers, that is "algorithmically organized software tools that autonomously collect and interpret data to make innovative design decisions" (Recker et al., 2023, p. 27). One prominent example is Moderna's SARS-CoV-2 vaccine, for which machine designers generated several mRNA vaccine candidates within days (Fang et al., 2022).

From the perspective of work design, these changes point to the central role of learning opportunities that should be provided as part of daily work as well as through on- and off-the-job training to improve workers' readiness to transition to new occupations. Thus, work design could complement companies' reskilling and upskilling efforts to get their workforce ready for AI-induced changes in jobs and occupations (Li, 2022). However, work design should also adopt a more dynamic perspective to better understand how people move between jobs and occupations and with what effects for their performance and well-being. Of particular interest is a closer look at changes in people's identity as their jobs and occupations become increasingly challenged by technological advances. Erich Dierdorff (2019) has argued that with more frequent job and organizational changes, occupations become a more important anchor for identity. Guri Medici and colleagues (2023) found that workers in apprenticeship-based occupations, such as polymechanics, cooks, or gardeners, were often able to harness technological change as a way to update their skills and remain motivated to develop and grow within their learned occupation.

Challenges to people's identity will also result from an even more fundamental question: With technological progress, how much human work will be needed at all to bring about the economic productivity and social welfare that societies are striving for (Hunnicut, 2020)? The hopes for new "paths to paradise" (Gorz, 1983) invoked in earlier waves of technology development are starting to resurface, as increasing numbers of companies and whole countries are experimenting with four-day work weeks (Gurchiek, 2023). Work design research and practice have much to offer in debates about future models of work which encompass general reduction of work hours, a new balance of paid and unpaid work, and unconditional basic income, all touching upon the coexistence of work's extrinsic value for individuals' livelihood and its intrinsic value as a source of meaning and growth. The two-year basic income experiment in Finland has illustrated that people receiving a basic income worked just as much (or as little) as people who were eligible for traditional social security payments (Kangas et al., 2021). The researchers found highly varied patterns of activities that were enabled by the basic income, such as topping up a low-income job, pursuing a creative career, returning to study, or undertaking volunteering or care work. Overall, these activities can be taken as an indication of people's intrinsic motivation to engage in meaningful work and to find a balance between paid and unpaid work that increases their sense of agency and well-being.

Approaching options for reducing the need for paid work through advanced technologies from a work design perspective can enrich discussions on the future of work by pointing to new opportunities for meaningful work, which may not necessarily be paid work. For instance, the general sense of urgency to employ robots to care for the elderly (Hsu et al., 2020; Suwa et al., 2020) may appear in a different light when people are partially freed from their paid work by robots or other forms of technology, allowing them to take over more care work. To date, such choices have not been systematically discussed and work design researchers would be ideally positioned to instigate and lead this debate. For example, Jessica Rodell (2013) explored the question of whether volunteering activities can compensate for the lack of job quality in paid work and found volunteering was more likely when a person perceived their paid work as less meaningful.

494 TRANSFORMATIVE WORK DESIGN

From these considerations, several important questions for future research arise: How is people's sense of identity affected by occupational changes? How can work design prepare people for occupational transitions? Can working with advanced technology create a new sense of identity based on feeling engaged in more future-oriented work? How can high levels of productivity be maintained in shortened work weeks without creating unhealthy levels of work intensification? With reduced hours spent with paid work, what new opportunities arise for meaningful unpaid work (e.g., through volunteering or care work)? How can work design principles be applied to unpaid work? What job choices do people make when their livelihood is secured by an unconditional basic income and how does that affect their sense of identity?

Understanding and Shaping Technology Developers' Work

Core to technology developers' work is creating technological innovation that enhances competitive advantage and economic success for their employer. If the technology targets retail customers as users, the importance of human-centered design for selling the technology is more obvious, although often not sufficiently addressed (Emmenegger & Norman, 2019; Gray, 2016). If firms are the customers, human-centered design usually becomes secondary to gains in efficiency (Norman & Euchner, 2023). In either case, technology development is usually driven by the assumption that the new systems will shape work processes and user behavior in predictable ways; that is, by a belief in technological determinism (Wyatt, 2008).

In their daily work, technology developers encounter many situations where the interests of different stakeholders collide, requiring them to take an ethical stance (Gray & Chivukula, 2019). For instance, Jenna Myers (2023) found that developers managed to address worker concerns in their designs, even against the interests of those workers' managers by using various techniques, such as stretching features of the technology, that were introduced for managerial control to also give workers choices. For instance, workers had to report operational problems to managers via standardized messages to which the technology developers added options that allowed workers to communicate issues they themselves wanted to be solved. Moreover, technology developers are likely to experience that counter to technological determinism users adapt technology to their needs and preferences in unpredictable ways (Orlikowski & Scott, 2008). Even for something as simple as invoice processing, Brian Pentland and colleagues (2010) found that the same software package was used very differently in the four companies they studied. Accordingly, technology developers need to engage with users early on to not only understand their preferences but also to decide whether they should deliberately create a malleable system.

In the case of AI, these challenges are exacerbated as the technology becomes intransparent even for technology developers themselves, making it more likely that it will be used in unforeseen ways, with increasing worries that new and uncontrollable risks are generated (McLean et al., 2023; Tabassi, 2023). The most recent example of the enormous uncertainties that come with AI are large language models (LLMs), such as Chat-GPT. These systems can easily produce faulty and misleading information and generate dangerous decision errors by human users (e.g., in medical diagnoses). In her analysis of development teams charged with producing software for the Amazon Social Chatbot Alexa to lead "engaging conversations" with humans, Prachee Jain (2023) was astonished to find that mostly more controllable rule-based algorithms rather than LLMs were used by the developers, thereby avoiding that conversations get out of hand. Another example more directly related to work design was reported by Lydia Hagtvedt (2019) in which AI developers lived up to their personal ethical standards by forecasting the impact of their creativity, both positive and negative, and by self-imposing constraints on their work to cope with the resulting ambivalence. For instance, one developer intentionally produced "clumsy assistants" that would require strong human involvement to make sensible decisions rather than being able to work autonomously. This example shows both how technology developers may become more responsive to questions of work design for the users of their technology, but also how they craft their own jobs to create more meaning for themselves.

To render technology development more ethical, Lucy Suchman (2002, p. 94) argued long ago already that technology developers must give up control over technology design and see themselves as entering an extended set of working relations for which the question at each next turn becomes: "How do we proceed in a responsible way?" Only if AI developers fully understand the impact of their work on the work of others and have the autonomy to shape AI in ways that foster high-quality jobs and the alignment of control and accountability across different actors involved in AI development and use, will responsible technological innovation be possible (Grote, Parker, & Crowston, 2024).

Work design research can support such work practices by specifying job characteristics for technology developers that foster human-centered system design. For instance, the necessary feedback loops with customers and users require more cross-disciplinary cooperation and the social skills to make such cooperation successful, such as perspective-taking to bridge engineers' rationalist worldviews engineers with users' sensemaking of the technology (Dingsøyr et al., 2012; Dönmez et al., 2016; Hess et al., 2017; McNair et al., 2008). These new demands can enrich the work of technology developers and can create a new sense of meaning as well, as in Myers (2023) research where technology developers saw themselves as brokers between different stakeholders.

To foster working conditions for technology developers that help them manage high uncertainty and ethical challenges on the way to human-centered design and high-quality jobs for workers, work design research should answer questions such as the following: How can interdisciplinary collaboration be facilitated during technology development? How can technology developers be supported in managing increasing amounts of uncertainty in their work? What technical and social support do technology developers need to manage the limits of their own control over the technology they produce, especially regarding ethical implications? How can technology developers be empowered to become brokers for worker interests?

Future Directions

AI has and will continue to change human work in increasingly fundamental ways. In this chapter, we have argued that work design research and practice are essential for shaping these changes in ways that foster human well-being and societal progress more broadly. We have emphasized the importance of better understanding work practices and meaning-making of technology developers themselves to create working conditions for them that support a concern for the job quality of technology users. A multitude of questions for work design research and practice arise from these considerations (see Table 19.1). In the following, we highlight some directions for future research and practice that we consider particularly important for a humane future of work in the age of AI.

First, we encourage work design researchers to tackle the foundational question of how human control over technology can be maintained with increasingly complex and opaque AI systems. The assumption that human operators of technology should stay "in the loop" (Endsley, 2023) becomes increasingly questionable when even AI developers do not fully understand the systems they have created (Berente et al., 2021; Castelvecchi, 2016). Given that accountability for system outcomes will have to stay with humans, and that accountability should be paired with control over what an actor is held accountable for (Boos et al., 2013; Bovens, 2007), either AI systems need to be kept sufficiently simple or new forms of controllability need to be found (Grote et al., 2024). Attempts to make AI more explainable are one way to address this conundrum (Kim & Doshi-Velez, 2021; Langer et al., 2021). Another is to explore how control and accountability might be shared among different actors, especially AI users and AI developers, and what implications this increased task interdependence has for the work design of both. If AI users get more involved in AI development and, in turn, AI developers engage more with users, new skills are required along with the changed job requirements (Bienefeld et al., 2023). Such transformations may represent an opportunity for increasing job quality across a broad range of occupations as there is hardly any type of work that will remain untouched by AI.

Second, we suggest that research on the impact of AI for work adopts a broad perspective on the meaning of work. Rather than focusing solely on paid work and how it might be changed and also endangered by new technologies, it would be important to incorporate paid and unpaid work to create a more complete picture of the quality of working life (Grote & Guest, 2017). Such research could offer important policy recommendations for managing reduced demands for human work in increasingly automated work systems (e.g., concerning new systems for securing social welfare) (Kangas et al., 2021). Moreover, it would open new avenues for understanding the relevance of work for personal and social identity. Michael Pratt and Blake Ashforth (2003) distinguished between role-based and membership-based identity related to the actual work activity and the organization within which the work is carried out. They argued that both types of identity can create the experience of meaningful work; that is, that the content and the context of work matter. Extending their framework by not only studying paid work in classic forms of employment but by examining the amalgam of identities created through paid and unpaid work activities in a wide range of settings would substantially deepen our understanding of the relevance of different work domains for identity and meaning. Depending on what we were to learn from such studies regarding the most important sources of identity and meaning, very different policy recommendations might result in shaping the future of paid and unpaid work.

Third, we recommend expanding on the emerging research that examines working conditions of technology developers themselves (Hagtvedt, 2019; Jain, 2023; Myers, 2023). Only if AI developers fully understand the impact of their work on the work of others and have the autonomy to shape AI in ways that foster high-quality jobs and the alignment of control and accountability across different actors involved in AI development and use, will responsible technological innovation be possible. Aniko Kahlert and Gudela Grote (2024) recently proposed to study technology developers' design mindsets to learn more about how they understand their own work and how the design of work for others might become part of their mindsets. These authors also investigated how technology developers define their own professional identity and found that more interdisciplinary professional identities might promote more holistic and impact-aware mindsets. This research might prove a useful base for identifying specific conditions that foster consideration of AI users' job quality during AI development, including the design of AI developers' own work.

Emerging technologies, and AI-based technologies in particular, bear both opportunities and challenges for the design of high-quality jobs. Work design researchers are perfectly positioned to support decision-makers in making effective choices for AI development and use. We hope we have been able to inspire researchers and practitioners alike to engage in a fruitful dialogue on shaping the future of work with AI.

References

Arntz, M., Gregory, T., & Zierahn, U. (2016). The risk of automation for jobs in OECD countries: A comparative analysis. OECD Social, Employment and Migration Working Papers, No. 189.

Accenture. (2023). A new era of generative AI for everyone. https://www.accenture.com/content/dam/accenture/final/accenture-com/document/Accenture-A-New-Era-of-Generative-AI-for-Everyone.pdf

Ayers, J. W., Poliak, A., Dredze, M., Leas, E. C., Zhu, Z., Kelley, J. B., Faix, D. J., Goodman, A. M., Longhurst, C. A., Hogarth, M., & Smith, D. M. (2023). Comparing physician and artificial intelligence chatbot responses to patient questions posted to a public social media forum. *JAMA Internal Medicine 183*(6), 589–596. https://doi.org/10.1001/jamainternmed.2023.1838

Berente, N., Gu, B., Recker, J., & Santanam, R. (2021). Managing artificial intelligence. *MIS Quarterly 45* (3), 1433–1450.

Bienefeld., N., Keller, E., Grote, G. (2024). Human-AI Teaming in the ICU: A Comparative Analysis of Data Scientists' and Clinicians' Assessments on AI Augmentation and Automation at Work. *J Med Internet Res.* http://dx.doi.org/10.2196/50130

Bienefeld, N., Keller, E., Grote, G. (2025). AI Interventions to Alleviate Healthcare Shortages and Enhance Work Conditions in Critical Care: Qualitative Analysis. J Med Internet Res;27:e50852. https://www.jmir.org/2025/1/e50852

Bienefeld, N., Boss, J. M., Lüethy, R., Brodbeck, D., Azzati, J., Blaser, M., Willms, J., & Keller, E. (2023). Solving the explainable AI conundrum by bridging clinicians' needs and developers' goals. *NPJ Digital Medicine 6*(1), 94. https://doi.org/10.1038/s41746-023-00837-4

Bienefeld, N., Kolbe, M., Camen, G., Huser, D., & Buehler, P. K. (2023). Human–AI teaming: Leveraging transactive memory and speaking up for enhanced team effectiveness. *Frontiers in Psychology 14.* https://doi.org/10.3389/fpsyg.2023.1208019

Boos, D., Grote, G., & Guenter, H. (2013). A toolbox for managing organisational issues in the early stage of the development of a ubiquitous computing application. *Personal and Ubiquitous Computing 17*(6), 1261–1279. https://doi.org/10.1007/s00779-012-0634-y

Bovens, M. (2007). Analysing and assessing accountability: A conceptual framework. *European Law Journal 13*(4), 447–468. https://doi.org/10.1111/j.1468-0386.2007.00378.x

Briône, P. (2020). My boss the algorithm: An ethical look at algorithms in the workplace. *ACAS.* https://www.acas.org.uk/my-boss-the-algorithm-an-ethical-look-at-algorithms-in-the-workplace/html

Brynjolfsson, E., Li, D., & Raymond, L. R. (2023). Generative AI at work (Working Paper 31161). National Bureau of Economic Research. https://doi.org/10.3386/w31161

Burnett, B. (2023). *Designing your new work life.* Random House.

Castelvecchi, D. (2016). Can we open the black box of AI? *Nature News 538*(7623), 20. https://doi.org/10.1038/538020a

Clegg, C. W. (2000). Sociotechnical principles for system design. *Applied Ergonomics 31*(5), 463–477. https://doi.org/10.1016/S0003-6870(00)00009-0

Davenport, T. H., & Patil, D. J. (2022, 15 July). Is data scientist still the sexiest job of the 21st century? Harvard Business Review. https://hbr.org/2022/07/is-data-scientist-still-the-sexiest-job-of-the-21st-century

Dierdorff, E. C. (2019). Toward reviving an occupation with occupations. *Annual Review of Organizational Psychology and Organizational Behavior 6*(1), 397–419. https://doi.org/10.1146/annurev-orgpsych-012218-015019

Dingsøyr, T., Nerur, S., Balijepally, V., & Moe, N. B. (2012). A decade of agile methodologies: Towards explaining agile software development. *Journal of Systems and Software 85*(6), 1213–1221. https://doi.org/10.1016/j.jss.2012.02.033

Dönmez, D., Grote, G., & Brusoni, S. (2016). Routine interdependencies as a source of stability and flexibility: A study of agile software development teams. *Information and Organization 26*(3), 63–83. https://doi.org/10.1016/j.infoandorg.2016.07.001

Eloundou, T., Manning, S., Mishkin, P., & Rock, D. (2023). GPTs are GPTs: An early look at the labor market impact potential of large language models (arXiv:2303.10130). *arXiv.* https://doi.org/10.48550/arXiv.2303.10130

Emmenegger, C., & Norman, D. (2019). The challenges of automation in the automobile. *Ergonomics 62*(4), 512–513. https://doi.org/10.1080/00140139.2019.1563336

Endsley, M. R. (2023). Supporting human–AI teams: Transparency, explainability, and situation awareness. *Computers in Human Behavior 140*, 107574. https://doi.org/10.1016/j.chb.2022.107574

Endsley, M. R., Cooke, N., McNeese, N., Bisantz, A., Militello, L., & Roth, E. (2022). Special issue on human–AI teaming and special issue on AI in healthcare. *Journal of Cognitive Engineering and Decision Making 16*(4), 179–181. https://doi.org/10.1177/15553434221133288

Fang, E., Liu, X., Li, M., Zhang, Z., Song, L., Zhu, B., Wu, X., Liu, J., Zhao, D., & Li, Y. (2022). Advances in COVID-19 mRNA vaccine development. *Signal Transduction and Targeted Therapy 7*(1), article 1. https://doi.org/10.1038/s41392-022-00950-y

Faraj, S., Pachidi, S., & Sayegh, K. (2018). Working and organizing in the age of the learning algorithm. *Information and Organization 28*(1), 62–70. https://doi.org/10.1016/j.infoandorg.2018.02.005

Felten, E., Raj, M., & Seamans, R. (2021). Occupational, industry, and geographic exposure to artificial intelligence: A novel dataset and its potential uses. *Strategic Management Journal 42*(12), 2195–2217. https://doi.org/10.1002/smj.3286

Felten, E., Raj, M., & Seamans, R. (2023). How will language modelers like Chat-GPT affect occupations and industries? (arXiv:2303.01157). *arXiv.* https://doi.org/10.48550/arXiv.2303.01157

Frank, M. R., Autor, D., Bessen, J. E., Brynjolfsson, E., Cebrian, M., Deming, D. J., Feldman, M., Groh, M., Lobo, J., Moro, E., Wang, D., Youn, H., & Rahwan, I. (2019).

Toward understanding the impact of artificial intelligence on labor. *Proceedings of the National Academy of Sciences 116*(14), 6531–6539. https://doi.org/10.1073/pnas.1900949116

Gallup. (2024). State of the global workplace report. *Gallup.com.* https://www.gallup.com/workplace/349484/state-of-the-global-workplace.aspx

Goldman Sachs. (2023). Generative AI report. *Goldman Sachs.* https://www.goldmansachs.com/intelligence/pages/generative-ai-could-raise-global-gdp-by-7-percent.html

Gorz, A. (1983). *Les chemins du paradis: L'agonie du capital.* Editions Galilée. https://cir.nii.ac.jp/crid/1130282271850406656

Grant, A. M., & Parker, S. K. (2009). 7 redesigning work design theories: The rise of relational and proactive perspectives. *Academy of Management Annals 3*(1), 317–375. https://doi.org/10.1080/19416520903047327

Gray, C. M. (2016). "It's more of a mindset than a method": UX practitioners' conception of design methods. Proceedings of the 2016 CHI Conference on Human Factors in Computing Systems, 4044–4055. https://doi.org/10.1145/2858036.2858410

Gray, C. M., & Chivukula, S. S. (2019). Ethical mediation in UX practice. Proceedings of the 2019 CHI Conference on Human Factors in Computing Systems, 1–11. https://doi.org/10.1145/3290605.3300408

Grote, G., Parker, S. K., & Crowston, K. (2024). Taming Artificial Intelligence: A Theory of Control-Acountability Alignment among AI Developers and Users. *Academy of Management Review,* (ja), amr-2023. https://doi.org/10.5465/amr.2023.0117

Grote, G., & Guest, D. (2017). The case for reinvigorating quality of working life research. *Human Relations 70*(2), 149–167. https://doi.org/10.1177/0018726716654746

Grote, G., Ryser, C., Waefler, T., Windischer, A., & Weik, S. (2000). KOMPASS: A method for complementary function allocation in automated work systems. *International Journal of Human-Computer Studies 52*(2), 267–287. https://doi.org/10.1006/ijhc.1999.0289

Gurchiek, K. (2023, 16 August). Is a 4-day workweek for you? Employers find what works. *SHRM.* https://www.shrm.org/hr-today/news/hr-news/pages/is-a-4-day-workweek-for-you-employers-find-what-works-.aspx

Hackman, J. R., & Oldham, G. R. (1976). Motivation through the design of work: Test of a theory. *Organizational Behavior and Human Performance 16*(2), 250–279. https://doi.org/10.1016/0030-5073(76)90016-7

Hagendorff, T., Fabi, S., & Kosinski, M. (2023). Thinking fast and slow in large language models. *arXiv.* https://doi.org/10.48550/arXiv.2212.05206

Hagtvedt, L. P. (2019). *Creating artificial intelligence: An inductive study of how creative workers forecast the future and manage present emotions* [Doctoral dissertation, Boston College]. http://dlib.bc.edu/islandora/object/bc-ir:108640

Hampel, N., Sassenberg, K., Scholl, A., & Reichenbach, M. (2022). Introducing digital technologies in the factory: Determinants of blue-collar workers' attitudes towards new robotic tools. *Behaviour & Information Technology 41*(14), 2973–2987. https://doi.org/10.1080/0144929X.2021.1967448

Hess, J. L., Strobel, J., & Brightman, A. O. (2017). The development of empathic perspective-taking in an engineering ethics course. *Journal of Engineering Education 106*(4), 534–563. https://doi.org/10.1002/jee.20175

Hollnagel, E., & Woods, D. D. (2005). *Joint cognitive systems: Foundation of cognitive systems engineering.* Taylor and Francis.

Hsu, E. L., Elliott, A., Ishii, Y., Sawai, A., & Katagiri, M. (2020). The development of aged care robots in Japan as a varied process. *Technology in Society 63*, 101366. https://doi.org/10.1016/j.techsoc.2020.101366

Hunnicut, B. (2020). *The age of experiences: Harnessing happiness to build a new economy.* Temple University Press.

IBM. (2024). The augmented workforce for an automated, AI-driven world. IBM. https://www.ibm.com/thought-leadership/institute-business-value/en-us/report/augmented-workforce

Jain, P. (2023). *The yellow brick road to artificial intelligence* [Doctoral Dissertation, Standford University].

Jarrahi, M. H., Newlands, G., Lee, M. K., Wolf, C. T., Kinder, E., & Sutherland, W. (2021). Algorithmic management in a work context. *Big Data & Society 8*(2), 20539517211020332. https://doi.org/10.1177/20539517211020332

Johnson, M., & Vera, A. (2019). No AI is an island: The case for teaming intelligence. *AI Magazine 40*(1), 16–28. https://doi.org/10.1609/aimag.v40i1.2842

Kahlert, A., & Grote, G. (2024). "Why should I care?" Understanding technology developers' design mindsets in relation to prospective work design. *European Journal of Work and Organizational Psychology 33*, 230–244.

Kangas, O., Jauhiainen, S., Simanainen, M., & Ylikanno, M. (Eds.). (2021). *Experimenting with unconditional basic income: Lessons from the Finnish BI experiment 2017–2018.* Edward Elgar Publishing. https://doi.org/10.4337/9781839104855

Karasek, R. A. (1979). Job demands, job decision latitude, and mental strain: Implications for job redesign. *Administrative Science Quarterly 24*(2), 285–308. https://doi.org/10.2307/2392498

Katz, D. M., Bommarito, M. J., Gao, S., & Arredondo, P. (2023). GPT-4 Passes the Bar Exam. *SSRN*, Scholarly Paper 4389233. https://doi.org/10.2139/ssrn.4389233

Kellogg, K. C., Valentine, M. A., & Christin, A. (2020). Algorithms at work: The new contested terrain of control. *Academy of Management Annals 14*(1), 366–410. https://doi.org/10.5465/annals.2018.0174

Kim, B., & Doshi-Velez, F. (2021). Machine learning techniques for accountability. *AI Magazine 42*(1), 47–52. https://doi.org/10.1002/j.2371-9621.2021.tb00010.x

Knight, C., & Parker, S. K. (2021). How work redesign interventions affect performance: An evidence-based model from a systematic review. *Human Relations 74*(1), 69–104. https://doi.org/10.1177/0018726719865604

Knight, C., Tims, M., Gawke, J., & Parker, S. K. (2021). When do job crafting interventions work? The moderating roles of workload, intervention intensity, and participation. *Journal of Vocational Behavior 124*, 103522. https://doi.org/10.1016/j.jvb.2020.103522

Kung, T. H., Cheatham, M., Medenilla, A., Sillos, C., Leon, L. D., Elepaño, C., Madriaga, M., Aggabao, R., Diaz-Candido, G., Maningo, J., & Tseng, V. (2023). Performance of ChatGPT on USMLE: Potential for AI-assisted medical education using large language models. *PLoS Digital Health 2*(2), e0000198. https://doi.org/10.1371/journal.pdig.0000198

Lane, M., Williams, M., & Broecke, S. (2023). *The impact of AI on the workplace: Main findings from the OECD AI surveys of employers and workers.* OECD. https://doi.org/10.1787/ea0a0fe1-en

Langer, M., Oster, D., Speith, T., Hermanns, H., Kästner, L., Schmidt, E., Sesing, A., & Baum, K. (2021). What do we want from explainable artificial intelligence (XAI)? A stakeholder perspective on XAI and a conceptual model guiding interdisciplinary

XAI research. *Artificial Intelligence 296*, 103473. https://doi.org/10.1016/j.artint.2021.103473

Lebovitz, S., Lifshitz-Assaf, H., & Levina, N. (2022). To engage or not to engage with AI for critical judgments: How professionals deal with opacity when using AI for medical diagnosis. *Organization Science 33*, 126–148. https://doi.org/10.1287/orsc.2021.1549

Lee, P., Bubeck, S., & Petro, J. (2023). Benefits, limits, and risks of GPT-4 as an AI chatbot for medicine. *New England Journal of Medicine 388*(13), 1233–1239. https://doi.org/10.1056/NEJMsr2214184

Li, L. (2022). Reskilling and upskilling the future-ready workforce for industry 4.0 and beyond. *Information Systems Frontiers, 26*, 1697–1712. https://doi.org/10.1007/s10796-022-10308-y

Mateescu, A., & Elish, M. (2019). AI in context: The labor of integrating new technologies (United States of America) [Report]. Data & Society Research Institute. https://apo.org.au/node/217456

McLean, S., Read, G. J. M., Thompson, J., Baber, C., Stanton, N. A., & Salmon, P. M. (2023). The risks associated with artificial general intelligence: A systematic review. *Journal of Experimental & Theoretical Artificial Intelligence 35*(5), 649–663. https://doi.org/10.1080/0952813X.2021.1964003

McNair, L. D., Paretti, M. C., & Kakar, A. (2008). Case study of prior knowledge: Expectations and identity constructions in interdisciplinary, cross-cultural virtual collaboration. *International Journal of Engineering Education 24*, 386–399.

Medici, G., Igic, I., Grote, G., & Hirschi, A. (2023). Facing change with stability: The dynamics of occupational career trajectories. *Journal of Career Development 50*(4), 883–900. https://doi.org/10.1177/08948453221133123

Meskó, B., & Topol, E. J. (2023). The imperative for regulatory oversight of large language models (or generative AI) in healthcare. *NPJ Digital Medicine 6*(1), article 1. https://doi.org/10.1038/s41746-023-00873-0

Microsoft. (2024, November). Microsoft 365 Copilot. https://www.microsoft.com/en-us/microsoft-365/copilot

Milanez, A. (2023). *The impact of AI on the workplace: Evidence from OECD case studies of AI implementation.* OECD. https://doi.org/10.1787/2247ce58-en

Möhlmann, M., & Henfridsson, O. (2019, 30 August). What people hate about being managed by algorithms, according to a study of Uber drivers. *Harvard Business Review.* https://hbr.org/2019/08/what-people-hate-about-being-managed-by-algorithms-according-to-a-study-of-uber-drivers

Myers, J. E. (2023). When big brother is benevolent: How technology developers navigate power dynamics among users to elevate worker interests. *Academy of Management Discoveries 10*(3). https://doi.org/10.5465/amd.2022.0111

Norman, D., & Euchner, J. (2023). Design for a better world. *Research-Technology Management 66*(3), 11–18. https://doi.org/10.1080/08956308.2023.2183015

OpenAI. (2024). GPT-4 [Computer software].

Orlikowski, W. J., & Scott, S. V. (2008). 10 sociomateriality: Challenging the separation of technology, work and organization. *Academy of Management Annals 2*(1), 433–474. https://doi.org/10.1080/19416520802211644

Parasuraman, R., & Manzey, D. H. (2010). Complacency and bias in human use of automation: An attentional integration. *Human Factors 52*(3), 381–410. https://doi.org/10.1177/0018720810376055

Parker, S. K., & Grote, G. (2020). Automation, algorithms, and beyond: Why work design matters more than ever in a digital world. *Applied Psychology 71*, 1171–1204. https://doi.org/10.1111/apps.12241

Parker, S. K., Morgeson, F. P., & Johns, G. (2017). One hundred years of work design research: Looking back and looking forward. *Journal of Applied Psychology 102*(3), 403–420. https://doi.org/10.1037/apl0000106

Pentland, B. T., Hærem, T., & Hillison, D. (2010). Comparing organizational routines as recurrent patterns of action. *Organization Studies 31*(7), 917–940. https://doi.org/10.1177/0170840610373200

Pratt, M. G., & Ashforth, B. E. (2003). Fostering meaningfulness in working and at work. *Positive Organizational Scholarship: Foundations of a New Discipline 309*, 327.

Recker, J., von Briel, F., Yoo, Y., Nagaraj, V., & McManus, M. (2023). Orchestrating human–machine designer ensembles during product innovation. *California Management Review 65*(3), 27–47. https://doi.org/10.1177/00081256231170028

Rodell, J. B. (2013). Finding meaning through volunteering: Why do employees volunteer and what does it mean for their jobs? *Academy of Management Journal 56*(5), 1274–1294. https://doi.org/10.5465/amj.2012.0611

Schmidt, G. B. (2015). Fifty days an MTurk worker: The social and motivational context for amazon mechanical turk workers. *Industrial and Organizational Psychology 8*(2), 165–171. https://doi.org/10.1017/iop.2015.20

Sheridan, T. B. (2012). Human supervisory control. In G. Salvendy (Ed.), *Handbook of human factors and ergonomics* (pp. 990–1015). John Wiley & Sons, Ltd. https://doi.org/10.1002/9781118131350.ch34

Shrestha, Y. R., Ben-Menahem, S. M., & von Krogh, G. (2019). Organizational decision-making structures in the age of artificial intelligence. *California Management Review 61*(4), 66–83. https://doi.org/10.1177/0008125619862257

Suchman, L. (2002). Located accountabilities in technology production. *Scandinavian Journal of Information Systems 14* (2), 91–105.

Suwa, S., Tsujimura, M., Kodate, N., Donnelly, S., Kitinoja, H., Hallila, J., Toivonen, M., Ide, H., Bergman-Kärpijoki, C., Takahashi, E., Ishimaru, M., Shimamura, A., & Yu, W. (2020). Exploring perceptions toward home-care robots for older people in Finland, Ireland, and Japan: A comparative questionnaire study. *Archives of Gerontology and Geriatrics 91*, 104178. https://doi.org/10.1016/j.archger.2020.104178

Tabassi, E. (2023). *Artificial intelligence risk management framework (AI RMF 1.0)*. National Institute of Standards and Technology (U.S.). https://doi.org/10.6028/NIST.AI.100-1

Traeger, M. L., Strohkorb Sebo, S., Jung, M., Scassellati, B., & Christakis, N. A. (2020). Vulnerable robots positively shape human conversational dynamics in a human–robot team. *Proceedings of the National Academy of Sciences 117*(12), 6370–6375. https://doi.org/10.1073/pnas.1910402117

Vaassen, B. (2022). AI, opacity, and personal autonomy. *Philosophy & Technology 35*(4), 88. https://doi.org/10.1007/s13347-022-00577-5

van den Broek, E., Sergeeva, A., & Huysman, M. (2021). When the machine meets the expert: An ethnography of developing AI for hiring. *MIS Quarterly 45*(3), 1557–1580. https://doi.org/10.25300/MISQ/2021/16559

Varanasi, L. (2023, 5 November). AI models like ChatGPT and GPT-4 are acing everything from the bar exam to AP Biology: Here's a list of difficult exams both AI versions have passed. *Business Insider*. https://www.businessinsider.com/list-here-are-the-exams-chatgpt-has-passed-so-far-2023-1

Walsh, S. M., & Strano, M. S. (2018). *Robotic systems and autonomous platforms: Advances in materials and manufacturing*. Woodhead Publishing.

Wang, B., Liu, Y., & Parker, S. K. (2020). How does the use of information communication technology affect individuals? A work design perspective. *Academy of Management Annals 14*(2), 695–725. https://doi.org/10.5465/annals.2018.0127

Wang, B., Liu, Y., Qian, J., & Parker, S. K. (2021). Achieving effective remote working during the COVID-19 pandemic: A work design perspective. *Applied Psychology 70*(1), 16–59. https://doi.org/10.1111/apps.12290

Waschull, S., Bokhorst, J. A. C., Wortmann, J. C., & Molleman, E. (2022). The redesign of blue- and white-collar work triggered by digitalization: Collar matters. *Computers & Industrial Engineering 165*, 107910. https://doi.org/10.1016/j.cie.2021.107910

Webb, T., Holyoak, K. J., & Lu, H. (2023). Emergent analogical reasoning in large language models. *Nature Human Behaviour 7*, 1526–1541. https://doi.org/10.1038/s41562-023-01659-w

Wiec, A. (2020, 10 June). UBI, owning your data, & donating $1 billion: Jack Dorsey on Yang Speaks. *Yang Speaks Podcast*. https://podcastnotes.org/yang-speaks/jack-dorsey/

Wood, A. J. (2021). Algorithmic management consequences for work organisation and working conditions (Working Paper 2021/07). *JRC Working Papers Series on Labour, Education and Technology*. https://www.econstor.eu/handle/10419/233886

World Economic Forum. (2024). Why there will be plenty of jobs in the future — even with artificial intelligence. World Economic Forum. https://www.weforum.org/stories/2024/02/artificial-intelligence-ai-jobs-future/

World Economic Forum. (2023). These are the jobs most likely to be lost—and created—because of AI. World Economic Forum. https://www.weforum.org/agenda/2023/05/jobs-lost-created-ai-gpt/

Wyatt, S. (2008). Technological determinism is dead; long live technological determinism. In E. Hackett, O. Amsterdamska, M. Lynch, & J. Wajcman (Eds.), Handbook of *science and technology studies* (pp. 165–180). MIT Press.

Yamamoto, I. (2019, 14 March). The impact of AI and information technologies on worker stress. Centre for Economic Policy Research. https://cepr.org/voxeu/columns/impact-ai-and-information-technologies-worker-stress

Reimagining Work Design in Contemporary Employment
The Disruptive Rise of the Gig Economy

James Duggan and Jérôme Sulbout

Introduction

The world of work is in a constant state of change. Debates on the "future of work" have been, and continue to be, dynamic and varied in their focus (Dries et al., 2023), yet the rapid emergence of new employment forms in recent decades has signaled that what was once commonly accepted as traditional employment is in decline (Barley et al., 2017; Jooss et al., 2022). In today's labor market, a growing component of the workforce is engaged in non-standard work—essentially, referring to any type of working arrangement that deviates from the standard employment model of full-time roles centralized within a singular organization (Harvey et al., 2017; ILO, 2016). Non-standard work often features contingent arrangements (Polivka & Nardone, 1989) involving workers that do not have an implicit or explicit understanding that the employment will be continuous, meaning the working relationship is typically tied to the completion of a specific task for a defined duration (McLean Parks et al., 1998). Consequently, the temporality, scope, and nature of roles and employment contracts within this categorization are extremely broad and wide-ranging (Eurofound, 2017).

Despite being considered by many scholars and policymakers as precarious and insecure, contingent labor is viewed as offering greater flexibility for those who partake, and not all work types in this category are necessarily ominous or risky (Sulbout et al., 2022). For example, while contingent work was traditionally concentrated in low-skill and low-wage industrial occupations, more recent forms have included highly skilled work arrangements, such as freelancing, subcontracting, flextime, and consultancy, in addition to the likes of seasonal work, zero-hours contracts, and temporary employment (Ashford et al., 2007; Kunda et al., 2002; Sulbout et al., 2022). While these arrangements

James Duggan and Jérôme Sulbout, *Reimagining Work Design in Contemporary Employment*. In: *Transformative Work Design*. Edited by: Edited by: Sharon K. Parker et al., Oxford University Press. © Society for Industrial and Organizational Psychology (2025). DOI: 10.1093/oso/9780197692554.003.0020

differ, sometimes in minor ways, a common feature is that they all diverge from the norm of standard, full-time employment (Felstead & Jewson, 1999). Studies suggest that non-standard work arrangements, in all forms, affect up to 75 percent of the global workforce, with some companies using contingent workers to form up to 30 percent of their workforce (Geller & Mazor, 2011; Harvey et al., 2017).

Following its advent around the time of the global financial crisis, the gig economy quickly emerged as perhaps the most widely debated and disruptive trend within the realm of contingent work. Offering contract-based work via the medium of digital platforms, the gig economy uses technology to digitally connect on-demand, freelance workers with customers to perform fixed-term tasks (Duggan et al., 2020; Kaine & Josserand, 2019). Work in the gig economy takes on many forms and operates across a diverse array of industries and sectors (Cropanzano et al., 2023; Wood et al., 2019). As a phenomenon, gig work is inherently controversial, with scholars, governments or policymakers, and media bodies all raising important concerns about the potential flaws and risks—whether legal, ethical, financial, or otherwise—associated with gig-style arrangements (Adams-Prassl, 2022; McGaughey, 2018). Work design, despite being underexplored in this context, is no exception, particularly given the fragmented nature of gig work and the unique, yet often opaque, involvement of multiple parties in the work arrangement (Keegan & Meijerink, 2022). Ostensibly, gig work is positioned as a form of self-employment, where individuals can engage freely and flexibly to suit their own needs. Yet, research has suggested that platform organizations exert significant levels of control over gig workers' activities and decisions (Bucher et al., 2021; Wood et al., 2019), and that other non-organizational actors and surveillance technologies also contribute to this control system (Duggan et al., 2023).

In this chapter, we examine the emergence of the gig economy and its associated work forms, with a particular focus on exploring the disruptive nature of gig work in reimagining work design norms and expectations. We begin by providing an overview of important trends in contemporary employment forms, wherein we trace the rise of the gig economy and outline its core characteristics. We then proceed to analyze the key work design features of two widely researched gig work variants, outlining the most prominent issues and debates that have dominated discourse in recent years. Finally, we conclude with a critical discussion of work design issues in gig work, highlighting elements such as the fragmented and isolating nature of tasks, tensions in the flexibility and autonomy afforded to gig workers, and important concerns as we look toward the future of this new economy.

The Changing Nature of Work

Contingent workers were traditionally used by companies who sought to outsource their workforce, either because work was generic and uncomplicated, or because work required a high degree of knowledge and skills not available within their internal labor market (Connelly & Gallagher, 2004; ILO, 2016). In the latter scenario, skilled contingent workers were often internalized to meet the company's needs for knowledge and skills, essentially allowing the worker to enter a more secure and conventional employment relationship (Felstead & Jewson, 1999). In today's workplace, this outcome is becoming less common as workers increasingly tend to remain within their contingent work arrangement, while the outsourcing of tasks to freelancers or consultants is on the rise (Sulbout et al., 2022; Keegan & Meijerink, 2022). Consequently, the nature of the employment relationship has changed: rather than involving a clearly defined employer and employee, the relationship has become triangular in nature, typically involving an independent worker, an intermediate organization, and a client or customer (Bonet et al., 2013; Sulbout et al., 2022).

The changing nature and increasing fragmentation of the employment relationship has received significant interest across scholarly literature (Ashford et al., 2007; Barley et al., 2017). Concerns have been raised about the potentially damaging implications for workers who enter these arrangements, with studies suggesting that opportunities for training and development are diminished (Duggan et al., 2021); progression pathways are difficult to pursue (Sulbout & Pichault, 2022); and employment protections and benefits such as pension schemes, sick pay, and unemployment insurance are increasingly challenging to access (Kaine & Josserand, 2019). Contrastingly, other narratives around the rise of non-standard work are more positively positioned as granting workers greater autonomy over their working lives and earning potential, ultimately serving to heighten flexibility and satisfaction as workers move freely between different roles and organizations (Pichault & McKeown, 2019).

The advent and advancement of new technologies have enabled much of the change witnessed in the design of work and in the labor market at large (Rosenblat, 2018; Waldkirch et al., 2021). Historically, work has been geographically bounded, with the labor process typically associated with or confined to the workplace (Graham et al., 2017). However, technology has been transformative in this context, allowing organizations to redesign the ways in which work activities are carried out, and temporally and spatially organized (Aroles et al., 2019). These technologies have enabled organizations to link workers directly with customers for the provision of services, with large gains in the quality, speed, and efficiency of service. For organizations, these technologies have also

508   TRANSFORMATIVE WORK DESIGN

played an important and strategic role in creating comprehensive surveillance and control systems, which have allowed work activities to be deconstructed into a series of individual tasks to be completed sequentially under the close supervision of workforce management technologies (Waldkirch et al., 2021; Wu et al., 2019), while simultaneously reducing labor and operations costs. Studies examining the implications of these technologies on workers—whether positive or negative—have surged in recent years (e.g., Schildt, 2020; Walker et al., 2021).

Although accounts of workers' experiences with these new technologies are becoming more common, it remains unclear whether the organizations who create and implement these systems intentionally set out to alter the design and organization of work, or whether the nature of work itself morphs and transforms as the world changes. According to Stephen Barley and colleagues (2017), both dynamics occur, and regardless of which dynamic takes precedence, the key issue lies in recognizing the reality of the changes and social consequences brought about by these developments. While reflecting on the implementation of new technologies at work is an important starting point, we also caution that these developments have not halted. Indeed, developments in automation and artificial intelligence are ongoing in discussions on the future of work (McLean Parks et al., 1998; Parent-Rocheleau & Parker, 2022), and it must be assumed that work design implications and transformations will continue to emerge in line with this.

Work in the Gig Economy

The gig economy, as a defining feature of contemporary labor markets, continues to reshape traditional employment models and introduce novel forms of contingent work. Characterized by its reliance on digital platforms to mediate tasks, the gig economy emphasizes flexibility and independence, but it also raises critical questions about job security, worker protections, and organizational control.

Emergence of gig work

Stemming from the uncertainties and insecurities of the evolving economic landscape, the gig economy emerged as a departure from traditional employment models and their associated protections (Pichault & McKeown, 2019). Originally coined in news and journalism circles, the term "gig economy" refers to various forms of contingent work that are facilitated through digital platform organizations (McDonnell et al., 2021; Meijerink et al., 2021). Each task or job in this context is referred to as a "gig," drawing parallels to the flexible and independent nature of a musician's free-spirited work life (Duggan et al., 2020). In many cases, the tasks, or "gigs," to be completed by workers are simply components of formerly full-time roles held by taxi drivers, couriers, translators, secretaries, and so on, with the noteworthy differences in gig work being that these tasks are digitally mediated by platform organizations, and importantly, that workers are classified as independent contractors rather than employees. This fluidity has allowed platform organizations to outsource and redistribute labor via the use of independent contractors and freelancers—in the form of gig workers—who complete short-term, ad-hoc tasks while remaining peripheral to the organization (Keegan & Meijerink, 2022). Consequently, gig working relationships are interdependent due to increased interactions with both the platform organization and external parties (e.g., customers or clients) (Cross & Swart, 2021), while also becoming more challenging to form and maintain with the increased prevalence of digital technologies throughout the relationship (Duggan et al., 2020).

The fluidity of the gig economy is reflected in how it has been conceptualized across scholarship to date. Definitions of gig work have varied, ranging from encompassing all non-standard and less structured work arrangements to focusing specifically on work performed through digital platforms and crowdsourcing marketplaces (Cropanzano et al., 2023; Duggan et al., 2020). In this chapter, we focus on gig work exclusively as it relates to labor that is performed via digital platforms, where work processes and the mediating role of technology are clearly identifiable. Our chapter proceeds by focusing on two of the most distinctive and widely studied forms of gig work: *app-work* and *crowdwork*. App-work refers to the provision of on-demand services in local markets, such as transportation (e.g., Uber, Lyft), food or grocery delivery (e.g., UberEATS, Post Mates), and housekeeping or repair-type services (e.g., Handy, TaskRabbit) (Duggan et al., 2022). Comparatively, crowdwork refers to the provision of remote and computer-based micro services such as, for example, translation, transcription, and graphic design by individuals anywhere in the world for requesters via platforms such as Fiverr and Amazon Mechanical Turk (Berg & Rani, 2018; Howcroft & Bergvall-Kåreborn, 2019).

The nature and design of gig work

As we learn more about gig work, we realize that the services on offer in this new economy are often fragments of more traditional roles and occupations that have been restructured or reimagined. Although there are suggestions that highly skilled roles may become more prevalent in the gig economy, the predominant focus largely centers on jobs that are traditionally considered to be low-skilled. In the gig economy, these roles are deconstructed into smaller, algorithmically managed tasks, which are then offered to workers on a highly precarious and often poorly compensated basis (Cropanzano et al., 2023). As self-employed workers, both app-workers and crowdworkers are promised the opportunity to "be your own boss" by having control over various aspects of their roles, including scheduling and task selection (Wood et al., 2019; Wu et al., 2019). For platform organizations, this classification holds significant importance as it exempts them from the obligations and protections typically associated with traditional employment, such as overtime payments, union representation, payroll taxes, and unemployment benefits (Meijerink et al., 2021; Pichault & McKeown, 2019).

Some studies have suggested that many gig workers enjoy the increased autonomy offered to them in their roles, particularly those who may engage in gig work as a side-hustle to supplement another role that they hold beyond the gig economy (Meijerink & Bondarouk, 2023). Yet, research has also revealed that gig workers operate in highly insecure and pressurized roles, striving to complete multiple, repetitive, short-term tasks as quickly as possible, devoid of long-term commitment and income stability (Bucher et al., 2021; Dunn, 2020). Such evidence casts doubt on the oft-cited promise of flexibility promoted by platform organizations, instead signaling the potential risks and drawbacks faced by workers operating in these roles (Graham et al., 2017; Heiland, 2021). For workers, the outcome is often that their roles are characterized by intense precarity and anonymity, with most workers never meeting their "employer" or any representative of the platform organization, in addition to having few, if any, interactions with their peers. Literature has highlighted the challenges of this scenario for gig workers, where the more relational aspects of work are eroded, and workers are left feeling isolated in their roles and estranged from platform organizations (Cropanzano et al., 2023; Heiland, 2021). Additionally, research has also examined gig workers' efforts to mobilize and collectivize to improve their working conditions (Cini, 2023; Tassinari & Maccarrone, 2020), although this is a complex challenge due to the highly precarious and geographically dispersed nature of roles (Walker et al., 2021).

Although the digital remediation of gig work is largely viewed as significant and transformative (Newlands, 2020; Waldkirch et al., 2021), and despite the broader trends and disruptions in the labor market at large, our understanding of work design has remained predominantly resistant to change (Reiche, 2023; Wang et al., 2020). Reflecting how work tasks, activities, relationships, and responsibilities are organized, performed, and altered (Grant & Parker, 2009), studies on work design have also remained surprisingly sparse in the gig work context, despite the novel and unique features of this work being on-demand

(Schroeder et al., 2021), deconstructed into micro tasks via new technologies (Reiche, 2023), involving of multiple parties (Duggan et al., 2023), and compensated on a dynamic piece-rate basis (McDonnell et al., 2021). Research by B. Sebastian Reiche (2023) identified and attempted to address this void by proposing new work design modes that more effectively capture the pace of change in the world of non-standard work. Within this updated conceptualization, gig work is said to represent a work design mode that is both external and formalized: that is, gig workers operate beyond the core boundaries of the organization, but their work-based activities are still monitored and controlled by the organization due to the need to meet organizational demands (Reiche, 2023).

Indeed, research consistently supports the notion that much of the autonomy purportedly granted to gig workers is largely symbolic and designed to attract workers to the platform or to fulfil legal requirements (Wood et al., 2019). In reality, platform organizations must avoid issuing direct commands to workers, which could indicate a legal employment relationship, while simultaneously exerting substantial control over the labor process by using algorithmic technologies that allocate tasks, monitor service delivery, and determine rewards (Keegan & Meijerink, 2022). Workers who are deemed by the algorithm to have failed to meet performance criteria may face penalties or repercussions at the behest of these technologies (Duggan et al., 2020; Wu et al., 2019). Consequently, the availability of tasks and income is highly unpredictable for workers (Heiland, 2021), and it perhaps becomes more apparent why studies on the experiences of gig workers encompass such a diverse array of issues and complexities (Duggan et al., 2023; Huang, 2022; Norlander, 2021). At once, organizational boundaries are designed to be intentionally fluid, making clear to workers that they are not core employees with the associated levels of commitment (Meijerink & Bondarouk, 2023), yet decision-making authority and control remain centrally enacted and comprehensively enforced (Reiche, 2023). This means that hiring or onboarding is short-term and task-based (Pichault & McKeown, 2019), work allocation is driven by algorithmic on-demand matching in digital markets (Waldkirch et al., 2021), training and development is often non-existent and wholly the responsibility of individual workers (Barley et al., 2017), performance management is customer-led (Veen et al., 2020), and rewards are often issued sporadically and dynamically (Duggan et al., 2023).

While this overview is intended to capture a broad spectrum of work design issues and complexities in gig work, we recognize that the gig economy represents a range of populations of digitally enabled workers, all engaged in a variety of roles. Thus, the intricacies of work design likely differ from one type of gig work to another, but also from one platform organization to another, given

512 TRANSFORMATIVE WORK DESIGN

the superficially similar but practically different work ecosystems in which they exist. While it would be impractical to explore work design features in all types of gig work, we continue by focusing specifically on the app-work and crowdwork variants.

Work Design in App-Work

In recent years, app-work has emerged as one of the most visible forms of labor in the gig economy. It represents a transformative approach to organizing work, where traditional employment relationships are replaced with algorithmically mediated interactions between workers, customers, and platform organizations. This section explores the distinctive features and complexities of app-work, examining its implications for work design and the experiences of app-workers.

Key features

Across existing scholarship, app-work is perhaps the most recognized and widely debated form of labor in the gig economy (McDonnell et al., 2021; Norlander et al., 2021). Referring to digitally transacted services that are offered in local markets, app-work involves platform organizations that operate by matching supply and demand between workers and customers (Duggan et al., 2020). As the term implies, this form of gig work is facilitated via smartphone applications (or apps) that are created, owned, and managed by platform organizations. It is through these apps that most aspects of the service delivery and labor process are facilitated: customers can search, request, and pay for services via the app; while the app also offers workers individual "gigs" to complete and, if they accept, workers are then given guidance on task completion within the app (Kellogg et al., 2020). In this way, the platform organization—through the medium of an app—both facilitates and mediates the working arrangement. As a result, although app-work mainly involves the provision of traditional services, the novelty of this arrangement lies in the re-design and digital remediation of work. For example, the organization of app-work is typically dictated by the platform and the algorithmic technologies it uses to remotely manage and coordinate workers' activities, meaning there is little focus on the relational components of the work, and subsequently, interactions between parties are heavily restricted (Kaine & Josserand, 2019; Keegan & Meijerink, 2022).

Compared to other types of gig work, app-work is strikingly visible in urban areas, and consequently app-workers tend to be easily recognizable to consumers due to the services they provide (e.g., food-delivery workers typically use platform-branded courier bags, while ride-hail drivers usually display a platform-branded badge or sticker on their vehicle's windshield). Because app-work occurs locally, workers must adapt to the fluctuating nature of customer demand in their specific location at any given time (Vallas & Schor, 2020). For example, in a typical ride-hail arrangement, workers log-in to the platform organization's app to begin working from their own personal vehicle but must then wait to be offered work opportunities when tasks are requested by customers (Duggan et al., 2021). The scenario is similar for food-delivery workers, who must wait for customers to place orders from restaurants before a delivery task then becomes available. Therefore, although app-workers usually have increased autonomy over the scheduling of their working hours, they constantly face the risk of low levels of demand—and consequently, low earnings—during their shifts (Veen et al., 2020; Wu et al., 2019).

When app-workers choose to accept the tasks offered to them, they are then provided with step-by-step guidance by the platform organization on how to proceed through the labor process to efficiently complete each task. For example, food-delivery workers receive precise notifications on when to travel to a particular restaurant to collect orders, and then receive in-app navigational guidance while traveling from the restaurant to the customer's address (Duggan et al., 2023). Likewise, ride-hail workers receive similar navigational guidance and recommended routes to ensure the customer reaches their destination as quickly as possible (Rosenblat, 2018). Although platform organizations position these prompts and guidance as being optional for workers, a widely studied feature of app-work is the use of surveillance technologies and algorithms to direct, manage, and control the activities of workers, with the goal of ensuring that performance standards are constantly upheld (Vallas & Schor, 2020; Veen et al., 2020). As discussed elsewhere in this collection, this process of monitoring and managing app-workers' activities has become known as *algorithmic management* and continues to be subject to widescale debate and controversy for its intense surveillance capabilities and potential to tightly control workers who are predominantly classified as being self-employed (Rodgers et al., 2022; Wood et al., 2019).

Complexities and issues

Research on app-work has identified and explored a wide range of complexities, issues, and dilemmas associated with this form of labor (Bader & Kaiser, 2019; Bucher et al., 2021; Cini, 2023). Central to these discussions is the unique structure of the working relationship found in this arrangement. App-work relationships are not rooted in traditional conceptualizations of a clearly defined employer and employee, but instead feature multiple parties contributing to a dynamic exchange agreement between three, or sometimes four different parties (e.g., platform organizations, app-workers, customers, and occasionally external suppliers such as restaurants) (Duggan et al., 2020). It is the app—representative of the platform organization—that connects and directs each party in the working arrangement, thereby functioning as a centralized mechanism governing the dynamics of this unique working relationship (Cennamo, 2019; Duggan et al., 2022).

The design of app-work is characterized by brevity and fragmentation—that is, the speed at which the working relationship is created, along with the speed at which the same relationship can be terminated, is striking (Graham et al., 2017; Heiland, 2021). In most cases, app-workers are hired and onboarded almost instantly, provided they meet a set of minimum criteria and agree to the terms outlined by the platform organization (Meijerink et al., 2021). However, the short-term nature of app-work—with no expectation of commitment to an ongoing relationship beyond the completion of each individual task—means that these arrangements remain heavily insecure (McGaughey, 2018). A range of studies have considered the experiences of app-workers, and how the fragmented nature of this working relationship may negatively impact upon them (e.g., Kaine & Josserand, 2019; Norlander et al., 2021).

Relatedly, the potential for app-workers to be immediately deactivated or removed from platforms further contributes to the insecurity of this arrangement. Research has explored how platform organizations use advanced technologies to continuously gather performance-related metrics and data on workers, in addition to aggregating and interpreting anonymous ratings submitted by customers of the platform (Duggan et al., 2023; Norlander et al., 2021). These data and evaluations can influence future task opportunities for workers, and more controversially, can also result in the platform's algorithm determining that certain workers should be removed from the platform entirely, essentially equating to the working relationship being terminated with immediate effect and without an opportunity for recourse or dialogue with the organization (Kellogg et al., 2020; Parent-Rocheleau & Parker, 2022).

While the potential deactivation of workers lies on the more extreme end of the issues associated with app-work, a more commonly cited concern relates to the levels of organizational control enacted upon app-workers, seemingly contradicting the purported autonomy and flexibility promised by platforms (Vallas & Schor, 2020). Notionally, the opportunity to "be your own boss" allows workers to balance app-work with other roles and personal commitments, but with the caveat of also needing to manage their own schedules and workloads. Yet, a growing body of research has challenged this notion, questioning whether app-workers possess any meaningful control over the design and execution of work processes (Veen et al., 2020; Waldkirch et al., 2021). Indeed, studies suggest that the platform organization dictates the parameters and requirements of each work task, leaving workers with minimal influence over how work is organized or executed (Meijerink & Bondarouk, 2023; Wang et al., 2020).

Work Design in Crowdwork

Crowdwork has emerged as a significant aspect of the gig economy, operating distinctly from app-work while also redefining traditional work structures. This section delves into the unique nature of crowdwork, emphasizing its remote and decentralized characteristics, and explores its implications for both workers and organizations.

Key features

Although app-work has been more prevalent in studies on gig work in the work and employment domain, the crowdwork variant has also garnered significant attention (Berg & Rani, 2021; Howcroft & Bergvall-Kåreborn, 2019; Huws et al., 2018). In many ways, crowdwork is almost the opposite of standard work (Harvey et al., 2017; ILO, 2016); that is, individuals engaged in crowdwork undertake a series of one-off macro- or micro-tasks for third-party clients or requesters, as independent contractors, on one or multiple digital platforms from any location in the world (Schmidt, 2017). This contrasts with app-work, where the service must be provided locally, and usually with some level of direct interaction with those requesting the service. Crowdwork originates from the outsourcing practices of companies and, more specifically, from outsourcing tasks to a mass of people (i.e., an online "crowd") for piece-rate remuneration (Howe, 2006; Huws et al., 2018). Thus, companies or individuals requiring services can easily access a vast, online marketplace filled with the skills and knowledge of masses of on-demand, hyperflexible workers (Altenried, 2020).

Academics and policymakers have grown increasingly interested in the crowdwork phenomenon (Eurofound, 2017; Huws et al., 2018), particularly as more major platform organizations have emerged and grown in this space (e.g., Fiverr, Amazon Mechanical Turk, Click Worker) (Berg & Rani, 2018). By its very nature and design, crowdwork is intrinsically concealed and remote (Altenried, 2020), with workers typically being "invisible" to the requester and elusive for researchers. While crowdwork is generally understood as one form of gig work, research has identified different crowdwork sub-variants (Howcroft & Bergvall-Kåreborn, 2019; Schmidt, 2017). These sub-variants are cloud-based crowdwork, where tasks can be completed remotely via the Internet; micro-tasking crowdwork, where each task is further subdivided into smaller units of work with each component remunerated individually; and contest-based crowdwork, where tasks are carried out simultaneously by a group of individuals but only one end-result is used and paid for.

Crowdworkers undertake human intelligence tasks that computers cannot perform, although these tasks generally require less training and experience than the work of cloud-based consultants or freelancers (Duggan et al., 2022; Vallas & Schor, 2020). Still, there are notable variations in the level of skills required, the type of tasks provided, the income generated, and the levels of autonomy and control afforded to workers by platforms and requesters (Howcroft & Bergvall-Kåreborn, 2019). For example, platforms offering micro-tasks require workers to possess only a very small set of basic skills and knowledge to complete the task (e.g., photo-tagging or feeding simple information into AI-based algorithms), indicating a work design that is less enriched due to the likely repetitive and monotonous nature of the tasks to be completed. In such scenarios, requests to perform tasks are usually made to several workers, mediated by the platform organization, and are therefore extremely ad-hoc and typically achievable within minutes or hours (Berg & Rani, 2021).

Contrastingly, macro-tasks are more advanced in their content and usually require workers to possess a greater array of skills and knowledge to success-fully complete tasks (Huws et al., 2018). Again, the range of potential job types associated with macro-tasks is hugely broad, but can include, for example, administrative assignments, projects, or creative work such as song writing, developing marketing strategies, website creation, and so on (Panteli et al., 2020; Vallas & Schor, 2020). Thus, the projects issued by requesters are usually only achievable in a longer time period than microtasks, often depending on the nature of the task and the demand-based needs of the requester. As a result, macro-tasks tend to be less parceled than microtasks, and they seem likely to encompass a more enriched and meaningful work design as a result.

From the perspective of user organizations or clients, crowdwork boasts the potential to cheaply disperse work that was once performed in-house, particu-larly for quick tasks that do not require significant instruction or supervision (Schmidt, 2017). On certain crowdwork platforms, the compensation for tasks is set by platforms themselves, while in other cases the remuneration is deter-mined directly by the requester who can assess the nature of the work to be completed (Duggan et al., 2020). Likewise, as requesters in this context can be either individuals or external companies who have a specific task or set of tasks to be completed, it is the platform organization who then hosts and mediates the relationship between requesters and workers, while also managing the financial transaction between parties (Huws et al., 2018).

Complexities and issues

A prominent feature of crowdwork is that this form of labor is designed to be completed remotely, from anywhere in the world, provided the worker can access the host platform's website (Huws et al., 2018). In some ways, this can be advantageous for workers because it notionally allows them to conveniently access work from anywhere and to reorganize their working hours according to their own needs, potentially facilitating a greater work–life balance. Yet, the potentially dark side of this feature is that the experience of being a crowdworker may be inherently isolating because those who are partaking in such work are less likely to build relationships with other workers or actors in the working arrangement due to the distant and anonymous nature of this work form. In combating this issue, research suggests that crowdworkers may seek to regain a collective sense of identity by engaging with other workers via online forums (Gerber & Krzywdzinski, 2019), where users can share tips and recommendations for skills to maximize their efficiency and earning potential (Elbanna & Idowu, 2022). These online communities may be developed informally by workers or directly by platform organizations. While the hyper-flexibility of crowdwork might indicate low commitment levels between workers and platforms, research has suggested that some workers may instead develop a degree of attachment or identification with the online communities associated with platforms (Panteli et al., 2020).

The use of algorithmic technologies in crowdwork, while still widespread, is notably different to app-work. In crowdwork, the platform organization's role is more heavily focused on matchmaking—essentially, to ensure that requesters are speedily matched with workers and that tasks are completed efficiently according to the requester's specific requirements (Howcroft & Bergvall-Kåreborn, 2019). Hence, algorithms are typically less directive and pervasive in crowdwork, and hence, hold less direct influence over the labor process (Gerber & Krzywdzinski, 2019). Some crowdwork platforms use algorithms that are designed to benefit requesters by lowering search times and costs, ultimately serving to ensure a perfect match between the supply of crowdworkers with the demand of requesters (Vallas & Schor, 2020). While this is beneficial for requesters, it presents a greater degree of uncertainty for workers, whose ability to access work can vary based on these algorithmic determinations.

Relatedly, as with app-work, the evaluation of crowdworkers via rating systems holds implications for work design (Gerber & Krzywdzinski, 2019). Internal algorithmic evaluations are often supplemented with evaluations from requesters, which for many workers represents a source of stress (Howcroft & Bergvall-Kåreborn, 2019), spurring a need to constantly seek out new tasks to increase their ranking and potentially countering the increased autonomy they are afforded in determining and selecting their work activities (Benlian et al., 2022). Yet, this is also structurally challenging on certain crowdwork platforms where workers can only bid for tasks for a finite period, potentially without any guarantee of being selected for that particular task.

From a job crafting perspective, the heavily structured and potentially monotonous nature of crowdwork—particularly micro-tasks—presents challenges for workers seeking to align their work activities with their values and objectives (Wong et al., 2021). While highly skilled crowdworkers completing macro-tasks may have some room to shape their work, most crowdworkers have little opportunity to do this, with tasks typically being entirely predefined by requesters and compliance strictly encouraged by platform organizations (Wong et al., 2021). Indeed, the redesign of traditional work into one-off microtasks has been criticized for encouraging the exploitation and commodification of labor (Howcroft & Bergvall-Kåreborn, 2019), particularly as many of these work forms are often invisible, poorly compensated, and heavily controlled, with little autonomy or agency granted to workers (Altenried, 2020; Huws et al., 2018). Likewise, research has reported that many workers engaged in crowdwork are often left frustrated with the low level of pay, the lack of a reliable and steady source of work, the unresponsiveness of platform organizations to workers' concerns, and the poor or sometimes abusive relationships that are formed with clients (Berg & Rani, 2018). While some laud the gig economy and crowdwork for minimizing entry barriers into the labor market and to access an income (Panteli et al., 2020), others argue that the risks associated with this labor form outweigh the benefits (Berg & Rani, 2018, Wood et al., 2019).

Implications of Gig Work

Reflecting broader trends in contemporary employment, the rise of the gig economy has attracted noteworthy attention for its rapid evolution and controversial work practices, and thus appears to be more disruptive than other contemporary employment forms. Ostensibly, the gig economy holds potential to be mutually beneficial for workers and organizations alike: those engaged in gig work gain increased flexibility and autonomy, while organizations can reduce labor-related costs and simultaneously increase efficiency (Huang, 2022; Vallas & Schor, 2020). Yet, the developments and features witnessed in the gig economy—particularly relating to hyper-flexibility and heightened insecurity—align firmly with broader trends in the labor market of employers seeking to distance themselves from employment-based responsibility toward workers by fragmenting and casualizing working arrangements (Ashford et al., 2007;

Cross & Swart, 2021; Eurofound, 2017). In gig work, these shifts are largely attributed to the technologies used by platform organizations, which have significantly shaped the type and quality of work on offer in this domain (Rodgers et al., 2022; Wang et al., 2020). Thus, by using these technologies, gig work is designed and organized to achieve the maximum possible level of standardization and efficiency—even if this is potentially at the detriment of workers' lived experiences and well-being (Newlands, 2020).

Despite the vast range of issues and controversies associated with the gig economy and its associated work forms, most stakeholders tend to agree that this new way of working is here to stay (Aroles et al., 2019; Bonet et al., 2013; Cennamo, 2019). Although specific details on the future of the gig economy are difficult to predict at this stage, and some EU rulings that could affect its future are still pending, it is expected that gig work will continue to grow and evolve into a broader array of industries and sectors (Cross & Swart, 2021; Dunn, 2020), and that it will remain an important component of the labor market in the future of work. From a work design perspective, the growth and apparent permanence of the gig economy highlights the radical changes seen in the world of work, emphasizing that organizations and workers alike still face significant challenges in structuring their work to reflect and adapt to these trends (Reiche, 2023; Wang et al., 2020).

While research on the gig economy has exploded in popularity over the last decade, studies explicitly exploring work design in this context remain limited. Yet, various features of gig work continue to be intensely debated, particularly those in which the perspective of gig workers is a focal point, and where concerns are raised about the potential for gig-style working arrangements to seep into more traditional work forms (Duggan et al., 2022). Despite the ongoing surge in research activity, the gig economy is fast-moving and remains somewhat elusive, particularly as the specific dimensions of gig work are often difficult to understand and examine, and because accessing and engaging with platform organizations continues to be challenging for researchers (McDonnell et al., 2021; Norlander et al., 2021).

Implications for workers

For gig workers, the organization of work brings about a daunting number of issues and complexities. Relating to some of the topics outlined throughout this chapter, these include autonomy-related concerns (Wood et al., 2019), legal challenges (Adams-Prassl, 2022), career and developmental hurdles (Duggan et al., 2021), and issues involving the potentially controlling nature of the surveillance technologies used by platform organizations (Kellogg et al., 2020).

Understandably, the breadth and scope of these issues has raised important questions about the sustainability of the gig economy and its novel work forms (Cropanzano et al., 2023; Dunn, 2020), and perhaps even more concerningly, the sustainability of the work-based trends and features on display in this new economy. By fragmenting labor into one-off, micro-tasks, gig work erodes the norms of conventional employment and increases the casualization of work (Felstead & Jewson, 1999; ILO, 2016). Currently, these trends represent risks for policymakers around the world, who continue in their efforts to effectively regulate the gig economy in all its forms (Adams-Prassl, 2022).

It is almost unheard of for gig workers to have regular, or even periodical engagement with a human representative of the platform organizations for whom they work. Although this appears to be a deliberate decision by organizations, this lack of engagement that characterizes the working relationship weakens social ties between parties and potentially indicates a careless approach toward workers who, in their isolated roles, ultimately perform core duties for the platform organization (Cennamo, 2019; Wang et al., 2020). The erosion of social ties and connections, and the isolation that workers may experience due to this, can impact negatively on well-being, and hence signals the existence of a work design that likely lacks relational elements (Grant & Parker, 2009). While appearing nonchalant toward the development of the working relationship, platform organizations' use of technology paradoxically signals an intensely different control-based approach to managing workers. From the beginning of the working arrangement, gig workers are submerged in a uniquely complex arrangement where most managerial processes and responsibilities are reconfigured via an obscure algorithm (Kellogg et al., 2020). This type of algorithmically enabled control and supervision system is highly distinctive, both for its encompassing and comprehensive nature throughout the labor process, and for its ability to influence workers' experiences and continuity in roles via the gathering and issuing of individualized performance metrics (Norlander et al., 2021).

Research suggests that while gig workers are often unclear about the type of data being collected and used by platform organizations, the internalization of the managerial function is potent enough to create an overall climate of discipline and control (McGaughey, 2018; Wu et al., 2019). Consequently, some have argued that the gig economy has prompted the emergence of a new type of rejuvenated and unregulated Taylorism (Altenried, 2020; McGaughey, 2018). In many ways, this argument holds logic: gig work seemingly reflects the re-emergence and normalization of what once constituted highly fragmented work—especially for crowdworkers—and poor or undesirable working conditions (Aroles et al., 2019; Barley et al., 2017). Likewise, the digital tools used by platform organizations allow for a dramatic, control-based reimagining of where and how work is completed (Ashford et al., 2018; Bucher et al., 2021; Duggan et al., 2023). Workers who find themselves at the center of such arrangements must remain constantly aware of the pressurized nature of gig work, ensuring they closely abide by the platform's guidance and strive for consistently positive evaluations from customers and clients to ensure continued access to work and income (McDonnell et al., 2021).

Although the potential for gig worker resistance likely represents a greater issue for platform organizations—and thus, is more comprehensively addressed in the next section—it is worth highlighting that several studies have identified power asymmetries in gig work, typically with the worker holding the least favorable position (Cini, 2023). For example, research by Michael Walker and colleagues (2021) describes the fragmentation, isolation, and resignation likely felt by gig workers who are on the receiving end of the advanced, digital control systems used by platform organizations. Scholarship has explored efforts by gig workers to resist these control systems, either individually or collectively (Cini, 2023; Wood et al., 2019). Yet, the dispersed and isolated nature of gig work makes it difficult for workers to collectivize, and subsequently, there is a limited number of formal worker associations or unions among gig worker populations (Duggan et al., 2022).

Finally, while the issues outlined are clearly concerning and important, we also exercise caution to refrain from assuming that the experiences of all gig workers are the same. For example, for workers who may be seeking a more casual arrangement or who engage in gig work to supplement income earned from another role (Ashford et al., 2018; Myhill et al., 2021), the fragmented nature of this work may be less problematic or potentially desirable in allowing increased flexibility to engage in the gig economy as a casual side-earner (Cennamo, 2019; Cropanzano et al., 2023; Vallas & Schor, 2020)—something that is particularly common among crowdworkers (Berg & Rani, 2018). Consequently, as the gig economy continues to evolve, it remains important to work toward developing a fuller understanding of the experiences, motivations, and perceptions of gig workers.

Implications for organizations

For platform organizations, the design of gig work presents significant strategic benefits. In a theoretical study of contemporary work design modes, Reiche (2023) outlines these strategic benefits in detail: by organizing work in a way that is both external and formalized, platform organizations can reduce labor costs at all junctures, while also restricting autonomy and retaining centralized control over work activities. In many ways, this approach solves the independent contractor issue for platform organizations, who can grant workers nominal flexibility over when and where to perform their work activities, but while ensuring the scope of work tasks remains prescribed and clearly bounded (Kellogg et al., 2020; Reiche, 2023). This is the one of the great struggles of the gig economy: what represents *strategic value and innovation* for platform organizations, instead represents *complexity and injustice* for gig workers.

Adopting a slightly different perspective, it is possible that the challenges faced by gig workers ultimately create corresponding challenges for platform organizations. For example, workers' efforts to spearhead regulatory change have created headaches and an abundance of negative publicity for platform organizations, who have faced scrutiny for their apparent unwillingness to engage with workers or make meaningful efforts to improve working conditions (Duggan et al., 2021; Griesbach et al., 2019). Likewise, the growing number of broadly negative accounts of gig workers' experiences in roles once again raise concerns, on the one hand, for the realization of decent work and career sustainability, but on the other hand, for the longevity and sustainability of platform organizations and the gig economy at large. In almost any other context, it would seem unimaginable that organizations experiencing such high turnover levels and sustained negative attention would be unconcerned with improving the experiences of their workers. Yet, much of the discourse on the gig economy has been one-sided, resulting in an extremely slow or stagnant pace of change.

As we learn more about the gig economy and the dynamics between platform organizations and workers, it becomes less surprising why solutions to "fix" gig work have not yet been agreed upon. Ultimately, gig work is designed to be inherently precarious and unstable: working relationships are fluid, work processes are highly fragmented, and neither work nor platform organizations are embedded to a particular place (Meijerink et al., 2021; Walker et al., 2021). This perhaps provides greater context as to why platform organizations seemingly have little interest in engaging with or trying to retain workers. Even from the outset of the working relationship, there appears to be little regard for ensuring "fit" between workers and organizations (Bérastégui, 2021; Duggan et al., 2020). While all of this seems highly unconventional, these practices have become close to the norm in the gig economy.

As previously mentioned, an emerging issue for platform organizations is the rise in resistance efforts from gig workers. Even where collective efforts may be hampered, research has shown that gig worker resistance can be more individualized and informal, with workers rebuffing the novel design of this labor with efforts to rework and resist organizational control strategies (Cini, 2023). For example, Tom Barratt and colleagues (2020) explain how gig workers may engage in a type of entrepreneurial agency, wherein they seek to reorganize their work activities and processes with the goal of materially improving their own individual conditions, rather than directly or collectively challenging the business models of platform organizations. Similarly, Sarah Kaine and Emmanuel Josserand (2019) describe how gig workers can develop "algorithmic competencies," which relate to a willingness to experiment, manipulate, and make sense of the algorithm. These informal resistance strategies or efforts may amount to a source of personal satisfaction for gig workers, with the use of tacit and covert disobedience demonstrating a type of informal solidarity with fellow workers.

Looking Ahead: The Future of Gig Work

The rapid emergence, continued development, and disruptive nature of platform organizations, as well as the potential forthcoming changes in regulatory systems governing gig work, make it difficult to forecast what lies ahead for the gig economy. Most studies on various forms of gig work—whether scholarly or otherwise—propose recommendations or solutions for addressing the various challenges associated with this new economy. Thus, efforts to chart the course for the future of gig work have considered a myriad of different perspectives and potential remedies, including, for example, legislative and regulatory avenues (Adams-Prassl, 2022), a further reimagining of work in this domain to enhance the experiences of workers (Keegan & Meijerink, 2022; McGaughey, 2018), and a potentially less intrusive role of technology and algorithms wherein these tools can still heighten service efficiency but without exerting such intense control over workers (Duggan et al., 2023; Parent-Rocheleau & Parker, 2022).

Yet, these grand issues and considerations—while potentially transformative —still leave many questions unanswered, notably in a work design context. For example, literature is still uncertain about who exactly works in the gig economy and their motivations for doing so, as well as whether all gig workers truly want to see the same, large-scale level of transformation and change in how their work is designed and organized. Across the app-work and crowdwork domains, are there differences in the types of changes or improvements that workers wish to see implemented? And assuming that the experiences and motivations of gig workers are not homogenous, do the specific characteristics and motivations of workers—ranging from previous professional experience to their level of engagement and dependency on gig work—influence their perceptions on the organization of work in this domain? Addressing these concerns leads to perhaps the grandest question of all for work and employment scholars in this context: is there potential to work toward creating a gig economy wherein its work forms can be mutually beneficial for workers and organizations alike? We propose that future research, rather than only seeking to measure the overall size of the gig economy, examines the various types or "profiles" of gig workers to more effectively understand their motivations, needs, and desires as key participants in this unique domain.

Likewise, any efforts to revise the nature of gig work would also benefit from greater insight on specific work design features and issues in these dynamic contexts, and in particular, from platform organizations who have led the way in shaping these labor arrangements (Bérastégui, 2021; Walker et al., 2021). For example, is there a conscious effort by these organizations to deconstruct and fragment work in such impactful ways? And are platform organizations concerned with the potentially negative implications of the work design transformations seen in this domain, particularly relating to concerns around the fair and ethical treatment of those who partake? Indeed, research has suggested that organizations play a critical role in shaping work design, even when workers are not direct employees (Parker et al., 2019). In the gig economy context, this appears to be the case, where platform organizations exert significant influence in how self-employed workers engage with and carry out work activities. Thus, we propose that exploring the perspective of these organizations—in addition to those of any other influential parties in various types of gig work arrangements (e.g., customers or clients)—holds notable importance in considering work design issues and potentially improving the quality of work for those who engage.

In many ways, the uncertainty surrounding the future of gig work resembles debates around the future of work more generally, where concerns about increased fragmentation and fluidity are rampant (Ashford et al., 2007; Grant & Parker, 2009). In the gig economy, these concerns have prompted an ongoing debate on decent work and job quality (Dunn, 2020). As detailed throughout this chapter, gig work is regularly associated with over-long working hours, reduced social protections, minimal union representation or collective voice opportunities, and little opportunity for training or development (Barratt et al., 2020; Bérastégui, 2021). So, we ask, is gig work a sustainable employment opportunity for those who partake? Or, indeed, is the gig economy model even sustainable for platform organizations in the longer term, especially given the myriad of criticisms and controversies that surround their operations? To advance understanding of job quality in this domain, scholarship must examine which specific characteristics and features of gig work either facilitate or inhibit the realization of decent work. Such lines of inquiry are especially important if gig-style work arrangements are to become more widespread in the labor market.

Overall, an encompassing issue in designing gig work is the struggle of balancing flexibility, sustainability, and opportunity for gig workers. Importantly, if the subjective experiences of gig workers vary across platform organizations, as well as in accordance with individual worker characteristics (e.g., those undertaking gig work as a primary or supplementary source of income) (Duggan et al., 2021; Kaine & Josserand, 2019), it becomes increasingly complex for organizations and policymakers to develop appropriate outcomes. In particular, what are the implications (if any) for workers arising from the erosion of social aspects of work in the gig economy? Do such arrangements truly represent opportunities as well as risks? Or are we witnessing the emergence of a new form of digital Taylorism where relational work design elements are predominantly ignored? We propose future studies that examine these concerns, with a particular focus on the well-being of those who partake in gig work.

References

Adams-Prassl, J. (2022). Regulating algorithms at work: Lessons for a "European approach to artificial intelligence." *European Labour Law Journal 13*, 30–50.

Altenried, M. (2020). The platform as factory: Crowdwork and the hidden labour behind artificial intelligence. *Capital & Class 44*(2), 145–158.

Aroles, J., Mitev, N., & de Vaujany, F.X. (2019). Mapping themes in the study of new work practices. *New Technology, Work and Employment 34*(3), 285–299.

Ashford, S. J., Caza, B. B., & Reid, E. M. (2018) From surviving to thriving in the gig economy: A research agenda for individuals in the new world of work. *Research in Organizational Behavior 38*, 23–41.

Ashford, S. J., George, E., & Blatt, R. (2007). Old assumptions, new work: The opportunities and challenges of research on nonstandard employment. *Academy of Management Annals 1*(1), 65–117.

Bader, V., & Kaiser, S. (2019). Algorithmic decision-making? The user interface and its role for human involvement in decisions supported by artificial intelligence. *Organization 26*(5), 655–672.

Barratt, T., Goods, C., & Veen, A. (2020). "I'm my own boss . . .": Active intermediation and "entrepreneurial" worker agency in the Australian gig economy. *EPA: Economy and Space 52*(8), 1643–1661.

Barley, S. R., Bechky, B. A., & Milliken, F. J. (2017). The changing nature of work: Careers, identities, and work lives in the 21st century. *Academy of Management Discoveries 3*(2), 111–115.

Benlian, A., Wiener, M., Cram, W. A., Krasnova, H., Maedche, A., Möhlmann, M., Recker, J., & Remus, U. (2022). Algorithmic management. *Business & Information Systems Engineering 64*, 825–839.

Bérastégui, P. (2021). *Exposure to psychological risk factors in the gig economy: A systematic review*. European Trade Union Institute.

Berg J., & Rani, U. (2018). Digital labour platforms and the future of work: Towards decent work in the online world. International Labour Organization. https://www.ilo.org/publications/digital-labour-platforms-and-future-work-towards-decent-work-online-world

Berg, J., & Rani, U. (2021). Working conditions, geography and gender in global crowdwork. In *Work and labour relations in global platform capitalism* (pp. 93–110). Edward Elgar Publishing.

Bonet, R., Cappelli, P., & Hamori, M. (2013). Labour market intermediaries and the new paradigm for human resources. *Academy of Management Annals* 7(1), 341–392.

Bucher, E. L., Schou, P. K., & Waldkirch, M. (2021). Pacifying the algorithm: Anticipatory compliance in the face of algorithmic management in the gig economy. *Organization* 28(1), 44–67.

Cennamo, C. (2019). Competing in digital markets: A platform-based perspective. *Academy of Management Perspectives* 35(2). https://doi.org/10.5465/amp.2016.0048.

Cini, L. (2023). Resisting algorithmic control: Understanding the rise and variety of platform worker mobilizations. *New Technology, Work and Employment* 38(1), 125–144.

Connelly, C. E., & Gallagher, D. G. (2004). Emerging trends in contingent work research. *Journal of Management* 30(6), 959–983.

Cropanzano, R., Keplinger, K., Lambert, B. K., Caza, B., & Ashford, S. J. (2023). The organizational psychology of gig work: An integrative conceptual review. *Journal of Applied Psychology* 108(3), 492–519.

Cross, D., & Swart, J. (2021). The (ir)relevance of human resource management in independent work: Challenging assumptions. *Human Resource Management Journal* 32(1), 232–246.

Dries, N., Luyckx, J., & Rogiers, P. (2023). Imagining the (distant) future of work. *Academy of Management Discoveries* 10(3). https://doi.org/10.5465/amd.2022.0130

Duggan, J., Carbery, R., McDonnell, A., & Sherman, U. (2023). Algorithmic HRM control in the gig economy: The app-worker perspective. *Human Resource Management* 62(6), 883–899.

Duggan, J., McDonnell, A., Sherman, U., & Carbery, R. (2022). *Work in the gig economy: A research overview*. Routledge.

Duggan, J., Sherman, U., Carbery, R., & McDonnell, A. (2020). Algorithmic management and app-work in the gig economy: A research agenda for employment relations and HRM. *Human Resource Management Journal* 30(1), 114–132.

Duggan, J., Sherman, U., Carbery, R., & McDonnell, A. (2021). Boundaryless careers and algorithmic constraints in the gig economy. *International Journal of Human Resource Management Journal* 33, 4468–4498.

Dunn, M. (2020). Making gigs work: Digital platforms, job quality and worker motivations. *New Technology, Work and Employment* 35(2), 232–249.

Elbanna, A., & Idowu, A. (2022) Crowdwork, digital liminality and the enactment of culturally recognised alternatives to Western precarity: Beyond epistemological terra nullius. *European Journal of Information Systems* 31(1), 128–144.

Eurofound. (2017). *Non-standard forms of employment: Recent trends and future prospects*. Publications Office of the European Union.

Felstead, A., & Jewson, N. (1999). Flexible labour and non-standard employment: An agenda of issues. In A. Felstead & N. Jewson (Eds.), *Global trends in flexible labour* (pp. 1-20). Macmillan.

Geller, J., & Mazor, A. H. (2011). *Global business driven HR transformation: The journey continues*. Deloitte.

Gerber, C., & Krzywdzinski, M. (2019). Brave new digital work? New forms of performance control in crowdwork. In S. P. Vallas & A. Kovalainen (Eds.), *Work and labor in the digital age* (pp. 121–143). Emerald Publishing Limited.

Graham, M., Hjorth, I., & Lehdonvirta, V. (2017). Digital labour and development: Impacts of global digital labour platforms and the gig economy on worker livelihoods. *Transfer: European Review of Labour and Research* 23(2), 135–162.

Grant, A. M., & Parker, S. K. (2009). Redesigning work design theories: The rise of relational and proactive perspectives. *Academy of Management Annals 3*, 273–331

Griesbach, K., Reich, A., Elliott-Negri, L., & Milkman, R. (2019). Algorithmic control in platform food-delivery work. *Socius 5*, 1–15.

Harvey, G., Rhodes, C., Vachhani, S. J., & Williams, K. (2017). Neo-villeiny and the service sector: The case of hyper flexible and precarious work in fitness centres. *Work, Employment and Society 31*(1), 19–35.

Heiland, H. (2021). Neither timeless, nor placeless: Control of food delivery gig work via place-based working time regimes. *Human Relations 75*, 1824–1848.

Howe, J. (2006). *The rise of crowdsourcing. Wired Magazine 14*(6), 1–4.

Howcroft, D., & Bergvall-Kåreborn, B. (2019). A typology of crowdwork platforms. *Work, Employment and Society 33*(1), 21–38.

Huang, H. (2022). Algorithmic management in food-delivery platform economy in China. *New Technology, Work and Employment 38*(2), 185–205.

Huws, U., Spencer, N., & Syrdal, D. S. (2018). Online, on call: The spread of digitally-organized just-in-time working and its implications for standard employment models. *New Technology Work & Employment 33*, 113–129.

International Labour Organisation. (2016). *Non-standard employment around the world: Understanding challenges, shaping prospects.* ILO.

Jooss, S., Duggan, J., & Parry, E. (2022). Technology in human resource functions: Core systems, emerging trends and algorithmic management. In P. Holland, T. Bartram, T. Garavan, & K. Grant (Eds.), *The Emerald handbook of work, workplaces and disruptive issues in HRM* (pp. 49–66). Emerald Publishing.

Kaine, S., & Josserand, E. (2019). The organization and experience of work in the gig economy. *Journal of Industrial Relations 61*(4), 479–501.

Keegan, A., & Meijerink, J. (2022). Dynamism and realignment in the HR architecture: Online labor platform ecosystems and the key role of contractors. *Human Resource Management 62*, 15–29.

Kellogg, K. C., Valentine, M. A., & Christin, A. (2020). Algorithms at work: The new contested terrain of control. *Academy of Management Annals 14*(1), 366–410.

Kunda, G., Barley, S. R., & Evans, J. (2002). Why do contractors contract? The experience of highly skilled technical professionals in a contingent labor market. *Industrial and Labor Relations Review 55*(2), 234–261.

McDonnell, A., Carbery, R., Burgess, J., & Sherman, U. (2021). Technologically mediated human resource management in the gig economy. *International Journal of Human Resource Management 32*(19), 3995–4015.

McGaughey, E. 2018. Taylorooism: When network technology meets corporate power. *Industrial Relations Journal 49*, 459–472.

McLean Parks, J., Kiddler, D. L., & Gallagher, D. G. (1998). Fitting square pegs into round holes: Mapping the domain of contingent work arrangements onto the psychological contract. *Journal of Organizational Behavior 19*, 697–730.

Meijerink, J., & Bondarouk, T. (2023). The duality of algorithmic management: Toward a research agenda on HRM algorithms, autonomy, and value creation. *Human Resource Management Review 33*, 1–14.

Meijerink, J., Boons, M., Keegan, A., & Marler, J. (2021). Algorithmic human resource management: Synthesizing developments and cross-disciplinary insights on digital HRM. *International Journal of Human Resource Management 32*(12), 2545–2562.

Myhill, K., Richards, J., & Sang, K. (2021) Job quality, fair work and gig work: The lived experience of gig workers. *International Journal of Human Resource Management* 32(19), 4110–4135.

Newlands, G. (2020). Algorithmic surveillance in the gig economy: The organization of work through Lefebvrian conceived space. *Organization Studies* 42(5), 719–737.

Norlander, P., Jukic, N., Varma, A., & Nestorov, S. (2021). The effects of technological supervision on gig workers: Organizational control and motivation of Uber, taxi, and limousine drivers. *International Journal of Human Resource Management* 32(19), 4053–4077.

Panteli, N., Rapti, A., & Scholarios, D. (2020). "If he just knew who we were": Microworkers' emerging bonds of attachment in a fragmented employment relationship. *Work, Employment and Society* 34(3), 476–494.

Parent-Rocheleau, X., & Parker, S. K. (2022). Algorithms as work designers: How algorithmic management influences the design of jobs. *Human Resource Management Review* 32(3), 100838.

Parker, S. K., Andrei, D. M., & Van den Broeck, A. (2019). Poor work design begets poor work design: Capacity and willingness antecedents of individual work design behavior. *Journal of Applied Psychology* 104(7), 907.

Pichault, F., & McKeown, T. (2019). Autonomy at work in the gig economy: Analysing work status, work content and working conditions of independent professionals. *New Technology, Work and Employment* 34(1), 59–72.

Polivka, A. E., & Nardone, T. (1989). On the definition of "contingent work." *Monthly Labor Review* 112(12), 9–16.

Reiche, B. S. (2023). Between interdependence and autonomy: Toward a typology of work design modes in the new world of work. *Human Resource Management Journal* 33, 1001–1017.

Rodgers, W., Murray, J. M., Stefanidis, A., Degbey, W. Y., & Tarba, S. Y. (2022). Human resource management review: An artificial intelligence algorithmic approach to ethical decision-making in human resource management processes. *Human Resource Management Review* 33, 100925.

Rosenblat, A. (2018). *Uberland: How algorithms are rewriting the rules of work.* University of California Press.

Schildt, H. (2020). *The data imperative: How digitalization is reshaping management, organizing, and work.* Oxford University Press.

Schmidt, F.A. (2017). *Digital labour markets in the platform economy: Mapping the political challenges of crowd work and gig work.* Friedrich-Ebert-Stiftung.

Schroeder, A. N., Bricka, T. M., & Whitaker, J. H. (2021). Work design in a digitized economy. *Human Resource Management Review* 31(1), 100692.

Sulbout, J., & Pichault, F. (2022). Free agents seeking career support: Exploring the expectations of skilled contingent workers via-à-vis labour market intermediaries. *Personnel Review* 52(9), 2304–2321.

Sulbout, J., Pichault, F., Jemine, G., & Naedenoen, F. (2022). Are skilled contingent workers neglected? Evidence from a cross-sector multiple case study on organisational career management practices. *European Management Journal* 40(3), 429–440.

Tassinari, A., & Maccarrone, V. (2020). Riders on the storm: Workplace solidarity among gig economy couriers in Italy and the UK. *Work, Employment, and Society* 34(1), 35–54.

Vallas, S., & Schor, J. B. (2020). What do platforms do? Understanding the gig economy. *Annual Review of Sociology 46*, 273–294.

Veen, A., Barratt, T., & Goods, C. (2020). Platform-capital's "app-etite" for control: A labor process analysis of food-delivery work in Australia. *Work, Employment & Society 34*, 388–406.

Waldkirch, M., Bucher, E., Kalum Schou, P., & Grünwald, E. (2021). Controlled by the algorithm, coached by the crowd: How HRM activities take shape on digital work platforms in the gig economy. *International Journal of Human Resource Management 32*(12), 2643–2682.

Walker, M., Fleming, P., & Berti, M. (2021). "You can't pick up a phone and talk to someone": How algorithms function as biopower in the gig economy. *Organisation 28*(1), 26–43.

Wang, B., Liu, Y., & Parker, S. K. (2020). How does the use of information communication technology affect individuals: A work design perspective. *Academy of Management Annals 14*(2). https://doi.org/10.5465/annals.2018.0127

Wood, A. J., Graham, M., Lehdonvirta, V., & Hjorth, I. (2019). Good gig, bad gig: Autonomy and algorithmic control in the global gig economy. *Work, Employment and Society 33*(1), 56–75.

Wong, S. I., Kost, D., & Fieseler, C. (2021). From crafting what you do to building resilience for career commitment in the gig economy. *Human Resource Management Journal 31*(4), 918–935.

Wu, Q., Zhang, H., Li, Z., & Liu, K. (2019). Labor control in the gig economy: Evidence from Uber in China. *Journal of Industrial Relations 61*(4), 574–596.

The Perils of Algorithmic Management for Work Design

Xavier Parent-Rocheleau

Algorithmic Management

Throughout the ages, technological advances have shaped the world of work. The steam engine, electricity, and computers have in turn had a structuring impact on work methods and processes, so much so that they are recognized as the markers of the first three industrial revolutions. Digital technologies such as big data, the Internet of Things (IoT), and artificial intelligence, markers of the fourth industrial revolution (Schwab, 2017), go further by allowing the total or partial automation of work management. This change may be defined as a digital paradigm shift as technology is no longer only used to support individuals at work but also to control and supervise them (Kellogg et al., 2020; Lee et al., 2015).

This shift is largely facilitated by the rise of increasingly sophisticated and complex algorithms. An algorithm is a "computational formula that autonomously makes decisions based on statistical models or decision rules without explicit human intervention, [such as] a sequence of instructions telling a computer what to do within a set of precisely-defined steps and rules designed to accomplish a task" (Duggan et al., 2020, p. 6). The use of such algorithms to entirely or partially carry out functions pertaining to the management of workers has been coined algorithmic management (AM), or "the use of computer-programmed procedures for the coordination of labour input in an organisation" (Baiocco et al., 2022). Also referred to as algorithmic control (Kellogg et al., 2020) or algorithmic human resources management (HRM) (Meijerink & Bondarouk, 2023), it is composed of two key processes across which algorithms take over management functions: algorithmic *monitoring* (or surveillance) of employees and their activities, and algorithmic *decision-making* regarding goal setting, scheduling, evaluation, compensation, and discipline (Kellogg et al., 2020; Parent-Rocheleau & Parker, 2022). These two processes are interdependent, such that algorithmic decisions, like targets, schedules, promotions, or rewards, are based on data collected through monitoring or

Xavier Parent-Rocheleau, *The Perils of Algorithmic Management for Work Design*. In: *Transformative Work Design*. Edited by: Sharon K. Parker et al., Oxford University Press. © Society for Industrial and Organizational Psychology (2025). DOI: 10.1093/oso/9780197692554.003.0021

surveillance of productivity, attendance, attitudes, behaviors, online activities, biometrics, location, and so on (Noponen et al., 2024; Wood, 2021).

The literature on algorithmic management has grown quickly since its initial conceptualization by Min Kyung Lee in 2015. It first caught the attention of researchers as the sole and dominant mode of organizing work in the platform (or gig) economy, where management is, in most cases, completely automated through algorithms (Fernandez et al., 2023; Jarrahi et al., 2021; Lippert et al., 2023; Wood, 2021). Monideepa Tarafdar and colleagues (2022) conceptualized algorithms in the gig economy as role senders and workers as role takers to illustrate the power and importance of an automated system in the control and coordination of work. More recently, scholars have started to examine the deployment of algorithmic management in traditional contexts of employment, where it is increasingly found, in more diverse and complex ways than in gig work. In sectors like warehousing, manufacturing, transport, retail, call centers, care work, hotels, banking, and engineering, algorithms are increasingly intertwined with human managers to monitor, coordinate, and control employees' work (Baiocco et al., 2022; Fernandez et al., 2023; Jarrahi et al., 2021; Lippert et al., 2023; Liu, 2023; Wood, 2021).

A recent European report indicates that 35 percent of workers in Spain and 20 percent in Germany consider that they are exposed to a certain degree of algorithmic management (Fernandez et al., 2023). Thus, algorithmic management may undoubtedly be seen as a growing phenomenon, representing new forms of organizing and optimizing. This rapid growth is concerning because research shows that current forms of AM lead to on-demand and unstable work, datafied and atomized tasks, exacerbated power imbalance between workers and employers, and intensified work (Baiocco et al., 2022; Fernandez et al., 2023; Newlands, 2023; Wood, 2021). Moreover, because of its obsession for efficiency, it has often been associated with a new and digital form of Taylorism (Jarrahi et al., 2021; Liu, 2023; Noponen et al., 2024).

Despite the fast-growing research on the topic, few authors have reviewed the literature on the links between AM and work design, and the existing or potential mechanisms to ensure that the former benefits the latter. Xavier Parent-Rocheleau and Sharon K. Parker (2022) reviewed nearly 50 studies and concluded that, according to these studies, the current forms and uses of algorithmic management tend to negatively impact work design. Aiming to extend and update this work, the objectives of this chapter are thus to summarize the current knowledge on the repercussions of algorithmic management on work design, including the most recent ones, along two main dimensions: work characteristics and work demands. To facilitate this analysis, we draw on Frederick P. Morgeson and Stephen E. Humphrey (2006)'s work design framework, categorizing work characteristics into tasks characteristics (i.e., autonomy, task variety, feedback from the job, task significance), knowledge characteristics (i.e., job complexity, problem-solving opportunities, skill variety, specialization), and social characteristics, focusing on various aspects of relatedness at work. We consider work design as a suitable framework to understand workers reactions to AM, following an implicit model by which algorithmic management influences work design which, in turn, has strong impact on various workers' outcomes (Parker et al., 2017).

Moreover, following the principles of socio-technical design, it is fundamental to keep in mind that the effects of technology are not predetermined, but rather shaped by organizational choices regarding the uses of this technology. Hence, after reviewing the evidence on the links between AM and work design, the chapter will elaborate on potential avenues for a more responsible implementation and use of AM in the workplace by outlining organizational choices around this technology that could shape its impact, as well as policy and regulation.

Algorithmic Management and Work Characteristics

More than simply automating many managerial activities, algorithmic management has profound and multifaceted implications for the nature of work. In this section, we focus on how it is transforming tasks, knowledge, and social characteristics, highlighting the main conclusions emerging from the literature.

Task characteristics (especially autonomy)

The use of algorithmic automation of management shapes employees' degree of agency in a complex and somewhat paradoxical manner (Meijerink & Bondarouk, 2023; Noponen et al., 2024; Wiener et al., 2021). On the one hand, such automation is often intended to reduce management, lessening the number and power of managers and redistributing this power to employees. In the gig economy, it supposedly also gives workers the ability to choose when and where they work and to get tips to autonomously maximize their income, with no boss around (Fernandez et al., 2023). On the other hand, this expected autonomy is seriously limited by several burdens pertaining to algorithmic management systems and where they are implemented.

First, in most cases, the strength and pervasiveness of the control exerted by algorithmic systems offset the gain of autonomy. Researchers have shown how, through algorithmic tracking, direction and coercion, such systems are used to ensure optimization of work execution in fields such as trucking (Levy, 2022), warehousing (Delfanti & Frey, 2021), banking (Perez et al., 2022), and data centers (Liu, 2023). Second, in the gig economy, workers have a high degree of dependence on the platform's algorithmic system, which fully controls the assignment and the remuneration of their work (Gagné & Parent-Rocheleau, 2022; Pignot, 2021). The purported freedom to choose tasks and schedules is thus mitigated by the high costs of refusing gigs and the obligation to work long hours to make an adequate living (Kellogg et al., 2020; Noponen et al., 2024; Rosenblat, 2018; Wiener et al., 2021). A study by Ngai Chan (2022) reported workers' feelings of lack of control and powerlessness due to the importance of customer ratings algorithmic metrics on their income and future work allocation by the platform. Third, because algorithmic systems are opaque black boxes, information about how data is collected and how decisions are made is generally unavailable or unintelligible (Gal et al., 2020; Kellogg et al., 2020). This generates a serious asymmetry of information and power between the workers who produce and collect the data and the companies who own and use this data to further optimize work through algorithmic decisions (Baiocco et al., 2022; Jarrahi et al., 2021; Wood, 2021). Consequently, this inability to understand and interact with the "role sender" algorithms limits workers' agency (Tarafdar et al., 2022).

Knowledge characteristics (job complexity and skill variety)

Scholars have also highlighted how algorithmically managed work can be characterized by deskilling and low stimulation. This is mostly due to the process of datafication, standardization, and atomization of work. Data fuels this type of system, and the more granular the data, informing on every stage, action, behavior, movement, or part of the work, the more efficient the system will be (Fernandez et al., 2023). However, this datafication (Gal et al., 2020; Schafheitle et al., 2020) or quantification of work (Moore, 2017; Moore & Robinson, 2016) is limited to the "objective truth" (Mateescu & Nguyen, 2019) and omits the intrinsic and idiosyncratic aspects that people may value the most in their work (Moore & Hayes, 2017), whittling work down to its quantifiable aspects and generating perceptions of reductionism (Newman et al., 2020).

Moreover, every aspect of the work must be predictable, with all this data being centralized and used to optimize companies' ability to make the best decisions in all circumstances. To attain this level of predictability, work must be routinized, standardized, exempt of subjectivities, with predetermined rules of actions (Baiocco et al., 2022; Gal et al., 2020). This automated Tayloristic process of granular division of work, fundamental to algorithmic management, has been coined the atomization of work (Baiocco et al., 2022) and is well documented, namely in the warehousing (Delfanti, 2021a), oil (Monteiro, 2022), and retail industries (Levy & Barocas, 2018; Vargas, 2021).

Besides rendering work less meaningful, this process can also "lead to a demand (from the organisation) and a need (of the worker) for skills that are very specific to discrete, short and very specific tasks to perform on an on-demand basis in a pre-defined (i.e., standardised) way, while diminishing and devaluing overarching competences and knowledge for the job" (Baiocco et al., 2022, p. 25). This devaluation of skills is compounded by another type of deskilling, in which workers must execute actions or decisions "that previously they had the power to shape" (Jarrahi et al., 2021, p. 6). In addition, researchers find that AM, by centralizing digitally collected and codified knowledge, exacerbates the power imbalance between workers and employers. Workers produce data that will then be owned by the company which, in turn, uses it to direct and control workers. Alessandro Delfanti and Bronwyn Frey (2021) named this process the "machinic dispossession" of knowledge, echoing Taylor's obsession with dividing the ones who know from the ones who do not.

Social characteristics

Although less documented, researchers have observed some potential effects, mostly negative, of the use of AM on the social characteristics of work. First, the atomization of work previously defined tends to isolate workers. When employees are siloed in their narrow parts or sections of a specific task, commonalities and opportunities for teamwork, or simply working together, are significantly reduced (Baiocco et al., 2022; Delfanti, 2021b; Todoli-Signes, 2021).

Second, because it is normally associated with less human intermediation, resulting in more distant or fewer human managers, the implementation of algorithmic managers diminishes the support the social environment can provide (Gagné et al., 2022; Parent-Rocheleau & Parker, 2022). In the gig economy, the low sense of belonging or relatedness to an organization combined with the individual nature of work and the total absence of managers was found to deprive workers of important social recognition and other resources (Cameron, 2022; Newlands, 2022; Petriglieri et al., 2019).

Third, the quantification of work necessary for AM creates favorable conditions for competitive rather than for cooperative behaviors. When, for example, promotions, shifts, pay raises or bonuses, and other rewards are distributed based on metrics, workers' competition for the highest positions in the rankings undermines the social environment and can lead to dehumanized workplaces and even to deviant behaviors (Liu, 2023). The gamification of work is very common in algorithmically managed workplaces and aims to enhance productivity by creating a competition-friendly environment; however, it can also be detrimental if it is not counterbalanced with cooperation incentives (Baiocco et al., 2022).

Algorithmic Management and Work Demands

Good work design is normally characterized by tolerable demands emanating from the tasks and the work environment. However, evidence suggests that employees under algorithmic management face significant and varied demands in terms of work intensity, intrusiveness, and insecurity, among others (Vignola et al., 2023). Moreover, employees often must invest additional efforts to develop strategies to cope with these demands.

This may be explained by a few factors. First, in many cases, AM is implemented with the aim of optimizing processes, time, or productivity (Newlands, 2023). The interiorization of this productivity pressure in a company's culture or practices, supported or enabled by an algorithmic system, is associated with an increased workload, an intensification of work (Felix et al., 2023; Liu, 2023; Newlands, 2023; Wood, 2021; Wu et al., 2023), and workers' experience of stress (Chan, 2022; Fernandez et al., 2023) or technostress (Cram et al., 2022). Second, data collection, fundamental to AM, is in many cases done in an ubiquitous, pervasive, or intrusive way (De Vaujany et al., 2021; Leclercq-Vandelannoitte, 2017). AI-driven technologies allow tracking of almost everything, relevant or not to the assessment of productivity, and sometimes without workers' consent or awareness (Chan, 2022; Elmholdt et al., 2021; Parent-Rocheleau & Parker, 2022). This constant, ever-present tracking can have a serious negative impact on workers' privacy and contribute to work–life blurring (Baiocco et al., 2022; Noponen et al., 2024; Vignola et al., 2023; Wood, 2021). Third, because AM allocates work (tasks, gigs, rides, and schedules) based on real-time or forecasted demand and/or employee performance (Parent-Rocheleau & Parker, 2022), adopting a just-in-time perspective to task allocation and goal setting, workflow, and income are often more unstable, unpredictable, and, consequently, precarious (Baiocco et al., 2022; Wood, 2021).

Coping with Algorithmic Management

As a consequence of poor work design, workers exposed to AM experience different outcomes and reactions. Notably, they are not passively accepting or integrating these altered work characteristics and high work demands. Researchers have examined the mechanisms and strategies developed by workers to cope with AM and thrive in their work (Chan, 2022; Wu et al., 2023). Some workers decide to "domesticate" the algorithmic systems, trying to manipulate, override, or work around the algorithms (Cram et al., 2022; Wiener et al., 2021). Others protest or resist, often at a high cost (Cameron & Rahman, 2022; Wood, 2021), or engage in "anthropotropism" (i.e., humanizing the machine to gain recognition) (Newlands, 2022), or in a complex process of sensemaking of their algorithmic and dehumanized work (Möhlmann et al., 2021; Möhlmannn et al., 2023). Furthermore, in the gig economy, workers often overcome social isolation by developing active virtual communities, used for collective resistance or simply to exchange advice (Kaine & Josserand, 2019; Wood et al., 2019), or they try to fulfill relatedness needs through risky or one-sided relationships with customers (Cameron, 2022). These strategies are far from effortless; they require additional cognitive or emotional resources from workers, and thus can be considered as additional work demands.

Can Algorithmic Management be Improved?

So far, the evidence summarized in this chapter undoubtedly paints a dark picture of the impacts of AM on work design and employee outcomes. Other scarce but noteworthy research reports, for their part, propose potential positive effects. Exposure to algorithmic management could, for instance, under certain conditions, be associated with greater customer-oriented behavior, work engagement, or continuance intention (Cram et al., 2022; Wang et al., 2022; Wiener et al., 2021).

These findings echo a nascent idea in the literature positing that AM could either deplete work design and lead to negative outcomes for workers or rather enable workers, eventually leading to higher autonomy and better work design (Meijerink & Bondarouk, 2023; Noponen et al., 2024). According to this perspective, better forms of algorithmic management could exist, depending on organizational choices surrounding its use and deployment, as informed by decades of research guided by the socio-technical systems (STS) perspective (Guest et al., 2022; Marabelli et al., 2021). AM systems are an exacerbated and technologically embedded illustration of the norms and cultures of the places where they are implemented (Jarrahi et al., 2021). Beyond organizational choices, some higher level societal, political, and economic considerations are thus worth mentioning.

Organizational choices

Parameters of the technological systems and of the context (i.e., the organization) can shape the resulting effects, hindering or enabling, of algorithmic management. Regarding the systems, there are two key elements. First, the transparency, explainability, and understandability of data collection and algorithmic decision-making is a boundary condition to enable employees' agency, autonomy and power (Gagné et al., 2022; Langer & König, 2023; Parent-Rocheleau & Parker, 2022). Antoine Bujold and colleagues (2022) observed, for instance, that the more truck drivers perceive AM (monitoring and performance evaluation) as transparent and understandable, the fairer they feel they are being treated and the more they intend to stay with the company, controlling for their level of exposure to algorithmic management. Second, human-centered and participatory designs of algorithmic systems, including the possibility for employees to opt out, question, or counteract an algorithmic decision, can also potentially represent safeguards of employees' agency and autonomy (Parent-Rocheleau & Parker, 2022). The exploratory work by Lee and colleagues (2021) and by Fangfang Zhang and colleagues (2022) reports elicitation models of intervention ideas designed by employees exposed to AM and aiming to uncover their preferences, improve their work conditions with platforms, rebalance power, and regain agency.

Regarding choices pertaining to the organizational contexts where AM is implemented, there is, unfortunately, a crucial lack of research and empirical evidence. However, following STS principles, technology is embedded in and reflects the values of the place it is used. It is thus reasonable to believe that organizational culture, leadership styles, as well as skills development and valuation are crucial. For instance, Marta Fana and Davide Villani (2023) observed that the type of innovation (process or digital) culturally embraced by firms plays an important role in the level of direct and indirect control experienced by employees. A study by Jenna Myers (2023) highlights that third-party developers can collaborate with the company in the configuration AM tool that integrates the interests and input of low-powered manufacturing workers, but that this collaboration depends on the companies' progressive culture.

Job crafting opportunities are also a promising insight. Fabienne Perez and colleagues (2022) show how bank employees exposed to AM were able to change their tasks and relationship boundaries and cognitively reframe their job after the introduction of AI algorithmic decision-making. In the gig economy, Xiaoya Wu and colleagues (2023) describe the case of a food delivery platform using a human–algorithm hybrid management mode (instead of algorithm only) to humanize platform work.

Overall, it is important to remember that Tayloristic practices, on-demand and performance-based management of workers, although common, are not inherent to algorithmic systems, but rather result from how companies decide to use algorithms.

Beyond organizations: Policy and regulation

The self-regulation of organizations and responsible practices of their use of algorithms for management decision-making is desirable and necessary, but it is only one part of the solution. The other part, equally essential, is public policy, regulations, research, and advocacy (Fernandez et al., 2023; Wood, 2021). Policy and regulations must define and protect the rights of workers in terms of decent work, dignity, job stability, privacy, and data collection and protection. This effort is ongoing but moves at highly different paces around the world. Specific to the gig economy is the legal battle around the status of the workers (employees vs. self-employed or users of the platform), which makes all the difference regarding their protection from the risks associated with algorithmic management. Beyond this battle, the increasing platformization, also coined Uberization, of many sectors of the economy (e.g., care work; Glaser, 2021) is worrisome. Authors have questioned whether this type of economy can at all be conjugated with decent work and good work design.

What predates policy and regulations, however, is research and advocacy, which will remain necessary for a long time to come. Advocacy, like *Algorithm Watch*, is necessary for a nonstop fight for workers' rights to decent work and a fulfilling work design.

Directions for Future Research

Research is, for its part, crucial to guide policy and guidelines for organizations. Although there are many others, we identify the following four avenues as priority research areas.

First, one important research avenue concerns *AM risk assessment*. Similar to environmental risk evaluation for big infrastructure projects like ports, mines, big factories, or roads, AM risk assessment aims to identify the potential deleterious impact of AM systems for work and workers. To analyze and assess the risks of an AM system, we first need a framework or classification of these risks along with measurement instruments. Whereas such frameworks are being developed for the more general use of AI (see, e.g., IFOW, 2023), research is still needed to conceptualize and validate specific tools for algorithmic management.

Second, research on *the antecedents of AM* is missing. Whereas the consequences of AM on workers have been the topic of an impressive number of studies over a short period of time, very little attention has been devoted to the factors that influence why and how AM tools are implemented (Marabelli et al., 2021). Several research questions can be raised and investigated, such

540 TRANSFORMATIVE WORK DESIGN

as: What distinguishes companies that implement responsible AM systems (i.e., associated with emancipating work design) from others that consider technology before humans? What leads a company to put humans at the center of AM systems in the first place, even prior to implementation? Which actors should be involved in the planning and implementation phases to ensure optimal work design? For instance, how can unions play a key role to maintain the quality of jobs in AM settings?

Third, the development of *algorithmic skills and literacy* is essential to maintain workers' autonomy and agency in the face of AM or more general AI (e.g., Khorakian et al., 2023; Liu et al., 2023), but very little is known about the nature of the required skills and the best development approaches. These questions represent a key research topic because, as a solution to opaque AM systems previously mentioned, transparent ones provide somewhat detailed explanations regarding algorithmic decision processes and data collection. Digital literacy is necessary for employees to absorb and mobilize such explanations and eventually maintain their autonomy. Such skills are also important to stay critical and alert to the possibility of intrusive and dehumanizing uses of AM systems.

Fourth, *job crafting opportunities* also represent a promising research avenue. Research has extensively shown the benefits of workers adapting and crafting their work to increase resources and reduce (or better manage) demands emanating from work (Knight et al., 2021; Zhang & Parker, 2019). Whereas some studies have investigated the opportunities for job crafting in gig work, which is highly exposed to AM (Mousa & Chaouali, 2022; Wong et al., 2021), we know very little about job crafting interventions to enhance the quality of work design in traditional settings where AM has been introduced. We urge scholars to conduct intervention studies in settings where AM is used extensively to explore how workers themselves can craft positive interactions with AM which enhance their work design.

In conclusion, responsible AM that promotes good work design is possible, but will largely depend on the capability of researchers, practitioners, and policymakers to work together to avoid the rise of a generalized neo-Taylorism.

References

Baiocco, S., Fernández-Macías, E., Rani, U., & Pesole, A. (2022). The algorithmic management of work and its implications in different contexts. European Commission. https://joint-research-centre.ec.europa.eu/publications/algorithmic-management-work-and-its-implications-different-contexts_en

Bujold, A., Parent-Rocheleau, X., & Gaudet, M.-C. (2022). Opacity behind the wheel: The relationship between transparency of algorithmic management, justice perception, and intention to quit among truck drivers. *Computers in Human Behavior Reports* 8, 1–14.

Cameron, L. D. (2022). "Making out" while driving: Relational and efficiency games in the gig economy. *Organization Science 33*(1), 231–252.

Cameron, L. D., & Rahman, H. (2022). Expanding the locus of resistance: Understanding the co-constitution of control and resistance in the gig economy. *Organization Science 33*(1), 38–58.

Chan, N. K. (2022). Algorithmic precarity and metric power: Managing the affective measures and customers in the gig economy. *Big Data & Society 9*(2), 1–13.

Cram, W. A., Wiener, M., Tarafdar, M., & Benlian, A. (2022). Examining the impact of algorithmic control on uber drivers' technostress. *Journal of Management Information Systems 39*(2), 426–453.

De Vaujany, F.-X., Leclercq-Vandelannoitte, A., Munro, I., Nama, Y., & Holt, R. (2021). Control and surveillance in work practice: Cultivating paradox in "new" modes of organizing. *Organization Studies 42*(5), 675–695.

Delfanti, A. (2021a). Machinic dispossession and augmented despotism: Digital work in an Amazon warehouse. *New Media & Society 23*(1), 39–55.

Delfanti, A. (2021b). *The warehouse: Workers and robots at Amazon.* Pluto Press.

Delfanti, A., & Frey, B. (2021). Humanly extended automation or the future of work seen through Amazon patents. *Science, Technology, & Human Values 46*(3), 655–682.

Duggan, J., Sherman, U., Carbery, R., & McDonnell, A. (2020). Algorithmic management and app-work in the gig economy: A research agenda for employment relations and HRM. *Human Resource Management Journal 30*(1), 114–132.

Elmholdt, K. T., Elmholdt, C., & Haahr, L. (2021). Counting sleep: Ambiguity, aspirational control and the politics of digital self-tracking at work. *Organization 28*(1), 164–185.

Fana, M., & Villani, D. (2023). Is it all the same? Types of innovation and their relationship with direct control, technical control and algorithmic management. *European Journal of Industrial Relations 29*(4), 367–391.

Felix, B., Dourado, D., & Nossa, V. (2023). Algorithmic management, preferences for autonomy/security and gig-workers' wellbeing: A matter of fit? *Frontiers in Psychology 14*, 1–12.

Fernandez, M. E., Urzi, B. M. C., Wright, S., & Pesole, A. (2023). *The platformisation of work.* Research Report of the Publications Office of the European Union. https://publications.jrc.ec.europa.eu/repository/handle/JRC133016

Gagné, M., & Parent-Rocheleau, X. (2022). The algorithmic management of pay for gig platform workers: Design considerations for higher work motivation. *Journal of Total Rewards 31*(4), 1–13.

Gagné, M., Parent-Rocheleau, X., Bujold, A., Gaudet, M.-C., & Lirio, P. (2022). How algorithmic management influences worker motivation: A self-determination theory perspective. *Canadian Psychology 63*(2), 247–260.

Gal, U., Jensen, T. B., & Stein, M.-K. (2020). Breaking the vicious cycle of algorithmic management: A virtue ethics approach to people analytics. *Information and Organization 30*(2), 1–15.

Glaser, A. L. (2021). Uberized care: Employment status, surveillance, and technological erasure in the home health care sector. *Anthropology of Work Review 42*(1), 24–34.

Guest, D., Knox, A., & Warhurst, C. (2022). Humanizing work in the digital age: Lessons from socio-technical systems and quality of working life initiatives. *Human Relations 75*(8), 1461–1482.

IFOW. (2023). Good work algorithmic impact. https://www.ifow.org/publications/good-work-algorithmic-impact-assessment-an-approach-for-worker-involvement

Jarrahi, M. H., Newlands, G., Lee, M. K., Wolf, C. T., Kinder, E., & Sutherland, W. (2021). Algorithmic management in a work context. *Big Data & Society 8*(2), 1–14.

Kaine, S., & Josserand, E. (2019). The organisation and experience of work in the gig economy. *Journal of Industrial Relations 61*(4), 479–501.

Kellogg, K., Valentine, M., & Christin, A. (2020). Algorithms at work: The new contested terrain of control. *Academy of Management Annals 14*(1), 366–410.

Khorakian, A., Jahangir, M., Rahi, S., Eslami, G., & Muterera, J. (2023). Remote working and work performance during the COVID-19 pandemic: The role of remote work satisfaction, digital literacy, and cyberslacking. Behaviour & Information Technology 43(10), 1938–1956.

Knight, C., Tims, M., Gawke, J., & Parker, S. K. (2021). When do job crafting interventions work? The moderating roles of workload, intervention intensity, and participation. *Journal of Vocational Behavior 124*, 1–20.

Langer, M., & König, C. J. (2023). Introducing a multi-stakeholder perspective on opacity, transparency and strategies to reduce opacity in algorithm-based human resource management. *Human Resource Management Review 33*(1), 1–13.

Leclercq-Vandelannoitte, A. (2017). An ethical perspective on emerging forms of ubiquitous IT-based control. *Journal of Business Ethics 142*(1), 139–154.

Lee, M. K., Kusbit, D., Metsky, E., & Dabbish, L. (2015). Working with machines: The impact of algorithmic and data-driven management on human workers. Proceedings of the 33rd Annual ACM Conference on Human Factors in Computing Systems, Seoul, Korea.

Lee, M. K., Nigam, I., Zhang, A., Afriyie, J., Qin, Z., & Gao, S. (2021). Participatory algorithmic management: Elicitation methods for worker well-being models. Proceedings of the 2021 AAAI/ACM Conference on AI, Ethics, and Society, Virtual Event.

Levy, K. (2022). *Data driven: Truckers, technology, and the new workplace surveillance.* Princeton University Press.

Levy, K., & Barocas, S. (2018). Refractive surveillance: Monitoring customers to manage workers. *International Journal of Communication 12*, 1166–1188.

Lippert, I., Kirchner, K., & Wiener, M. (2023). Context matters: The use of algorithmic management mechanisms in platform, hybrid, and traditional work contexts. Proceedings of the 56th Hawaii International Conference on System Sciences.

Liu, H. Y. (2023). Digital Taylorism in China's e-commerce industry: A case study of internet professionals. *Economic and Industrial Democracy 44*(1), 262–279.

Liu, J., Wu, D., & Guo, Q. (2023). Are we different? Analyzing the role of algorithmic curation and algorithmic literacy during online shopping from a gender differences perspective. Behaviour & Information Technology 43(10), 1990–2006.

Marabelli, M., Newell, S., & Handunge, V. (2021). The lifecycle of algorithmic decision-making systems: Organizational choices and ethical challenges. *Journal of Strategic Information Systems 30*(3), 101683.

Mateescu, A., & Nguyen, A. (2019, 6 February). Algorithmic management in the workplace. *Explainer Issue.* https://datasociety.net/output/explainer-algorithmic-management-in-the-workplace/

Meijerink, J., & Bondarouk, T. (2023). The duality of algorithmic management: Toward a research agenda on HRM algorithms, autonomy and value creation. *Human Resource Management Review 33*(1), 1–14.

Möhlmann, M., Zalmanson, L., Henfridsson, O., & Gregory, R. W. (2021). Algorithmic management of work on online labor platforms: When matching meets control. *MIS Quarterly 45*(4), 1999–2022.

Möhlmannn, M., Alves de Lima Salge, C., & Marabelli, M. (2023). Algorithm sensemaking: How platform workers make sense of algorithmic management. *Journal of the Association for Information Systems 24*(1), 35–64.

Monteiro, E. (2022). *Digital oil*. MIT Press.

Moore, P. (2017). *The quantified self in precarity: Work, technology and what counts*. Routledge.

Moore, P., & Robinson, A. (2016). The quantified self: What counts in the neoliberal workplace. *New Media & Society 18*(11), 2774–2792.

Moore, S., & Hayes, L. (2017). Taking worker productivity to a new level? Electronic Monitoring in homecare—the (re) production of unpaid labour. *New Technology, Work and Employment 32*(2), 101–114.

Morgeson, F. P., & Humphrey, S. E. (2006). The Work Design Questionnaire (WDQ): Developing and validating a comprehensive measure for assessing job design and the nature of work. *Journal of Applied Psychology 91*(6), 1321–1339.

Mousa, M., & Chaouali, W. (2022). Job crafting, meaningfulness and affective commitment by gig workers towards crowdsourcing platforms. *Personnel Review 52*(8), 2070–2084.

Myers, J. E. (2023). When big brother is benevolent: How technology developers navigate power dynamics among users to elevate worker interests. *Academy of Management Discoveries 10*(3). https://doi.org/10.5465/amd.2022.0111.

Newlands, G. (2022). Anthropotropism: Searching for recognition in the Scandinavian gig economy. *Sociology 56*(5), 821–838.

Newlands, G. (2023). The algorithmic surveillance of gig workers: Mechanisms and consequences. In I. Ness (Ed.), *The Routledge handbook of the gig economy* (pp. 64–73). Routledge.

Newman, D. T., Fast, N. J., & Harmon, D. J. (2020). When eliminating bias isn't fair: Algorithmic reductionism and procedural justice in human resource decisions. *Organizational Behavior and Human Decision Processes 160*, 149–167.

Noponen, N., Feshchenko, P., Auvinen, T., Luoma-aho, V., & Abrahamsson, P. (2024). Taylorism on steroids or enabling autonomy? A systematic review of algorithmic management. *Management Review Quarterly 74*, 1695–1721.

Parent-Rocheleau, X., & Parker, S. K. (2022). Algorithms as work designers: How algorithmic management influences the design of jobs. *Human Resource Management Review 32*(3), 1–14.

Parker, S. K., Morgeson, F. P., & Johns, G. (2017). One hundred years of work design research: Looking back and looking forward. *Journal of Applied Psychology 102*(3), 403–420.

Perez, F., Conway, N., & Roques, O. (2022). The autonomy tussle: AI technology and employee job crafting responses. *Relations industrielles/Industrial Relations 77*(3), 1–19.

Petriglieri, G., Ashford, S. J., & Wrzesniewski, A. (2019). Agony and ecstasy in the gig economy: Cultivating holding environments for precarious and personalized work identities. *Administrative Science Quarterly 64*(1), 124–170.

Pignot, E. (2021). Who is pulling the strings in the platform economy? Accounting for the dark and unexpected sides of algorithmic control. *Organization 28*(1), 208–235.

Rosenblat, A. (2018). *Uberland: How algorithms are rewriting the rules of work.* University of California Press.

Schafheitle, S. D., Weibel, A., Ebert, I. L., Kasper, G., Schank, C., & Leicht-Deobald, U. (2020). No stone left unturned? Towards a framework for the impact of datafication technologies on organizational control. *Academy of Management Discoveries 6*(3), 455–487.

Schwab, K. (2017). *The fourth industrial revolution.* Crown Publishing.

Tarafdar, M., Page, X., & Marabelli, M. (2022). Algorithms as co-workers: Human algorithm role interactions in algorithmic work. *Information Systems Journal 33*(2), 232–267.

Todoli-Signes, A. (2021). Making algorithms safe for workers: Occupational risks associated with work managed by artificial intelligence. *Transfer: European Review of Labour and Research 27*(4), 433–452.

Vargas, T. L. (2021). Consumer redlining and the reproduction of inequality at dollar general. *Qualitative Sociology 44*(2), 205–229.

Vignola, E. F., Baron, S., Abreu Plasencia, E., Hussein, M., & Cohen, N. (2023). Workers' health under algorithmic management: Emerging findings and urgent research questions. *International Journal of Environmental Research and Public Health 20*(2), 1239–1253.

Wang, C., Chen, J., & Xie, P. (2022). Observation or interaction? Impact mechanisms of gig platform monitoring on gig workers' cognitive work engagement. *International Journal of Information Management 67*, 102548.

Wiener, M., Cram, W., & Benlian, A. (2021). Algorithmic control and gig workers: A legitimacy perspective of Uber drivers. *European Journal of Information Systems 32*(3), 485–507.

Wong, S. I., Kost, D., & Fieseler, C. (2021). From crafting what you do to building resilience for career commitment in the gig economy. *Human Resource Management Journal 31*(4), 918–935.

Wood, A. J. (2021). Algorithmic management consequences for work organisation and working conditions. *JRC Working Papers Series on Labour, Education and Technology.*

Wood, A. J., Graham, M., Lehdonvirta, V., & Hjorth, I. (2019). Networked but commodified: The (dis)embeddedness of digital labour in the gig economy. *Sociology 53*(5), 931–950.

Wu, X., Liu, Q., Qu, H., & Wang, J. (2023). The effect of algorithmic management and workers' coping behavior: An exploratory qualitative research of Chinese food-delivery platform. *Tourism Management 96*, 1–13.

Zhang, A., Boltz, A., Wang, C. W., & Lee, M. K. (2022). Algorithmic management reimagined for workers and by workers: Centering worker well-being in gig work. *Proceedings of the 2022 CHI Conference on Human Factors in Computing Systems.*

Zhang, F., & Parker, S. K. (2019). Reorienting job crafting research: A hierarchical structure of job crafting concepts and integrative review. *Journal of Organizational Behavior 40*(2), 126–146.

Understanding Why, When, and How Virtual Work Works through the Lens of a Work Design Perspective

Bin Wang, Xiang Fang, and Yi Zhao

Virtual work[1] is "a broader term often used to describe individuals, groups, or organizations who do not interact face-to-face because of geographic dispersion yet who interact using technology" (Allen et al., 2015). The idea about virtual work traces back to the term "telecommuting" proposed by Jack Nilles in the 1970s. Scholars at that time encouraged employees to work from home or from remote workstations to cope with the challenges of energy crisis and traffic problems. Along with the development of information communication technology (ICT), opportunities for telecommuting increased and further sparked a great theoretical interest in this new way of working (e.g., Bailey & Kurland, 2002; Gajendran & Harrison, 2007; Raghuram et al., 2019). Especially since the unprecedented outbreak of COVID-19 in 2020, working away from the central office has become the "new normal," and has significantly challenged our understanding of when, where, and how we work (McPhail et al., 2023). Considerable virtual work practices have shown that employees can successfully adapt to the virtual workspace (Schlaegel et al., 2023). In the current post-COVID era, more and more people believe that virtual work is no longer a "privilege"; instead, it is a right for an employee.

However, in addition to the well-documented benefits of virtual work (Gajendran & Harrison, 2007; Martin & MacDonnell, 2012), recent studies have also revealed a set of challenges in the virtual work context, such as procrastination, poor communication, lower creative performance, work–family conflict, isolation, and so on (e.g., Hill et al., 2022; McPhail et al., 2023; Wang et al., 2021; Wang & Parker, 2023). Because of the dark sides of virtual work, some employers, following the pandemic in 2022, required their workers to

---

[1] Virtual work could be referred to as telework, remote work, distributed work, and other constructs (Allen et al., 2015).

Bin Wang et al., *Understanding Why, When, and How Virtual Work Works through the Lens of a Work Design Perspective*. In: *Transformative Work Design*. Edited by: Sharon K. Parker et al., Oxford University Press. © Society for Industrial and Organizational Psychology (2025). DOI: 10.1093/oso/9780197692554.003.0022

546   TRANSFORMATIVE WORK DESIGN

return to the office and reduce remote positions. For example, Elon Musk asked Tesla employees to spend at least 40 hours in the office per week (Mac, 2022). Given the mixed effects of virtual work practices on organization and employee outcomes, we argue that it is more important to investigate a way to improve virtual work effectiveness (Gohoungodji et al., 2023), rather than arbitrarily dismiss virtual work. This is because various challenges of virtual work could be alleviated through a careful design of jobs/tasks and technologies (Miglioretti et al., 2022). That said, both employers and employees can maximize the advantages of virtual work, while avoiding pitfalls in the virtual workplace (Wang & Parker, 2023).

To obtain a more comprehensive understanding of virtual work practices, this chapter will introduce a work design perspective to integrate fragmented virtual work research, thereby understanding *why*, *when*, and *how* virtual work works. Work design or job design refers to "the content and organization of one's work tasks, activities, relationships, and responsibilities" (Parker, 2014, p. 662), with a central focus on impacts of key work characteristics on individuals (Morgeson & Humphrey, 2006; Parker, Morgeson, et al., 2017). The work design perspective has been widely used to understand the changing nature of work in the current digital workplace (Parker & Grote, 2022a, 2022b; Wang et al., 2020, 2021). Based on the work design perspective, this chapter will conduct a state-of-the-art review to illustrate what work characteristics link the effects of virtual work practices with employee outcomes (e.g., work effectiveness and well-being) (i.e., the *why* question), which type of job is suitable for virtual work (i.e., the *when* question), and how to improve virtual work effectiveness (i.e., the *how* question). The relationship of three research streams is depicted in Figure 22.1. Based on this review, we conclude by outlining promising opportunities and directions for future research.

Why Virtual Work Matters

The existing body of literature approaches the concept of virtual work from several theoretical perspectives. Sumita Raghuram and colleagues (2019) conducted a co-citation analysis with 1,769 articles and identified three major research clusters. The first cluster of studies primarily focuses on the extent to which virtual work (also known as telecommuting) is adopted by employees/organizations and examines the potential influence of virtual work frequency or intensity (Allen et al., 2015). The second stream of research, informed by the virtual team tradition, characterizes virtual work in terms of technology dependence and dispersion (Hill et al., 2022). The third cluster centers

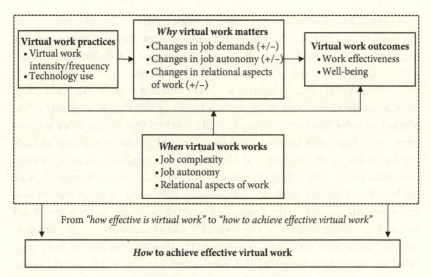

Figure 22.1 The Relationship of Three Research Streams

its research on computer-mediated communication, investigating the influence of specific technology usage behaviors in virtual work settings (Wang et al., 2020). Although research interests vary across three clusters, scholars all focus on the impacts of virtual work practices on employees' working experiences (Raghuram et al., 2019).

Following Raghuram and colleagues (2019), this chapter will review the broad virtual work literature. In this section, we, through the lens of work design, will discuss how virtual work practices shape a set of work characteristics (i.e., job demands, job autonomy, and relational aspects of work).

Changes in job demands

Virtual work practices exert mixed effects on job demands defined as "physical, social, or organizational aspects of the job that require sustained physical or mental effort" (Demerouti et al., 2001, p. 501). Early research primarily underscored the beneficial impacts of virtual work on reducing job demands. For instance, virtual work practices can alleviate employees' physical demands of commutes by working from home (Baruch, 2000). Besides, virtual workers are expected to experience less work–family conflict because they have more boundary control to coordinate their work and family responsibilities (Duxbury et al., 1992; Morganson et al., 2010).

548 TRANSFORMATIVE WORK DESIGN

However, as the scholarship in virtual work continues to develop, a growing body of research has indicated that virtual work may also introduce new demands, such as work intensification, technology-related demands, work–family conflict, and role ambiguity (Hill et al., 2022; Ingusci et al., 2021; Sardeshmukh et al., 2012; Thulin et al., 2019; Villamor et al., 2023). Specifically, work intensification is one of the unanticipated consequences of virtual work. Marie-Colombe Afota and colleagues (2023) reveal that virtual work leads to longer working hours because employees feel obliged to be available outside regular hours. Clare Kelliher and Deirdre Anderson (2010), moving beyond involuntary work intensification, identify that virtual workers may reciprocate the benefits of flexible working arrangements with working more intently and intensively. In addition to the demand of working overtime, technology-related demands are also prevalent (Wang et al., 2020). In virtual work settings, employees need to navigate various ICTs to ensure the smooth operation of daily work activities, resulting in increased ICT hassles and learning requirements (Ayoko et al., 2012; Dias et al., 2022; Golden & Gajendran, 2019). In addition, scholars have found that technology dependence exposes virtual workers to more information or ICT-related interruptions than they can process, ultimately leading to information overload and work overload (Venz & Boettcher, 2022; Wang, Liao, et al., 2023).

Furthermore, virtual work practices could blur the boundary between work and personal domains and exacerbate inter-role conflict (e.g., work–family conflict). Virtual workers usually find themselves being always connected and needing to respond to work messages after hours, which hinders them from fulfilling family roles (Allen et al., 2021; Cho et al., 2020; Choroszewicz & Kay, 2020; Wöhrmann & Ebner, 2021). Finally, virtual work may increase role ambiguity (i.e., a lack of clear information about the expectation associated with a role, methods for fulfilling role expectations, and outcomes of role performance). Lawrence Whitman and colleagues (2005) compared the differences in communication between face-to-face work and virtual work. Results from their study show that virtual workers often have more difficulty defining their roles, because they usually infer roles from written text (e.g., email) due to the absence of visual communication cues. This ambiguity could be further enhanced by the simultaneous receipt of multiple ICT-mediated messages, creating competing demands and causing confusion (Bean & Eisenberg, 2006; Pianese et al., 2023).

In sum, previous studies have revealed the mixed effects of virtual work practices on job demands. Although virtual work helps to reduce physical demands of daily commutes and work–family conflict, scholars have also identified that virtual work may increase other types of demands, including work intensification, technology-related demands, inter-role conflict, and role ambiguity.

Changes in job autonomy

Job autonomy refers to the degree of control an employee has over their work (Spreitzer, 1995). Job autonomy is a multidimensional construct, which includes work scheduling autonomy, decision-making autonomy, and work methods autonomy (Morgeson & Humphrey, 2006). Previous studies have revealed the effects of virtual work practices on job autonomy are contingent on a set of organizational and employee outcomes (Hill et al., 2022; Wang et al., 2020). First, virtual work usually can grant employees greater autonomy to decide when and where to work. Interestingly, Ravi Gajendran and colleagues (2015) identified the moderating role of the workgroup virtual work (telecommuting) norm, such that the positive effect of virtual work on job autonomy was stronger when the virtual work norm was low compared to when it was high. This is because employees who are allowed to work virtually are likely to feel privileged when the virtual work norm is low. However, when group members take virtual work practices to be normalized within the workgroup, the advantage of virtual work will be diminished (Gajendran et al., 2015). In addition to the positive effects on job autonomy, virtual work sometimes could hamper scheduling autonomy through the increase of boundaryless working hours. According to Anne Marit Wöhrmann and Christian Ebner's (2021) research, the flexibility of virtual work can erode the traditional temporal boundaries of work, as it may induce overtime work and a constant sense of availability. In other words, intensive virtual work risks transforming the freedom to work "anytime and anywhere" into an obligation to work "all the time and everywhere" (Mazmanian et al., 2013).

Secondly, due to limited micromanagement in a virtual work context, employees usually have discretion over the way to complete their tasks. Yet, the effect of virtual work practices on work method autonomy is contingent on employees' knowledge, abilities, skills, and organizational support. For example, Paulo Dias and colleagues (2022) found that employees lacking ICT skills might encounter more technological stress and struggle to handle work as skillfully as they could in an office environment. Additionally, Janet Marler and John Boudreau (2017) shed light on the critical role of organizational support. Their study indicates that without sufficient technical training and resources, employees might be unable to fully leverage the autonomy provided by virtual work arrangements.

Changes in relational aspects of work

The relational aspects of work focus on "how work structures can provide more or fewer opportunities for employees to interact with others" (Parker, 2014, p. 668). As Adam Grant and Sharon K. Parker (2009) identified in their review, representative relational and social characteristics include support, task inter-dependence, interpersonal interaction, impacts on others, and so on. Virtual work practices have substantially altered the social and relational aspects of work due to limited face-to-face interactions and informal communications (Hill et al., 2022). According to Media Richness Theory (Daft & Lengel, 1986), the diminished social and informational cues in ICT-mediated communications (e.g., Zoom meetings and emails) can hinder the frequency and quality of information exchange, complicating the maintenance and development of inter-personal relationships among virtual workers (Fonner & Roloff, 2010). Conse-quently, it is unsurprising that existing studies have shown that virtual workers often report lower quality relations with their coworkers and supervisors than their counterparts who engage in work less frequently (e.g., Golden, 2006; Wöhrmann & Ebner, 2021); this could, in turn, result in decreased social sup-port and greater isolation at work (Sardeshmukh et al., 2012; Vander Elst et al., 2017).

Despite these challenges, the nature of virtual work is not entirely detrimen-tal to relational aspects of work. Alison Collins and colleagues (2016) probed deeper into the social process in virtual work settings and their findings indeed supported the social disconnection between virtual workers and office-based staff. Yet, their research also illuminated the potential positive effects. The spatial distance in virtual work helps employees to distance themselves from nega-tive relationships, mitigating interpersonal conflicts and negative politics in the workplace. Additionally, ICT-mediated communications can enable timely and efficient connections with others (Wang, Liu, et al., 2023). Although the connec-tion between virtual workers and office-based staff generally has been weakened, participants in Collins and colleagues' (2016) study developed greater social support relationships with other virtual workers. That means virtual workers still have opportunities to expand and develop supportive relationships in the virtual space.

When Virtual Work Works

The second stream of literature strives to discern the types of jobs that align well with the virtual work form. Specifically, this research stream implicitly assumes that one's work characteristics are stable, and conceptualizes work char-acteristics as moderators in the relationship between virtual work practices and employee outcomes (Wang et al., 2021). Scholars argue that employees with jobs possessing certain characteristics (e.g., lower levels of task interdependence) are more likely to benefit from virtual work practices (Golden & Gajendran,

2019; Golden & Veiga, 2005). Conversely, making a virtual shift may present substantial challenges for jobs lacking these characteristics.

Job complexity as a boundary condition

Job complexity refers to "the extent to which the tasks on a job are complex and difficult to perform" (Morgeson & Humphrey, 2006, p. 1323). Given that complex jobs usually require more cognitive resources, people in these job positions will benefit from extended and uninterrupted periods to perform complex tasks. Compared to their counterparts in the central office, virtual workers might still face electronic interruptions but they have more control over how and when to manage these interruptions at work (Golden & Gajendran, 2019). Therefore, when it comes to highly complex jobs, virtual work forms can help employees better concentrate on their primary tasks, leading to higher job performance (Bailey & Kurland, 2002). This argument has been supported by Timothy Golden and Gajendran's (2019) research. The authors identified a moderating role of job complexity in the positive relationship between virtual work intensity and job performance. Specifically, virtual work is more effective and can lead to greater performance when job complexity is at higher levels.

Job autonomy as a boundary condition

According to the well-established work design literature, job autonomy is conducive to alleviating work–family conflict for employees who work in a central office (Michel et al., 2011). However, the effects of job autonomy on work–family conflict are sometimes not significant in virtual workplaces (Wang et al., 2021), suggesting the necessity for a more nuanced examination of job autonomy in this unique context. Golden and colleagues' (2006) study showed that virtual work can reduce work–family conflict; and this effect was stronger for employees high in work scheduling autonomy and low in decision-making autonomy. In other words, those with more decision-making autonomy did not experience an expected reduction in work–family conflict in virtual work. Sara Perry and colleagues (2018) provided one plausible explanation for this result. They agreed with the argument that decision-making autonomy is a job resource for virtual workers to cope with various demands, but personality determines how people manage and use resources. Their study revealed that high-emotional stability employees with high decision-making autonomy reported the lowest levels of strain in virtual work; however, low-emotional stability employees

552 TRANSFORMATIVE WORK DESIGN

who also have high decision-making autonomy were more susceptible to strain. This means high job autonomy may not necessarily be positive for virtual work practices because the value of autonomy may vary from individual to individual.

Relational aspects of work as a boundary condition

Employees' opportunities to interact with their supervisors, workers, and customers (i.e., relational aspects of work) also influence the effectiveness of virtual work. In virtual work environments, the visibility of employee efforts and devotions to leaders is often reduced due to the absence of face-to-face social interactions. Thus, the intensity of virtual work is expected to be negatively related to individuals' promotions and salary growth (Golden & Eddleston, 2020). Golden and Kimberly Eddleston's (2020) study supports this argument, and further reveals that face-to-face contact with supervisors can mitigate the detrimental impacts of virtual work on objective career success (i.e., promotions and salary growth). That is, these negative effects were greater when face-to-face contact was low in comparison to when it was high.

However, the above findings do not imply that jobs with positive social characteristics are always ideal for virtual work settings. For instance, employees with unsupportive relationships at work may not necessarily desire face-to-face interactions, and, therefore, they may prefer working remotely. According to Golden and Gajendran's (2019) study, virtual work was positively associated with job performance when social support was low rather than high. The authors speculated that virtual work may provide more motivational benefits for employees with unsupportive relationships at work (i.e., lower levels of perceived social support) because working away from the office can help them avoid undesirable social interactions with their colleagues.

Task interdependence is another relational factor that influences the relationship between virtual work and employee outcomes

Highly interdependent jobs require more communication and interaction with others at work (Morgeson & Humphrey, 2006). In a virtual work environment, employees heavily rely on ICTs (e.g., enterprise social media) to collaborate in an electronic way. However, individuals often don't receive feedback or responses in time in ICT-mediated interpersonal communications (e.g., communicating with colleagues using email or apps like Slack/Teams), which may reduce the effectiveness of virtual work (Bailey & Kurland, 2002). In other words, the virtual work form is more effective for independent jobs, which is supported by Golden and colleagues' study (Golden & Gajendran, 2019). Based on matched data collected from virtual workers and their supervisors in an organization with a voluntary telecommuting program, Golden and Gajendran (2019) identified a more positive impact of virtual work intensity on job performance for employees with lower levels of task interdependence.

How to Achieve Effective Virtual Work

The first two research streams aim to understand the effects of virtual work practices (e.g., intensity or frequency) on organizational and employee outcomes. Departing from early research, the third stream of literature frames virtual work as a research *context* rather than an independent variable, and has mainly focused on various factors (e.g., work, technology, and home characteristics) in shaping virtual work outcomes (Gohoungodji et al., 2023). The meaning of work design in the third stream is different from its counterparts in the first two streams, because it particularly refers to characteristics of one's virtual work (i.e., what does one's virtual work look like) (Wang et al., 2021).

According to our review, most research findings are consistent with the well-established work design literature (e.g., Wilkinson et al., 2022; Wood et al., 2023). The basic tenet from that literature is that "good" work designs are conducive to work effectiveness and well-being, playing a crucial role in achieving success in virtual work (Klonek & Parker, 2021). Therefore, managers are encouraged to design virtual work in a SMART way; that is, making virtual work Stimulating, promoting Mastery, supporting human Agency, increasing Relational features, and keeping job demands Tolerable (Wang & Parker, 2023). In this section, we will discuss a set of crucial virtual work characteristics as antecedents that can significantly influence employee outcomes.

Relational aspects of virtual work

Given the limited social cues in virtual work context, the relational aspect of work has attracted considerable theoretical attention. Cristina Gibson and colleagues' (2011) study showed that the relationship between task significance and experienced meaningfulness was greater when perceived virtuality was at higher levels (i.e., high electronic dependence and low copresence). In other words, relational features (e.g., task significance) become more important in virtual work settings. Following Gibson and colleagues (2011), scholars further examined other relational aspects of work. Consistent with previous research, workplace social support is positively associated with virtual workers' performance, job attitudes, and well-being outcomes (Mihalache & Mihalache, 2022; Smollan et al., 2023; Wood et al., 2023); social isolation, on the contrary, will lead to a set of detrimental effects (Aitken et al., 2023; Wong et al., 2022). Scholars also identified that the influence of these relational features is more pronounced for employees with specific traits. Taking Mashiho Mihalache and Oli Mihalache's (2022) study as an example, support from the organization and one's supervisor during the pandemic was associated with positive changes in employees' affective commitment to their organization, and those relationships were stronger for employees with low core self-evaluation and high future focus. Similarly, Bin Wang and colleagues (2021) found the effect of social support on procrastination was more positive for individuals who were less disciplined.

However, research results about task interdependence are mixed. As discussed in the last section, early scholars believed that highly interdependent jobs are not suitable for the virtual work form because frequent online communications may increase misunderstandings and conflicts in interpersonal collaborations (Golden & Veiga, 2005). Ward van Zoonen and colleagues (2021) further argued that virtual workers who perceive a higher degree of interdependence are likely to experience time pressures, loss of control, and a decline in personal productivity (Suh & Lee, 2017). In contrast, employees who can complete work tasks independently are expected to experience greater adjustment to virtual work. Based on data collected from 5,452 Finnish employees, Zoonen and colleagues' research results revealed a positive relationship between task independence and adjustment to virtual work, supporting the negative role of task interdependence.

Nevertheless, recent studies have revealed the bright side of interdependence in the virtual work context, which is not in line with studies conducted prior pandemic (Klonek & Parker, 2021). According to Christina Fuchs and Astrid Reichel's (2023) qualitative study conducted during the outbreak of COVID-19, employees with high levels of interdependence are more likely to fully use ICT affordances, and, therefore, can have more effective communications and collaborations in virtual work settings. In other words, for jobs high in interdependence employees would maximize the benefits of ICTs to support their work. To reconcile previous mixed outcomes and obtain a more comprehensive understanding, we encourage more empirical efforts to investigate the "double-edged sword" effect of interdependence for virtual workers.

Job autonomy in virtual work

The effects of job autonomy for virtual workers are also debated. Virtual work provides considerable autonomy to employees to decide when, where, and how to work (Wang et al., 2020). Although empirical evidence has supported the desirable outcomes of job autonomy or job control in virtual work settings (Becker et al., 2022; Wood et al., 2023), Gibson and colleagues' (2011) study showed that the positive effects of autonomy became weaker when perceived virtuality was at higher levels. This might be because "too much" autonomy may lead to side effects. For instance, Lars Uhlig and colleagues (2023) discussed the cognitive demands induced by autonomy in flexible work practices, including the autonomy for planning of working times, planning of working places, structuring of work tasks, and coordinating with others. The authors framed these cognitive demands of flexible work as challenge stressors. Results from their two-wave study revealed the positive impacts on cognitive flexibility and work engagement, while the expected effects on fatigue were not significant. In other words, their findings are consistent with prior challenge stressors literature, suggesting that cognitive demands of flexible work can motivate virtual workers.

Moving beyond the employee-centered perspective, too much autonomy in virtual work sometimes may lead to increased managerial control (e.g., intensive monitoring at work) (Jeske, 2022). In the early stages of the COVID-19, Parker and colleagues (2020) identified the challenge of manager mistrust and close monitoring during the large-scale transition to home office. A recent study has further examined the effects of supervisor daily monitoring on virtual workers (Zheng et al., 2023). Xiaotong Zheng and colleagues (2023) conducted two daily diary studies and found that focal employees' daily felt trust mediated the indirect effects of supervisor daily monitoring on daily vigor and exhaustion. Interestingly, the negative relationship between supervisor daily monitoring and employee daily felt trust was significant when monitoring variability was higher but not when it was lower. That is, uncertainty in monitoring behaviors may amplify the detrimental impact of daily monitoring.

Technology and home characteristics in virtual work

In addition to traditional task/work characteristics, scholars have incorporated a work design perspective to theorize and examine the influence of technology and home characteristics (e.g., a dedicated work space in one's home) on virtual work outcomes (Smollan et al., 2023; Wang & Parker, 2023; Wood et al., 2023). According to Frederick P. Morgeson and Stephen E. Humphrey's (2006) work design framework, technology and home characteristics can be grouped into work context aspects of work, with a focus on equipment use, work conditions, and ergonomics. In virtual work settings, employees usually work in the home office, and their tasks and interactions are mainly mediated by ICTs. Thus, home and technology characteristics now play a significant role in predicting virtual working experiences (Wood et al., 2023). Based on the job demands-resources model, Krystal Wilkinson and colleagues (2022) and Roy Smollan and colleagues (2023) theorized technology factors (e.g., ICT support and challenge) and home/non-work factors (e.g., household conflict and support from household members) as the sources of job demands and resources, which will further influence work performance and well-being. The work design perspective not only helps to understand the consequences of technology and home characteristics, but also provides a useful framework to improve these factors. For instance, Wang and Parker (2023) discussed the potential to re-design the technical system with a SMART work design approach to motivate virtual workers, such as creating technical features/functions that meet one's needs to challenge, facilitate social interactions, support user autonomy, and so on.

Taken together, a burgeoning number of studies have explored factors that predict virtual work success since the outbreak of COVID-19 pandemic (e.g., Gohoungodji et al., 2023; Wang & Parker, 2023). Based on the work design perspective, our review shows that some work characteristics (e.g., task significance and social support) become more valuable for virtual workers; however, other factors are worth further investigation (e.g., job autonomy and interdependence) to confirm potential undesirable outcomes. Additionally, although France Bélanger and colleagues (2013) have pointed out the socio-technical system nature of virtual work, scholars usually study influencing factors in work, technology, and home domains from different angles, with limited cross-fertilization (Raghuram et al., 2019). Work design theories (e.g., job demands-resources model) have recently been used to integrate different research clusters (e.g., Smollan et al., 2023; Wilkinson et al., 2022; Wood et al., 2023), and provided a powerful framework to understand and improve technology and home characteristics in virtual work settings.

Future Research Agenda

To further update and expand both virtual work and work design literature, based on our review, we propose several promising directions for future investigation. In particular, we call for more attention to research on novel work characteristics, creative performance, crafting behaviors, leadership behaviors, cultural variances, and the dynamic process in virtual work settings.

Temporal work characteristics in virtual work

The existing literature has focused on classical task and social characteristics (e.g., job demands, autonomy, and relational aspects of work) in virtual work settings (Hill et al., 2022). Scholars are starting to explore novel job characteristics in the virtual workplace (e.g., Xie et al., 2019). Given the geographically dispersed and asynchronous nature of virtual work, we encourage more empirical efforts to examine how virtual work practices shape temporal work design characteristics and their subsequent impacts on virtual workers (Zhao et al., 2022). Temporal predictability and task segmentation are two crucial temporal work characteristics (Zhao et al., 2022). Temporal predictability refers to the extent to which a job minimizes unpredictable waiting periods before a task or event. Task segmentation refers to the extent to which a large chunk of time at work is divided into several smaller blocks by temporal markers with a distinguishable nature (Zhao et al., 2022). Temporal work design in virtual settings could significantly differ from temporal work onsite because of geographic dispersion. For instance, due to the inability to monitor coworkers' progress directly, virtual workers may find it hard to predict waiting periods and will perceive lower levels of temporal predictability. On the other hand, task segmentation can be socially constructed, self-initiated, or externally imposed. In the virtual work context, people have considerable autonomy to alter task segmentation based on their own preferences, and their task segmentation could also be influenced by cross-domain factors (e.g., family demands). Given the significance of temporal work designs, more empirical research is warranted to thoroughly explore these propositions, and more importantly, to identify strategies for redesigning temporal characteristics to achieve success in virtual work.

Creativity in virtual work

Recent practices and research have demonstrated employees can remain productive in the virtual workplace. However, the existing literature fails to reach a consensus on the relationship between virtual work and creative performance (Gohoungodji et al., 2023). Some scholars argue that virtual work will contribute to creative performance by increasing virtual workers' positive psychological states (e.g., intrinsic motivations) (Martínez-Sánchez et al., 2007, 2008). Another stream of research, on the contrary, has raised concern about the negative effects of virtual work on spontaneous communication and collaboration (e.g., Brucks & Levav, 2022; Yang et al., 2022). Given that creativity is more of a result of close collaboration and teamwork, scholars and practitioners believe that virtual work is making creativity harder. To reconcile the inconsistent findings in the existing literature, we recommend systematically exploring the underlying mechanisms between virtual work practices and employees' creative performance, and more importantly, investigating how to facilitate creativity through re-designing the work and technological sub-systems (Wang & Parker, 2023). For example, collaboration tools (e.g., Microsoft Teams) have developed several virtual games for virtual workers, which could be used to boost creativity (Wang & Parker, 2023).

Leadership in virtual work

The existing literature has predominantly focused on virtual workers' experiences, while the leader perspective has been omitted. To achieve effective virtual work, it is practically and theoretically important to consider the significant role of leaders (Venz & Boettcher, 2022). Managerial support has been demonstrated to be conducive for virtual workers to overcome a set of challenges (Lautsch et al., 2009; Stoker et al., 2022). However, some managers report relatively negative attitudes toward virtual work and workers, which further shape their leadership behaviors (Kowalski & Ślebarska, 2022). During the early phase of the COVID-19 epidemic, almost one-third of surveyed managers reported not trusting the competence of their own employees (Parker et al., 2020). Even after the large scale "work-from-home experiment," there are still considerable business leaders and managers (e.g., Elon Musk) questioning whether their employees can be as efficient at home as in the office (Mac, 2022). Mistrust may further lead to more micro-management and monitoring, resulting in lower virtual work quality (Zheng et al., 2023). Accordingly, we encourage researchers to investigate antecedents of managers' attitudes toward virtual work, and how it influences virtual work characteristics via their managerial behaviors (Parker et al., 2019).

Cross-domain crafting behaviors/strategies

Job crafting refers to self-initiated change behaviors that employees engage in with the aim to align their jobs with their own preferences, motives, and passion (Tims et al., 2012; Wrzesniewski & Dutton, 2001). Except for the top-down work design approach, people also can proactively craft their jobs to improve job quality in a "bottom-up" manner (Parker, Van den Broeck, et al., 2017). Given that blurred boundaries occur in a virtual work context, employees' crafting behaviors are not limited to the work domain. According to Jaimee Caringal-Go and colleagues' (2022) study conducted during the pandemic, employees' crafting strategies include balancing demands and seeking resources in both work and non-work domains. Results from Erica Bailey and colleagues' (2022) multi-day experiments also support the effects of crafting behaviors in non-work domains on work outcomes. They found that even slightly changing clothing choices in the home office can produce work-related benefits. Following a recent study on home crafting behaviors (Demerouti et al., 2020), we recommend more research on cross-domain crafting behaviors or strategies, such as work-oriented family crafting (i.e., changing family demands and resources to meet work-related goals) and family-oriented work crafting (i.e., changing work demands and resources to meet family-related goals).

Cross-cultural variances

Previous studies have shown that cultural background can differentiate people's understanding of virtual work practices, further influencing the adoption of virtual work (Peters et al., 2016) and their subsequent performance and well-being (Adamovic, 2022; Peretz et al., 2018; Schlaegel et al., 2023). However, most data in previous studies were collected in developed and/or western countries, while individuals and organizations from developing countries and other cultural contexts are greatly under-represented. The biased sample could be problematic because employee responses to specific work characteristics can vary with the cultural context. For example, some interviewed Chinese employees in Wang and colleagues' (2021) study believed that monitoring was necessary and useful in their virtual work, which may not be supported in other countries. Thus, research on virtual work would be strengthened if the sample studied is better represented. Besides, scholars have examined the effects of individual cultural values and societal (or national) cultural values respectively (e.g., Adamovic, 2022; Peters et al., 2016). However, especially in culturally diverse countries, employees' values are not necessarily consistent with their embedded societal cultures (e.g., an Asian worker in Australia), which increases the difficulty of interpersonal collaboration and virtual team management. Therefore, we also call attention to the multi-level nature of cultures in the virtual work context.

A process perspective

Most previous research findings indicate the relatively short-term effects of virtual work practices because of the cross-sectional nature of research design or

560 TRANSFORMATIVE WORK DESIGN

short time intervals. When taking temporal factors into consideration, challenges identified at the early stage of virtual work (e.g., poor communication) are expected to be overcome over time. As Ned Kock (2004) argued, human brains are plastic and people can adapt themselves to the virtual form of work. For instance, employees may develop their knowledge, abilities, and skills for virtual collaboration (Schulze & Krumm, 2017). Masayuki Morikawa and colleagues' (2023) research on the productivity dynamics of remote work during the pandemic in Japan has supported these learning effects. However, new virtual work challenges may emerge if virtual or hybrid work becomes a new normal, such as lower levels of organizational commitment and identity (Ashforth et al., 2022). According to our review, only a few studies have adopted a longitudinal design to investigate this dynamic process (Klonek et al., 2022; Morikawa, 2023; Schulze et al., 2023). We believe that a process perspective can contribute to the virtual work literature by sparking a series of important research questions, such as will virtual work characteristics change over time? How would appropriate work designs facilitate adaptation and socialization in the virtual workplace?

Concluding Remarks

Based on the work design perspective, this chapter integrates the existing literature on virtual work, thereby addressing *why*, *when*, and *how* virtual work works. Our review indicates that virtual work practices can shape the nature of work (i.e., changing various crucial work characteristics), and jobs with specific characteristics are indeed more suitable for virtual work. More importantly, we also identified that scholars have shifted their attention from "how effective is virtual work" to "how to achieve effective virtual work," namely, exploring antecedents of effective virtual work (Wang & Parker, 2023). In addition to the crucial role of virtual work characteristics, scholars have expanded the work design perspective to consider the influence of technology and home characteristics in the virtual work context (e.g., Smollan et al., 2023; Wang & Parker, 2023; Wilkinson et al., 2022).

References

Adamovic, M. (2022). How does employee cultural background influence the effects of telework on job stress? The roles of power distance, individualism, and beliefs about telework. *International Journal of Information Management 62*, 102437. https://doi.org/10.1016/j.ijinfomgt.2021.102437

Afota, M.-C., Provost Savard, Y., Ollier-Malaterre, A., & Léon, E. (2023). Work-from-home adjustment in the US and Europe: the role of psychological climate for face time and perceived availability expectations. *The International Journal of Human Resource Management, 34*(14), 2765–2796. https://doi.org/10.1080/09585192.2022.2090269

Aitken, J. A., Kaplan, S. A., & Kuykendall, L. (2023). Going with(out) the flow at home: day-to-day variability in flow and performance while teleworking. *European Journal of Work and Organizational Psychology 32*, 662–677. https://doi.org/10.1080/1359432X.2023.2211271

Allen, T. D., Golden, T. D., & Shockley, K. M. (2015). How effective is telecommuting? Assessing the status of our scientific findings. *Psychological Science in the Public Interest 16*(2), 40–68. https://doi.org/10.1177/1529100615593273

Allen, T. D., Merlo, K., Lawrence, R. C., Slutsky, J., & Gray, C. E. (2021). Boundary management and work-nonwork balance while working from home. *Applied Psychology 70*(1), 60–84. https://doi.org/10.1111/apps.12300

Ashforth, B. E., Caza, B. B., & Meister, A. (2022). My place: How workers become identified with their workplaces and why it matters. *Academy of Management Review 49*(2). https://doi.org/10.5465/amr.2020.0442

Ayoko, O. B., Konrad, A. M., & Boyle, M. V. (2012). Online work: Managing conflict and emotions for performance in virtual teams. *European Management Journal 30*(2), 156–174. https://doi.org/10.1016/j.emj.2011.10.001

Bailey, D. E., & Kurland, N. B. (2002). A review of telework research: Findings, new directions, and lessons for the study of modern work. *Journal of Organizational Behavior 23*(4), 383–400. https://doi.org/10.1002/job.144

Bailey, E. R., Horton, C. B., & Galinsky, A. D. (2022). Enclothed harmony or enclothed dissonance? The effect of attire on the authenticity, power, and engagement of remote workers. *Academy of Management Discoveries 8*(3), 341–356. https://doi.org/10.5465/amd.2021.0081

Baruch, Y. (2000). Teleworking: Benefits and pitfalls as perceived by professionals and managers. *New Technology, Work and Employment 15*(1), 34–49. https://doi.org/10.1111/1468-005X.00063

Bean, C. J., & Eisenberg, E. M. (2006). Employee sensemaking in the transition to nomadic work. *Journal of Organizational Change Management 19*(2), 210–222. https://doi.org/10.1108/09534810610648915

Becker, W. J., Belkin, L. Y., Tuskey, S. E., & Conroy, S. A. (2022). Surviving remotely: How job control and loneliness during a forced shift to remote work impacted employee work behaviors and well-being. *Human Resource Management 61*(4), 449–464. https://doi.org/10.1002/hrm.22102

Bélanger, F., Watson-Manheim, M. B., & Swan, B. R. (2013). A multi-level socio-technical systems telecommuting framework. *Behaviour and Information Technology 32*(12), 1257–1279. https://doi.org/10.1080/0144929X.2012.705894

Brucks, M. S., & Levav, J. (2022). Virtual communication curbs creative idea generation. *Nature 605*(7908), 108–112. https://doi.org/10.1038/s41586-022-04643-y

Caringal-Go, J. F., Teng-Calleja, M., Bertulfo, D. J., & Manaois, J. O. (2022). Work–life balance crafting during COVID-19: Exploring strategies of telecommuting employees in the Philippines. *Community, Work and Family 25*(1), 112–131. https://doi.org/10.1080/13668803.2021.1956880

Cho, S., Kim, S., Chin, S. W., & Ahmad, U. (2020). Daily effects of continuous ICT demands on work–family conflict: Negative spillover and role conflict. *Stress and Health 36*(4), 533–545. https://doi.org/10.1002/smi.2955

Choroszewicz, M., & Kay, F. (2020). The use of mobile technologies for work-to-family boundary permeability: The case of Finnish and Canadian male lawyers. *Human Relations 73*(10), 1388–1414. https://doi.org/10.1177/0018726719865762

Collins, A. M., Hislop, D., & Cartwright, S. (2016). Social support in the workplace between teleworkers, office-based colleagues and supervisors. *New Technology, Work and Employment 31*(2), 161–175. https://doi.org/10.1111/ntwe.12065

Daft, R. L., & Lengel, R. H. (1986). Organizational information requirements, media richness and structural design. *Management Science 32*(5), 554–571. https://doi.org/10.1287/mnsc.32.5.554

Demerouti, E., Bakker, A. B., Nachreiner, F., & Schaufeli, W. B. (2001). The job demands-resources model of burnout. *Journal of Applied Psychology 86*(3), 499–512. https://doi.org/10.1037/0021-9010.86.3.499

Demerouti, E., Hewett, R., Haun, V., De Gieter, S., Rodríguez-Sánchez, A., & Skakon, J. (2020). From job crafting to home crafting: A daily diary study among six European countries. *Human Relations 73*(7), 1010–1035. https://doi.org/10.1177/0018726719848809

Dias, P., Lopes, S., & Peixoto, R. (2022). Mastering new technologies: Does it relate to teleworkers'(in) voluntariness and well-being? *Journal of Knowledge Management 26*(10), 2618–2633. https://doi.org/10.1108/JKM-01-2021-0003

Duxbury, L. E., Higgins, C. A., & Mills, S. (1992). After-hours telecommuting and work-family conflict: A comparative analysis. *Information Systems Research 3*(2), 173–190. https://doi.org/10.1287/isre.3.2.173

Fonner, K. L., & Roloff, M. E. (2010). Why teleworkers are more satisfied with their jobs than are office-based workers: When less contact is beneficial. *Journal of Applied Communication Research 38*(4), 336–361. https://doi.org/10.1080/00909882.2010.513998

Fuchs, C., & Reichel, A. (2023). Effective communication for relational coordination in remote work: How job characteristics and HR practices shape user–technology interactions. *Human Resource Management 62*(4), 511–528. https://doi.org/10.1002/hrm.22161

Gajendran, R. S., & Harrison, D. A. (2007). The good, the bad, and the unknown about telecommuting: Meta-analysis of psychological mediators and individual consequences. *Journal of Applied Psychology 92*(6), 1524–1541. https://doi.org/10.1037/0021-9010.92.6.1524

Gajendran, R. S., Harrison, D. A., & Delaney-Klinger, K. (2015). Are telecommuters remotely good citizens? Unpacking telecommuting's effects on performance via i-deals and job resources. *Personnel Psychology 68*(2), 353–393. https://doi.org/10.1111/peps.12082

Gibson, C. B., Gibbs, J. L., Stanko, T. L., Tesluk, P., & Cohen, S. G. (2011). Including the "I" in virtuality and modern job design: Extending the job characteristics model to include the moderating effect of individual experiences of electronic dependence and copresence. *Organization Science 22*(6), 1481–1499. https://doi.org/10.1287/orsc.1100.0586

Gohoungodji, P., N'Dri, A. B., & Matos, A. L. B. (2023). What makes telework work? Evidence of success factors across two decades of empirical research: A systematic and critical review. *International Journal of Human Resource Management 34*(3), 605–649. https://doi.org/10.1080/09585192.2022.2112259

Golden, T. D. (2006). The role of relationships in understanding telecommuter satisfaction. *Journal of Organizational Behavior 27*(3), 319–340. https://doi.org/10.1002/job.369

Golden, T. D., & Eddleston, K. A. (2020). Is there a price telecommuters pay? Examining the relationship between telecommuting and objective career success. *Journal of Vocational Behavior 116*, 103348. https://doi.org/10.1016/j.jvb.2019.103348

Golden, T. D., & Gajendran, R. S. (2019). Unpacking the role of a telecommuter's job in their performance: Examining job complexity, problem solving, interdependence, and social support. *Journal of Business and Psychology 34*(1), 55–69. https://doi.org/10.1007/s10869-018-9530-4

Golden, T. D., & Veiga, J. F. (2005). The impact of extent of telecommuting on job satisfaction: Resolving inconsistent findings. *Journal of Management 31*(2), 301–318. https://doi.org/10.1177/0149206304271768

Golden, T. D., Veiga, J. F., & Simsek, Z. (2006). Telecommuting's differential impact on work-family conflict: Is there no place like home? *Journal of Applied Psychology 91*(6), 1340–1350. https://doi.org/10.1037/0021-9010.91.6.1340

Grant, A. M., & Parker, S. K. (2009). Redesigning work design theories: The rise of relational and proactive perspectives. *Academy of Management Annals 3*(1), 317–375. https://doi.org/10.1080/19416520903047327

Hill, N. S., Axtell, C., Raghuram, S., & Nurmi, N. (2022). Unpacking virtual work's dual effects on employee well-being: An integrative review and future research agenda. *Journal of Management 50*(2), 752–792. https://doi.org/10.1177/01492063221131535

Ingusci, E., Signore, F., Giancaspro, M. L., Manuti, A., Molino, M., Russo, V., Zito, M., & Cortese, C. G. (2021). Workload, techno overload, and behavioral stress during COVID-19 emergency: The role of job crafting in remote workers. *Frontiers in Psychology 12*(April), 1–11. https://doi.org/10.3389/fpsyg.2021.655148

Jeske, D. (2022). Remote workers' experiences with electronic monitoring during COVID-19: Implications and recommendations. *International Journal of Workplace Health Management 15*(3), 393–409. https://doi.org/10.1108/IJWHM-02-2021-0042

Kelliher, C., & Anderson, D. (2010). Doing more with less? Flexible working practices and the intensification of work. *Human Relations 63*(1), 83–106. https://doi.org/10.1177/0018726709349199

Klonek, F. E., Kanse, L., Wee, S., Runneboom, C., & Parker, S. K. (2022). Did the COVID-19 lock-down make us better at working in virtual teams? *Small Group Research 53*(2), 185–206. https://doi.org/10.1177/10464964211008991

Klonek, F., & Parker, S. K. (2021). Designing SMART teamwork: How work design can boost performance in virtual teams. *Organizational Dynamics 50*(1), 100841. https://doi.org/10.1016/j.orgdyn.2021.100841

Kock, N. (2004). The psychobiological model: Towards a new theory of computer-mediated communication based on Darwinian evolution. *Organization Science 15*(3), 327–348. https://doi.org/10.1287/orsc.1040.0071

Kowalski, G., & Ślebarska, K. (2022). Remote working and work effectiveness: A leader perspective. *International Journal of Environmental Research and Public Health 19*(22), 15326. https://doi.org/10.3390/ijerph192215326

Lautsch, B. A., Kossek, E. E., & Eaton, S. C. (2009). Supervisory approaches and paradoxes in managing telecommuting implementation. *Human Relations 62*(6), 795–827. https://doi.org/10.1177/0018726709104543

Mac, R. (2022, 1 June). Elon Musk to workers: Spend 40 hours in the office, or else. *The New York Times.* https://www.nytimes.com/2022/06/01/technology/elon-musk-tesla-spacex-office.html

Marler, J. H., & Boudreau, J. W. (2017). An evidence-based review of HR Analytics. *International Journal of Human Resource Management 28*(1), 3–26. https://doi.org/10.1080/09585192.2016.1244699

Martin, B. H., & MacDonnell, R. (2012). Is telework effective for organizations? *Management Research Review 35*(7), 602–616. https://doi.org/10.1108/01409171211238820

Martínez-Sánchez, A., Pérez-Pérez, M., De-Luis-Carnicer, P., & Vela-Jiménez, M. J. (2007). Telework, human resource flexibility and firm performance. *New Technology, Work and Employment 22*(3), 208–223. https://doi.org/10.1111/j.1468-005X.2007.00195.x

Martínez-Sánchez, A., Pérez-Pérez, M., José Vela-Jiménez, M., & de-Luis-Carnicer, P. (2008). Telework adoption, change management, and firm performance. *Journal of Organizational Change Management 21*(1), 7–31. https://doi.org/10.1108/09534810810847011

Mazmanian, M., Orlikowski, W. J., & Yates, J. A. (2013). The autonomy paradox: The implications of mobile email devices for knowledge professionals. *Organization Science 24*(5), 1337–1357. https://doi.org/10.1287/orsc.1120.0806

McPhail, R., Chan, X. W. (Carys), May, R., & Wilkinson, A. (2023). Post-COVID remote working and its impact on people, productivity, and the planet: An exploratory scoping review. *International Journal of Human Resource Management 35*, 154–182. https://doi.org/10.1080/09585192.2023.2221385

Michel, J. S., Kotrba, L. M., Mitchelson, J. K., Clark, M. A., & Baltes, B. B. (2011). Antecedents of work-family conflict: A meta-analytic review. *Journal of Organizational Behavior 32*(5), 689–725. https://doi.org/10.1002/job.695

Miglioretti, M., Gragnano, A., Simbula, S., & Perugini, M. (2022). Telework quality and employee well-being: Lessons learned from the COVID-19 pandemic in Italy. *New Technology, Work and Employment 38*, 548–571. https://doi.org/10.1111/ntwe.12263

Mihalache, M., & Mihalache, O. R. (2022). How workplace support for the COVID-19 pandemic and personality traits affect changes in employees' affective commitment to the organization and job-related well-being. *Human Resource Management 61*(3), 295–314. https://doi.org/10.1002/hrm.22082

Morganson, V. J., Major, D. A., Oborn, K. L., Verive, J. M., & Heelan, M. P. (2010). Comparing telework locations and traditional work arrangements: Differences in work-life balance support, job satisfaction, and inclusion. *Journal of Managerial Psychology 25*(6), 578–595. https://doi.org/10.1108/02683941011056941

Morgeson, F. P., & Humphrey, S. E. (2006). The work design questionnaire (WDQ): Developing and validating a comprehensive measure for assessing job design and the nature of work. *Journal of Applied Psychology 91*(6), 1321–1339. https://doi.org/10.1037/0021-9010.91.6.1321

Morikawa, M. (2023). Productivity dynamics of remote work during the COVID-19 pandemic. *Industrial Relations: A Journal of Economy and Society 62*(3), 317–331. https://doi.org/10.1111/irel.12327

Parker, S. K. (2014). Beyond motivation: Job and work design for development, health, ambidexterity, and more. *Annual Review of Psychology, 65*(1), 661–691. https://doi.org/10.1146/annurev-psych-010213-115208

Parker, S. K., Andrei, D. M., & Van den Broeck, A. (2019). Poor work design begets poor work design: Capacity and willingness antecedents of individual work design behavior. *Journal of Applied Psychology 104*(7), 907–928. https://doi.org/10.1037/apl0000383

Parker, S. K., & Grote, G. (2022a). More than "more than ever": Revisiting a work design and sociotechnical perspective on digital technologies. *Applied Psychology 71*(4), 1215–1223. https://doi.org/10.1111/apps.12425

Parker, S. K., & Grote, G. (2022b). Automation, algorithms, and beyond: Why work design matters more than ever in a digital world. *Applied Psychology 71*(4), 1171–1204. https://doi.org/10.1111/apps.12241

Parker, S. K., Knight, C., & Keller, A. (2020, 30 July). Remote managers are having trust issues. *Harvard Business Review.* https://hbr.org/2020/07/remote-managers-are-having-trust-issues

Parker, S. K., Morgeson, F. P., & Johns, G. (2017). One hundred years of work design research: Looking back and looking forward. *Journal of Applied Psychology 102*(3), 403–420. https://doi.org/10.1037/apl0000106

Parker, S. K., Van den Broeck, A., & Holman, D. (2017). Work design influences: A synthesis of multilevel factors that affect the design of jobs. *Academy of Management Annals 11*(1), 267–308. https://doi.org/10.5465/annals.2014.0054

Peretz, H., Fried, Y., & Levi, A. (2018). Flexible work arrangements, national culture, organisational characteristics, and organisational outcomes: A study across 21 countries. *Human Resource Management Journal 28*(1), 182–200. https://doi.org/10.1111/1748-8583.12172

Perry, S. J., Rubino, C., & Hunter, E. M. (2018). Stress in remote work: Two studies testing the Demand-Control-Person model. *European Journal of Work and Organizational Psychology 27*(5), 577–593. https://doi.org/10.1080/1359432X.2018.1487402

Peters, P., Ligthart, P. E. M., Bardoel, A., & Poutsma, E. (2016). "Fit for telework?" Cross-cultural variance and task-control explanations in organizations' formal telework practices. *International Journal of Human Resource Management 27*(21), 2582–2603. https://doi.org/10.1080/09585192.2016.1232294

Pianese, T., Errichiello, L., & da Cunha, J. V. (2023). Organizational control in the context of remote working: A synthesis of empirical findings and a research agenda. *European Management Review 20*(2), 326–345. https://doi.org/10.1111/emre.12515

Raghuram, S., Hill, N. S., Gibbs, J. L., & Maruping, L. M. (2019). Virtual work: Bridging research clusters. *Academy of Management Annals 13*(1), 308–341. https://doi.org/10.5465/annals.2017.0020

Sardeshmukh, S. R., Sharma, D., & Golden, T. D. (2012). Impact of telework on exhaustion and job engagement: A job demands and job resources model. *New Technology, Work and Employment 27*(3), 193–207. https://doi.org/10.1111/j.1468-005X.2012.00284.x

Schlaegel, C., Gunkel, M., & Taras, V. (2023). COVID-19 and individual performance in global virtual teams: The role of self-regulation and individual cultural value orientations. *Journal of Organizational Behavior 44*(1), 102–131. https://doi.org/10.1002/job.2671

Schulze, J., & Krumm, S. (2017). The "virtual team player": A review and initial model of knowledge, skills, abilities, and other characteristics for virtual collaboration. *Organizational Psychology Review 7*(1), 66–95. https://doi.org/10.1177/2041386616675522

Schulze, J., Krumm, S., Eid, M., Müller, H., & Göritz, A. S. (2023). The relationship between telework and job characteristics: A latent change score analysis during the COVID-19 pandemic. *Applied Psychology 73*, 3–33. https://doi.org/10.1111/apps. 12461

Smollan, R. K., Morrison, R. L., & Cooper-Thomas, H. D. (2023). Working from home during lockdown: The impact on performance and wellbeing. *Journal of Management & Organization 2023*, 1–22. https://doi.org/10.1017/jmo.2023.9

Spreitzer, G. M. (1995). Psychological empowerment in the workplace: Dimensions, measurement, and validation. *Academy of Management Journal 38*(5), 1442–1465.

Stoker, J. I., Garretsen, H., & Lammers, J. (2022). Leading and Working from Home in Times of COVID-19: On the Perceived Changes in Leadership Behaviors. *Journal of Leadership & Organizational Studies 29*(2), 208–218. https://doi.org/10.1177/15480518211007452

Suh, A., & Lee, J. (2017). Understanding teleworkers' technostress and its influence on job satisfaction. *Internet Research 27*(1), 140–159. https://doi.org/10.1108/IntR-06-2015-0181

Thulin, E., Vilhelmson, B., & Johansson, M. (2019). New telework, time pressure, and time use control in everyday life. *Sustainability 11*(11). https://doi.org/10.3390/su11113067

Tims, M., Bakker, A. B., & Derks, D. (2012). Development and validation of the job crafting scale. *Journal of Vocational Behavior 80*(1), 173–186. https://doi.org/10.1016/j.jvb. 2011.05.009

Uhlig, L., Korunka, C., Prem, R., & Kubicek, B. (2023). A two-wave study on the effects of cognitive demands of flexible work on cognitive flexibility, work engagement and fatigue. *Applied Psychology 72*(2), 625–646. https://doi.org/10.1111/apps.12392

van Zoonen, W., Sivunen, A., Blomqvist, K., Olsson, T., Ropponen, A., Henttonen, K., & Vartiainen, M. (2021). Factors influencing adjustment to remote work: Employees' initial responses to the COVID-19 pandemic. *International Journal of Environmental Research and Public Health 18*(13), 6966. https://doi.org/10.3390/ijerph18136966

Vander Elst, T., Verhoogen, R., Sercu, M., Van den Broeck, A., Baillien, E., & Godderis, L. (2017). Not extent of telecommuting, but job characteristics as proximal predictors of work-related well-being. *Journal of Occupational and Environmental Medicine 59*(10), e180–e186. https://doi.org/10.1097/JOM.0000000000001132

Venz, L., & Boettcher, K. (2022). Leading in times of crisis: How perceived COVID-19-related work intensification links to daily e-mail demands and leader outcomes. *Applied Psychology 71*(3), 912–934. https://doi.org/10.1111/apps.12357

Villamor, I., Hill, N. S., Kossek, E. E., & Foley, K. O. (2023). Virtuality at work: A doubled-edged sword for women's career equality? *Academy of Management Annals 17*(1), 113–140. https://doi.org/10.5465/annals.2020.0384

Wang, B., Liao, Y., Chen, M., Zhang, L., & Qian, J. (2023). Work and affective outcomes of social media use at work: A daily-survey study. *International Journal of Human Resource Management 34*(5), 941–965. https://doi.org/10.1080/09585192. 2021.2012711

Wang, B., Liu, Y., & Parker, S. K. (2020). How does the use of information communication technology affect individuals? A work design perspective. *Academy of Management Annals 14*(2), 695–725. https://doi.org/10.5465/annals.2018.0127

Wang, B., Liu, Y., Qian, J., & Parker, S. K. (2021). Achieving effective remote working during the COVID-19 pandemic: A work design perspective. *Applied Psychology: An International Review 70*(1), 16–59. https://doi.org/10.1111/apps.12290

Wang, B., Liu, Y., Qian, J., & Parker, S. K. (2023). How can people benefit, and who benefits most, from using socialisation-oriented social media at work? An affordance perspective. *Human Resource Management Journal 33*, 1035–1052. https://doi.org/10.1111/1748-8583.12504

Wang, B., & Parker, S. K. (2023). Embracing the digital workplace: a SMART work design approach to supporting virtual work. In L. L. Gilson, T. O'Neill, & M. T. Maynard (Eds.), *Handbook of virtual work* (pp. 403–424). Edward Elgar Publishing Ltd. https://doi.org/10.4337/9781802200508.00032

Whitman, L. E., Malzahn, D. E., Chaparro, B. S., Russell, M., Langrall, R., & Mohler, B. A. (2005). A comparison of group processes, performance, and satisfaction in face-to-face versus computer-mediated engineering student design teams. *Journal of Engineering Education 94*(3), 327–337. https://doi.org/https://doi.org/10.1002/j.2168-9830.2005.tb00857.x

Wilkinson, K., Collins, A. M., & Antoniadou, M. (2022). Family status and changing demands/resources: The overlooked experience of solo-living employees transitioning to homeworking during the COVID-19 pandemic. *International Journal of Human Resource Management 34*, 3585–3611. https://doi.org/10.1080/09585192.2022.2142064

Wöhrmann, A. M., & Ebner, C. (2021). Understanding the bright side and the dark side of telework: An empirical analysis of working conditions and psychosomatic health complaints. *New Technology, Work and Employment 36*(3), 348–370. https://doi.org/10.1111/ntwe.12208

Wong, S. I., Berntzen, M., Warner-Søderholm, G., & Giessner, S. R. (2022). The negative impact of individual perceived isolation in distributed teams and its possible remedies. *Human Resource Management Journal 32*(4), 906–927. https://doi.org/10.1111/1748-8583.12447

Wood, S., Michaelides, G., Inceoglu, I., Niven, K., Kelleher, A., Hurren, E., & Daniels, K. (2023). Satisfaction with one's job and working at home in the COVID-19 pandemic: A two-wave study. *Applied Psychology 72*(4), 1409–1429. https://doi.org/10.1111/apps.12440

Wrzesniewski, A., & Dutton, J. E. (2001). Crafting a job: As active employees revisioning crafters of their work. *Academy of Management Review 26*(2), 179–201. https://doi.org/10.2307/259118

Xie, J. L., Elangovan, A. R., Hu, J., & Hrabluik, C. (2019). Charting new terrain in work design: A study of hybrid work characteristics. *Applied Psychology 68*(3), 479–512. https://doi.org/10.1111/apps.12169

Yang, L., Holtz, D., Jaffe, S., Suri, S., Sinha, S., Weston, J., Joyce, C., Shah, N., Sherman, K., Hecht, B., & Teevan, J. (2022). The effects of remote work on collaboration among information workers. *Nature Human Behaviour 6*(1), 43–54. https://doi.org/10.1038/s41562-021-01196-4

Zhao, H. H., Deng, H., Chen, R. P., Parker, S. K., & Zhang, W. (2022). Fast or slow: How temporal work design shapes experienced passage of time and job performance. *Academy of Management Journal 65*(6), 2014–2033. https://doi.org/10.5465/amj.2019.1110

Zheng, X. (Janey), Nieberle, K. W., Braun, S., & Schyns, B. (2023). Is someone looking over my shoulder? An investigation into supervisor monitoring variability, Subordinates' daily felt trust, and well-being. *Journal of Organizational Behavior 44*(5), 818–837. https://doi.org/10.1002/job.2699

Designing Work to Retain an Aging Workforce

Robin Umbra and Ulrike Fassbender

Designing Work to Retain an Aging Workforce

Organizations are under pressure to retain older workers (Harris et al., 2024). One approach is to optimize work design characteristics (Truxillo et al., 2012, 2015; Zacher & Schmitt, 2016), which represent the quantity and quality of organizational resources available to people at work (Morgeson & Humphrey, 2006). Essentially, organizations adjust work design characteristics to benefit older workers' work outcomes (Truxillo et al., 2015), particularly their intention to continue working (Fassbender et al., 2014), possibly even beyond the mandatory or typical retirement age (i.e., bridge employment; Beehr & Bennett, 2015; Fassbender et al., 2016; Truxillo et al., 2012).

This chapter summarizes the theoretical and practical underpinnings of aging in the workplace, with the goal of understanding which work design features are most effective in retaining older workers. The focus is on identifying work design characteristics that directly affect the retention of older workers, as well as those that promote their health and productivity and have a direct impact on the continuation of their working lives. Additionally, the relationship between these characteristics and other factors such as job satisfaction is analyzed.

Theoretical Background

The work design characteristics were identified by J. Richard Hackman and Greg Oldham (1975) and Frederick P. Morgeson and Stephen E. Humphrey (2006). The primary work design characteristics include *skill variety* (job's hard skill requirements), *task identity* (job's clarity), *task significance* (job's meaningfulness vs. expediency), *autonomy* (job agency level), *feedback from the job* (job-related information received on the job), *feedback from others* (peer-related info during job performance.), and *dealing with others* (job's soft skill requirements). Morgeson and Humphrey (2006) refined these work design characteristics

---

Robin Umbra and Ulrike Fassbender, *Designing Work to Retain an Aging Workforce*. In: *Transformative Work Design*. Edited by: Sharon K. Parker et al., Oxford University Press. © Society for Industrial and Organizational Psychology (2025). DOI: 10.1093/oso/9780197692554.003.0023

and added new constructs, such as *job complexity* (task complexity and interconnectivity), *information processing* (data manipulation needed for a job), *problem-solving* (innovativeness for complex job tasks), *specialization* (hard skill depth for a job) *task variety* (job flexibility requirements), *work scheduling autonomy* (job agency in terms of task timing), *decision-making autonomy* (job agency in terms of decision making), *work-methods autonomy* (job agency in terms of work-methods), *social support* (organizational peer group interconnectedness during job), *interaction outside the organization* (organizational peer group interconnectedness outside job), *initiated interdependence* (dependency level of remote jobs on focal job execution), *received interdependence* (dependency level of focal job on remote jobs execution), *ergonomics* (facilitating good posture and movement in the workplace), *physical demands* (physical effort required for a job), *work conditions* (job safety and hospitality level), and *equipment use* (tool supply level of a job). These work design characteristics are organized into four overarching categories: task characteristics, knowledge characteristics, social characteristics, and work context.

Low work design characteristics are harmful to workers' psychological states and work outcomes (Hackman & Oldham, 1975; Morgeson & Humphrey, 2006). High values are beneficial. Low values are associated with increased job strain (Bakker & Demerouti, 2007; Karasek, 1979; Morgeson & Humphrey, 2006), which occurs when there is not enough job resources (degree of skills and knowledge provided by a job) to fulfill job demands (degree of skills and knowledge required for a job). Work design characteristics may indirectly affect older workers' intention to remain in the workforce through job strain (Bakker & Demerouti, 2007; Hackman & Oldham, 1975; Karasek, 1979; Morgeson & Humphrey, 2006).

Defining "older worker" is contentious. Legal definitions say 40+ (Age Discrimination in Employment Act, 1967), but scholars disagree (Bohlmann et al., 2018), claiming aging is a continuous process. Jean McCarthy and colleagues (2014) found individuals aged 50+ are viewed as older workers in practice. We use this definition, acknowledging that aging is continuous and take a lifespan development perspective when relevant.

Systematic Literature Review

We conducted a comprehensive literature review to synthesize findings, considering the number and heterogeneity of studies in work design and workplace aging. Our review included English articles that were peer-reviewed, contained quantitative or qualitative data, included workers aged 50 or older (Bohlmann et al., 2018; McCarthy et al., 2014), and simultaneously measured age and a work design characteristic from Morgeson and Humphrey's (2006) or Hackman and Oldham's (1975) frameworks. We excluded meta-analyses and articles that conceptualized work design characteristics solely as outcomes.

We searched for citations in work design and workplace aging literature using a comprehensive string: (*"work design" OR "job design" OR "work characteristic" OR "work characteristics" OR "job characteristic" OR "job characteristics" OR "job demands" OR "job content" OR "work scheduling autonomy" OR "decision-making autonomy" OR "work methods autonomy" OR "task variety" OR "task significance" OR "task identity" OR "feedback from job" OR "job complexity" OR "information processing" OR "problem solving" OR "skill variety" OR "specialization" OR "social support" OR "initiated interdependence" OR "received interdependence" OR "interaction outside organization" OR "feedback from others" OR "ergonomics" OR "physical demands" OR "work conditions" OR "equipment use") AND ("old" OR "older" OR "ageing" OR "ageing" OR "aged"*). To ensure external validity, we used string terms from Morgeson & Humphrey's (2006) framework. We searched abstracts in APA PsycNet, ProQuest, and EBSCO Business Source Premier without any time constraints to maximize the sample size of articles.

Findings

Our screening flowchart is shown in Figure 23.1. We compared 9,001 articles to our inclusion criteria, resulting in 158 distinct articles. We assessed the full texts of these articles to determine their eligibility for inclusion in our synthesis, selecting 64 articles. Details of our findings are presented in Table 23.1, at the end of this chapter.

The findings were organized according to the theoretical frameworks employed. When encountering an article with unclear theoretical basis, the theoretical framework was reevaluated. The results were integrated into one of the well-established frameworks reviewed in this chapter, taking into consideration their theoretical proximity.

Our investigation uncovered two meta-theoretical approaches that have influenced theorizing in this field: the retention-push and retention-pull approaches. Most studies cannot be perfectly categorized into one approach due to the role of individual perceptions and individual differences as moderators. However, the retention-push approach focuses on self-generated motivation for the employee to stay, while the retention-pull approach emphasizes the environment-generated motivation that affects the employee's decision to stay. We provide a theoretical overview of these approaches, and the models used alongside them, followed by a review of work design characteristics with

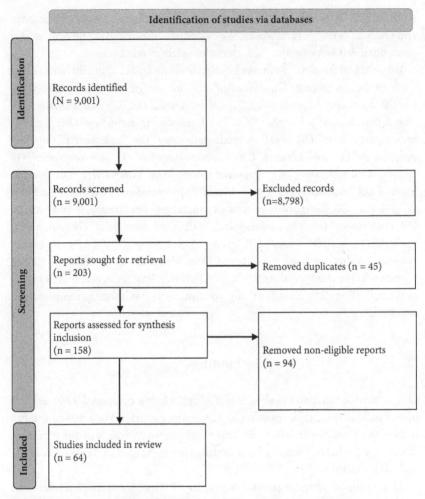

Figure 23.1 Screening Flowchart

empirical evidence supporting their beneficial or detrimental impact on work outcomes for older workers.

Retention-push approach (lifespan development focus)

Researchers used the retention-push approach, deploying theoretical frameworks that propose changes in a person's perception of work design characteristics can intrinsically motivate an older worker to stay in the workforce. The frameworks used are based on the *socioemotional selectivity framework*

Table 23.1 Overview of Findings

No.	Year	Authors	Research Type	Research Design	Moderator	x	Predictor	y	Mediator	z	Outcome
1	2018	Alcover & Topa	Quantitative	Cross-sectional	Age	0	Task characteristics	+			Psychological work ability
2	1984	Abush & Burkhead	Quantitative	Cross-sectional			Feedback from job	–			Job strain
							Job autonomy	–			Job strain
							Task significance	–			Job strain
3	2022	Axelrad et al.	Quantitative	Cross-sectional			Decision-making autonomy	+			Job satisfaction
							Working hours	0			Job satisfaction
							Income satisfaction	+			Job satisfaction
							Additional benefits	+			Job satisfaction
							Job significance	+			Job satisfaction
							Appraised discrimination	–			Job satisfaction
							Task identity	+			Job satisfaction
							Job safety	0			Job satisfaction
							Job security	+			Job satisfaction
							Feeling-at home	+			Job satisfaction
							Work–life balance	+			Job satisfaction
4	2020	Beier et al.	Quantitative	Cross-sectional	Worker abilities	+	Job complexity	–			Health
					Worker abilities	–	Job complexity	+			Work exit

continued

Table 23.1 *continued*

No.	Year	Authors	Research Type	Research Design	Moderator	x	Predictor	y	Mediator	z	Outcome
5	2011	Bennett et al.	Quantitative	Cross-sectional			Age	0			Absolute working heart rate
							Age	0			Recovery heart rate
6	2017	Berglund et al.	Quantitative	Longitudinal (cross-lagged)	Work capacity	−	Physical demands	+			Turnover intention
							Sports during working hours	−			Turnover intention
7	2013	Besen et al.	Quantitative	Cross-sectional	Age	−	Workplace friendship	+			Job satisfaction
					Age	−	Task variety	+			Job satisfaction
8	2013	Bos et al.	Quantitative	cross-sectional			Task variety	+			Job satisfaction
9	2011	Boumans et al.	Quantitative	Cross-sectional	Age	+	Job motivating potential	+			Motivation
					Age	−	Career opportunities	+			Motivation
10	2009	Brougham & Walsh	Quantitative	Cross-sectional			Importance of personal goals	0			Intention to retire early
11	2014	Brown et al.	Quantitative	Cross-sectional	Job autonomy	+	Job demands	−			Job satisfaction
					Social support	0	Job demands	−			Job satisfaction
12	2020	Cavanagh et al.	Quantitative	Cross-sectional	Age	+	Job autonomy	+			Job satisfaction
					Age	+	Annual income	+			Job satisfaction

13	2022	Choi et al.	Quantitative	Cross-sectional		Physical demands	−	Cognitive function
14	2022	Christensen & Knardahl	Quantitative	Cross-sectional		Job autonomy	−	Turnover intention
						Positive challenges	−	Turnover intention
						Job demands	+	Turnover intention
						Role conflict	+	Turnover intention
						Role ambiguity	+	Turnover intention
						Work-life conflict	+	Turnover intention
						Social support	−	Turnover intention
15	1995	Davis et al.	Quantitative	Cross-sectional		Job stress	+	Fibrinogen levels
						Supervisor support	−	Fibrinogen levels
16	2020	de Breij et al.	Quantitative	Longitudinal (cross-lagged)		Physical demands	−	Health
						Psychosocial demands	+	Health
						Task variety	+	Health

continued

Table 23.1 *continued*

No.	Year	Authors	Research Type	Research Design	Moderator	x	Predictor	y	Mediator	z	Outcome
17	2000	De Jonge et al.	Quantitative	Cross-sectional			Job strain	+			Psychosomatic health complaints
							Job strain	+			Physical health symptoms
							Job strain	+			Emotional exhaustion
							Job strain	–			Job satisfaction
18	2021	Den Boer et al.	Qualitative	Cross-sectional			Job autonomy	+			Intention to stay
							Working hours	–			Intention to stay
							Task significance	+			Intention to stay
							Social support	+			Intention to stay
							Social interaction	+			Intention to stay
19	2015	Drabe et al.	Quantitative	Cross-sectional	Age	–	Job autonomy	+			Job satisfaction
					Age	–	Advancement opportunities	+			Job satisfaction
					Age	–	Interesting job	+			Job satisfaction
					Age	–	Income	+			Job satisfaction
					Age	0	Job security	+			Job satisfaction
20	2007	Elovainio et al.	Quantitative	Cross-sectional			Job autonomy	–			Early retirement thoughts
							Job demands	+			Early retirement thoughts

21	2009	Fraser et al.	Qualitative	Cross-sectional	Physical demands	+			Intentions to retire
					Social support	–			Intentions to retire
					Task identity	–			Intentions to retire
22	2016	Frins et al.	Quantitative	Longitudinal (time-lagged)	Job demands	+			Emotional exhaustion
					Job demands	0			Dedication
					Job demands	+	Emotional exhaustion	–	Desired retirement age
					Job demands	0	Dedication	–	Desired retirement age
					Job resources	+	Dedication	–	Desired retirement age
					Job demands	+			Emotional exhaustion
					Job resources	–			Emotional exhaustion
					Job resources	+			Dedication
					Job resources	–	Emotional exhaustion	–	Desired retirement age
					Job resources	+			Dedication
					Job resources	–			Emotional exhaustion

continued

Table 23.1 *continued*

No.	Year	Authors	Research Type	Research Design	Moderator	x	Predictor	y	Mediator	z	Outcome
23	1989	Greenwald et al.	Quantitative	Cross-sectional	Age	0	Work scheduling autonomy	+			Efficiency
					Age	0	Physical demands	+			Work disability
					Age	0	Work scheduling autonomy	+			Employment
24	2016	Guglielmi et al.	Quantitative	Longitudinal (cross-lagged)	Job demands	+	Job satisfaction	+	Work engage-ment	+	Job satisfaction
					Age	–	Job satisfaction	+	Work engage-ment	+	Job satisfaction
25	1982	Hardy	Quantitative	Cross-sectional			Job strain	–			Health
26	1996	Hayslip et al.	Quantitative	Cross-sectional	Age	–	Laissez faire supervision	0			Job attitudes
27	1985	Hayward & Hardy	Quantitative	Longitudinal			Job complexity (social)	–			Early retirement intentions
28	2019	Hernaus et al.	Quantitative	Cross-sectional	Age	–	Job complexity	+			Innovative work behavior
					Age	+	Job innovation requirements	+			Innovative work behavior
29	2013	Jones et al.	Quantitative	Cross-sectional			Work conditions	–			Perceived health risk
							Work conditions	–			Health complaints
							Work conditions	–			Injury

					Work conditions	−	Mental & physical health problems
					Work conditions	−	Sickness absence
					Work conditions	−	Fatigue
30	2017	Korsakienė et al.	Quantitative	Cross-sectional		Decision making autonomy	+	Job engagement
					Feedback from job	+	Job engagement
					Work schedule autonomy	+	Job engagement
31	2016	Li et al.	Quantitative	Cross-sectional		Job demands	−	Job resources
					Job demands	−	Work ability
					Job resources	+	Work ability
32	2016	Lichtenthaler & Fischbach	Quantitative	Cross-sectional		Burnout	−	Motivation to work after retirement
33	2010	Marquié et al.	Quantitative	Cross-sectional	Age +	Shift work	−	Sleep quality
34	2015	McGonagle et al.	Quantitative	Longitudinal (time-lagged)		Job demands	0	Perceived work ability
					Job resources	0	Perceived work ability
35	2014	Nilsen et al.	Quantitative	Longitudinal (cross-lagged)		Job demands	0	Serious health problems

continued

Table 23.1 *continued*

No.	Year	Authors	Research Type	Research Design	Moderator	x	Predictor	y	Mediator	z	Outcome
							Job demands	−			Serious health problems
					Gender (f; m)	+	Job autonomy	0			Serious health problems
							Job strain	+			Serious health problems
							Job demands	+			Mobility problems
					Gender (m; f)	+	Job demands	+			Late-life physical functioning
							Job autonomy	0			Mobility problems
							Job autonomy	0			Lung function
							Job demands	+			Mobility problems
							Job strain	+			Limited physical performance
36	2022	Nivalainen	Quantitative	Cross-sectional			Work ability	−			Retirement intentions
							Organizational layoffs	+			Intentions to retire
							Organizational layoffs	−			Intention to work post-retirement age
							HR age-oriented practices	+			Intention to work post-retirement age

#	Year	Author	Method	Design	Moderator	Effect	Predictor	Effect	Outcome
37	2013	Oakman & Wells	Quantitative	Cross-sectional			Job autonomy	0	Retirement intentions
							Job demands	0	Retirement intentions
							Social cohesion	+	Retirement intentions
38	2014	Padyab et al.	Quantitative	Cross-sectional			Job demands	0	Cardiovascular disease mortality
							Job strain	0	Cardiovascular disease mortality
39	2017	Palumbo et al.	Quantitative	Cross-sectional			Physical demands	+	Physical limitations
							Job complexity	–	Physical limitations
40	2016	Parkes	Quantitative	Cross-sectional	Job demand	+	Age	+	Sleep duration
					Job demand	–	Age	+	Sleep quality
41	2022	Pirzadeh et al.	Quantitative	Longitudinal (cross-lagged)			Work conditions	0	Mental health
					Age	–	Job demands	0	Mental health
					Age	–	Job complexity	0	Mental health
42	2021	Piszczek & Pimputkar	Quantitative	Longitudinal (cross-lagged)	Age	+	Work scheduling autonomy	0	Health

continued

Table 23.1 *continued*

No.	Year	Authors	Research Type	Research Design	Moderator	x	Predictor	y	Mediator	z	Outcome
					Age	−	Work scheduling autonomy	0			Sick day use
					Age	+	Work scheduling autonomy	0			Health perceptions
					Age	+	Work scheduling autonomy	0			Absenteeism
					Age	+	Work scheduling autonomy	0			Job engagement
43	2014	Qin et al.	Quantitative	Experimental	Age	+	Physical demands	+			Muscle fatigue
	2013	Reynolds et al.	Qualitative				Long commutes	+			Age-related discomfort
44	2022	Rice et al.	Quantitative	Cross-sectional	Age	+	Job autonomy	+			Job satisfaction
					Age	−	Job security	+			Job satisfaction
45	2022	Rinsky-Halivni et al.	Qualitative	Cross-sectional			Job demands	+			Productivity
							Job autonomy	+			Productivity
46	2018	Roy et al.	Qualitative	Cross-sectional			Exit norm	−			Intention to stay
							Resource shortages	+			Absenteeism

					Physical demands	−		Intention to stay
					Supervisor support	+		Job satisfaction
47	2003	Schnorpfeil et al.	Quantitative	Cross-sectional	Job demands	+		Allostatic load
48	2009	Sekine et al.	Quantitative	Cross-sectional	Job strain	−		Physical functioning
49	2022	Sousa-Ribeiro et al.	Qualitative		Supervisor support	+		Job satisfaction
					Supervisor support	+		Intention to stay
					Work schedule autonomy	+		Job engagement
50	2018	Stansfeld et al.	Quantitative	Longitudinal (cross-lagged)	Job demands	+		Permanent sickness
					Job autonomy	−		Work-exit
					Job demands	−		Work-exit

continued

Table 23.1 *continued*

No.	Year	Authors	Research Type	Research Design	Moderator	x	Predictor	y	Mediator	z	Outcome
							Work support	–			Work-exit
							Job insecurity	+			Work-exit
51	2017	Stynen et al.	Quantitative	Longitudinal (cross-lagged)			Job autonomy	–			Intention to retire early
							Social support	–			Intention to retire early
							Personal mastery	–			Intention to retire early
52	2006	Tsutsumi et al.	Quantitative	Longitudinal (time-lagged)			Job autonomy	0			Mortality
53	2020	Van der Heijden et al.	Quantitative	Longitudinal (time-lagged)			Work conditions	–			Burnout
							Task significance	+			Job satisfaction
							Age-related HR practices	+			Subjective career success
					Career commitment	0	Age-related HR practices	+			Subjective career success

54	2016	Van Droogen-broeck & Spruyt	Quantitative	Cross-sectional		Job autonomy	–		Psychological fatigue
						Job autonomy	0		Job satisfaction
						Psychological fatigue	+		Retirement intentions
						Physical demands	+		Retirement intentions
						Supervisor support	–		Psychological fatigue
						Supervisor support	+		Job satisfaction
						Task variety	–		Psychological fatigue
						Task variety	+		Job satisfaction
55	2021	Vélez-Coto et al.	Quantitative	Longitudinal (cross-lagged)		Job complexity	+		Executive functioning
						Job complexity	+		Overall cognition
						Job complexity	–		Cognitive decline post-retirement

continued

Table 23.1 *continued*

No.	Year	Authors	Research Type	Research Design	Moderator	x	Predictor	y	Mediator	z	Outcome
56	2018	Veth et al.	Quantitative	Longitudinal (cross-lagged)			Social support	+			Health
							Social support	+			Job engagement
							Social support	+			Employability
57	2021	Vigoureux et al.	Quantitative	Longitudinal (cross-lagged)			Job autonomy	−			Cognitive decline
							Job strain	+			Cognitive decline
58	2017	Viotti et al.	Quantitative	Cross-sectional			Job resources	+	Work ability	−	Emotional exhaustion
							Job demands	−	Work ability	−	Emotional exhaustion
59	2014	Virtanen et al.	Quantitative	Longitudinal (cross-lagged)			Work schedule autonomy	+			Intention to work post-retirement age
60	2021	Visser et al.	Quantitative	Cross-sectional			Phasing out agreement	0			Job satisfaction
							Job demotion	−			Job satisfaction
							Job training	+			Job satisfaction

61	2021	Wilckens et al.	Quantitative	Cross-sectional			Ergonomics	+		Intention to work post-retirement age
							Job demands-job resources fit	+		Intention to work post-retirement age
							Workplace autonomy	+		Intention to work post-retirement age
							Work schedule autonomy	+		Intention to work post-retirement age
							Work schedule autonomy	−		Intention to quit job
							Work location autonomy	−		Intention to quit job
62	2018	Yang & Matz-Costa	Quantitative	Cross-sectional	Supervisor age	−	Employee-Supervisor-Age-Fit	−		Job engagement

continued

Table 23.1 *continued*

No.	Year	Authors	Research Type	Research Design	Moderator	x	Predictor	y	Mediator	z	Outcome
63	2021	Yeung et al.	Quantitative	Cross-sectional			Perceived age discrimination	–			Job resources
							Perceived age discrimination	+			Job strain
							Perceived age discrimination	0			Job engagement
							Perceived age discrimination	0			Intention to stay
							Perceived age discrimination	+			Job demands
							Perceived age discrimination	–	Social support	+	Job engagement
							Perceived age discrimination	–	Social support	+	Intention to stay
							Perceived age discrimination	+	Emotional demand	–	Job engagement
							Perceived age discrimination	+	Emotional demand	+	Intention to stay
							Perceived age discrimination	+	Workload	–	Job engagement
							Perceived age discrimination	+	Workload	+	Intention to stay

					x		y		z	
64	2017	Zacher et al.	Quantitative	Cross-sectional	Job resources		Perceived age discrimination	0		Job engagement
					Job resources		Perceived age discrimination	+		Job strain
					Job resources		Perceived age discrimination	0		Intention to stay
							Feedback from job	+		Job attraction
					Age	–	Feedback from job	+		Job attraction
							Job autonomy	+		Job attraction
					Age	0	Job autonomy	+		Job attraction
							Task significance	+		Job attraction
					Age	–	Task significance	+		Job attraction
							Task variety	+		Job attraction
					Age	–	Task variety	+		Job attraction
					Age	–	Task variety	+		Job attraction

Note: x = interaction effect of moderator and predictor. *y* = relationship between predictor and outcome. If a mediator is included, then *y* represents the relationship between predictor and mediator. *z* = relationship between mediator and outcome. +/0/– = positive/no/negative relationship.

590 TRANSFORMATIVE WORK DESIGN

(Carstensen et al., 2003), *selection, optimization, and compensation framework* (Baltes, 1987), and *successful aging at work framework* (Kooij et al., 2020; Zacher, 2015).

Socioemotional selectivity framework

As individuals age and perceive a decline in remaining time, they are likely to shift personal resources from growth to meaning-oriented goals (Carstensen et al., 2003; see also Fassbender et al., 2019). An aging plumber who receives a cancer diagnosis may redirect resources from generating revenue toward training their apprentice. This infers that perceived remaining time may impact older workers' outcomes.

Some researchers have presented evidence that contradicts the socioemotional selectivity framework (Besen et al., 2013; Piszczek & Pimputkar, 2021). Despite the framework's suggestion that friendships at work become more important as individuals age, empirical evidence does not support this idea (Besen et al., 2013). In fact, social bonds formed outside of work become more crucial for older adults, while those formed within the workplace may become less so. The inconsistent results of these theories may be due to methodological issues, such as biased comparisons or underpowered samples.

Research suggests a connection between schedule autonomy, job attitudes, and well-being throughout the lifespan. As individuals age, having control over work scheduling becomes more important. These findings are consistent with the socioemotional selectivity framework (Carstensen et al., 2003), which proposes that greater autonomy over one's work schedule enables individuals to prioritize meaning-oriented goals and allocate their personal resources toward them.

The investigation shows that a limited range of work design characteristics were studied in the context of the socioemotional selectivity framework. To expand the research scope, future studies may explore more work design characteristics with this framework. Additionally, studies using this framework overlooked a crucial element: changes over time and differences between time periods. This omission appears to contradict the foundation of the framework as a *lifespan development* framework.

Selection, optimization, and compensation framework

Based on the selection, optimization, and compensation framework (Baltes, 1987), older workers experiencing a decline in the input–output relationship at work will establish a new equilibrium using adaptive coping strategies (Freund & Baltes, 2002; Rudolph, 2016). These strategies may include selecting goal preferences, optimizing resource usage, or shifting resources between different life domains (Fassbender et al., 2022). For example, an older logger with declining physical fitness may allocate resources from work to family. Thus, perceived disequilibrium in the input–output relationship could affect work outcomes for older workers.

The socioemotional selectivity framework has limited support in work design, but the assumptions of the selection, optimization, and compensation framework hold firm based on evidence (Beier et al., 2020; Korsakienė et al., 2017; Palumbo et al., 2017; Stynen et al., 2017; Wilckens et al., 2021). Reduced job demands, increased autonomy, social support, feedback, and job demands–job resources fit are consistently associated with positive work attitudes and improved health.

Contradictory evidence exists for the framework (Palumbo et al., 2017; Yang & Matz-Costa, 2018). For instance, the framework suggests that a better person–environment fit should lead to positive work attitudes. However, this may not be the case for leader–follower fit, where the relationship seems to be negative (Yang & Matz-Costa, 2018). These paradoxical findings do not support the framework and future research could explore whether the perceived imbalance in input–output relationship increases curvilinearly (Bohlmann et al., 2018). Perhaps "too much" equilibrium is detrimental to worker's attitudes, possibly due to inertia. This assumption could provide an explanation for the contradictory results.

Our review found that few work design characteristics were examined in this context. As a framework that considers lifespan development, we expected studies using this framework to explore various age groups and changes over time in perceived imbalances. However, we found that studies insufficiently investigated within-time changes or differences between time periods.

Successful aging at work framework

The successful aging at work framework suggests that aging-induced changes in situational interpretation can impact work outcomes (Kooij, 2015; Zacher, 2015). For example, an older worker's negative relationship between physical disability and work performance may be influenced by their appraisal of supervisor support, resulting in a weaker relationship with high perceived supervisor support. Similarly, aging may lead to increased fatigue appraisal, which could contribute to declining work outcomes. Thus, age-induced changes in situational interpretation can affect older workers' work outcomes.

Researchers found evidence supporting the efficacy of the successful aging at work framework (Jones et al., 2013; Nivalainen, 2022; Roy et al., 2018). Situational construal changes were linked to improved work attitudes and health among older workers when they felt more supported in a resource-supplying work context. However, the study designs did not adequately capture the "aging"

592 TRANSFORMATIVE WORK DESIGN

component of "changes in situational interpretation induced by agsing." This poses a challenge to interpreting the results, as it is unclear whether the changes were due to aging or other factors. A study by Ruby Brougham and David Walsh (2009) found evidence against the assumption that changes in situational construal were solely due to aging. The study found that personal goals, assumed to change over the lifespan according to Laura Carstensen and colleagues (2003), did not relate to work attitudes. Additional research is necessary to draw accurate conclusions regarding the moderating impact of aging on the relationship between situational construal, work design characteristics, and work attitudes.

Studies examining age as a moderator found limited evidence for aging's impact on the relationship between work design characteristics and work outcomes. Bridget Rice and colleagues (2022) discovered that age moderates the association between job autonomy and job satisfaction, with the relationship becoming more robust as age increases. In contrast, Carlos-Maria Alcover and Gabriela Topa (2018) did not observe such a moderation effect, presumably due to sample size (171 vs. 5,038).

Retention-pull approach (person–environment fit focus)

The retention-pull approach uses theoretical models to propose that external factors, such as work design characteristics, motivate older workers to continue working. The frameworks used include the *job demands-resources* (Bakker & Demerouti, 2007; including De Vos et al., 2020; Karasek, 1979) and *work design* (Morgeson & Humphrey, 2006; including Hackman & Oldham, 1975) frameworks.

Job demands-resources framework

The sustainability of a person's career depends on the balance between their demand for work characteristics (such as agency, meaning, and complexity) and their supply in the work environment, according to the job demands-resources framework (Bakker & Demerouti, 2007; including De Vos et al., 2020; Karasek, 1979). If the organization fails to provide these characteristics, the work outcomes may decline, affecting the sustainability of the career. For instance, a construction worker's career may be more sustainable if they perceive their job provides sufficient meaning. Therefore, the equilibrium between a worker's demand for work characteristics and their environment's supply can impact the work outcomes of older workers.

The retention-pull approach and the job demands-resources framework were compared regarding the level of support for their respective models. The models in the retention-pull approach showed a clear level of support, while the job demands-resources framework did not. A majority of effect sizes aligned with the framework (Berglund et al., 2017; Bos et al., 2013; Brown et al., 2014; de Breij et al., 2020; De Jonge et al., 2000; Elovainio et al., 2007; Frins et al., 2016; Guglielmi et al., 2016; Hayward & Hardy, 1985; Li et al., 2016; Lichtenthaler & Fischbach, 2016; Van der Heijden et al., 2022; Van Droogenbroeck & Spruyt, 2016; Veth et al., 2018; Vigoureux et al., 2021; Viotti et al., 2017; Visser et al., 2021; Yeung et al., 2021), while the rest did not (Frins et al., 2016; McGonagle et al., 2015; Nilsen et al., 2014; Oakman & Wells, 2013; Padyab et al., 2014; Pirzadeh et al., 2022; Van der Heijden et al., 2022; Van Droogenbroeck & Spruyt, 2016; Visser et al., 2021; Yeung et al., 2021).

Age is rarely studied as a moderator in the connection between work design characteristics and work outcomes for older workers. Instead, gender (Nilsen et al., 2016), commitment (Van der Heijden et al., 2022), and work design characteristics (Brown et al., 2014; Guglielmi et al., 2016; Yeung et al., 2021) are often studied as moderators. Although this was expected given the focus of the literature review, it was surprising to see that a lifespan development perspective was mostly absent from the research, despite the theoretical advancements in the aging at work literature and the sample characteristics of the studies.

Some studies (Guglielmi et al., 2016; Marquié et al., 2010; Pirzadeh et al., 2022) found that as workers age, the relationship between work design characteristics (such as job complexity; Pirzadeh et al., 2022) and work outcomes (well-being and health) becomes more significant. This supports the suggestion of combining the job demands-resources framework and lifespan development frameworks. However, when studying the connection between work design characteristics and work outcomes for older workers, the aging construct must be considered to avoid relying on age-based cutoffs and failing to consider the continuous aging process (Bohlmann et al., 2018).

Studies using the job demands-resources framework had a different theoretical focus than those using the retention-push approach. Lifespan development frameworks primarily examined predictor–outcome relationships, while job demands-resources studies emphasized mediator analyses. They aimed to identify the mechanisms underlying the connection between work design characteristics and work outcomes in older workers (Frins et al., 2016; Guglielmi et al., 2016; Viotti et al., 2017; Yeung et al., 2021).

Work design framework

The work design framework (Morgeson & Humphrey, 2006; Hackman & Oldham, 1975) suggests that work design characteristics, such as autonomy and social support, can impact worker outcomes, including well-being, health, and performance. For example, an older blacksmith may perform better if their supervisor provides greater autonomy over their schedule. Thus, the overall supply of work design characteristics can affect the work outcomes of older workers.

Comparing the work design framework with the job demands-resources framework, we found overwhelming support for the former. Evidence brought forward by researchers corroborates the work design framework (Abush & Burkhead, 1984; Axelrad et al., 2022; Boumans et al., 2011; Cavanagh et al., 2020; Choi et al., 2022; Christensen & Knardahl, 2022; Davis et al., 1995; Den Boer et al., 2021; Drabe et al., 2015; Greenwald et al., 1989; Hernaus et al., 2019; Sekine et al., 2009; Stansfeld et al., 2018; Vélez-Coto et al., 2021; Zacher et al., 2017), albeit with some exceptions (Axelrad et al., 2022; Stansfeld et al., 2018). These findings attest to the work design framework as a valid representation of the underlying mechanisms between work design characteristics and work outcomes in older workers.

Studies exploring age as a moderator (Boumans et al., 2011; Cavanagh et al., 2020; Drabe et al., 2015; Greenwald et al., 1989; Hernaus et al., 2019; Zacher et al., 2017) are more prevalent than those investigating actual work design characteristics (Parkes, 2016), despite the latter being the focus of the work design framework. The distribution of publication dates of studies on aging suggests an increasing interest in the subject in the work design literature. Some studies have found that aging moderates the relationship between work design characteristics and work outcomes among older workers (Boumans et al., 2011; Cavanagh et al., 2020; Drabe et al., 2015; Greenwald et al., 1989; Hernaus et al., 2019; Zacher et al., 2017), although there are exceptions (Drabe et al., 2015; Greenwald et al., 1989; Zacher et al., 2017). Generally, work design characteristics that are favorable, such as job autonomy (Cavanagh et al., 2020; cf., Drabe et al., 2015), become more influential in shaping work attitudes, including job satisfaction, as individuals grow older. The concept of aging is becoming increasingly established in the work design framework literature based on accumulated evidence. However, the work design literature tends to focus on direct predictor–outcome relationships, with less emphasis on mediator analyses.

Work Design Characteristics Affecting the Retention of an Aging Workforce

This section provides an overview of the observed patterns regarding the work design characteristics that impact the retention of older workers. We caution against interpreting these results as absolute truths due to high levels of heterogeneity in empirical evidence.

We found six work design characteristics that help retain older employees: job autonomy, complexity, task variety, significance, identity, work context conditions, social support, and feedback. Two overarching factors, job demands and resources, connect work design characteristics and work outcomes for older workers.

Job autonomy is the most studied factor in keeping older workers motivated and engaged. Work scheduling autonomy is particularly important when it comes to maintaining their motivation (Abush & Burkhead, 1984; Axelrad et al., 2022; Berglund et al., 2017; Cavanagh et al., 2020; Christensen & Knardahl, 2022; Den Boer et al., 2021; Elovainio et al., 2007; Greenwald et al., 1989; Korsakienė et al., 2017; Marquié et al., 2010; Piszczek & Pimputkar, 2021; Rinsky-Halivni et al., 2022; Sousa-Ribeiro et al., 2022; Stansfeld et al., 2018; Stynen et al., 2017; Van Droogenbroeck & Spruyt, 2016; Vigoureux et al., 2021; Virtanen et al., 2014; Wilckens et al., 2021; Zacher et al., 2017; cf., Nilsen et al., 2016; Oakman & Wells, 2013; Piszczek & Pimputkar, 2021; Tsutsumi et al., 2006; Van Droogenbroeck & Spruyt, 2016; Visser et al., 2021). Our findings show that giving older workers the freedom to choose how, where, and when to perform their job has a significantly positive impact on their well-being, health, and productivity. This is consistent with the socioemotional selectivity theory (Carstensen et al., 2003) and work design (Morgeson & Humphrey, 2006; Hackman & Oldham, 1975) frameworks.

The second finding suggests that job complexity can counterbalance negative job demands if the older worker has sufficient coping resources (Christensen & Knardahl, 2022; Hayward & Hardy, 1985; Hernaus et al., 2019; Palumbo et al., 2017; Vélez-Coto et al., 2021; cf., Pirzadeh et al., 2022). Job complexity was found to be beneficial for older workers and aligns with the selection, optimization, and compensation (Baltes, 1987) and job demands-resources (Bakker & Demerouti, 2007; De Vos et al., 2020; Karasek, 1979) frameworks. Therefore, assigning older workers jobs that align with their mental and social capabilities can enhance their well-being, health, and productivity.

The third finding highlights the crucial role of task characteristics in promoting the well-being and health of older workers (Abush & Burkhead, 1984; Alcover & Topa, 2018; Axelrad et al., 2022; Besen et al., 2013; Bos et al., 2013; Boumans et al., 2011; Brougham & Walsh, 2009; de Breij et al., 2020; Den Boer et al., 2021; Drabe et al., 2015; Fraser et al., 2009; Van der Heijden et al., 2020; Van Droogenbroeck & Spruyt, 2016; Zacher et al., 2017). Task characteristics significantly drive job satisfaction and the intention to continue working. The analysis aligns with the retention-pull approach models, such as the job demands-resources (Bakker & Demerouti, 2007; De Vos et al., 2020; Karasek, 1979) and work design (Morgeson & Humphrey, 2006; Hackman & Oldham, 1975) frameworks. Assigning tasks that align with older workers' values and provide a sense of fulfillment can aid in supporting and retaining them in the workplace.

The fourth observation suggests that work context impacts the job attitudes of older workers (Axelrad et al., 2022; Cavanagh et al., 2020; Drabe et al., 2015; Jones et al., 2013; Lichtenthaler & Fischbach, 2016; Nivalainen, 2022; Reynolds et al., 2013; Rice et al., 2022; Stansfeld et al., 2018; Van der Heijden et al., 2020; Wilckens et al., 2021; Yeung et al., 2021; cf., Pirzadeh et al., 2022; Van der Heijden et al., 2020; Yang & Matz-Costa, 2018). When older workers feel safe at work, they are more likely to stay in their current job. Poor working conditions, on the other hand, can negatively affect their well-being, health, and productivity. This analysis aligns with the retention-pull approach paradigms, specifically the job demands-resources framework (Bakker & Demerouti, 2007; De Vos et al., 2020; Karasek, 1979).

The fifth point suggests that social support motivates older workers (Besen et al., 2013; Christensen & Knardahl, 2022; Davis et al., 1995; Den Boer et al., 2021; Fraser et al., 2009; Roy et al., 2018; Sousa-Ribeiro et al., 2022; Stansfeld et al., 2018; Stynen et al., 2017; Van Droogenbroeck & Spruyt, 2016; Veth et al., 2018; cf., Hayslip et al., 1996). When they receive help from peers and value it, their intentions to work beyond retirement age and overall health improve. Social support is a crucial factor in promoting job satisfaction and retention among older workers, aligning with the work design framework (Morgeson & Humphrey, 2006; Hackman & Oldham, 1975).

The final point highlights the impact of feedback on the well-being and work attitudes of older workers (Abush & Burkhead, 1984; Korsakienė et al., 2017; Roy et al., 2018; Zacher et al., 2017). Receiving feedback on job performance can enhance job attitudes such as engagement and intention to stay. However, feedback on organizational exit norms from peers can decrease the intention to stay. The interpretation of the results is consistent with the successful aging at work framework (Kooij, 2015; Zacher, 2015). Therefore, we conclude that the content of feedback has a significant impact on the retention of older workers in the workplace.

On a higher level of abstraction, job demands are a barrier to retaining older workers in the workplace, but their hindrance is not solely due to job demands themselves (see Choi et al., 2022; Christensen & Knardahl, 2022; Davis et al., 1995; de Breij et al., 2020; De Jonge et al., 2000; Den Boer et al., 2021; Elovainio et al., 2007; Fraser et al., 2009; Frins et al., 2016; Greenwald et al., 1989; Hardy, 1982; Li et al., 2016; Nilsen et al., 2014, 2016; Oakman & Wells, 2013; Palumbo et al., 2017; Schnorpfeil et al., 2003; Sekine et al., 2009; Stansfeld et al., 2018; Van Droogenbroeck & Spruyt, 2016; Vigoureux et al., 2021; Viotti et al., 2017; Wilckens et al., 2021; cf., Axelrad et al., 2022; McGonagle et al., 2015; Padyab et al., 2014; Pirzadeh et al., 2022; Rinsky-Halivni et al., 2022; Stansfeld et al., 2018). Instead, their interaction with job autonomy and job resources plays a crucial role. High job demands, along with low job autonomy or low job resources, result in high job strain, which is the primary cause of the negative relationship between job demands and well-being, health, and productivity. This finding aligns with the job demands-resources framework (Bakker & Demerouti, 2007; De Vos et al., 2020; Karasek, 1979) previously reviewed.

Job resources are both a hygiene and motivating factor for older workers (see Axelrad et al., 2022; Boumans et al., 2011; Drabe et al., 2015; Frins et al., 2016; Li et al., 2016; Nivalainen, 2022; Roy et al., 2018; Viotti et al., 2017; Visser et al., 2021; cf., McGonagle et al., 2015). Sufficient job resources are required to counterbalance the perceived strain caused by job demands. Exceeding this threshold can enhance the well-being of older workers. Adequate perceived job resources can help retain older workers in the workplace, and additional job resources can increase their job satisfaction. This aligns with the retention-pull approach frameworks, specifically the job demands-resources (Bakker & Demerouti, 2007; including De Vos et al., 2020; Karasek, 1979) and work design (Morgeson & Humphrey, 2006; Hackman & Oldham, 1975) frameworks.

Discussion

The chapter aimed to provide an overview of the theoretical and practical foundations of aging in the workplace. The objective was to comprehend the work design characteristics that facilitate the retention of older workers and to identify the factors that can impede or jeopardize it. To achieve this, we conducted a systematic literature review, considering the vast number and diversity of studies on work design and aging in the workplace.

Summary of evidence

Figure 23.2 summarizes our findings. We identified two meta-theoretical perspectives that have influenced theories in this area: the retention-push and retention-pull approaches. Some researchers adopted the retention-push approach, testing theoretical frameworks proposing that changes within an individual stimulate an older worker to either continue working or leave the workforce. The theoretical models used in this approach are founded on the socioemotional selectivity (Carstensen et al., 2003), the selection, optimization, and compensation (Baltes, 1987), and the successful aging at work (Kooij et al., 2020; Zacher, 2015) frameworks. Other researchers adopted a retention-pull approach, assessing theoretical frameworks that suggest work design features

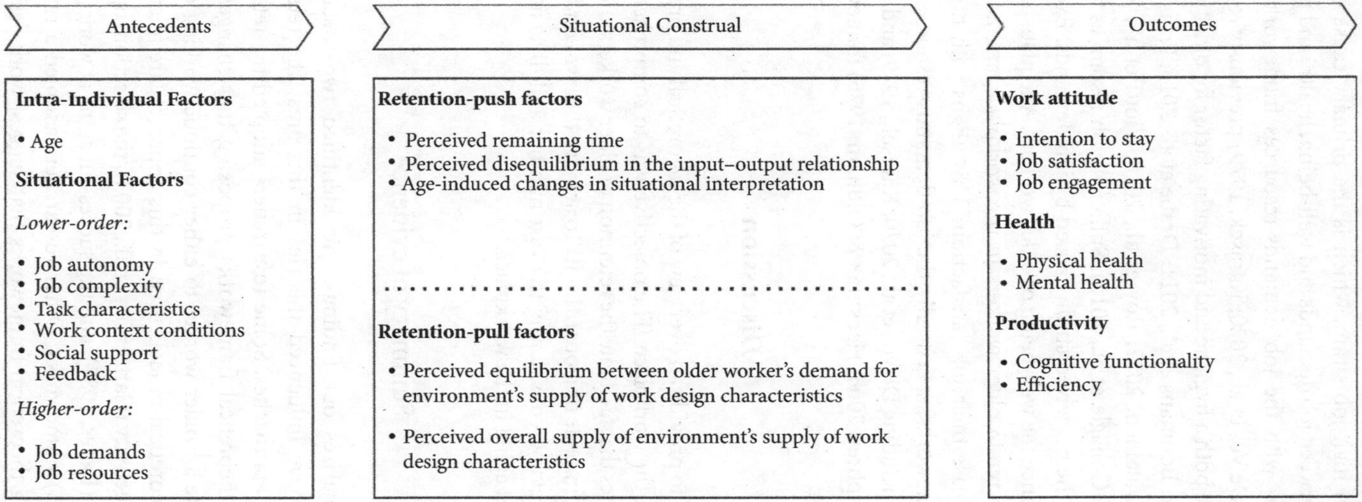

Antecedents	Situational Construal	Outcomes

Intra-Individual Factors

- Age

Situational Factors

Lower-order:

- Job autonomy
- Job complexity
- Task characteristics
- Work context conditions
- Social support
- Feedback

Higher-order:

- Job demands
- Job resources

Retention-push factors

- Perceived remaining time
- Perceived disequilibrium in the input–output relationship
- Age-induced changes in situational interpretation

. . . .

Retention-pull factors

- Perceived equilibrium between older worker's demand for environment's supply of work design characteristics

- Perceived overall supply of environment's supply of work design characteristics

Work attitude

- Intention to stay
- Job satisfaction
- Job engagement

Health

- Physical health
- Mental health

Productivity

- Cognitive functionality
- Efficiency

Figure 23.2 Results of Systematic Literature Review: Retention of Older Workers Framework

encourage older workers to remain in the workforce. The theoretical frameworks used in this approach comprise the job demands-resources (Bakker & Demerouti, 2007; De Vos et al., 2020; Karasek, 1979) and work design (Morgeson & Humphrey, 2006; Hackman & Oldham, 1975) frameworks.

Support for the frameworks varied when confronted with empirical evidence. The socioemotional selectivity framework was mostly unsupported regarding the retention of older workers. The selection, optimization, and compensation framework, the successful aging at work framework, and the work design framework were mostly backed by evidence. Support for the job demands-resources framework was inconsistent. Studies using a retention-push approach only examined a limited set of work design features related to work outcomes in older workers. In contrast, retention-pull studies evaluated a wider range of work design characteristics.

Researchers rarely investigated aging. When aging was incorporated into their model testing, certain work design characteristics, such as job autonomy, became more significant in enhancing work outcomes as individuals aged. However, these findings are only minimally reproducible.

Limited variability in relationships was found. Most studies tested predictor-outcome relationships, with few exceptions. Job demands-resources framework studies were exceptions, as mediator analyses played a crucial role.

We summarized the work design features that can facilitate, impede, or damage the retention of older workers. Six such characteristics were identified: job autonomy, job complexity, task characteristics, work context conditions, social support, and feedback. The interplay between job demands and job resources appears to have a significant impact on the retention of older workers.

Theoretical Implications

The findings suggest that the selection, optimization, and compensation, successful aging at work, and work design frameworks are reliable for examining the relationship between work design characteristics and work outcomes among older workers. The socioemotional selectivity framework appears less dependable for retaining older workers, while the job demands-resources yielded inconsistent results. The varying validity among different theoretical frameworks implies that future researchers should prioritize using the reliable frameworks for a better understanding of effective work design characteristics for retaining older workers in the workforce.

Assumptions about the impact of work design on older workers' outcomes, attributed to age-related changes, lack reliable evidence from previous studies.

600 TRANSFORMATIVE WORK DESIGN

Although many theoretical frameworks account for lifespan development, particularly the retention-push approach, this aspect is rarely tested, raising questions about its validity. Our research supports the theoretical differences between younger and older employees regarding work design and outcomes, as seen in various frameworks (e.g., Kooij, 2015; Zacher, 2015). However, testing assumptions of within-person change requires additional research.

Practical Implications

Our study suggests that certain work design characteristics can support and retain older workers. Providing autonomy over work arrangements, aligning skills with job demands, offering resources for professional development, ensuring safe work conditions with social support opportunities, and providing regular job performance feedback, while discouraging traditional exit norms, motivate older workers to continue contributing. By implementing these practices, practitioners can encourage older workers to generate value, resulting in sustainable outcomes.

Future Research Directions

Our systematic literature review revealed that many studies lack a sufficient investigation of the aging process, possibly due to the difficulty in recruiting working individuals for longitudinal studies. Targeting populations that are easier to access and retain may help to address this issue. If within-person designs are not possible, recruiting a relatively sizable group of "younger" and "older" individuals can help to investigate between-person differences. Scholars may also use existing data sets, such as the European Working Conditions Survey (EWCS) or the Survey of Health, Aging and Retirement in Europe (SHARE). Apart from methodological recommendations, it is relevant to note that age is just a proxy for age-related processes (e.g., physical, cognitive, and socioemotional changes) that require our attention to better understand how an aging workforce can be retained through work design.

In this regard, we found that most studies focused on examining predictor–outcome relationships, with only a few exceptions. Studies within the job demands-resources framework stood out as they also incorporated mediator analyses. We thus recommend testing for potential mediators between work design characteristics and work outcomes among older workers. Specifically, scholars may draw on the careers and lifespan development literature (for an overview see Zacher & Froidevaux, 2021) to gain insights on the potential mechanisms that link work design characteristics to retaining older workers.

Furthermore, future research could examine the cognitive and affective mechanisms that, in synergy with work design characteristics, promote older workers' health, and productivity. Previous research has mainly focused on the motivational and behavioral components that synergize with work design or are affected by it. Because cognition and affect are the primary facilitators of these components (Lazarus, 1991), future research may concentrate more on the cognitive-affective mechanisms that impact the retainment of older workers in the workforce, and the quality of their time during this prolonged work period.

Finally, based on our review, we found that most studies have focused on a limited range of work design characteristics. For instance, future studies could investigate the impact of the work design characteristic of specialization, which is presumed to become more important and stable with age (see selection, optimization, and compensation framework; Baltes, 1987), on the retention and work life quality of older workers. Therefore, to widen the scope of research, future studies may consider applying the reviewed frameworks to a broader range of work design characteristics, and also examine their dynamic interplay.

Conclusion

Due to global population aging, it is important to retain older workers in the workforce. This chapter provides insights into how work can be designed to benefit older workers' health, productivity, and work attitudes. Integrating frameworks from the aging and work design literature, this chapter presents a systematic literature review. The findings are organized along a retention-push and retention-pull approach, paving the way for future research.

References

Abush, R., & Burkhead, E. J. (1984). Job stress in midlife working women: Relationships among personality type, job characteristics, and job tension. *Journal of Counseling Psychology 31*(1), 36–44. https://doi.org/10.1037/0022-0167.31.1.36

Alcover, C. M., & Topa, G. (2018). Work characteristics, motivational orientations, psychological work ability and job mobility intentions of older workers. *PLoS ONE 13*(4). https://doi.org/10.1371/JOURNAL.PONE.0195973

Axelrad, H., Yirmiyahu, A., Axelrad, H., & Yirmiyahu, A. (2022). Who wants to work and why? Workplace practices, job satisfaction and the will to work. *National Accounting Review 4* (3), 287–309. https://doi.org/10.3934/NAR.2022017

Bakker, A. B., & Demerouti, E. (2007). The Job Demands-Resources model: State of the art. *Journal of Managerial Psychology 22*(3), 309–328. https://doi.org/10.1108/02683940710733115

Baltes, P. B. (1987). Theoretical propositions of life-span developmental psychology: On the dynamics between growth and decline. *Developmental Psychology 23*(5), 611–626. https://doi.org/10.1037/0012-1649.23.5.611

Beehr, T. A., & Bennett, M. M. (2015). Working after retirement: Features of bridge employment and research directions. *Work, Aging and Retirement 1*(1), 112–128. https://doi.org/10.1093/WORKAR/WAU007

Beier, M. E., Torres, W. J., Fisher, G. G., & Wallace, L. E. (2020). Age and job fit: The relationship between demands-ability fit and retirement and health. *Journal of Occupational Health Psychology 25*(4), 227–243. https://doi.org/10.1037/OCP0000164

Bennett, A. I., Hanley, J., Buckle, P., & Bridger, R. S. (2011). Work demands during firefighting training: does age matter? *Ergonomics 54*(6), 555–564. https://doi.org/10.1080/00140139.2011.582540

Berglund, T., Seldén, D., & Halleröd, B. (2017). Factors affecting prolonged working life for the older workforce: The Swedish case. *Nordic Journal of Working Life Studies 7*(1), 19–36. https://doi.org/10.18291/NJWLS.V7I1.81396

Besen, E., Matz-Costa, C., Brown, M., Smyer, M., & Pitt-Catsouphes, M. (2013). Job characteristics, core self-evaluations, and job satisfaction: What's age got to do with it? *International Journal of Aging and Human Development 76*(4), 269–295. https://doi.org/10.2190/AG.76.4.A

Bohlmann, C., Rudolph, C. W., & Zacher, H. (2018). Methodological recommendations to move research on work and aging forward. *Work, Aging and Retirement 4*(3), 225–237. https://doi.org/10.1093/WORKAR/WAX023

Bos, J. T., Donders, N. C. G. M., Schouteten, R. L. J., & van der Gulden, J. W. J. (2013). Age as a moderator in the relationship between work-related characteristics, job dissatisfaction and need for recovery. *Ergonomics 56*(6), 992–1005. https://doi.org/10.1080/00140139.2013.789553

Boumans, N. P. G., De Jong, A. H. J., & Janssen, S. M. (2011). Age-differences in work motivation and job satisfaction. the influence of age on the relationships between work characteristics and workers' outcomes. *International Journal of Aging and Human Development 73*(4), 331–350. https://doi.org/10.2190/AG.73.4.D

Brougham, R., & Walsh, D. (2009). Early and late retirement exits. *International Journal of Aging and Human Development 69*(4), 267–286. https://doi.org/10.2190/AG.69.4.B

Brown, M., Pitt-Catsouphes, M., McNamara, T. K., & Besen, E. (2014). Returning to the workforce after retiring: A job demands, job control, social support perspective on job satisfaction. *International Journal of Human Resource Management 25*(22), 3113–3133. https://doi.org/10.1080/09585192.2014.919951

Carstensen, L. L., Fung, H. H., & Charles, S. T. (2003). Socioemotional selectivity theory and the regulation of emotion in the second half of life. *Motivation and Emotion 27*(2), 103–123. https://doi.org/10.1023/A:1024569803230/METRICS

Cavanagh, T. M., Kraiger, K., & L. Henry, K. (2020). Age-related changes on the effects of job characteristics on job satisfaction: A longitudinal analysis. *International Journal of Aging and Human Development 91*(1), 60–84. https://doi.org/10.1177/0091415019837996

Choi, E., Kim, S. G., Zahodne, L. B., & Albert, S. M. (2022). Older workers with physically demanding jobs and their cognitive functioning. *Ageing International 47*(1), 55–71. https://doi.org/10.1007/S12126-020-09404-8

Christensen, J. O., & Knardahl, S. (2022). "I'm too old for this!": A prospective, multilevel study of job characteristics, age, and turnover intention. *Frontiers in Psychology 13*, 1015313. https://doi.org/10.3389/FPSYG.2022.1015313

Davis, M. C., Matthews, K. A., Meilahn, E. N., & Kiss, J. E. (1995). Are job characteristics related to fibrinogen levels in middle-aged women? *Health Psychology 14*(4), 310–318. https://doi.org/10.1037/0278-6133.14.4.310

de Breij, S., Huisman, M., & Deeg, D. J. H. (2020). Work characteristics and health in older workers: Educational inequalities. *PLoS ONE 15*(10), e0241051. https://doi.org/10.1371/JOURNAL.PONE.0241051

De Jonge, J., Bosma, H., Peter, R., & Siegrist, J. (2000). Job strain, effort-reward imbalance and employee well-being: A large- scale cross-sectional study. *Social Science and Medicine 50*(9), 1317–1327. https://doi.org/10.1016/S0277-9536(99)00388-3

De Vos, A., Van der Heijden, B. I. J. M., & Akkermans, J. (2020). Sustainable careers: Towards a conceptual model. *Journal of Vocational Behavior 117*, 103196. https://doi.org/10.1016/J.JVB.2018.06.011

Den Boer, H., van Vuuren, T., & de Jong, J. (2021). Job design to extend working time: Work characteristics to enable sustainable employment of older employees in different job types. *Sustainability (Switzerland) 13*(9), 4719. https://doi.org/10.3390/SU13094719

Drabe, D., Hauff, S., & Richter, N. F. (2015). Job satisfaction in aging workforces: An analysis of the USA, Japan and Germany. *International Journal of Human Resource Management 26*(6), 783–805. https://doi.org/10.1080/09585192.2014.939101

Elovainio, M., Forma, P., Kivimäki, M., Sinervo, T., Sutinen, R., & Laine, M. (2007). Job demands and job control as correlates of early retirement thoughts in Finnish social and health care employees. *Work & Stress 19*(1), 84–92. https://doi.org/10.1080/02678370500084623

Fassbender, U., Deller, J., Wang, M., & Wiernik, B. M. (2014). Deciding whether to work after retirement: The role of the psychological experience of aging. *Journal of Vocational Behavior 84*(3), 215–224. https://doi.org/https://doi.org/10.1016/j.jvb.2014.01.006

Fassbender, U., Vignoli, M., & Topa, G. (2022). Understanding how aging experiences shape late career development. *Career Development Quarterly 70*(3), 174–189. https://doi.org/https://doi.org/10.1002/cdq.12301

Fassbender, U., Wang, M., Voltmer, J.-B., & Deller, J. (2016). The meaning of work for post-retirement employment decisions. *Work, Aging and Retirement 2*(1), 12–23. https://doi.org/10.1093/workar/wav015

Fassbender, U., Wöhrmann, A. M., Wang, M., & Klehe, U. C. (2019). Is the future still open? The mediating role of occupational future time perspective in the effects of career adaptability and aging experience on late career planning. *Journal of Vocational Behavior 111*, 24–38. https://doi.org/10.1016/J.JVB.2018.10.006

Fraser, L., McKenna, K., Turpin, M., Allen, S., & Liddle, J. (2009). Older workers: An exploration of the benefits, barriers and adaptations for older people in the workforce. *Work 33*(3), 261–272. https://doi.org/10.3233/WOR-2009-0874

Freund, A., & Baltes, P. (2002). Life-management strategies of selection, optimization and compensation: Measurement by self-report and construct validity. *Journal of*

Personality and Social Psychology 82, 642–662. https://doi.org/10.1037//0022-3514. 82.4.642

Frins, W., van Ruysseveldt, J., van Dam, K., & van den Bossche, S. N. J. (2016). Older employees' desired retirement age: A JD-R perspective. *Journal of Managerial Psychology 31*(1), 34–49. https://doi.org/10.1108/JMP-05-2013-0133/FULL/PDF

Greenwald, H. P., Dirks, S. J., Borgatta, E. F., McCorkle, R., Nevitt, M. C., & Yelin, E. H. (1989). Work disability among cancer patients. *Social Science and Medicine 29*(11), 1253–1259. https://doi.org/10.1016/0277-9536(89)90065-8

Guglielmi, D., Avanzi, L., Chiesa, R., Mariani, M. G., Bruni, I., & Depolo, M. (2016). Positive aging in demanding workplaces: The gain cycle between job satisfaction and work engagement. *Frontiers in Psychology 7*, 1224. https://doi.org/10.3389/FPSYG. 2016.01224

Hackman, J. R., & Oldham, G. R. (1975). Development of the job diagnostic survey. *Journal of Applied Psychology 60*(2), 159–170. https://doi.org/10.1037/H0076546

Hardy, M. A. (1982). Job characteristics and health: Differential impact on benefit entitlement. *Research on Aging 4*(4), 457–478. https://doi.org/10.1177/ 0164027582004004003

Harris, A., Davenport, M. K., & Fassbender, U. (2024). Exploring the role of uncertainty regulation strategies to demystify the link between person–environment misfit and late-career outcomes. *Work, Aging and Retirement.* https://doi.org/10.1093/workar/ waae008

Hayslip, B., Miller, C., Beyerlein, M. M., Johnson, D., Metheny, W., & Yeatts, D. (1996). Employee age and perceptions of work in self-managing and traditional work groups. *International Journal of Aging and Human Development 42*(4), 291–312. https://doi. org/10.2190/XB1F-DRV4-878U-PTCW

Hayward, M. D., & Hardy, M. A. (1985). Early retirement processes among older men: Occupational differences. *Research on Aging 7*(4), 491–515. https://doi.org/10.1177/ 0164027585007004001

Hernaus, T., Maric, M., & Černe, M. (2019). Age-sensitive job design antecedents of innovative work behavior: The role of cognitive job demands. *Journal of Managerial Psychology 34*(5), 368–382. https://doi.org/10.1108/JMP-10-2018-0478/FULL/PDF

Jones, M. K., Latreille, P. L., Sloane, P. J., & Staneva, A. V. (2013). Work-related health risks in Europe: Are older workers more vulnerable? *Social Science & Medicine 88*, 18–29. https://doi.org/10.1016/J.SOCSCIMED.2013.03.027

Karasek, R. A. (1979). Job demands, job decision latitude, and mental strain: Implications for job redesign. *Administrative Science Quarterly 24*(2), 285. https://doi.org/10.2307/ 2392498

Kooij, D. (2015). Successful aging at work: The active role of employees. *Work, Aging and Retirement 1*(4), 309–319. https://doi.org/10.1093/WORKAR/WAV018

Kooij, D., Zacher, H., Wang, M., & Heckhausen, J. (2020). Successful aging at work: A process model to guide future research and practice. *Industrial and Organizational Psychology 13*(3), 345–365. https://doi.org/10.1017/IOP.2020.1

Korsakienė, R., Raišienė, A. G., & Bužavaitė, M. (2017). Work engagement of older employees: Do employee and work-related factors matter? *Economics and Sociology 10*(4), 151–161. https://doi.org/10.14254/2071-789X.2017/10-4/12

Lazarus, R. S. (1991). *Emotion and Adaptation.* Oxford University Press.

Li, H., Liu, Z., Liu, R., Li, L., & Lin, A. (2016). The relationship between work stress and work ability among power supply workers in Guangdong, China: A cross-sectional study. *BMC Public Health 16*(1). https://doi.org/10.1186/S12889-016-2800-Z

Lichtenthaler, P. W., & Fischbach, A. (2016). Job crafting and motivation to continue working beyond retirement age. *Career Development International 21*(5), 477–497. https://doi.org/10.1108/CDI-01-2016-0009/FULL/PDF

Marquié, J. C., Foret, J., & Quéinnec, Y. (2010). Effects of age, working hours, and job content on sleep: A pilot study. *Experimental Aging Research 25*(4), 421–427. https://doi.org/10.1080/036107399243896

McCarthy, J., Heraty, N., Cross, C., & Cleveland, J. N. (2014). Who is considered an "older worker"? Extending our conceptualisation of "older" from an organisational decision maker perspective. *Human Resource Management Journal 24*(4), 374–393. https://doi.org/10.1111/1748-8583.12041

McGonagle, A. K., Fisher, G. G., Barnes-Farrell, J. L., & Grosch, J. W. (2015). Individual and work factors related to perceived work ability and labor force outcomes. *Journal of Applied Psychology 100*(2), 376–398. https://doi.org/10.1037/A0037974

Morgeson, F. P., & Humphrey, S. E. (2006). The Work Design Questionnaire (WDQ): Developing and validating a comprehensive measure for assessing job design and the nature of work. *Journal of Applied Psychology 91*(6), 1321–1339. https://doi.org/10.1037/0021-9010.91.6.1321

Nilsen, C., Agahi, N., & Kåreholt, I. (2016). Work stressors in late midlife and physical functioning in old age. *Journal of Aging and Health 29*(5), 893–911. https://doi.org/10.1177/0898264316654673

Nilsen, C., Andel, R., Fors, S., Meinow, B., Darin Mattsson, A., & Kåreholt, I. (2014). Associations between work-related stress in late midlife, educational attainment, and serious health problems in old age: A longitudinal study with over 20 years of follow-up. *BMC Public Health 14*(1), 1–12. https://doi.org/10.1186/1471-2458-14-878/TABLES/4

Nivalainen, S. (2022). From plans to action? Retirement thoughts, intentions and actual retirement: An eight-year follow-up in Finland. *Ageing and Society 42*(1), 112–142. https://doi.org/10.1017/S0144686X20000756

Oakman, J., & Wells, Y. (2013). Retirement intentions: What is the role of push factors in predicting retirement intentions? *Ageing and Society 33*(6), 988–1008. https://doi.org/10.1017/S0144686X12000281

Padyab, M., Blomstedt, Y., & Norberg, M. (2014). No association found between cardiovascular mortality, and job demands and decision latitude: Experience from the Västerbotten Intervention Programme in Sweden. *Social Science and Medicine 117*, 58–66. https://doi.org/10.1016/J.SOCSCIMED.2014.07.033

Palumbo, A. J., Anneclaire, J., Cannuscio, C., Robinson, L., Mossey, J., Weitlauf, J., Garcia, L., Wallace, R., & Michael, Y. (2017). Work characteristics associated with physical functioning in women. *International Journal of Environmental Research and Public Health 14*(4), 424. https://doi.org/10.3390/IJERPH14040424

Parkes, K. R. (2016). Age and work environment characteristics in relation to sleep: Additive, interactive and curvilinear effects. *Applied Ergonomics 54*, 41–50. https://doi.org/10.1016/J.APERGO.2015.11.009

Pirzadeh, P., Lingard, H., & Zhang, R. P. (2022). Job quality and construction workers' mental health: Life course perspective. *Journal of Construction Engineering and Management 148*(12), 04022132. https://doi.org/10.1061/(ASCE)CO.1943-7862.0002397

Piszczek, M. M., & Pimputkar, A. S. (2021). Flexible schedules across working lives: Age-specific effects on well-being and work. *Journal of Applied Psychology 106*(12), 1907–1920. https://doi.org/10.1037/APL0000844

Qin, J., Lin, J. H., Buchholz, B., & Xu, X. (2014). Shoulder muscle fatigue development in young and older female adults during a repetitive manual task. *Ergonomics 57*(8), 1201–1212. https://doi.org/10.1080/00140139.2014.914576

Reynolds, F., Farrow, A., & Blank, A. (2013). Working beyond 65: A qualitative study of perceived hazards and discomforts at work. *Work 46*(3), 313–323. https://doi.org/10.3233/WOR-121547

Rice, B., Martin, N., Fieger, P., & Hussain, T. (2022). Older healthcare workers' satisfaction: Managing the interaction of age, job security expectations and autonomy. *Employee Relations 44*(2), 319–334. https://doi.org/10.1108/ER-07-2020-0346

Rinsky-Halivni, L., Hovav, B., Christiani, D. C., & Brammli-Greenberg, S. (2022). Aging workforce with reduced work capacity: From organizational challenges to successful accommodations sustaining productivity and well-being. *Social Science and Medicine 312*, 115369. https://doi.org/10.1016/J.SOCSCIMED.2022.115369

Roy, D., Weyman, A., George, A., & Hudson-Sharp, N. (2018). A qualitative study into the prospect of working longer for physiotherapists in the United Kingdom's National Health Service. *Ageing and Society 38*(8), 1693–1714. https://doi.org/10.1017/S0144686X17000253

Rudolph, C. W. (2016). Lifespan developmental perspectives on working: A literature review of motivational theories. *Work, Aging and Retirement 2*(2), 130–158. https://doi.org/10.1093/WORKAR/WAW012

Schnorpfeil, P., Noll, A., Schulze, R., Ehlert, U., Frey, K., & Fischer, J. E. (2003). Allostatic load and work conditions. *Social Science & Medicine 57*(4), 647–656. https://doi.org/10.1016/S0277-9536(02)00407-0

Sekine, M., Chandola, T., Martikainen, P., Marmot, M., & Kagamimori, S. (2009). Socioeconomic inequalities in physical and mental functioning of British, Finnish, and Japanese civil servants: Role of job demand, control, and work hours. *Social Science and Medicine 69*(10), 1417–1425. https://doi.org/10.1016/J.SOCSCIMED.2009.08.022

Sousa-Ribeiro, M., Lindfors, P., & Knudsen, K. (2022). Sustainable working life in intensive care: A qualitative study of older nurses. *International Journal of Environmental Research and Public Health 19*(10), 6130. https://doi.org/10.3390/IJERPH19106130

Stansfeld, S. A., Carr, E., Smuk, M., Clark, C., Murray, E., Shelton, N., & Head, J. (2018). Mid-life psychosocial work environment as a predictor of work exit by age 50. *PLoS ONE 13*(4), e0195495. https://doi.org/10.1371/JOURNAL.PONE.0195495

Stynen, D., Jansen, N. W. H., & Kant, J. (2017). The impact of work-related and personal resources on older workers' fatigue, work enjoyment and retirement intentions over time. *Ergonomics 60*(12), 1692–1707. https://doi.org/10.1080/00140139.2017.1334094

Truxillo, D. M., Cadiz, D. M., & Hammer, L. B. (2015). Supporting the aging workforce: A review and recommendations for workplace intervention research. *Annual Review of Organizational Psychology and Organizational Behavior 2*, 351–381. https://doi.org/10.1146/ANNUREV-ORGPSYCH-032414-111435

Truxillo, D. M., Cadiz, D. M., Rineer, J. R., Zaniboni, S., & Fraccaroli, F. (2012). A lifespan perspective on job design: Fitting the job and the worker to promote job satisfaction, engagement, and performance. *Organizational Psychology Review 2*(4), 340–360. https://doi.org/10.1177/2041386612454043/ASSET/IMAGES/LARGE/10.1177_2041386612454043-FIG1.JPEG

Tsutsumi, A., Kayaba, K., Hirokawa, K., & Ishikawa, S. (2006). Psychosocial job characteristics and risk of mortality in a Japanese community-based working population: The Jichi Medical School Cohort Study. *Social Science and Medicine 63*(5), 1276–1288. https://doi.org/10.1016/J.SOCSCIMED.2006.03.028

Age Discrimination in Employment Act 29 U.S.C. §§ 621–634. (1967). https://uscode.house.gov/view.xhtml?req=granuleid:USC-prelim-title29-section621&num=0&edition=prelim

Van der Heijden, B. I. J. M., Houkes, I., Van den Broeck, A., & Czabanowska, K. (2020). "I just can't take it anymore": How specific work characteristics impact younger versus older nurses' health, satisfaction, and commitment. *Frontiers in Psychology, 11*, 762. https://doi.org/10.3389/FPSYG.2020.00762

Van der Heijden, B. I. J. M., Veld, M., & Heres, L. (2022). Does age matter? Examining career commitment as a moderator in the relationship between age-related HR/D practices and subjective career success for younger versus older academic staff. *Human Resource Development Quarterly 33*(4), 405–425. https://doi.org/10.1002/HRDQ.21463

Van Droogenbroeck, F., & Spruyt, B. (2016). I ain't gonna make it. Comparing job demands-resources and attrition intention between senior teachers and senior employees of six other occupational categories in Flanders. *International Journal of Aging and Human Development 83*(2), 128–155. https://doi.org/10.1177/0091415016647729

Vélez-Coto, M., Andel, R., Pérez-García, M., & Caracuel, A. (2021). Complexity of work with people: Associations with cognitive functioning and change after retirement. *Psychology and Aging 36*(2), 143–157. https://doi.org/10.1037/PAG0000584

Veth, K. N., Van der Heijden, B. I. J. M., Korzilius, H. P. L. M., De Lange, A. H., & Emans, B. J. M. (2018). Bridge over an aging population: Examining longitudinal relations among human resource management, social support, and employee outcomes among bridge workers. *Frontiers in Psychology 9*, 574. https://doi.org/10.3389/FPSYG.2018.00574

Vigoureux, T. F. D., Nelson, M. E., Andel, R., Small, B. J., Dávila-Roman, A. L., & Crowe, M. (2021). Job strain and late-life cognition: Findings from the Puerto Rican Elderly Health Conditions Study. *Journal of Aging and Health 33*(3–4), 273–284. https://doi.org/10.1177/0898264320977329

Viotti, S., Guidetti, G., Loera, B., Martini, M., Sottimano, I., & Converso, D. (2017). Stress, work ability, and an aging workforce: A study among women aged 50 and over. *International Journal of Stress Management 24*, 98–121. https://doi.org/10.1037/STR0000031

Virtanen, M., Oksanen, T., Batty, G. D., Ala-Mursula, L., Salo, P., Elovainio, M., Pentti, J., Lybäck, K., Vahtera, J., & Kivimäki, M. (2014). Extending employment beyond the pensionable age: A cohort study of the influence of chronic diseases, health risk factors, and working conditions. *PLoS ONE, 9*(2). https://doi.org/10.1371/JOURNAL.PONE.0088695

Visser, M., Lössbroek, J., & Van Der Lippe, T. (2021). The use of HR policies and job satisfaction of older workers. *Work, Aging and Retirement 7*(4), 303–321. https://doi.org/10.1093/WORKAR/WAAA023

Wilckens, M. R., Wöhrmann, A. M., Deller, J., & Wang, M. (2021). Organizational practices for the aging workforce: Development and validation of the later life workplace index. *Work, Aging and Retirement* 7(4), 352–386. https://doi.org/10.1093/WORKAR/WAAA012

Yang, J., & Matz-Costa, C. (2018). Age diversity in the workplace: The effect of relational age within supervisor–employee dyads on employees' work engagement. *International Journal of Aging and Human Development* 87(2), 156–183. https://doi.org/10.1177/0091415017709798

Yeung, D. Y., Zhou, X., & Chong, S. (2021). Perceived age discrimination in the workplace: The mediating roles of job resources and demands. *Journal of Managerial Psychology* 36(6), 505–519. https://doi.org/10.1108/JMP-04-2020-0185/FULL/PDF

Zacher, H. (2015). Successful aging at work. *Work, Aging and Retirement* 1(1), 4–25. https://doi.org/10.1093/WORKAR/WAU006

Zacher, H., Dirkers, B. T., Korek, S., & Hughes, B. (2017). Age-differential effects of job characteristics on job attraction: A policy-capturing study. *Frontiers in Psychology* 8, 1124. https://doi.org/10.3389/FPSYG.2017.01124

Zacher, H., & Froidevaux, A. (2021). Life stage, lifespan, and life course perspectives on vocational behavior and development: A theoretical framework, review, and research agenda. *Journal of Vocational Behavior 126*, 103476. https://doi.org/10.1016/J.JVB.2020.103476

Zacher, H., & Schmitt, A. (2016). Work characteristics and occupational well-being: The role of age. *Frontiers in Psychology 7*, 1411. https://doi.org/10.3389/FPSYG.2016.01411/BIBTEX

Text Analysis Using Artificial Intelligence as a Tool for Job Analysis and Job Design

Emily D. Campion and Michael A. Campion

Organizational scientists are finding many uses of artificial intelligence (AI) in human resource management and organizational behavior. Applications range from facilitating basic research, such as discovering and measuring constructs, to developing tools, such as selection procedures, training programs, and decision aides. Research reviewed in this chapter will show that AI can be promising in the improvement of measurement and prediction. One meaningful way in which this can occur is through the use of text data, which is an underused source of information relevant to many human resource (HR) functions. The purpose of this chapter is to discuss the emerging trend of using text analysis enabled by AI for job analysis and job design purposes. The potential benefits including analyzing new data (text) and doing so more objectively than historical qualitative methods of text analysis to identify new constructs, measure them more precisely, save researcher time and effort, and often not require any additional data collection.

Text analysis using AI refers broadly to a family of machine learning techniques for identifying and measuring topics, themes, or other dimensions of interest in a corpus of text (Campion & Campion, 2020; Kobayashi et al., 2018). Predominant among the techniques is natural language processing (NLP). Sometimes referred to as computational linguistics, NLP involves extracting the meaningfulness of narrative information by analyzing words and relationships among words. Probably the most straightforward technique is using dictionaries developed rationally or empirically to count the frequencies of words that reflect a construct (most popularized by the dictionaries developed by Pennebaker et al., 2001). More advanced techniques identify and measure phrases and combinations of words using more sophisticated machine learning algorithms to be described. Both approaches are promising for job analysis and job design.

Job analysis refers to a systematic research process for collecting information on what workers do (job duties and tasks) and the job requirements to do the work (knowledge, skills, abilities, and other characteristics [KSAOs])

Emily D. Campion and Michael A. Campion, *Text Analysis Using Artificial Intelligence as a Tool for Job Analysis and Job Design*. In: *Transformative Work Design*. Edited by: Sharon K. Parker et al., Oxford University Press. © Society for Industrial and Organizational Psychology (2025). DOI: 10.1093/oso/9780197692554.003.0024

610   TRANSFORMATIVE WORK DESIGN

(Morgeson et al., 2019). The purpose of gathering this information is to develop HR procedures, processes, and programs that are job related, such as hiring procedures, compensation plans, training programs, appraisal procedures, promotion criteria, and so on. This not only ensures they are relevant and accurate, but this is the primary defense against discrimination claims in some countries (e.g., the United States). A well-done job analysis is a multi-stage process that requires engagement from a number of informants including incumbents, supervisors, and HR professionals. It usually includes reviewing existing information on the jobs, and then conducting observations, interviews, and focus groups to identify the tasks and KSAOs, and finally using questionnaires to collect ratings (for an example of one of the first popularized job analysis surveys, see McCormick et al., 1972). Job analysis typically results in extensive lists of tasks and KSAOs and data on their importance and other quantitative descriptors, which is then used to develop many HR procedures (e.g., job descriptions, selection assessments, training materials, performance appraisals). Most organizations have a significant amount of job analysis information on their unique jobs, and open-source archives contain job analysis data collected on the full range of occupations in the labor market, such as the Occupational Information Network (O*NET) developed by the US Department of Labor (Peterson et al., 2001; https://www.onetonline.org/) and the European Skills, Competences, Qualifications and Occupations (ESCO), developed by the European Commission (https://esco.ec.europa.eu/en/about-esco/what-esco).

Conducting job analyses is labor intensive, involving the collection of textual data (e.g., existing job information, interview transcripts, answers to open-ended survey questions, written notes, and observations) and the analysis and synthesis of both quantitative and qualitative information from various sources. As such, there are many opportunities throughout the process to leverage AI to improve the methodological efficiency of job analysis. Some of these are noted in Figure 24.1. In the following section, we review these opportunities and present example studies illustrating these uses.

Opportunities for Artificial Intelligence in Job Analyses

There are at least five steps to conducting a typical job analysis (see Figure 24.1): (1) reviewing existing information (e.g., existing job descriptions, appraisal forms, training materials, etc.), (2) identifying subject matter experts (SMEs), (3) collecting new job information, (4) analyzing the data, and (5) creating products (e.g., updated job description, hiring assessments, training materials, compensable factors, etc.). Steps 1 and 2 include processes prior to data collection and analyses but will be relevant in data analysis. In Step 3, HR

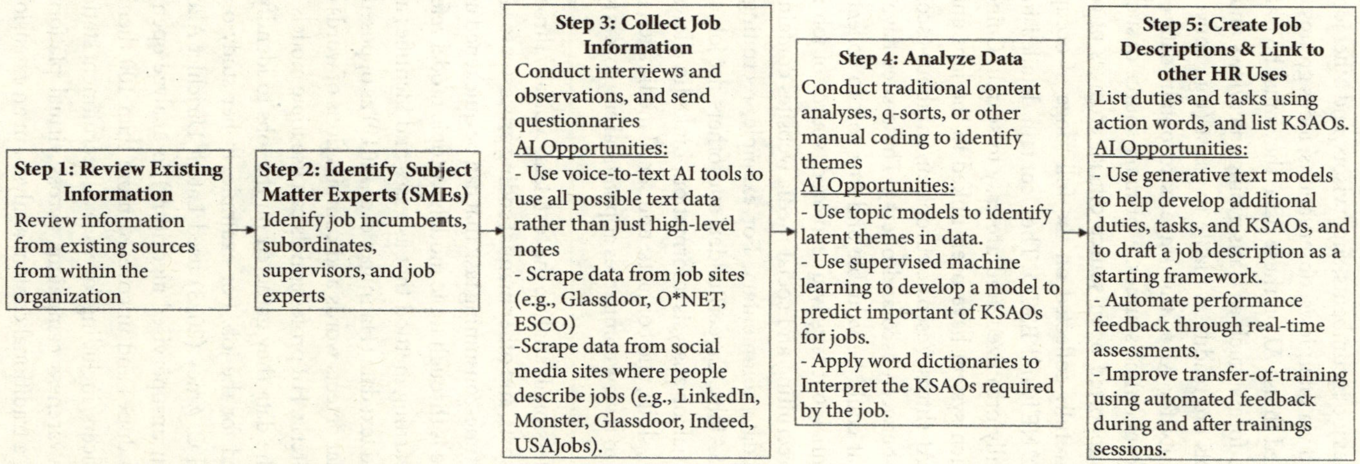

Step 1: Review Existing Information

Review information from existing sources from within the organization

Step 2: Identify Subject Matter Experts (SMEs)

Identify job incumbents, subordinates, supervisors, and job experts

Step 3: Collect Job Information

Conduct interviews and observations, and send questionnaries

AI Opportunities:
- Use voice-to-text AI tools to use all possible text data rather than just high-level notes
- Scrape data from job sites (e.g., Glassdoor, O*NET, ESCO)
- Scrape data from social media sites where people describe jobs (e.g., LinkedIn, Monster, Glassdoor, Indeed, USAJobs).

Step 4: Analyze Data

Conduct traditional content analyses, q-sorts, or other manual coding to identify themes

AI Opportunities:
- Use topic models to identify latent themes in data.
- Use supervised machine learning to develop a model to predict important of KSAOs for jobs.
- Apply word dictionaries to Interpret the KSAOs required by the job.

Step 5: Create Job Descriptions & Link to other HR Uses

List duties and tasks using action words, and list KSAOs.

AI Opportunities:
- Use generative text models to help develop additional duties, tasks, and KSAOs, and to draft a job description as a starting framework.
- Automate performance feedback through real-time assessments.
- Improve transfer-of-training using automated feedback during and after trainings sessions.

Figure 24.1 Job Analysis Framework with Artificial Intelligence Opportunities

612 TRANSFORMATIVE WORK DESIGN

professionals collect job information, often from SMEs identified in Step 2, which usually includes job incumbents, supervisors, and other job experts. Data are typically collected via interviews, observations, focus groups, and question-naires. If it is intended to use AI on these data, they must be transformed into a computer readable format such as transcribing interviews and observations digitally, and AI tools are readily available to assist (e.g., converting voice to text). One opportunity for AI at this stage is to obtain data on the jobs or highly related jobs from online sources. A primary source of such information is the government-supported open-source official archives of comprehensive job analysis data carefully collected on the full range of occupations in the economy, such as O*NET and ESCO. They contain detailed information on jobs, are systematically organized, and are easy to search. Coincidentally, the jobs and skills in each system have been linked to the jobs and skills in the other system using AI (https://esco.ec.europa.eu/en/about-esco/data-science-and-esco/crosswalk-between-esco-and-onet#). These sites have a plethora of text data on jobs that could be valuable and low cost to collect for organiza-tions. Another potential, but largely unexplored, source of job information is to scrape the many recruiting and social media websites containing job adver-tisements and candidate commentary. For example, recruiting websites like Monster, Indeed, USAJobs, CareerBuilder, and others list job advertisements that contain substantial job analysis information; LinkedIn allows professionals to describe their jobs, skills, and contacts; and social media sites, like Glassdoor, allow job candidates to review companies as potential employers to inform other job seekers.

In Step 4, HR professionals analyze the text data, typically through traditional content analyses, q-sorts, and other manual coding processes to identify themes. This is an extremely time-consuming task that can be quickened using NLP. One way this can be done is through topic models. A topic model refers to an unsu-pervised machine learning method that assesses and identifies a latent pattern of topics in unlabeled text data (Hannigan et al., 2019) as opposed to supervised machine learning that detects words and combinations of words based on their relationship with criteria. HR professionals can use topic models to uncover the themes present in the data they gathered on the jobs to identify duties, tasks, and KSAOs required for the job. For example, in her study on occupational descriptions, Rachel C. Amey (2023) used Latent Dirichlet Allocation (LDA; Blei et al., 2003) (an unsupervised algorithm) to analyze open-ended survey questions about job duties and uncovered more than 100 themes across jobs held by US Army officers, including "oversee all recruitment station operations" and "create Army awareness campaigns across virtual platforms" in signifi-cantly less time than a traditional content analysis. In an extension of this work,

Ryan Royston and Nai Lin (2023) used topic modeling to uncover how jobs differ by leadership level (e.g., supervisor, middle manager, executive).

In addition to using unsupervised methods to uncover latent themes within text data, researchers have also shown how to develop supervised models to predict the KSAOs required of jobs. In one example of this, Dan Putka and colleagues (2023) built a language model to predict the importance of KSAOs to jobs. They reasoned that job analysts make inferences about attribute requirements based on the words used to describe the job tasks. For example, words like "cooperation," "interaction," and "working with others" might reflect interpersonal skills. They extracted n-grams (combinations of words within text) from the descriptions and tasks of jobs in O*NET and then used supervised machine learning to select and weigh these variables based on their prediction of the attribute requirements data in O*NET collected from samples of representative job incumbents in the labor market. The result was a language model that predicted job requirement scores with good accuracy that can be used to facilitate job analysis.

Logan Lebanoff and Charles Newton (in press) conducted a highly similar study for the same purpose. They sought to train a computer model to predict the most relevant KSAO requirements based on job descriptions. However, they used somewhat different methods. For one, they focused on a subset of jobs of interest to the organization (US Army civilian jobs). For another, they developed a corpus of job analysis information to train the model by using analysts to select the KSAO requirements for each job. These two steps ensured the model would be tailored to the jobs of interest to the organization. Another difference is they used a highly complex type of computer algorithm to analyze the corpus to predict the KSAOs called Bidirectional Encoder Representations from Transformers (BERT; Devlin et al., 2019), which is a deep-learning approach that uses a transformer to analyze language. BERT is an algorithm that is pre-trained based on vast amounts of English text (e.g., Wikipedia and books). Because it uses neural networks, it does not produce a dictionary of words like the other methods, but the content scored by the models can be understood based on specialized output of the model features that represent composites of the information extracted. The model had similar prediction accuracy to that of human raters. The results were generally similar although slightly better than other less complex AI approaches.

Another way to leverage AI when analyzing job data is using a more rudimentary method: word dictionaries. Word dictionaries are likely one of the simplest methods of automated text analysis. Essentially, dictionaries are lists of words that have been empirically or rationally determined to represent the construct of interest. These can be applied to job analysis text data to infer the KSAOs

614   TRANSFORMATIVE WORK DESIGN

required of the job. While not directly used on job analysis data, Andrew Speer and colleagues (2019) developed a series of dictionaries to measure a generic set of competencies called the Great Eight (Bartum, 2005) using text analysis in the performance appraisal context. This research represents a reasonable way in which dictionaries can be developed and applied to text data within HR functions. Speer and colleagues (2019) developed the dictionaries by extracting words and combinations of two and three words (bigrams and trigrams) using automated text mining from a corpus of text describing job performance from appraisals in a financial organization. They used the common "bag of words" approach that extracts *n*-grams, ignoring other semantic information such as grammar, punctuation, syntax, parts of speech, and other linguistic features. Thus, it only determines the content of the text (like the concepts mentioned) and not how it is written. It uses stemming or lemmatizing to reduce words to their base forms so different versions of the words will be recognized as the same (e.g., talk, talked, talking). They then had human raters judge the relationship between the extracted words and the definitions of the competencies. The resulting dictionaries included several hundred words for each competency. The dictionaries were then used to score the written performance appraisals by giving one point for each word from the dictionary used and then dividing by the total number of words. The resulting total summed scores showed adequate reliability and construct validity with other dictionary scores and performance ratings.

Although this study was conducted in the context of performance appraisal, dictionaries could be applied to any corpus of job-related text to measure the competencies reflected. This taxonomy of competencies includes attributes required of, or desired for, many jobs: leading and deciding, supporting and cooperating, interacting and presenting, analyzing and interpreting, creating and conceptualizing, organizing and executing, adapting and coping, and enterprising and performing. As such, the dictionaries could be used for job analysis by applying them to job descriptions or lists of tasks to determine the competencies required by the job. The dictionaries are available publicly in their article (Speer et al., 2019). The work of Vladimer Kobayashi and colleagues (2018) should also be noted. In a tutorial on the use of text mining in a research methods journal, they illustrated the techniques by extracting skills from job descriptions. They did not validate their results against normal job analysis methods such as human ratings or develop a tool to conduct job analyses, but they illustrated the applicability of text analysis in a job analysis context.

In Step 5 of the job analysis process, HR professionals create HR products like job descriptions, assessment questions, and other products. For example, job descriptions are often developed by taking the results of Step 4 and creating lists of duties and tasks using action words. A prime opportunity to use AI at this stage is to use generative text models to help create lists of duties and tasks. These models can provide examples of duty and tasks statements and can be instructed to generate similar items.

In addition to using generative models to supplement duties and tasks uncovered in the job analysis, researchers can create a draft of a job description that can be used in the development of a fuller job description. An example of a job description generated by ChatGPT can be found in Figure 24.2 where the authors instructed ChatGPT to "Write a job description for a human resource specialist" (OpenAI, 2023). The job description is vague, but it provides an initial version that can be used as a starting point. Additional information on tasks and technical skills should be added to develop a more complete job description.

An example of using AI to create assessment questions is Ivan Hernandez and Jared Nie's (2022) recent work using GPT-2 to develop a pool of items that capture personality (the Big Five), self-efficacy, and curiosity. In their research, they generated one million personality items and then trained a neural network-based classification model using BERT to refine the list of personality items to a smaller pool of the most predictive ones. They found that their AI-optimized scales had reliability, validity, and model structure fit similar to those optimized using traditional analytic methods.

As another example of using AI with job analysis to facilitate the development of assessments, the same AI used to identify KSAOs in Step 4 can be used to identify KSAOs in candidate applications, letters, and interview responses. The words candidates and others use to describe their credentials and accomplishments can be analyzed using the same job analysis dictionaries to infer KSAOs possessed by the candidates. Moreover, this has other benefits as a selection tool, such as not requiring the candidate to complete any additional selection procedures and being a non-invasive and non-reactionary way to measure personality that will be less fakable than personality tests.

AI could also use job analysis for a range of other HR purposes, like measuring job performance from narrative information in appraisal comments, presenting training content and providing feedback, and providing career development feedback by comparing an employee's past job tasks and KSAOs to those of higher-level jobs and identifying gaps or opportunities. For example, AI could be used to automate performance evaluations using job analysis data and comparing to employee metrics. Notably, we are not suggesting managers should be eliminated from this process. However, employees may find regular automated feedback more immediately palatable than supervisor feedback. Real-time feedback where employees can track themselves empowers them to course-correct without requiring individual meetings with their manager. Similarly, AI could be used to provide feedback during and after training to improve transfer-of-training.

616 TRANSFORMATIVE WORK DESIGN

Job Title: Human Resource Specialist

Job Summary:
We are seeking an experienced Human Resource Specialist to join our team. The ideal candidate will be responsible for providing support to the HR department in areas such as recruitment, employee relations, performance management, benefits administration, and compliance with employment laws and regulations. The HR Specialist will be expected to work closely with management and employees to ensure that our company's human resources policies and procedures are consistently applied and comply with all applicable legal requirements.

Key Responsibilities:
- Coordinate and manage the recruitment process, including developing job descriptions, screening resumes, conducting interviews, and making job offers.
- Assist in the development and implementation of HR policies and procedures, ensuring compliance with all applicable laws and regulations.
- Manage employee relations issues, including investigations and resolution of complaints, and support the development of effective communication and conflict resolution strategies.
- Manage the performance management process, including conducting performance evaluations and providing feedback to employees and managers.
- Administer employee benefits programs, including health, dental, and retirement plans.
- Maintain accurate employee records, including tracking employee time off, salary changes, and other HR related data.
- Assist with the preparation and delivery of training programs for employees and managers on a variety of HR-related topics.

Qualifications:
- Bachelor's degree in Human Resources or related field
- At least 3–5 years of experience in Human Resources, with a focus on recruitment, employee relations, and compliance
- Knowledge of federal, state, and local employment laws and regulations
- Strong communication and interpersonal skills, with the ability to effectively communicate with all levels of employees and management
- Ability to manage multiple projects and priorities, with excellent attention to detail and organizational skills
- Proficiency in HRIS and Microsoft Office Suite
- Ability to maintain confidentiality and handle sensitive information with discretion

If you are passionate about Human Resources, have a strong attention to detail, and enjoy working in a dynamic and fast-paced environment, we encourage you to apply for this exciting opportunity!

Figure 24.2 Example Job Description of "Human Resource Specialist" from ChatGPT

Note: The authors ran this job description through a plagiarism checker and found only minor potential similarities to other sources on the internet but not rising to the level of plagiarism.

Although the application of AI-based text analysis to job analysis is in its infancy, AI clearly offers a number of promising opportunities that are certain to have a major impact on the practice of job analysis because it automates the cumbersome and time-consuming process of collecting KSAO judgments from incumbents or analysts. Several other observations on this trend should be noted. First, these job analysis tools can be tailored to the organization to provide more organizationally specific information (e.g., unique technical skills), or developed to apply to all the major occupations in the economy to provide more general information that can be compared across-jobs. Second, the analytic approaches vary widely, including the extraction of text features and combining the features to produce scores. The more complex methods may be more accurate, but the difference is small and there may be a sacrifice in model interpretability, as well as accessibility to researchers who are not programmers. Third, these tools will not definitively replace humans in the job analysis process or traditional job analysis completely. A human-in-the-loop is still required to derive meaning from topic models, make sense of and develop rational word lists, and interpret output.

Potential Applications of Text Analysis to Job Design

To our knowledge, only a few papers have sought to use text analysis to better understand job design. In their study on virtual job design, Cristina Gibson and colleagues (2011) developed word dictionaries to measure features of J. Richard Hackman and Greg Oldham's (1976) job characteristics model—task significance, autonomy, feedback—as well as virtual features of a job such as perceptions of electronic dependence, intimacy, copresence, and identification. They captured these variables in research interview transcriptions. With some text variables, they were able to offer construct validity evidence using proxy variables (i.e., time zones for copresence), and other-reports (i.e., independent external ratings of electronic dependence). While these researchers captured several job design variables, the dictionary approach provided a valuable method for measuring a host of other relevant job design variables including variety, skill usage, importance of the work, challenge, decision making, and most any other motivational job design characteristics. In another example, Speer and colleagues (2022) used NLP to develop measures of attitudes and perceptions in open-ended comments in employee surveys. Many of the measures are job design characteristics such as autonomy, job complexity, identity, significance, variety, and others. The measures are made available to other researchers to use.

Aside from these two studies, some related studies have measured job design types of characteristics for other purposes that suggest the potential. For example, Sheela Pandey and Sanjay Pandey (2017) used NLP to measure organizational culture in annual reports and letters to shareholders. Some of the

618   TRANSFORMATIVE WORK DESIGN

culture dimensions they extracted are similar to job design characteristics, such as control (similar to the job design characteristics of autonomy and responsibility), competitiveness (similar to importance and challenge), innovation and learning orientation (similar to skill usage), and customer and team orientation (similar to social aspects of job design). Similarly, Boris Kabanoff and colleagues (1995), while not machine learning, used a dictionary text analysis approach applied to annual reports, company internal magazines, and corporate value statements to measure organizational culture along many dimensions that are like job design characteristics, such as authority, rewards, participation, and teamwork. In yet another study of organizational culture, Theresa Schmiedel and colleagues (2019) illustrated the application of topic modeling by applying it to reviews of companies posted on Glassdoor. Many of the topics identified are related to job design characteristics, such as career opportunities, work-life balance, flexibility, work atmosphere, and management quality. Although these studies used organizational-level text corpuses, the constructs measured are somewhat similar to job design characteristics suggesting these methods might be used at the individual jobholder level.

Text analysis could also be used to measure all interdisciplinary approaches to job design from industrial engineering (e.g., repetition, specialization), to human factors (e.g., input requirements, memory requirements, lighting, safety), to ergonomics (e.g., physical comfort, lifting, postural requirements, tool design) (Campion, 1988; Campion & Thayer, 1985). Being highly similar, team design characteristics would also lend themselves to measurement by text analysis, including interdependence, composition, context, job, and process variables (Campion et al., 1993; Morgeson & Campion, 2021). John E. Mathieu and colleagues (2022) did something similar by developing word dictionaries to measure team processes including transition, action, and interpersonal. Another possible application would be to use text analysis to measure words reflecting the various types of job crafting like work role expansion and reduction, work organization, adoption, metacognition, and withdrawal (Bruning & Campion, 2018).

A Brief How-To Guide for Using Text Analysis in Job Design Research

Given the strongly theoretical nature of job design, these dictionaries would likely be rationally and deductively developed to measure the key words representing the relevant characteristics. The process might consist of the following steps, which could be performed by any researcher without any advanced knowledge of machine learning:

1. Identify the key words representing the job design characteristic from the theories, existing survey measures, and other sources of descriptors.
2. Use thesauruses to expand the list into all possible synonyms.
3. Perhaps use lexical databases like WordNet (https://wordnet.princeton. edu/) to identify words that are semantically related to the synonyms.
4. Because the previous step will produce a great number of related words, many of which are not conceptually related, use human judges with knowledge of the job design characteristics to review the lists and select those to retain.
5. Apply the dictionary to representative samples of text (further described below) using the many available word counters (such as Linguistic Inquiry Word Count [LIWC]) to evaluate the words for their frequency of usage and ability to create a reliable score for each characteristic. Often, many of the words will have very low frequencies and may thus not be as useful for measurement, and it may take a fairly long dictionary to achieve an acceptable internal consistency reliability (often several hundred words per construct measured).
6. Validate the dictionary using typical methods such as convergent and discriminant validity with existing measures of the characteristics (e.g., existing survey measures) and correlating with other outcomes of interest (e.g., satisfaction, performance, etc.).

The text corpuses relevant to job design are widely varying. They might include narrative comments collected on surveys, both those collected for the purpose of job design but also those collected for other purposes that yield job-related comments such as opinion or engagement surveys. Text relevant to job design might be collected or currently exist in suggestions systems or grievances. Text analysis could also be applied to narrative data collected in focus groups or interviews with incumbents. Any text that contains comments on jobs from employees might be explored to measure job design characteristics.

Another potential role is to use supervised machine learning to train a model to score a particular construct. For example, if we wanted to build a model to score the Big Five personality characteristics—Openness to Experience, Conscientiousness, Extraversion, Agreeableness, and Neuroticism—we could gather data from individuals with self- or other-reports of the Big Five using existing quantitative measures, and then also collect text data from them perhaps describing themselves in various scenarios (e.g., at work, with friends, with family). We could then build a language model using the self-reports or other-reports of personality as the criterion against which to train the model to score the Big Five. In an example of this, Joseph Harrison and colleagues (2019) built a language model to score CEO Big Five personality traits using earnings calls and other-reports of CEO personality (also see Fan et al., 2023). A similar model could be built on a variety of other job requirements.

How Language Usage Represents Job Features

The logic of how automated text analysis can represent job features depends on the purpose. Broadly speaking, there are two purposes: summarizing the content of the text and inferring underlying constructs from the text, including constructs about the job such as skill requirements and job design characteristics, and constructs about the person such as skills possessed, personality, sentiment, emotions, and the like.

When summarizing content, text analysis extracts words and combinations of words that reflect the verbal expressions one might use to describe the relevant behaviors, activities, tasks, outcomes, descriptions, features, or other content of the construct. For example, when measuring leadership skills, the verbal expressions might include descriptions of leadership behavior like action, authorize, build team, business decision, coordinate, confidence, direct reports, drive, empower, and so on. In their study on former US President George W. Bush's pre- and post-9/11 speeches and media coverage, Michelle Bligh and colleagues (2004) summarized the content of the text data according to existing text dictionaries on optimism, collective language, faith, patriotism, ambivalence, and aggression.

When inferring underlying constructs, the process is similar, but the verbal expressions extracted and measured are induced instead of imposed. In the example using supervised machine learning, it is possible that the words or terms extracted and retained in the model may sometimes appear as indirect indicators of the underlying construct. This occurs because it was developed inductively rather than deductively. For example, when measuring enthusiasm, the verbal expressions might include aspire, cheerful, eager, emotional, enjoy, impatience, intense, and other expressions that are indirectly related to enthusiasm such as these associated behaviors or outcomes rather than direct synonyms.

Obviously, the two purposes overlap and may be indistinguishable or are simultaneous goals in a given application. Perhaps it is best to view them as a continuum, ranging from direct synonyms of the construct to indirect indicators that can be used to infer the presence of a construct. As with many psychological measures, constructs are indexed by having a great many indicators that are imperfect individually, but the composite creates a reliable metric. As previously illustrated, these measures will often have hundreds of verbal expression indicators. Moreover, aside from ensuring reliable measurement, many indicators are needed because people use a wide range of words to describe the same phenomena. A dictionary or model that measures many hundreds of verbal expressions may only detect a couple dozen in any given text sample.

It is also important to recognize that the corpus used and the manner in which it was collected also determines what is measured and the inferences possible. For example, is the text a description of the job or the employee's reactions to the job, or is the application information a description of the candidate's past work experience or a description of the candidate's claimed skills? Another critical factor is the size of the text sample. A more accurate measurement will be obtained from responses to a one-hour interview, which may yield a text sample of 2,000 words, compared to written comments in a survey, which may only yield a text sample of 20 to 50 words. Finally, answer length itself may be meaningful. As opposed to simply reflecting verbosity, a respondent who takes 200 words to describe some feature of a job probably has more content to express than a respondent who takes 50 or 100 words. For example, our research has shown that candidates with longer answers on applications and interviews will receive higher ratings from recruiters because they are describing more skills and experience as captured by more content categories mentioned in their answers. Thus, length is likely to capture an individual's depth of knowledge or experience rather than their talkative tendencies.

Future Research Directions

Applications of AI-enabled text analysis in HR are in their infancy. Most of the published illustrations to date have been in personnel selection (e.g., Banks et al., 2019; Campion & Campion, 2020; Campion et al., 2016; Hickman et al., 2022; Sajjadiani et al., 2019) and appraisal (Speer, 2018). A special issue on machine learning and personnel selection has increased the amount of information we have on the application of machine learning to HR functions. The editors of the special issue (Campion & Campion, 2023a) summarize the current potential applications of machine learning in selection, including those using automated text analysis, and introduce the special issue that contains four articles reporting 11 primary studies.

The existing research in job analysis and job design was previously summarized. Another potential role of text analysis in job design, aside from measurement of known characteristics, is its use to discover what characteristics of job design are important to employees but perhaps not captured by existing theories and measures. The potential inductive value of analyzing narrative data is key because it may provide insight as to what is important to employees, which may not be the assumed features from theories of work design. The way employees express their reactions to their jobs in words may represent inductive messaging about what is important to them that is heretofore undiscovered in traditional survey job designs that only measure predetermined characteristics. As such, it may be used for discovery, at least initially, as opposed to measurement. In a comprehensive literature review of the use of text analysis in organizational psychology and management, Emily Campion and Michael Campion (2023b) found that text analysis has been used to discover or measure 250 different constructs. Until now, most of this research has not used automated text analysis. However, now that it is available, the contributions of text analysis to discovery are certain to accelerate. Such an inductive approach would likely apply topic models rather than dictionaries. As noted previously, topic models are a form of unsupervised machine learning that can uncover patterns in unlabeled data. This means that there is no indication in the data of what exactly is being measured. Instead, the algorithm identifies latent patterns, and it is the responsibility of the research or HR professional to make sense of the results. This can be thought of as an automated content analysis (e.g., Hannigan et al., 2019). Such an inductive approach may offer new ideas for the redesign of current jobs or reactions to current or redesigned jobs, which may be better identified inductively as expressed in the employees' own words, as opposed to deductively measured using existing questionnaire measures.

Conclusion

In conclusion, AI, and particularly NLP, has been shown to be potentially invaluable to job analysis. Job analyses can be a very time-consuming process and using AI can help reduce resources spent collecting and analyzing text data, and perhaps also generating job descriptions. Job analyses are crucial to all functions of HR, so leveraging AI to improve job analyses has lasting positive consequences for recruitment, selection, performance evaluation, and training and development. In the context of job design, the use of NLP is largely unexplored, but holds great potential. We call for more research using text mining and text analysis in job analysis and job design.

References

Amey, R. C. (April, 2023). *Utilizing natural language to optimize occupational descriptions.* Symposium presented at the Annual Conference of the Society for Industrial and Organizational Psychology. Boston, MA.

Banks, G. C., Woznyj, H. M., Wesslen, R. S., Frear, K. A., Berka, G., Heggestad, E. D., & Gordon, H. L. (2019). Strategic recruitment across borders: An investigation of multinational enterprises. *Journal of Management 45*(2), 476–509.

Blei, D. M., Ng, A. Y., & Jordan, M. I. (2003). Latent dirichlet allocation. *Journal of Machine Learning Research, 3*(Jan), 993–1022.

Bligh, M. C., Kohles, J. C., & Meindl, J. R. (2004). Charting the language of leadership: A methodological investigation of President Bush and the crisis of 9/11. *Journal of Applied Psychology 89*(3), 562–574. https://doi.org/10.1037/0021-9010.89.3.562

Bruning, P., & Campion, M. A. (2018). A role-resource approach-avoidance model of job crafting: A multi-method integration and extension of job crafting theory. *Academy of Management Journal 61*, 499–522.

Campion, M. A. (1988). Interdisciplinary approaches to job design: A constructive replication with extensions. *Journal of Applied Psychology 73*, 467–481.

Campion, E. D., & Campion. M. A. (2020). Using computer-assisted text analysis (CATA) to inform employment decisions: Approaches, software, and findings. *Research in Personnel and Human Resources Management 38*, 287–327.

Campion, E. D., & Campion, M. A. (2023a). Machine learning applications to personnel selection: Current illustrations, lessons learned, and future research. *Personnel Psychology 76*, 993–1009.

Campion, E. D., & Campion, M. A. (2023b). *A review of text analysis contributions to construct identification, theory building, and paradigmatic diversity in the psychology of people at work.* Manuscript submitted for publication.

Campion, M. C., Campion, M. A., Campion, E. D., & Reider, M. H. (2016). Initial investigation into computer scoring of candidate essays for personnel selection. *Journal of Applied Psychology 101*, 958–975.

Campion, M. A., Medsker, G. J., & Higgs, C. (1993). Relations between work group characteristics and effectiveness: Implications for designing effective work groups. *Personnel Psychology 46*, 823–850.

Campion, M. A., & Thayer, P. W. (1985). Development and field evaluation of an interdisciplinary measure of job design. *Journal of Applied Psychology 70*, 29–43.

Devlin, J., Chang, M.-W., Lee, K., & Toutanova, K. (2019). BERT: Pre-training of deep bidirectional transformers for language understanding. *Proceedings of the Conference of the North American Chapter of the Association for Computational Linguistics.* https://doi.org/10.48550/arXiv.1810.04805

Fan, J., Sun, T., Liu, J., Zhao, T., Zhang, B., Chen, Z., Glorioso, M., & Hack, E. (2023). How well can an AI chatbot infer personality? Examining psychometric properties of machine-inferred personality scores. *Journal of Applied Psychology 108*, 1277–1299. https://doi.org/10.1037/apl0001082

Gibson, C. B., Gibbs, J. L., Stanko, T. L., Tesluk, P., & Cohen, S. G. (2011). Including the "I" in virtuality and modern job design: Extending the job characteristics model to include the moderating effect of individual experiences of electronic dependence and copresence. *Organization Science 22*(6), 1481–1499. https://doi.org/10.1287/orsc.1100.0586

Hackman, J. R., & Oldham, G. R. (1976). Motivation through the design of work: Test of a theory. *Organizational Behavior and Human Performance, 16*, 250–279.

Hannigan, T. R., Haans, R. F., Vakili, K., Tchalian, H., Glaser, V. L., Wang, M. S., Kaplan, S. & Jennings, P. D. (2019). Topic modeling in management research: Rendering new theory from textual data. *Academy of Management Annals 13*(2), 586–632. https://doi.org/10.5465/annals.2017.0099

Harrison, J. S., Thurgood, G. R., Boivie, S., & Pfarrer, M. D. (2019). Measuring CEO personality: Developing, validating, and testing a linguistic tool. *Strategic Management Journal 40*(8), 1316–1330. https://doi.org/10.1002/smj.3023

Hernandez, I., & Nie, W. (2023). The AI-IP: Minimizing the guesswork of personality scale item development through artificial intelligence. *Personnel Psychology 76*(4), 1011–1035.

Hickman, L., Bosch, N., Ng, V., Saef, R., Tay, L., & Woo, S. E. (2022). Automated video interview personality assessments: Reliability, validity, and generalizability investigations. *Journal of Applied Psychology 107*(8), 1323–1351.

Kabanoff, B., Waldersee, R., & Cohen, M. (1995). Espoused values and organizational change themes. *Academy of Management Journal 38*(4), 1075–1104.

Kobayashi, V. B., Mol, S. T., Berkers, H. A., Kismihok, G., & Den Hartog, D. N. (2018). Text mining in organizational research. *Organizational Research Methods 21*(3), 733–765.

Lebanoff, L., & Newton, C. (In press). Naturalistic extraction of knowledge, skills, abilities and other characteristics using natural language processing with human-level proficiency. *Personnel Psychology.*

Mathieu, J. E., Wolfson, M. A., Park, S., Luciano, M. M., Bedwell-Torres, W. L., Ramsay, P. S., Klock, E. A., & Tannenbaum, S. I. (2022). Indexing dynamic collective constructs using computer-aided text analysis: Construct validity evidence and illustrations featuring team processes. *Journal of Applied Psychology 107*(4), 533–559. https://doi.org/10.1037/apl0000856

McCormick, E. J., Jeanneret, P. R., & Mecham, R. C. (1972). A study of job characteristics and job dimensions as based on the Position Analysis Questionnaire (PAQ). *Journal of Applied Psychology 56*(4), 347.

Morgeson, F. P., Brannick, M. T., & Levine, E. L. (2019). *Job and work analysis: Methods, research, and applications for human resource management.* SAGE.

Morgeson, F. P., & Campion, M. A. (2021). Job and team design. In G. Salvendy & W. Karwowski (Eds.), *Handbook of human factors and ergonomics* (5th ed., pp. 383–413). Wiley.

OpenAI. (2023). *ChatGPT* (3 May Version) [Large language model]. https://chat.openai.com/chat

Pandey, S., & Pandey, S. K. (2017). Applying natural language processing capabilities in computerized textual analysis to measure organizational culture. *Organizational Research Methods 22*(3), 765–797.

Pennebaker, J. W., Francis, M. E., & Booth, R. J. (2001). *Linguistic inquiry and word count: LIWC 2001.* Lawrence Erlbaum Associates.

Peterson, N. G., Mumford, M. D., Borman, W. C., Jeanneret, P. R., Fleishman, E. A., Levin, K. Y., Campion, M. A., Mayfield, M. S., Morgeson, F. P., Pearlman, K., Gowing, M. K., Lancaster, A., & Dye, D. (2001). Understanding work using the occupational information network (O*NET): Implications for practice and research. *Personnel Psychology 54*, 451–492.

Putka, D. J., Oswald, F. L., Landers, R. N., Beatty, A. S., McCloy, R. A., & Yu, M. C. (2023). Evaluating a natural language processing approach to estimating KSA and interest job analysis ratings. *Journal of Business and Psychology 38*, 385–410.

Royston, R. P., & Lin, N. (April, 2023). *Applying topic modeling to narrative statements to determine how job responsibility descriptions differ by leadership level and experience.* Symposium presented at the Annual Conference of the Society for Industrial and Organizational Psychology. Boston, MA.

Sajjadiani, S., Sojourner, A. J., Kammeyer-Mueller, J. D., & Mykerezi, E. (2019). Using machine learning to translate applicant work history into predictors of performance and turnover. *Journal of Applied Psychology 104*, 1207–1225.

Schmiedel, T., Müller, O., & vom Brocke, J. (2019). Topic modeling as a strategy of inquiry in organizational research: A tutorial with an application example on organizational culture. *Organizational Research Methods 22*(4), 941–968.

Speer, A. B. (2018). Quantifying with words: An investigation of the validity of narrative-derived performance scores. *Personnel Psychology 71*(3), 299–333.

Speer, A. B., Perrotta, J., Tenbrink, A. P., Wegmeyer, L. J., Delacruz, A. Y., & Bowker, J. (2022). Turning words into numbers: Assessing work attitudes using natural language processing. *Journal of Applied Psychology* 108(6), 1027–1045.

Speer, A. B., Schwendeman, M. G., Reich, C. C., Tenbrink, A. P., & Siver, S. R. (2019). Investigating the construct validity of performance comments: Creation of the great eight narrative dictionary. *Journal of Business and Psychology 34*, 747–767.

CONCLUSION

Where is the Future of Work Design Research Heading?

A Roadmap for Key Topics To Be Investigated

Fangfang Zhang, Caroline Knight, Florian E. Klonek,
and Sharon K. Parker

While this book has highlighted the significant progress in our understanding of work design, this chapter aims to highlight the challenges and opportunities lying ahead. In a new era of work, characterized by volatility, uncertainty, complexity, and ambiguity, work has become more complex and dynamic than ever. Considering this, each chapter has provided insightful future research directions that will shape and move the future of work design research forward. This concluding chapter will not repeat all future directions proposed in previous chapters, although these are summarized in the Appendix, but instead will synthesize the key themes, highlighting the main opportunities and challenges that lie ahead. We hope this chapter will inspire researchers, practitioners, and policymakers to think about how they can shape a future of work that is both productive and fulfilling for all.

Theme 1: Expanding the Scope of Work Design

Several scholars in this book have strongly advocated for expanding the scope of work design beyond traditional motivational factors. This is a crucial step for a more comprehensive and impactful understanding of how work design affects individuals and organizations when considering how the nature of work is changing. Anja Van den Broeck, Lorenz Verelst, and Hans de Witte (Chapter 2) highlighted that, while classic motivational models have been valuable in focusing on many important job characteristics, these models neglect crucial aspects of work design such as aspects concerning social relations, remuneration and the work environment. Similarly, Sabine Sonnentag (Chapter 4) discussed the scarcity of research on how "stimulating" and "mastery" features

---

Fangfang Zhang et al., *Where is the Future of Work Design Research Heading?*. In: *Transformative Work Design*. Edited by: Sharon K. Parker et al., Oxford University Press. © Fangfang Zhang, Caroline Knight, Florian E. Klonek, and Sharon K. Parker (2025). DOI: 10.1093/oso/9780197692554.003.0025

of a job from Sharon K. Parker & Caroline Knight's (2023) SMART Work Design Model influence employees' well-being. Giverny De Boeck, Maïlys George, and Aušrinė Vyšniauskaitė (Chapter 6) indicated a lack of research on the impact of knowledge and contextual work characteristics on identity.

Moreover, we see an emergence of novel work characteristics that are tied to the fourth industrial revolution, such as techno-overload, techno-uncertainty, techno-insecurity, techno-invasion, and techno-complexity. These new work demands have emerged due to the technological changes (e.g., AI, robotics, big data, etc.) permeating across industries and affecting work (Tarafdar et al., 2019). This trend of changes also makes some aspects of work design such as cognitive factors (e.g., information processing, job complexity, problem-solving) and social characteristics (e.g., interdependence and interactions outside the organization) more important than ever before. This is because technological advances increase cognitive demands on workers as they learn to apply new technologies to their tasks. Technological interactions also change the very social nature of work, as we have seen an uprise in working-from-home, where workers reduced their work-related interactions in the office, but increasingly rely on technology to interact with others or complete tasks that would otherwise have involved direct contact. This points to important questions: When, how and why do these work-related trends contribute to mental health issues, such as feelings of isolation and loneliness? How do flexible work arrangements affect the work design of teams who have to process tasks from different locations and using novel technologies.

Altogether, going beyond the predominant focus on job resources and demands, or motivational features to include these new work factors, is an important extension of existing research to provide a more nuanced understanding of the impact of work design in contemporary jobs.

Theme 2: Re-examining and Broadening the Outcomes of Work Design

Another insight from this book is that it is crucial to go beyond the traditional focus of work design outcomes on well-being and task performance to include a broader range of outcomes such as employees' learning and development, adaptivity, and proactivity. These outcomes are increasingly important in contemporary work, as discussed by Sandra Ohly and Laura Venz (Chapter 5) and Van den Broeck and colleagues (Chapter 2). In addition, identity and personality are two key outcomes highlighted in this book that are just beginning to be explored from the perspective of work design; for example, see De Boeck and colleagues (Chapter 6) and Chia-Huei Wu and Ying Wang (Chapter 7).

WHERE IS THE FUTURE OF WORK DESIGN RESEARCH HEADING? 631

In terms of identity, De Boeck and colleagues (Chapter 6) discuss how autonomy and feedback contribute to the development of individuals' future work selves, while relational work characteristics shape individuals' self-growth by encouraging a view of the self as "expert." Moving away from individual identities, working in groups in close physical proximity can also promote group identity. However, the processes underlying these relationships, and the degree and types of identities shaped by work design, are yet unclear.

Likewise, Wu and Wang (Chapter 7) expand the outcomes that work design is suggested to impact by proposing that work design can shape motivations and behaviors over the shorter and longer term. For example, being employed in a specific role or occupation, even if it wasn't an intentional choice, can shift individuals' personality traits toward traits that facilitate that profession (e.g., frequent public speaking engagements can increase extraversion). Being required to engage in challenging tasks at work can develop mastery and self-determination beliefs, increasing individual locus of control. Wu and Wang (Chapter 7) go further to suggest that proactive job crafting can shape personality traits further, yet further research is needed to unpack whether, when, and how this might transpire.

In terms of how work design affects individuals' cognition, readers could refer to the review paper by Parker and colleagues (2021). The authors synthesized research from work design, human factors, learning, occupational health, and lifespan perspectives to show how work design (job complexity, job autonomy, relational work design, job feedback, and psychosocial demands) can affect employees' short-term cognitive outcomes (e.g., learning, knowledge/skill acquisition) and long-term cognitive outcomes (e.g., development of expertise). But as these authors discussed, there are crucial research gaps, especially in terms of unpacking and demonstrating the long-term cognitive repercussions of work design.

The impact of job characteristics can be complex, occurring at different levels and shaping different outcomes through multiple mechanisms (e.g., Parker et al., 2017). But there is more to uncover. For example, Van den Broeck and colleagues (Chapter 2) highlight the need to move beyond simply assuming that "more is always better" when it comes to motivational work design. This idea aligns with the "Vitamin Model" proposed by Warr (2013), suggesting that certain work characteristics, like autonomy or variety, can be beneficial up to a certain point, but beyond that, they can become detrimental, resulting in a "too much of a good thing" effect. Thus, researchers should go beyond the linear assumption of the impact of work design and adopt curvilinear analysis techniques to examine the relationships between different work characteristics and outcomes, particularly those that are expected to show inverted U-shape patterns. Additionally, the inflection point, the point at which the positive

632 TRANSFORMATIVE WORK DESIGN

relationship between a work characteristic and an outcome begins to decline, might be different depending on individuals' preferences and characteristics. For example, people who prefer high autonomy at work may not find a high level of job autonomy overtaxing. Future research could investigate how individual characteristics moderate the relationship between work design and outcomes, which will help identify the optimal levels of work characteristics for different individuals.

Furthermore, scholars in this book (e.g., Ohly & Venz; Sonnentag; Van den Broeck et al.) have suggested that it is important to consider the complex effects of some specific work design characteristics. For example, stimulating work, characterized by task variety, skill variety, job complexity, problem-solving demands, and information processing, could be motivating and cognitively exhausting at the same time. On the one hand, stimulating work benefits employees' work engagement, job satisfaction, and a sense of meaningfulness. On the other hand, overly stimulating work might lead to cognitive overload, mental fatigue, and even burnout, especially when stimulating work characteristics are excessive or not adequately balanced with other resources. Recognizing the dual nature of some work design aspects and the different mechanisms could help explain the inconsistent and contradictory effects of these job characteristics on a variety of outcomes.

Theme 3: Work Design in an Era of Artificial Intelligence

This book has provided significant insights into the implications of emerging trends like artificial intelligence (AI) and the gig economy for work design. As these trends are continuously reshaping how, where, and why we work, it is crucial to prioritize research that addresses the complex interplay between these emerging trends and work design.

This is even more critical when considering the strong evidence for the importance of good work design—work which is high in resources such as autonomy, support, and task significance, with manageable demands—for well-being and proactivity. Nadine Bienefeld and Gudela Grote (Chapter 19) highlight that it is imperative to deliberately consider how AI is and will influence work design so that proactive steps can be taken to ensure that AI has a positive influence on work design in the future.

As indicated by Bienefeld and Grote, AI is not simply about automating tasks; instead, it is about transforming entire occupations and redefining the meaning and value of work itself. Future research could investigate how specific occupations are being reshaped by AI and the new skills and knowledge required for workers to remain relevant in these evolving roles. This leads to

WHERE IS THE FUTURE OF WORK DESIGN RESEARCH HEADING? 633

another important research direction: human–AI collaboration. While AI can automate routine tasks and free up human workers to focus on more complex and meaningful activities, it can also lead to algorithmic control systems that restrict worker agency and create a sense of deskilling. Thus, future research could investigate how work systems can be designed to ensure that humans maintain meaningful control over AI-powered processes, particularly when AI systems become increasingly complex, lack transparency and are unpredictable. Bienefeld and Grote propose exploring new forms of controllability, such as explainable AI and shared accountability models, to foster user trust and understanding. Additionally, research on work design and learning is beneficial for fostering a culture of continuous learning and adaptability, helping employees develop the skills they need to navigate a rapidly changing technological landscape.

Similarly, James Duggan and Jérôme Sulbout (Chapter 20) call for more research on how work design principles can be applied to address the specific AI challenges of non-traditional work arrangements in the gig economy such as algorithmic exploitation. Algorithmic exploitation can limit the autonomy of gig workers, forcing them to work specific hours and to meet specific targets which may not be reasonable or feasible, with poor implications for well-being. Redesigning the use of algorithmic management systems to improve worker autonomy and performance management systems would help mitigate these negative effects. However, it is important to keep in mind the diverse motivations and needs of gig workers to address research questions in this area properly.

Theme 4: Work Design for Diversity and Inclusion

The future of work demands a more inclusive approach to work design, recognizing the diverse needs and preferences of a workforce that increasingly spans generations, engages in a variety of work arrangements, and contributes value through both paid and unpaid activities. Several chapters in this book have highlighted key areas where work design research can promote diversity and inclusion by focusing on specific population groups and their unique work experiences. For example, in Chapter 23, Robin Umbra and Ulrike Fassbender acknowledge that older workers may have different needs and preferences than their younger counterparts. For example, older workers may experience declining physical capacity and increased fatigue which could restrict the type of work they can do, or they be more interested in working beyond retirement age because they receive support, for mentoring younger workers or creating meaningful connections at work. Future research should investigate how work

634 TRANSFORMATIVE WORK DESIGN

design preferences change across the lifespan, moving beyond age-based cutoffs (such as those aged forty-five years and older being considered the "aging workforce") to consider how employers can maintain older workers and contribute to a solution of demographic changes. This will help organizations create work designs that are responsive to the evolving needs of older workers.

Duggan and Sulbout (Chapter 20) also call for more research on how work design principles can address inclusion and diversity challenges observed in non-traditional work arrangements in the gig economy, such as the lack of job security, and social isolation, both of which we know to lead to poor well-being. Additionally, future research could explore how work design principles can be applied to both paid and unpaid work due to technological progress. Bienefeld and Grote suggest that the demand for human labor may decline due to AI-driven productivity meaning unpaid work, such as caregiving, volunteering, and community involvement, could be potentially fulfilling alternative avenues for individuals to find meaning and purpose. Thus, future research could investigate how the principles of work design, traditionally applied to paid employment, can be adapted to enhance the meaningfulness and motivation associated with unpaid work. It is also important to investigate how individuals balance their time and energy between paid and unpaid activities, and how individuals' identities and sense of purpose will be shaped by a changing balance between paid and unpaid work. This could increase participation in the workforce, improving well-being and productivity.

Theme 5: Proactive Employees Who Craft Their Jobs

Beyond the traditional top-down perspective on work design, several chapters illuminate the potential for employees to actively influence their work experiences, particularly when dealing with rapid technological advancements and evolving work arrangements. This emphasis on employee proactivity highlights a crucial shift in the field, recognizing individuals not as passive recipients of their work, but as having agency in actively creating conditions that help them to work more effectively and dealing with novel demands.

Proactive adaptation to technological change. Drawing on the insights presented by Irene de Pater (Chapter 11) on the antecedents of developmental challenges, future research could investigate the individual and contextual factors that facilitate or hinder proactive adaptation to technological change. This leads to a number of important questions that have yet to be explored. For example, what personality traits promote proactive crafting in the context of new technology? Do people engage in different job crafting behaviors depending on differences in motivational orientations (such as approach or avoidance orientation)? What is the contextual role of effective leadership in the context of job crafting? What can leaders do to help or sustain crafting that is beneficial for the individual and their team? How does the organizational culture and climate influence employees' willingness to engage with new technologies? Drawing on the insights from Maria Tims and Melissa Twemlow (Chapter 16) and Evangelia Demerouti, Maria Peeters, and Machteld van den Heuvel (Chapter 17) that job crafting is an individual-driven bottom-up strategy that workers use to more proactively shape their work experiences, future research could explore how job crafting strategies can be adapted to support employees in finding meaning and purpose work environments where many tasks are being handled by AI-augmented technology. For example, under what conditions do employees use job crafting to proactively identify and develop new skills that complement AI capabilities? On the counterpart, we need to understand when AI-enabled work leads to deskilling, knowledge decline, or problems in safety-related jobs.

The dark side of employee proactivity and job crafting. While emphasizing the importance of employee proactivity and bottom-up work redesign behaviors like job crafting, this book has also identified potential risks and downsides. As discussed by Tims and Twemlow (Chapter 16) and Arnold B. Bakker and Yuri S. Scharp (Chapter 18), some forms of job crafting could have unintended consequences, such as work intensification, role conflict, and even burnout. Future research needs to explore the potential "dark side" of proactivity and develop strategies for mitigating these risks. The wise proactivity framework proposed by Parker and colleagues (2019) could be adopted to facilitate future research questions in this area. Specifically, Parker and colleagues (2019) proposed that wise proactivity involves the balanced consideration of the task and strategic context (e.g., whether the proactivity is appropriate given the tasks that employees are expected to do, or given the organization's strategic goals), social and relational aspects (e.g., whether the proactivity affects others' interests), and one's own self-regulation (e.g., whether proactivity fits the individuals' interests, expertise, and resources). We also need more research that looks at the consequences of individual job crafting behaviors in groups and teams. Particularly, when workers have high level of interdependence, then individuals who job craft may create conditions that potentially disadvantage others (e.g., by shifting workload to others). Particularly, when workers try to reduce hindering demands and manage their workload, coworkers could see this as social loafing and group tensions if job crafters are seen as "free riders."

Theme 6: Leaders as Work Designers

This book repeatedly underscores the powerful role of managers and leaders in making decisions that affect work design and, which consequently trickle down

636   TRANSFORMATIVE WORK DESIGN

to, employee experiences. From allocating tasks and setting expectations to implementing self-managing teams which fosters empowerment and a positive work environment. Leaders can act as "work designers"; that is, they influence the structure and meaning of work for their subordinates. Several future research directions can be considered.

First, leaders can actively change and adapt the work design of their subordinates. Building on the recommendations by Caroline Knight and Florian E. Klonek (Chapter 12), effective work re-design involves participatory interventions. This means that not only leaders need to effectively engage with their staff members to get in the co-creation of better work design. For example, this could mean seeking employee input on what aspects of their work they would like to change and how that could realistically be achieved (e.g., creating more team autonomy but giving teams more control over decision-making). However, we need a better understanding of this complex interplay regarding the top-down and bottom-up processes that govern these strategies. Additionally, as indicated by Kevin Daniels, David Watson, Rachel Nayani, and Helen Fitzhugh (Chapter 13), more efforts need to be made to improve the resources and training for leaders in work design. Future research could explore the effectiveness of training resources or leadership development programs focused on work design, examining how these resources and programs influence leaders' behaviors and their employees' work experiences. Leaders can also actively help to promote worker proactivity and bottom-up strategies in and of itself. As indicated by Tims and Twemlow (Chapter 16) and Bakker and Scharp (Chapter 18), leaders can encourage job crafting and other proactive behaviors that promote positive changes in work design by providing autonomy support, fostering a psychologically safe environment for experimentation, and encouraging employees to take ownership of their work.

Third, leaders could work toward creating a more dynamic, diverse and inclusive workforce, which links to Theme 4, discussed earlier. A dynamic workforce means that organizations can adapt quickly to changing customer, economic and social trends, and remain competitive. A diverse workforce means that employees of all ages and sectors of society, with different skill and from different cultures are included in the workforce, promoting inclusion, well-being, and innovation. Building on insights from Duggan and Sulbout (Chapter 20) and Bin Wang, Xiang Fang, and Yi Zhao (Chapter 22) on the challenges of virtual and hybrid teams, future research could explore the specific leadership behaviors and strategies that are most effective in these contexts, such as building trust remotely, fostering communication and collaboration, and providing support for work–life balance. With the prevalent aging problem in many countries, future research could investigate how leaders can effectively manage and support an aging workforce, making adaptations to work design that better suits the unique needs and preferences of older workers.

Fourth, leaders play a key role in facilitating effective human–AI collaboration. Building on insights from Bienefeld and Grote (Chapter 19) on the need to develop new skills for human–AI collaboration, future research could explore what specific leadership behaviors are needed to foster responsible AI development and implementation, ensure worker agency and control, and promote ethical decision-making in AI-augmented work environments. In terms of the importance of explainable AI, future research could examine how leaders can communicate effectively with employees about AI systems, fostering transparency and trust in algorithmic decision-making processes.

Theme 7: Methodological Advancements

This book has also covered the key methods that researchers are using to study work design. While some of these methods are quite matured, we do see novel methods emerging that allow to study work design and its outcomes from multiple angles as well as tracking changes over time.

Measurement. One limitation of many work design studies which has been identified in the chapter by Anita Keller and Tina Armasu (Chapter 8) is the heavy reliance on self-report measures. The authors pointed out some key problems, such as social desirability bias, recall bias, and common method bias. In this book, Keller and Armasu suggested using a broader range of measurement techniques, such as observations of work behaviors and environments, existing data sources (e.g., performance metrics, email logs, activity trackers), physiological measures, and cognitive assessments to improve limitations of self-report measures.

Moreover, new measures are needed to better drive work design research forward. For example, researchers need to develop new measures for new work characteristics arising from the changing nature of work such as the gig economy, algorithmic management, and AI.

Rather than focusing on AI as a substantive construct, Emily Campion and Michael Campion (Chapter 24) turn things upside down, and provide some interesting directions for the future. The authors suggest that AI focused text analyses could be used as a novel way to conduct job analyses and measure work characteristics. These suggestions could be solutions for the problems identified by David Holman and Anthony Rafferty (Chapter 9) who indicated the lack of appropriate measures restricted the use of national surveys to investigate how national and global factors shape work design. Cory M. Eisenhard and

638 TRANSFORMATIVE WORK DESIGN

Frederick P. Morgeson (Chapter 3) also pointed out that team-level characteristics are not simply aggregations of individual characteristics but require unique conceptualizations and measurements.

Holistic (whole jobs) versus atomistic perspectives (work design dimensions). While much research has looked at single dimensions of job characteristic and its unique impact on employees (thus taking a more atomistic view), there have been calls to look at work design more holistically (e.g., by studying configurations, or sets of work characteristics operating together in a whole job as they exhibit a collective impact on worker experiences). The holistic versus atomistic views on work design are both important to address different research questions. For example, Sonnentag (Chapter 4) suggested a more holistic perspective on job design can offer new insights into how work design affects individuals' well-being as specific combinations of job characteristics may be particularly beneficial for well-being. On the contrary, De Boeck and colleagues (Chapter 6) called for investigating job characteristics separately to test different mechanisms between work design and identity. Similarly, Duggan and Sulbout (Chapter 20) recommended investigating specific work design features that facilitate or inhibit the quality of gig work. For emerged new work design characteristics in new work contexts (e.g., the implementation of AI and algorithm management, virtual work, etc.) or less investigated work design areas (e.g., work design and identity), it is necessary to investigate the effects of specific job characteristics to provide a solid foundation for future research. In research areas (e.g., work design and well-being) where the effects of specific work design features have been studied thoroughly, it will benefit to adopt a holistic approach to investigate the effects of different configurations of job characteristics to provide deeper insights into the impact of work design.

Multi-level perspective. This book has also highlighted that work design needs to be investigated more from a multi-level lens. Many scholars in this book have advocated the multi-level perspective to investigate factors that shape work design and impacts of work design at different levels. For example, regarding the antecedents of work design, scholars in the book (Andrei et al.; de Pater; Holman & Rafferty) have suggested conducting multi-level studies to investigate how the interplay of national, occupational, organizational, managerial, and work group factors in shaping individual-level work design. In terms of outcomes, more research is needed that goes beyond individual-level outcome, but that looks at higher level of analysis (team-level and organizational-level outcomes). Future research could investigate how organizational factors and team-level characteristics not only trickle down to individual well-being, but also how these higher-level work design factors shape team and organizational performance (see Eisenhard and Morgeson, Chapter 3). This multi-level perspective is also important in work redesign processes and interventions.

For example, as employees are embedded in work groups and organizations, there could be interplay between individual crafting and social context (Tims & Twemlow, Chapter 16). Work redesign interventions also need to take wider organizational environments into account and investigate the complex interplay between changes at organizational, team, and individual levels (Knight & Klonek, Chapter 12).

Non-static lens on work design processes. As indicated in this book, work design is not static, and it could be reciprocally correlated with antecedents and outcomes. Thus, it is important to conduct longitudinal studies to capture the changes of work design and the temporal dynamics between work design changes and other factors. For example, while job characteristics could affect employee well-being (Sonnentag, Chapter 4), identity (De Boeck et al., Chapter 6), and personality (Wu & Wang, Chapter 7), these factors could also affect future job characteristics. Longitudinal research enables investigation of reciprocal relationships between work design and these factors and uncover how long the positive or negative effects of work design could be reflected in outcomes and vice versa. Another important view in work design research is that employees are not passive recipients of their work design, but they can proactively craft their jobs for the better. Tims and Twemlow (Chapter 16) pointed out a lack of research on how work design shapes employees' job crafting and the actual changes in work design due to job crafting. Longitudinal research could shed light on the temporal dynamics between work design and job crafting.

Further, multi-level analyses are critical to establish how wider organizational (e.g., policies and procedures, degree of centralization), cultural (e.g., social context and norms), and leadership (e.g., leader behaviors) factors affect work design at the team and individual level. While there is some research which has integrated individual and team levels of analysis, Eisenhard and Morgeson (Chapter 3) highlight that there is much less which has integrated the organizational level with team and individual levels. Eisenhard and Morgeson consider work design at the organizational level in terms of sets of work characteristics which work together to achieve desired outcomes. These include sets of work characteristics associated with scientific management, lean production, socio-technical systems, and high performance work systems, among others, which were all designed with the aim of increasing performance. Future research is required to delve into the sets of work characteristics that exist in current organizations and how they holistically influence team and individual work design.

In summary, the future research directions presented in this concluding chapter represent a roadmap for advancing the field of work design and shaping a future of work that is both productive and fulfilling for all. By addressing these critical gaps in our understanding and using innovative methodologies,

640 TRANSFORMATIVE WORK DESIGN

academics can contribute to knowledge that helps solve critical current issues, such as designing work for an aging workforce and sustaining meaningful work in the face of AI and increased workforce mobility.

References

Parker, S. K. & Knight, C. (2023). The SMART model of work design: A higher order structure to help see the wood from the trees. *Human Resource Management 63*, 265–291. https://doi.org/10.1002/hrm.22200

Parker, S. K., Van den Broeck, A., & Holman, D. (2017). Work design influences: A synthesis of multilevel factors that affect the design of jobs. *Academy of Management Annals 11*(1), 267–308. https://doi.org/10.5465/annals.2014.0054

Parker, S. K., Wang, Y., & Liao, J. (2019). When Is Proactivity Wise? A Review of Factors That Influence the Individual Outcomes of Proactive Behavior. *Annual Review of Organizational Psychology and Organizational Behavior 6*(1), 221–248. https://doi.org/10.1146/annurev-orgpsych-012218-015302

Parker, S. K., Ward, M. K., & Fisher, G. G. (2021). Can high-quality jobs help workers learn new tricks? A multidisciplinary review of work design for cognition. *Academy of Management Annals 15*(2), 406–454. https://doi.org/10.5465/annals.2019.0057

Tarafdar, M., Cooper, C. L., & Stich, J. F. (2019). The technostress trifecta—techno eustress, techno distress and design: Theoretical directions and an agenda for research. *Information Systems Journal 29*(1), 6–42. https://doi.org/10.1111/isj.12169

Warr, P. (2013). Jobs and job-holders: Two sources of happiness and unhappiness. In I. Boniwell, S. A. David, & A. C. Ayers (Eds.), *Oxford handbook of happiness* (pp. 733–750). Oxford University Press. http://dx.doi.org/10.1093/oxfordhb/9780199557257.013.0054

Appendix
A Summary of Future Research Directions in Each Chapter

Chapter 2: The Evolution of Work Design Theory and Research

- Clarify assumptions about who benefits from motivational work design and why.
- Broaden the scope of job characteristics studied to gain a broader understanding of factors influencing employee outcomes.
- Expand the scope of work design outcomes to include learning and development, ambidexterity, and performance.
- Increase focus on the antecedents of work design (e.g., personality traits, managers' role in work redesign).

Chapter 3: Multi-level Work Design: Integrating Work Characteristics Across Individual, Team, and Organizational Levels of Analysis

Team Level:

- Conduct more comprehensive and careful reviews of the team autonomy literature.
- Investigate the potential costs of team autonomy and decentralization relating to coordination when considering the interdependence between teams.
- Examine the impact of modern AI and work-from-home policies on team-level work characteristics.

Organizational Level:

- Conduct research on how organizational level factors shape the meaning of work at lower levels.
- Perform an integrative review of the literature on HR constructs that interact with work design.
- Examine work design alongside other organizational design considerations to understand which decisions around work design are most important.

642 TRANSFORMATIVE WORK DESIGN

Chapter 4: Job-Design and Well-Being: A Review of the Empirical Evidence

- More integrative research: Conduct meta-analyses focused on neglected work characteristics and provide a more holistic perspective on work design.
- More explicit inclusion of time: Investigate how job design influences well-being over different time intervals using rigorous longitudinal designs.
- Explore the relationship between job design and eudaimonic well-being, including experienced meaning and growth satisfaction, and underlying mechanisms.

Chapter 5: Work Design and Performance

- Disentangle the mechanisms underlying the effects of work design on performance (e.g., explore motivation, learning, and cognitive capacity).
- Examine how work design influences performance when considering the distinction between primary and secondary tasks.
- Investigate how work design impacts IT safety and security, particularly in the context of high workloads.
- Explore the potential for work design characteristics to have both positive and negative effects on different performance types.
- Investigate how work design can hinder or facilitate knowledge sharing and learning, specifically considering the role of social work characteristics in knowledge hiding.
- Study how the interplay of AI and work design affects different types of performance and identify potential challenges.

Chapter 6: Work Design and Identity: Taking Stock of What We Know and Charting Pathways for Future Research

- Investigate how technology and virtual workplaces shape job complexity and information processing, ultimately affecting workers' identities.
- Investigate how identity affects work characteristics: Explore the antecedents of work design through a focus on the role of identity.
- Further investigate the influence of work design on more stable elements of the self and non-work identities.

A SUMMARY OF FUTURE RESEARCH DIRECTIONS IN EACH CHAPTER   643

- Study the impact of work design on identities beyond organizational and occupational identity, including leader identity, team identity, and role identity.
- Enrich the temporal understanding of the relationship between work design and identity.
- Explore work characteristics as triggers of identity opportunities: Investigate how work design can facilitate positive self-evaluations and help people establish harmonious identity networks.
- Explore how work design affects identity conflict and vice versa.
- Conduct research that directly examines the role of identity processes in mediating the relationship between work design and its outcomes.
- Unpack the complex processes at play to understand how work design shapes identity.
- Investigate the work design–identity relationship across different geographical/cultural contexts.

Chapter 7: What you do makes who you are: The role of work design in personality change

- Explore the function of the bottom-up work design approaches in shaping personality change processes (e.g., job crafting).
- Design and build longitudinal datasets purposefully for addressing questions of work and personality change.
- Conduct cross-cultural research to understand how work design drives personality change trajectories across different social systems and cultures.

Chapter 8: Methodology in Work Design Research: The Past, Present, and (Longitudinal) Future

- Conduct more studies testing the effects of work redesign interventions.
- Emphasize longitudinal research designs to examine temporal processes, change dynamics, and reciprocal relationships between variables.
- Use objective measures of work design and outcomes (e.g., observations, tracking data, cognitive assessments, and biomarkers).
- Pay more attention to social dynamics by incorporating social network analysis and other techniques to analyze how work design impacts social interactions and relationships.
- Leverage technologies like augmented and virtual reality to study work design in complex and dynamic environments.

644 TRANSFORMATIVE WORK DESIGN

Chapter 9: Global and National Factors Shaping Work Design

- Develop a comprehensive framework for national and global effects on work design.
- Unpack the mechanisms through which national and global factors shape work design.
- Explore the interplay between national and global factors and the role of national institutions in mediating these effects.
- Extend research to cover a broader range of factors (e.g., climate change, migration) and geographic areas.

Chapter 10: Occupational, Organizational, Managerial, and Work Group Factors

- Conduct more cross-level research between work design antecedents, teams and work groups, and individual work design.
- Investigate the "trickle-up" effects of work design by studying how work design at lower levels impacts higher-level factors such as organizational structure and occupational norms.
- Explore how work design changes for individual employees over time and investigate potential asymmetric relationships across different levels of work design.

Chapter 11: On the Creation of Developmental Jobs

- Explore leadership behaviors that stimulate employees to choose and negotiate for developmental challenges (e.g., empowering and inclusive leadership).
- Examine factors that influence supervisors' task allocation decisions (e.g., supervisor perceptions of employee performance, self-efficacy, the quality of the supervisor-subordinate relationship, and stereotypes and biases).
- Investigate how team diversity influences the negotiation for and engagement in developmental challenges.

Chapter 12: How and Why do Top-Down Work Redesign Interventions Impact Well-being and Performance?

- Conduct multi-organizational, industry-wide research to inform policy and practice.

A SUMMARY OF FUTURE RESEARCH DIRECTIONS IN EACH CHAPTER   645

- Investigate how work design interventions affect performance-relevant team processes (e.g., psychological states).
- Examine the complex interplay between changes at different organizational levels (e.g., organizational, team, department, individual) and the mechanisms by which these changes impact work design and outcomes.
- Adopt a person-centered approach by considering the constellations of work characteristics that individuals experience and how these change following interventions.

Chapter 13: Implementing and Sustaining Work Redesign

- Examine how jobs evolve over time in relation to organizational values, how job redesign may influence organizational culture, and the impact of job redesign on planned and unplanned changes within organizations.
- Examine the implementation and sustainability of coordinated job redesign activities across multiple organizations and industrial sectors
- Explore alternative methodologies, for example, by borrowing methods from strategic change and organizational culture change research and considering using large databases or simulation studies to forecast the effects and evolution of work redesign.

Chapter 14: Unleashing Magic: A PARRTH to Participatory Work Redesign

- The PARRTH model provides a structured, participatory framework for work redesign, emphasizing stakeholder involvement, data-driven decision-making, and a phased approach (Prepare, Assess, Reflect, Redesign, Track, and Habituate) to ensure sustainable improvements in work quality, employee well-being, and organizational outcomes.
- Prepare: Lay the groundwork by securing commitment from stakeholders, forming a diverse steering group, and developing a clear communication strategy to ensure alignment and support for the redesign.
- Assess: Diagnose the current situation, gather baseline data, and identify key issues to address through surveys, interviews, and observations while fostering broad participation.
- Reflect: Synthesize and share assessment findings with stakeholders, enabling collective understanding of problems, clarifying redesign focus, and maintaining trust and engagement.
- Redesign: Generate and evaluate multiple work redesign ideas using criteria linked to project goals, selecting and planning actionable changes while addressing root causes.

646   TRANSFORMATIVE WORK DESIGN

- Track: Monitor the implementation process, assess the intervention's impact on individuals and groups, and document lessons learned to improve future change efforts.
- Habituate: Embed the redesign into the organization through alignment of systems, ongoing support, and potential scaling while ensuring sustainability and continuous improvement.

Chapter 15: Understanding the Outcomes of Work Transformations: Evaluation of Organizational Interventions

- Conduct research that identifies and tests CMO-configurations (context + mechanism = outcome) to understand the conditions under which interventions work, including exploring mechanisms and using coincidence analysis to determine the most important factors contributing to intervention outcomes.
- Implement ongoing process evaluation to identify adjustments needed to improve intervention effectiveness and ensure that changes are maintained over time.
- Conduct meta-analyses of organizational interventions to synthesize evidence on the effects of interventions, considering mediators, moderators, and contextual factors.
- Use the FRAQOI (Framework for Reporting and Assessing the Quality of Organizational Interventions) to improve the reporting and evaluation of organizational interventions.

Chapter 16: Job Crafting Theory and Perspectives

- Conduct research that examines the antecedents and outcomes of each of the eight distinct job crafting constructs.
- Explore how specific work characteristics, including task interdependence and organizational support, influence different types of job crafting.
- Investigate which job demands and resources are most likely to change because of job crafting and explore how different types of crafting affect specific job characteristics.
- Explore how job crafting by one person impacts the work of others, particularly in interdependent work contexts.

Chapter 17: Job Crafting Interventions

- Include other stakeholders and broader data sources to better understand organizational needs and determine the most appropriate interventions.

A SUMMARY OF FUTURE RESEARCH DIRECTIONS IN EACH CHAPTER   647

- Develop multi-level interventions.
- Train leaders in the principles of job crafting.
- Explore the use of digital tools and AI, such as coaching chatbots, to enhance the delivery and effectiveness of job crafting interventions.
- Apply rigorous research designs by using randomized controlled trials or quasi-experimental designs.
- Tailor interventions and measurement instruments to meet the needs of specific employee groups and work contexts.
- Investigate the role of different mechanisms, including those based on SDT and social exchange theory, in mediating the relationship between job crafting interventions and outcomes.
- Examine the moderating effects of individual, organizational, team, and leadership-level factors on the effectiveness of job crafting interventions.
- Include a wider range of outcomes (e.g., creativity, innovation, customer service, potential unintended consequences).

Chapter 18: It Pays to Play: Playful Work Design

- Investigate how leadership behaviors and workplace characteristics can influence the adoption of playful work design strategies.
- Develop training programs aimed at teaching employees about playful work design and how to implement it effectively.
- Investigate potential negative consequences of playful work design, such as misinterpretation or over-extension in demanding contexts.
- Conduct longitudinal research to understand the long-term effects of habitual playful work design on employee well-being and performance.
- Explore how playful study and sport design can be used to enhance learning and training, respectively.

Chapter 19: Artificial Intelligence: How It Changes the Landscape for Work Design Research and Practice

- Investigate the effects of AI automation and augmentation on job characteristics such as job autonomy, skill variety, and relational aspects of work.
- Explore how to design AI systems that enhance human autonomy and control while minimizing the risks of dehumanization.
- Examine how accountability for errors in human–AI interaction should be distributed across different stakeholder groups when control is shared.
- Explore the impact of AI on whole occupations and the skills and knowledge required for success in a rapidly evolving labor market.

648 TRANSFORMATIVE WORK DESIGN

- Investigate the implications of AI-driven productivity gains for the overall meaning of work.
- Investigate the challenges faced by AI developers and how work design can support human-centered system design, ethical decision-making, and user-aware technology development.

Chapter 20: Reimagining Work Design in Contemporary Employment: The Disruptive Rise of the Gig Economy

- Examine the various types or "profiles" of gig workers in terms of motivations, needs, and desires to understand how these factors influence work design perceptions.
- Investigate how platform organizations design and organize work, and the role they play in shaping the gig economy.
- Investigate whether and how the gig economy can be redesigned to improve work quality, and benefit both workers and organizations.

Chapter 21: The Perils of Algorithmic Management for Work Design

- Identify the potential negative impacts of algorithmic management systems on work and workers and create tools for assessing and mitigating these risks.
- Explore the factors that influence the implementation of algorithmic management tools and the organizational contexts that facilitate responsible algorithmic management.
- Study the skills and knowledge needed to interact effectively with algorithmic systems and develop strategies for training and education.
- Explore how workers can use job crafting to enhance their work design and agency in the presence of algorithmic management.

Chapter 22: Understanding Why, When, and How Virtual Work Works through the Lens of a Work Design Perspective

- Examine the impact of virtual work practices on temporal work design characteristics (e.g., temporal predictability, task segmentation).
- Explore the relationship between virtual work and creative performance.
- Investigate the role of leadership in virtual work, such as studying the impact of leadership attitudes and behaviors on virtual work design, and the development of effective leadership practices for virtual teams.

A SUMMARY OF FUTURE RESEARCH DIRECTIONS IN EACH CHAPTER   649

- Investigate how employees craft their work across different domains, such as work and family, and the impact of these cross-domain crafting strategies on virtual work outcomes.
- Conduct research in a wider range of countries and cultural contexts to understand the influence of cultural values on virtual work experiences and outcomes.
- Conduct longitudinal studies to investigate the dynamic processes of virtual work and explore how work design changes over time in response to new challenges and opportunities.

Chapter 23: Designing Work to Retain an Aging Workforce

- Explore a wider range of work design characteristics in the context of the socioemotional selectivity framework (e.g., investigate how different work design characteristics influence the priorities and goals of older workers).
- Conduct longitudinal studies to assess changes in work design preferences and outcomes as individuals age.
- Examine the potential for a curvilinear relationship between perceived input–output balance and work attitudes, such as investigating whether "too much" equilibrium between job demands and resources can be detrimental to worker attitudes.
- Explore the role of aging in shaping how individuals interpret and respond to different work design features.
- Explore the moderator and mediator effects of age on the relationship between work design characteristics and work outcomes

Chapter 24: Text Analysis Using Artificial Intelligence as a Tool for Job Analysis and Job Design

- Expand applications beyond selection, for example, by exploring the use of AI-enabled text analysis for performance management, training, engagement, and organizational culture.
- Use text analysis to identify employee preferences that are not captured by traditional measures, leading to better job design and satisfaction.
- Develop and validate automated content analysis methods to efficiently analyze employee feedback and gain valuable insights.
- Address ethical issues by ensure fairness, bias mitigation, transparency, and responsible data use in AI-driven text analysis for HR.
- Explore the synergy and benefits of combining AI-enabled text analysis with other HR technologies like people analytics and talent management systems.

Index

For the benefit of digital users, indexed terms that span two pages (e.g., 52–53) may, on occasion, appear on only one of those pages.

Tables and figures are indicated by an italic *t* and *f* following the paragraph number.

Abildgaard, Johan, 394
ability. *See also* knowledge, skills, abilities, and other characteristics; knowledge, skills, and abilities
  meta-cognitive, 490–491
  variation in, 371
absence, 312, 379
  peer norms, 181
absenteeism, 34
Accenture, 488–489
achievement motivation, 289
Ackley, Betty, 389–392
action plans, 386–388
  adherence to, 401*t*
  developing, 376
  program theory, 401*t*
action regulation theory, 152
active labor market policies, 240–241
active learning, 152, 154
adaptive behavior, 155
adaptive performance, 154–155, 163
adaptivity, 148–149, 427–428
affect
  circumplex model of, 97–98
  cognition and, 153–154
  feedback and, 122
Afota, Marie-Colombe, 548
agency hindrances, 472
agile HRM, 268–269
agile organizations, 264
agile work, 161
aging population, 22
  work redesign and, 343–344
aging workforce, 569, 633–634
  feedback and, 596
  findings on, 571–594
  future research directi3ons, 600–601, 649
  job autonomy and, 595–597
  job complexity and, 595
  job demands and, 596–597
  job resources and, 596–597

literature review for, 570–571
  practical implications, 600
  social support and, 596
  task characteristics and, 595
  theoretical background for, 569–570
  theoretical implications, 599–600
  work context and, 596
  work design characteristics and retention of, 594–597
agonistic play, 466
AI. *See* artificial intelligence
AI chatbots, 488–489
Albertsen, Karen, 391–392
Alcover, Carlos-Maria, 592
Alexa, 495
algorithmic competencies, 522–523
algorithmic decision making, 531–532, 537–538
algorithmic management (AM), 21, 268–269, 490, 531–533
  antecedents of, 539–540
  autonomy and, 533–534
  coping with, 536–537
  future research directions, 539–540, 648
  in gig economy, 509–511, 513, 517, 532, 533–534
  growth of, 532
  improving, 537–539
  initial conception of, 532
  job crafting and, 538, 540
  knowledge characteristics and, 534–535
  organizational choices and, 537–538
  policy and regulation and, 539
  risk assessment for, 539
  social characteristics and, 535–536
  work characteristics and, 533–536
  work demands and, 536
  work design and, 532–533
algorithmic monitoring, 531–532
algorithmic skills and literacy, 540
algorithms, 160–161

652 INDEX

alternative causes, 390
AM. *See* algorithmic management
Amazon, employee surveillance by, 3
Amazon Mechanical Turk, 20, 509, 515–516
Amazon Social Chatbot Alexa, 495
AmazonTurk, 491
ambivalent sexism theory, 287–288
Amey, Rachel C., 612–613
Anderson, Deirdre, 548
Andrei, Daniela, 13–14
antecedents of work design
    future research directions for, 274–276
    leadership, 272–274
    local work group, 269–274
    occupation, 260–263
    organization, 263–269
approach-avoidance behavioral
        crafting, 423–427
approach-avoidance motivation theory, 419
approach behavioral resource crafting, 421
approach cognitive crafting, 428
approach crafting, 427–428
approach motivation, 419, 429
approach resources crafting
        behaviors, 424–425
app-work, 20–21, 509–510, 523–524
    autonomy in, 514–515
    complexities and issues in, 513–515
    deactivation of workers in, 514
    key features of, 512–513
    speed of arrangements for, 514
    work design in, 512–515
AR. *See* augmented reality
Armasu, Tina, 12, 637
Arthur, Jeffrey B., 83
artificial intelligence (AI), 15, 19–20, 160–161,
        483, 531, 609
    algorithmic management and, 490
    autonomy and, 489–490, 497–498
    complex exams and, 490
    future research directions, 496–498,
        647–648
    in healthcare, 488, 491
    in job analysis and job design, 23, 610–617,
        611*f*
    job crafting and, 456
    job performance and, 163
    job quality changes from, 488–492
    occupation and meaning of work changes
        from, 492–494
    risks of, 495
    skills for collaborating with, 490–491
    team-level work and, 641

text analysis with, 609, 637–638
    work design and, 632–633
ASA. *See* Attraction-Selection-Attrition
Ashforth, Blake, 497
Askenazy, Philippe, 251–252
assessment questions, 615
Assess phase, 367–370
asymmetric effects, 216–217
atomization, 534
attention, 152–153
Attraction-Selection-Attrition (ASA), 196–197
attribute requirements, 613
Audenaert, Mieke, 423, 430–431
augmented reality (AR), 228–229
authenticity, 343–344
automated management, 21
automaticity, 152, 156
automation, 19, 160–161, 488–489
    algorithmic management and, 533
autonomous teams
    conditions for high performing, 228
    interdependence in, 82–83
    performance feedback and, 72
    STS and, 79
    task characteristics and, 63
autonomous work, 104–106, 105*t*
    experimental lab studies on, 122–123
    field interventions studies on, 127
autonomy, 33–34, 60*t*, 147–148, 163, 312–313,
        362, 378, 631
    AI and, 489–490, 497–498
    algorithmic management and, 533–534
    in app-work, 514–515
    channeled, 72
    decision-making, 551–552
    downsizing and, 265
    efficiency improvement and, 324
    feedback and, 72
    flexible work arrangements and, 267–268
    formalization and, 265
    in gig work, 510–511
    hedonic wellbeing and, 100–104
    individual, within teams, 64
    job enrichment and enlargement and, 312
    measuring changes in, 215
    motivation and, 34
    performance and, 64, 150
    scheduling, 549, 551–552
    SMTs and, 315, 325–326
    stress and, 67, 104, 122
    team, 63–65, 82–83, 159, 270–272
    TPS and, 56
    virtual work and, 549, 551–552, 554–555

wellbeing and, 122–123
avoidance motivation, 419, 429
Axtell, Carolyn, 127, 312–313
"bag of words" approach, 613–614

Bailey, Erica, 558–559
Bakker, Arnold, 19, 36–39, 415, 417–418, 429, 471–473, 635
Balance Theory of Job Design, 79–80
Bamberger, Peter A., 122, 181
Bamforth, Ken, 31–32
Barley, Stephen, 508
Barratt, Tom, 522–523
Barrick, Murray, 64–65
basic income, 493
Bélanger, France, 556
Bellego, Maxime, 240, 251–252
beneficiary contact, 42
Berg, Justin, 427–428, 444–445
Bidirectional Encoder Representations from Transformers (BERT), 613, 615
Bienefeld, Gudela, 19–20, 637
Bienefeld, Nadine, 488, 632, 634
big data, 492, 531
Big Five traits, 11, 619–620
    career roles and, 194
    occupational characteristics and, 194
biomarkers, 224–225, 209t
Birdi, Kamal, 159
Biron, Michal, 122, 181
Bizzi, Lorenzo, 428
Björk, Janina, 126
Bligh, Michelle, 620
blinding, 398
Blume, Brian, 404
Blustein, David, 118
BMW, 371, 376
Bond, Frank, 127
bottom-up work redesign, 17–19, 219–220, 415
    personality and, 643
    SMTs and, 314–315
Boudreau, John, 549
brain drain, 248–249
Brenninkmeijer, Veerle, 418–419
Brougham, Ruby, 591–592
Bruning, Patrick, 419
Bujold, Antoine, 537–538
Bunce, David, 127
bureaucracies, 264
burnout, 15, 635
Burns, Tom, 57–58
Bush, George W., 620

call centers
    AI and, 488–489
    algorithmic management and, 21
    chat bots and, 160–161
    interdependence in, 369
    job enrichment and enlargement interventions in, 312–313
    performance predictors in, 150
    work redesign and, 359
Campbell, John, 147, 152
Campion, Emily, 23, 621–622, 637–638
Campion, Michael, 23, 58, 419, 621–622, 637–638
Cao, Jie, 295–296
capitalism, 239, 243
cardiovascular indicators, 225
CareerBuilder, 610–612
career development, developmental challenge and, 286
career identity, 177
career roles, Big Five traits and, 194
Caringal-Go, Jaimee, 558–559
Carstensen, Laura, 591–592
Carter, Kameron, 316–318
Caspi, Avshalom, 10
causal inference, 390
causality, 212–213
Cendales-Ayala, Boris, 218
centralization, 264–265
    of decision making, 264
Centre for Transformative Work Design, 98
challenge demands, 112, 154
challenge-hindrance frameworks, 46
challenging work experiences. See developmental challenge
Chan, Ngai, 533–534
change
    communication importance to, 366
    describing and explaining trajectories of, 215–216
    effective facilitation of, 380–381
    longitudinal research designs and measuring, 214
    readiness for, 391
    root causes and systemic, 373
    spreading, 380
change facilitation, 380–381
channeled autonomy, 72
chat bots, 160–161, 488–489, 491, 495
Chat-GPT, 483, 495
    job description created with, 615, 616f
Chen, Gilad, 271
Chen, Yaru, 261–262

654 INDEX

Chiaburu, Dan, 118
Christina, Sian, 267, 322, 324
circumplex model of affect, 97–98
Clarke, Sharon, 158
Click Worker, 515–516
climate change, 249–250, 238t
cloud-based crowdwork, 515–516
CMO-configurations, 393, 395, 400–405, 401t,
    646
coal mining, 315
*Cochrane Handbook for Systematic
    Review*, 397
Cockburn, Bethany, 225–226
coercion, 340–341
    algorithmic management and, 533–534
cognition
    affect and, 153–154
    assessments of, 225–226
    creativity and, 156
    employment regimes and, 244
    job complexity and, 551
    job control and, 225–226
    wellbeing and, 153
    work design and, 11–12, 152–154, 631
cognitive assessment, 209t
cognitive capacity
    performance and, 152–154
    technology and, 160–161
cognitive crafting, 429–430, 440–441, 468
cognitive demands, 35, 150–151
    of flexible work, 554–555
    occupations and, 260–261
    safety behaviors and, 158
    social democratic regimes and, 244
Cohen, Stanley, 312
coincidence analysis, 404–405
collaborative work, 161
colleague support, 421, 430–431, 447
collective decision making, 320
collective team crafting, 373
Collins, Alison, 550
common method bias, 213, 222, 637
communication
    in change processes, 366
    of early redesign successes, 377
    with stakeholders, 366
    virtual work and, 548, 552–553
communion hindrances, 472
competition, 472
    designing, 467, 467t
conflict
    fracturing and, 342
    inter-role, 548

role, 635
    team, 271–272
    work-family, 551–552
confounders, 397–398
conscientiousness, 471
conservation of resources theory (COR
    theory), 38, 323, 452
consultancy, 505–507
content analysis, 612–613
contest-based crowdwork, 515–516
contextual characteristics, 259
    identity and, 181
    at team level, 73–74
continental regimes, 243–244
contingency theory, 57–58
contingent labor, 505–507. *See also* gig work
continuous performance monitoring, 490
continuous task improvement, 77–78
contract-based work, 506
control, 9–10
co-option, 340–341
coordinating functions, 340–341
coordination activities, interdependence
    and, 160
Cordery, John, 318–319
COR theory. *See* conservation of resources
    theory
Costa, Paul, 191, 196
Costantini, Arianna, 450
Courtright, Stephen, 71, 296
covariation, 390
COVID-19 pandemic, 19, 227, 268–269,
    275–276, 545
    as discrete context, 397–398
    playful work design during, 472–473
    remote and hybrid work and, 21–22
    virtual work during, 554–556, 558
    working conditions and, 388
co-workers
    AI and changes between, 491
    dyadic studies and, 228
    influence of, 196–197
crafting interventions, 18
creativity, 148–149, 155–156, 163
    occupational, 194–195
    role clarity and, 162
    in virtual work, 557–558
critical incident techniques, 373
critical thinking, 490–491
cross-sectional research designs, 209t

crowdwork, 20–21, 509–510, 523–524
  complexities and issues in, 517–518
  job crafting and, 518
  key features of, 515–516
  macro-tasks in, 516, 518
  matchmaking in, 517
  micro-tasks in, 516, 518
  rating systems in, 517–518
  as remote work, 517
  as side work, 521
  work design in, 515–518
Cruz, Kevin, 271
Cullinane, Sarah-Jane, 78, 428
culture
  contextual factors and, 397–398
  job redesign outcomes and, 338
  learning, 290
  occupations and, 261–262
  service, 423–424
  supervisor task allocation decisions
    and, 295–296
  virtual work variances across, 559
Cummings, Thomas G., 66

Dai, Hengchen, 223–224
daily diary studies, 220–221
Daniels, Kevin, 15–16, 306–307, 336–337, 339,
  340–341, 351–352, 636
datafication, 534
De Beer, Leon, 427
De Boeck, Giverny, 10–11, 177–179, 629–631,
  638
decentralization, 264–265, 641
DeChurch, Leslie A., 67
decision making
  algorithmic, 531–532, 537–538
  autonomy in, 42, 551–552
  centralization of, 264
  collective, 320
  in healthcare work, 421–422
  task interdependence and, 341–342
  work design and, 274
De Dreu, Carsten, 67–68
De Fruyt, Filip, 194
de Jonge, Jan, 43
Delfanti, Alessandro, 535
delivery context, 340–341
Demand-Control Model, 7–8
Demand Induced Strain Compensation Model
  (DISC), 43
Demerouti, Evangelia, 18, 29, 33, 36–39,
  418–419, 441, 453–454, 456, 634–635
Dengler, Katharina, 241–242

De Pater, Irene, 14, 287–290, 293, 634–635
depersonalization, 128
Design Thinking, 373
De Simone, Stefania, 125–126
deskilling, 534
developmental challenge, 285–286
  antecedents of, 14, 287–294
  choosing, 288–290
  future research directions, 294–296, 644
  gender differences in, 287–288, 291–292
  job crafting and, 288
  leadership and, 295
  managerial skills and, 286
  negotiating for, 291–292
  supervisor assignment of, 292–296
de Wit, Frank, 67–68
De Witte, Hans, 7–8
De Witte, Lorenz, 629–630
Dhar, Rajib, 451–454, 457
Dickinson, Peter, 346
Dierdorff, Erich, 260–262, 275, 492–493
digitalization, 19, 21
digital platform organizations, 521–523
  changes to gig work and, 524
  data collection by, 520–521
  employment classification and, 509–510
  employment relationship and, 511
  engagement with, 520
  gig economy facilitated by, 508–509
  matchmaking by, 517
  speed of arrangements with, 514
Ding, He, 423
D'Innocenzo, Lauren, 67–68
DISC. See Demand Induced Strain
    Compensation Model
discrete contextual factors, 339–341, 344,
  397–398
Dishon-Berkovits, Miriam, 471–472
dissatisfaction, 32
distributed work, 160
diverse thinking, 374–375
diversity, 633–634, 636–637
  SMTs and team, 319
  team performance and, 291
division of labor, 30, 62
dominant voices, 369–370
Dong, Yanan, 421
Dong, Yuntao, 296
Dormann, Christian, 43
downsizing, 265
Dreison, Kimberly, 125–126
dropout, 221, 398, 401t
dual-task performance, 163

656 INDEX

Dubbelt, Lonneke, 451–452
Duggan, James, 20–21, 633, 634, 638
Dutton, Jane, 415, 417, 418, 429, 440–441, 449
dyads, 228
  task allocation in, 291–292
dynamic workforce, 636–637

Earle, Fiona, 122–123
early retirement, 15
Ebner, Christian, 549
Eddleston, Kimberly, 552
education
  approach resources crafting behaviors
    in, 424–425
  formative evaluation and, 396
  job crafting in, 424–426
  team crafting in, 426
  training systems and, 241–242
effective change facilitation, 380–381
Effective Public Health Practice Project
    (EFPPH), 397–398
efficiency, 7–8
  increasing, 324
effort ratio, 375
EFPPH. *See* Effective Public Health Practice
    Project
Eisenhardt, Corey, 8–9, 637–639
electrodermal indicators, 225
Elovainio, Marko, 181–182
email, 549–550
emerging adverse working conditions, 388
emotional demands, 43, 130–131, 223,
    242–243, 267–268, 473
employee job performance, 292
employee surveillance, 3
employee wellbeing, 268–269
Employment Charters, 346
employment policies, 240–241, 238t
employment practices, work design
    and, 306–307
employment protection legislation, 240–241
employment regime theory, 239, 243–244
employment relationship
  changes in, 507
  digital platform organizations and, 511
  external shocks and, 342–344
  in gig work, 508–509
empowering leadership, 290, 474, 476
empowerment, 271. *See also* team
    empowerment
endocrinological indicators, 225
engagement surveys, 369–370
entrepreneurial identity, 177

equipment use, 60t
  at team level, 74
ergonomics, 60t
  at team level, 73
ESCO. *See* European Skills, Competences,
    Qualifications and Occupations
Esser, Ingrid, 240
ethical judgment, 490–491
  technology development and, 494–495
eudaimonic wellbeing, 97–98, 130
  autonomous work and, 106
  relational work and, 112
  tolerable work and, 118
European Skills, Competences, Qualifications
    and Occupations (ESCO), 609–612
European Union (EU), trade unions in, 240
European Working Conditions Survey
    (EWCS), 600
evaluation planning, 401t
EWCS. *See* European Working Conditions
    Survey
expansion-oriented crafting, 440–441
experiential learning theory, 450–452
experimental research designs, 217–220, 209t
external shocks, 342–344
external validity, 218, 390, 392, 397
extrinsic motivation, 155–156

family identity, 177
Fana, Marta, 538
Fang, Xiang, 21–22, 636–637
Fasbender, Ulrike, 22–23, 633–634
faultlines, 319–320
fault rectification, 323–324
feedback, 9–10, 33–34, 60t, 100–104, 631
  affect and, 122
  aging workforce and, 596
  autonomy and, 72
  challenges in, 372
  from job, 66
  leader, 72
  learning and, 154, 323–324
  mastery and, 121–122
  from others, 72
  performance and, 150
  Reflect phase and, 371–372
  task, 147–148
  at team level, 72
feedback loops, 216
Feeney, Brooke, 465–466
Felten, Edward, 490
Feng, Jie, 179–180
field experimental studies, 218–219

INDEX

field intervention studies, 124–130
field study, 209t, 213
FIFO. See fly-in-fly-out work arrangements
FigShare, 403
Fischbach, Andrea, 419
Fischer, Agneta, 289–290
Fisher, Gwenith G., 11–12
Fitzhugh, Helen, 15–16, 636
Fiverr, 20, 509, 515–516
fixed-term tasks, 506
flexible work arrangements, 267–268
    health and wellbeing outcomes, 336–337
flextime, 505–506
fly-in-fly-out work arrangements (FIFO), 325
focus groups, 369–370
Fong, Christine, 420
food-delivery work, 512–513, 538
formalization, 264–265
formative evaluation, 396, 401t
fourth industrial revolution, 630
Fox, Kimberly, 336–337
fracturing, 15–16, 341, 342, 344
Framework for Reporting and Assessing the
        Quality of Organizational Interventions
        (FRAQOI), 16–17, 385–386, 400, 401t,
        646
    practice implications, 405–406
    research implications, 403–405
Frazier, M. Lance, 63
freelance workers, 20, 505–507
Frese, Michael, 192
Frey, Bronwyn, 535
Fuchs, Christina, 554
Fuller, Paul, 337–338
fun, designing, 467, 467t
functional job analysis, 373
future of work, 505
    gig work, 523–525
future work, 19–23

Gajendran, Ravi, 549, 551, 552
gamification, 535–536
Ganster, Daniel, 127
GDP. See gross domestic product
gender
    developmental challenge and, 287–288,
        291–292
    task allocation and, 291–292
general training, 241–242
generative AI, 483
generative models, 615
genetic indicators, 225
George, Maïlys, 10–11, 629–630

Gestalting, 15–16, 341, 342, 344
Ghitulescu, Brenda, 428
Gibson, Cristina, 553–555, 617
Giessner, Steffen, 218–219
gig economy, 268–269, 506, 632. See also
        app-work; crowdwork
    algorithmic management in, 509–511, 517,
        532–534
    future research directions, 648
    implications of, 518–519
    regulatory change and, 522
    Taylorism and, 520–521
    work in, 508–512
gig work, 20–21, 268–269
    algorithmic management and, 21, 513
    autonomy in, 510–511
    digital remediation of, 510–511
    emergence of, 508–509
    future of, 523–525
    implications for organizations, 521–523
    implications for workers, 519–521
    implications of, 518–523
    nature and design of, 509–512
    performance management and, 511
    precarity of, 522
    resistance efforts in, 522–523
    strategic benefits of, 521–522
    surveillance technology and, 519–520
Glassdoor, 23, 610–612, 617–618
global factors, 12–13, 237, 238t
    climate change, 249–250
    future research directions and, 251–253
    migration, 247–249
    supply chains, 246–247
global financial crisis, 506
goal interdependence, 71
goal-setting theory, 449–450, 452
Golden, Timothy, 551–552
Gonzalez-Mulé, Erik, 225–226
Good Jobs Project, 16, 346–347
Gordon, Heather, 422–423, 443–444, 450
GPT-2, 615
grafting, 15–16, 341–342, 344
grand resignation, 491–492
Grant, Adam, 106, 179–180, 314, 549–550
Great Eight competencies, 613–614
Green, Francis, 240
Greenan, Nathalie, 246
green behavior, 163
greening, 250
Greer, Lindred, 67–68
Griffeth, Rodger, 313
Griffin, Mark, 10, 147

658 INDEX

Griffin, Ricky, 273–274
gross domestic product (GDP), 245–246
Grote, Gudela, 497–498, 632, 634
Grote, Nadine, 19–20, 637
group cohesion, 321
group factors, 270–272
group identity, 181
group think, 369–370
growth hypothesis, 35–36

Habituate phase, 379–380
Hackman, J. Richard, 29, 33–34, 39, 63,
    99–100, 104, 569–570, 617
Hagtvedt, Lydia, 495
Hammer, Leslie, 219–220
Hamori, Monika, 295–296
Handy, 509
hard regulation, 344–345
Harju, Lotta, 420, 431–432
Harrison, Joseph, 619–620
Hawaii Personality and Health Cohort, 194
Hawthorne studies, 31, 62, 453
Hay, Georgia, 262, 321–322
Health and Safety Executive (HSE), 345–346
healthcare
    AI in, 488, 491
    decision making in, 421–422
    interdependence in, 423–424
    job crafting in, 421–424
    leadership in, 423
health-impairment process, 37–38
health outcomes
    job design and, 335–336
    state of evidence on, 336–338
    success factors for, 339
health & safety regulations, 238t
Heaney, Catherine, 128
hedonic wellbeing, 97–98, 130
    autonomy and, 104
    mastery-oriented work and, 100–104
    relational work and, 106–112
    stimulating work and, 100
    tolerable work and, 112–118
Hekkert-Koning, Marleen, 418–419
Helson, Ravenna, 194–195
Hernandez, Ivan, 615
Herzberg, Frederick, 32–33, 39–42, 47, 285
hierarchies of evidence, organizational
    intervention evaluation and, 389–390
high performance work practices
    (HPWPs), 311, 322
high-performance work systems
    (HPWS), 80–81

hindrance demands, 112, 153, 154
    playful work design and, 472
Hockey, G. Robert J., 122–123
Holland, John, 194
Holman, David, 12–13, 21, 126–127, 196,
    312–313, 374–375, 637–638
Holocracy, 79
home characteristics, virtual work
    and, 555–556
Homo Ludens (Playing Man) (Huizinga), 466
horizontal alignment, 266–267
House, James, 192–193
HPWPs. See high performance work practices
HPWS. See high-performance work systems
HR data, 12
HRM. See human resource management
HR practices, 83
HSE. See Health and Safety Executive
Hu, Qiao, 423–424
Hughes, David, 196
Huizinga, Johan, 466
human-centered design, 483, 494
human intelligence tasks, 516
human resource management (HRM), 55–57,
    311, 322
    alignment of, 266–268
    indirect pathway effects, 268
    strategies, policies, and practices, 266–269
humble leadership, 423
Humphrey, Ronald, 287–290
Humphrey, Stephen E., 55–56, 147–148, 175,
    532–533, 555–556, 569–570
Huselid, Mark A., 80–81
Huyghebaert-Zouaghi, Tiphaine, 430–431
hybrid work, 21–22, 268–269

IBM, 490–491
identified motivation, 151–152
identity, 630–631
    AI and, 493
    career, 177
    contextual characteristics and, 181
    family, 177
    future research directions for, 182–185,
        642–643
    group, 181
    membership-based, 497
    occupational, 176–177, 262–263, 642–643
    occupational changes and, 494
    organizational, 176–177, 642–643
    practice implications, 185–186
    role, 179, 181
    role-based, 497

INDEX 659

satisfaction and, 179
social characteristics and, 180–181
task characteristics and, 177–179
technology and, 493, 642–643
types of, 176–177
work design and, 10–11, 185–186, 642–643
work-related, 176–177
work teams, 176
identity threat
job crafting and, 417
occupational, 177
IGLOO model, 445–446
Iida, Mako, 423–424
Ilies, Remus, 122
inclusion, 633–634, 636–637
Indeed, 610–612
individual autonomy, 64
individual differences, 212–213, 222–223, 287, 571–572
individual empowerment, 271
individual interventions, 387–389
categories of, 446
individual level, 57–59
developmental challenge choice and, 288–290
work characteristics at, 60t
work design at, 59, 60t
Industrial Revolution, 30
industry-specific health and safety guidance, 346
informal groups, 62
information exchange, 549–550
information processing, 60t
at team level, 69–70
institutional regimes, 12–13, 237, 238t
national, 243–245
institutions
national, 239–243
work design and, 237
Integrated Realist Evaluation Model for Organizational Interventions, 403–404
intensive longitudinal studies, 209t
interaction, 60t
interdependence, 60t, 150, 373–374
assessing, 369
coordination activities and, 160
defining, 70
in healthcare, 423–424
job crafting and, 432
outcome, 71
reciprocal processes and, 216
task, 319, 321, 552–553
at team level, 70–71

workflow patterns and, 70–71
interdependent work designs, 261–262
internal validity, 219, 390, 391–392, 397
International Federation of Robotics, 223–224
International Organization for Standardization (ISO), 345
International Standard Classification of Occupations (ISCO-88), 223
international supply chains, 246–247
Internet of Things (IoT), 531
inter-role conflict, 548
intervention integrity, 398–399
intervention processes
explaining, 401t
need to understand, 385–386
program theory, 401t
understanding, 393–396
intervention quality
assessing and reporting, 397–406
dropout and, 398
internal and external validity and, 390
intervention research designs, 217–220, 209t
interviews, 442
intra-team processes, 321
intrinsic motivation, 151–152, 155–156
IoT. *See* Internet of Things
ISCO-88. *See* International Standard Classification of Occupations
ISO. *See* International Organization for Standardization
IT safety, 10
IT security, safety behaviors and, 163

Jackson, Paul R., 64–65
Jain, Aditya, 242–243
Jain, Prachee, 495
James, William, 191
JCE. *See* Job Crafting Exercise
JCM. *See* Job Characteristics Model
JDCM. *See* Job Demand-Control Model
JDCSM. *See* Job Demand-Control Support Model
JD-R. *See* Job Demands-Resources model
Jehn, Karen, 67–68
Jiang, Winnie Yun, 118
jingle-jangle fallacy, 447–448
JIT. *See* Just-in-Time approach
job analysis
AI and, 23
artificial intelligence in, 610–617, 611f
defining, 609–610
future research directions, 648
process of, 609–612

660 INDEX

job analysis (*Continued*)
  tools for, 373
job autonomy, 10–11, 312–313
  aging workforce and, 595–597
  AI and, 19–20, 488–489
  distributed work and, 160
  downsizing and, 265
  SMTs and, 315–316
  task characteristics and, 195
  team autonomy and, 271
  virtual work and, 549, 551–552, 554–555
Job Challenge Profile, 285–286
job characteristics, 33, 147, 631–632
  antecedents of, 47
  broadening scope of studied, 41–44
  job crafting and, 444–445, 450–451
  motivation and, 34, 150
  personal characteristics and, 45–46
Job Characteristics Model (JCM), 7–8, 29,
      33–34, 39, 41, 43, 55, 99–100, 104, 106,
      147, 175, 346–347
  SMTs and, 316
  word dictionaries for, 617
job complexity, 19, 60t
  aging workforce and, 595
  algorithmic management and, 534–535
  future research directions on, 162
  task characteristics and, 195
  at team level, 67–68
  virtual work and, 551
job control, 35, 127
  cognition and, 225–226
job crafting, 17–18, 415, 429–430, 439–440,
      634–635
  algorithmic management and, 538, 540
  approach and avoidance motivation
      and, 419
  assignments for, 443t
  blueprint for interventions, 441–445
  categorizing and defining
      interventions, 445–449
  coals in, 443–444
  crowdwork and, 518
  defining, 440–441
  developmental challenge and, 288
  in education, 424–426
  future research directions, 430–432,
      455–458, 646–647
  generalizability of, 416
  in healthcare, 421–424
  impact of interventions, 451–453
  improving intervention
      methodology, 456–458

increasing intervention
    effectiveness, 455–456
integrating perspectives of, 418–420
interdependent work contexts and, 432
interviews for, 442
job characteristics and, 450–451
job demands and, 417
job redesign through, 440–441
job resources and, 447
leadership and, 273, 423, 455–456
in manufacturing, 427–428
needs assessment and, 455
occupations and, 454
personality change and, 198
playful work design and, 468
practice implications of, 432
as proactive behavior, 416
process evaluation of, 453–455
promotion and prevention focus
    and, 418–419
role overload and, 427–428
social impact of, 432
within social perspective, 420–421
strategies in, 441
studying dimensions of, 430
technology and, 456
theoretical background for
    interventions, 449–451
theories and perspectives of, 416–421
virtual work and, 558–559
work changes through, 431–432
work context and, 388–389, 421–428
work engagement and, 422, 454
work-identity fit and, 181–182
workshops, 442–443
Job Crafting Boosts, 443–444
Job Crafting Exercise (JCE), 442–445
Job Crafting Plans, 451–452
Job Demand-Control Model (JDCM), 29,
      35–36, 39–41, 43, 44–46, 104, 122–123
Job Demand-Control Support Model
      (JDCSM), 35, 323
job demands, 35, 37, 38
  aging workforce and, 596–597
  crafting, 418
  job crafting and, 417
  performance and, 150–151
  promotion and prevention focus
      and, 418–419
  safety institutions and, 242–243
job demands, virtual work and, 547–548

Job Demands-Resources model (JD-R), 7–8, 18, 29, 36–40, 43, 44–46, 147, 326, 416–417, 439–441, 452, 592–593
job crafting interventions and, 441–445, 449, 450–451
playful work design and, 469, 473–475
task characteristics and, 195
job descriptions, 373, 614–615, 616f
text analysis of, 23
job design, 29, 335
AI and, 23
local work group factors, 269–274
text analysis and, 617–620
wellbeing and, 642
job-design interventions
field studies of, 125–126
SMART framework and, 126–129
Job Diagnostic Survey, 34
job discretion, 244
job enlargement, 15, 32–33, 308–309, 312–313, 308t
defining, 312
job enrichment, 15, 32–33, 308–313, 308t
defining, 312
job features, 97. See also SMART Work Design Model
autonomy and, 104
language usage and, 620–621
mastery and, 98–99
wellbeing and, 120
job performance
AI and, 163
changes in, 160–161
developmental challenge assignment and, 292
model of, 148–150
work design and, 10, 150–154
job quality
AI-induced changes in, 488–492
technology and, 488
job redesign, 335
authenticity in, 343
contextual factors for outcomes of, 337–338
delivery context, 340–341
discrete and omnibus organizational contexts, 339–340
evidence on health and wellbeing outcomes, 336–338
follow-up period of studies, 339
fracturing and, 342
future research directions, 348–352
Gestalting and, 342

good practices for implementing and sustaining, 349t
good practices for policy makers of, 351t
grafting and, 341–342
implementation impact on outcomes, 337
implementing and evolving, 339–344
through job crafting, 440–441
managing for beneficial outcomes, 336
across organizations, 344–348
shocks and, 342–343
success factors for health and wellbeing initiatives, 339
sustainability of, 338
job resources, 37, 125, 195, 323
aging workforce and, 596–597
crafting, 418
decision-making autonomy as, 551–552
job crafting and, 447
promotion and prevention focus and, 418–419
safety institutions and, 242–243
job rotation, 32–33, 308t
job satisfaction, 312
design outcomes and, 369–370
leadership and, 218–219
Johns, Gary, 317, 339–340
Josserand, Emmanuel, 522–523
Journal of Applied Psychology, 3
Judge, Timothy A., 122
Jumelet, Jacqueline, 179, 181
Just-in-Time approach (JIT), 77

Kabanoff, Boris, 617–618
Kahlert, Aniko, 497–498
Kaine, Sarah, 522–523
Kaizen, 373, 378
Karabey, Canan, 428
Karasek, Robert, 29, 33, 35–36, 39, 41–42, 104, 122–123
Kark, Ronit, 179
Keller, Anita, 12, 637
Kelliher, Clare, 548
Kerse, Gokhan, 428
Khan, Muhammad, 474, 476
Kiggundu, Moses N., 70–71
Kipfelsberger, Petra, 179
Kirkman, Bradley L., 65–66
Kivimäki, Mika, 181–182
Klonek, Florian, 13–15, 23, 215, 636
Knight, Caroline, 15, 23, 128, 306–307, 323, 336–337, 442–444, 447, 452, 629–630, 636

662 INDEX

knowledge
 creativity and, 156
 machinic dispossession of, 535
 performance and, 152
 social transfer of, 323–324
knowledge, skills, abilities, and other
  characteristics (KSAOs), 609–610,
  612–613, 615, 616–617
knowledge, skills, and abilities (KSAs), 66–67
 diversity in teams of, 68
 HPWS and, 80–81
knowledge characteristics, 179–180
 algorithmic management and, 534–535
 at team level, 66–70
Kobayashi, Vladimer, 614
Kock, Ned, 559–560
Kohn, Melvin, 225–226
Kolb, David, 450
Kooij, Dorien, 426, 454
KSAOs. *See* knowledge, skills, abilities, and
  other characteristics
KSAs. *See* knowledge, skills, and abilities
Kukenberger, 67–68

laboratory study, 209*t*
labor market policies, 240–241
lack-of-fit model, 293
Lambert, Brittany, 445, 447
Langfred, Claus, 64, 271–272
language models, 613
language usage, job features and, 620–621
large language models (LLMs), 495
latent change score mode, 216
Latent Dirichlet Allocation (LDA), 612–613
latent growth curve models, 215
Lawler, Edward, 71
Lazazzara, Alessandra, 181–182, 447–448
LDA. *See* Latent Dirichlet Allocation
Leach, Desmond, 323–324
leader feedback, 72
leadership
 developmental challenges and, 295
 empowering, 290, 474, 476
 in healthcare, 423
 humble, 423
 job crafting and, 273, 423, 455–456
 job satisfaction and, 218–219
 perceptual pathway of, 273–274
 playful work design and, 474, 476
 Prepare phase and, 365
 safety performance and, 157
 self-efficacy, 296
 structural pathway of, 273

transformational, 273, 474, 476
 in virtual work, 558
 work design factors, 272–274, 635–637
leadership support, 455–456
Leana, Carrie, 426
lean production (LP), 77–78, 264, 373
learning
 developmental challenge and, 286
 encouraging, 323–324
 experiential learning theory, 450
 feedback and, 154, 323–324
 formative evaluation and, 396
 organizational culture of, 290
 from redesign, 378–379
 social context of, 449–450
 team, 291
 technology and, 160–161
 training transfer, 388–389
 transferring, 388
 work characteristics and, 152
 work design and, 152
learning goal orientation, 289, 293, 294
Lebanoff, Logan, 613
Lee, Min Kyung, 532, 537–538
lemmatizing, 613–614
lexical databases, 618
Li, Wen-Dong, 195–196, 215
liberal regimes, 243–244
Lichtenthaler, Philipp, 419
lifespan development focus, 572–592
Lin, Nai, 612–613
Linguistic Inquiry Word Count (LIWC), 618
LinkedIn, 610–612
link organizations, 346
Liu, Wei, 477
Lively, Kathryn, 192–193
LIWC. *See* Linguistic Inquiry Word Count
LLMs. *See* large language models
local trusted intermediaries, 347–348
local work group factors, 269–274
Locke, Edwin, 312
Locke, Richard, 246–247
Logan, Mary, 127
longitudinal research designs, 213–217, 209*t*
 change trajectories and, 215–216
 measuring change with, 214
longwall mining approach, 315
longwall mining machines, 31–32
low strain jobs, 35
LP. *See* lean production
ludic play, 466, 471
lump of labor fallacy, 248
Luu, Tuan, 423–424

INDEX 663

Lyft, 509

machine learning, 609
machinic dispossession of knowledge, 535
macroergonomics, 79–80
macro-tasks, 516, 518
Mainka, Danina, 421
Mäkikangas, Anne, 422, 424
Management Standards for Work-Related
    Stress, 345–346
manager feedback, 72, 305
  automated feedback and, 615
managerial antecedents, 13–14
managerial skills, developmental challenge
    and, 286
manager mistrust, 554–555, 558
managers
  job design influence of, 346–347
  Prepare phase and, 365
  work design by, 305
manager support, 337–338
  for interventions, 399–400
manufacturing
  algorithmic management in, 21
  energy efficiency in, 250
  job crafting in, 18, 416, 427–428
  mechanistic work design in, 30
  teamwork in, 159
market liberalization, 245
Marler, Janet, 549
Maslow, Abraham, 32
mastery-oriented work, 100–104, 102t, 362
  experimental lab studies on, 121–122
  feedback and, 121–122
  field interventions studies on, 127
  longitudinal studies and, 120
matchmaking, 517
Mathieu, John, 67–68
Mattarelli, Elisa, 181–182
Mayo, Elton, 31
McCarthy, Jean, 570
McCauley, Cynthia, 285–286
McChesney, G. G., 3
McCrae, Robert, 191
McGregor, Douglas, 39–40
McLeod, Jane, 192–193
Meagher, Gabrielle, 251–252
meaning, of work, 497
meaningfulness, 98, 151–152
measurement
  of change, longitudinal research designs
    and, 214
  of changes in autonomy, 215

of changes in proactive behavior, 216
observation measures, 222–223, 209t
of organizational culture, 617–618
other report measures, 222–223, 209t
of playful work, 469
self-report measures, 213, 222–223, 209t
of work design, 222–224, 637
mechanistic work design, 9, 56–57
  organizational level and, 75–78
Media Richness Theory, 549–550
Medici, Guri, 492–493
Meier, Laurenz, 216–217
Mell, Julija, 218
membership-based identity, 497
mental health
  design outcomes and, 369–370
  regulation and, 344–345
Mesmer-Magnus, Jessica R., 67
metabolic indicators, 225
meta-cognitive abilities, AI collaboration
    and, 490–491
method autonomy, 42
method control, 64–65, 98–99, 104
micromanagement, in virtual work, 549
micro services, 509
Microsoft 365 Copilot, 488–489
micro-tasking crowdwork, 515–516
micro-tasks, 510–511, 516, 518–520
migration, 247–249, 238t
Mihalache, Mashiho, 553–554
Mihalache, Oli, 553–554
Milanez, Mareike, 488–489
mindfulness training, 446
Miraglia, Mariella, 387–388, 390–391
Moderna, 492
Monday Blues hypothesis, 215–216
monitoring
  algorithmic, 531–532
  virtual work and, 554–555
Monster, 610–612
Morgeson, Frederick, 8–9, 55–56, 175,
    260–262, 275, 532–533, 555–556,
    569–570, 637–639
Morikawa, Masayuki, 559–560
Morse, Nancy, 309
motivation, 631
  achievement, 289
  approach and avoidance, 419
  autonomy and, 34
  forms of, 155–156
  importance of, 32–33
  job characteristics and, 34, 150

664 INDEX

motivation (*Continued*)
  job crafting process evaluation
    and, 453–454
  proactivity and, 155–156
  work performance and, 151–152
motivational process, 37–38
motivational work design, 29
  assumptions of benefits of, 39–41
  background of, 29–33
  future directions for, 39–48
  models for, 33–39
mRNA vaccines, 492
Mukherjee, Tulika, 451–454, 457
Mullarkey, Sean, 64–65
Musk, Elon, 545–546
mutual gains perspective (mutuality), 342–344
Myers, Jenna, 494–495, 538

Nabe-Nielsen, Kirsten, 391
national economy, 12–13, 245–246, 238*t*
national employment policies, 240–241
national factors
  economic, 245–246
  future research directions and, 251–253
  institutions and regimes, 239–245
National Institute of Health and Social
    Care, 345
national institutional regimes, 243–245
national institutions, 12–13, 237, 239–243,
    238*t*
national training systems, 241–242
national workplace safety
    institutions, 242–243
natural language processing (NLP), 609,
    617–618
  text data analysis with, 612–613
Nayani, David, 15–16
Nayani, Rachel, 636
Neal, Andrew, 147
needs assessment, 455
networks
  social, 228
  study design and, 228
Newton, Charles, 613
n-grams, 613
Nie, Jared, 615
Nielsen, Karina, 16–17, 127, 128, 345,
    387–392, 394, 396–398, 405
Nilles, Jack, 545
NLP. *See* natural language processing
Noblet, Andrew, 405
non-research data, 223–224

non-standard work arrangements, 20,
    268–269, 505–507, 510–511
Nordic advantage, 13
Norwich Good Economy
    Commission, 346–347

observation measures, 222–223, 209*t*
OCB. *See* organizational citizenship behavior
occupational antecedents, 13, 259
occupational characteristics
  Big Five traits and, 194
  personality in childhood and, 194
occupational classifications, 209*t*, 223
occupational codes, 209*t*, 223
occupational creativity, 194–195
occupational factors, 260–263
  future research directions on, 644
occupational identity, 176–177, 262–263,
    642–643
Occupational Information Network
    (O*NET), 12, 23, 223, 609–613
occupational socialization, 261–262
occupations
  AI-induced changes in, 492–494
  cognitive demands and, 260–261
  cultural features of, 261–262
  defining, 260
  job crafting and, 454
  professional, 260–261
  task significance and, 260–261
Ohly, Sandra, 10, 19, 630
older workers, defining, 570
Oldham, Greg, 29, 33–34, 39, 63, 99–100, 104,
    569–570, 617
omnibus contextual factors, 339–341, 344,
    397–398
on-demand work, 19, 510–511
O*NET. *See* Occupational Information
    Network
ongoing process evaluation, 396
on-the-job training, 241–242
Oprea, Bogdan, 126, 451–452, 454
optimizing demands, 441
organizational antecedents, 13–14, 259
organizational behavior, 55
organizational changes, 308–309, 311,
    321–322, 308*t*
organizational choices, algorithmic
    management and, 537–538
organizational citizenship behavior
    (OCB), 72, 149–150
  humble leadership and, 423
  organizational identification and, 424–425

organizational context, 74
 delivery, 340–341
 discrete and omnibus, 339–341, 344,
  397–398
 job redesign and, 339–340
organizational culture, 261–262
 job redesign and changing, 338, 342,
  348–350, 352
 measuring, 617–618
 rituals and routings as manifestations
  of, 338
 task allocation and, 295–296
 technology and, 538
organizational design, 74
organizational factors, 263–269
 future research directions on, 644
 work redesign alignment with, 327
organizational identification, 181, 424–425,
  427, 642–643
organizational identity, 176–177
organizational interventions, 445–446
 assessing and reporting quality of, 397–406
 defining, 386–387
 evaluation of, 386–392
 evidence-based levels of hierarchy, 389–390
 future research directions, 646
 participation in, 386–387
 pitching, 387–389
 practice implications, 405–406
 quality criteria guidelines for, 399–400
 RCT design challenges in, 390–392
 realist evaluation of, 393–395
 research implications, 403–405
 understanding processes in, 393–396
organizational level, 57–59
 future research directions at, 83, 641
 mechanistic work design and, 75–78
 performance and, 158–159
 work characteristics and, 74, 75t
 work design at, 9, 56–57, 74–81
organizational psychology, 192
organizational restructuring, 265
organizational rituals and routines, 338
organizational strategy, 266–267
organizational structure, 263–266
 specialization and, 264
organizational support, 425, 549
organizational values, 268
organizational work designs
 implications and future research
  directions, 82–83
 types of, 9
organization learning culture, 290

organizations
 control groups and differences between, 391
 job redesign across, 344–348
 self-managing, 79
other report measures, 222–223, 209t
outcome interdependence, 71
outcomes
 evaluating designs for impact on, 375
 theory of change and, 367

Pan, JiaLiang, 424
Pandey, Sanjay, 617–618
Pandey, Sheela, 617–618
panel and cohort studies, 209t, 214
Parent-Rocheleau, Xavier, 21, 532–533
Parker, Sharon, 11–12, 16, 23, 64–65, 147, 262,
  265–266, 295–296, 306, 314, 323, 325,
  336–337, 419–420, 532–533, 549–550,
  629–631, 635
PARRTH Model, 16, 360
 Assess phase, 367–370
 change facilitation and, 380–381
 future research directions, 645–646
 Habituate phase, 379–380
 overview of, 363–364, 364f
 phases of, 363
 Prepare phase, 364–366
 Redesign phase, 372–376
 Reflect phase, 370–372
 Track phase, 376–379
participation, 361f
 direct processes, 360–362
 indirect effects, 362
 in organizational interventions, 386–387
 self-efficacy and, 362
 in work redesign, 360–363
participatory interventions, 439–440, 636
 phases of, 386–387
Pasmore, William A., 79
passive jobs, 35
pay-for-performance schemes, 268
PCP. See Personal Crafting Plan
peer absence norms, 181
Peeters, Maria, 18, 441, 634–635
Pentland, Brian, 494–495
Perez, Fabienne, 538
performance
 adaptive, 154–155
 autonomy and, 64
 in changing world, 159–164
 cognitive capacity and, 152–154
 future research directions, 161–164, 642,
  644–645

666 INDEX

performance (*Continued*)
  job demands and, 150–151
  job design and, 335
  KSAs and, 152
  organizational identification and, 181
  proficiency and, 154
  SMTs and, 316–317, 320–321
  task significance and, 314
  team-level and organizational
    level, 158–159
  wellbeing and, 151–152
  work characteristics and, 150–151
  work design and, 10, 642
performance feedback, autonomous teams
    and, 72
performance management, 311
  gig work and, 511
performance management systems, 340–341
performance related pay, 341–342
Perry, Sara, 551–552
personal characteristics
  job characteristics and, 45–46
  work characteristics and, 192
Personal Crafting Plan (PCP), 442–444
personality, 619–620, 630
  bottom-up work redesign and, 643
  in childhood, occupational characteristics
    and, 194
  defining, 191
  developmental challenge and, 14
  future research directions, 643
  play and, 471
  playful work design and, 471
  proactive, 288–289
  social structure and, 192–193
  vocational choice and, 193–194
  work design and, 11, 191, 643
personality change
  future research directions, 197–200
  methodological challenges and, 199–200
  practice implications, 200–201
  relational characteristics and, 196–197
  task characteristics and, 195–196
  theoretical foundations of, 192–193
  vocational characteristics and, 193–195
  volitional, 198
  work design and process of, 197–198
  work design characteristics and, 193–197
  work environment and, 192
personal resources, 38
person-centered approaches, 326
person-environment fit, 449, 591, 592–594
Petelczyc, Claire, 471

Petrou, Paraskevas, 418–419
physical demands, 60t
  at team level, 73
physical space, 73
Pil, Frits, 271
Pindek, Shani, 215–216
Pitchforth, Jegar, 219
play
  defining, 465–466
  personality and, 471
  traits and, 471
  types of, 466
playful work design, 19, 465
  cognitive crafting and, 468
  defining, 466–469
  empirical evidence for, 471–473
  fun and competition in, 467, 467t
  future research directions, 475–477, 647
  generalizability of, 477
  JD-R and, 469
  leadership and, 474, 476
  personality and, 471
  practice implications of, 473–474
  psychological need satisfaction and, 473
  situational factors and, 476
  theoretical background for, 465–466
  work environment and, 475–476
play initiatives, 468–469, 470f
political functions, 340–341
population growth, 248
Post Mates, 509
Pratt, Michael, 497
pre-event or intervention data collection, 221
Prepare phase, 364–366
prevention focus, 418–419
primary interventions, 446
proactive behavior, 5, 148–149, 155–156, 163,
    416, 427–428, 634–635
  AI and, 488–489
  developmental challenge and, 288–289
  job crafting interventions and, 447
  measuring changes in, 216
  playful work design and, 468
problem solving, 60t
  AI collaboration and, 490–491
  at team level, 69
process evaluation, 393
  adherence to, 401t
  formative evaluation and, 396
  ongoing, 396
productivity pressure, 536
professional occupations, 260–261
proficiency, 147–149, 163

task performance and, 154
work characteristics and, 154
program theory, 393, 401t
promotion focus, 418–419
psychological capital, 428
psychological need satisfaction, 473
Public Health England, 345
Putka, Dan, 613

Qi, Jipeng, 427
q-sorts, 612–613
qualitative research designs, 209t
Quality Assessment Tool for Quantitative
Studies, 397
quasi-experimental studies, 218–219

Rafferty, Anthony, 12–13, 21, 637–638
Raghuram, Sumita, 546–547
Rail Safety and Standards Board, 346
Ram, Monder, 347–348
RAMESES standards, 395
Randall, Raymond, 127–128, 391–392, 396,
397–398
random intercept cross-lagged panel model
(RI-CLPM), 216
randomized control trial (RCT), 385–386,
389–390
organizational interventions and challenges
in design of, 390–392
rating systems, 517–518
RCT. *See* randomized control trial
readiness for change, 391
RE-AIM model, 394–395
realist evaluation, 393–396, 403–404, 447–448
realist synthesis, 395–396
Reay, Trish, 261–262
recall bias, 213, 222, 637
reciprocal processes, 216–217
recovery interventions, 446
recruiting websites, 610–612
recruitment, 401t
Redesign phase, 372–376
reducing demands, 441
reduction-oriented crafting, 440–441
Reflect phase, 370–372
regulation, 245
algorithmic management and, 539
hard, 344–345
mental health and, 344–345
regulatory focus theory, 418–419
Reh, Susan, 223
Reiche, B. Sebastian, 510–511
Reichel, Astrid, 554

Reimer, Everett, 309
reinforcer patterns, 261–263
relational characteristics, 196–197, 362
relational crafting, 440–441
relational interventions, 308–309, 311,
313–314, 308t
relational job architecture, 106
relational team functions, 71
relational work, 106–112, 107t
AI and, 491
experimental studies on, 123
field interventions studies on, 128–129
virtual work and, 549–550, 552, 553–554
relational work design, 156, 313–314, 524–525
relational work redesign, 15
relationships
crafting, 418
employee actions shaping, 417
supervisor-subordinate, 293
relative deprivation theory, 421
remittances, 248–249
remoteness, supervisory control and, 181
remote work, 19, 21–22, 160, 268–269,
275–276
crowdwork as, 517
repeated measures
longitudinal studies and, 214, 227
methodological considerations for, 220–221
of playful work design, 472–473
research designs, 12, 207–208
definitions for, 209t
future directions for, 227–229
longitudinal, 213–217, 209t
social context of, 228
reskilling, 492–493
resources, seeking, 441
resource theories, 323
restructuring, 265
retention, 569, 601
aging and, 22
retention-pull approach, 592–594
retention-push approach, 572–592
reward and pay systems, 311
Rice, Bridget, 592
Richardson, Katherine, 125–126, 387–390
RI-CLPM. *See* random intercept cross-lagged
panel model
ride-hail work, 512–513
Riva, Egidio, 246
robots, 160–161, 493
Roczniewska, Marta, 404–405
Rodell, Jessica, 493
role ambiguity, 265

role-based identity, 497
role clarity, 127, 162
role conflict, 635
role congruity theory, 287–288
role creation, 374
role harmony, 362
role identity, 179, 181
role overload, 8, 42, 112, 314, 427–431
role performance
  in-role and extra-role, 417–418
  organizational identification and, 181
role-resource approach-avoidance model, 419,
    447–448
role theory, 147
Romis, Monica, 246–247
Roodbari, Hamid, 337–338, 395, 403–404
root causes, 373–374
Rosen, Christopher, 216–217, 226
Rothstein, Hannah, 125–126, 387–390
Royston, Ryan, 612–613
rumination, 472–473
Rydstedt, Leif, 129
Ryu, J. Woon, 64

safety behaviors, 80, 149
  future research directions for, 163
  IT security and, 163
safety design, 157–158
safety performance, 149, 153, 157–158, 163
  fracturing and, 342
safety practices, 80
safety protocols, 80
safety regulations, 242
Sarmah, Pallavi, 274
SARS-CoV-2 vaccines, 492
satisfaction, 32
  design outcomes and, 369–370
  identity and, 179
  leadership and, 218–219
Scharp, Yuri, 19, 469–473, 635
Schaubroeck, John, 127
scheduling autonomy, 549, 551–552
Schmiedel, Theresa, 617–618
Schooler, Carmi, 225–226
scientific management, 7–8, 29, 30
  organizational level and, 75–76
screening, for conditions to change, 386–387
SDT. See self-determination theory
seasonal work, 505–506
secondary interventions, 446
seeking challenges, 441
selection, optimization, and compensation
    framework, 572–591

selection bias, 397, 401t
self-concept, 196–197
self-confidence, 293
  supervisor, 294
self-determination, 195
self-determination theory (SDT), 104, 106,
    179–180, 473
self-discipline, 471
self-efficacy, 5, 14, 37, 155–156
  developmental challenge and, 289–293
  employee, 293
  empowering leadership and, 290
  leadership, 296
  participation and, 362
self-employment, 506, 509–510
self-improvement, 415
self-initiating behaviors, 17–18, 415
self-leadership, team, 64–65
self-management
  task identity and, 66
  team, 64–66
self-managing organizations (SMOs), 79
self-managing teams (SMTs), 15, 270–271,
    308–311, 314–321, 308t
  future research directions for, 325–326
  performance improvement in, 320–321
  team learning and, 319
  when to implement, 318–319
  where to implement, 317–318
  who to implement for, 319–320
self-monitoring, 449–450
self-regulation, 198, 449–450
  safety regulations, 242
self-report measures, 213, 222–223, 209t
SELN. See Situated Experiential Learning
    Narratives
semi-autonomous teamworking, 341–342
sense making, 273–274
service culture, 423–424
service work, mechanistic work design in, 30
Shang, Weiwei, 425
SHARE. See Survey of Health, Aging, and
    Retirement in Europe
Shepherd, Rose, 388–389
shocks
  external, 342–344
  fracturing and, 342
  job redesign and, 342–343
SHRM. See strategic HRM theory
silence, 369–370
simulation research designs, 209t, 218
Sinclair, Robert, 421

Situated Experiential Learning Narratives
(SELN), 450–451
situational factors
developmental challenge choice and, 290
playful work design and, 476
skill development, 152
skill utilization, 428
AI and, 490
skill variety, 60t
AI and, 490
algorithmic management and, 534–535
LP and, 77–78
at team level, 68
Slattery, Jeffrey P., 179–180
SMART Work Design Model, 4, 8–9, 42,
97–99, 360, 629–630
assessing impact of changes and, 377–378
Assess phase and, 367
experimental lab studies on, 120–124
field intervention studies on, 124–130
future research directions for, 132–134
job crafting and, 442–443
job-design interventions addressing features
within, 126–129
longitudinal research on, 119–120
meta-analyses for, 99–119, 101t, 102t, 105t,
107t, 113t
participation in redesign and, 360, 362
practical implications of, 134
role creation and, 374
tensions in research area, 130–132
virtual work and, 553
SMEs. See subject matter experts
Smith, Adam, 30
Smollan, Roy, 555–556
SMOs. See self-managing organizations
SMTs. See self-managing teams
social categorization theory, 262
social characteristics
algorithmic management and, 535–536
identity and, 180–181
at team level, 70–73
virtual work and, 552
social cognitive theory, 287–288, 449–451
social connection
gig work and, 520
work and, 10–11
social contact, 98–99, 375–376, 491
social context
of learning, 449–450
of study design, 228
social democratic regimes, 13, 243–244
social desirability bias, 213, 222, 637

social environment, 535–536
social exchange, 342–343
social identity theory, 262
social information processing theory, 292
socialization
occupational, 261–262
virtual workplace and, 559–560
social media, 610–612
social networks, 228
social robots, 491
social role theory, 287–288
social stressors, 106–112
social structure, 192–193
social support, 60t, 128
aging workforce and, 596
intervention evaluation and, 392
at team level, 72
virtual work and, 550
social transfer of knowledge, 323–324
social welfare, 493, 497
social work characteristics, 150
agile work and, 161
AI and, 491
cardiovascular indicators and, 225
safety performance and, 157–158
socioemotional selectivity
framework, 572–590
socio-technical structures, 264
socio-technical system design principles, 488
socio-technical systems approaches, 9, 56–57,
309–311
team learning and, 319
socio-technical systems theory (STS), 31–32,
62, 63, 147, 263–264, 321–322
algorithmic management and, 537–538
autonomy and, 63–64
organizational level and, 78–80
Solberg, Elizabeth, 427–428
Sonnentag, Savine, 9–10, 629–630, 638
specialization, 60t
efficiency improvement and, 324
organizational structure and, 264
at team level, 69
work design and, 264–265
Speer, Andrew, 613–614, 617
sports
agonistic play and, 466
playful design in, 477
spreading changes, 380
stakeholders
action plans and, 376
communication with, 366
Prepare phase and, 365

670 INDEX

stakeholders (*Continued*)
  Reflect phase and, 371
  in steering groups, 365–366
Stalker, George, 57–58
standardization, 534
state regulation model, 37–38
steering groups, 365, 370–371
stemming, 613–614
stereotypes, 293
Stewart, Greg L., 64–65, 316–317
stimulating work, 99–100, 101*t*, 362
  experimental lab studies on, 121
  field interventions studies on, 126–127
  longitudinal studies and, 120
strain hypothesis, 35–36
strategic change, 337–338
strategic HRM theory (SHRM), 266–267
strategic HR systems approaches, 9, 80–81
stress
  algorithmic evaluations and, 517–518
  autonomy and, 67, 104, 122
  biomarkers and, 12, 225
  interventions to reduce, 446
  JDCSM and, 35–37, 41, 44
  job crafting and, 469
  large-scale sources of, 268–269, 275–276
  performance and, 154, 156
  personality change and, 198
  play and, 465–466, 471–472
  relational task features and, 123
  relational work and, 106–112
  SMART framework and, 98–99
  technology impact and, 42–43
  time demands and, 195–196
  tolerable task features and, 123–124
  tolerable work and, 112–118
stress adaptation model, 37–38
stress appraisal theory, 46
stress management training, 446
Stroop test, 226
subcontracting, 505–506
subject matter experts (SMEs), 610–612
successful aging at work framework, 572–592
Suchman, Lucy, 495
Sulbout, Jérôme, 20–21, 633, 634, 638
summative evaluation, 396
supervised models, 613
supervisor ratings, 12
supervisors
  developmental challenge assignment by, 292–296
  influence mechanisms, 196–197
  task assignment by, 287–288

supervisor-subordinate relationships, 293
supervisor support, 36, 106, 127–128, 157, 181, 185, 428
  proactive personality and, 197
supervisory control
  automated systems and, 488
  remoteness and, 181
supply chains, 12–13, 246–247, 238*t*
supporting actions, 379
surveillance technology, 519–520
Survey of Health, Aging, and Retirement in Europe (SHARE), 600
surveys, 222–223
  in Assess phase, 369–370
  screening conditions with, 386–387
Suß, Stefan, 421
Sutin, Angelina, 196
symbolic functions, 340–341
systemic change
  root causes and, 373
  top-down work redesign and, 15
systems level approaches. *See* socio-technical systems theory
system-wide changes, 308–309, 321–322, 308*t*
  fracturing and, 342

Tafvelin, Susanne, 267
Tagliaventi, Maria Rita, 181–182
Tarafdar, Monideepa, 532
task allocation, 291–292
task analysis, 374
task assignment, 287–288
task automation, 488–489
task characteristics, 63–66, 195–196
  aging workforce and, 595
  algorithmic management and, 533–534
  identity and, 177–179
task complexity
  approach behavioral crafting and, 428
  at team level, 68
task crafting, 440–441
task discretion, 295–296
task division, 287–288
task feedback, 147–148
task fit, 371
task functions
  task interdependence and, 71
  team autonomy and, 64
  technology and, 488
task identity, 33–34, 60*t*, 66, 147–148, 313
  performance and, 150
task interdependence, 319, 321
  decision making and, 341–342

in education, 424–425
virtual work and, 552–553
task inventories, 373
task performance, 163
dual-task, 163
proficiency and, 154
TaskRabbit, 20, 509
task significance, 33–34, 65–66, 60t, 128–129, 147–148
occupations and, 260–261
performance and, 150, 314
relational work design and, 314
task team functions, 71
task variety, 33–34, 60t, 65
Tavistock Institute, 31–32
Taylor, Frederick Winslow, 30, 75–76
Taylorism, 30–31
algorithmic management and, 534–535
gig economy and, 520–521
safety and, 157–158
teaching
job crafting interventions in, 426
job demands of, 424
team approach crafting, 423–424
team autonomy, 82–83, 159, 270, 272, 641
individual job autonomy and, 271
SMTs and, 315
team performance and, 64
team conflict, 271–272
team crafting, 415, 426
collective, 373
team diversity, 319
team empowerment, 271, 320
team factors, 270–272
negotiating for developmental challenges and, 291
team learning, 291
SMTs and, 319
team level, 57–59
autonomy at, 63–65
contextual characteristics, 73–74
feedback at, 72
future research directions at, 82–83, 641
information processing at, 69–70
interaction outside organization, 72–73
interdependence at, 70–71
job complexity at, 67–68
knowledge characteristics at, 66–70
performance and, 158–159
problem solving at, 69
skill variety at, 68
social characteristics at, 70–73
social support at, 72

specialization at, 69
work characteristics at, 8–9, 60t
work design at, 59, 62–74, 60t
team performance
diversity and, 291
SMTs and, 316–317, 320–321
team autonomy and, 64
uncertainty and, 318–319
team processes, 325–326
teams
faultlines in, 319–320
study design and, 228
task division among members, 287–288
task interdependence of, 319
team self-leadership, 64–65
team self-management, 64–66
team service recovery performance, 423–424
team skill variety, 68–69
teamwork
intervention evaluation and, 392
participation in redesign and, 363
safety performance and, 157
semi-autonomous, 341–342
skills of, 67
technical support systems, 323–324
technological determinism, 494–495
technology
changes in work and, 507–508
identity and, 493, 642–643
"in the loop" human operators of, 496–497
organizational culture and, 538
proactive adaptation to, 634–635
surveillance, 519–520
understanding and shaping work in, 494–496
virtual work and characteristics of, 555–556
work characteristics and, 630
technostress, 536
telecommuting, 545
telework, 160
temporal work characteristics, virtual work and, 557
temporary employment, 505–506
tertiary interventions, 446
Tesla, 545–546
text analysis, 23, 609, 637–638
future research directions, 621–622, 648
job design and, 617–620
job features and, 620–621
word dictionaries for, 613–614
text data, 609
analyzing, 612–613
Theorell, Tores, 36

672 INDEX

theory of change, 367, 368*f*
theory of planned behavior, 450–451
Theory X, 39–40
Theory Y, 39–40
third-party observers, 222–223
Thompson, James D., 70–71
Thorsen, Sannie, 386
Tian, Amy Wei, 13–14
time-lagged research designs, 209*t*
time lags, 220–221
time-order relationship, 390
time pressure, 35, 112, 158, 163, 265, 271, 272, 421–422, 424
timing autonomy, 42, 64–65
Tims, Maria, 17–18, 415, 417–418, 423–424, 429, 431–432, 634–635, 639
tolerable work, 112–118, 113*t*, 362, 371, 378
  experimental studies on, 123–124
  field interventions studies on, 129
Ton, Zeynep, 379
Topa, Gabriela, 592
top-down job redesign, 335
  future research directions, 644–645
  PARRTH Model as, 363
top-down work redesign, 15–17, 219–220, 305, 306
  future research directions, 325–326
  history of, 309–313
  intervention types, 308–309, 308*t*
  practice implications, 327–328
topic models, 612–613
Toyota Production System (TPS), 56, 76–78
tracking data, 223–224, 209*t*
Track phase, 376–379
trade barriers, 245
trade unions, 13, 239–240, 238*t*
training interventions, 387–388
  job crafting interventions as, 447
  playful work design in, 473–474
training systems, 241–242, 238*t*
training transfer, 388–389, 404
traits, 191
  play and, 471
transformational leadership, 273, 474, 476
transformative, defining, 10–11
Tris, Eric, 31–32
TST theory. *See* socio-technical systems theory
Turner, Nick, 64–65
Turney, John, 312
turnover, 34, 80–81, 83, 179, 185, 369–370, 398, 417–418
Twemlow, Melissa, 17–18, 634–635, 639
2-factor theory, 32–33, 39–40

Tyers, Claire, 345–346

Uber, 20, 491, 509
UberEATS, 509
Uhlig, Lars, 554–555
Umber, Robin, 22–23, 633–634
uncertainty
  adaptive behavior and, 155
  job complexity and, 162
  SMTs and, 15, 318–319
  team performance and, 318–319
  technology and, 42–43
  workplace change and, 148–149
  work redesign and, 365–366
uncertainty regulation model, 149
unconditional basic income, 493
unemployment, 245–246
United Kingdom
  coal mining in, 31–32
  job design and health practices, 345–348
  safety regulation in, 150
  trade unions in, 240
unit grouping, 264
upskilling, 492–493
USAJobs, 610–612

validity
  external, 218, 390, 392, 397
  internal, 219, 390, 391–392, 397
  intervention quality and, 390
  playful work measurement and, 469
  self-report assessments and, 213
  simulation studies and, 218
value-congruent actions, 343
Van Den Broeck, Anja, 7–8, 629–632
van den Huevel, Machteld, 18, 443–444, 634–635
van der Klink, Jac, 387–390
Vangrieken, Katrien, 216
van Mierlo, Heleen, 270–271, 316–317
Van Vianen, Annelies, 287–290
Van Vleet, Meredith, 465–466
van Windgerden, Jessica, 426, 442–443, 453–454, 472–473
van Zoonen, Ward, 554
Venz, Laura, 10, 19, 630
Verelst, Hans, 629–630
Verelst, Lorenz, 7–8, 456
Verijmeren, Sarina, 477
Vermeerberge, Lander, 13–14
vertical alignment, 266–267
Villani, Davide, 538
virtual reality (VR), 228–229

INDEX 673

virtual work, 21–22, 275–276, 545–546
  achieving effective, 553–556
  boundary between work and personal
    domains and, 548
  communication and, 548, 552–553
  creativity in, 557–558
  cross-cultural variances in, 559
  cross-domain crafting behaviors and
    strategies and, 558–559
  future research directions, 556–560,
    642–643, 648–649
  job autonomy and, 549, 551–552, 554–555
  job complexity and, 551
  job crafting and, 558–559
  job demands and, 547–548
  leadership in, 558
  micromanagement in, 549
  process perspective on, 559–560
  relational aspects of work and, 549–550,
    552, 553–554
  relevance of, 546–550
  research streams on, 546–547, 547f
  SMART model and, 553
  social characteristics and, 552
  task interdependence and, 552–553
  technology and home characteristics
    in, 555–556
  temporal work characteristics in, 557
  types of jobs working well with, 550–553
vitamin model, 40, 631–632
vocational characteristics, 193–195
vocational training, 241–242
volitional personality change, 198
volunteer identity, 177
volunteering, 493
Volunteer Work Model, 179–180
VR. See virtual reality
Vysniauskaite, Ausrine, 10–11, 629–630

Waldman, David, 67–68
Walker, Michael, 521
Wall, Toby, 324
Walsh, David, 591–592
Wang, Bin, 21–22, 553–554, 636–637
Wang, Danni, 67–68
Wang, Haijiang, 455–456
Wang, Huatian, 477
Wang, Shenghui, 293
Wang, Ying, 11, 630, 631
Wang, Zhonghao, 425
Ward, M. K., 11–12
warehousing, algorithmic management
  and, 21, 532, 533–535

Warr, Peter, 40, 631–632
wastewater treatment plants, 318–319
Watson, David, 636
Watson, Gwendolyn, 421
Watson, Rachel, 15–16
WDM. See Work Design Model
WDQ. See Work Design Questionnaire
Weingart, Laurie, 67–68
WEIRD contexts, 457
welfare, 240–241
wellbeing, 268–269
  autonomy and, 122–123
  cognition and, 153
  concept of, 97–98
  experimental lab studies for job design
    and, 120–124
  future research directions, 642, 644–645
  job design and, 642
  performance and, 151–152
  SMTs and, 316
  state of evidence on, 336–338
  success factors in initiatives for, 339
  work characteristics and, 216–217
  work design and, 9–10
Western Electric Company, 31
Whitman, Lawrence, 548
Wiernik, Brenton, 147
Wihler, Andreas, 162
Wilkinson, Krystal, 555–556
Wille, Bart, 194
Williams, Helen, 64–65
Woehler, Meredith, 228
Wöhrmann, Anne Marit, 549
Wong, Sut, 427–428
Woods, Stephen, 194
word counters, 618
word dictionaries, 613–614, 617, 618
WordNet, 618
work
  atomization of, 534
  changing nature of, 507–508
  fragmentation of, 520–521
  future of, 505
  gamification of, 535–536
  in gig economy, 508–512
  meaning of, 497
  technology and changes in, 507–508
work adjustment, 261–262
work characteristics, 5, 7–8, 569–570, 631–632
  AI and, 491
  algorithmic management and, 533–536
  at individual level, 60t

674 INDEX

work characteristics (*Continued*)
  job enrichment and enlargement
    interventions and, 313
  learning and, 152
  Mondays and, 215–216
  organizational level and, 74, 75t
  outcomes and, 9–10
  performance and, 150–151
  personal characteristics and, 192
  personality change and, 193–197
  proficiency and, 154
  relational, 106–112
  SMART framework and, 97
  team-level, 8–9
  at team level, 60t
  technology and, 630
  transformative outcomes, 10–11
  wellbeing and, 216–217
work conditions, 60t
  at team level, 73
work context
  aging workforce and, 596
  training transfer and, 388–389
work demands
  algorithmic management and, 536
  outcomes of, 630–632
work design, 3–4. *See also* playful work design
  action plans for implementing, 376
  aging workforce retention and
    characteristics of, 594–597
  AI and, 19–20, 632–633
  algorithmic management and, 532–533
  analyzing, 372–373
  antecedents of, 5–7, 12–14, 46–48, 638–639
  in app-work, 512–515
  changes in, 160–161
  characteristics for, 569–570
  climate change and, 249–250
  cognition and, 11–12, 152–154, 631
  in crowdwork, 515–518
  decision making and, 274
  defining, 57, 175
  diversity and inclusion and, 633–634
  employee participation in, 306–307
  employment practices and, 306–307
  expanding scope of, 629–630
  foundations of, 7–9
  future directions for research
    methods, 227–229, 641
  future work and, 19–23
  health and wellbeing outcomes, 9
  holistic and atomistic perspectives on, 638
  identity and, 10–11, 185–186, 642–643

  identity types studied in relation
    to, 176–177
  at individual level, 59, 60t
  institutions and, 237
  integrative framework for, 4–7
  interdependent, 261–262, 6f
  job performance and, 10, 150–154
  leadership and, 272–274, 635–637
  learning and, 152
  levels of analysis in, 56–59
  LP and, 77–78
  macro influences on, 12–13
  measuring, 222–224, 637
  mechanisms linking performance
    to, 151–154
  methodological choices for research
    in, 208–213
  motivational, 29–33
  multi-level perspectives, 638–639, 641
  national and global influences on, 237, 238t, 644
  non-static view of processes of, 639
  occupational factors in, 260–263
  organizational factors in, 263–269
  organizational level, 9, 56–57, 74–81
  organizational structure and, 263–266
  outcomes of, 5, 9–12
  performance in changing world
    and, 159–164, 642
  personality and, 11, 191, 643
  personality change and, 192–193
  personality change process and, 197–198
  physiological markers and cognitive
    processes linked to, 224–227
  playful, 19
  rating systems and, 517–518
  reconsidering scope of outcomes, 44–45
  research methods in, 207–208, 643–644
  reskilling or retraining and, 492–493
  safety performance and, 157–158
  study methods for, 12
  at team level, 59, 62–74, 60t
  wellbeing and, 9–10
work design framework, 593–594
Work Design Model (WDM), 175, 177, 181–182
Work Design Questionnaire (WDQ), 55, 222
work discretion
  approach behavioral crafting and, 428
  in education, 424–425
work engagement, 427–428
  job crafting and, 422, 454
work environment

climate change and, 249–250
job crafting and, 447–448
personality and, 192
playful work design and, 475–476
simulating, 228–229
work-family conflict, 551–552
workflow patterns, interdependence
and, 70–71
workgroup antecedents, 13–14, 259, 269–274
workgroup factors
future research directions on, 644
job design and, 269–274
work-identity fit, 181–182
working conditions
COVID-19 pandemic and, 388
emerging adverse, 388
work intensification, 635
workload, 3–4, 35, 46, 112, 161, 163, 216, 218,
245–246, 272, 378
job crafting and, 431–432, 441, 452, 454
tolerable job features and, 129
tolerable task features and, 112
work motivation, 323
work performance
AI and, 163
future research directions for, 161–164
mechanisms linking design to, 151–154
motivation and, 151–152
work characteristics and, 150–151
workplace health and safety
standards, 345–346
workplace safety institutions, 242–243
Workplace Wellbeing Charter, 345
work quality, 359–360
work redesign. *See also* bottom-up work
redesign; top-down work redesign
assessing impact of changes, 377–378
assessment before, 327
common mechanisms in, 323–324
direct processes in, 360–362
employee participation in, 327
evaluating options, 375–376
evaluating outcomes, 385–386
evaluation of, 16–17
future research directions, 325–326, 645

generating multiple options for, 374
indirect effects of participation, 362
learning from, 378–379
organizational factor alignment with, 327
participation in, 360–363, 361*f*
practice implications of top-down, 327–328
relational, 15
supporting actions for, 379
tracking process of, 377
work-related identities, 176–177
work schedule flexibility, 380–381
workshops
action planning, 387–388, 394–395
industry, 346
job crafting, 422–423, 426, 442–443
in organizational interventions, 386–387
in participatory job design, 359, 365
work simplification
mechanistic work design and, 152
TPS and, 56
work systems, 321–322
analyzing, 374
work tasks
crafting, 418
employee actions shaping, 417
work team identity, 176
work teams
early forms of, 62
interdependence in, 70
Wrzesniewski, Amy, 415, 417, 418, 429,
440–441, 449
Wu, Chia-Huei, 11, 45–46, 195–196, 630, 631
Wu, Xiaoya, 538

Xerox, 371, 380–381

Yam, Paola, 223–224

zero-hour contracts, 505–506
Zhang, Fangfang, 23, 419–420, 427, 537–538
Zhang, Zhen, 67–68
Zhao, Yi, 21–22, 636–637
Zheng, Xiaotong, 554–555
Zilstra, Fred, 374
Zoom, 549–550